D0712459

THE CONFEDERATE REPUBLIC

Civil War America

Gary W. Gallagher, editor

The Confederate
REPUBLIC

A REVOLUTION AGAINST POLITICS

George C. Rable

The University of North Carolina Press | Chapel Hill and London

© 1994 The University of North Carolina Press
All rights reserved
Manufactured in the United States of America

The paper in this book meets the guidelines for
permanence and durability of the Committee on
Production Guidelines for Book Longevity of the
Council on Library Resources.

Library of Congress Cataloging-in-Publication Data
Rable, George C.
   The Confederate republic: a revolution against politics /
by George C. Rable.
      p. cm.—(Civil War America)
   Includes bibliographical references and index.
   ISBN 0-8078-2144-6 (cloth : alk. paper)
   1. Confederate States of America—Politics and
government. 2. Political culture—Confederate States of
America. I. Title. II. Series.
E487.R18   1994
973.7'13—dc20   93-36491
                                      CIP

98 97 96 95 94   5 4 3 2 1

For Kay, Anne, and Katie

and for the faculty and

graduate students of the

History Department at

Louisiana State University,

with fond memories of

1972–1978—and beyond

CONTENTS

A section of illustrations will
be found following page 110.

As this project lengthened in both pages and time, so did the list of the author's obligations to family, friends, and colleagues. The people mentioned below deserve much more than a thank you and (for the unlucky ones) a free copy of this book, but they must also realize that if such debts can be repaid at all, they can only be repaid in kind.

My wife, Kay, has shown amazingly little interest in Confederate political culture. But she cheerfully (more or less) read proofs, offered occasional but valuable suggestions on sticky points of style, and applied her superb skills as a librarian to tracking down some elusive sources. She has also reminded me often and gently that there is much more to life than writing but at the same time tolerates (and even encourages) my often compulsive behavior.

Daughters Anne and Katie have enjoyed bursting into the study for an endless variety of reasons. Their "interruptions" have been welcome most of the time. Games of various types, tennis, catch, bike rides, movies, track meets, swim meets, a few hands of euchre, softball games, basketball games, and conversations have not really delayed the completion of this project and have infinitely enriched my life. Even their disdain for visiting historical sites has a certain exasperating charm.

A National Endowment for the Humanities Summer Stipend provided time for writing the first three chapters. The faculty development committee at Anderson University through its Falls Fund was a steady source of support for travel. At several places, most notably Duke University, the

University of North Carolina, the University of Georgia, and Emory University, archivists cheerfully and efficiently aided in the research.

It has been a pleasure to work with Trudie Calvert as a copyeditor once again. Her excellent stylistic suggestions and remarkable eye for detail greatly improved the manuscript.

My colleague Doug Nelson gave me good leads in studying the literature on political culture and even tolerated critical comments on the dense prose of his fellow political scientists. As a department chair and, more important, as a friend, he has always encouraged my work while offering his wry (and occasionally valuable) observations on any number of subjects.

Once again, William J. Cooper, Jr., generously provided comments and suggestions. In addition, his own important work on Southern politics has shaped my thinking on many issues discussed in this book. I doubt that Bill will fully approve what I have to say about Jefferson Davis (or about Joseph E. Johnston), but he always manages to ask tough and useful questions.

Richard E. Beringer and Gary W. Gallagher read the manuscript for the University of North Carolina Press. Their full, generous, and helpful comments proved valuable in the final round of revisions. For both their encouragement and suggestions, I am grateful.

Michael Perman may have regretted his generous offer to tackle this manuscript, but I did not. His penetrating criticism and recommendations led to several additional but also valuable and necessary months of reworking and rewriting. On matters large and small, his advice was unfailingly shrewd and helpful.

For twenty years now, Thomas E. Schott has been a valued friend, and though he has assumed the onerous burden of reading two manuscripts for me, he remains so. As usual his comments on both substance and style (often expressed in acerbic language) forced changes on nearly every page (more accurately, nearly every paragraph). We have discussed Confederate politics for almost two decades, and though he does not endorse several of the interpretations presented here, his strongly held opinions and vast knowledge have greatly influenced my thinking on innumerable issues. His intermittent correspondence and unfailing friendship have meant more than I can express.

George C. Rable
Anderson, Indiana

Confederate politics has hardly been a neglected topic in Civil War history. Biographies and monographs have probed the operations of the Confederate government, analyzed the conflicts between Jefferson Davis and his critics, dissected the issue of states' rights, and examined the workings of the Confederate Congress. More recently, as part of a broader effort to reassess the causes for Confederate defeat, scholars have interpreted political conflicts as sources of ambiguity and weakness in Southern nationalism. Yet there has been no comprehensive work on Confederate politics itself because historians have generally neglected the interplay of ideology and practical politics during the war and have not thoroughly evaluated the complex interaction of state and "national" politics in the Confederacy.

This book will explore Confederate political culture in its own right rather than as a reflection of the problematic character of Southern nationalism or as a possible factor in Confederate defeat. The emphasis is on both the assumptions, values, and beliefs that laid the foundation for a Confederate political culture and on the immediate questions and problems that bedeviled Southern leaders. From the secession crisis through the end of the war, competing visions of the Southern nation's political future, and especially the emergence of rival political cultures, forced Confederates constantly to reconsider their most fundamental political assumptions even as they wrestled with more immediate economic and military crises. What is termed here a "revolution against politics" did not entirely succeed in transforming political behavior. A major theme that runs through the chapters that follow is the constant tug between political ideology and political practice that formed the basis for conflict and exacerbated differences between often ambitious and highly individualistic political leaders. Although antiparty (and, more broadly speaking, antipolitical) ideology is the thread that holds the argument together, most chapters deal in one way or another with the tensions and contradictions between political ideals and political behavior. In the same vein, contemporaries often talked about a Confederate "revolution," and I have chosen to retain the term "revolution" while carefully noting its often peculiar usage, including its conservative and sometimes reactionary elements.

Official ideology placed great emphasis on both political unity and social harmony. Although some readers will surely object that this is hardly surprising in the midst of a fight for survival, the war itself reinforced already powerful impulses toward creating a political culture based on a vision of purified republicanism, and this process was well under way before the first shots were ever fired. To the extent that Confederate nationalism existed, it meant primarily the struggle for Confederate independence with a strong (though not always consistent) emphasis on national unity and, as the war dragged on, the necessity for expanded government power. Libertarian dissenters, however, offered a quite different definition of the Confederate cause. Given traditional Southern assumptions about the importance of individual and communal liberty (and limited government), it is hardly surprising that many politicians and their constituents strenuously objected to any centralizing tendencies in the Confederacy. Nor were expressed fears of "consolidation" usually empty rhetoric or political ploys. Broader than a mere defense of states' rights, libertarian arguments formed the basis for an alternative political culture. Those speaking for national unity and their libertarian opponents (not to mention moderates searching for some middle ground) all claimed to be the true defenders of a genuine Southern republicanism as well as a nascent Confederate nationalism.

But despite heated arguments and no little friction between the competing political cultures of unity and liberty, antiparty ideology and broader fears about politics in general shaped civic life. These beliefs could obviously not eliminate partisanship or prevent Confederates from holding on to and exploiting old political prejudices. Indeed, some states, notably Georgia and North Carolina, remained political tinderboxes throughout the war. Even the most bitter foes of the Confederate government, however, refused to form an opposition party, and the Georgia dissidents, to cite the most prominent example, avoided many traditional political activities. Only in North Carolina did there develop anything resembling a party system, and there the central values of the Confederacy's two political cultures had a far more powerful influence on political debate than did organizational maneuvering.

David Potter and other historians have long warned about the hazards of hindsight in historical analysis of the antebellum sectional conflict, and the same can be said for the Civil War. This book therefore attempts to interpret Confederate political culture on its own terms and not primarily as the story of the rise and fall of the Confederate States of America. In a limited sense the book is counterfactual: it deals with how Confederates tried to envision their political future—assuming the existence of an independent Southern nation—without the corrupting influences of parties. The difficulty lies in concentrating on the political culture Confederate leaders attempted to create without always having one eye turned to the outcome of the war.

The concept of political culture carries with it several analytical problems. Although there are numerous (and sometimes contradictory) definitions of political culture, the focus in this work is on the beliefs, attitudes, and values expressed through political statements and behavior. Some aspects of political culture can be implicit and unspoken, and these often resist historical analysis, but in the Confederacy the rational, emotional, and symbolic dimensions of political culture appeared often in speeches, editorials, sermons, pamphlets, textbooks, and even in private documents. This rich body of evidence reveals common assumptions about the legitimacy of the political process in general and about the role of government in particular. Most Confederates viewed the war through the lens of their political culture, but the war itself also altered, or perhaps distorted, fundamental political attitudes. Too often political scientists have used political culture simply as a way to describe and categorize a society's political values. Although useful, this approach tends to exaggerate continuity and gives politics a misleadingly static quality. Obviously, Confederates entered the war with certain core beliefs that formed the basis for a political culture, but events (such as campaigns, battles, and elections), policies, and leaders all brought about subtle changes in political values. A Confederate political culture was not simply created, it evolved in an atmosphere of crisis and conflict. Therefore, rather than isolating and examining particular political ideas or adopting a topical organization, I have chosen to write an analytical narrative that explores the interactions among political culture, events, and leadership.

More so than their Northern counterparts, antebellum Southerners had been skeptical about the supposed virtues of political parties. Many Southern leaders remained deeply ambivalent about political organization and even about the electoral process. The secession crisis heightened this wariness and marked the beginning of a revolution against politics. Although specific discussion of the South's political future was not always central to the battle between immediate secessionists and cooperationists, a strongly antipolitical ideology appeared before the war began. Even taking into account the usual bombast and opportunism, Southerners of various political origins and views made denunciations of partisanship, demagoguery, patronage, and corruption central to their understanding of political culture. At the same time, their political behavior sometimes lagged behind their more idealistic aspirations.

In drafting the Confederate Constitution, the delegates at Montgomery did more than simply graft specifically proslavery provisions onto the United States Constitution; they deliberately sought to purge their politics of the degrading and dangerous influences of partisanship. Students of the Confederacy have often emphasized the basic conservatism of the Confederate Constitution, but if this document did not exactly offer a blueprint for revolution, neither was it pallid or unimaginative. Instead, it embodied the fundamental paradox of the Confederate experiment—the bold and at the same time circumscribed attempt to make a conservative or even a reactionary revolution, a revolution against the old political system.

Yet like any new political entity, the Confederacy faced a legitimacy crisis. The first state and national elections and the selection and inauguration of Jefferson Davis as Confederate president addressed this question by short-circuiting traditional political practices. Optimists declared that the new Confederate government was well on its way to restoring a simpler and purer republicanism; the hacks, lobbyists, and other money changers would be driven from the temples of public life. In theory, this new political culture rested on an organic sense of community and national solidarity that would be nourished by public faith in Confederate leadership. And it was up to Jefferson Davis and other Confederate spokesmen to handle the intractable problems of defining the nature of the Confederate revolution while constructing a new political order. By drawing elaborate parallels between the Confederate and American revolutions, Southerners staked a historical claim for their announced goal of perfecting the work of the founding fathers. Even military policy along with the complex factionalism in the Confederate high command reflected and was influenced by the widespread suspicion of political maneuvering.

Not only did politicians and newspaper editors specifically call for a sharp break with recent political practices—including conventions, election oratory, editorial feuds, and partisan wrangling—other influential Confederates broadened the movement into a cultural crusade. Preachers explicitly connected a purified Southern republic to the divine will; educators called for the training of children in the values of a new age. More specifically, wartime sermons (and some political speeches as well) often became Confederate jeremiads, and the Southern fire-eaters' dream of instructing Southern students from Southern textbooks came to fruition. By sternly lecturing and occasionally lashing the pious and by giving some attention to the political socialization of the young, Confederates worked to build a model republic.

Of course, these halcyon days, this Indian summer of the Confederate States of America, would be short-lived. By the spring of 1862—that season of military disasters and harsh realities—new worries, new political values, and an alternative political culture would emerge. Once easily made statements about God smiling on the Confederacy rang hollow. Ideological denunciations of political manipulation ran up against the persistence of unseemly ambition, personal prejudice, and bitter disputes over wartime policies. Critics of the Confederate government seemed to crop up everywhere, emphasizing individual liberty and playing on fears of centralized power. Cries would be raised not only against a despotic Abraham Lincoln but against a despotic Jefferson Davis. A new debate about the future course of the Confederate republic, and indeed about the character of the Southern people, would begin. This debate would wax and wane but would persist up through the final days of the Civil War and beyond.

CHAPTER 1

The Old South

A Political Culture in Crisis

He knew the right chords to strike. The years of restless, relentless preparation seemed to be over. Bitter clashes with his Yankee preacher stepfather, the disastrous attempts to manage his wife's property in South Carolina, his brief imprisonment for murdering her uncle in a street brawl, his stormy political career in Alabama amid mounting sectional conflict, his dismay over the willingness of fellow Southerners to sacrifice sacred principles for the sake of Union, party, and compromise: all these unpleasant memories could be set aside. In 1858, William Lowndes Yancey believed that the time had at last arrived to "fire the Southern heart—instruct the Southern mind—give courage to each other, and at the proper moment, by one organized, concerted action we can precipitate the cotton States into a revolution."[1] How many times would his political enemies North and South cite this passage to prove the existence of a secessionist conspiracy?

Much more to the point is how in this famous letter (addressed to his young Georgia friend James S. Slaughter), Yancey presented a blueprint of sorts for a Southern revolution. In words that reverberated among citizens grown increasingly wary of the political process, the Alabama firebrand bluntly asserted: "No National Party can save us; no Sectional Party can do it." What, then, could save the South? The answer lay in the past, in the glorious memories of an eighteenth-century revolution, in the political culture of a younger, more innocent American republic, in a vision of a golden age of political purity and unity. Once Southerners had taken these historical lessons to heart, Yancey believed, they would "organize

Committees of Safety all over the cotton states."[2] Gone would be the conventions and party caucuses, the trimmers and place hunters. In their place would rise a more perfect republic that even the founding fathers of the once great American Union might have envied.

Southerners who read Yancey's brief remarks had to flesh out the meaning for themselves. Indeed the entire letter rested on a series of unspoken assumptions that had shaped the politics of the antebellum South.[3] The antiparty rhetoric, the terse reference to the American Revolution (a period during which political parties had been noticeably absent), the call for Southern unity—all spoke to long-standing beliefs and fears. Unfortunately for Yancey, his audience, and the cause of Southern nationalism, little else aside from these basic propositions could be taken for granted. What a Southern nation might look like—even if the fire-eaters' dreams came to fruition—was anybody's guess. Southern political and social traditions shaped public responses to the sectional tensions of the antebellum years but never produced a coherent vision of the South's political future in or outside the Union. The absence of a well-defined "national" identity, divisions among Southerners, limited expectations for government, and a striking lack of faith in political decision making gave calls for Southern independence an ominously nebulous quality.[4]

Determining the essential characteristics of a Southern nation divided Yancey's contemporaries and has baffled historians ever since. David Potter has convincingly argued that a complex and shifting collection of national, local, family, and individual loyalties hardly formed the basis for a separate and distinct Southern culture. Even the fire-eaters, the most rabid proponents of Southern rights, who should have been able to offer a coherent and compelling vision of the future, fell into hopeless disagreement when trying to define Southern nationalism with any precision.[5] Too often they resorted to a fuzzy romanticism that obscured far more than it revealed. The Texas firebrand Louis T. Wigfall boasted that Southerners were a peculiar people, an agrarian people, who had no use for cities, manufacturing, or even literature and who would stake their economic future on King Cotton. Edmund Rhett, brother of leading radical Robert Barnwell Rhett, basically shared Wigfall's worldview but also believed that agrarianism and slavery afforded Southerners the leisure to "cultivate the arts, the graces, and accomplishments of life, to develop science, to apply our selves to the duties of government, and to understand the affairs of the country." Besides the obvious contradictions and inconsistencies in these statements, neither Wigfall nor Rhett dealt with the realities of Southern life. Their portrait of a bucolic, agrarian civilization created a Southerner as ideal type, a disembodied paragon of classical virtues. Such rhetoric has misled historians into exaggerating Southern cultural distinctiveness, while neglecting the sometimes narrowly political nature of Southern nationalism.[6]

After all, the South's dilemma was primarily political, and whatever its economic and cultural effects, secession was a political decision—a decision shaped by the region's political traditions but also by recent and painful experience. Sectional conflict and the strident politics of slavery had certainly alienated Southerners from partisanship, elections, and political agitation. Yet because of their cautious conservatism and occasional paranoia, Southerners—and especially their political leaders—instinctively feared revolution. However alluring disunion and the creation of a Southern nation might appear, the potential dangers were equally apparent. In an age of "disorder, socialism, communism, rabid democracy and open atheism," Presbyterian minister James Henley Thornwell maintained, forming new governments and new constitutions would be "perilous in the extreme."[7]

The difficulties of nation building became especially acute in a volatile political atmosphere and in a political culture fraught with ideological and practical incongruities. The Northern public and a fair number of Southerners described politics below the Mason-Dixon line as elitist and planter-dominated. And indeed, most Southern politicians stoutly defended property rights and were hypersensitive about both real and imaginary threats to slavery. Ambitious young men, as they moved up the rungs of the political ladder, acquired their own land and slaves while assiduously cultivating the patronage of their wealthier neighbors. Ideally, such striving for success fostered political, economic, and social stability by building broad-based support for slavery.

During the 1850s, slaveholder representation in state governments increased across the lower South. Even in North Carolina, with its large nonslaveholding population, most legislators of both parties owned slaves. Although race and sectional questions often overrode class considerations, a resentment against aristocratic nabobs sometimes seethed beneath the surface of state and local politics. The wealthy gobbled up the best lands, lived in fancy houses, monopolized higher education, and haughtily disdained social inferiors, all the while worrying about the fragility of their elite-dominated political culture.[8] To the extent that class antagonisms threatened political stability, many Southern politicians rightfully worried that any attempt to secure "home rule" against Yankee usurpation might well degenerate into a battle over which Southerners would rule at home. Therefore, Whigs and most Democrats shied away from appeals to class interests, skittish about arousing popular passions even for short-term political gains.

Jean Baker has argued that slavery caused the South's political culture to diverge markedly from the North's, and clearly many Southern politicians distrusted democratic political practices long accepted elsewhere in the nation. Keeping in mind the historical temptation to exaggerate sectional differences, there is some truth in this assertion. Denunciations of treating the voters with whiskey or wagering on elections along with condemnations of electioneering in general often appeared in newspaper editorials, stump speeches, and private correspondence. To counter the perceived excesses of democracy, critics of the political system proposed longer terms of office for public officials and a reduced number of elected offices. A Georgia editor suggested a life term for the state's governor, tighter franchise requirements, and abolishing popular election of judges.[9] Constitutional debates had enlivened Southern politics since the 1820s, but the sectional conflict of the 1850s and the possibility of forming a Southern nation reopened old questions about political democracy.

For all their criticism of current political practices, however, Southern white men had fully participated in the democratization of American politics during the first half of the nineteenth century. The Southern states had embraced and often taken the lead in the dramatic opening up of American politics. Elimination of property requirements for voting, reapportionment of state legislatures, the increased number of elective offices, and even attempts at breaking up the old courthouse cliques all promised to transform public life. By the 1840s, high voter turnout in elections at all levels gave evidence of growing popular participation and enthusiasm. Even in supposedly aristocratic Virginia, George Cary Eggleston recalled, "not to know the details of the vote of Connecticut in any given year was to lay oneself open to a suspicion of incompetence; to confess forgetfulness of the 'ayes and noes' on an important division in Congress was to rule oneself out of the debate as an ignoramus."[10]

Incessant political activity fostered public knowledge and interest. Spring elections, nominating conventions, picnics, barbecues, debates, speeches, fall canvassing, election day, postmortems, and winter strategy meetings followed a seasonal pattern readily understandable to farmers and planters wedded to the regular cycles of plowing, planting, hoeing, weeding, and harvesting. Tumult, excitement, and no small amount of frenzy characterized state and local politics from Virginia to Texas and even—to cite the least obvious example—in South Carolina. Despite the Palmetto State's restrictions on the number of elective offices, a generally elitist approach to public policy, and the absence of well-organized parties, a vigorously competitive politics prevailed from the days of nullification through the secession crisis. Promising young men hitched their political stars to a local magnate, but they still had to campaign hard, ever wary of the treacherous shoals of democratic politics. On the stump, at political barbecues, and even at dances, in up-country and low country alike, ambitious leaders of various stripes expounded an ideology based on long-standing notions of republican liberty that had broad popular appeal far beyond any narrow defense of the planters' interests.[11]

Even within what William J. Cooper, Jr., has called the "politics of slavery," Southerners sustained a two-party system. Competition between Democrats and Whigs reflected no clear regional, sectional, or class divisions but instead suggested how political, social, and even religious life blended into an amalgam of energy, ritual, ceremony, and organization. Precinct or beat meetings, county conventions, district conclaves, state conventions, legislative caucuses, party central committees—a full panoply of activity publicized and promoted by party newspapers—had spread rapidly across the South.[12]

Appearances, however, were somewhat deceiving. The new politics of participation (and entertainment) had modified but had not transformed political values. In a state such as North Carolina, where party competition became notably intense, traditional antiparty ideology originating in eighteenth-century republicanism and continuing through the Federalist-Republican era declined but did not disappear. Old suspicions that parties and party leaders were selfish and even despotic survived in the midst of intense partisan excitement.[13] Politicians and voters could accept parties as necessary evils or even occasionally as desirable without embracing the party system as a positive good. Ambivalence continued to characterize attitudes about political parties. An apparently firm commitment to the second American party system was qualified and tentative, and Northern attacks on slavery or on Southern influence in national politics could quickly revive latent antiparty sentiment.

Therefore, what at first appears to be contradictory—an elitist politics permeated with democratic practices; strong party organizations in some states, weak ones in others; elements of strikingly different political cultures coexisting at the same time and place—simply shows that the triumph of both democracy and political parties in the Old South was far from complete. For years, fire-eaters had been damning political parties and warning about the dangers partisanship posed to Southern interests. The dominance of the party men, those politicians who believed that a national political party was the best protection for Southern interests, had often thwarted efforts to unite the South against Northern antislavery forces. Much to the dismay of those seeking Southern unity, a running debate between so-called party men and would-be Southern nationalists punctuated by sharp electoral contests persisted up to the eve of the Civil War and beyond.[14] Even after the demise of the Whig party in the early 1850s, Southern Democrats still struggled to persuade skeptical voters that a national party, and more specifically Northern Democratic leaders, could be trusted to safeguard Southern interests.[15]

Paradoxically, the same politics of slavery that strengthened party organization also weakened it. So long as Southern politicians were able to convince Southern voters that their party best protected the people's welfare, they could sustain party loyalty. But working to preserve party unity and win national elections inevitably led to compromises that seemed to sacrifice Southern interests to political expediency.[16] So the very efforts to build and maintain political parties within a slave-based political culture undermined faith in political organizations and nourished antiparty ideology.

If partisanship may have indirectly threatened slavery, it also clashed with the Southern cult of honor. As a value that permeated Southern society and dominated Southern politics, honor became inextricably linked to slavery.[17] To defend slavery was to defend honor—whether the honor of an individual, a family, a state, or the South. Failure to uphold the South and slavery against internal or external enemies was to court disgrace. Party leaders in particular faced the formidable task of preserving both slavery and honor within a national political system. The realities of power and proslavery ideology exposed serious contradictions and difficulties. Broad-based parties by their nature can ill afford to press matters of principle and honor too far, but during the 1850s the old tactics of negotiation and compromise appeared increasingly outmoded and heretical in a political culture succumbing to the forces of extremism. Parties survived only on their ability to smooth ruffled feathers and hold together bickering factions.

Continuing competition between Whigs and Democrats—especially concerning the economic issues that had helped form the second party system—sometimes raised, if only rhetorically and tangentially, the dangerous issue of class in a society where class unity was an indispensable myth. Indeed, much of the proslavery argument rested on the convenient and powerful fiction that race always overrode class interests, that an organic unity among whites preserved social peace in the South. Therefore, politicians not only had to show how their party best safeguarded slavery and Southern rights but also to emphasize that the humblest white citizen had just as vested an interest in slavery as the richest planter. Yet even proslavery ideology could not entirely mute questions of class. James Henry Hammond of South Carolina admitted that in all countries there were two classes, "the rich and poor, the educated and ignorant." In Hammond's South, the enslaved blacks certainly qualified as poor and ignorant. But he conveniently overlooked the poor whites and struggling yeomen, the absence of public education, and the occasional outbursts of resentment against slaveholders' wealth and power.[18] Obviously party competition that divided the electorate into fiercely competing groups militated against Hammond's vision of social unity. As outside pressure against slavery mounted, partisanship seemed even more divisive and dangerous.

This is not to say that party leaders did not fight long and hard to convince voters that a national political organization—in this case the Democratic party—could serve Southern interests. Indeed, the relatively narrow support for the fire-eaters and their secessionist remedies until the late 1850s suggests some success in these efforts. Likewise, habit and tradition remained powerful influences on political behavior so long as Southerners continued to exert substantial influence in national politics and could deal with external threats to slavery. But sustaining popular faith in political parties in an increasingly volatile political atmosphere became more difficult than many party leaders could have predicted.

For politicians who had invested their careers in the great political battles of the 1830s and 1840s, jettisoning political parties might be painful if not impossible, but antiparty elements grew stronger. The most powerful ideological impetus apart from the defense of slavery was the South's commitment to its own version of republicanism. Admittedly, historians for the past several decades have used the concept of republicanism so broadly and carelessly that it has lost much of its originality, analytical rigor, and interpretative power.[19] If every group and nearly every individual embraces "republican" values, the concept becomes so all-encompassing that it ends up explaining nothing and describing little.

One problem is that republicanism was not a static ideology. Evolving from colonial political disputes (greatly influenced by European political thought) that had culminated in the American Revolution, republicanism in the United States showed considerable staying power and flexibility. Politicians, parties, preachers, businessmen, workers, women, and slaves all laid claim to the language of this powerfully evocative ideology. The question is not whether the adult white males who participated in Southern political life worshiped at the shrine of republicanism but rather to which republican "denomination" they belonged.

Southern politicians of every stripe appealed to republican tradition—at least selectively. While claiming to cherish the public good over personal advancement, newspaper editor, Unionist, and ardent Democrat William W. Holden labeled his Whig opponents enemies of republicanism. At the other end of the political spectrum, the fire-eaters were equally insistent that their views embraced classical notions of honor and liberty. Masterfully portraying themselves as martyrs to conviction and enemies of expediency, they perfected the dramatic gesture of resigning from public office and then retiring to private life with their vaunted principles intact. Denials of personal ambition, warnings of corruption and conspiracies—Southerners well understood the language of republicanism.[20] But their oratory and their convictions remained rooted in eighteenth-century republicanism rather than the more partisan varieties that held sway in the rest of the country. In contrast to their Northern counterparts, who more easily reconciled republicanism with partisanship, Southern politicians preferred appeals to liberty rather than appeals to party. With a faith in agrarian simplicity, suspicions of power, and fears of government usurpation, Southern intellectuals, fire-eaters, and even some party politicians sounded as out of place in the mid-nineteenth century as John Randolph of Roanoke had in the age of Andrew Jackson.

Besides being tied to a more static set of beliefs, Southerners spurned the shibboleths of Northern republicanism. Unlike some Whigs, and later many Republicans such as Abraham Lincoln, who revered the American Union, many Southerners remained deeply ambivalent about the national compact. South Carolina radicals denounced a Union that had become a monster devouring the people's liberties. Throughout his career, John C. Calhoun had argued for preservation but not worship of the Union. And by the 1850s ardent Southern Democrats such as Jefferson Davis admitted valuing liberty more than Union, even at the price of severing relations with their Northern party brethren. By the same token, even Southerners who declared their love for the Union often called for restoring the early republic's supposedly purer political culture. In every Southern state, some politicians and newspaper editors also expressed reservations about the seemingly irresistible growth of political democracy.[21]

More important, Southern leaders from Calhoun's era forward vigorously upheld the ideals of a slaveholders' republic. However sophisticated historians have become in delineating the nature of Southern distinctiveness, most interpretations eventually return to matters of race and slavery. Unfortunately, historians have too often attempted to read twentieth-century guilt and uncertainty back into the nineteenth century, even though few Southern whites in the antebellum decades saw slavery and republicanism as incompatible. In fact, Southerners viewed Northern attempts to stop the expansion of slavery as a serious threat to white liberty because it denied slaveholders an equal opportunity to carry their property into the national territories. At the same time, Southern defenders of slavery proclaimed the superiority of their society. Slavery fostered class harmony, paternalism ameliorated the exploitation of labor, and a slaveholding society secured the personal independence of slaveholder and nonslaveholder alike. The real threat to liberty, then, came from Northern abolitionists, free-soilers, and other fanatics who would enslave white Southerners by denying them their sacred rights in the American Union. Such a contradictory and self-serving ideology may be a flimsy foundation for nation building, but as Benedict Anderson has cogently observed, a nation is an "imagined political community," an idealistic construct that omits or rationalizes the injustice and inequality that may well characterize the society.[22] So for some white Southerners to affirm both their faith in a slaveholding republic and their own version of republicanism was hardly remarkable.

Politicians (and their parties) therefore much preferred to portray themselves as guardians of Southern republican values than as men skilled in handling difficult, delicate questions requiring a recognition of complexity and a willingness to compromise. Even party leaders such as Jefferson Davis and Howell Cobb often had to distance themselves from political practices that made them appear too beholden to Northern allies. Partisanship, then, became not so much a defense of one's party (and certainly not a paean to the efficacy and benefits of parties) but rather a means to link the opposition to supposed threats against republican liberty. In both argument and tone, Southern political debates sounded much like the partisan warfare of the 1790s in which Federalists and Republicans had condemned each other as enemies of the republic. But mounting sectional tension beginning in the 1830s forced spokesmen for Southern republicanism to pay as much attention to external as to internal dangers. In turn, the question of Southern rights tempted politicians to exploit the sectional crisis for partisan advantage.[23]

There was little danger, however, that such partisanship would overshadow the politics of slavery. Indeed, partisanship encouraged ever more extreme defenses of Southern rights, which in turn weakened the parties and made both Southern unity and a Southern nation seem more plausible and necessary. Not only did each party watch its opponent with a jaundiced eye, ever alert for signs of some deep-seated conspiracy against liberty, but Southerners had grown up with an eighteenth-century suspicion of political power. Yet power was an unavoidable reality in the household, on the plantation, and in political life. Given this tension between theory and practice, politicians had to wield power without appearing powerful and pursue their ambitions without seeming ambitious. As hard as it might be to conceal both ambition and power, Southerners regularly equated the exercise of power with oppression. In light of the emphasis on limited government, strict construction of the Constitution, and separation of powers derived from the teachings of Thomas Jefferson and John C. Calhoun, it is not surprising that Southerners did everything possible to confine political power within narrow boundaries.[24]

Eighteenth-century notions of liberty and power reinforced public skepticism about political parties and politics in general. Southern republicanism came to mean an obsessive concern with liberty, a fear of political power, and a passion for individual, state, and even sectional independence. Yet political parties could undermine if not destroy these political values. Nationally, antiparty values had persisted long after the rise of the second American party system—especially in the Whig party.[25] In the North conservative Whigs continued to deplore partisan agitation, and abolitionists denounced parties for sacrificing political principles. But Northern Democrats and the new antislavery Republican party partially restored their constituents' confidence in the ability of the political system to deal with the slavery question and offered voters what appeared to be real choices. The South's politics, however, moved in a radically different direction. After Henry Clay's waffling on the Texas question in 1844, Zachary Taylor's support for the admission of California and other western territories as free states in 1849, and Winfield Scott's lackluster and free-soil-tainted presidential campaign in 1852, Southern Whigs had little reason to mourn their party's demise or hope for its revival. For Southern Democrats, disillusionment was slower but just as sure. The fiasco over the

Lecompton Constitution in Kansas, the disaffection of Stephen A. Douglas and his Northern followers, and the vacillation of President James Buchanan steadily eroded their confidence in the party.[26]

By the latter half of the 1850s, many white Southerners stood largely outside the national political culture. After more than a decade of rancorous sectional conflict—conflict often exacerbated by partisan maneuvering—the antiparty diatribes of the fire-eaters carried more weight with the electorate and had even picked up support from Democratic party leaders. Curiously, radical Southern rights men had always exaggerated the evils of party as well as the strength of party sentiments in the South, but now their long ignored warnings appeared prophetic, and agitators suddenly became statesmen. The events of the 1850s brought the party men and the fire-eaters together as the secession crisis approached.[27] Democratic leaders now had to downplay party loyalty, and especially any alliances with Northerners of doubtful orthodoxy. This process of purification, as Southern nationalists would have called it, further weakened the bonds of Union and pushed the Southern states toward a future without parties.

Even veteran politicians now appeared to elevate honor over compromise, principle over expediency, and slavery over Union. Any lingering attachment to parties would threaten the independence not only of the Southern states but of the Southern people. Thus both personal and Southern honor were jeopardized when party organizations and government could no longer manage the slavery question or foster social and political harmony. In short, what had always been a weak commitment to political parties grew weaker.[28]

At the same time, the outcries against politicians reached a crescendo, reflecting a critical disillusionment with the political process. In this new, or, more accurately, refurbished, credo of Southern politics, politicians were viewed axiomatically as demagogues shamefully trimming their sails with each shifting breeze of public sentiment, ever ready to surrender Southern interests to self-interest. Traditional fears of both politicians and power spread and grew as the old Calhounite rhetoric against political spoilsmen gained credibility and popular favor.[29] Robert Barnwell Rhett regretted that men who could have forcefully campaigned for secession sought federal offices, thereby avoiding any bold stand for Southern rights. Edmund Ruffin agreed. Too many Southern politicians, he believed, had their eyes on the presidency and would eagerly cooperate with Stephen A. Douglas and others to "buy northern votes."[30]

Cries against demagoguery and spoilsmen originated in ancient fears of political corruption. Reservations about democracy—notably the "tyranny of numbers"—along with worries about the security of both liberty and property contributed to this dissatisfaction. Scandals in state government and especially in Washington during the Buchanan administration revived old apprehensions about the abuse of political power. Legislative bodies became sinkholes of corruption; elections proved how susceptible the people—or "mudsills" as the more candid Southern extremists labeled them—were to partisan trickery. The ultimate nightmare was that the corruption, which had so tainted the Northern states and the national capital, would overwhelm Southern liberty and honor.[31]

In 1857, when a committee of the United States House of Representatives launched an inquiry into bribery charges against several members of Congress, Edmund Ruffin summed up the reaction of self-righteous Southerners: "As a body, the majority of the northern members of congress are as corrupt, & destitute of private integrity as the majority of southern members are the reverse." Ruffin also sharply contrasted the equally degraded constituents of these Northern congressmen with virtuous Southerners. The only way to avoid contamination was for the Southern states to leave the Union, in effect establishing a moral quarantine. Alarms about corruption exacerbated sectional tensions because no honorable man could trust the promises of Northern spoilsmen—whether Democrat or Republican. The scandals of the Buchanan administration merely confirmed prevailing Southern notions about the real workings of the national government.[32] The fire-eaters' attacks on Northern placemen seemed more believable when public thievery received extensive and sensational coverage in Southern newspapers.

In the past, many Southern voters might have ignored this extremist rhetoric and followed the lead of traditional party leaders. But Southern Democrats by the late 1850s were clearly losing control of their party, and they could now agree with the fire-eaters that political parties could no longer safeguard Southern rights. A conjunction of principle and ambition had begun to create widespread support for or at least acquiescence to secession. To paraphrase William Lowndes Yancey in a different context, the men and the hour had met.

The presidential election of 1860 marked the culmination of this political evolution. As always, the fire-eaters fussed and fumed over the influence of party men who would again abandon Southern rights in the interests of presidential candidates. In January 1860, Robert Barnwell Rhett was planning a walkout from the Democratic national convention as a means to wreck the "spoils democracy."[33] This time, however, Southern radicals should not have sounded so gloomy because their blasts against partisanship enjoyed a much larger, more receptive audience. The Democratic party, claimed the editor of the *Savannah Republican* a little over two months before the convention in Charleston, "presents no security either for the rights of the South or the peace of the country." By June, even so loyal a party man as Jefferson Davis acknowledged that a "grog-drinking, electioneering Demagogue [Stephen A. Douglas]" had fatally wounded his party. At the other end of the political spectrum, former Whigs campaigning for Constitutional Union candidate John Bell agreed that the entire mechanism of political parties, from partisan wire-pullers to treacherous spoilsmen to mercenary newspaper editors, was sounding the death knell of a once glorious Union.[34]

The breakup of the Democratic party naturally gave new hope to secessionists. Rhett's *Charleston Mercury* proclaimed political party conventions "more or less fraudulent" because they had always lacked constitutional sanction. Thus the demise of party might well prove an enormous blessing. Partisanship had long delayed the fulfillment of Calhoun's dream for a united South, but the almost certain election of Lincoln promised to accomplish what years of radical agitation had failed to achieve. No longer would party considerations serve as roadblocks to secession. South Carolinians could lead the Southern states out of the Union, Congressman Laurence M. Keitt declared, because "the absence of party spirit enables us to do so."[35] More ominous still, old party leaders who in the past had pleaded for toleration and forbearance no longer disagreed with Rhett and Keitt.

So the moment of truth, the time for action, had come. Or had it? The election returns in the Southern states hardly constituted a ringing endorsement for Southern separatism. During the campaign, the Bell and Douglas men had of course opposed secession, and even John C. Breckinridge, the Southern Democratic candidate, had not run as an avowed disunionist. Nagging questions about Southern unity added to the confusion. Given the bitterness of the election campaign, James Henry Hammond doubted that a Southern confederacy could be formed. The prospect for more debate among Southerners threatened to delay once again what the fire-eaters saw as the day of deliverance. South Carolina congressman William Porcher Miles epitomized the radicals' impatience. "Let us act if we mean to act without talking," he told the cautious Hammond. "Let it be a word and a blow—but the blow first."[36] Endless discussion would further divide Southerners and, more important, raise difficult and dangerous questions. For once in their lives, the hotspurs seemed to be the most practical of politicians.

Yet for all their passion, militant statements hardly offered a blueprint for the South's political future. By 1860, Southern politicians had a much clearer idea of what they were against than what they were for. Strong antiparty sentiments, disgruntlement with politics as usual, and fragments of eighteenth-century republicanism spoken in a Southern accent were hardly the basis for a coherent political ideology. Even longtime believers in Southern nationalism often lacked a clear picture of what should follow secession. In forming a new nation, politicians would try to build a distinctive political culture, a vitally important matter that had thus far barely been considered. Too often personal ambition and disappointment, a constant sense of crisis, and a narrow vision focused on immediate or merely local problems had discouraged clear thinking about the political needs of this nebulously defined Southern nation. The immediate future seemed to promise little but confusion, conflict, and perhaps political disintegration.

CHAPTER 2

Through a
Glass Darkly

Secession and the Future

of Southern Politics

Preoccupation with past grievances and fears about the future dominated Southern thinking during the secession crisis. Worries about external threats and internal divisions, often expressed in strikingly similar language by secessionists and cooperationists, prevented Southerners from meditating much about the political future. Impassioned debates over secession, endless diatribes against Lincoln, and fears of lingering Unionism—especially in the border states—distracted politicians from considering the South's political destiny. Worries about unity (or its absence) became a major political theme.

Ardent secessionists seeking to dissolve the Union paid little attention to the long-run consequences. The most earnest Southern "nationalists" (if they can even be called that) spoke and wrote in only the vaguest terms about their "nation's" characteristics and prospects.[1] Despite their flaming rhetoric, they had no more of a blueprint for the future than did cooperationists, who appealed to conservatism, caution, and fear of revolution.

This omission involved more than a mere failure of vision or even of nerve. Perceptive Southerners were all too aware of the divisions among themselves. States of the upper and lower South viewed each other through lenses of mutual suspicion and economic competition. The Gulf states would likely favor free trade, while border states such as Virginia and Maryland would insist on protection for manufacturing. The same tariff debates that had helped disrupt the Union might make a Southern nation unworkable.[2] Cooperationists in particular emphasized the costs of secession, especially for state and local governments. James G. Taliaferro believed that the Mississippi River bound Louisiana more firmly to the border states than to the Deep South and argued that "an alliance in a weak government with the Gulf state [Mississippi] east of her, is unnatural and antagonistic to her obvious interests and destiny." And who would pay the higher taxes needed to finance this new Southern nation? Where would the all-but-certain war be fought? Which groups would benefit and which would suffer? A skeptical Virginian could foresee only high taxes and corruption because the secessionists would "fill the lucrative offices and secure rich appointments. . . . They will luxuriate on two or three or four hundred dollars per month, with horses, and servants, and rations to match."[3]

In decrying oppressive taxation and standing armies, border state men relied on the arguments and imagery of eighteenth-century republicanism. In this view a Southern government might become as expensive and tyrannical as the worst Yankee administration. And yet the upper South states faced a classic dilemma. If they refused to leave the Union, a Gulf states confederacy might reopen the African slave trade and stop importing slaves from the border states. This possibility raised explosive issues of class and race that threatened to abort any experiment in Southern nationalism. In an unusually blunt assessment, the vituperative editor of the *Knoxville Whig* and onetime Methodist preacher, William G. "Parson" Brownlow, warned that the people of the upper South risked becoming "hewers of wood and drawers of water for a set of aristocrats." Even Virginia's moderate governor, John Letcher, asserted that if the cotton states were "looking to their interests alone," the border states should do likewise.[4]

Intrasectional distrust made a unified commitment to Southern nationalism problematic at best. As the Deep South states began leaving the Union, fire-eaters questioned the loyalty of the upper South. In January 1861 Robert Barnwell Rhett saw no reason to conciliate border state politicians, who in all likelihood would try to patch up the wreck of the old Union.[5] Indeed, as Southern radicals gained a larger following during the secession crisis, their prominence as catalysts for disunion made the formation of a Southern nation that much more difficult.

But secessionists and cooperationists alike, whether from South Carolina, Georgia, or Virginia, all agreed that politicians had brought on the crisis. One of the strongest arguments for South Carolina taking the lead in secession and for separate state action elsewhere was the expectation that self-seeking politicians would sell the South's birthright for a thin mess of compromise potage. There were Southern senators in Washington, Rhett declared, "begging, kneeling, like very mendicants, for Yankee charity." In contrast to the small-minded politicians, secessionists claimed to represent a mass movement that would sweep the time-serving party men aside and make way for statesmen of unbending principle. "The people are ahead of the politicians" was a cry often heard in the winter months of 1861, as the radicals worked to turn this bit of wishful thinking into reality.[6]

Cooperationists of all stripes—from those who would follow the lead of their states to outright Unionists—joined in excoriating the politicians for stirring up sectional antagonism. Denunciations of secessionist leaders grew increasingly strident in the upper South because conditional Unionists were searching for a political escape hatch. As the center of Southern extremism, South Carolina naturally became a lightning rod for conservative anger. "If I had the power," a Virginia legislator fumed, "I would seize South Carolina and sink her into the depths of the fathomless ocean never again to be resurrected."[7] In Georgia, a state with a substantial cooperationist minority, Alexander H. Stephens branded many politicians as "disunionists *per se*" with no interest whatsoever in sectional reconciliation. Offering a markedly different assessment of public opinion than the fire-eaters, conservatives claimed that a coterie of agitators had been steadily plotting to force a reluctant majority out of the Union.[8]

Cooperationists' analysis of secessionists' motivation was equally forceful. Turning the radicals' condemnation of corruption on its head, conservative leaders claimed that disunionists expected to monopolize the public offices in any new Southern nation. Catchwords and phrases such as "demagogues," "corrupt politicians," and "loaves and fishes" often cropped up in correspondence and speeches. Sam Houston carefully distinguished between those misguided Texans who honestly favored secession and a much smaller group of men pursuing personal "aggrandizement."[9]

Throughout the winter and spring of 1860–61, both sides used remarkably similar arguments because they shared similar political values. Paradoxically, as the secession crisis divided Southerners, it also laid a partial foundation for national unity based on shared political assumptions. Experiences during the past decade had clearly fueled suspicions of parties and party leaders. Moreover, the developing antiparty political culture could easily accommodate a range of opinions. Classical republicanism was a spacious ideology: even its Southern version left plenty of room for everyone from the most rabid fire-eater to the most hesitant Unionist. At the same time, the very amorphous and abstract character of Southern republicanism was bound to create misunderstandings, rival claims to political rectitude, and often bitter disputes over the meaning of language.

Though neither cooperationists nor secessionists favored "revolution" in any abstract sense, disunionists did not hesitate to endorse a *Southern* revolution against Yankee usurpation. For Laurence Keitt and other South Carolina radicals, Lincoln's inauguration would launch a frightful experiment in quondam democracy comparable to the French Revolution.[10] Such assertions suggested reactionary tendencies in secessionist thinking that could prove politically dangerous. The fire-eaters had to be wary of going too far in denouncing either democracy or politicians. They might have to suppress their aspersions on popular majorities temporarily to persuade Southern voters of the imperative need for disunion while sidestepping the unintended consequences of political change.

Cooperationists, by contrast, had to pull fewer punches in cautioning the Southern people about the inherent evils of revolution. Men of naturally conservative temperament, such as Robert E. Lee, equated secession with anarchy; others worried that the Southern states had started down the road taken by revolutionary France.[11] In the large, wealthy state of Georgia, articulate cooperationists warned of political and social upheaval, accusing secessionists of attempting to carry the state toward a dangerous future without adequate discussion or preparation. Secession might destroy the social harmony of the organic Southern community. In an important public letter, Alexander H. Stephens prophesied disaster: "Revolutions are much easier started than controlled, and the men who begin them, seldom end them." Pointing to the history of ancient republics, Stephens noted that well-meaning leaders had often been consumed by their own revolutions. Reiterating these sentiments to the Georgia legislature in November 1860, he pleaded with his neighbors to heed the voices of reason over the cries of passion. In his view, the United States Constitution remained the best in the world. For the Southern states to embark on a bold and uncertain experiment in revolutionary government would be to cast aside an invaluable heritage. Like Edmund Burke and other conservative nationalists, Stephens could approve only those revolutions designed to restore or preserve great historical traditions.[12] In drawing fine distinctions between acceptable and unacceptable revolutions, Stephens strained the meaning of the word "revolution" but also kept the door open for eventually supporting a properly conservative Southern nation.

Largely directed at politicians, intellectuals, and avid newspaper readers, these philosophical discussions must have seemed arid, academic, and irrelevant to many Southerners. Hence conservatives had to make their fears of the future more tangible by linking them to popular assumptions and prejudices about the nature of politics. Besides stating their general abhorrence of revolution, they also accused disunionists of preparing a coup d'état. Alarming tales about the activities of "minute men" and other radical bands spread through South Carolina and Georgia. James Henry Hammond described a "reign of terror" in the countryside and claimed that radicals had threatened to hang a cooperationist who was campaigning for a seat in the South Carolina convention. Rumor had it that Georgia firebrands were preparing to take their state out of the Union without even the formality of an election or, as Thomas R. R. Cobb reportedly bragged, "without waiting to hear from the cross roads and grog shops."[13]

Cooperationists, with varying emphases, described a train of woes that would surely follow the disruption of the Union: secession would produce anarchy and eventually despotism; radical politicians would secure special privileges for the elite while destroying the remnants of democracy in the Southern states. In establishing a ruling oligarchy, these radicals would disregard freedom of speech, unleash mobs against dissenters, and seize control of the press.[14] Encapsulating several of these dire predictions, a cooperationist petition from Upson County, Georgia, declared that radicals aimed to "overthrow our present republican form of Government" and establish a "Constitutional monarchy." The disunion movement originated in "disappointed partisans who vainly imagine that the government and all its offices and honors rightfully belong to the favored few, who are 'afraid of conventions,' and are unwilling 'to wait to hear from the people.' "[15]

A heaping serving of eighteenth-century assaults on aristocracy with a dash of Jacksonian rhetoric tossed in for seasoning, such arguments made for a filling if not always flavorful political dish. The missing ingredient, the spice that tickled Southern palates, was slavery. Persistent charges that secessionists planned to establish a slaveholders' junto struck at the heart of class harmony and social consensus. In North Carolina, a state caught geographically and politically between radical South Carolina and cautious Virginia, such accusations embittered political discourse. "The Cotton Oligarchs," wrote a skeptical Tar Heel, were trying to "dragoon" the upper South into secession.[16] Resentment against the pretensions of slaveholding nabobs and against the claims of Gulf state politicians to speak for the entire South clearly strengthened the cooperationists.

Politicians soliciting the votes of yeoman farmers in the February and April elections to the North Carolina secession convention claimed that a slaveholding aristocracy was hell-bent on snatching up the best land and driving middling whites into poverty. For their part, secessionists had to downplay the protection of slavery and instead emphasize a more inclusive defense of white liberty and property.[17] When skeptical yeomen suggested that if war broke out, poor men would do most of the fighting, they touched a raw nerve.

Once class suspicions and antagonisms had been aroused, they could easily shift the grounds of political discussion toward the economics of war. In North Carolina, long smoldering dissatisfaction over the incidence of taxation lit a fire under some politicians. William W. Holden claimed that secessionist leaders would never agree to higher taxes on their slaves and would instead raise the poll tax. Poor men who could not afford these additional levies would then see their land auctioned off to wealthy speculators. Discussions of direct taxation under a Southern government (as opposed to a revenue tariff) implied that new burdens would fall heavily on the already hard-pressed yeomanry.[18]

Although they were significant, it would be easy to exaggerate the importance of these controversies. In many cases, desperate cooperationists were simply searching for any argument—no matter how risky—that might delay secession. For the time being, soothing words and a crisis atmosphere might paper over differences. After all, both secessionists and cooperationists (the latter almost by definition) believed Southern unity essential. The occasional resort to class rhetoric as an electioneering device was therefore far less significant than the persistence of appeals against party and politicians.

To cooperationists the secessionist case for Southern nationalism was simply political humbug. Unscrupulous demagogues roamed the countryside hoodwinking unwary voters, raising false issues, and concealing their true motives. Politicians, newspaper editors, and even ministers of the gospel misled the people into believing secession was justified and that it would be peaceful. Such men not only would manipulate public opinion but also would attempt to cow the weak and if necessary control the polls. Humble and unsophisticated citizens too readily believed what they heard and read. "While the people may be capable of self-government," a Virginia Unionist lamented, "they do not exercise self-government."[19]

Reason could prevail only if the voters took their political responsibilities more seriously, argued the cooperationists. The times demanded careful deliberation whereas secessionists insisted on haste.[20] Yet many cooperationists were former Whigs who had spent years denouncing the cheap demagoguery of their Democratic foes and privately disparaging popular delusions. Even during the presidential election campaign, these conservatives had revealed ambivalent views about the people at large. They claimed to respect common sense even as they wondered whether most folks had much. With characteristic melancholy, Alexander H. Stephens thought that people had lost their "character and principles" and were heading toward the same fate as the Greeks, the Romans, and the French. "Selfishness and ambition" among the voters, along with the activities of wily politicians who "generally hated their enemies or rivals more than they love their country," were driving the South toward the abyss of revolution and war.[21] If, as the founding fathers believed, republican government depended on the virtue of its citizens, then republican government was doomed.

In their own way, secessionists shared some of these hopes and fears. The more optimistic maintained that the Southern people fully supported disunion and would force their reluctant leaders to act. According to the novelist William Gilmore Simms, "The people will not suffer the politicians any longer. They are neither to be deluded, nor coaxed nor cajoled." In states where secessionists held substantial majorities, they even chided cooperationists for being afraid to test public sentiment.[22] But more candid and perhaps more realistic radicals had serious reservations. Admitting that the "common people" hardly understood what was at stake, Alfred P. Aldrich, a member of the South Carolina legislature from Barnwell District, asserted that revolutions never waited on public sentiment and that Southern leaders must act and "force them [the people] to follow."[23] Many fire-eaters realized that they must still push reluctant politicians and their constituents toward disunion.

Ironically, the very success of the secession movement spelled danger because the public excitement might carry the Southern revolution into dangerous political waters. South Carolina's James Henry Hammond, whose onetime radicalism had greatly cooled, refused to celebrate what he saw as an illegitimate marriage of Southern nationalism with radical democracy: "The little great men who would seek notoriety by proposing to elect Judges, Senators, and Representatives annually by universal suffrage must be kept from putting their hand upon our Constitution or we shall soon have the guillotine at work upon good men."[24] Revolution, despotism, monarchy, demagoguery, anarchy: the secession debate had revealed many internal dangers.

But if Southern nationalism was to triumph, the rhetorical emphasis would have to be on external threats. Secessionists hoping to unite the Southern people in a crusade for independence stressed the hazards the hated Yankees posed to Southern civilization. Their list of complaints was long: the exclusion of slavery from the national territories, tariff discrimination, subsidies for Northern industry, the inciting of slave insurrections. Lincoln's election marked the culmination of these accumulated grievances.[25] Anticipating the course of the new administration, worried Southerners described a series of horrors that would soon befall the land. The Republican triumph would forever consign the Southern states to a minority status in the Union. Lincoln would use patronage to build Republican strength in the South, and unprincipled Southerners who accepted appointments from a "Black Republican" would become the entering wedge for abolition. Emancipation, free labor, political equality, amalgamation, rapine, murder, and race war would quickly follow.

Secessionists decided to wage a propaganda war against the Union first and address the problem of internal dissent later.[26] Lincoln's election as an immediate menace to slavery became their clarion call. To submit to the rule of a Black Republican administration would be disgraceful; abolition threatened the interests of slaveholder and nonslaveholder alike. However often cooperationists downplayed such dangers, secessionists inevitably replied that the honor of every white man and the future of slavery were inextricably linked.[27] Perceived threats to liberty made secessionist arguments more persuasive and allowed the fire-eaters' rhetoric to bridge the gaps between rich and poor, between slaveholder and nonslaveholder, between the privileged and the common folk.

In language curiously reminiscent of Northern attacks on the Southern slave power, disunionists charged that the Republicans intended to enslave the Southern people and establish a tyranny that would shame the worst despots of the ancient and modern world.[28] Such hyperbolic statements suggested how much the secession crisis had become a struggle based on symbols. By using elements of eighteenth-century republicanism, proslavery rhetoric, and antiparty ideology, secessionists built their case on traditional arguments that awakened old anxieties and aroused new fears for the future. The emphasis on irreconcilable differences between North and South transformed the Republicans and large segments of the Northern population into an antislavery monolith. Black Republicanism itself evolved into a powerful abstraction to be manipulated at will, thereby hopelessly confounding perception and reality. To distinguish tangible threats from imaginary dangers became both impossible and irrelevant. The signs of the times were all too clear. Through an oversimplified analysis of both cause and motives, disunionists claimed to have discovered deep-laid conspiracies to destroy Southern liberties. The fanatical and hypocritical Yankee archetype, tirelessly laboring to subdue and oppress the South, became the most potent symbol in fire-eater propaganda.[29]

Political hostilities also reflected a widening cultural and historical gulf between the two sections. The notion of Northern Puritan versus Southern Cavalier became much more than a stock literary device. According to the secessionists' version of American history, from the seventeenth century onward, the bigotry and intolerance of New England Puritanism had driven liberty-loving people to the South, where courage and chivalry flourished along with African slavery. The election of Lincoln—though the freethinking, storytelling Illinois rail-splitter hardly fit the stereotype of the ultra Yankee—gave the Southern people a magnificent opportunity to cast off the influence of a foreign and hostile civilization. For extremists who still harbored reservations about political democracy, this meant repealing the three-fifths clause and giving slave property full representation in national councils, restricting the franchise, and elevating liberty over the chimera of a false equality.[30] Should Southerners fail to throw off the shackles of the old Union and refuse to break free from Northern fanaticism, they would find themselves infested by all the "isms" that had sapped the nation's strength and virtue. The Republicans, charged one Mississippi convention delegate, would not only incite slave insurrections but also bring feminism, infidelity, and who knew what other evils into the South.[31] That such twisted perceptions appeared not only in public statements but also in private correspondence shows the power exerted by pervasive images of a debauched Northern people supporting a wholly malevolent administration presiding over a government about to collapse in financial and moral ruin.

These prophets of disaster also played on familiar fears of corruption. From Washington, to the state capitals, to the great cities, the prevalence of public thievery symbolized the general demoralization of Northern society. The United States Congress had become a den of thieves scrambling after the spoils of power. Regular readers of Southern newspapers might have concluded that Republicans would even abandon their dream of an abolition empire in their single-minded pursuit of patronage. To raid the treasury and to distribute offices were apparently the chief desiderata.[32]

Besides the obvious exaggerations, such strong statements also contained hints of insecurity. While excoriating the Yankees, secessionists occasionally revealed their own worst nightmare—that native Southerners might be seduced by Republican blandishments. Once the government "passed into Black Republican hands," Governor Joseph E. Brown warned his fellow Georgians, "a portion of our citizens must, if possible, be bribed into treachery to their section, by the allurements of office; or a hungry swarm of abolition emissaries must be imported among us as officeholders, to eat out our substance, insult us with their arrogance, corrupt our slaves . . . and do all in their power to create in the South a state of things which must ultimately terminate in a war of extermination between the white and black races." This deft combination of eighteenth-century political ideology and racial phobia proved powerful and pliable, as useful against cooperationists and outright Unionists as against Northern politicians. Opponents of secession in Tennessee, claimed the editor of the *Memphis Appeal,* had formed a coalition held together only by the search for public "plunder."[33] Equating secession with disinterested patriotism transformed the opposition into self-seeking knaves.

Once the Southern people stood up to Yankee bluster and stopped their own bickering, they could escape contaminating Northern influences and reestablish political purity. Secessionists reveled in their vision of a glorious political future, however general and imprecise it might be. Sharply contrasting Southern virtue to Northern vice, they promised to form a new government based, as one editor phrased it, on "safe and salutary ideas of republican simplicity and economy." No longer would selfish men make politics a profession; a glorious past of wise statesmanship would be restored. Low taxes, limited government, and civic virtue would characterize a perfected republic built on the twin foundations of white liberty and black slavery.[34]

Rejecting a model of politics based on competition and compromise, secessionists hoped to construct a commonwealth resting on social harmony, political consensus, and unquestionable legitimacy.[35] Public life would become an arena for public service rather than public thievery; virtuous leaders would wield power to serve the interests of the entire community. Parties and patronage would have no place in this purified political culture. Despite the reforming and moralistic character of this new system, radicalism would be avoided, and secessionists continued to struggle with the paradoxes of a "conservative revolution." Paternalism, social hierarchy, and a careful balance of elitism and democracy still shaped any blueprints for the South's political future.

Yet such lofty aspirations meant little in the absence of Southern unity. Clever Northern politicians would first divide, then conquer, and finally impose their tyranny on the Southern states and people. Therefore, invocations of harmony and calls for cooperation between old political enemies were neither pro forma nor empty. They formed the warp and woof of an emerging nation woven together by powerful strands of traditional republican beliefs about power and liberty. In words that had profound meaning in a culture greatly influenced by evangelical Protestantism, Governor Andrew B. Moore implored the people of Alabama to act as "brethren," to "stand shoulder to shoulder in the great work before us." Even some cooperationists, who conceded the inevitability of disunion, prepared for the unavoidable. Acquiescence, or accepting the verdict of the people, or bowing to the need for unity became watchwords for these men and their constituents.[36]

Proclaiming the need for harmony and the burial of old political quarrels struck a responsive note among a people increasingly disgusted with political parties. Secessionists especially stressed the dangers to liberty posed by the Republican party with conventional warnings about the tyranny of an antislavery majority and the prospect of enslavement to a sectional party. More important, they urged their own people to abandon old party loyalties. No longer would Southerners be Democrats or Whigs, or even secessionists or cooperationists. Instead, the South would become a harmonious political culture without the divisive influence of partisanship. More than a decade of disillusioning encounters with national parties and their leaders had led many Southerners to embrace secession without following the cautionary advice of once powerful and respected party men.[37] At last the people were heeding old warnings about the dangers of party. Clever demagogues had lost their mesmerizing influence, and the South would now assume her rightful place among the nations of the world—a model of political rectitude and a beacon to anyone seeking escape from politics as usual. Again fire-eaters and veteran politicos alike could rally around an antiparty ideology.

From Virginia to Georgia, from South Carolina to Texas, the "no party" cry rang out as Southerners deliberated the wisdom of secession. In speeches, petitions, and editorials, they vowed to abandon partisan warfare.[38] Although secession sentiment was strongest in the Deep South states, where the old party system had nearly disappeared, the relationship between secession and party was reciprocal. If the absence of party encouraged sectional extremism, sectional extremism also helped complete the destruction of political parties.

By the beginning of 1861, secessionists and cooperationists tried to outdo one another in denouncing the evils of partisanship while accusing their opponents of promoting divisiveness. Secessionist Democrats, the leading editorial spokesman for North Carolina Whiggery declared, had always lived on "party issues, party cries and caucuses, party conventions, party proscriptions, and party spoils." Their appeals for harmony rang hollow and hypocritical. Unionist William W. Holden—himself a tireless Democratic wire-puller—feared that parties would plague and bedevil any Southern confederacy, leading to endless controversies, high taxes, slave insurrections, and military despotism.[39]

The survival of party competition in the upper South slowed the progress of secession because many cooperationists still believed traditional political mechanisms were capable of securing a Union-saving compromise. Attacks on secessionist Democrats carried weight in states where remnants of the Whig and American (Know-Nothing) parties still constituted a potent opposition. Yet however much upper South cooperationists of various stripes might cling to old loyalties, they hardly sang the praises of political parties.[40] By necessity, the opponents of secession engineered coalitions without regard to party, patching up old quarrels in hope of delaying disunion. Just as secessionists had urged their followers to cast aside party considerations to unite the South, so cooperationists advised the people, as Holden put it, to "rise above party" to save the Union. What seems most notable about the entire secession debate is that both sides resorted to similar arguments expressed in nearly identical language. Warnings about corruption, demagoguery, and above all the influence of party appeared in the speeches and writings of Southerners of all political persuasions.[41] Little wonder Southern voters felt confused and uncertain as they cast their ballots during the elections for the secession conventions.

Nor is it surprising that the results of these elections bewildered contemporaries and have baffled historians ever since. Some candidates ran unopposed; in highly competitive districts, candidates sometimes retreated from their earlier, more extreme positions or simply dodged the central question of disunion. Because there was little time for campaigning, distinctions between secessionism and the varying shades of cooperationism could not have been entirely clear even to political sophisticates.

Many voters must have looked for the familiar names of candidates they had supported in the past. In the absence of extensive canvassing and often with confusion about a candidate's position, party affiliations provided the Southern electorate with at least some direction. Especially in the upper South, voters still looked to old party leaders for guidance.[42]

Yet in the midst of all this confusion (which probably goes a long way toward explaining the sharp drop-off in voter turnout from the presidential election), party considerations no longer determined electoral choices. Thus despite strong correlations between Whig and cooperationist strength in the border states, the influence of party grew steadily weaker. A coalition of Whiggish slaveholders and nonslaveholding Whigs and Democrats gave Unionism considerable strength in the upper South, but this tenuous alliance could survive only if a sectional peace settlement was negotiated quickly, and secessionists could afford to bide their time. In the lower South, former Whigs were divided, and Democratic unity was more apparent than real. In some states, the secession debates nearly obliterated party lines, a political development welcomed by fire-eater and conservative alike.[43] All across the South, the more ardent secessionists took advantage of political fragmentation, hesitation, and the sense of crisis to press their case.

If Southern voters failed to speak in a clear voice during the convention elections, the secession conventions themselves only added to the confusion. Because the legislatures continued to meet in all the Southern states, the conventions occupied a constitutionally anomalous position. Although secessionists had long maintained that only sovereign conventions could take a state out of the Union, beyond making this decision their authority was nebulous. Theoretically, these state conventions acted in the interests of the people and would not wrangle about patronage, per diems, or other extraneous matters; statesmanship rather than low politics was supposed to characterize the proceedings. But governors and legislatures sooner or later grew suspicious, especially when conventions proceeded to rewrite state constitutions, enact military legislation, make appointments, and steadily encroach on executive and legislative authority.[44] As a result, the already established branches of state government became embroiled with the secession conventions in battles for political control.

In states with solid secessionist majorities, cooperationists typically argued that the conventions were not sovereign bodies, that they lacked even the authority to make a final decision on disunion. Nevertheless, many of the conventions loosely and expansively defined their own powers with little consideration for constitutional niceties. In North Carolina, the resulting political tensions ran so high by the fall of 1861 that members of the legislature were threatening to abolish the convention, and convention members considered doing the same to the legislature. Behind the arid legal controversies, ambitious politicians maneuvered for advantage. Any hostile action by the legislature, claimed Weldon N. Edwards, president of the secession convention, "savors of revolution." To allow the legislature to abolish the convention would be to surrender to the illegitimate force of "popular majorities." Should that happen, the "days of the republic are numbered."[45]

Despite their often technical nature, these discussions sounded several ominous notes. A rhetoric of liberty had driven the South toward secession, but obviously the same rhetoric could be turned against the secessionists. Differences between secessionists and cooperationists could perhaps be put aside in the early euphoria of independence or in the initial outburst of patriotism after Fort Sumter, but the persistence of dissent signified lingering disagreement over the new nation's political culture. In only a short time, libertarians would turn their oratorical guns on the Confederate government.

Delegates in the Deep South and, after Lincoln's call for troops, those in the upper South as well, supported secession by fairly lopsided majorities, though this apparent unanimity was deceiving, and on preliminary roll calls the results were often close. Most cooperationists, however, soon gave up (sometimes in defiance of the wishes of the people who had elected them) and voted for the ordinance of secession. One Alabamian admitted doing so even though he considered disunion little better than treason.[46] The uncertain outcome of the elections and the convoluted parliamentary maneuvering of the conventions revealed critical fault lines in what at first glance appeared to be a solid bedrock of determination.

One of the most serious fissures was the continuing dispute between secessionists and cooperationists on the philosophical but all-important question of sovereignty. For radicals to speak of sovereign conventions was no mere constitutional fine point, as their opponents well understood. In virtually all the states, perhaps merely as a delaying tactic but also out of conviction, cooperationists moved to submit ordinances of secession to the people for ratification. Typically, cooperationists could marshal more support for this proposition than any other during convention roll calls.[47] Secessionists refused to be sidetracked by such maneuvers, and though the elections that had taken place early in 1861 had slowed the momentum for secession in some states, it is doubtful whether letting the voters decide would have reversed the decision of any convention.

Sporadic newspaper discussion kept questions of sovereignty and ratification before the public. Few precedents for limiting the powers of the secession conventions existed because antebellum constitutional conventions in the Southern states had routinely exceeded their delegated authority. Naturally the fire-eaters could not openly express distrust of the people when outraged cooperationists insisted the voters had to approve the decision for secession. One embittered Unionist even made the dubious claim that most South Carolinians actually opposed the Southern revolution.[48] Disputes over whether the Southern people preferred immediate secession or some form of cooperative action intensified suspicion about the antidemocratic character of disunion.

All the old cooperationist fears welled to the surface. How could the radicals claim to be riding the crest of public opinion when they were unwilling to let the people render the final verdict? Why did conventions meet in secret sessions unless a destructive and noisy minority was plotting to override the will of a conservative majority? A Virginia editor compared his state's secession convention to the Federalist-controlled Hartford Convention held during the War of 1812; a Louisiana newspaper proclaimed the convention there a "Star Chamber, where the light of the sun never reaches"; a Mississippi journalist blasted the delegates meeting in Jackson as a "dictatorial oligarchy." Showing they could match secessionist rhetoric about despotism and corruption, cooperationists charged that politicians long steeped in the ways of Washington wire-pulling and jobbery were now maneuvering to seize the offices in any new confederacy and lining up to raid the treasury.[49] Although such arguments might have further divided Southerners and probably alarmed the more nervous Southern rights men, they actually indicated the political weakness and desperation of the cooperationists more than any die-hard opposition to secession.

Most conservatives simply went along with the decisions of the secession conventions because continued insistence on popular ratification laid them open to charges of "submissionism." In the Alabama convention, one cooperationist after another, though admitting to still having reservations about secession, pledged support for the ordinance once it was enacted and promised stout resistance to Black Republicanism. This impressive show of unity could not, however, entirely assuage old political enmities. Yancey deemed secession an "irresistible tide" and denied there was any reason to submit the decision of the Alabama convention to the people. Moreover, in a republic—as opposed to a democracy based on the "tyranny" of mere numbers—there was no precedent for restricting the authority of a sovereign convention. Despite Yancey's reputation as a radical agitator, such arguments were effective. Even the thirty-three delegates in the Alabama convention who at first refused to sign the ordinance of secession denied any intention of promoting public opposition once the convention adjourned.[50]

Indecisive leadership and divisions in their own ranks plagued cooperationists throughout the early months of 1861. Men who should have been pillars of strength, such as Alexander H. Stephens, fell silent. Conservative politicians suddenly manifested a strange passivity, a debilitating lassitude that allowed the secessionists to seize the initiative. In pleading with William A. Graham to oppose secession more openly and vigorously, Burgess Gaither admitted that North Carolina had few "reliable" men who would "stand firm, and stem the current of misrule in wild and revolutionary times like the present." Instead, the reticence of Union men—and for Gaither this especially meant former Whigs—allowed "locofocos" to plot the "downfall of our government." Nor could cooperationists afford to wait long for their leaders to act. Fearing that South Carolina would be the "head" and his own Texas the "tail" of any new Southern government, Robert H. Taylor looked back fondly on the days when Whig and Democratic leaders had been determined to preserve the Union at all costs.[51] This longing for the politics of the past suggested resignation, bewilderment, and perhaps hopelessness among the cooperationists.

Even in the upper South after Lincoln's inauguration, the opposition appeared demoralized and unable to muster its full strength against secession. The confusion of labels—"conservative," "cooperationist," "Unionist"—symbolized the difficulty. Some border state leaders were unconditional Unionists, others opposed secession but would resist any attempt to coerce the seceding states back into the Union, and still others adopted more complex positions. When the unyielding attitudes of both Republicans and Gulf state secessionists shattered hopes for sectional compromise, cooperationist leaders could not hold their fragile coalitions together.[52]

About the best cooperationists could hope for was to delay secession or win minor concessions. Yet timing was everything, and conservatives could ill afford to drag their feet too long once disunion had become an accomplished fact—especially when fire-eaters and other secessionists kept tightening the political screws. Ever since the presidential election, both sides had downplayed their differences and emphasized a common commitment to Southern interests. Cooperationists had stoutly denied being submissionists who would kowtow to a Black Republican administration. By the same token, secessionists generally tried to placate the opposition by appealing to state and regional patriotism.

Such conciliatory efforts, however, often failed to alleviate persistent bitterness and suspicion. In the Alabama convention, the cooperationist minority bristled when Yancey denounced as a traitor any delegate who continued to oppose secession after the convention's vote. Yancey also branded his opponents "Tories" and accused them of being in league with Northern abolitionists. This potent juxtaposition of republicanism (in the historical reference to the American Revolution) with the politics of slavery gave voice to what other, more judicious secessionists were thinking and perhaps saying privately. Rising to the bait, outraged conservatives objected to such language and again criticized their opponents for refusing to submit the ordinance of secession to the people. Angry delegates from northern Alabama even hinted at the possibility of armed resistance.[53]

Elsewhere, talk of political proscription became commonplace. Cooperationists suspected that Breckinridge Democrats planned to consign Douglas and Bell supporters to political exile, and they continued to blast disunionists as corrupt patronage-seekers. For all their hyperbole, these attacks did not entirely miss the mark. In states such as North Carolina, secessionists did try to exclude their opponents from positions of public trust and especially positions of profit. As early as December 1860, the legislature had taken the state printing contract away from outspoken Unionist William W. Holden and awarded this plum to his secessionist rival John Spelman. Some editors even suggested hanging fainthearted men who hesitated to support the Southern cause.[54]

Such wild talk only generated more political heat without addressing the critical question of how to restore unity once disunion had occurred. Some states required public officials to take a simple loyalty oath or certify that they had not sworn an oath of allegiance to the United States Constitution or government since the passage of the state's secession ordinance. For North Carolinians this question produced a brief political ruckus. At the end of 1861, the bolder secessionists pushed for a test oath. Any adult white male who refused to take the oath would be banished from the state. Although the convention voted the measure down overwhelmingly, its mere consideration revealed gaping political wounds left in the wake of a rancorous secession debate. In a carefully prepared and powerful speech, William A. Graham denounced loyalty tests as "antiquated instruments of oppression and despotism . . . wholly at war with all our ideas of free republican government." Such measures would be ineffective against traitors, would dishearten many loyal men, and would allow "a faction in the possession of temporary power, to convert the government into an oligarchy, expel their opponents from the State, and riot upon the substance they had left." For Southerners to imitate the practices of English and Yankee tyrants would be to sacrifice both liberty and honor. After the proposed test oath was defeated, Holden congratulated North Carolinians on standing united against Northern aggression, thereby rendering any effort to limit civil liberties unnecessary.[55] The sarcasm in this editorial reflected a renewed scramble for political—and in North Carolina one might even say partisan—advantage. The act of secession had failed either to purify the political process or lay to rest political, economic, and social conflicts in the Tar Heel State or elsewhere.

Continuing political warfare made fire-eaters and conservatives alike even more jittery about the possible course of a Southern revolution. For example, class appeals in deeply divided states revived proposals for the ad valorem taxation of slaves. This was especially true in North Carolina, where slaveholders had traditionally paid a poll tax on their slaves, receiving liberal exemptions for children and elderly blacks. Comparatively, more valuable slaves were lightly taxed. The so-called Opposition party (primarily former Whigs) had come out in favor of taxing slaves according to their value (the ad valorem principle) to finance a mushrooming state debt. Even though Democrats hysterically decried ad valorem taxation as the first step toward abolition, Whigs made substantial gains throughout the state in the 1860 elections. The secession crisis and the later wartime need for even more revenue brought the issue to the fore once again. The North Carolina convention eventually adopted a watered-down version of ad valorem taxation, but the controversy remained lively throughout the war's first year.[56]

As Unionists had been quick to point out, secession clouded the economic future of the South after a decade of unprecedented prosperity. Besides the always contentious matter of taxation, depressed markets and uncertain credit created alarm from Virginia to Texas. In something of a panic, secession conventions and state legislatures hastily passed stay laws temporarily suspending debt collections. Such measures, which often gave special consideration to soldiers' families, generally expired at the end of 1861 but in most states were eventually extended for the duration of the war. Angry merchants, lawyers, and many newspaper editors claimed that stay laws would ruin business and violate the sacred rights of contract.[57] Consideration of relief for debtors, moreover, exacerbated class tensions and hampered efforts to build public support for the new Confederate and state governments.

During the fall and winter of 1861, discussion of the stay law in North Carolina created arguments reverberating from the moral economy of republicanism and old Jacksonian controversies over money and credit. John McMannen, a minister and manufacturer of corn shellers, warned William A. Graham that without a workable stay law the convention risked a "Revolution at home." But defenders of property rights raised a formidable outcry. The beneficiaries of credit relief, declared veteran politico Bartholomew F. Moore, "are the profligate, the spendthrifts, [and] reckless insolvents." Heeding such opposition, the state convention in early 1862 voted to postpone the consideration of a stay law.[58]

Stay laws, ad valorem taxation, and test oaths barely touched the lengthening list of problems arising from the disruption of the Union. State and Confederate leaders faced not merely a political crisis but a constitutional one. Military and financial questions, of course, commanded most of their attention, but they also had to address explosive political issues. Not only would a Confederate government have to be constructed from the ground up, but the states would also have to wrestle with the constitutional implications of disunion.

Yet politicians were ill-prepared for the task, often having only the haziest notions about the South's political future. The rhetoric of classical republicanism, with its incessant warnings about usurpation and corruption, had set the political tone during the secession crisis. Most Southerners better understood the sort of government they wished to avoid than the sort they hoped to create. The messages of both secessionists and cooperationists had been largely negative. Ambivalence about democracy, competing definitions of Southern republicanism, class antagonisms, and even uncertainties about the precise relationship of slavery to Southern separatism left many important political questions hanging. Whether as delegates in the secession conventions rewriting state constitutions or as Confederate representatives meeting in Montgomery to draft an organic law for the seceding states, these leaders would have to begin charting the South's political destiny. Fire-eaters and cooperationists alike had come to embrace antiparty ideology and calls for political purification. Like the founding fathers of the American republic, they had the priceless opportunity of being present at the creation of a new nation.

CHAPTER 3

The Crisis of Southern Constitutionalism

The memoirs and other writings of Confederate politicians seem dry and inaccessible to modern readers because of their obsession with constitutional minutiae. For many Southerners, that favorite phrase of Charles Dickens's Mr. Snagsby, "Not to put too fine a point upon it," had no application to constitutional questions. From Calhoun's day onward, no constitutional point was too fine, too small, or too subtle to escape notice of men capable of spinning out elaborate arguments around the slightest historical precedent or obscure technicality.

The birth of a Southern nation began with the creation of organic law for both the states and the Confederacy. The timing for such a vast, uncertain enterprise could hardly have been worse as the possibility of civil war loomed. The state secession conventions and the Montgomery convention met when Southerners were divided over disunion and the future status of the border states hung in the balance. Projects for reconstructing the old Union were still afoot, and old party quarrels and burning ambition made for short tempers and sharp debate.

Even before delegates assembled in Montgomery to draft a Confederate constitution, the secession conventions began amending the state constitutions. Apparently minor changes signaled the beginning of a revolution against politics. On January 18, 1861, the Florida convention enacted an ordinance reducing the governor's term from four years to two but also providing that the present governor (John S. Milton) serve until 1865.[1]

With this step, the convention simultaneously struck a blow against executive power and spared people the distraction of a gubernatorial canvass in the midst of a possible civil war.

Perhaps Southerners could escape the supposed evils of the old political order. For planter-aristocrats, conservative Whigs, and anyone else who had deplored the democratization of Southern politics, secession offered an opportunity to reverse the historical tide. Private laments about universal suffrage and democratic excesses percolated into public discussions of constitutional reform. Cooperationists in the Arkansas convention, for example, suspected disunionists of planning to restore property requirements for officeholding and voting. Delegates in several states proposed ending the popular election of judges. Of course, anyone sensitive to public opinion, especially in the politically volatile border states, would not push reactionary proposals too far, but sometimes prejudice overrode judgment. When Arkansas's gubernatorial election was moved from August to October, a Whig waggishly remarked that holding the election in colder weather would at least force the Democrats to wear shoes when they voted.[2] Few politicians could openly condemn democracy, and fewer still seriously favored restrictions on the franchise, but the tensions between elitist and popular politics persisted throughout the Confederacy's brief life.

Shifting political alliances, general disarray, and voter apathy further complicated the process of constitutional revision. The discussion of constitutional questions occurred either behind closed doors or before a largely indifferent public. Immediate secessionists and cooperationists eyed each other warily, and remnants of the old party system made reaching any consensus more difficult.

The result was often constitutional and political stalemate. For example, the former Whigs who controlled the writing of a new constitution in Georgia proved to be timid. Perhaps cooperationist reservations about both the sovereignty of the Georgia secession convention and its authority to draft a new state constitution made most delegates hesitant to press for far-reaching constitutional changes. Despite much discussion about the nature of representation (a few delegates even favored returning to the old British concept of virtual representation), the most significant suggestion was to enlarge state senatorial districts from one county to three. Provisions for appointing rather than electing state judges and for denying the legislature's right to amend the constitution received little notice outside the convention.[3]

In the summer of 1861, when war news absorbed public attention, discussion of the new constitution was sporadic. Newspaper editors could not even decide whether the old constitution's three-fifths basis for apportioning representation had been repealed. After praising the reduction in the senate's size, the editor of the *Savannah Republican* decided that the constitution should not be ratified because slaveholders would not be adequately represented. Less than 20 percent of the eligible voters bothered to cast ballots in the July ratification election, and the constitution was approved by a margin of only 795 votes.[4] The new constitution had little effect on wartime politics, and future constitutional discussion would focus almost entirely on the relationship between Georgia and the Confederacy.

To the extent that secessionists in other states worked for a counter-revolution, they met with little success. Some fire-eaters still grumbled that democratic politics weakened the South and strengthened abolitionism, but converting such sentiments into organic law proved impossible. Virginia Whigs, led by Alexander H. H. Stuart, tried to undo the democratic reforms of the antebellum period. In a June 19 committee report to the state convention, Stuart boldly called for an end to the "despotism of king numbers." Arguing that government should primarily protect persons and property, he proposed to insulate Virginia from abolitionism, religious skepticism, free schools, and other Yankee heresies. Denouncing the twin evils of universal suffrage and popular elections, he revived the eighteenth-century argument that men who paid no taxes had no real stake in the community and held up the Virginia constitution of 1776 as a proper model for government.[5]

To Stuart and other conservatives, limiting the franchise to taxpayers and reducing the number of elected offices was vital. "Let us have no more prostitution of free principles, no more deification of popular ignorance," proclaimed the *Richmond Dispatch*, "but the sound, constitutional liberty which was the product of the wisdom and patriotism of the sages and heroes of the Revolution . . . but which have been cast away in an hour of madness for the apples of Sodom, which Yankee innovators have palmed off upon us."[6] Such striking tributes to an older republican tradition (with its skepticism about popular wisdom) led these Virginians to see themselves reclaiming and perfecting the legacy of the founding fathers.

But whatever the virtues of this program, it hardly promoted political harmony. When Stuart's committee attempted to restore franchise qualifications that had been repealed thirty years before, editor John M. Daniel of the *Richmond Examiner* exploded in a burst of Jacksonian indignation.

Whigs who had dragged their feet on secession, refused to join the army, and now sought "commissions and fat offices" would deprive poor soldiers of their liberty. Setting class against class by denying freemen their political birthright, these submissionists would destroy popular support for a Southern republic.[7]

Replying to Daniel's strictures, Whig conservatives claimed universal suffrage meant that public officials seldom looked beyond the next election. This cheapening of the franchise turned voting into a "matter of bargain and sale"—a coarsening of public life that had even corrupted the judiciary. Although delegates from the western counties defeated proposals to have the legislature choose the governor and lieutenant governor, the convention made most judgeships appointive. Many local officials would be selected by the courts, the governor, or a local council. Such halfway measures disappointed those seeking a return to the political culture of eighteenth-century Virginia. But even Edmund Ruffin conceded that if nonslaveholders were both disfranchised and drafted to fight in a war, this would "give ground for the demagogue clamor of the poor being required to defend or protect the slaves of the rich." He soon despaired of efforts to reform the state government and bewailed the influence of gutless and crooked politicians. Other constitutional conservatives, led by the *Richmond Daily Whig*, kept up a drumfire against universal suffrage and the excessive number of elected offices.[8]

Despite their disappointments at halfway measures, these men had little choice but to endorse the modest constitutional changes made by the convention and urge the voters to ratify the new constitution. Perhaps because of their reservations about the new constitution, conservatives campaigned for ratification with amazing ineptitude. In an editorial bound to anger nonslaveholders, Robert Ridgeway of the *Richmond Whig* described any man who could not pay taxes as "either too indolent, or too dishonest, or too indifferent to the welfare of the community to be made a depository of political power." Five days later, Ridgeway added that the new Southern Confederacy should "consist exclusively of gentlemen and negroes." In the March 1862 election, less than one-fifth the usual number of votes were cast, and the constitution was defeated by less than seven hundred votes.[9]

Once again the forces of political reaction had failed to place their stamp on the Southern revolution. The advent of war forestalled more extended consideration of constitutional revision, and the states' constitutional debates probably had little effect on the delegates to the Confederate convention. When these political leaders met for the first time on February 4, 1861, in Montgomery, Alabama, they began to define Southern constitutionalism on a national stage.

A small inland city with little elegance or charm, Montgomery nevertheless had an impressive neoclassical capitol that seemed a fitting birthplace for a Southern republic. Like the founding fathers of the United States over eighty years before, the delegates conducted most of their business in secret sessions. Reporters grumbled about a shortage of reliable information, but few people at first objected to the closed-door meetings, and experienced politicians hoped to avoid any public display of differences.[10]

The delegates embodied the diverse political impulses of the secession winter. To some observers, they seemed earnest Yankee-haters; to more sympathetic eyes, they personified what a Richmond editor termed an "unaffected republican simplicity." Veteran Georgia politician and influential cooperationist Alexander H. Stephens described the Confederacy's founding fathers as men of substance, character, and, most of all, impeccable conservatism. From a more radical perspective, Mary Boykin Chesnut declared that the ideal Southern politician for a new age must be "young and vigorous" and worried that too many timid old fogies long corrupted by experience in Washington would blunt the force of the Southern revolution.[11] Such contradictory hopes and expectations reflected real differences in how various Southerners envisioned their political future.

Lawyers and planters with substantial political experience dominated the convention. About 60 percent of the delegates were Democrats and 40 percent Whigs; secessionists outnumbered cooperationists by a roughly three-to-two margin. A mixture of careful thinkers, impetuous hotspurs, ambitious plotters, and political ciphers, the delegates represented a broad cross section of the South's traditional political leadership.[12] Although some delegates such as Stephens and Robert Barnwell Rhett, to cite two extreme examples, knew what sort of government they hoped to create, most had spent little time during the secession uproar pondering such questions.

Their task was daunting because in drafting a constitution they would establish new political ground rules. The uncertain attitudes of the border states required that this be done with considerable care but also with a clear, compelling vision. To break with the past and strike out boldly into a future fraught with unanticipated dangers or to play it safe and retain as much of the old constitutional system as possible seemed the most likely options.

Yet staking out a position engendered a host of complex philosophical and practical problems. At one level, the convention's mandate was clear. The secession conventions had expressed a decided and hardly surprising preference for basing any new government on the United States Constitution. Cooperationists still worried about the possibility of revolution believed that the fewer changes the better. But at the very least, a new constitution should remove the troubling ambiguities that had so disturbed the peace of the old Union. Therefore, the delegates in Montgomery could repair the defects of the original Constitution by applying the lessons of history and recent experience.[13] The difficulty was to strike the proper balance between respect for tradition and the need for innovation. This fundamental dilemma perhaps reflected the unreasonable desire of many Confederate politicians to bring about a conservative revolution—in several senses an oxymoron.

The notion of "revolution" bedeviled Southern leaders from the beginning, and even some South Carolinians believed that the representatives from their notoriously extremist state should perhaps defer to the judgment of more moderate colleagues. "In all revolutions," a Georgia editor warned, "there are sure to arise many crotchety men, with new fangled notions, and utopian dreams, offering new schemes and reforms in government."[14]

If conservatives feared revolution, the more ardent secessionists dreaded reconstruction. Although Howell Cobb confidently reported that no member of the Provisional Congress favored reunion, as might be expected, radicals such as Rhett still worried that the lukewarm and conservative men might be negotiating with Northern Democrats or other sympathetic parties. As Laurence Keitt—no moderate himself—complained, the *Charleston Mercury* considered everyone but Rhett a submissionist at heart. Rumor had it that both Stephens and Jefferson Davis held out hope for a sectional adjustment, and Virginia leaders especially looked to Montgomery for signs of moderation.[15] Although many of these fears had little basis, they nevertheless sowed seeds of division and distrust. Gossip in the corridors of the Alabama capitol revealed that serious political (and no doubt personal) animosities seethed beneath a publicly harmonious facade.

Naturally the gathering of so many veteran party leaders aggravated radicals long bred to a visceral hatred of the old party system. For the fire-eaters, Montgomery seemed too much like Washington, a place teeming with men of elastic principles. The dominance of such politicians perhaps signified politics as usual, and most of the carping and handwringing remained private. For the time being, a hopeful reporter could applaud those brave souls who had "left the Babylon of American politics to seek the far-famed Canaan of Southern desire."[16]

Fears of revolution, of reconstruction, and of Washington politicians made unity all that more imperative. Calls for harmony by both secessionists and cooperationists greeted the arriving delegates and reached a crescendo during the early spring. The secrecy of the Provisional Congress, including its special sessions as a constitutional convention, helped establish the appearance of concord. Yet old habits died hard. Thomas R. R. Cobb, a skilled lawyer and member of a powerful Georgia Democratic family, wrote to his wife after the first day of the convention that the influence of South Carolina firebrands on the one hand and Alabama reconstructionists on the other threatened to disrupt the proceedings. Nearly two months later, however, Cobb delivered a speech in Atlanta celebrating the goodwill displayed at Montgomery. Urging the people to rally around the new Southern government, he declared that the mere absence of antislavery agitators in the Confederacy would foster social and political peace. All across the South, citizens pointed to the example set by their leaders in Montgomery as a model for the Southern people.[17]

As the delegates went about their work, what made these calls for unity so necessary but also problematic was the amorphous character and uncertain intensity of Southern nationalism. Drew Faust is right that historians have too often probed the weaknesses of Confederate nationalism merely as a means to explain why the South lost the Civil War.[18] But defining Southern nationalism also involves evaluating its strength and ultimately whether it proved to be an asset or a liability to the struggling Confederacy. Historians who have dismissed Southern nationalism as a fledgling, anemic phenomenon that could not sustain wartime morale have too often rested this reasonably plausible conclusion on the doubtful premise that ambivalence and guilt over slavery planted deadly seeds of doubt and discord. Their evidence, however, is thin and unpersuasive. These same historians have more convincingly argued that many Southerners carried their reservations about secession into the war.[19] True enough, but persistent divisions and uncertainties are characteristic of most revolutions, especially movements of national liberation. To expect Southern nationalism to be the exception to the rule is to hold the Confederacy accountable to an unreasonable and ahistorical standard of judgment.

It is necessary also to remember that the foundations for Southern independence had barely been laid when the Civil War began. If the Confederacy's fighting effectiveness was hampered by a reluctant commitment to Southern nationalism, it is even more true that lost territory, heavy casualties, and economic woes ensured that the Confederates and later historians would never know whether Southern nationalism could have flourished if given a longer gestation period. Nor, as David Potter has observed, does national loyalty grow in isolation. It coexists and competes with various commitments to family, community, religion, and region. So too the lack of a common culture or other supposedly vital qualities of nationalism will not necessarily prevent a people from revolting against a colonial regime or striking a blow for "national" independence—even if the "nation" itself remains ill-defined and its prospects for success doubtful. Building on this point, Don Fehrenbacher has suggested an appropriate comparison between Confederate nationalism and the nationalism of the thirteen colonies at the beginning of the American Revolution. In neither case was there initially a strong sense of common purpose, but in both cases national identity evolved during a prolonged war despite the persistence and even the growth of internal disaffection.[20]

Nor is Fehrenbacher's analogy merely a modern historical construct. References to the spirit of '76 and the right of the people to revolt against tyranny enlivened speeches and writings of the fire-eaters and by the 1850s had become a rhetorical commonplace. By associating Northern society with French Jacobinism and other brands of radicalism, ardent Confederates laid claim to the American Revolution for themselves.[21]

Not only did the South's existence as a separate nation originate in the history of an eighteenth-century revolution, but it also promised to fulfill the shattered Union's once bright and shining promise of liberty. Suitable analogies came readily to mind. The English Parliament's logical successor was the Yankee Congress, and George III's heir apparent was Abraham Lincoln. The familiar history of the American Revolution offered a convenient framework for interpreting the unfolding story of the Southern revolution. In claiming the Fourth of July as a holiday consecrated to the celebration of "state sovereignty," the editor of the *New Orleans Picayune* simply but profoundly observed that the "Confederate States of 1861 are acting over again the history of the American Revolution of 1776."[22]

Although the Provisional Congress narrowly rejected Thomas R. R. Cobb's motion to name the new country the Republic of Washington, the delegates at Montgomery paid homage to their revolutionary forebears. Whatever its political, economic, social, and cultural weaknesses, the Confederate nation rested firmly on a well-defined historical tradition. The character of this new revolution and its national soul sprang from a reservoir of memories, from sacred images of revered patriots. The right of self-determination, deeply rooted in eighteenth-century nationalism, helped many Southerners broaden their affection for kin and local community into a powerful sense of loyalty to a cause that would eclipse differences of class and even of political ideology.[23] Confederate patriotism became alive and concrete, something real to be expressed in ways that would evoke not only emotion but action.

Language is a powerful revolutionary tool, an instrument of political and social transformation. In the act of secession, Southerners commonly used in a traditional, almost eighteenth-century, sense such words as "rights," "contract," "virtue," "corruption," and even "slavery." Sounding the tocsin, they warned of imminent danger to liberty posed by a Yankee conspiracy to enslave white Southerners by placing them under the heel of black Southerners. But their attacks on laggard politicians and their praise for ordinary people who could more easily grasp such dangers carried serious liabilities. As Lynn Hunt has commented about the French Revolution's political culture, antipolitical rhetoric can become self-defeating by fomenting hostility to all politics, including revolutionary politics. To prevent attacks on politicians, parties, and the political process from going too far, Southerners had to pledge their best efforts to restoring a mythic Eden, the ideal republic of the founding fathers.[24] In laying claim to old national holidays or in creating new ones, in commemorating selected events of the American Revolution, in pounding these images into the heads of young and old alike, the Confederates would somehow link their revolution to *the* Revolution.

At first, they simply appealed to an abstract right of revolution. Although fire-eaters had seldom if ever praised Thomas Jefferson's political doctrines (being especially leery of his assertions about human equality), they often used the Declaration of Independence to defend the right of an oppressed people to rebel against a tyrannical government.[25] The nature of this Southern rebellion, however, remained ill-defined. The right of revolution was such a latitudinarian idea that by implication it might well lead to the kind of radical—and if one dared think it—Jacobinical revolution that the cooperationists had warned against and secessionists feared.

As South Carolina was about to leave the Union, David F. Jamison, president of its secession convention, had quoted with approval the words of the French revolutionary Georges Jacques Danton: "To dare! and again to dare! without end to dare!"[26] Was he serious? Did secession mean revolution, did it mark the beginning of a bold experiment in republicanism, Southern style? Although this idea may seem paradoxical to historians, contemporary Southern leaders embraced the notion of a "conservative revolution." Indeed, Southerners could redefine revolution to suit their present situation. "Submission is revolution; Secession will be conservatism," Richmond editor John M. Daniel announced in appropriately Orwellian language. "To escape revolution in fact we must adopt revolution in form. To stand still is revolution—revolution already inflicted on us by our fanatical, unrelenting enemies." A Southern revolution would presumably harmonize with Southern traditions of state sovereignty, individual liberty, and slavery.[27]

Faith in their ability to build an ideal republic gave the Confederate revolution a hint of universalism. Perhaps the Southern states held the last best hope for liberty; perhaps the Confederacy would survive as one of the few remaining refuges from the oppression of both tyrannical monarchies and despotic majorities. This did not make Confederates into messianic crusaders bent on conquering and remaking the world, but it ennobled their cause by lending an air of broader purpose to an essentially conservative movement. In the view of one Georgia editor, the Confederacy offered the prospect of a unique experience, a revolution without a war or any "sensible shock."[28] Other Southerners of course doubted that independence could be won without bloodshed, but Confederate leaders adopted political theories designed to cushion the effects of change.

Perhaps the Confederate revolution of 1861 could replicate the revolution of 1776 without producing overblown and dangerous notions of equal rights. The proslavery ideologue George Fitzhugh even called for a return to Aristotle's belief in the natural inequality of men. Denying the existence of a social contract, he feared the triumph of a radicalism that would destroy not only order but religion. Thus the Confederates dared subscribe only to the "natural" and "conservative" elements of the American Revolution. An anonymous pamphleteer warned that the Declaration of Independence contained the seeds of democracy, a "fallacious theory" of utopian origin that undermined the divinely ordained foundations of government. Should the Confederates follow the lead of the North and build a political system based on a misplaced faith in weak and sinful human beings, Southerners would soon bring anarchy down upon their heads. For Confederate fanatics, biblical and historical analogies offered harsh judgments against their own democratic politics. Although explicit defenses of aristocracy were relatively rare—especially considering the fragility of the Confederate coalition—many Southerners longed for a monarch or a Caesar or a Napoleon to ensure national salvation.[29]

Yet even for many extremists, the reality of politics forced much trimming and backtracking. Given the inroads of democratic politics in the old South, few politicians dared openly disparage the people's wisdom. A balancing of ideology and practicality gave peculiar twists to what appeared at first to be simple antidemocratic rhetoric. Traditional republican theory, for example, held that governments resting on numerical majorities could not adequately represent or protect property. An essayist in the *Southern Literary Messenger* alarmingly described a democracy of paupers developing in Massachusetts, where the "shoe-maker [Henry] Wilson, and low demagogue [Charles] Sumner fill the places of [Daniel] Webster and [Edward] Everett." But the slaveholding South had fortunately adopted "universal" suffrage for only half the population and therefore could avoid ruinous conflict between capital and labor. These generalizations conveniently ignored the question of how white democracy actually functioned in the Southern states. Privately, Robert Barnwell, who served in both the provisional and permanent Confederate Congresses, admitted that politicians from the South Carolina low country could shun deceptive electioneering because they represented only "immense estates and negroes."[30] By implication, these rotten boroughs preserved slaveholders' political hegemony beneath a veneer of democracy.

But rather than stirring up the fears of proud yeomen and suspicious cooperationists by arousing sensitive social and class feelings, the more prudent secessionists—no matter how reactionary their private convictions—used antiparty rhetoric as a unifying force. Even if party organizations were necessary to free governments, their invariable tendency undermined what the author of an important article in *De Bow's Review* called "any well-regulated scheme of liberty." Through their control of political patronage, parties became the "ready instruments of despotic power." The new Southern government therefore needed to cast aside "factionists, village lawyers, pot-house politicians, and party myrmidons." For if the young Confederacy ever fell under the sway of the "hirelings of party or the venal apologists for licentiousness and excess, its career as a nation will be as brief and inglorious, and the night of its degradation will commence with its rising sun."[31]

Delegates to the Montgomery convention would have largely agreed with such sentiments, but the pressing nature of their work precluded extensive debate on the finer points of political theory. The early decision to draft both provisional and permanent constitutions, to create both provisional and permanent governments, placed a premium on acting with dispatch. Christopher G. Memminger of South Carolina had arrived in Montgomery with a draft proposal for a provisional constitution. Designed to relieve border state anxieties about the reportedly revolutionary designs of the secessionists, Memminger's document closely resembled the United States Constitution. A committee of the Provisional Congress tinkered with it for only two days, and on February 8, 1861, the Provisional Constitution received the unanimous approval of the convention.[32]

On its face, the drafting of a permanent Confederate constitution appears to have been equally simple. On February 9, the Provisional Congress appointed a committee of twelve; on February 28 the committee presented its report to the Provisional Congress sitting as a constitutional convention; on March 11, following extended discussion and the adoption of several amendments, the convention unanimously approved the final draft.[33] But neither the political dynamics nor the significance of the document have been well understood. Looking at how closely the Permanent Constitution resembled the United States Constitution, historians have concluded that more sober politicians seized the reins of power from the fire-eaters in Montgomery.[34]

Yet Robert Barnwell Rhett chaired the committee that drafted the Permanent Constitution, and he had come to Alabama eager to transform his region's politics. Rhett believed that the Confederacy must be a slaveholders' republic in the purest sense. This meant eliminating the constitutional prohibition against the African slave trade, repealing the three-fifths clause, and excluding free states from the Confederacy. Rhett also hoped to establish the right of secession firmly in the constitution, secure the principle of free trade, and end federal judicial review of state court decisions. He could not persuade enough other delegates on most of these points, but this hardly meant that Rhett considered either himself or the Permanent Constitution a failure.

As the *Charleston Mercury* observed shortly before the convention assembled, the real task of the Southern Congress was to frame a truly republican government free from Northern perversions. This meant an end to the "vulgar and irresponsible tyranny of the majority of voters . . . trampling the minority under their feet as opportunity and inclination urge." The editorial concluded with a warning and a challenge: "It now remains to be seen whether, with slave institutions, the master race can establish and perpetuate free government."[35] Eliminating old abuses of political power and preempting the formation of political parties became just as important as fulfilling the dreams of proslavery ultras.

More down-to-earth practical political considerations held sway as well. Two months before the Montgomery convention assembled, a conservative South Carolinian described Rhett as "so damned impractical, that I am afraid he will kick up hell in the [South Carolina] convention." Even ardent secessionist T. R. R. Cobb, who admired Rhett as a "generous hearted and honest man," worried that he had a "vast quantity of cranks and a small proportion of common sense." Indeed, Rhett's program promised to wreak havoc in the border states. Free trade, reopening the African slave trade, and eliminating the three-fifths clause horrified upper South conservatives already skeptical of disunion. If South Carolina extremists controlled the new government, why should Virginia or North Carolina even consider joining the Confederacy?[36]

Searching for a way to placate the slaveholding states still in the Union became the focus of discussion in the Provisional Congress. The more inflexible members called for the convention to remedy the defects of the old government without regard to opinion outside the seceding states. Less than a week before the firing on Fort Sumter, Thomas R. R. Cobb still maintained a studied indifference to the future of the border states and even worried that their admission to the Confederacy might shatter the harmony of the new government. Other delegates displayed a political tactlessness guaranteed to irritate folks from Arkansas to Virginia. Congressman William T. S. Barry of Mississippi, for instance, suggested the Confederate states stop purchasing slaves from any state that refused to leave the Union. He saw no reason for doing business with people who wished to dump their surplus slave population while maintaining allegiance to an abolition government.[37]

Such statements reinforced fears of border state moderates that Deep South radicals might gain political ascendancy. The most compelling evidence was the debate over reopening the African slave trade—a measure sure to send prices for slaves in the upper South plummeting. For much of the 1850s, the slave trade question had been the hobby of a small but articulate group of extremists who had sought to hasten disunion by forcing Southerners to stand for a measure sure to alienate the entire North, much of the upper South, and any lukewarm secessionists in the Gulf states.[38] After Lincoln's election, advocates of the slave trade redoubled their efforts in what many Southern rights men saw as defiance of political expediency and common sense.

At a time when soothing the fears of the border states seemed primary, this dangerous question refused to die. It first arose when the state conventions drafted instructions for their Montgomery representatives. Even secessionists who thought it politically unwise to reopen the trade claimed to have no moral qualms about the traffic. In the Alabama convention, the delegates wrangled over whether to condemn the African slave trade on grounds of policy or principle. On January 25, 1861, a brief debate occurred that touched on all the sensitive questions. Would reopening the trade depress cotton prices and flood the state with a large black population? In the name of consistency, how could slavery be defended and the slave trade condemned? What obligation did Alabama have to serve as a market for border state slaves, especially if these same states refused to leave the Union? Even Yancey doubted the wisdom of reopening the African slave trade, but he proposed a ban on importing slaves from outside the Confederacy.

Other delegates looked for cover behind a general statement extolling slavery as a "moral, social, and political blessing." With only three delegates opposed, the convention finally agreed to an innocuous resolution condemning the international slave trade strictly on policy grounds and instructing the state's Confederate delegation to oppose any motion to reopen the trade.[39] Despite the compromise, a fuse had been lit to a keg of political dynamite.

For the time being, however, an explosion was averted. All across the Deep South, Southern rights men worked diligently to contain the damage caused by a handful of extremists. It was no easy task. A brief floor debate in the Mississippi convention ended in confusion and anger all round; in Louisiana, the delegates could not even agree to dodge the issue. The Georgia convention adopted an ordinance continuing the federal ban on the African slave trade but reducing the penalties for violators. Commissioners from the Gulf states assured border state politicians that no one seriously expected the African slave trade to reopen. Hoping to escape from what a Mississippi editor termed a great political "humbug," most secessionists loudly, publicly, and hopefully declared the matter settled.[40]

Still trying to delay if not prevent secession, some cooperationists seized on the slave trade question to keep the fears of Deep South radicalism alive. Ignoring the many secessionists who had vigorously opposed reopening the trade, cooperationists accused disunionists of conniving to make border state slaves worthless. Taking a much different tack, an enraged Virginian charged that slave traders in Richmond were raising money to spread secessionist propaganda. Whatever the inconsistency in these arguments, many upper South politicians believed that any effort by the Confederate government to reestablish the international slave trade would be politically suicidal.[41]

They need not have worried. Most of the delegates to the Montgomery convention regretted that the issue had ever been raised. On March 5, a motion to remove the slave trade prohibition from the Permanent Constitution received no support outside South Carolina and Florida. Although many border state moderates must have breathed a sigh of relief, the always troublesome William W. Holden charged that the Confederacy was already being divided by the "rule or ruin" South Carolinians.[42]

The crushing defeat of the program to revive the slave trade briefly angered and alienated Southern extremists. Rhett's *Mercury* considered the action of the Provisional Congress "shortsighted, weak, sentimental." Zealots believed that reopening the slave trade was crucial to their hopes for a slaveholders' republic, and arguments for moderation in the interest of enlarging the new Confederacy carried little weight. It all came down to a matter of principle. "Either Negro slavery is a beneficent, merciful, God-chartered institution, or it is not," claimed William Gilmore Simms. "If beneficent, why limit it?"[43] But such foolish consistency, for such it was, attracted little support. Even Rhett and the *Mercury* crowd dropped the question once the convention approved the Permanent Constitution.

Most Southerners believed that with perfectly clear conscience and sound reasoning they could oppose the international slave trade *and* uphold slavery. After all, the Confederacy created at Montgomery *was* a slave republic. The "cornerstone" of the new government, declared Alexander Stephens in a much-quoted speech delivered on March 21, 1861, in Savannah, "rests upon the great truth, that the negro is not equal to the white man; that slavery—subordination to the superior race—is his natural and normal condition." Jefferson Davis and other Confederate leaders may not have welcomed this bald pronouncement of Southern racial dogma, preferring to stress constitutional questions and independence, but they could hardly deny that Stephens had accurately stated a central tenet of orthodox Southernism.[44]

In calls for unity, secessionists typically referred to the Southern states' "common institutions." Less euphemistically, a Richmond editor asserted that slavery "strengthened and improved" national character by purifying Southern life and insulating it from the "universal liberty and equality, universal elections, absolute majorities, eternal demagogism, and free competition, [that] have leveled, degraded, demoralized, and debased Northern society."[45]

Although proslavery intellectuals had routinely referred to the horrors of emancipation, secession exacerbated racial, class, and ideological anxieties. Besides the usual references to Santo Domingo or Haiti and appeals to racial phobias, many secessionists agreed with the Louisiana physician who declared that the Southern states could either build their own nation based on slavery as the "integral link in the grand progressive evolution of human society" or face "Africanization." Should white Southerners supinely submit to the dictates of a Black Republican administration, they would become, in the words of a young Georgian, Susan Cornwall, "as degenerate as our slaves, to be whipped into obedience at the command of our self-styled masters."[46] Such language evoked the grimmest nightmare of a slaveholding society, but it also laid the groundwork for sustaining an independent national identity.

The foundations of Southern republicanism and of an emerging Confederate political culture rested on slavery. Constitutional liberty, states' rights, and political virtue itself, so ran the argument, depended on the delicately balanced relations between races, classes, families, and communities found in a slave society.[47] If the Southern people were to be rallied behind this dream of national greatness, social harmony must be safeguarded. For those with an unshakable faith in slavery, this posed no theoretical and few practical problems. To Georgia governor Joseph E. Brown, slavery promoted "virtue and intelligence" in the people by making every white man part of the "ruling class." Because abolition would depress wages and prove ruinous to poor whites, "it naturally follows that our whole social system is one of perfect homogeneity of interest, where every class of society is interested in sustaining the interest of every other class."[48]

In lyrical tributes to the organic unity of Southern society, many Confederates deftly sidestepped troublesome class considerations by asserting that all white men belonged to the slave states' only true aristocracy. Thus the common whites should never be misled by Northern abolitionists or Southern traitors trying to stir up envy and class prejudice. Governor Francis W. Pickens of South Carolina hoped that the South would create a republic based on labor by an "inferior caste" and founded on "conservative principles."[49]

Did nonslaveholders buy these arguments? Many contemporary Southerners thought so, and even though historians have disagreed over whether to emphasize primarily the racial or class aspects of slavery, they generally have concluded that the yeomen and poor whites posed no immediate threat to slavery at the beginning of the Civil War.[50] This apparent support was of course tentative. Even before secession, some men announced that they would never fight to protect rich folks' slaves and lampooned the planters' social pretensions. Because political democracy failed to provide the "stability" needed to preserve the Southern social order, a conservative Georgian, J. Henly Smith, feared that slavery was doomed once "the poor men of the South . . . begin to calculate . . . [its] value . . . to them." From the other side of the class divide, a Mississippi artisan, B. C. Warner, pointedly wondered whether a slaveholding republic would best secure all people's interests. Warner complained that although the Confederacy's Permanent Constitution specifically protected slavery in the states and territories, white mechanics were already suffering by having to compete with slaves. Maintaining that slaves should perform "menial labor only," he proposed a constitutional amendment stating that "Negro Slaves Shall Not Be allowed to work in the arts of Mechanism or Be taught any arts and sciences in any What Ever." Yet in asserting that "white Men is free and Equal in this Country," Warner also tacitly accepted the central argument of proslavery ideologues.[51] For the time being, the B. C. Warners could protest these injustices without overtly challenging the peculiar institution because the general defense of slavery encompassed a wide range of opinion and interests.

Despite general agreement on securing the future of slavery, defining the exact nature of a slave republic raised more difficult problems. The balance of power between the cotton states and the rest of the South, not to mention the intricate connections of political stability, white mobility, and class relations, posed serious difficulties for the Confederacy's founding fathers. Even an opponent of reopening the African slave trade worried about the loyalty of common whites and advised the South's political leaders to "watch and control them, permitting them to have as little political liberty as we can, without degrading them."[52]

Eliminating the three-fifth basis of representation in the new Congress would have been the most logical way to increase slaveholders' influence while reducing the political power of the yeomen and poor whites. William Gilmore Simms worried that the growing white population of the border states might "overslough" the cotton states unless "we . . . make our *negroes* count as an integral part of our society and on equal terms with all." Simms even wanted to restore the old division between East and West Florida, creating another state to forestall upper South domination of a Confederate Senate. The delegates at Montgomery never seriously considered this idea, but they did struggle with the apportionment question. After a series of parliamentary maneuvers, the convention rejected Laurence Keitt's motion to repeal the three-fifths clause by a vote of four states to three.[53] Again an effort to restrain white democracy ran head-on into political reality. With the future status of the border states in doubt, most Confederate leaders hoped to avoid stirring up needless antagonism among nonslaveholders.

In early March, George Saunders, an associate of Stephen A. Douglas, was in Montgomery discussing a possible reconstruction supposedly based on the new Confederate Constitution. Determined Southern separatists acted quickly to scotch this movement. On March 8, Tom Cobb moved to prohibit the admission of nonslaveholding states to the Southern republic. But Cobb's own Georgia delegation was divided, with Stephens and Robert Toombs leading the opposition. After three days of debate the motion failed. The delegates eventually agreed to a compromise allowing for the admission of free states but requiring a two-thirds vote of approval from both House and Senate.[54] This result gave new life to reports of sentiments for compromise in the convention and greatly alarmed the fire-eaters. Both sides probably attached too much importance to this matter because it was unlikely that any free states would want to join the Confederacy, and in any case, the new nation's commitment to slavery was embedded in the Constitution.

Despite explicit acknowledgment of states' rights in the new Constitution, the delegates at Montgomery also created a potentially powerful and sovereign nation.[55] Yet even though this new government had fairly broad powers, there was a paradox woven into the Confederate Constitution. While the delegates forged a strong central government, they also restricted its authority in several politically significant ways.

Laboring to improve on the old Union and perfect their own notions of republicanism, they applied lessons of statecraft learned through painful historical experience. Fear of corruption, for example, conditioned their approach to taxation and spending. Many delegates believed that tariff laws and appropriations bills in the U.S. Congress had drained the treasury for private profit. Although Southerners differed sharply over trade policy, the Permanent Constitution prohibited protective tariffs. It also eliminated bounties for industry and, except for rivers and harbors bills, prohibited expenditures for internal improvements. Most important, a two-thirds vote in both houses was required for the passage of any appropriations not requested by the executive.

This bold attempt to end congressional logrolling and other traditional practices received wide support and seemed to portend a cleansing of Southern politics. Alexander Stephens welcomed the constitutional bans on protective tariffs and aid to internal improvements: "The question of building up class interests, of fostering one branch of industry to the prejudice of another under exercise of the revenue power, which gave us so much trouble under the old constitution, is put at rest forever under the new." So, too, limits on congressional spending would prevent the "extravagance and profligacy that existed under the old government."[56]

To curtail needless expenditures and control the congressional appetite for pork-barrel projects, delegates at Montgomery expanded the president's budgetary authority. Besides the two-thirds majority restriction on appropriations initiated by the Congress, the president also received a line-item veto that further shifted budget decisions from the legislative to the executive branch.[57] The new government could exercise its substantial powers in only limited areas. The Confederate Constitution would halt the expansion of government interference in the economy and restore a more pristine ideal of state authority. Worries about corruption and the tendency of politicians to wield power in potentially tyrannical ways suggested the influence of eighteenth-century republicanism and especially its emphasis on the dangers of unchecked rulers and the need for public rectitude.

Nor, given the antimonarchist nature of republican tradition, would the Confederacy's founding fathers establish an all-powerful chief magistrate. So even though they increased the president's executive authority, they sharply restricted his political power by fixing the length of the presidential term. By extending the term of office beyond the customary four years, many delegates hoped to insulate the president from congressional and outside political pressures, thus making him more independent. Although one Georgia delegate suggested a term of eight years, the convention eventually settled on a single six-year term. The president could therefore administer the government for a substantial period without worrying about reelection and without having to respond to every momentary political pressure. Restricting the president to a single six-year term would supposedly remove temptations of power and ambition. Alexander Stephens optimistically predicted that the president would single-mindedly seek "the good of the people, the advancement, prosperity, happiness, safety, honor, and true glory of the confederacy."[58]

Besides reducing the president's political influence, the convention struck an indirect blow against political parties and a direct one against popular democracy. For conservatives, presidential elections with their incessant canvassing, partisan warfare, and low tone had long been a national disgrace. Such campaigns aroused popular excitement without eliciting popular wisdom. During the early days of the republic, when, according to an anonymous Alabamian, "every man was a patriot," presidential elections had caused few problems. But the rise of political parties and their attendant demagoguery had debased public life. As a Georgia editor put it, presidential elections, along with even more frequent congressional contests, had dangerously increased the influence of "tricksters, ninnies, and nincompoops."[59] Such statements expressed the widely held conviction that the Confederate president—like that paragon of eighteenth-century republican virtue George Washington—should stand above petty partisan politics.

Merely reforming presidential elections, however, could hardly purify the government if the executive controlled too much patronage. Even in Jefferson's day, the president had spent an inordinate amount of time dealing with importunate politicians about piddling appointments. By the 1850s, Southern revulsion against the spoils system (especially should it fall into the hands of Republicans) had profoundly shaped political and constitutional attitudes even among party leaders. The Confederacy's Permanent Constitution therefore provided that the president could dismiss cabinet members and diplomats at will but could remove lower officials only on grounds of "dishonesty, incapacity, inefficiency, misconduct, or neglect of duty," subject to senatorial review. In addition, presidential appointees rejected by the Senate could not receive *ad interim* appointments during a congressional recess.[60] The titanic struggles over postmasterships in obscure villages were over; the age of the spoilsmen had ended and the age of the statesmen had begun. Or so it was hoped.

Robert Toombs noted perceptively that the most important changes in the new Constitution dealt with the presidency. Recent students of these constitutional debates have either emphasized the strengthening of the executive's fiscal authority or the weakening of his political influence.[61] But both are essential to understanding Confederate politics. The Confederacy's founding fathers initially had few qualms about creating a powerful presidency—or at least a powerful executive branch. The possibility of war naturally influenced their thinking, but antebellum political assumptions and experience also affected their decisions. Secessionists and cooperationists alike agreed that the president should not be a party leader but instead should stand as a patriot rallying the people to the cause of Southern independence.

"The ablest instrument ever prepared for the government of a free people," declared Howell Cobb in describing the Confederate Constitution. Others agreed that the delegates at Montgomery had dissipated fears of revolution by spurning wild theorizing in favor of accumulated historical wisdom. Believing that the Confederate Constitution preserved the best of the eighteenth-century Constitution, Stephens also praised its many improvements: "The old Constitution had been made an engine of power to crush out liberty; that of the Confederate States to preserve it."[62] With this new document, the conservative revolution seemed well launched.

Suitably enough, Robert Hardy Smith, a Whig cooperationist turned conservative secessionist, penned the most extensive exposition of the Confederate Constitution. Hoping to assuage any lingering doubts among his fellow Alabamians, he praised the "unanimity, confidence, and stability" that had characterized the Montgomery convention. "Revolution has been accomplished without anarchy," Smith exulted. Although a bit defensive about the secrecy of the Montgomery convention, he nevertheless reported that the delegates had freely discussed important constitutional questions without worrying about the misrepresentations of "news mongers and sensation telegrams." His lengthy pamphlet described how the Confederate Constitution both closely followed and significantly improved on the original Constitution. Pointing out the important changes in the presidency, Smith welcomed the end of party caucuses, platforms, and electioneering.[63] Other passages revealed a persistent antipolitical ideology, making this apologia for the Confederate Constitution a key document in understanding the evolution of Confederate politics.

Although most Southerners—including many newspaper editors—were too busy worrying and writing about the prospects of war to pay careful attention to the details, those who examined the new Constitution found much to approve. Many editorialists commended the framers for avoiding the extremes of both democracy and aristocracy. Even politicians with serious reservations about particular provisions refused to nitpick and denigrated any carping over details.[64]

The political innovations in the document won considerable praise. Several editors pronounced the old spoils system dead; others applauded reforms in the presidency. Government would become less expensive and less corrupt; republican simplicity would prevail.[65] In cataloging the virtues of their new political order, many Southerners let fancy take flight, but in the spring of 1861 the future appeared bright. The new Constitution promised the perfection of Southern republicanism, the creation of an ideal commonwealth.

Besides the grumbling of Rhett and a few other fanatics, what discontent remained focused on the process of ratification. With his usual flair for exaggeration, William W. Holden accused Confederate leaders of forcing the people to accept a Constitution they had not even read. Other critics discerned creeping despotism in the decision to have the Constitution ratified with little public discussion. Once again the secessionists had shown distrust of the people, preferring secrecy to genuine democracy. Bypassing the voters, declared one Louisiana editor, "bends not only the masses, but the property holders also, to the level of the brute creation. They must work and pay taxes, but they must not have a word to say about the adopting of a constitution or the enactment of laws."[66] Despite their obvious political purpose, such statements raised anew the fundamental question of sovereignty. Nor did the new Constitution's bow to states' rights settle the question of political legitimacy.

This sensitive issue made border state politicians even more leery of joining a government that some feared would be dominated by ambitious parvenus and cotton snobs. The North Carolina Unionist Robert P. Dick ridiculed the notion that the "hasty legislators at Montgomery" had somehow surpassed the wisdom of the founding fathers. Failing to submit the Constitution to the voters would mark the "Rubicon of public liberty." If the people truly supported disunion, as the secessionists kept telling everyone, why not hold a ratification election whose results could only strengthen the Southern cause? Several members of the Virginia convention scorned the pretensions of Confederate leaders who denounced Yankee tyranny while mistrusting their own people. Turning secessionist rhetoric on its head, former cooperationists (and in some cases future

Unionists or Confederate dissidents) accused their opponents of undermining republican government by usurping power.[67]

Spurning calls for ratification elections, Confederate leaders hauled out their most potent rhetorical weapons. Only a submissionist could doubt that the Southern people approved the Confederate Constitution, and further agitation would only play into the hands of Black Republicans. To cry "popular sovereignty" when the duly elected members of the secession conventions stood ready to speak for the people was dangerously irresponsible. At this late date, asserted one New Orleans editor, anyone who believed that Louisiana should hesitate to ratify the constitution must be an "abolitionist."[68] The all-purpose expletive had finally entered into public discussion as secessionists moved to crush their opponents by branding them traitors to the South. The tactic was as old as the politics of slavery.

Confederate leaders had momentum on their side and wherever possible gave short shrift to any protests. Infuriated cooperationists lashed out in frustration at their inability to win concessions. One Alabama delegate deprecated the "self-complacent and defiant air with which members flippantly declare that it is our duty to lead, and not to follow the people." But even parliamentary resourcefulness only postponed the inevitable. In the Louisiana convention, cooperationists successively moved to submit the Constitution to the voters, to elect a ratification convention, and to reserve the right of the state to withdraw from the Confederacy, but went down to defeat each time. The pattern held across the South. Conventions brushed aside all efforts at procedural delays and ratified the new Constitution with near unanimity.[69]

Only the South Carolina convention thoroughly discussed the merits of the Constitution. Uncompromising firebrands presented a long list of objections and needed amendments: foreclosing the admission of free states to the Confederacy, ending the three-fifths basis of representation, limiting the government's authority to levy direct taxes, granting Congress the power to prohibit the African slave trade as a matter of policy rather than principle, and abolishing the government postal monopoly. Nevertheless, Rhett along with 137 other delegates voted to ratify the Confederate Constitution. There were only 21 dissenters, but the debate reaffirmed South Carolina's reputation for impractical radicalism though even the *Mercury* conceded that the result had never been in doubt.[70] The ratification of the Constitution brought the first phase of the Confederate constitutional debate to a close. Despite extensive discussion of individual liberty and states' rights, Confederate leaders had hardly said the last word on these endless sources of contention.

They had also left two other nagging questions about the new political order unresolved. Tom Cobb addressed both in his efforts to establish the ethnic and religious purity of the new nation. Appealing to the remnants of Southern Know-Nothingism with references to the "corrupt" foreign vote, he proposed extending the naturalization period in the Constitution to ten years. Throughout the war, newspapers discussed other possible methods of restricting immigration. Bills to limit suffrage to the native-born were introduced in the conventions, legislatures, and the Confederate Congress. Some newspaper editors even warned about a possible flood of Northern immigrants who would head South, bringing with them latent abolitionism along with other noxious political and religious heresies. Franchise restrictions would supposedly discourage this migration as well as halt the spread of ignorance and crime. The Reverend Joseph Stiles even believed that God commanded the exclusion of drunken voters and the party hacks who sought their votes.[71]

Pious Southerners also hoped to make the Confederacy a holy commonwealth. Unlike the original Constitution, the Confederate instrument invoked "the favor and guidance of Almighty God." Although Cobb failed to have restrictions on Sunday labor added to the document, simple acknowledgment of divine providence boded well for the future. The creation of a Southern nation in itself signified divine blessing because the Confederate founding fathers had shunned the deism of their eighteenth-century forebears. Lieutenant Charles C. Jones, Jr., of the First Georgia Artillery rejoiced that the Confederate Constitution had been "born of prayer," unlike the old "godless" federal Constitution. On public days of fasting, humiliation, and prayer, preachers ritualistically invoked the themes of national sin and redemption. In celebrating the "conservative character" of the Confederate Constitution, Georgia's Episcopal bishop Stephen Elliott attributed its success to the "overruling spirit of God."[72]

Whatever involvement the Lord may have had in the birth of the Confederacy, Southern leaders had launched their new country onto stormy seas. Secessionists, cooperationists, Democrats, Whigs: all contributed to the effort but had not buried old political rivalries. Confederate constitutionalism mirrored the continuing theoretical and practical divisions among Southerners.

Historians have usually ignored the state constitutional debates and have described the Confederate Constitution as merely a conservative gloss on the old Constitution.[73] Yet even though the Confederacy's founding fathers revered the old Constitution, they were remarkably innovative. Changes in the presidency and restrictions on the power of Congress reduced popular influence on public policy. Had they not had to worry about the reaction of the border states, the delegates at Montgomery and perhaps in some of the state conventions might have gone much farther toward creating an elitist government.[74] Without satisfying the radicals who longed for a more purely slaveholders' republic, they had nevertheless established a distinctly Southern republic.

The question again, however, was not the South's commitment to republicanism but Southern definitions of republicanism. The republicanism embodied in the Confederate Constitution looked back into the eighteenth century before the formation of national parties. By removing slavery as a source of political division and explicitly placing it at the heart of Southern organic law, Confederate leaders had attempted to lay the foundations for social harmony. The constitutional revisions made at Montgomery were both progressive and reactionary, designed both to reform politics and to restore a mythic past.[75]

This persistent paradox of a conservative revolution would trouble the Confederacy throughout its short life. In the spring of 1861, this complex and often contradictory set of ideas was held together by the strength of antiparty ideology.[76] From antidemocratic fire-eaters, to Whiggish cooperationists, to skeptical spokesmen for a traditional yeoman democracy, Southern leaders shared a common disillusionment with American political institutions. Campaigning, stump speeches, patronage, and demagoguery had seriously weakened the Union, nearly destroyed public virtue, and fatally alienated the sections. And although Southerners could not and would not reach agreement on any detailed blueprint for their political future, they had turned their backs on the politics of their own era. The new Constitution provided a framework for a new political system, but the struggle for political legitimacy had just begun.

Establishing
Political Legitimacy

S hortly after the election of Jefferson Davis and Alexander H. Stephens as provisional president and vicepresident of the Confederate States of America, the Florida General Assembly rejoiced over the "burial of former political differences which is so much to be desired by all true lovers of their country."[1] These words reaffirmed the antiparty character of the secession movement, and for once even fire-eaters were pleased. Edmund Ruffin applauded selections made "without any previous electioneering . . . difficulty or opposition." The Montgomery delegates had avoided even the appearance of political jobbery. Stephens and Davis, Ruffin claimed, were men "who for intellectual ability and moral worth are superior to any President and Vice President elected together . . . since Madison's administration." Ruffin hoped that the Confederacy could eventually "get rid of the baleful influence of universal suffrage and popular election."[2] Although this reactionary gloss was not widespread, Southerners clearly expected Davis to become both a national statesman and a revolutionary hero.

Perhaps Jefferson Davis could be the Confederate George Washington, a man of unbending integrity and unquestionable rectitude who could rise above the partisan squabbling that had weakened the old Union. Revolutions require charismatic leadership, and although Davis by instinct and personality could hardly be a Lenin, or a Ho Chi Minh, he possessed the quiet dignity if not quite the commanding presence that had made Washington a natural leader. But even though the secession conventions had wrestled with the question of political legitimacy, Davis's task remained formidable: building a new sense of national identity among people used to thinking of themselves as citizens of small communities, of states, and of the old Union. As Lynn Hunt has cogently observed, every political culture has a "sacred center," but revolutions by their very nature attack and attempt to destroy the sacred center of the old regime. Long-standing reverence for the American Union had delayed secession and still threatened to abort the experiment in Southern separatism. It therefore became critical for the Confederates to define their own sacred center in order to justify their existence as a new republic. By appropriating the history of the American Revolution—both ideologically and symbolically—Southerners grounded their independence movement in a familiar historical tradition.[3] Yet they also needed to carve out their own version of republicanism, to create their own national icons, and, most of all, to establish the legitimacy of their government.

At the center of this new political order would stand the president of the Confederate States of America. Even before the delegates arrived in Montgomery, astute politicians were handicapping presidential candidates. Davis, Howell Cobb, Robert M. T. Hunter, Toombs, Rhett, Yancey, even Joe Brown were mentioned as possible choices. Texas fire-eater Louis T. Wigfall preferred Alexander Stephens because he could win over cooperationists and Unionists, but T. R. R. Cobb and other secessionists considered Stephens a reconstructionist at heart. Other delegates and newspaper editors agreed that only an original secessionist would do.[4] The secrecy of the selection process fueled speculation and made the election of a provisional president confusing to contemporaries and equally baffling to historians. The paucity of reliable contemporary evidence has only added to the mystery.

What is clear, however, is that after the initial round of speculation and some jockeying at Montgomery, the choice boiled down to Howell Cobb, Jefferson Davis, or Robert Toombs. In many respects, Cobb was a logical candidate. A Democrat and secessionist, but no radical, Cobb was a skillful politician and might have been an effective president. But the Georgian lacked solid support in his own state's delegation; his service as James Buchanan's secretary of the treasury had added to his reputation as a wire-puller; Toombs and Stephens were old foes and possible presidential aspirants in their own right. Even more important, Howell Cobb did not aggressively seek the office and perhaps did not want it. Although the lack of ambition expressed in a letter to his wife (and typical of Cobb at various stages of his political career) was conventional and perhaps not to be taken seriously, Tom Cobb believed that his brother "shrinks from the responsibility of the position."[5] Howell did nothing to advance his cause and inadvertently squandered his state's powerful influence.

Jefferson Davis's name appeared on every short list of likely candidates. Two weeks before the Montgomery convention had assembled, South Carolina governor Francis Pickens advised Davis that the officers of the new Southern government should be "high-toned gentlemen of exemplary honesty and firmness of character with full and thorough statesmanship and no demagogism." Pickens hardly needed to say so, but Davis seemed to fill the bill, and even though the Mississippian had served as congressman, secretary of war, and senator, he would be—again in Pickens's words— "free from the vulgar influences that have debauched and demoralized the government at Washington."[6] At the same time, Davis's vast experience would help the Confederacy handle political and diplomatic problems.

Many delegates, for instance, believed that the selection of Davis would ease upper South fears of political upheaval. Virginia cooperationists had warned that the new government would be dominated by extremists such as Rhett and Yancey. Confederate commissioners sent to the border state conventions offered public words of reassurance and private pledges of moderation.[7] Such tactics mollified cooperationists but alarmed the radical South Carolinians, already smarting from several floor defeats on constitutional questions. At the beginning of the Montgomery convention, the *Charleston Mercury* saw the Davis boom as a prelude to reconstructing the Union. The South Carolina delegation probably preferred Cobb or Toombs for president; James Chesnut, Jr., and apparently the moderate Robert Barnwell favored Davis. Unenthusiastically endorsing Cobb, Rhett dubbed the movement for Davis a "Washington-politician" plot.[8]

With Mississippi solidly behind Davis and Florida and Alabama inclined to follow suit, only Georgia could have prevented his election. On February 8, Tom Cobb sadly noted that his brother's name had been "almost withdrawn" from consideration. But when the Georgians caucused that evening, Stephens and several others strongly endorsed Toombs. Whether this was a serious move to stop Davis or merely reflected Stephens's and Toombs's old political hostility to Cobb, it came too late. Indeed, the Georgians could not decide whether they preferred Cobb, Toombs, or Stephens. After what Tom Cobb dubbed a "counting of noses," Howell "announced his wish that Davis should be unanimously elected." The Georgians had heard that Alabama, Mississippi, and Florida would go for Davis and that

South Carolina was divided. Stephens later claimed that these delegations actually favored Toombs and would have supported Cobb, but no contemporary evidence supports this assertion.[9] The conflicting accounts show instead the confusion prevailing in Montgomery and the reluctance of many delegates to wrangle over the presidency. The next day Davis was elected unanimously.

The process had largely dictated the result. The secrecy, the lack of party organization, and the absence of campaigning all favored Davis—a man of experience and solid reputation who had few determined opponents in the convention. Cobb's long history as a Democratic partisan, Toombs's mercurial temperament and drinking problems, Stephens's well-known opposition to secession and rumored reconstructionist leanings, and Rhett's fanaticism had all proved fatal handicaps. In making Davis the first consensus choice for president since George Washington, the delegates had gone a long way toward restoring the model political system of the early American republic. By avoiding electioneering, bargaining, and at least the appearance of secret maneuvering, they not only presented a united front to their constituents, the border states, and the Lincoln administration, but they also avoided the evils of partisanship.

The election of Davis along with the selection of his vice-president, widely respected former Whig Alexander H. Stephens, represented to many Southerners the burial of past political differences. A man of enormous intelligence and frail body, the diminutive Georgian was a constitutional hairsplitter par excellence. His high-pitched voice, habitual melancholy, and occasionally sharp tongue called to mind John Randolph of Roanoke.[10] And like the witty and eccentric Virginian, Stephens directed his tart lectures on "principles" at friend and foe alike. Despite being a cooperationist and reluctant Confederate, he had helped draft the Confederate Constitution in the hope that it would safeguard states' rights and individual liberty.[11]

Still unable to quell his fear of revolution, Stephens accepted his new position reluctantly. By serving as vice-president he sought to promote "harmony" among the people and above all wished to prevent "strife, factions, and civil discord." Stephens's election was clearly a sop to the cooperationists, though Howell Cobb dismissed the gesture as an "empty compliment." Perhaps so, but Cobb conceded that the elevation of his old rival was a "bitter pill" for original secessionists. Tom Cobb deplored the "maudlin disposition to conciliate the Union men" and scathingly remarked that Stephens had become "arrogant in his oracular announcements of what we should and should not do."[12] Most politically active Confederates, however, had confidence in the new president and vice-president; the experiment in Southern republicanism had begun auspiciously enough.

For the task of building a Southern nation, Jefferson Davis must have seemed almost too good to be true. His career as a West Point graduate, Mexican War veteran, Southern rights spokesman, and Mississippi planter exemplified Southern society's most widely shared ideals. Davis had not attended the Montgomery convention and was in the rose garden of his plantation near Vicksburg with his wife, Varina, when a messenger arrived to announce his election. When he received the not entirely unexpected news, his face momentarily grew ashen, and he seemed to shrink from the awesome responsibility, but quickly recovering, he quietly accepted what he deemed the call of duty. Though not exactly Cincinnatus throwing down his plow, Davis departed from his Brierfield plantation the next morning much as George Washington had reluctantly left Mount Vernon on several famous occasions.

Greeted upon his arrival in Montgomery by Yancey's famous bon mot "the man and the hour have met," Davis understood what the occasion required. Briefly addressing an enthusiastic welcoming party, he proclaimed that "we shall have nothing to fear at home, because at home we shall have homogeneity." In a striking biblical analogy, the recently divided Southerners became "brethren not in name merely, but in fact—men of one flesh, of one bone, of one interest, of one purpose, and of identity in domestic institutions." This organic unity—implicitly identified with slavery—combined with a high sense of moral purpose would serve Confederates in gaining their independence. "If war should come," Davis declared, "if we must again baptize in blood the principles for which our fathers bled in the Revolution, we shall show that we are not degenerate sons, but will redeem the pledges they gave to preserve the sacred rights transmitted to us, and show that Southern valor still shines as brightly as in the days of '76."[13] Jefferson Davis had come to claim the Confederacy's birthright as the legitimate heir to the republic of the founding fathers.

The citizens of Montgomery, as well as others who had crowded into the Alabama capital to watch the birth of a Southern nation, were anxious to see their new president. Contemporary descriptions emphasize Davis's erect military posture, spare frame, high cheekbones, and hollow jaw. Dignified without being handsome, at the age of fifty-two, the Mississippian had a wrinkled forehead that showed traces of strain and the marks of poor health. One sightless eye appeared covered with a film while the other eye, gray in color, according to North Carolina secessionist David Schenck, "is full of fire and intelligence." A sufferer from chronic dyspepsia and neuralgia, the president already looked haggard and careworn.[14] His polished manners and natural reserve impressed those meeting him for the first time, but more familiar associates found him sometimes aloof. Those looking for historical analogies or favorable portents might have noted that Davis's demeanor closely resembled the dignified and tightly controlled model established by Washington.

Indeed, as Washington had done in New York, Davis rode to his inauguration on February 18 in a large carriage drawn by six gray horses. Several thousand people crowded the streets and lined the balconies to catch a glimpse of their new hero and to shower him with flowers on his way to the capitol. After the swearing-in ceremony, Davis delivered his inaugural address in a strong, clear voice.[15]

Too stiff and formal to be an effective speaker, too reserved and reticent to express powerful emotions, Davis lacked both the passion and eloquence of a revolutionary leader. Some contemporaries thought he also lacked the common touch, the ability to move crowds and inspire sacrifice. Yet for all his love of abstraction and legalism, Davis believed in the Southern cause with all his heart and could expound its basic themes with conviction and some fervor.

On this bright February day, his words may not have been memorable, but they captured the essence of a nascent Southern political culture. Because a statesman should shun low ambition and personify selfless devotion, he accepted the presidential office with "humble distrust of my abilities," admitted there would be "many errors to forgive," but promised that the Southern people "shall not find in me either want of zeal or fidelity to the cause." These words must have been difficult for a man of intense pride and quietly burning fires of ambition, but Davis made the mandatory obeisance to antipolitical prejudices. He then struck a chord that would resound across the Confederacy for the next four years. With the unintentional irony that kept cropping up throughout the slaveholding republic's short life, Davis averred that all legitimate government "rests on the consent of the governed." After several other references to the Declaration of Independence, he predicted that the "impartial and enlightened verdict of mankind will vindicate the rectitude of our conduct." In this crisis, "the courage and patriotism of the people of the Confederate States will be found equal to any measure of defense which their honor and security may require." Sounding a call for unity that would become a dominant theme in his public addresses, Davis pointed to the necessity for "homogeneity" to make the "welfare of every portion . . . the aim of the whole." This awkward allusion to Calhoun's concurrent voice suggested that only the slaveholding border states could be added to the original Confederacy, but Davis also claimed that Southerners were true sons of the founding fathers. He fervently prayed that a people "united in heart" should "invoke the God of our fathers to guide and protect us in our efforts to perpetuate the principles which by his blessing they were able to vindicate, establish, and transmit to their posterity."[16]

Davis threw himself into this cause with all his energy. As befit the president of a republic, he conducted public business in a hotel parlor, where, according to Thomas Cooper DeLeon, he received both high officials and casual visitors "without ceremony." Arriving at this temporary office at nine each morning, he returned home at six each evening—by Varina's account—"exhausted and silent." Sleeping little and eating less, Davis reserved an hour each evening for informal receptions, but he could never quite unwind. Ill at ease—again rather like Washington at Martha's famous levees—Davis stiffly greeted his visitors but then hastened back to work, poring over papers late into the night.[17]

A stickler for detail, Davis drove his cabinet, his generals, and other officials as compulsively as he drove himself. Though too distant to develop intimate friendships, Davis could command loyalty from a few close associates. Never doubting his own patriotism and seldom questioning his own judgment, he could not understand why others failed to rally around the administration with a simple, unaffected devotion.

Even Varina Davis considered her husband excessively sensitive to criticism. Fanatical opponents such as the journalist Edward A. Pollard described Davis as an egomaniac, jealous of his advisers. But more judicious observers also noted the president's tendency toward self-righteousness and his refusal to admit error. When irritated, Davis could be needlessly abrasive, lashing out at anyone he suspected of disloyalty. Impatient and sometimes imperious, Davis was simultaneously stubborn and indecisive. Vulnerable to flattery, blind to the faults of his friends, and unforgiving of anyone who crossed him once, Davis could not forget a slight or work with people he disliked. Once engaged in a quarrel, Davis would pursue it to a conclusion and if necessary browbeat his opponent into submission. Failing to learn from mistakes, Davis lacked the capacity to grow in office.[18]

Yet few of these faults were immediately apparent, and in the spring of 1861, Davis's unquestionable patriotism and statesmanlike demeanor made him an ideal leader. His first tasks involved delicate matters of administration. Fire-eaters watched carefully to see who would take control of the Southern revolution; Whigs and Democrats, secessionists and cooperationists eyed each other warily, jockeying for position and positions. Ever the pessimist Tom Cobb dourly remarked that the Confederate "movement" had become "nothing but office seeking." Already disappointed with the Provisional Constitution and with Davis's election, Rhett immediately felt alienated from the new administration.[19]

For a man like Davis, with great confidence in his own abilities and little faith in others, choosing a cabinet must have been agonizing. His approach seemed odd at the time and has received much criticism even from sympathetic historians. In the absence of political parties, Davis decided that each state of the Confederacy should be represented in the cabinet. Although he would have hotly denied any lingering partisan prejudices, the president favored Democrats and original secessionists in making his first appointments.[20] Yet despite legitimate criticism of selections that later proved to be either mediocre or misplaced, Davis's criteria made sense in a nation devoted to states' rights. The most critical requirement both for a successful revolution against the corrupt politics of the recent past and for maintaining Southern independence was to build a broadly based and united administration.

In another break with traditional political practices, Davis refused to consign potential political rivals to the outer darkness. The appointment of Robert Toombs as secretary of state placed the right man in the wrong position but showed respect for the Georgian's abilities as well as his political influence. Toombs reluctantly accepted the post—perhaps realizing his inherent unfitness for anything remotely connected to diplomacy—but he apparently hoped to become something of a prime minister in the new administration. Unfortunately, Toombs's transparent ambition immediately rubbed Davis the wrong way. Blustering, swearing, and sometimes drinking heavily, Toombs lacked the necessary tact to get along with the president, and his outspoken proslavery views hurt the Confederacy abroad. Argumentative by nature, "Bob Toombs disagrees with himself between meals," one wag suggested. Compared to his own impetuousness and impatience, the secretary of state soon decided that Davis worked too "slowly." Frustrated and feeling his talents wasted, by late July Toombs had resigned, entered the army, and devoted his energies to pursuing an always elusive martial glory—and increasingly damning Jefferson Davis and all his works.[21]

Davis never seriously considered Rhett for a cabinet post, and so the South Carolina delegation recommended Christopher G. Memminger for the treasury portfolio. Some fire-eaters doubted Memminger's fervor and financial acumen; Pollard later claimed that Memminger spent more time scouring bookstores for works on obscure theological disputes than dealing with the Confederacy's knotty financial problems.[22] Memminger was competent but unassertive in a post demanding considerable energy, initiative, and imagination.

The new secretary of war, Leroy P. Walker of Alabama, was likewise a political cipher and soon proved to be an administrative liability. Largely unknown outside his home state, Walker was nevertheless a strong secessionist and had the support of Wigfall and Clement C. Clay, Jr. Politically astute observers suspected that Davis planned to run the department himself and therefore had no interest in choosing an independent-minded secretary.[23] In any case, Walker was soon over his head and would be gone by the fall.

Before the imposition of the Union blockade, few people paid much attention to Davis's selection of Floridian Stephen R. Mallory as secretary of the navy. Mallory became a capable administrator but also generated controversy. Two of the three Florida representatives in the Provisional Congress objected to Mallory's cooperationism and managed to hold up the nomination. Both the Florida and Texas delegations eventually voted against confirmation. Rumored to be a rake, Mallory was convivial and witty; his notoriety and suavity wickedly fascinated Montgomery's provincial society.[24] The daunting task of constructing a navy almost literally from the water up made Mallory a tempting target for political sniping.

The Texas representative in the cabinet was Postmaster General John H. Reagan, who established a reasonably efficient postal system. In cabinet meetings, Reagan frankly stated his views but apparently exerted little influence and quarreled with several other cabinet members. By May 1861, he had already angered powerful editors by persuading Congress to double postal rates on newspapers.[25] The resulting outcry led to accusations that Davis was trying to squelch opposition and destroy civil liberties.

The selection of an attorney general hardly seemed to matter. This traditionally minor position required some legal knowledge but offered little scope for ability or ambition—except of course for the intelligent and the clever. Davis's choice—Judah P. Benjamin of Louisiana—was both and much more. A skilled attorney and experienced politician, Benjamin oozed charm, erudition, and worldly wisdom. A social lion in the Confederacy, he relished good food, fine wine, Havana cigars, and, most of all, clever conversation.

His Jewish ancestry, separation from his wife (she maintained a residence in Paris), and purported weakness for gambling made Benjamin an exotic in the piously Protestant South. Unruffled by criticism and displaying a sangfroid in the face of disaster that seemed odd if not sinister to hot-blooded Confederates, Benjamin viewed himself and his society with a certain wry detachment. Admirers praised his wit, but critics—some of whom could not conceal their anti-Semitism—described his ever-present smile as more of a sneer and probably a sign of a conniving and hypocritical nature.[26] Jefferson Davis, however, appreciated Benjamin's coolness and above all his loyalty, and the more congressmen and newspapers criticized him, the more Davis relied on his counsel.

Although the Provisional Congress quickly confirmed Davis's cabinet selections, harsh invective arose over the distribution of other political loaves and fishes. Despite the safeguards in the new Constitution and the antipolitical ideology of many Confederate leaders, the scramble for patronage poisoned the atmosphere in Montgomery. Denizens of Washington seemed to have descended in droves on the Confederate capital. Rather than providing opportunity for the young and energetic, the Southern revolution offered places for "worn-out politicians," Mary Chesnut complained. "Whenever there is an election they hunt up some old fossil ages ago laid on the shelf. There never was such a resurrection of the dead and forgotten."[27]

A walk through the Alabama capitol building confirmed at least the partial truth of such laments. Eager applicants filled the halls and offices; each day's mail brought more requests for jobs. Howell Cobb ruefully remarked that "it really seems as if half Georgia were here after office and the other half were at home writing letters here on the same subject."[28] The continual hubbub, the constant press of visitors, and importunate letters kept the city buzzing with tales of old-fashioned political horse-trading. "A War of Secession . . . will end a War for the Succession of Places," Mary Chesnut acerbically commented. In a similar vein, British journalist William Howard Russell described Montgomery as filled with "placemen with or without places, and a vast number of speculators, contractors, and the like, attracted by the embryo government." Ever attuned to the dangers of corruption, secessionists raged against all manner of threats to republican purity. "The atmosphere of this place is absolutely tainted with selfish, ambitious schemes for aggrandizement," Tom Cobb huffed. Where were the men who held the interests of the nation above low intrigue?[29]

Where, indeed, for at the same time that Cobb was bemoaning the decline of public morality, he was assiduously seeking appointments for family and friends, including a military commission for his young, inexperienced, and alcoholic brother-in-law. What bothered Cobb and other Southern rights men was not patronage itself but rather the distribution of the choicest plums to cooperationists, border state politicians, and even recently arrived Yankees. "The best claim to distinction under the existing regime," he wrote in disgust, "seems to be either to have opposed secession or have done nothing for it."[30] Kowtowing to border state interests, doling out jobs to known reconstructionists, and ignoring men who had long labored for Southern rights smacked of betrayal and petty politics.

As always, definitions of partisanship remained in the eye of the beholder. Cooperationists, former Whigs, and conservatives generally were just as convinced that they had received the short end of the patronage stick. One Mississippi editor cynically suggested that the Confederate Constitution's restrictions on executive removal of public officials would help partisan Democrats hang on to their offices indefinitely. However exaggerated and self-serving these charges were, as early as May 1861, a ruckus had already erupted over the attempted removals of postmasters in South Carolina and Georgia.[31] The Confederacy may have been founded in a reaction against partisan politics, but old habits died hard.

The cries of double-dealing and hypocrisy also reflected the anxieties of a nation on the brink of war. For if Rhett and his followers denounced Davis's appointments, they worried even more about the possibility of a last-minute compromise and still feared that Davis was a reconstructionist. There is some evidence that the president felt compelled to attack Fort Sumter both to assert Confederate independence and to convince skeptical radicals of his commitment to the cause.[32]

Riding a crest of indignation and enthusiasm in the wake of Lincoln's call for troops, Davis informed the Provisional Congress that "a people thus united and resolved cannot shrink from any sacrifice." All the Southern people asked was "to be let alone." Historians have cited this statement as a prime example of the weakness of Confederate nationalism and have criticized Davis for failing to explain the causus belli in a more memorable way. Davis lacked Lincoln's flair for evocative and inspiring language, but he firmly believed that Southerners now stood as the last defenders of republicanism (defined as self-rule for white men) in a hostile world, and he expressed these deeply held convictions in a dignified and persuasive fashion. The new nation would survive, he avowed, "however long and severe may be the test of their determination to maintain their birthright of freedom and equality as a trust it is their duty to transmit undiminished to their posterity." The Confederates would prevail because they maintained a "firm reliance on that Divine Power which covers with its protection the just cause, and we will continue to struggle for our inherent right to freedom, independence, and self-government."[33]

Davis's religious language underscored a crucial component of Confederate nationalism. Politicians and clergy often described the war for Southern independence as a righteous crusade. Sermons, denominational magazines, and church publications exuded patriotism—magnifying successes, downplaying defeats, and holding out hope for ultimate victory. Meeting in Savannah less than a month after the attack on Fort Sumter, the Southern Baptist Convention not only invoked divine favor for the Confederate cause but expressed unbounded confidence in the president, cabinet, and Congress.[34]

The God preached in Southern churches directly intervened in human affairs: battlefield victories were signs of divine solicitude and defeats merely momentary chastisement for a sinful but still chosen people. In the spring and summer of 1861, the theology seemed simple enough. The Reverend Charles Colcock Jones—one of Georgia's most prominent Presbyterian ministers—admitted that the Northern and Southern people had been "sinning . . . as a nation for seventy or eighty years" and that "the Lord may use us as rods of correction to each other," but he averred that the Southern people "can commend our cause to His protection and blessing with the assured expectation that we shall eventually triumph." His son—serving as a lieutenant in a Savannah artillery battery—was even more confident that the "God of Battles" would bless the Southern cause and just as surely punish the vile Yankees, who "set at naught all rules of equality, or right, and of honor."[35]

Forgetting their former strictures against Northern clergymen meddling in politics, Southern preachers helped create a new civil religion.

A Virginia minister, O. S. Barten, praised the Confederacy for acknowledging God in its Constitution and honored Congress for opening its sessions with prayer. Warming to his theme, he unequivocally asserted that the Confederate government was a "Christian government" and that the "votes of Christian men will call such to fill our offices as will bring honor and glory to the government they serve. . . . We will have Christian Presidents and Christian Governors, and our delegates will act on Christian principles." The devout rejoiced over newspaper reports of Davis's newfound religious fervor and attendance at Episcopal services, lauding him as a Christian statesman and an instrument of God.[36]

The president regularly issued calls for days of fasting, humiliation, and prayer, and although war-weary Southerners eventually grew indifferent or even cynical about such occasions, in 1861 they joined in heartfelt expressions of thanksgiving and renewed pledges of patriotism. On May 28, Davis pointed out the "manifest proofs of the Divine blessing" bestowed on the Confederacy in the great contest for liberty. Yet like other orthodox Christians, Davis also realized that "none but a just and righteous cause can gain the Divine favor."[37] Perhaps this qualification was pro forma, but it portended a more complex and disturbing examination of the relationship between wartime vicissitudes and God's purposes.

Southern clergymen did not know whether to admit the complicity of Southern politicians in the great saturnalia of national corruption and cheap demagoguery that had wrecked the old Union or simply to applaud the rectitude of Confederate leaders. This ambivalence appeared long before Confederate armies had suffered any serious setbacks. On June 13, 1861, in a fast-day sermon, Augustus Baldwin Longstreet, Methodist minister, president of the University of South Carolina, and pioneer Southern humorist, delivered the first Confederate jeremiad. After briefly surveying the history of republican governments, Longstreet claimed that in almost all cases "liberty soon degenerated into license." Corruption became endemic. Anarchy, despotism, and aristocracy quickly followed. Only a national religion based on Jesus Christ could prevent republics from rapidly descending this path to destruction. Longstreet echoed ancient prophetic warnings against political sins: "Now go on, as you and they [Northerners] have gone, scrambling for office and wrangling about men, seeking place for profit, and profit for sin; putting up the available and pulling down the meritorious; trifling with oaths, buying and selling votes, and spreading iniquity broad-cast, in all its horrid forms, over the land— and your new republic will soon share the fate of the old, and probably die in more shocking convulsion than now agonizing it."[38] Apostasy to republicanism had thus become faithlessness to God. Should the Southern revolution against politics fail, or even falter, divine retribution would surely follow.

Efforts to square the cause with God's will made the new Confederate politics even more intensely antiparty. The corrupt nature of parties (and many Southerners reverted to using the eighteenth-century term "factions") was a given. Even newspaper editors asserted that the Confederacy should live without professional politicians and without the needless agitation of caucuses, conventions, and campaigning. "Let us for once have an election without the interference of the wire-puller and the corrupting influence of party strategy," an Alabamian demanded. Others talked of dispensing with elections altogether. An Atlanta newspaper praised the closed sessions of the Provisional Congress for preventing "discord and dissension" because "the demagogue has no chance to harangue the galleries or consume business hours in Buncombe declamation." Even Southerners who normally accepted the usefulness and even the necessity for political opposition maintained that partisanship had no legitimate place in wartime.[39] Emphasizing the danger of discord during a national emergency simply reinforced the general aversion to politics that had received such clear expression during the secession crisis.

Yet calls for unity and the defense of liberty could not entirely heal old political wounds or paper over persistent divisions and rivalries. Disaffected Whigs and cooperationists in northern Alabama and Mississippi apparently considered running their own tickets in the fall elections or even agitating for the repeal of the secession ordinances. In areas isolated from the plantation economy, yeoman farmers may well have felt a greater loyalty to their local community than to either the state or Confederate governments.[40] Despite the initial enthusiasm and support for the war, devotion to the larger cause of Southern nationalism remained tentative and conditional.

Especially in the border states, where cooperationists and outright Unionists retained considerable strength, political harmony proved elusive. Virginia governor John Letcher's appointment of moderates and cooperationists to civil and military posts angered secessionists. John M. Daniel of the *Richmond Examiner* repeatedly demanded the proscription of submissionists. Though hoping to avoid factional strife, even the more moderate *Richmond Enquirer* advised Virginia voters to spurn "timeservers, political trimmers who will give a lukewarm support to States' rights and State sovereignty." To placate all factions, one delegate to the Virginia convention suggested distributing the state's congressional seats among the recent supporters of Breckinridge, Bell, and Douglas, and the state's delegation to the Provisional Congress was roughly divided between Democrats and Whigs and between secessionists and cooperationists.[41] Despite some continued carping, a political truce took hold after the spring elections.

In neighboring North Carolina a combination of traditional partisanship, residual dismay over secession, and strong personalities produced politics reminiscent of the highly competitive heyday of the second party system. Although public meetings held after Lincoln's call for troops denounced any continuation of party squabbling, the most fervent advocates of unity were the minority of disunionist Democrats. For example, the *Raleigh Register*'s conciliatory attitude toward old Unionists reflected the weakness of secessionists in North Carolina.[42]

Even when North Carolina joined the Confederacy, the convention there mirrored the tenuous balance between secessionists and cooperationists. The delegates chose three secessionist Democrats, four Unionist Whigs, one secessionist Whig, and one Unionist Democrat to serve in the Provisional Congress.[43] Cooperationists, however, claimed their opponents' no-party cry had become merely a mask for jobbery. "Give them [secessionists] the plunder of the Government," declared one veteran Union Whig, "and they care but little for the interest of the people. I have no confidence in the men who lead in this rebellion. . . . There is not a more corrupt set of men living." Even if the Southern states won their independence, prominent conservative Jonathan Worth believed that "our late political opponents will regard us as subjugated vassals."[44] Such invective recalled the party battles of Andrew Jackson's era, and North Carolina newspapers continued to carry partisan editorials and reports of political meetings.

Though much more subdued, political conflict persisted in other states, especially in the upper South, where Whigs retained some strength. Politicians naturally preferred the habitual and the familiar even as they celebrated the advent of a new, and some hoped, purer political culture.

The decision to move the Confederate capital to Richmond, Virginia, not only altered military strategy, but, just as important, shifted the center of Southern politics and shaped the Confederacy's political history. Suspicious fire-eaters worried that Richmond offered more opportunities for upper South conservatives to win appointments. The Rhetts feared a plot to draw more border states into the Southern nation preliminary to a reconstruction of the old Union.[45] Along with the government's official papers and other baggage, political machinations and petty social rivalries followed Confederate officials and their families to Richmond.

The president soon discovered that patronage problems only multiplied. Congressmen scurried from office to office seeking appointments for friends and relatives; the War Department became a hive of military preparations, buzzing with talk of commissions and intrigue. The Southern nationalist and Presbyterian minister Benjamin M. Palmer issued a stern warning to Confederate leaders: "What of the political brokerage which trades in this dreadful immorality [e.g., party platforms] and sets up offices of government virtually at public outcry to the highest bidders? . . . For the love of God and Country, let us strive to bring back the purer days of the republic; when the honest merit waited, like Cincinnatus at his plow, to be called forth for service, and before noisy candidates cried their wares at the hustings like fisherwomen in the market—when a ribald press did not thrust its obtrusive gaze into the sanctities of private life, and the road to office did not lead through the pillory of public abuse and scandal—and when the votes of the people expressed their virtuous unbiased will."[46] Accepting such idyllic descriptions of a lost utopia, Southerners with a bent for historical analogies realized that their new nation faced the kinds of temptations that had often enervated and eventually destroyed earlier republics.

The danger seemed both real and immediate. New parties—new engines of corruption—might arise from the patronage battles already raging in Richmond. Whigs, cooperationists, and various other conservatives still believed that Breckinridge Democrats had received the most lucrative offices. Democrats, secessionists, and fire-eaters were just as certain that the opposite was true. "A great multitude of lazy drones, worthless cormorants, and pensioned vagabonds of the Buchanan administration, are now under pay with us," claimed an outraged letter writer in the *Richmond Whig.* "The 'red tape' philosophy—the brokerage, favoritism, and lobbyism of Washington, would seem to have been transferred." Should placemen and their minions come to dominate the new government, the Confederacy would become little better than a South American republic, a decadent state ripe for Yankee plucking.[47]

The Davis administration admittedly had looked for men with experience under the United States government to fill many jobs. As a practical matter, federal postmasters in the seceding states began working for the Confederate government; many former United States Treasury officials joined Memminger in Richmond.[48] This transfer of officeholders, which administration critics believed favored undeserving Northerners, probably reduced the scramble for patronage and made many positions decidedly less political.

Believing that he had risen above petty squabbling over appointments, Davis either hesitated or simply did not use patronage effectively to build support for his administration. Often indifferent to local politics, the president sometimes ignored the wishes of senators and congressmen.[49] Because he was unable to placate enemies or satisfy friends, Davis's approach to patronage worked against the formation of political parties but also alienated some powerful politicians.

Davis's and Memminger's financial policies showed little economic or political imagination. Relying on several loans and a modest tariff that proved adequate only until the middle of 1861, the administration failed to prepare the country for the economic dislocations and mounting costs of a rapidly expanding war. More ominously, the Confederate government began funding larger and larger portions of its mushrooming national debt through the issue of treasury notes not redeemable in specie.[50] Although Toombs, Stephens, and several newspaper editors believed that the Confederacy needed to raise taxes, there was substantial opposition to internal taxation, and the administration never pressed forcefully for tougher measures. With limited understanding of long-term needs and perhaps worried that new taxes might undermine public support for their fledgling nation, both Davis and Congress instead floated the government on a sea of increasingly worthless paper.[51]

At the end of the war's first summer, Herschel V. Johnson concluded that Congress and the administration had displayed a "timid and temporizing spirit. They seem to fear the patriotism of the people, to doubt their willingness to acquiesce in the pecuniary burdens which must be borne before this war can be closed and our revolution a success." Yet good Democrat that he was, Johnson fretted about the "money power" producing "reckless extravagance [and] public corruption" and hoped that a "simple, cheap, honest government" could be maintained even during a costly war.[52]

Because so many Southern politicians adhered to the financial truisms of their partisan past, it was impossible for Congress and the president to grapple with or even acknowledge the South's economic weaknesses. Patronage quarrels and simmering discontent over the administration's cautious economic measures dampened hope that the government could escape political turmoil.

Deferring to the judgment of the powers that be at the beginning of any war is a nearly universal tendency, and Southerners naturally placed much faith in Jefferson Davis. Ignoring their past political differences, Herschel Johnson applauded the president's good sense and "never doubted his patriotism or military genius." Throughout the war, the opinions of moderates such as Johnson were important indicators of Davis's performance and popularity. Even John M. Daniel, the caustic editor of the *Richmond Examiner*, who would later become the administration's most unrelenting critic, scoffed at fears of executive usurpation and proposed granting Davis dictatorial powers. To the president's credit, he paid little heed to such counsel and also discouraged talk of a short war.[53]

Davis's evaluation of Confederate resources, the goal of winning Southern independence, and political considerations all dictated a defensive military strategy. But at the same time, a rising war spirit, the aggressiveness of young hotspurs, exaggeration of Southern fighting ability, and perhaps overconfidence in Davis produced impatience and frustration. If Lincoln heard cries of "On to Richmond," to a lesser extent Davis faced steady pressure to carry the war into enemy territory. Besides the always aggressive Rhetts, other Southerners wondered why the president could not send hordes of volunteers to defeat the Yankees in one great campaign.[54] These criticisms neglected the practical problems of logistics and organization by overrating the importance of esprit.

Cooler heads disparaged such thoughtless overconfidence but neglected a more ominous future problem.[55] Would the mass of Southerners who owned no slaves fight for the cause of a slaveholders' republic, and if so, for how long? Plato had long ago concluded that oligarchical societies may well hesitate to call out the "common people" to fight because "they will have more to fear from the armed multitude than from the enemy."[56] In the late spring and early summer of 1861, there was concern in Richmond that poor whites were already disgruntled; malcontents played on class fears and proclaimed themselves the true friends of the nonslaveholding masses. With more bravado than conviction, a Louisiana editor declared that "demagogues can never array the poor against the rich upon the subject of slavery." This rhetoric of class unity was not entirely effective when yeomen noticed that some wealthy men avoided joining the army. The president of the Alabama secession convention warned Davis that too many men in the Alabama hill country had recently acquired "improper and unfounded jealousies" and had come to believe that the war was being fought solely to preserve title to slave property. The disaffected openly declared that they would never "fight for no rich man's slaves."[57] During the war's first months, these scattered complaints hardly threatened the military effort, but Confederate leaders nevertheless groped for ways to strengthen public morale.

In brief remarks at the Richmond fairgrounds in late May, Davis down-played the defense of slavery and ignored class resentments. Looking over a sea of young faces—the enthusiastic recruits of an embryonic national army—the president saw "a determination never to surrender—a determination never to go home but to tell a tale of honor." Disparities in numbers, training, and resources meant little to such patriots. The president also tried to arouse the proper fighting spirit with graphic descriptions of enemy barbarism. In a message to the Provisional Congress the day before the battle of First Manassas, he claimed that for Yankees, "rapine is the rule." A "brutal soldiery" had already ransacked and burned private homes, committed "outrages" on "defenseless females," and deliberately prevented medicine from reaching desperately ill mothers and children.[58] However stirring such calls to service may have been to common soldiers, they could not prevent the appearance of factionalism in the Confederate high command.

As Brigadier General Irvin McDowell's Federal army moved toward Manassas Junction, Virginia, Davis and other administration officials began making strategic and tactical decisions that would have far-reaching political consequences. Rejecting Brigadier General Pierre Gustave Toutant Beauregard's impractical plan to concentrate thirty-five thousand Confederate troops for a northward march to threaten Washington, the president stuck to a defensive strategy.[59] This decision reflected the government's cautious approach to building a Southern nation: a costly offensive, even if partly successful, might further strain both the economy and the political system.

Beauregard repeatedly recommended that the Confederates concentrate their forces in the face of an advancing enemy, and Davis eventually ordered Brigadier General Joseph E. Johnston's army from the Shenandoah Valley to join Beauregard's troops at Manassas. The ensuing battle resulted in a surprising rout of the Federals. Recriminations and petty jealousies, however, quickly soured the taste of victory. Davis and his friends at first praised Beauregard while slighting Johnston; later the president grew wary of Beauregard's sudden fame and popularity.[60] With three hypersensitive egos involved, hard feelings were bound to follow.

At the time, everyone had agreed that the troops were too exhausted and disorganized to pursue the fleeing Yankees, but many people assumed the Confederates could have captured Washington, and the more sanguine talked of invading Pennsylvania and Ohio. A public controversy soon erupted between Beauregard and the president over whether a shortage of supplies had prevented the army from advancing after Manassas. Speculation about Beauregard as a future presidential candidate along with several indiscreet statements from the general's staff also rankled Davis.[61]

Adding to the administration's problem with Beauregard, a quarrel between Davis and Johnston erupted that would rage off and on for the rest of the war and long afterward. Alternately cooperative and uncommunicative, self-effacing and egotistical, bold and cautious, the baffling and contradictory Joseph E. Johnston has always attracted a host of admirers and detractors. Possessed of a sound strategic sense and a decided preference for defensive warfare, Johnston commanded both the affection and the respect of his officers and men. He was quietly stubborn, willing to argue small points at length, and occasionally paranoid about his superiors. It is thus no wonder that he clashed with the equally resolute, combative, and sometimes insecure president.[62]

Although the exact origin of their feud remains obscure, it evidently did not break out in full force until some time after the battle of Manassas. In late June, Johnston was still urging the president to take the field and thus "appear in the position General Washington occupied during the revolution."[63] Davis probably dismissed this suggestion as flattery or sycophancy because his distrust of Johnston quickly became obvious. Rather than trying to work with and use this difficult subordinate, Davis seemed determined to alienate him. Their problems grew from the president's obsession with strategic and even tactical detail combined with Johnston's habit of either ignoring or intentionally misinterpreting orders. Davis's interference with organization and operations dismayed Johnston, but the real break came on the last day of August, when Davis announced the appointment of five generals for the Confederate army.

Adjutant General Samuel Cooper was named the senior Confederate general, followed by Albert Sidney Johnston, Robert E. Lee, Joseph E. Johnston, and Beauregard. Although Davis later claimed that he had carefully considered both line and staff positions held in the old army, his ranking of these five officers was inconsistent even by his own standards. The whole process appeared political, personal, and arbitrary. Johnston drafted a six-page protest, a letter bristling with well-founded objections, legal quibbles, and righteous indignation. Whatever strength his case may have had, the document's lecturing and insubordinate tone infuriated the president, who considered "its arguments and statements utterly one-sided; and its insinuations as unfounded as they are unbecoming."[64] With the Confederate high command rent by personal and strategic rifts, day-to-day operations became more difficult and careful strategic planning nearly impossible.

Public impatience with the government's failure to take advantage of the enemy's disarray after Manassas mounted. Johnston and Beauregard proposed an offensive and estimated that with sixty thousand men they could move into Maryland. Never deterred by practical objections or un-pleasant realities (in this case a shortage of arms), Beauregard suggested that troops be removed from coastal defense or from parts of the Con-federacy remote from any Federal forces.[65] Davis could ill afford to with-draw troops from the Confederacy's western line in Kentucky and Ten-nessee or weaken the coastal defenses of North Carolina. The tenuous loyalty of the border states and the political volatility of the Tar Heel State gave Davis little choice but to reject Beauregard's grandiose scheme.

Strengthening public devotion to the Confederacy initially meant adopt-ing a defensive strategy because political objectives had to shape military policy. By the same token, the natural centralization of political authority and the influence of powerful generals led to cries of "military despotism," and traditional republican fear of standing armies cropped up in political discussions. Because the Confederate Constitution had created a powerful presidency—an "elective King" according to the editor of the *Richmond Whig*—only public vigilance could preserve liberty. Ideology sparked op-position to the administration but received added force from men who simply could not trust Jefferson Davis.[66]

Such criticism in part reflected dissatisfaction with the president's mili-tary appointments. As the old saw would have it, awarding any office makes one friend and many enemies. Like Abraham Lincoln, Davis se-lected his share of political generals, preferring Democrats and secession-ists as well as old political or army associates. Yet Democrats and Whigs, secessionists and cooperationists all protested that their friends had been slighted.[67] Though Davis tried to balance military and political qualifications, his efforts, often clouded by unreasoning hostilities and unshakable friendships, pleased no one.

The Confederate commitment to states' rights further complicated the task. The president's division of the army command into small geographical departments and the dispersal of troops along the perimeters of the Confederacy may not have made much military sense, but it reflected the political constraints felt by the leader of a decentralized government. Any time he made an appointment, Davis risked upsetting some powerful state politician. And the governors not only offered plenty of advice but also kept their hands in Confederate military affairs.[68] They tried to funnel volunteers into the Confederate army through their state organizations, retain their power to commission officers in volunteer regiments, and take credit for defending their states. Therefore, if Davis transferred troops, or worse, chose officers for state military units after they had entered Confederate service, he had to run a dangerous political gauntlet.

Governors sometimes kept men in their states for local defense, or hoarded supplies for their own troops, or handed over skeleton regiments with a full complement of officers and few enlisted men. Not even the selection of junior officers escaped their notice. Florida governor John Milton, for instance, complained that a "pet" of former governor Madison Perry had won a rigged company election in a Florida infantry regiment. Protesting the results of one election in a company of a single regiment carried political interference too far, but governors had good reason to scrutinize appointments. After prodding Davis to choose several Whig generals in Tennessee to balance the Democrats who had already received commissions, Governor Isham G. Harris pointed out that he would be "held responsible here [Nashville] for your appointments" whether he had been consulted or not. The president naturally denied that partisan considerations influenced military appointments and claimed that all "good and true men" belonged to the "*one party* of the South."[69] Some friction was unavoidable and for the time being manageable. Milton and Harris and even the irascible Joe Brown strongly supported the Confederacy and more often than not cooperated with the government. At this early stage, the president himself well understood the political pressures and generally handled the governors with some tact.

Unfortunately, Jefferson Davis had to worry about more than the tender egos of his generals, the politics of military appointments, and the governors' occasional complaints. In June 1861, potentially destructive opposition began to emerge from several quarters. The Rhetts had always been suspicious of Davis, but other South Carolinians also began blasting the administration. Hotheaded Laurence Keitt dismissed Davis as an abysmal failure, and by midsummer, several South Carolina politicians railed against the president and his supposedly weak cabinet. Premature talk of an organized opposition spread in fashionable Richmond salons. Private grumbling gave way to public attacks when the Rhetts launched an editorial barrage in the *Mercury*.[70] Although public opinion in South Carolina had by no means turned against Davis, many firebrands refused to sacrifice their vaunted independence and often quirky principles to the common cause.

The resignation of Secretary of State Robert Toombs in early July and his unfortunate appointment as a brigadier general signaled division in Davis's official family and marked the beginnings of serious political trouble in Georgia. An equally important defector was Texas firebrand Louis T. Wigfall. Elected to the Provisional Congress but, like Toombs, eager for action and glory, Wigfall refused to run for a seat in the Permanent Congress. He served for a time on the president's staff even though his wife, Charlotte, made social relations with the Davises difficult. Despite talk in July of a falling-out, the Texan continued to support the administration in Congress.[71]

Wigfall, however, was not diplomatic enough to work with Davis or even keep his family from entering the Richmond social wars. Blustering by nature and with a weakness for alcohol, Wigfall also had a large capacity for hatred. In an otherwise unremarkable face, his piercing eyes, which reminded William Howard Russell of a "wild beast," revealed a ferocious disposition and a capacity for "pitiless anger" that had made Wigfall a stock villain in the Northern press and a formidable political foe in the South. During the summer of 1861, the Texan drifted out of the Davis orbit, disgruntled over the government's failure to launch a military offensive after Manassas and sympathetic to Joe Johnston in his quarrel with the president. Yet Wigfall cagily concealed his hand and in November received a brigadier's commission from Davis.[72] For all his fanaticism and violent outbursts, Wigfall understood politics and realized the president's popularity in the country. He could afford to bide his time.

Despite its vehemence, the South Carolina opposition along with the more privately expressed discontent of Toombs and Wigfall failed to shake the widespread confidence in Jefferson Davis. Even the *Richmond Examiner*, which would soon vie with the *Mercury* in vituperative assaults on the administration, deplored efforts to form an opposition party in Congress. In a classical warning against corruption and partisanship, John M. Daniel conceded that the Davis government was the best that could have been made for the new Confederacy.[73] This was not exactly a ringing endorsement, but for the moment Davis could ignore his enemies and bask in the people's continuing confidence.

The president still seemed the beau ideal of the Southern leader and, for many of his countrymen, had come to symbolize the Confederacy. His unanimous selection at Montgomery, his pristinely republican inauguration, and even his flawed attempts at building national unity offered a popular rallying point and marked an important epoch in the political history of the nascent Southern republic. The secession elections, conventions, and sessions of the Provisional Congress had also worked to promote public support for this experiment in Southern independence, but in their uncertainty about the future and the vicissitudes of war, people looked to their president for reassurance and security. Whatever his difficulties, no doubt compounded by bouts of ill health in the summer and fall of 1861, Jefferson Davis, more by public perception than by his policies, had gone a long way toward establishing the legitimacy of the Confederate government. In Lyndhurst, Louisiana, seventeen-year-old Sarah Wadley fully believed that Davis epitomized the highest ideals of Southern statesmanship: "Wise, moderate, and just in council, cool, brave and gallant in battle; firm, energetic, and instant in performance of his executive duties, truly we have in him a second Washington."[74]

CHAPTER 5

A New Political Universe

The Confederate voter is the forgotten man of Civil War history. Many knowledgeable students of the conflict are only vaguely aware that the Confederate and state governments held elections; even scholars of the Confederate Congress have given short shrift to congressional elections. This neglect is striking but hardly surprising and something of a tribute to Confederate success in creating an antiparty (and in many ways an antipolitician) political culture. Yet these elections revealed the Confederacy's central beliefs, values, and symbols that served both to regulate and limit public debate and participation.[1]

Although the war naturally reduced political activity, considerable effort was made to eliminate the more unseemly features of elections. If the revolution against politics succeeded, Confederates would be able to see the results: the absence of public agitation or even electoral competition would be a sure sign of political health.

Wartime distractions and antipolitical ideology explain how the Confederacy's only presidential election passed almost unnoticed. In constitutional law and political theory, elections had become troublesome. Robert Ridgeway, editor of the *Richmond Whig*, suggested that the presidential election be delayed for at least a year and that the provisional government be continued much as the old Continental Congress had operated under the Articles of Confederation during the revolutionary war. With so many voters in the army, the country hardly needed the distraction of a presidential contest.[2] Popular confidence in Davis reinforced these attitudes, but ironically so did concern over executive despotism and electoral corruption.

The *Charleston Mercury* repeated the often-made claim that presidential elections had undermined the old Union. Party divisions had subverted the intentions of the founding fathers by destroying the independence of the electoral college. Although Rhett could not convince his fellow delegates in Montgomery either to scrap or reform the electoral college, some leaders still hoped that the Confederate electors might exert a restraining influence on the voters and elevate the presidency above low politicking.[3]

The Confederate Constitution circumscribed the voters' influence by limiting the president's political powers. Governor Francis Pickens of South Carolina, for example, believed that the old government had suffered from a disease fatal to most republics—divisions over the selection of a "chief magistrate." The electoral college had degenerated first into a "simple democracy" and finally into a "consolidated democracy." By restricting the president to a single six-year term and by reducing executive patronage, the delegates at Montgomery had steered a course between anarchy and military despotism—dangers sure to beset the Northern government as an abolitionist administration consolidated its power.[4]

Yet the vigorous canvasses so familiar to Southern voters since the days of Jackson had not only expressed the fundamental values of the old politics but had set important precedents for popular participation. In the North, the rituals of nineteenth-century politics, including conventions, ratification meetings, serenades, and rallies, had multiplied. Election day had developed into a curious combination of solemn rite and frenzied celebration. In the South, not only was politics less elaborately organized, but the people remained much more ambivalent about the political system and even about parties and elections. The sectional conflict had simultaneously focused voter attention on national issues while alienating Southerners from national politics.[5] Yet even for Southerners, voting affirmed membership in a community, and in the new Confederacy, elections might begin molding these communities into a nation.

The Provisional Congress decreed the first Wednesday in November as election day for the permanent executive officers as well as for members of the Permanent Congress. Either the voters or the state legislatures could choose the presidential electors who were to meet on the first Wednesday of December to cast their ballots for president and vice-president.[6] But there would be no nominating conventions, no letters of acceptance, no committee meetings, no rallies, no speeches, and, most important, no opposition candidates. In short, there would be an election without a campaign; voting would be a simple patriotic exercise unsullied by partisanship and hoopla.

The absence of formal nominating procedures made any criticism of the Davis-Stephens ticket appear captious, and electioneering would be needlessly divisive and dangerous. Even the *Richmond Examiner* lauded the president as a true defender of Southern independence. The vice-president, however, was another matter. Stephens's succession to the presidency would be a "public calamity" and would "make our revolution logically an absurdity." As a Douglas supporter and a submissionist, Stephens had become the "pet, the idol, the hope of every corrupt spoilsman and jobber in the South," and the *Examiner* favored dumping him from the ticket.[7]

This brief controversy raised the most serious issue of the "campaign," but the response was swift and unequivocal. In language that strikingly paralleled the *Examiner*'s while arriving at opposite conclusions, a Tennessee editor dismissed the attack on Stephens as a "contemptible scrambling for patronage and power." Dredging up the political past only proved that overzealous demagogues would still jeopardize national unity by proscribing anyone who had not supported secession immediately after Lincoln's election. Some conservatives conceded that it might have been more politic to have chosen a border state man for vice-president, but they rallied to Stephens's defense and urged the people to rise above petty partisan and sectional considerations. Other Richmond newspapers ridiculed the *Examiner*'s position and deplored any questioning of Stephens's patriotism.[8]

In the midst of this flap, Herschel Johnson worried about the formation of political parties "for the mere promotion and elevation of *men*." Such organizations were "always bitter, intolerant, and soon degenerate into factions." Again the language of eighteenth-century antiparty republicanism helped define the new political culture. Selfish political maneuvering had destroyed the old government and now endangered the new one. "We are all slaveholders—all Southern States—all under the government of the Confederate States," an Atlanta editor reminded his readers in language that emphasized the new nation's distinctive character. The people should therefore heed George Washington's warnings about sectional and party divisions.[9]

Everyone agreed that a contested presidential election would not serve the public interest, and political discussion stressed one overriding theme—the burial of partisan differences. Perhaps a new "era of good feelings" had dawned in Southern politics. Secessionists and cooperationists alike could forget the past and celebrate their newfound unity at the polls. Without rival candidates, the election would mark, according to a Richmond editor, O. Jennings Wise, "merely the formal and authoritative declaration of the choice [of the president and vice-president] by acclamation." Even Governor Joseph E. Brown of Georgia, an early critic of the administration, admitted there was no serious opposition to the Davis-Stephens ticket.[10]

In most states, the slate of presidential electors exemplified this newfound political harmony. Whigs and Democrats, secessionists and cooperationists were all represented. Names of old political enemies appeared side by side, patriots standing together on a single platform of Southern independence. "The war should be the serpent swallowing all other controversies," one enthusiastic Louisianian believed, "and our age, experience, wisdom, and vigor combined, should constitute our civil authority." Attempts to hold state conventions or get up rival electoral tickets received little newspaper coverage and attracted even less public interest.[11]

As election day approached, "unity" remained the watchword. Newspapers urged Confederate citizens to express their patriotism by going to the polls because a large turnout would send a clear message to the Yankees that there was no lingering Unionism in the South. According to a Mississippi editor, Davis and Stephens had been "touched by Providence" to lead the nation.[12] In this shining moment of harmony, it seemed as if the revolution against politics was about to succeed; a purified republic deserving the allegiance of all Southerners was being born.

Some politicians worried, however, that efforts to promote harmony might instead produce an embarrassingly low turnout.[13] Election day was the quietest in anyone's memory. Although there are no reliable numbers on turnout, most Confederates appeared to ignore the election. The *New Orleans Picayune* reported a heavy vote in the city but also noted the absence of the usual election day bustle and excitement. Citizens reportedly approached the polls with "a grave dignity becoming the grandeur of the occasion." Despite the indifference of many voters, the appearance of harmony was the most important consideration. Even in factious South Carolina the legislature voted unanimously for Davis and Stephens.[14] Perhaps this uneventful election portended a return to the ideals of the early American republic.

The same day Southerners formally selected their president and vice-president, they also voted for members of the Permanent Congress. These contests attracted more interest and were considerably more complicated than the presidential election. Localism, old political habits, and partisan loyalties influenced the results in many districts, but even here hostility to many traditional political practices and especially to political parties shaped political behavior.

Like the United States Constitution, the Confederate Constitution prohibited members of Congress from holding any other national office, including military commissions. The ban on plural officeholding hearkened back to eighteenth-century worries about corruption and also reflected republican fears of concentrated power in general and of military despotism in particular. Whether state army or militia officers were barred from holding seats in Congress, however, was unclear, an ambiguity that allowed Southerners to engage their penchant for legal hairsplitting. According to some, patriotism proved by military service should be an important qualification for office. A correspondent of the *Richmond Enquirer* trumpeted the heroism of William Smith, who had "rushed to the tented field to fight your battles to defend your wives and children . . . under the whistle of enemy bullets." Brave men in uniform presented a striking contrast to the stay-at-homes whose only courage had been of the rhetorical variety. No true Confederate should favor a skulker over a candidate who had enlisted at the beginning of the war.[15]

Without conventions or other formal nominating procedures, newspaper letters and advertisements were about the only means available to place candidates' names before the public. This especially favored army officers, who typically evoked the call of duty as an excuse to avoid a traditional canvass. Their civilian opponents in turn felt pressured to limit their campaigning or even withdraw.[16]

Perhaps resenting this seemingly unfair advantage, candidates running against army officers appealed to the principles of classical republicanism to even the contest. Plural officeholding was unhealthy by its very nature. The ambition of military officers was especially dangerous because of their undue influence over enlisted men. Edmund Ruffin feared an officer would be "tempted . . . to seek popularity with his soldiers to secure their votes . . . and so prostitute his service and duties to advance his self-interest."[17] This would inevitably tarnish elections, weaken the army, and even lead to military despotism.

Responding to these ideological objections, some officers hid behind legal technicalities, claiming to hold commissions under state rather than Confederate authority. Others promised to resign from the army if elected to Congress. But their military experience may have suggested that the best defense against such attacks was a good offense. Responding to criticism from Whig cooperationists, secessionist Roger A. Pryor seized the high moral ground by denying that volunteer officers should be disqualified from taking congressional seats "to insure a monopoly of public offices to those who remained at home."[18]

In many congressional districts, the question of military men running for Congress became the most hotly debated issue. John Goode had enlisted as a private in the Confederate army (though he had been quickly promoted to a colonel on General Jubal Early's staff) and therefore claimed the right to run for Congress in Virginia's Sixth District. Deftly noting that his opponents campaigned while he remained with his regiment, he also touted his early support for secession. Whenever the other three candidates spoke, one of his friends would stand up in the audience and announce that Goode "cannot be here today because he is down at the front with the other boys in the army."[19] This clever strategy no doubt enraged his rivals but also helped him win election with ease.

Whatever the strictures against plural officeholding and fears of military interference in politics, there is little doubt that a commission was a great advantage—even for candidates running against opponents with powerful political allies. When Herbert Fielder raised these issues against Colonel Lucius J. Gartrell in their contest for the seat in Georgia's Eighth District, Gartrell sharply suggested that Fielder show his dedication to the Confederate cause by joining the army. Despite Fielder's attempt to enlist the aid of his friend Joe Brown and despite Gartrell's lackluster record (discipline in his regiment was so lax that court-martial proceedings began shortly after the November election), Gartrell was an easy victor.[20] Aside from other considerations, a candidate's military service offered a clear reference point in a new and uncertain political environment with few other signposts to guide public opinion.

Although procedures for selecting and promoting candidates reflected chaotic wartime conditions, they also marked a return to the less organized and more informal political procedures of the early republic. In most states, would-be congressmen simply announced their candidacies in brief advertisements; many of these notices appeared in the classifieds. Candidates published campaign letters in newspapers and occasionally as broadsides. This limited communication with the voters carried Confederate politics back to the preparty period of the late eighteenth century.

Even in factious North Carolina, nominating conventions took place in only a few districts. Holden charged that secession Democrats, having lost faith in the people, had become Hartford Convention Federalists maneuvering to place future elections under the control of "oligarchs." Yet such calls for untrammeled nonpartisan democracy were often seconded by secessionists, who also opposed county caucuses and district conventions. Few newspapers made editorial endorsements or placed the names of favorites on mastheads.[21]

Although standard calls for political unity during wartime also appeared outside the Confederacy, Northern editors gave much more attention to normal political activity than did their Southern counterparts. If Northern readers might sometimes find it hard to believe that a war was going on in the midst of all the election excitement, in many Confederate newspapers, even careful readers might not realize that an election was taking place. The lack of demand for campaign portraits and posters in the absence of political parties may also have discouraged lithography and other types of print production in the Confederacy.[22] Compared to the robust, highly charged, and often partisan campaigns in the United States, Confederate elections seemed extremely tame.

Indeed, the number of uncontested races raised hopes for national unity and the avoidance of partisan bickering. Candidates running unopposed evinced an absence of party feeling (or at least competition). Conversely, the absence of party organization was equally apparent in districts where as many as six candidates ran for one seat.[23] Nor would the voters receive much guidance before election day. Many candidates proudly pointed to their refusal to campaign in the midst of a war or welcomed an end to the bitter contests of the recent past. In most districts candidates did not give speeches, and if they did, the newspapers seldom covered them.[24]

These practices naturally gave considerable advantage to well-known individuals who had been prominent in either state or national politics. Then as now, name recognition was critical.[25] Former party affiliation probably also helped voters sort out the candidates, but antiparty themes remained strong. In some districts, Whigs and Democrats went out of their way to praise each other's devotion to the cause. Writing to the leading newspaper organ of Virginia Whigs, "Powhatan" urged Whig voters to support M. L. Hopkins, a Democrat from Petersburg, to end partisan divisions. Patriots did not need parties, and voters should judge congressional candidates by their loyalty to the Confederacy, not by their political antecedents.[26]

Many citizens must have wondered what to make of this political love feast, welcome as a temporary halt to partisan squabbling might be. Realistic commentators conceded that the Confederacy might develop parties someday, but ambitious politicians seeking the spoils of office had no legitimate place in wartime. And if parties were ever formed, they should be based solely on conflicts over important principles of government.[27] But even these observers talked vaguely about a party of national unity and often seemed ambivalent and contradictory about the role of political opposition. They greatly feared the rise of "factions" and hardly deviated from antiparty orthodoxy.

Julian Hartridge, candidate for a Georgia congressional seat, claimed that because of the irrelevance of party distinctions, there could be no real differences on issues between himself and his opponent. By implication, this meant that voters would have to base their choice on personal preference, though even on that score Hartridge disclaimed any "superiority." Candidates typically denied personal ambition and made special efforts to appear as selfless patriots.[28] Such appeals conveniently avoided controversial issues and allowed politicians to hide behind innocuous statements of support for the Confederate war effort. Endless references to letting the people decide begged the question of whether the people had much to decide with so many uncontested races and candidates who had so little to say.

In Louisiana, where factions led by John Slidell and Pierre Soulé had long battled for ascendancy, Sam C. Reid caught the spirit of a new day. His vacuous but revealing election announcement declared that in "all cases the clearly expressed will of the people should be permitted to prevail, free from dictation by combinations of men or cliques of parties, and unfettered by sectional feeling, which the immortal Washington warned our people against and the ceaseless agitation of which has proved destructive to the vitality of all communities." Should the voters ignore this advice, partisanship would inevitably undermine the Confederacy just as it had destroyed the Greek and Roman republics as well as the United States government.[29] Suitably proselytized with eighteenth-century warnings against the dangers of faction, voters had to be constantly on the lookout for political cabals.

Whigs and Democrats regularly accused their opponents of rekindling party feuds but also tried to take advantage of previous loyalties without triggering charges of proscription or opportunism. Southern rights Democrat Martin J. Crawford had served in the Provisional Congress and was running for the Permanent Congress from Georgia's Third District. A wealthy slaveholder who could have comfortably retired from politics, Crawford, however, could not stomach the idea of letting his equally well-off Whig rival Hines Holt win by default. He especially resented efforts to rally old Know-Nothing forces against him. Elsewhere there were subtle references to party affiliation in candidates' announcements and editorials, and remnants of party organization probably helped candidates in some districts, though any precise assessment of their influence is impossible.[30]

Not only did old party divisions continue to influence voters in many districts, but a few candidates still harped on the issues of the 1830s and 1840s. In a long letter to voters of Arkansas's Third Congressional District, B. C. Harley celebrated the death of the old party system and praised the Confederate Constitution for perfecting the work of republicanism. Styling himself a "plain farmer," he also pointed to his record as a states'-rights Democrat, including his unyielding opposition to bounties and tariffs. What Whig could mistake the tenor of these remarks? Likewise, the *Richmond Examiner* accused congressional candidate William H. McFarland of promoting the interests of his bank while scheming to draw two salaries at the same time. This explicit class appeal echoed Jacksonian rhetoric with warnings against the insidious "money influence." The *Examiner* crowed when former president John Tyler—a Whig with impeccable anti-bank credentials—crushed the hapless McFarland. Such demagoguery attracted some support but nevertheless rubbed a sensitive nerve. Any effort to "array classes against each other," warned a Georgia country editor, would divide the people, revive the old political parties, and soon weaken the Confederacy.[31]

Recent battles between immediate secessionists and cooperationists promised to have an even more disruptive effect on the congressional elections. Secessionists emphasized their early support for Southern independence. The friends of Colonel Roger A. Pryor bragged that their candidate had come out for resistance to any Northern attempt at coercion immediately after Lincoln's election and had been at Fort Sumter while the Virginia convention was still debating whether to leave the Union. Even in areas carried by conservatives in the convention elections, some voters may well have supported a moderate secessionist for the sake of unity.[32]

Although some secessionist editors explicitly called on the people to forget past political differences, few could refrain from twitting candidates who had so recently favored equivocation and delay. As the *Examiner* put it, "Old fogies are of no use. Give us men who have the spirit of the Revolution, earnest, practical, up to the times with blood and energy in them." Why should elderly men risk their delicate health in drafty Richmond hotels when younger and more eager men could better serve in Congress? Editor Daniel's sarcasm reflected persistent fears of counterrevolution and reconstruction. If the Whigs and Union men returned to power, a North Carolina soldier wrote, the state is "sold out to Lincoln." He urged his friends at home to make sure that no "old Union slop" would represent his district.[33] Aspiring congressmen who had been slow to endorse secession aroused suspicion.

Cooperationists, vulnerable to accusations of submissionism, especially in closely contested districts, therefore had to champion the Confederate cause and avoid being put on the political defensive. Seizing the initiative with time-tested tactics, they warned against a secessionist conspiracy to monopolize lucrative offices. Now that the war was under way, they could also quote with telling effect the predictions of peaceable secession made by Southern firebrands.[34]

Such battles grew particularly heated in the upper South states. In North Carolina's Fifth Congressional District, Archibald Arrington, despite his moderately cooperationist background, trumpeted his defense of Southern rights and tried to turn the congressional election into a belated referendum on secession. His competitor, Josiah Turner, Jr., had resisted secession even after the firing on Fort Sumter but had then enlisted as a cavalry captain. Turner counterattacked by sharply suggesting that men who had been so anxious for secession should now join him in the Confederate army. Yet Turner still had to deny being a reconstructionist and repeatedly explain why he had opposed arming state troops before North Carolina left the Union. The contest became even more lively when a debate between the two candidates in Wake County nearly ended in a riot.[35] Arrington barely won the election, and Turner's surprisingly strong showing indicated that many North Carolinians still had doubts about secession.

Yet simply weighing the relative strength of Democrats and Whigs or even secessionists and cooperationists oversimplifies these elections. The breakdown of political organization and the lack of campaign excitement resulted in many races turning on personalities or local issues. Some candidates stressed the military needs of their districts or even of single counties. Others accused their opponents of everything from land speculation (how many prominent nineteenth-century politicians could have avoided that charge?), to financial mismanagement of a railroad, to ruthless foreclosures of mortgages.[36]

In races lacking such issues, candidates hid behind meaningless generalities. Their public letters exuded patriotism without addressing the Confederacy's pressing military and financial problems. John Tyler, for instance, offered a lengthy defense of states' rights and wrapped his candidacy in the Confederate flag. The perfect campaign notice contained roughly equal portions of patriotic banalities, denials of personal ambition, and vague calls for political unity. And of course all candidates claimed to favor the vigorous prosecution of the war, though they seldom discussed ways and means.[37]

"In a period of peace and prosperity," intoned the editorial spokesman for conservative Virginians, "the people are too apt to give countenance to demagogues, political tricksters and harlequins, who amuse them with their buffoonery on the hustings. But now the public demand grave, sensible, earnest men—men who comprehend the importance of their position, and have the talent and manliness to meet it." Yet this supposed newfound wisdom hardly comforted those who could always find reason to fret about public ignorance and the excesses of democracy, and the congressional races still gave considerable scope for political trimmers and place hunters. Disgusted with what he saw as rampant lust for office among most members of the North Carolina convention, David Schenck feared that the "days of Republican government ended with Republican simplicity."[38] Some Confederates already despaired of the political future.

Several articles in the *Southern Literary Messenger* and *De Bow's Review* discussed the long history of corruption in both the ancient and modern world, noting how republics had often fallen prey to demagoguery and office-seeking. Conveniently ignoring the practices of Washington's day, "Virginius" admonished Southerners to stop "treating" the voters because plying them with alcohol appealed to men's "worst passions." Such a thinly disguised attempt at bribery "corrupted the elective franchise" and ultimately contaminated free institutions. These gloomy warnings, however, could not suppress many people's natural pride in the new Confederate government. Pointing to the supposedly rampant corruption of the Lincoln regime, one commentator praised the Davis administration for exemplifying the values of moral and patriotic gentlemen, the highest products of Southern civilization. He added significantly that "domestic slavery elevates the character of all men."[39]

Nevertheless, confidence in virtuous leaders and a just cause could not entirely overcome fears that the new nation might face serious internal divisions. A sense of danger permeated public discourse. Newspaper editors and congressional candidates alike echoed general anxieties over the lingering effects of partisanship and patronage. From his historic home at Chatham (where the godlike Washington had once slept) across the Rappahannock River from Fredericksburg, Virginia, J. Horace Lacy wrote a letter accepting the call of "many citizens" to stand for a seat in Congress. The only way to "preserve our Government from . . . corruption . . . [is] by limiting the power of patronage, by regarding honesty, capacity, and fidelity as the indispensable and only qualification for office, and inaugurating a rigid economy in our public administration, which would disburse millions for defense but not a cent for favor."[40]

Such sentiments resonated in many quarters. Religious leaders denounced factional divisiveness and partisan ambition. The *Nashville Christian Advocate* advised voters to shun drunkards, gamblers, adulterers, and time-serving demagogues. "How is it that so few public men are good men?" asked the Reverend Henry Tucker, a professor of literature at Mercer University. Perhaps because ordinary people lacked virtue: "Every voter who allows personal interests or preferences, or prejudices, or party zeal or anything else, to influence his suffrage in favor of a bad man in preference to a good one . . . is doing what he can to banish virtue from our councils and God from our support." Less than a month after the election, in a sermon preached at Greensboro, North Carolina, J. Henry Smith delivered a classic jeremiad to stiff-necked Tar Heels: "The man that attempts directly or indirectly by insinuation of 'secessionism,' 'unionism,' 'democracy,' 'whiggery' and such like to fan up the differences and make future political capital of the past, will be as guilty in his soul before heaven and earth [as] . . . the cowardly ingrate and fiend incarnate, who promotes civil war and who robs and murders his aged father and mother."[41]

These solemn warnings seemed strangely out of place in an election campaign that failed to attract much public interest or arouse popular passions. The war remained the all-absorbing question, and many Southerners believed that the real statesmen were already in the Confederate army. Would-be congressmen too often seemed little more than amiable mediocrities or eloquent nonentities who feigned surprise when anyone suggested they run for office. Given such candidates, who would actually go to the polls? Since the best citizens were in uniform, Edmund Ruffin drew the obvious conclusion: "A government like ours of universal suffrage will be a government of & by the *worst* of the people."[42] These first congressional elections, however, hardly marked the transfer of power to sans-culotte mobs. Instead, political apathy and the absence of many yeomen and poor whites (and no small number of planters) in the army left the power of local elites largely intact. The calm of election day also reflected support for the Davis administration, faith in the Confederacy, and hope for the future. The lack of interest in the presidential election, the large number of uncontested congressional races, obsession with war news, and general indifference kept many voters at home. Confederates who had crusaded against partisanship and demagoguery could temporarily rejoice.

Because few returns are extant, quantitative analysis of these elections is impossible. Scattered reports indicate that turnout was no more than half that of a normal election and in many districts lower.[43] Secessionists won about three-fifths of the races, and Democrats captured approximately the same proportion of seats. Amid considerable apathy and confusion, these first Confederate elections disrupted old voting patterns, and the party complexion of a district had little influence on the results. Traditionally Democratic districts were nearly as likely to choose a Whig as a Democrat, and the same was true for many old Whig strongholds.[44] Declining partisanship reflected a natural desire for political peace as well as the influence of antiparty ideology. Early in the war voters preferred secessionists or former cooperationists who strongly supported the Confederacy and who had some experience in office. Political organization and even campaigning had fallen into disfavor; unity and patriotism had become the central values of the new political order.

The selection of Confederate senators produced even less public excitement than the congressional elections but also offered more opportunity for political wire-pulling. Old rivalries, partisan feuds, complex factionalism, and personal ambition naturally appeared. In the interest of political harmony, some legislatures chose one Democrat and one Whig or followed the antebellum practice of assigning Senate seats by sections. Occasionally party and geographical considerations clashed. The Mississippi legislature picked a leading secession Democrat, Albert Gallatin Brown, to represent the southern and eastern portions of the state. Some members believed that a Whig should have been chosen for the other seat, but legislators from northern Mississippi could not settle on a candidate. Consequently, a Democrat, James Phelan, was elected.[45] In states where the Whig opposition had nearly disappeared, Democrats captured both senatorships. Besides old party considerations, mending divisions over disunion also became important, especially in the upper South. Arkansas, Florida, Georgia, North Carolina, Tennessee, and Virginia each chose one cooperationist and one secessionist; in the rest of the states, both new senators were secessionists.[46]

On closer examination, however, these selections seem more complex and confusing. In a political culture based on national unity (that consequently disparaged party organization), choosing senators sometimes seemed nearly impossible. Between the end of November and the middle of December, the Florida legislature cast over forty ballots. Scattered votes among a multitude of candidates marked the breakdown of traditional party discipline; whether an aspirant's party background or even his position on secession mattered is anyone's guess. The choice of James M. Baker and Augustus E. Maxwell signified both resignation and exhaustion. Baker was an obscure jurist and Whig cooperationist, Maxwell a veteran Democratic legislator and congressman with an undistinguished record. Both men were clearly second, third, or more likely fourth choices of the fragmented legislature.[47]

The uncertain course of Confederate and state politics, calls for harmony, and a general disillusionment with politicians may have temporarily sobered legislative leaders, but old divisions and strife had not disappeared. The "Family" Democrats in Arkansas managed to elect Robert W. Johnson to the Senate, but C. W. Mitchel, a cooperationist, anti-Family Democrat, and enemy of Governor Henry M. Rector, won the other seat. Feuding between Arkansas Democrats (with the Whig minority generally aligned against the "Family" Democrats) continued for several months.[48]

Though party and factional competition survived in some states, fluidity generally characterized wartime politics. Alliances and loyalties changed more rapidly than ever, especially as politicians reacted to political and military events. The Byzantine politics of Alabama, for instance, took another peculiar turn. Snubbed earlier by the Alabama convention but with the secessionists riding a wave of war fervor, Yancey easily won a Senate seat. His triumph hardly signaled a fire-eater rout of the conservative opposition because cooperationist Democrats and their Whig allies then tried to block the election of Southern rights man Clement Claiborne Clay as Alabama's other senator. False reports circulated that Clay (and other secessionists) had not contributed to the Confederate produce loan. Miffed at not being elected until the tenth ballot and appalled at the surprisingly strong opposition, the sensitive Clay considered refusing the now dubious honor. One friend begged him not to "give a victory to selfish . . . intriguers over your own tried friends." Another supporter listed the many legislators who had worked hard for Clay's election. Such counsel and its attendant flattery persuaded him to accept the post.[49] Secessionists and supporters of the Davis administration had temporarily prevailed. Yancey and Clay, however, would both pursue increasingly independent courses, and the Whig-cooperationist faction had survived to fight another day.

Weighing the relative influence of state sectionalism, secession politics, old party quarrels, and personal ambition on these contests is tricky given the dearth of detailed information. Shifting legislative blocs caucused behind closed doors, and newspaper coverage was sparse. Virginia was a partial exception to this pattern. After Toombs's early exit from the cabinet, Davis had chosen Robert M. T. Hunter as secretary of state. A reluctant secessionist and a Democrat with a reputation as a political trimmer, Hunter never lost the itch for higher office. Though loyal to Davis, he hoped to win election to the Senate, then leave the cabinet, and perhaps position himself for the 1867 presidential election.

But these plans did not proceed smoothly. The *Examiner* complained that Virginia would lose a cabinet seat simply to satisfy Hunter's presidential ambitions and denounced his "selfishness, calculation and cunning." Several letters in the *Richmond Whig* accused Hunter of underestimating the importance of his cabinet post, belittled his political record, and condemned such blatant jobbery. Supporters of cooperationist Democrat James A. Barbour claimed that Hunter depended on the machinations of a political clique, disparaged his unseemly office-seeking, and inaccurately denounced him as a rabid secessionist.

By January 1862, old-line Democrats regretted the growing public acrimony. Without mentioning Hunter's name, the *Richmond Enquirer* advised the legislature to make selections calmly and patriotically—much as the state's voters had done during the recent congressional elections. Hunter's enemies, however, could not remain calm. The *Examiner* continued its almost daily attacks on this prototypical Washington spoilsman, and when Barbour withdrew and Hunter at last prevailed, editor Daniel hinted at bribery. Public disgust over the entire affair was evident. According to War Department official Robert G. H. Kean, "The legislature has wasted two months in wretched squabbles over the senatorship while a powerful and artful enemy has been drawing his lines closer and closer around us on every side."[50]

The election of such a prominent Davis ally as Hunter, however, showed the administration's political strength. Across the Confederacy, most newspapers condemned the president's early critics as "croakers." Rhett's friends still held out hope that the "father of secession" might yet occupy an office worthy of his talents, but the Carolina firebrand's intemperate attacks on the government were politically costly. In fact, many members of the South Carolina legislature appeared to be in a remarkably conciliatory and conservative mood. Bypassing Rhett, James Henry Hammond (who was virulently anti-Davis), and even the moderate James Chesnut, Jr., they selected Davis supporter Robert Barnwell. The fire-eaters were even more appalled by the election of their longtime enemy and so-called National Democrat James L. Orr to the other Senate seat.[51] Apparently moderation and the dread spirit of reconstruction still threatened the young republic.

A strong political reaction had set in against the Rhetts and other malcontents. Party balance, the end of ideological bickering, and above all simple patriotism had become the touchstones of Confederate politics, and even the most cautious cooperationists were falling into line. Although many Georgia Whigs complained that Democrats had received the Confederacy's choicest appointments, they had good reason to welcome the selection of moderate cooperationist Benjamin Hill as their state's first Confederate senator. So did Davis. On the first ballot, Hill had easily defeated chronic complainer and troublemaker Robert Toombs. Yet not all moderates were satisfied. Herschel Johnson protested the continued discrimination against Douglas Democrats and observed that "the distinctions of party have [merely] taken on new names." Johnson himself was a good case in point. Self-righteous and priggish, he routinely accused political rivals of low intrigue. And though he pointedly forswore office-seeking, he hoped against hope that the legislature would turn to him. Realizing his own slim chances, however, Johnson decided that the demagoguery and corruption of the present generation would surely bring forth divine retribution.[52] In other words, the Georgia secessionists deserved God's punishment for bypassing Herschel Johnson.

But Johnson's frustration and the strong showing of ardent Southern rights man Alfred Iverson on the early ballots were only sideshows in Milledgeville. In the center ring of this political circus stood the irascible Toombs. After the ignominious defeat by Hill, Toombs's supporters worked hard to secure his election to the short-term (two-year) Senate seat and won out on the sixth ballot. Toombs, however, was furious. With lordly disdain, he declared that "the manner in which the legislature thought proper to confer this trust relieves me from any obligation to sacrifice either my personal wishes or my convictions of public duty in order to accept it." Toombs's stilted language barely concealed his thwarted ambition. Privately, he fulminated against the "Know-Nothing" supporters of "that scoundrel Davis" who had conspired to humiliate him. His behavior disgusted some Georgia politicians and even shocked his friends.[53] The Georgia legislature had belatedly recognized Toombs's considerable intelligence and raw talent without sanctioning his opposition to the Davis administration. For his part, Toombs had spurned the senatorship as a spoiled child might throw aside a favorite toy during a temper tantrum.

How much the average Confederate citizen understood or cared about these contests is difficult to gauge. The senatorial elections had occurred with little fanfare in most states. Newspaper editors did not even bother to speculate on whether the Senate (or the House for that matter) would stand behind administration policies. Neither the party composition nor even the secessionist-cooperationist mix of the new Congress elicited much comment.

Perhaps the best talent had gone into the army and the relative obscurity of many new lawmakers was a good sign. North Carolinian David Schenck objected that the very process of choosing senators had rekindled party passions, but if so they had quickly cooled.[54] Confederate, or what now might be called national, politics had assumed a decidedly placid appearance, but in a few states a combination of traditional partisanship or factional combativeness and early wartime controversies threatened to dash hopes for political harmony.

The values and practices of an emerging Confederate political culture also had a powerful and immediate impact on state elections. Especially in the Deep South, where Whiggery had grown feeble during the 1850s, the conservative forces were fragmented. Personal factions might occasionally appear, but the electoral machinery had grown rusty. Bristling at the mere suggestion of holding nominating conventions for state legislative races, a Shreveport editor made a classic antiparty appeal: "Let our offices be left open and free to all who aspire for such honors or profits—no more log-rolling. Let the free and untrammeled voice of the people be heard." Such a simple call for democracy was also a formula for political chaos, but the death of party rivalries and an end to the unbecoming scramble for minor offices seemed the best way to show support for the cause and solidarity with the troops in the field.[55]

Condemnations of partisanship and the decline of many traditional political practices characterized Confederate politics even at the state level. Texas Democrats could neither settle on a gubernatorial candidate nor discover any significant issues for a canvass. In a campaign broadside, Thomas Jefferson Chambers waxed eloquent on the Confederacy's bright future but said nothing about his qualifications for office or about any public questions. Francis Lubbock declared himself a states'-rights Democrat, a friend of Jefferson Davis, and a democratic politician. Because neither Lubbock, Chambers, nor the incumbent Edward Clark did much campaigning, Texans had trouble making a choice. Lubbock eked out a narrow victory over Clark with Chambers finishing a respectable third in a contest that could easily have passed unnoticed.[56]

Across the Confederacy, political opposition had become suspect. Incumbent governors and other state officials seemed safely ensconced in their offices—sometimes regardless of their performance. During the spring of 1861 a surfeit of poorly armed, clothed, and fed volunteers with plenty of time to gripe spelled trouble for Governor John J. Pettus of Mississippi. Residents of Gulf Coast counties accused the governor of leaving them defenseless against Federal attack. Whigs groused that too many Democrats had received commissions and vice versa. Nonetheless, a Democratic convention met in July to renominate Pettus for governor. Remnants of the Whig party and some disgruntled Democrats turned to the state's quartermaster general, Madison McAfee, who had often clashed with Pettus and the state military board. Yet even the governor's critics doubted the desirability of a campaign when Confederate fortunes were so precarious.[57]

After Pettus cleverly sent McAfee to Richmond for consultations with the War Department, opposition to the governor quickly evaporated. Though McAfee disapproved of many of the appointments made by the military board, he had no stomach for a political battle. Defensive about charges that Whig Unionists had engineered his candidacy, McAfee claimed that party distinctions now meant nothing because all factions had fought side by side on the plains of Manassas. He therefore withdrew his name from the governor's race but did not endorse Pettus. Although candidates for the legislature sometimes ran against the governor's policies, calls for electing these men without opposition showed the strength of political apathy and antiparty sentiments even at the county level. Despite the chronic dissatisfaction over patronage, Pettus captured over 87 percent of the votes cast.[58] The victory of a governor who had seemed vulnerable only a few months earlier and who even in the fall had not become a popular figure reaffirmed the politics of patriotic unity.

Secessionist Democrats now dominated politics in much of the Gulf South and even in states with once formidable cooperationist minorities. In early discussion of the approaching gubernatorial election, Alabama newspaper editors rejected holding a convention or organizing opposition against either the Confederate administration or Democratic candidate John Gill Shorter. The defense of liberty against Yankee aggression became a rallying cry even in the hill country. Some Whigs and disaffected Democrats nominated the conservative Whig Thomas H. Watts for governor, and, given their obvious political weakness, naturally called for burying past party differences.

The Southern rights men were firmly in control, however, and the fractured opposition had no chance. Watts refused to campaign and even tried to withdraw from the race. Adroitly tying his candidacy to the Davis administration, Shorter handily defeated Watts by nearly ten thousand votes in the August election. Shorter lost some Whig strongholds in southern Alabama but ran surprisingly well in counties that had been dominated by cooperationists only a few months before. Secessionists also won a majority of seats in the new legislature.[59] Although in Alabama, as in most of the other Confederate states, the gubernatorial election passed quietly, disenchantment with "wire workers" remained strong, and many potential voters were in army camps rather than at the polls. The prospects for a powerful political coalition that would sustain the war effort and the Davis administration appeared as bright as the gleam of the volunteers' new bayonets.

Georgia politics would paradoxically reinforce these trends while giving rise to dissonant voices in Confederate politics. Not only had Robert Toombs become an implacable enemy of the Davis administration, but Governor Joseph E. Brown appeared increasingly troublesome. Despite his popularity with the white masses, Brown was no country rube or demagogic spellbinder. A bean pole of a man at five feet, ten inches in height and weighing only 135 pounds, at age forty, with his balding head and cropped beard, he looked more like a Baptist preacher than a politician. At once pious and opportunistic, humorless and intelligent, stubborn and clever, sober and argumentative, Brown was the consummate politician.

He was a self-made man whose ambition always burned brightly.[60] Although Southern state governors often had tightly circumscribed authority and commonly served but a single term, Brown had first won election in 1857 and kept winning.

A master at cultivating popularity, Brown recoiled at the slightest threat to his position and jealously protected his power base in Georgia. His provincialism was at once his most notable strength and his most glaring weakness. Even before the war began, Brown was determined to control the composition and disposition of Georgia troops. In proffering regiments to the Confederacy, he stipulated that the government retain the officers he had appointed. Equally solicitous about the arms and supplies his state contributed, Brown always insisted that Georgians not be forced to bear more than their fair share of wartime burdens.

The governor did more than stand on his prerogatives and defend state interests. He pursued these objects with a petulance that soon exasperated Confederate officials. Brown's steady stream of telegrams and letters to the War Department were filled with excuses for either not meeting government troop requisitions or ignoring army regulations.[61] The governor's sturdy independence seemed more annoying than dangerous at this early stage of the war, and he had not yet directly crossed swords with Jefferson Davis.

A month before the attack on Fort Sumter, speculation about Brown's political future was already rife. Would he seek a third term as governor? Brown was not saying. At first, he seemed inclined to retire and honor the state's two-term tradition. In a series of editorials, the *Milledgeville Southern Federal Union* advised Georgians to stick with their governor in such perilous times, and by July his name appeared on the paper's masthead. Brown's friends declared old party ties dead and warned that a full-fledged campaign would serve no good purpose. They accused the governor's enemies of trying to revive strife between original secessionists and cooperationists and even claimed to face strong opposition from bankers who had always feared any honest Democrat. Brown's supporters dismissed the third-term issue as a smoke screen put up by unscrupulous opponents but also denied that their man was a monarchist.[62]

On August 13, Brown at last declared his intention to seek another term though at first glance his prospects for reelection seemed slim. All but two newspapers in the state opposed the governor, and many of his supporters were pessimistic. The rules of the political game, however, had changed; no longer would organization or newspaper support prove decisive. Seeing beyond the sound and fury of hostile editorials, Brown confidently maintained that "the masses of the people are with me and continue to sustain me."[63]

For Brown, incumbency proved to be a double advantage in an antiparty political culture. To run for reelection, all he had to do was draft a public letter, but the opposition had no easy way to challenge him. Almost any campaign effort smacked of dangerous partisanship. Even an anti-Brown editor agreed that conventions only increased the power of selfish "cliques." Brown dismissed calls for a political convention as a desperate ploy by "politicians and office-seekers." When plans were announced to hold a meeting in Milledgeville, a pro-Brown newspaper charged that the Lincoln administration would surely welcome the defeat of the patriotic Georgia governor and predicted that only 13 of 133 counties would bother sending delegates to a gathering of political renegades.[64]

Such appeals infuriated and frustrated Brown's adversaries. Although Brown, Toombs, and Howell Cobb had all worked together for secession against the Stephens brothers and other cooperationists, by the spring and summer of 1861, a realignment in Georgia politics had begun. Toombs and the more cautious Stephenses allied with Brown. Cobb supported the Davis administration in its struggle with the governor over the control of Georgia troops and hoped to "thoroughly put down the miserable demagogue who disgraces the executive chair of Ga." Cobb stood ready to work with his old rival Ben Hill and anyone else who opposed Brown. A Savannah editor suggested that the opposition press should choose one man to run against Brown, but the problem was not that simple.[65]

Several papers issued a call for a nominating convention to meet on September 11 in Milledgeville. Some forty counties officially sent delegates, though enough self-appointed ones showed up to provide some representation for around fifty-eight counties. The opposition press lamely asserted that this assemblage embodied the popular will. The delegates unanimously nominated Eugenius A. Nisbet for governor. A onetime Whig, Know-Nothing, and Douglas Democrat in 1860, "Judge Nisbet," as he was usually called, was a firm friend of the Davis administration.[66] Even Brown supporters had few objections to the colorless Nisbet, but then he was hardly a formidable opponent.

The convention probably did the governor more good than harm by handing him a ready-made issue: aversion to political wire-pulling. "We fear that these professional politicians and bush fighters are creeping back to their old dirty sewers," wrote one outraged Georgian to an anti-Brown newspaper, "trying to keep the people from learning that they have brains enough in their heads to take care of themselves, and that they are only fit for laborers and fighters. We think if the people do not understand and appreciate their rights, it is getting time that they were educated up. If the question of caucus and convention is to be dug up, we want it done squarely and boldly, and not to sneak like a serpent through the grass, under the guise of 'no party.'" Predicting that the election would complete the obliteration of old party lines, Brown supporters dismissed the Milledgeville meeting as a rump convention of disappointed office-seekers and happily noted the public indifference to Nisbet's candidacy. Brown felt more confident than ever and saw no reason to campaign.[67]

Stressing their supposed harmony and popular appeal, Nisbet's friends immediately raised the third-term issue. Rotation in office—a rhetorical staple of early Jacksonian democracy—became their political hobbyhorse. Brown's "love of office," asserted the *Savannah Republican*, was the driving force behind his bid for reelection. The opposition also zeroed in on Brown's character: his egotism, which would be laughable if it did not threaten the people's liberties; his hypocrisy in denouncing conventions and caucuses, the very means of his own elevation to political power; and his vanity, already hamstringing Confederate recruiting in Georgia. The governor's "sole ambition," declared one angry citizen, "is self-promotion and aggrandizement."[68] If this campaign rhetoric were taken seriously, threats to republicanism—in the form of selfish and potentially despotic politicians—came from both sides.

Brown privately expressed shock at the bitterness of the attacks against him and claimed to prefer withdrawing from the race if he could have done so with "honor." More likely he must have secretly rejoiced over the opposition's ineptitude and relished their prospective humiliation at the polls. In fact, old party divisions and even the recent conflicts between secessionists and cooperationists had become increasingly confused and apparently insignificant. Brown's allies charged that the old Whig and Know-Nothing influence had engineered Nisbet's candidacy, overlooking the Cobb brothers' leading role in the opposition.[69]

Brown capitalized on the weakness of the jerry-built alliance against him to win over 58 percent of the vote in the October election. The victory was a tribute to Brown the governor and the politician but hardly a setback for the Davis administration. Brown might have won by an even wider margin had he been more flexible in dealing with Confederate authorities. As it was, a majority of members in the newly elected legislature had backed Nisbet, and they would frustrate the governor on many issues. Georgians at large seemed to have been favorably disposed toward Brown and the president.

In some ways, both men came to represent the Confederate cause. Davis was the great symbol of national power and harmony, the source of Confederate authority, the new republic's only genuine political hero. The first Confederate elections had reaffirmed patriotism, harmony, and faith in the government. Antiparty ideology and wartime necessity had begun to forge a politics based on the central value of national unity. This political dynamic had gone a long way toward destroying the remnants of the second American party system in the South and healing or at least covering over the old quarrels of the secession crisis. Even Joe Brown had not dared openly to criticize the Confederate government during the election campaign. Political activity had become suspect though the gap between ideology and reality remained wide. Partisan feeling, personal ambition, and political recrimination had not disappeared. And the apparent political consensus harbored seeds of dissension that would eventually germinate and finally blossom (with the help of Joe Brown) into an alternative political culture that exalted liberty over unity.

Confederate States of America.

FOR PRESIDENT,
JEFFERSON DAVIS,
Of Mississippi.

FOR VICE PRESIDENT,
ALEX. H. STEPHENS,
Of Georgia.

ELECTORS.

FOR STATE AT LARGE,
CHARLES DERBIGNY, of Orleans.
ALBERT G. CARTER, of E. Feliciana.

FIRST DISTRICT,
DONATIEN AUGUSTIN, of Orleans.

SECOND DISTRICT,
JAMES P. FRERET, of Orleans.

THIRD DISTRICT,
EDWARD DUFFEL, of Ascension.

FOURTH DISTRICT,
WM. R. BARROW, of West Feliciana.

FIFTH DISTRICT,
B. EGAN, SR., of Bienville.

SIXTH DISTRICT,
S. L. CHAMBLISS, of Carroll.

FOR CONGRESS—FOURTH-DISTRICT,
LUCIUS J. DUPRE, of St. Landry.

Ballot used in Louisiana for the first Confederate elections
(Special Collections, Robert W. Woodruff Library, Emory University)

The Confederate president and vice-president, who exemplified the competing values of national unity and libertarianism

Jefferson Davis
(Library of Congress)

Alexander H. Stephens
(Library of Congress)

Louis T. Wigfall
(Library of Congress)

Joseph E. Johnston
(Library of Congress)

William Lowndes Yancey
(Southern Historical Collection, Wilson Library, University of North
Carolina at Chapel Hill)

Robert Barnwell Rhett, Sr.
(South Caroliniana Library, University of South Carolina)

Joseph E. Brown
(Library of Congress)

Robert Toombs
(Hargrett Rare Book and Manuscript Library, University of Georgia)

Two politicians who sought to steer a moderate course

Zebulon Vance
(North Carolina Division of Archives and History)

Herschel V. Johnson
(Georgia Department of Archives and History)

William W. Holden, leading peace advocate
(North Carolina Division of Archives and History)

CHAPTER 6

Origins of
Political Crisis

T
he new Confederate politics soon became an amalgam of unity and divisiveness, harmony and contentiousness, apathy and anger. In addition to lingering partisan feeling, contradictions between ideology and political practice soon appeared. Political conflict took place under a broad umbrella of Southern republicanism with its general antipathy to a wide range of political activity.

Another ingredient was the sheer cantankerousness of Confederate leaders who had imposing egos and an appalling inability to cooperate with anyone who disagreed with them. Indeed, the notion of honest differences seemed utterly foreign to men like Toombs, T. R. R. Cobb, and the Stephens brothers. A basic touchiness, a hypersensitivity, along with a frequent obsession with personal honor made for prickly relationships among the Confederate elite. If Jefferson Davis often appeared stubborn and unyielding, so did many of his opponents and supporters.

During the transition to the permanent government and in the absence of strong congressional leadership, the president became the focus of both adulation and criticism. Whether he would be a rallying point for beleaguered Confederates became more doubtful by the spring of 1862, when a series of military defeats and political disputes severely tested a political culture dependent on economic, social, and political harmony.

Shortly after Davis's election as permanent Confederate president, a brief but sharp controversy erupted over supposedly well-settled constitutional questions. Declaring the Confederate Constitution a patched-together compromise satisfying no one, Robert Ridgeway of the *Richmond Whig* warned against yielding too much power to the executive. His vision of a purified republic included setting a salary cap of $1,000 for all Confederate officials, requiring the president and Congress to serve without pay, and handing over military and naval defense to the states. These bizarre and unworkable proposals of course got nowhere. Blasting them as "anti-republican," the *Memphis Appeal* pointed out that the Confederate Constitution already curtailed political patronage and protected the people from presidential usurpation.[1] Yet such unresolved constitutional questions suggested ideological confusion and promised future political disaffection.

The antipolitician rhetoric of the secession crisis threatened to cause a more general loss of faith in government. Raising the shopworn cries of proscription and corruption, some former Whigs mourned the demise of their political principles. A Virginia Presbyterian minister, Thomas V. Moore, lamented the persistence of jealousies, animosities, and rivalries between the "border, and cotton, and gulf, and western States" but at the same time vigorously defended his state against the slanders of Deep South fire-eaters. Perhaps the war would mold these disparate elements into a new union, but many vices of the old order survived. Following the sinful example of Yankee speculators, greedy Southerners were already reaping undeserved profits from the common suffering.[2] Moore spoke for many other former cooperationists who supported the Confederate experiment with considerable trepidation.

From veteran Whigs to young fire-eaters, editors and politicians still railed against the excesses of democracy. Georgian Eugenius Nisbet considered a liberal franchise an "impracticable dream." The evils of the old Union—"a licentious press, ignorance among the large voting masses, the revival of old party animosities, and a low grade of representation in our legislatures state and national"—were already enervating the Southern nation. To Mary Chesnut, a republic meant "everybody jawing, everybody putting their mouths in, nothing sacred, all confusion of babble, crimination, and recrimination." Doubting the strength of the Confederate system, she cried, "Hurrah for a strong one-man government." In a remarkably candid speech in Richmond, Alabama congressman Jabez Lamar Monroe Curry denied that the Confederate government should seek "the greatest good of the greatest number." "Enlarged liberal Christian statesmanship" should protect liberty against both numerical majorities and executive encroachment, he declared, because "representation is a check on popular passion; restrains popular prejudice; and secures the triumph of reason, deliberation, and accountability."[3]

Although reactionary sentiments seldom received such vehement public expression, many Confederates firmly believed that their new nation was becoming if not the last bastion at least the best hope for the survival of ordered liberty. They particularly emphasized the virtues of a political culture that avoided the evils of partisanship. Even veteran party leaders now embraced antiparty attitudes. Ideally, political antecedents were irrelevant: the only real test of patriotism was support for the Confederacy. "Dissension now is death," the usually critical and highly partisan Thomas R. R. Cobb announced. Making the wish father to the thought, politicians even claimed that an end to traditional political divisions had largely been achieved.[4]

On January 17, 1862, at the capitol building in Austin, Texas, two judges delivered speeches that wove together many of these threads of early Confederate political ideology. Secession had become necessary, asserted Thomas J. Devine, because the grievances of the South in 1861 were far more serious than those of the American colonies in 1776. "No party in opposition to a cause so sacred will be permitted to exist in safety, or will dare to raise its serpent head with impunity in the South," he warned. Judge A. W. Terrill agreed that the right to dissent should not extend to Southerners who maintained allegiance to a "foreign" power: "With such men liberty of speech has no rational meaning. They have been deluded by the catch-words of 'liberty, equality, and fraternity' which deluged France in blood. . . . There is a bastard liberty which is the twin brother of Anarchy, and its advocates are among those, who would cloak incipient treason under the garb of liberty of speech."[5]

But for the Confederacy to limit the right of free speech meant abandoning both the high moral ground and a powerful propaganda tool. Davis and other leaders had repeatedly contrasted the Lincoln administration's behavior with the Confederacy's scrupulous observance of civil liberties through the early months of the war. The *Richmond Whig* even recommended striking any reference to the suspension of habeas corpus from the Confederate Constitution. Yet at the same time, military necessity prompted some newspaper editors to call for press censorship in the interests of security and unity. A Louisianian proposed that Black Republican sympathizers be deported from the Confederacy.[6] Tolerance for dissent and even for criticism had grown thin; the pressures of war brought new demands for the suppression of "treason."

Nor were the apprehensions of ardent Confederate patriots unfounded. Pockets of Unionism and even occasional resistance to Confederate authority plagued state and national officials at the end of the war's first year. Several bridges in East Tennessee were burned by Unionist guerrillas. In Arkansas, Governor Henry M. Rector ordered the arrest of 117 members of the Arkansas Peace Society. Under repeated attack from anti-Family politicians and newspapers, Rector conflated disloyalty with political opposition. In a fire-breathing message to the legislature, he deplored the "libelous 'traduction' of its [Arkansas's] authorities, gloatingly sought for, and swallowed by snarling cormorants of newspaper filth." This "vehicle for undeveloped treason" had become a "dire curse" to the state.[7]

Near Hillsboro, North Carolina, a candidate in an election for constable openly avowed his Unionist sympathies, and his supporters cast ballots emblazoned with an American eagle. Local militia refused to muster under the Confederate flag, defying anyone to arrest them. "It may be very imprudent to make public that there is *any* disappointment among our people," William K. Ruffin commented, "but persons who deny it in private are either totally ignorant of the state of feeling in their region of the State or are themselves unsound." In North Carolina, distinctions among disloyalty, disaffection, and partisanship became murky.[8]

The trouble was that loyalty to the Confederacy did not necessarily translate into support for the government (or even the abandonment of partisan goals). The men who had succeeded "in destroying the old government," the prominent North Carolina Whig Augustus S. Merrimon complained, "are wholly unfit to establish a permanent new one or to mold its policy." Merrimon defined incapacity to govern as a failure to adopt Whiggish measures. He favored a Confederate national bank, a protective tariff, and, aware of latent Know-Nothingism among many Whigs, the exclusion of foreigners from voting or holding office until they had lived in North Carolina for twenty-one years.

Dissatisfaction with Confederate policies, however, extended far beyond differences in political philosophy. There were constant complaints about increased taxes and favoritism in granting military commissions. Disgusted with the incessant politicking in his regiment, the son of one powerful North Carolina conservative considered leaving the army, getting married, and taking up farming because "if we are to be ruled by democrats let them fight for the government." By the same token, North Carolina secessionists remained suspicious of cooperationists' motives and even their loyalty. An innocuous resolution condemning partisanship never came to a vote in the North Carolina convention because disunionist Democrats saw it as a veiled attack on Jefferson Davis and Governor Henry T. Clark.[9]

Factionalism in the states often spilled over into national politics; Confederate questions in turn affected state and local politics. Of course this interplay had long characterized federalism, but the absence of political parties at once hastened and complicated the development of a distinctly Confederate political system.

In what must have seemed a dangerous development to students of ancient and modern republics, disputes about military policy and leadership became heavily politicized. Joe Brown still objected to the president's appointing officers for Georgia's volunteer regiments. "This is an imperial power," he warned the legislature, that would enable a popular president "to trample under foot all restraints and make his will the supreme law of the land." Although professing confidence in Jefferson Davis, Brown nevertheless worried about future presidents practicing Bonapartism. But the governor confronted a more immediate threat in Milledgeville, where a hostile legislature tended to side with the Confederate War Department. Brown angrily accused lawmakers of acting out of "party considerations . . . personal hatred, or personal favoritism." A House committee countered that the governor had gotten up protest petitions from various regiments to intimidate the legislature. Yet eventually, both the House and Senate agreed with Brown that state troops should not be forced into Confederate service without their consent or their officers. The governor's supporters claimed that a coterie of Whigs and Know-Nothings were making political capital out of this issue, but Brown got in the final lick. He vetoed a legislative pay raise along with a cleverly spiteful measure that would have reduced the salaries of state judges and the governor by one-third. He also ordered state militia officers to seize any salt held by speculators, though he would have howled in protest had Davis exerted such executive authority.[10]

In the power struggles between the legislatures, governors, and state conventions, the politics of unity gave way to a politics of liberty, all sides claiming to defend the people's rights against would-be despots. Despite everyone's fervid appeals to republicanism—whether defined as traditional political prerogatives, the defense of self-government, or the avoidance of executive and military usurpation—it had become much more difficult to distinguish principled opposition from rank opportunism.

Conflicts over military appointments and broader disputes between state and Confederate authorities obliterated traditional distinctions between military and political questions. Secretary of War Benjamin blamed governors who would not "trust the common defense to one common head."[11] Political pressures (including legitimate concern about civilian morale) greatly influenced strategic and even logistical decisions. A cabinet meeting in early January 1862 considered several requests from governors concerning the return of arms to their states. Francis Pickens of South Carolina, John Milton of Florida, and Brown had been especially insistent. An exasperated Davis remarked that the government had best sue for peace because the war could not long continue with such obstructive governors.[12] The enormous task of defending so much territory and consequent debates over strategy confirmed the truth of Karl von Clausewitz's famous dictum on the inextricable linkage between war and politics.

Davis's continuing disputes with several generals—especially Beauregard and Joe Johnston—carried broad political overtones. During the fall Davis had tried to soothe Beauregard and had even appealed to the general's considerable vanity: "The country needs all of your mind and your heart; you have given cause to expect all which men can do, and your fame and her interests require that your energies should have a single object." Even as he wrote, Davis must have known that some of Beauregard's friends were working to make the Louisianian the next president. Still, Davis's efforts might have succeeded had the Manassas controversy not erupted again shortly before the presidential election. Beauregard's official report of the battle—parts of which appeared in newspapers before the full text reached the War Department—implied that the president had prevented Confederate forces from advancing after the Federal rout. In a sharply worded note of October 30, Davis accused Beauregard of trying "to exalt yourself at my expense." A week later, the *Richmond Whig* published Beauregard's vainglorious response. The general disdained answering slanders against his name (save of course with gallant victories over the enemy) and expressed complete indifference to office-seeking. But several newspapers were already lambasting the administration for the failure to follow up on the Manassas victory, and Beauregard appeared to be supplying grist for their mills. The general hardly helped himself by commenting to Davis that "I have always pitied more than I have envied those in high authority."[13]

The strained relations between Davis and Joe Johnston also had far-reaching political ramifications. Increasingly Johnston and Beauregard appeared to challenge Davis's authority as commander in chief and complicated his relations with Congress. Wigfall, Stephens, and a host of other politicians admired Johnston; the Rhett family, along with many of Johnston's friends and Davis's critics, likewise supported Beauregard.[14] Ambition, politics, and ego all contributed to these quarrels, but there was more at work than mere pettiness. Beauregard, Johnston, and Davis also had strongly held views on military strategy that carried considerable political baggage.

Publicly, the president maintained that victories at Manassas and in lesser engagements "checked the wicked invasion . . . and has proved that numbers cease to avail when directed against a people fighting for the sacred right of self-government and the privileges of freemen." As Confederate prospects brightened, ambitious men naturally took stock of their own political futures. Rumor had it that public confidence ran so high after Manassas that Beauregard, R. M. T. Hunter, and others were angling to succeed Davis.[15] At the same time, such optimism produced unrealistic expectations for battlefield victories. Although the government lacked both the weapons and transportation to conduct aggressive operations, to its critics the administration appeared lethargic and reluctant to risk an offensive.

A defensive posture frustrated hot-blooded Southerners. The *Richmond Examiner* and the *Charleston Mercury* called for an advance on Washington or even a massive invasion of the Northern states. Robert Toombs grumbled that cautious generals had brought on military paralysis. The newly elected Mississippi congressman Reuben Davis blamed Benjamin for placing too much stock in foreign intervention. Others believed that West Point timidity with its emphasis on training and bureaucratic detail had dampened the volunteers' enthusiasm.[16]

Offensive-minded Confederates had great faith in Beauregard. Though even an amateur like Toombs believed in the principle of concentration, Beauregard's strategic thinking centered on this widely accepted maxim of warfare. Arguing that the dispersal of forces across the Confederacy would be calamitous, Beauregard advised the government to concentrate its available men to meet any Union thrust or to mount an attack before the enemy became even more powerful. He appeared oblivious to the political imperatives behind dispersion and the sound strategic and logistical reasons for a defensive posture.[17]

Whatever the deficiencies of Beauregard's thinking, he had pinpointed a serious military and political problem. East of the Appalachian Mountains, with a relatively small territory to protect, a defensive strategy could work well. In contrast, the great expanse west of the Appalachians, where several rivers formed natural invasion routes, created overwhelming strategic difficulties. On September 10, Davis assigned his old West Point and army colleague Albert Sidney Johnston to command of an enormous department that included Tennessee, Arkansas, Kentucky, western Mississippi, Missouri, and Kansas. Johnston could muster no more than forty thousand poorly armed men in his widely scattered command to oppose some ninety thousand Union troops.[18]

Even more than additional regiments or arms, Johnston, like most military men, wanted clear lines of communication and centralized control. In an important dispatch to the War Department, he suggested that Congress consider "the necessity of augmenting the executive authority" to meet the increasing threat of Federal invasion. This oblique proposal for a dictatorship included a grandiose restructuring of the Confederate military system: "If necessary, let us convert our country into one vast camp of instruction for the field of every man able to bear arms, and fix our military establishment upon a permanent basis. Whenever a people will make the necessary sacrifices to maintain their liberty they need have no fear of losing it."[19] But to most Southerners, increased executive authority and an expanded army meant sacrificing rather than safeguarding liberty. Johnston like many other generals offered political advice without political understanding. His extraordinary recommendations show that he knew little about the history of republics in general and even less about Confederate political values.

Johnston's advice also reflected a sense of desperation, military weakness, and political turmoil in the western theater. Confederate sympathizers in Missouri grumbled that the administration had written off their state, and so they pressed for the appointment of the dashing and popular Sterling Price to command Confederate forces in the Trans-Mississippi. The president, however, had little faith in Price's military talent and knew the government lacked the resources for a full-scale campaign in Missouri. When Davis proposed putting Brigadier General Henry Heth, a Virginian, in charge of the Trans-Mississippi, Missouri politicians became apoplectic. Their objections to Heth as an impractical West Pointer irritated Davis, who testily replied that he preferred men with military training. After the Missouri congressional delegation moved to block his promotion to major general, Heth declined the new command. The appointment eventually went to Major General Earl Van Dorn—an aggressive, raucous Mississippian, a West Pointer, and a friend of Davis. The Missourians tolerated Van Dorn so long as their favorite, Price, agreed to serve under him.[20] Davis had offended and then mollified the Missourians, but the military situation in the West steadily deteriorated, raising new questions about the president's leadership.

By December 1861, politicians of various stripes sounded deeply pessimistic. The Confederate government seemed to be on the defensive both militarily and politically; much of the Southern coastline lay open to attack, and financially the new nation was adrift. "Yet the administration at Richmond," the moderate Herschel Johnson complained, "so far as the public can see, exhibits no special solicitude to prevent the catastrophe." Davis seemed increasingly withdrawn and reportedly obsessed with a newfound religious faith. Not unexpectedly the *Mercury*'s Richmond correspondent described the president as "cold, haughty, peevish, narrow-minded, pigheaded, *malignant*." Even Robert H. Smith of Alabama, a dependable administration supporter in the Provisional Congress, considered Davis "narrow minded, ill tempered, unwilling to be advised, without energy of view or action."[21]

Although Attorney General Thomas Bragg deemed Congress "full of factions," the president and his critics agreed on the necessity for public harmony and the virtues of a political system without parties. "As a nation we should be united, forbearing to one another, frowning upon all factious opposition and censorious criticisms, and giving a trustful and generous confidence to those selected as our leaders in the camp and council-chamber."[22] This passage from a public address to the "People of Georgia" issued by Howell Cobb, Thomas R. R. Cobb, Martin J. Crawford, and Robert Toombs on February 18, 1862, shows how even veteran politicians had adjusted to the demands of a new day. For all their private carping, these intense partisans temporarily assumed the public role of antiparty patriots and peacemakers. Aversion to political conflict, however, could prove frustrating and constraining. Ambitious politicians would find it hard to advance their careers without running afoul of growing popular prejudice against politicians, and those with serious reservations about government policies would have to couch their criticisms in language and behave in ways that avoided the appearance of factious opposition.

At this early date, however, such dilemmas seemed manageable. Speaker of the House Thomas S. Bocock declared that "our new system is designed to avoid the errors of the old; certainly it is founded on a different system of political philosophy and is sustained by a peculiar and more conservative state of society." State politicians, though often manifesting a latent partisanship against old political enemies, likewise paid homage to the antiparty political culture. Newly elected Alabama governor John Gill Shorter claimed to take office "untrammeled by personal or party combinations." In a farewell speech as president of the Provisional Congress on February 17, Howell Cobb carefully and fully expounded on the character of Confederate republicanism. In contrast to "revolutions," when the "excited passions of the people" led to "anarchy and discord," Southerners had deliberately chosen to "escape from the very anarchy they see impending [in the old Union] and to preserve those conservative principles of the fathers of the Republic, which were fast being overwhelmed by popular fanaticism." The Provisional Congress had further solidified these sacred values because "the spirit of party has never shown itself for an instant in your [the members'] deliberations." Such statements may have been poor history, but they well captured the ideals of the Confederate revolution, and Cobb's address appeared in newspapers all across the South.[23]

The president explicitly connected this political transformation to divine favor by portraying his fellow countrymen as the true defenders of freedom. In a proclamation issued only two days before his inauguration as permanent Confederate president, Davis declared that Southerners could be grateful that everywhere law "reigned supreme" with "personal liberty and private rights . . . duly honored." He rejoiced that "a tone of earnest piety has pervaded our people, and the victories which we have obtained over our enemies have been justly ascribed to Him who ruleth the universe." Yet with news coming in of an apparent collapse of the Kentucky line, including the loss of Forts Henry and Donelson, as well as the considerable gloom caused by the successful Federal assault on Roanoke Island off the North Carolina coast, Davis could not be entirely sanguine. He admitted that God "has prescribed affliction as the discipline of nations as well as of individuals." As was typical of early Confederate jeremiads, Davis closed on a somber though hopeful note: "Our faith and perseverance must be tested, and the chastening which seemeth grievous will, if rightly received, bring forth its appropriate fruit."[24]

In attempting to define Confederate nationalism, Jefferson Davis, along with Toombs, Rhett, Stephens, and more practical politicians such as Howell Cobb and Herschel Johnson, continued to stress ideological as opposed to pragmatic themes.[25] A search for republican purity and an effort to quarantine the Southern world from the plague of Northern radicalism, infidelity, and abolitionism dominated editorials, speeches, and public ceremonies. Such appeals could foster unity and build patriotism while discouraging political controversy and for a time stifling opposition.

The inauguration of Jefferson Davis as permanent president became an event fraught with symbolic significance. It revealed what anthropologist Clifford Geertz has called the "imaginative universe" of a people and the "conceptual world" of a society—in this case the Southern leadership class. Confederates naturally rejected many symbols of the old Union—the flag, the eagle, the great seal of the United States—but they appropriated the history of the American Revolution for their own use. Seizing upon Washington as the exemplar of republicanism, Davis and other prominent Confederates created their own iconography—beginning with Washington on horseback on the Confederate seal—that fused their new nation to an eighteenth-century revolution.

But words were the primary symbols. Confederate leaders carefully chose theirs to promote public identification with the Confederate government, to reforge national identity, and it was hoped, to destroy any lingering affection for the old Union. Proclamations and speeches also served temporarily to unify or at least minimize differences among Southern leaders. Thus the rhetorical manipulation of symbols would inspire people to make sacrifices and to submerge individual desires into a higher purpose.[26]

Because the Confederacy had no political parties to train citizens through elaborate organizations and rituals, that burden increasingly fell to the Southern political elite.[27] Contemporaries therefore paid particular attention not only to Davis's inaugural address but to the ceremony itself as both symbol and portent. In many ways this second inauguration in Richmond seemed more important than the one held a year earlier in Montgomery. The launching of the permanent government made the decision to form the Confederate States of America appear irrevocable and the dread spirit of reconstruction at last laid to rest.

Around noon on February 22, 1862, Davis rode in a carriage to Richmond's Capitol Square. In his plain black suit, the pale and sickly president looked the model of ascetic republicanism. Outside the Virginia capitol, a canvass awning had been erected over a speaker's platform next to the statue of George Washington. Despite torrential rain that showed no signs of slacking, Davis insisted on proceeding with the ceremony. Hats and coats dripped; some spectators wrapped themselves in blankets that soon became soggy; mud caked the men's boots and bespattered the women's long dresses. The president read his inaugural address in a strong voice though most of the crowd could barely hear over the rain beating against carriages and umbrellas. For a time, the water trickled off the edge of the awning onto Davis's head until someone held an umbrella over him so that he could finish speaking.[28]

Some would later claim that the chilly dampness and relentless rain had proved an ill omen for the young nation, but Davis in many ways had risen to the requirements of the occasion. By holding the inauguration on Washington's birthday, the Confederates had shown that "under the favor of Divine Providence, we hope to perpetuate the principles of our revolutionary fathers." Davis thus linked the occasion to a hallowed revolutionary tradition (and its eighteenth-century republican values). In words paralleling Yancey's earlier and more famous statement in Montgomery, the president also announced that "the day, the memory, and the purpose seem fitly associated." He extolled the justice of the Southern cause while arraigning the Northern government for recklessly violating civil and religious liberty by suspending the writ of habeas corpus and filling "Bastilles" with political prisoners. Southerners had struck for independence because a "sectional majority" had so twisted the principles of voluntary Union by shackling the South to a "despotism of numbers." Acknowledging recent military setbacks, Davis warned that though the young republic would still face many "trials and difficulties," its ultimate triumph was certain. Viewing the Confederacy as a culmination in the history of republican government, he offered a clear, succinct, and even eloquent summary of the ideological components of Confederate nationalism: "The tyranny of an unbridled majority, the most odious and least responsible form of despotism, has denied us both the right and the remedy [against future violations of Southern rights in the Union]. Therefore we are in arms to renew such sacrifices as our fathers made to the holy cause of constitutional liberty. At the darkest hour of our struggle the Provisional gives way to the Permanent Government. After a series of successes and victories, which covered our arms with glory, we have recently met with serious disasters. But in the heart of a people resolved to be free these disasters tend but to stimulate to increased resistance. To show ourselves worthy of the inheritance bequeathed to us by the patriots of the Revolution, we must emulate that heroic devotion which made reverse to them but the crucible in which their patriotism was refined."[29]

The appeals to history, the candor about recent defeats, and the powerful defense of the Southern cause had set just the right tone. Even those who still saw Davis as a partisan secessionist deeply prejudiced against Whigs and Union men generally praised the speech and resolved at least for the time being to support the administration. For less ambivalent patriots, the whole affair seemed a marvelous vindication of Confederate honor. Judith McGuire, a refugee from Alexandria, Virginia, wondered if there had ever "been a day since the Fourth of July, 1776, so full of interest, so fraught with danger, so encompassed by anxiety, so sorrowful, and yet so hopeful, as this 22nd day of February, 1862?"[30]

The defining moment of the Southern republic had arrived, and its gauge was the American Revolution. All the nation's financial and military and political problems had precedents in the struggles of eighteenth-century patriots. The analogy offered comfort during times of doubt (the "Valley Forge" of despair) and buttressed the people against loss of faith (by remembering how an earlier revolutionary generation had relied on divine providence). "The last experiment of republican government is now to be made," the *Richmond Dispatch* declared in almost apocalyptic language. Having betrayed their birthright, the Yankees no longer had any right to celebrate the birthday of that great rebel and slaveholder George Washington. According to the *New Orleans Picayune*, Southerners were "defending the memory of Washington from obloquy, and the work of his great mind and heart from destruction. If we fail, we may indeed say Washington will have labored and lived in vain."[31]

Yet Washington's legacy was an ambiguous one. The exemplar of republicanism, the Cincinnatus of the Revolution, Washington had also been an aloof and reserved aristocrat, a man who expected and received the deference of lesser mortals, and a statesman with little understanding of political opposition. Merely revering Washington, the founding fathers, and the memory of the American Revolution could not resolve the inherent tensions between the Confederacy's robustly democratic legacy from the antebellum South and its aristocratic pretensions.

Some conservatives still worried that the new political system contained too many of the old Union's democratic vices. Episcopal bishop Stephen Elliott marveled at the rapid "moral deterioration" of the United States "in philosophy, in letters, in ethics, in religion . . . in politics . . . commerce and trade, and finance and social life" during the past forty years. Expediency, demagoguery, and a misguided belief in human equality had proved fatal in public life. "Man is not capable of self government because he is a fallen creature, and interest, passion, ambition, and lust sway him far more than reason and honor." Even so, the doctrine of majority rule had infected the South, and Confederate politicians hesitated to challenge popular beliefs about the political wisdom of ordinary people. The solution to this problem and the republic's hope for salvation, according to Elliott, was a return to the biblical standard that recognized an inherent need for hierarchy.[32] Elliott's political point could scarcely be missed. The Confederates now had to live with the implications of their ideology. Yet practical problems, personal ambition, greed for office, and financial and military crises would make philosophical consistency an expensive luxury.

For the Confederate political dilemma had become and would remain how to create and sustain a firm political and cultural identity in the midst of a bloody civil war while at same time showing enough flexibility to meet unanticipated demands on resources and will. In the spring of 1862, the political system appeared hardly up to the task. Paradoxically, the government seemed both too weak and too strong, the president vacillating and indecisive but also arbitrary and despotic.

The first session of the Permanent Congress hardly resolved these dilemmas or inspired confidence. The newly elected representatives and senators were comparatively inexperienced and, knowledgeable observers believed, decidedly mediocre. Echoing complaints widely heard during the fall election campaign, many Confederates concluded that the best talents had gone into the army.[33]

In one respect, however, Congress embodied the ideals of the Southern republic: the spirit of party seemed nearly extinguished. Roll calls in the first Congress showed few signs of Democrat-Whig or even secessionist-cooperationist divisions. The events of the past year had eclipsed many traditional political loyalties, and no longer did caucuses, conventions, or newspapers help draw party lines.[34] In reality, petty quarrels, ideological rigidity, and plain stubbornness often slowed the legislative machinery. So, too, parliamentary maneuvering along with endless debate made Congress seem inefficient and irresponsible. Whether such bickering might be worse than partisanship was not yet an issue.

Congress held its sessions in the suitably classical Virginia capitol designed by Thomas Jefferson. On closer inspection, however, his impressive-looking building proved grimy and uncomfortable. The Confederate House occupied a spartan, cramped room on the first floor while the Senate met in the state senate chamber. But when that body was in session, Confederate senators crowded into the adjutant general's office on the third floor. Having no desks, the members sat behind long tables, shivering in winter and sweltering in summer. A few rows of hard benches served as galleries, and spectators sat so close that everyone complained of the noise. According to one newspaper report, well-dressed young ladies and many older women sometimes "ogled" the lawmakers and distracted them from public business.[35]

Representatives and senators lived in various parts of the city, often sharing rooms to cut down expenses. What voters deemed a princely salary of $2,760 per year—or as a Georgia country newspaper complained, more money per day than a Confederate soldier earned in two months—did not go far in wartime Richmond. In the grip of the capital's hyperinflation, congressmen became especially strapped when sessions dragged on longer than expected. Yet in a time of general austerity, official salaries naturally drew criticism for extravagance. People expected congressmen to set an example of self-sacrifice or, like Washington during the revolutionary war, to serve without compensation. Some newspaper editors conceded that the members of Congress should be paid above bare subsistence and even sympathized with those trying to cope with Richmond's spiraling prices, but lawmakers did not dare vote themselves a pay raise until June 1864. By that time, living costs had skyrocketed out of control, and Confederate prospects had grown so gloomy that no one cared enough to complain.[36]

By conducting so much of its business in closed sessions, Congress aroused public suspicion. The security of sensitive military and political information supposedly justified this practice, though as the journals of both houses show, members erred on the side of caution. The *Charleston Mercury* and *Richmond Examiner* accused both the executive and legislative branches of trying to hide their blunders. After all, even the Northern Congress conducted the lion's share of its business in open session. Worse, secrecy violated an important principle of representative government and made Confederate claims to political virtue appear hypocritical.[37] Although secrecy heightened dissatisfaction over specific pieces of legislation, it also inhibited the formation of organized factions and made politics more deferential. Secrecy limited public knowledge of important questions and also limited public access to congressmen. A dearth of reliable and detailed information hardly prevented criticism of Congress but certainly made that criticism less effective. Citizens lacking real understanding of Congress's inner workings could either become hypercritical, apathetic, or simply willing to accept unthinkingly the judgments of their political leaders.

In the absence of a Supreme Court, the Confederacy's two-branch federalism amplified the normal legislative-executive conflict. War policies and related constitutional questions that caused friction between the state and Confederate governments also tipped the power balance in Davis's favor. Congress never developed the leadership or organization to effectively challenge executive prerogatives or shape government policies except on financial questions. And even on matters of taxation and currency, Congress usually reacted to administration recommendations rather than initiating its own measures. Antiparty ideology and war-driven pressures for national unity promoted expansion of presidential power even as a passion for individual, local, and state liberty made Southerners wary of centralization.

In the spring of 1862, Congress seemed willing to follow the president's lead, but secret sessions and the absence of extensive public debate did not mask widespread unease. Impatience with Davis and his generals naturally arose when an overconfident people found hopes for an easy victory dashed. Shocking reports of defeats in Tennessee along with the disgraceful loss of Roanoke Island caused great dismay. Vice-President Stephens began to lose hope and wondered if Davis's heart was in the cause (a question that many Confederates continued to ask about Stephens). Even the moderate James L. Orr joined in the chorus of criticism, and some firebrands talked of deposing Davis in favor of a military dictator, perhaps Beauregard.[38]

By early March, a few newspapers were firing editorial salvos at the president. With equal portions of self-righteous indignation and smug arrogance, the *Mercury* accused the administration of trying to shift the blame for military setbacks to its innocent though prescient critics. Even editors who had never had much good to say about democracy suddenly decided that the average citizen better understood the necessities of the hour than the president and his sycophantic advisers.[39] This supposed dichotomy between the virtuous masses and their failed leaders became a favorite rhetorical device for dissenters, though defenders of the government sometimes turned it against opposition politicians.

This scattered criticism apparently had little effect on Congress or on public opinion. Even South Carolinians preferred to give Davis the benefit of the doubt and discounted the wisdom of newspaper strategists.[40] Indeed, a rising war spirit swept across the Confederacy in the wake of all the bad news from the armies. Reconstruction was impossible, congressmen affirmed, because the Lincoln administration waged war against the sacred principle of government by consent. The strongest expression of this militant spirit came from the border South. Senator William E. Simms of Kentucky predicted that the Southern people would fight "to the last man and the last dollar." Senator John B. Clark of Missouri believed that the war should continue until the enemy had been "expelled from every foot of soil." These politicians worried that a peace settlement recognizing Confederate independence might leave their states under Federal control, but several Deep South senators reassuringly replied that no true Confederate would ever trade territory for peace. By March 11, both the House and Senate had officially endorsed Clark's statement of war aims.[41] In reaffirming its uncompromising support for the cause, Congress implicitly approved Davis's strategy of defending the Confederate perimeter.

Better than many of his critics, Davis could see the larger strategic and political picture. Despite his obvious ties to Mississippi, Davis was more cosmopolitan and more nationalistic than politicians who prattled endlessly about states' rights and individual liberty. For Davis, service to the Confederacy meant looking beyond the neighborhood, the county, or even the state.[42] But Southern provincialism forced him to spread limited military resources too thin. Although he was sometimes insensitive to the demands of local defense and the political problems of state governors, Davis nevertheless realized that to abandon territory for some larger strategic objective would sap morale and have potentially disastrous political consequences. The president believed that the success of the Confederate cause best assured the survival of liberty, including states' rights.

Yet victory seemed far off in early 1862, and the string of recent debacles sent shock waves through official Richmond. Davis responded to the deepening gloom by reevaluating his strategy. Meeting with the North Carolina congressional delegation on February 15, 1862, a week after the loss of Roanoke Island and on the eve of Fort Donelson's surrender, the president admitted that much of the Confederate coastline could not be adequately defended. He implored the congressmen to explain to their constituents the necessity for sending North Carolina troops outside the state. He also assured the president of the North Carolina convention and other leaders of his concern for the defense of their state.[43] Promises here, a few more troops there, shuffling department commanders: such measures proved mere stopgaps. Responding to pressure from one quarter only led to more pressure from another.

Trying to put the best possible face on a rapidly deteriorating military situation, Davis informed Congress that "events have demonstrated that the Government had attempted more than it had power successfully to achieve." The effort to protect "the whole of the territory of the Confederate States" had met with "serious disasters." Short-term enlistments and furloughs had severely weakened the Confederate army, but the president had faith that the redoubled efforts of the Southern people would drive back the invaders. Attorney General Bragg noted that the president's message "expresses a confidence which truth to say none of us feel." And for good reason. The Confederate military system—command, communications, and supply—was so defective that the War Department had trouble grasping the extent of the disaster in the West. The multiplication of military departments gave too much discretion to politically naive generals such as Leonidas Polk, Gideon Pillow, Albert Sidney Johnston, and the hapless Benjamin Huger, who had neglected the Roanoke Island defenses. Dependent on often delayed, fragmentary, and misleading dispatches from the front as well as ubiquitous newspaper rumors, Davis and his advisers could make neither timely nor wise decisions.[44]

After the Confederate evacuation of Nashville in late February and the retreat toward Corinth, Mississippi, in early March, Tennessee congressmen angrily called for the removal of Albert Sidney Johnston. For the rest of the war, political pressure and military intrigue would characterize operations in the Confederate heartland. The group that historians Thomas Connelly and Archer Jones have called the "western concentration bloc" would continually push for offensives in Tennessee and Kentucky. This complex network of interrelated families and ambitious generals included such inveterate administration opponents as Beauregard, Joe Johnston, and Wigfall.[45] Disagreements over strategy thus became tied up in the complexities of Confederate politics. The movements of Rebel armies fundamentally shaped public debate, making Davis a political hostage to the successes or failures of his generals.

During three days in the early spring of 1862, Davis responded to the mounting public criticism in ways that would typify his behavior throughout the war. On March 12, he assured Sidney Johnston of his continued support "as friendship prompted, and many years of acquaintance justified." He urged Johnston to provide full reports of his recent campaign because "the public . . . have no correct measure for military operations, and the journals are very reckless in their statements." The following day, Davis composed a long letter to the president of the Alabama convention.

Again conceding the folly of trying "to defend all the frontier, seaboard and inland," he still maintained that this strategy would have succeeded had the government received the expected numbers of men and arms. With obvious pique, he denied pursuing a purely defensive strategy and noted that many people exaggerated both the size and capability of Confederate forces. Downplaying disagreements with Beauregard, Johnston, and Sterling Price, Davis argued that most denunciations of the government came from men disappointed that army appointments were being awarded for military rather than political qualifications. "If we can achieve our independence," he self-righteously concluded, "the office seekers are welcome to the one I hold." With his finely tuned sense of punctilio, Davis bristled at congressional interference in military administration. On March 14, he vetoed a bill that would have created a commanding general for the Confederate armies. Jealous of his prerogatives as commander in chief, Davis saw this measure not only as an affront to his strategic judgment but also as a dangerous attempt to undermine presidential authority.[46]

Many critics believed Davis treated his cabinet just as imperiously. According to the *Richmond Examiner*, the president had tried "to administer the government himself with the aid of a cabinet of dummies." Davis had somewhat allayed cooperationist fears by appointing North Carolina conservative Thomas Bragg as attorney general, though the selection of yet another Democrat sparked more charges of party favoritism. "Whigs are not relished among the highest official circles," one editor complained, "and it is said that with some secretaries, a Yankee fresh from Barnstable, reeking with the odors of garlic and codfish, is more acceptable than a Southern Whig."[47] Normally, such grousing could be dismissed as the sour grapes of disappointed partisans, but the recent military setbacks had opened the floodgates for new criticism of the cabinet.

Secretary of the Navy Mallory became an ideal scapegoat for anyone appalled by the weakness of Confederate coastal defenses. That this diligent and capable Floridian could hardly have built an adequate navy in less than a year failed to impress those convinced of his incompetence. Yet despite caustic editorials and a congressional investigation of the operations around Roanoke Island, on March 18, 1862, the Senate voted thirteen to six to confirm Mallory as secretary of the navy under the permanent government.[48]

Secretary of War Judah Benjamin came under even sharper attack. According to Congressman Henry S. Foote—a longtime Davis enemy and the administration's most strident critic in the House—Benjamin had been largely "responsible for our national calamities." In truth, Benjamin's performance had been lackluster. He had quarreled with Joe Johnston, Beauregard, and Thomas J. "Stonewall" Jackson, and his legalistic approach to administration easily offended other general officers. Perhaps, as a hostile Virginian later recalled, the problem was that Benjamin "had more brains and less heart than any other civic leader in the South."[49]

His intelligence, wit, and charm may also have stirred envy and jealousy in Richmond's hothouse social and political atmosphere. Benjamin was probably too cosmopolitan for many Confederates. Gossips said that he received a steady stream of Yankee visitors and maintained memberships in several exclusive Boston and New York clubs. But Benjamin also faced considerable anti-Semitism. After receiving what he considered a "pettifogging order," Milledge Luke Bonham ripped into the secretary as a "casuistical Jew." Both Bonham and the censorious Tom Cobb claimed that Benjamin was a "eunuch" who had taken a wife only for appearance's sake. She had had a child, later separated from Benjamin, and was reportedly living with a "paramour" in Paris.[50]

Davis could ignore such vicious talk, but he could not so easily brush aside more serious congressional opposition, including a committee investigation into Benjamin's role in the Roanoke Island fiasco. Yet rather than trying to conciliate his enemies, the president promoted Benjamin to secretary of state on March 18, 1862. After brief consideration, the Senate voted thirteen to eight to confirm the nomination.[51] The president's maneuver infuriated some politicians, but in his first serious clash with Congress, Davis had prevailed rather easily and with a minimum of public controversy. Because there was no political party to coalesce the opposition, the president could afford to stick by his controversial friend.

Davis had handled the Benjamin matter with finesse, and the formation of a new cabinet under the permanent government had generated little discussion. The president pleased the sensitive Virginians by appointing George W. Randolph to replace Benjamin in the War Department and, after Bragg resigned, moved to conciliate Unionist Whigs by selecting Thomas Hill Watts of Alabama as the new attorney general. Chronic complainers still did so—John M. Daniel of the *Richmond Examiner* could never abide Benjamin's presence in the cabinet and sourly remarked that "the representation of the Synagogue is not diminished; it remains full"— but most newspaper comment was favorable. Rhett and others might flail away at Davis, Mary Chesnut noted, but he remained the man of the hour.[52]

The military situation, however, only grew more critical. In the spring of 1862, Confederates were staring at defeat and an early end to the dream of a Southern nation. Davis had failed to solve the command problems in the army, and the need for more men and supplies had reached a crisis point. In these dark days, references to the American Revolution and George Washington took on new meaning and maybe even buoyed morale. Politically, the Confederates had succeeded in turning the clock back but not to the idyllic republican past so idealized in Southern political thought. With a strong president, a disorganized opposition, a vituperative press, and what was fast becoming a poisoned political atmosphere, the Confederates had in many ways reverted to the politics of the 1790s—to the intensely personal and vicious preparty politics of the founding fathers.

Desperate Times,
Desperate Measures,
Desperate Politics

T he President is annoyed, has lost his temper, and seems distressed and almost gloomy," wrote Thomas Bragg the day after his departure from the cabinet. As the military situation grew desperate in February and March 1862, Davis appeared increasingly beleaguered. "All is lost," Bragg feared. "Our people are dispirited and losing confidence."[1] He no doubt exaggerated. The spirit of self-sacrifice had by no means disappeared, and calls for throwing back the Yankee invaders and even taking the offensive echoed across the Confederacy.

A combination of despair over recent defeats, criticism of the government, and continuing faith in Jefferson Davis tested the mettle of a political system that had little place for legitimate opposition. Pockets of disloyalty had appeared in several states, attacks on the administration had become more vocal, debates on strategy had intensified, and the need for strong war measures had grown apace. Yet the prevalence of antiparty attitudes prevented administration critics from coalescing into an effective opposition. During the spring of 1862 enactment of the first conscription law and the suspension of habeas corpus raised questions that revealed anew the intimate and complex relationship between Confederate policies and state politics, as well as fundamental differences over the meaning of the Confederate revolution.

After the loss of Roanoke Island, reports of subversive Unionism appeared. Along the coast and in the mountainous western counties of North Carolina, men were refusing to enlist in the army and even raising white flags in public meetings. Davis continued to reassure Governor Henry T. Clark that the government would never "slight" the Tar Heel State, but rumors of dissension in the upper South and especially reports of class divisions made official Richmond nervous.[2] Disaffection ran strongest among the yeomen and poor whites as Confederates began to reassess what might be called the moral calculus of the war. More than simply blaming the rich for not giving up enough for the cause, disgusted cooperationists could easily point to prominent secessionists in their neighborhoods whose patriotism had lagged once the shooting started.[3] Democrats and Whigs, cooperationists and secessionists all gauged their opponents' contributions to the cause, and equality of sacrifice became the elusive ideal that fostered political recrimination. With such a sensitive barometer, social resentments were bound to fester.

As leaders of opinion, newspaper editors hardly dared mention signs of class conflict and generally supported the war with great fervor. After all, their success depended on the success of the Southern nation. Of the eight hundred newspapers published in the Confederacy, half or more had gone out of business by early 1862, and the surviving sheets had trouble finding paper, ink, and most of all paying subscribers. Students of the Confederacy, who seem to have spent most of their time scanning the *Richmond Examiner* and the *Charleston Mercury*, have exaggerated the extent of newspaper opposition to the Davis administration. Although hardly exempt from provincialism and selfishness, the Southern press generally sustained the president and worked to build a national consciousness.[4] Newspapers were a prime source of political information in a predominantly rural society and shaped a political culture still dependent on the oral transmission of news and opinion.

Yet editorial opposition exerted influence through the sheer stridency of its rhetoric. Vilifying the "pimps and parasites" who supported the Richmond government and denouncing the "venal self-seekers or base panderers to executive power," Robert Barnwell Rhett sought to make the president's reputation "subservient to . . . the redemption and salvation of the Confederate States." Or in other words, make Jefferson Davis subservient to Robert Barnwell Rhett. Even Edmund Ruffin, no friend of the president, believed that Rhett spoke from "feelings of neglect and disappointed ambition."[5]

Such comments suggested a return to the vitriolic journalism of the late eighteenth century. Rhett sarcastically suggested that Davis stop trying to be a Washington, a Jackson, or a Calhoun and instead seek his "proper level" as a Tyler or a Polk. Then the president could select a better cabinet (i.e., Rhett or his followers) and leave military strategy to the generals, or at least to generals approved by Palmetto State radicals. Instead, Davis had surrounded himself with "flatterers and sycophants," lorded it over the Congress, and exalted his supposed administrative and military genius. Other critics blasted the government for general incompetence.[6]

Too many of these malcontents either wore political and military blinders or lived in a dream world. South Carolina congressman William W. Boyce suggested replacing Davis with a cumbersome provisional government composed of the "ablest men" from each state who would in turn choose better-qualified generals. With equally little logic, Boyce also proposed summoning a convention of the states to make Sterling Price or Robert Toombs dictator. Ironically, the same men who berated Davis for dominating the cabinet and Congress favored one-man rule. Referring to the possibility of impeachment, Tom Cobb remarked that Davis would "be deposed if the Congress had any faith in Stephens."[7]

This early opposition was most remarkable for its isolation from the mass of still enthusiastic Confederates who defended the president and even wanted to expand his authority. After suggesting that Congress should adjourn for the duration of the war, a New Orleans editor proposed that Davis take the field with one of the armies. Preachers, civilians, many politicians, and editors deplored carping against the president no matter how many mistakes had been made or how serious the military crisis was. The expected calls for political harmony often contained references to the American Revolution that carried an unmistakable antiparty flavor. Disappointed office-seekers naturally assailed the president, a Georgia editor charged, just as a similar "cabal" had hounded Washington. Therefore, unity became the essence of patriotism: "The man who strikes at him [Davis] strikes at the heart and head of the Confederacy. The man who weakens his influence with the people strikes at the cause in which we are engaged and is a deadly enemy of every man in the Confederacy."[8] In his own eyes as well as those of many other Southerners, Jefferson Davis stood above politics, a pure, disinterested statesman who embodied the nation itself.

This idealized perspective sheds new light on the president's relationship with Congress during the first half of the war. In another analogy to the American Revolution, the editor of the *Savannah Republican* claimed that Davis exerted more control over Congress than "George III ever aspired to [in his] palmiest days." Historians have often faulted the president for his stiff and high-handed dealings with Congress and his inability to curry the favor of powerful representatives and senators.[9] Yet the president of the Confederacy was not supposed to be a party leader, and he usually shunned political negotiation. Both the Confederate Constitution and prevailing notions of executive authority held that the president should lead the nation through example, with Congress and the people deferring to his wisdom.

Old habits, however, along with the unfulfilled promise of a revolution against politics, made the reality of wartime leadership much messier. The nation had fallen prey to the political "wire-worker," warned Methodist bishop George F. Pierce. The Southern people were "victims . . . of this ungodly traffic in vice, of unscriptural theories of government, of fiendish schemes of power." Pierce hoped that the Confederacy might become a Christian nation but worried that its government retained too many evils of the old federal system. Therefore a political revolution required a structural as well as an ideological cleansing. Forgetting how weak the government had been during the American Revolution, the *Richmond Examiner* recommended dispensing with executive authority altogether and creating a Continental Congress for the Confederacy.[10]

Although the magnitude of patronage problems had been much reduced because many federal post office and treasury officials had joined the new government, the president and Congress still wrangled over civil offices. While eager applicants sought to influence congressmen, Davis had to wend his way through the mine fields of state and local politics. Exaggerating the president's power, Robert Toombs charged that Davis would use the many appointments at his disposal to manipulate and intimidate the Congress.[11] In fact, Davis—hardly a political innocent when it came to patronage—could not stand above the fray. Preoccupied with military problems, he naturally looked to old political associates in making appointments.

Administration supporters deplored simplistic efforts to count how many Democrats or Whigs received appointments. Party antecedents, an Atlanta editor hoped, belonged to the "dim (and should be) forgotten past." But Confederate politics had not yet been purged of partisanship. Even after receiving an appointment as a treasury agent, an Arkansas Whig still complained that the administration valued party over merit.

The president's efforts at evenhandedness ended up displeasing both conservative Whigs and fire-eaters.[12]

His military appointments aroused even more furor. Complex political and geographical considerations competed with the president's own notions of military fitness. From his camp in Virginia, Lieutenant Colonel John T. Morgan recommended that the selection of a Unionist commander for troops from northern Alabama would conciliate conservative hill country men. From a somewhat broader perspective, Senators Clement Clay and William L. Yancey complained that Davis had passed over qualified Alabama men in appointing generals to lead brigades from that state. The president returned their letter with a frosty endorsement, asserting his sole authority to make nominations and refusing to discuss the merits of his selections.[13] If each state demanded its share of general officers, politics would hopelessly ensnarl the Confederate command structure.

Politics also intruded on strategic decisions when the defeats in the spring caused much finger-pointing. Maryland and Missouri had already been lost, Congressman Boyce gloomily observed, and Tennessee was "slipping from our grasp," all because of "West Point red tape" and a haughty president who had neglected the border states. The administration had been too slow in raising troops, in gathering supplies, in acquiring arms and ammunition, and in building a navy. Much of this criticism, however, ignored the government's limited resources. As late as June 1862, the *Savannah Republican* maintained that the Confederates should have followed up their "victory" at Shiloh by marching toward Louisville and Cincinnati and after Manassas should have captured Washington and maybe even Boston.[14]

Political and military pressure on the president mounted. Governors, congressmen, and generals all demanded more men, arms, and supplies for their particular corner of the Confederacy, and each saw his bailiwick as the linchpin of Southern fortunes. The vision of a Confederate Kentucky, for example, refused to die. The collapse of the Confederate line in the Bluegrass State and the retreat through Tennessee produced an angry search for a political scapegoat. Congressman Eli M. Bruce, who had recently been chosen to represent northeastern Kentucky's ninth district, could never forgive Albert Sidney Johnston for his "errors of omission, commission, and delay." Davis also came in for considerable censure, and heated debate could not be confined to secret congressional sessions. The discontented who lacked reliable information or pet schemes of their own could always accuse the administration of not having a coherent military policy.[15]

In early April, Confederate prospects in the Mississippi River Valley temporarily brightened. Davis had reinforced Johnston's army by stripping Confederate coastal defenses and dispatching these troops to Corinth, Mississippi. A Confederate offensive at the battle of Shiloh came close to driving Grant's army into the Tennessee River. A federal counterattack the next day had turned a tactical Confederate victory into a costly strategic defeat.[16]

Many Confederates would have agreed with T. S. Eliot that April is the cruelest month. Close on the heels of Shiloh—and the death of Albert Sidney Johnston—the unexpected surrender of New Orleans sent morale plummeting. Almost as bad, the politics of local defense continued to hamstring strategy in the western theater. Louisiana's governor, Thomas O. Moore, pointedly asked, "How much longer is Louisiana to be considered without the protection or beneath the considerations of the Confederate Government?" Although it would take the Federals more than a year to take Vicksburg, pessimists believed the Mississippi River was already lost and the Confederacy riven in two.[17]

In the East, where Joe Johnston commanded the Confederate defenses but not the president's confidence, the situation had become, if anything, even more precarious. During a meeting on February 19, 1862, Davis and Johnston had decided that the Confederate defensive line along the Potomac River was untenable. Though consenting to the abandonment of Manassas, the president worried about irreplaceable field guns falling into enemy hands and urged Johnston to take every precaution. "Recent disasters have depressed the weak, and are depriving us of the aid of the wavering," the president advised. "Traitors show the tendencies, heretofore concealed, and the selfish grow clamorous for local and personal interests. At such an hour, the wisdom of the trained, and steadiness of the brave, possess a double value. The military paradox that impossibilities must be rendered possible had never better occasion for its application."[18] This oddly philosophical dispatch probably put the already suspicious Johnston on his guard, and the breakdown in communication between the commander in chief and one of his most important generals was nearly complete.

Fearing leaks from the cabinet and the War Department, Johnston kept the administration in the dark about his movements. As they hurriedly left the Manassas area, soldiers had to burn several days' rations and spike their heavy guns. Davis complained about Johnston's silence since their late February conference and bemoaned the loss of equipment and provisions in the "precipitous retreat."[19] Meanwhile, George B. McClellan's formidable army inched its way up the Virginia Peninsula toward Richmond.

On May 2, Johnston began the evacuation of Yorktown and for the next two weeks moved ever closer to Richmond. Wondering all the while where Johnston intended to fight, Davis continued to badger him about shuffling regiments between various brigades. Newspapers blamed Davis for the retreat. One Georgia editor even suggested a rapid advance of Confederate forces through Maryland to force McClellan's withdrawal from the Peninsula. Added to the military threats and criticism of the administration, rumor had it that several generals were conspiring to overthrow Davis and make Johnston a military dictator.[20] Official Richmond and the public generally were in a panic as military losses threatened to spread political disaffection.

The series of disasters in the West and looming disaster in the East plainly exposed the Southern nation's weaknesses in men, weapons, and perhaps even will. Politicians in Richmond, in the state capitals, and undoubtedly in county seats and crossroads stores now had to confront practical and ideological questions about ends and means. More than a simple conflict between those prepared to create a consolidated, revolutionary state and those unwilling to sacrifice states' rights to military necessity, this new debate marked the beginning of a long contest between a politics of national unity and a politics of individual, community, and state liberty.

The most immediate problem was manpower. In April, May, and June the terms of service for the twelve-month volunteers would expire. The newly appointed secretary of war, George W. Randolph, saw conscription as the only solution, and many soldiers agreed. An Alabama colonel, E. D. Tracy, offered some pointed advice to Senator Clay: "Despotism is the soul of efficient military organization, and our people must be made to feel that the whole country needs their services as soldiers, they must temporarily submit to absolute discipline, as a part of the price of permanent civil liberty."[21]

Tracy's comments cut to the heart of the matter because conscription raised difficult questions for Southerners sensitive to the slightest threats to individual freedom. A draft exposed both the connections and tensions between political culture and public policy.[22] To sacrifice liberty in order to preserve it: this paradox summed up the Confederate dilemma. The competing and sometimes contradictory emphases on national authority and individual liberty set the terms for the debate over conscription and in turn sparked a broader discussion of the Confederacy's national character.

If conscription was required to maintain Confederate independence, Alabama governor John Gill Shorter could "almost despair of our ultimate triumph." Only the manly, independent, liberty-loving citizens who would unhesitatingly make any sacrifice for their country could save the cause. But such idealism—rooted in classical notions of republican virtue—ignored political and military reality. Voluntarism had failed though the mere mention of conscription stirred defiant opposition.[23]

As was his wont, Jefferson Davis approached these matters obliquely and a bit awkwardly. Even when praising the spirit of cooperation that had characterized relations between Richmond and the state governors, he did not fully explain the military situation or the need for conscription. Instead, he abruptly proposed that all white males between the ages of eighteen and thirty-five "shall be held to be in military service of the Confederate States, and that some plain and simple method be adopted for their prompt enrollment and organization."[24] Perhaps the urgency was obvious, but Davis had neither issued a ringing call to arms nor dealt with possible objections to a draft.

By votes of fifty-three to twenty-six in the House and nineteen to five in the Senate, Congress adopted a conscription act. Although the debate was brief and mostly in secret session, it focused on important ideological concerns. Opposing a draft, Texas senator Williamson S. Oldham pleaded that "we can accomplish our deliverance without violating our fundamental law." In response, Wigfall urged Southern leaders to "cease this child's play." Downplaying republican fears of military centralization, he argued that "it will not do to talk about the justice of our cause, the favor of Providence, or the aid of foreign nations. We must have heavy battalions." Such blunt realism typified Wigfall's slashing style in debate but infuriated his fellow Texan. In no mood for a lecture, Oldham retorted that only European "despotisms" had resorted to conscription.[25] Nevertheless, lawmakers of various political stripes voted for a measure that only a few months earlier would have been unthinkable. With Davis providing somewhat uncertain leadership, the Confederacy moved toward creating a consolidated national state.

The first Conscription Act (adopted April 16, 1862) followed Davis's sketchy recommendations. All white men between the ages of eighteen and thirty-five would be placed in Confederate service unless exempted. Those already enlisted would serve for three years dating from their original enlistment and would retain the privilege of electing officers. With the consent of the governors, the president could use state officers, or if necessary, Confederate officers to enroll men.[26]

The draft question accelerated political fragmentation because old party alignments and even opinions about Davis mattered little on this question. The usually hypercritical Rhetts could only chide the president for not recognizing the necessity for a draft before Kentucky and Tennessee had been lost. Yet for many fire-eaters and for moderate secessionists, to force freeborn Southern men into the army might have presented insuperable difficulties. The trick was to fit conscription into the evolving definition of Southern republicanism. The delicate juggling sometimes produced contradictory and unworkable political positions. Although arguing that a draft probably should have been adopted sooner, an Atlanta editor favored having the states enroll soldiers, who would then be mustered into Confederate service.[27] As if clinging to states' rights would make conscription any less threatening to individual liberty.

Politicians and editors who defended conscription repeated one word again and again: "necessity." Even a levee en masse was preferable to subjugation, a proposition that helped the reluctant to swallow their scruples. Indeed, the usual objections to government coercion carried much less weight when national survival was at stake. Predictably, an Arkansas editor maintained that once conscription had been enacted, it was "unpatriotic to offer any captious opposition to its immediate execution."[28]

But for other Confederates, condemning conscription became the patriot's highest duty. Besides placing far too much power in the hands of the president, conscription would inexorably lead to military government and destroy republicanism.[29] The initial shock over the enactment of the Confederacy's first draft law showed how deeply the passion for individual liberty had permeated the political culture despite pleas for national unity. In Arkansas, Confederate treasury official John W. Brown, borrowing rhetoric from the eighteenth century, remonstrated against "officers and their vast salaries and their hirelings consuming the substance of the country, while these poor men [the conscripts] are forced to leave everything dear to them to be sacrificed to the ambition of wicked men." Thus the draft widened fundamental differences over the meaning of the Southern experiment. In an eloquent description of the inextricable link between individual liberty and Confederate identity, R. C. Puryear of North Carolina condemned conscription as "unnecessary, unequal, unjust, and tyrannical." What had become of "that great paramount doctrine of states' rights which in fact was the prime cause of this revolution? It is repudiated and trodden underfoot and the germ of consolidation is already springing up on its ruins." All history proved that "consolidation leads to despotism."[30]

The vividness and historical richness of these images illustrate the inadequacy of positing a simple conflict between centralization and states' rights as the key to understanding Confederate political history. Whether states' rights fatally weakened or actually strengthened the Confederate cause has received considerable historical attention without shedding much light on wartime politics.[31] For many Confederates, defending liberty meant preserving personal freedoms and community rights; for these Southerners, even state governments appeared as distant and potentially dangerous agents of illegitimate power. Appeals to states' rights might mediate rival claims of national authority and local or individual autonomy but could not encompass the wide-ranging, disunited, and often bewildering forms of dissent in the Confederate nation. Broader libertarian arguments subsumed a host of individuals and groups that had little in common except their aversion to the exercise of political power. Even those who endorsed conscription remained alert to its dangers. Reluctant politicians might agree to a draft out of necessity, but they could not elevate that necessity into a virtue.

Yet despite often serious reservations, there was at first little serious political opposition. During the congressional discussions, the *Milledgeville Southern Federal Union* cited several historical precedents to show that conscription had always been autocratic and cries of necessity the "tyrant's plea in every age," but once conscription became the law of the land, this same editor advised the people to obey. Governor John Letcher of Virginia considered a draft the "most alarming stride towards consolidation that has ever occurred" but would not press the issue because "harmony, unity, and conciliation are indispensable to success now." Herschel Johnson agreed that conscription violated states' rights, discouraged volunteering, and showed weakness and desperation in the face of the enemy but conceded that the experiment had to be made.[32] Many states'-rights stalwarts echoed these views.

A notable exception was Joe Brown. The Georgia governor denounced conscription as an outrageous measure of centralization aimed at destroying the state governments. Even though Congress had provided for exemptions, he complained that the Confederate government would forcibly enroll legislators, executive officers, and various skilled tradesmen.[33] Brown's protest appeared at once bold, hasty, and confusing. His private secretary claimed that the governor would not hinder the enforcement of the law; Brown would bow to the inevitable without abandoning his belief that conscription violated the Confederate Constitution. His apparent acquiescence, however, was hedged. On the one hand, he promised Secretary of War Randolph to "throw no obstacles" in the way of executing the Conscription Act; on the other, he ordered the arrest of any enrolling officers who attempted to conscript a state militia officer.[34]

The problem was that Brown shifted back and forth from philosophical to practical objections, from grudging cooperation to higgling obstructionism. He began a lengthy correspondence with the president that dragged on from April through July. In May, Brown sent Davis an especially long and complaining letter. Denying any need for a draft in Georgia, he summarily dismissed the notion that revolutionary times demanded revolutionary measures. Constitutional privileges must be preserved, phony pleas of necessity notwithstanding. For Brown, every male of draft age in the state of Georgia was part of the militia by definition and therefore not subject to call by the national government. This expansive definition of militia also would have preserved the governor's authority to dispense military commissions, but this was a highly technical point that Georgia's many constitutional hair-splitters could argue about endlessly.

Whether all this expenditure of paper and ink served any purpose was another matter, but once an argument had begun Davis could be every bit as tenacious (or pigheaded) as Brown. Emphasizing how the Southern states had united against a common foe, the president could discover no limits to the congressional power of raising armies. Making the dubious assertion that conscription was constitutional because it was designed to achieve a constitutional purpose, Davis also maintained that the Confederate government could draft citizens regardless of whether they were members of the militia.

Such arguments carried little weight with Brown when individual liberties (and his own prerogatives) were at stake. Conscription was nothing but a "bold and dangerous usurpation by Congress of the reserved rights of the States and a rapid stride toward military despotism." These seemingly abstract objections raised troublesome questions for some Confederates. If the Southern states were fighting a just war, the people would readily sacrifice their lives and treasure; if not, conscription could never salvage an unholy cause.

To many Confederates, Brown sounded nit-picking if not factious, and even in Georgia newspapers stopped publishing the governor's tiresome letters. In the spring of 1862 calls for harmony still carried more weight than appeals to individual liberty. The editor J. Henly Smith publicly assailed the governor's "obstinacy," dismissing his arguments as "ridiculous and untenable." Privately Smith went further, describing Brown as a "very unsafe man, governed . . . by vindictiveness, mulishness, and other bad impulses." At best, Brown's tendentiousness seemed irrelevant and ill-timed; at worst, he appeared determined to foment opposition for selfish purposes.[35] Yet the governor's own determination and strongly held opinions largely shaped the character of the Georgia opposition, and Brown's enemies dared not underestimate his political savvy or popular appeal.

However much they might try to conceal it, many Davis supporters also found conscription disconcerting. Even the Northern "consolidationists" had not yet resorted to a draft. From the beginning of the war, warnings against Yankee tyranny and pride in the Southern commitment to white freedom had been the twin themes of Confederate propaganda. In a political tract designed to kindle the fighting spirit of Confederate soldiers, Robert Armistead claimed that the Yankees would soon replace the American eagle with the boa constrictor. Virginia governor John Letcher, in a telling analogy, accused the Lincoln administration of following in the footsteps of George III.[36] Yet such rabid statements also hinted at dangers closer to home. Confederate conscription made it harder to hold the high moral ground in the contest over which side better preserved republican liberties.

By the standards of Christian orthodoxy, excessive pride also set up the Confederacy for a fall from grace. No one better expressed this damning hubris than Jefferson Davis. After Lincoln's suspension of habeas corpus, the Confederate president had exulted that "we have forever severed our connection with a government that thus tramples on all the principles of constitutional liberty." And only five days before the Confederate Congress authorized Davis himself to suspend the writ, he was still decrying military arrests and Yankee Bastilles.[37]

Such statements too closely identified Confederate nationalism with constitutional forms. Davis had painted himself into a legalistic corner and had not prepared citizens for wartime restrictions on traditional liberties. What if it suddenly became necessary, for example, to limit freedom of the press? Administration opponents could readily turn the president's arguments against him. Public debate would delay and perhaps water down if not block passage of the required legislation.

Yet Davis's claims for Southern constitutional probity were neither disingenuous nor hypocritical. Even after the Confederacy suspended habeas corpus on a limited basis, these arguments retained some plausibility. Southern newspapers, for example, remained unfettered and editors freely denounced the mildest efforts at censorship.[38] Despite much provocation, the Davis administration never suspended publication of any newspaper, no matter how disloyal its editorial policies. Congress considered but never passed a sedition act. This achievement is all the more remarkable because wars seldom promote respect for political dissent. In the interest of conformity, new states typically resort to one-party rule if not outright dictatorship. The temptations of power can subvert the original goals of any revolution, but political polarization also may fatally weaken fragile regimes.[39]

Confronting the dangers of division and despotism, the Confederate system both permitted and discouraged political activity. Citizens felt free to criticize the government and often did; editors regularly disagreed with administration policies. But again the antiparty character of the political culture combined with wartime calls for unity prevented the organization of an effective political opposition and limited opportunities for public debate.

Ironically, demands for uniformity came as much from outside as from inside the government. The war reinforced suspicions of political parties and advanced the revolution against politicians and their practices. "The spirit of faction is even more to be dreaded than the spirit of avarice and plunder," the prominent Presbyterian minister James Henley Thornwell maintained. "The man who now labors to weaken the hands of the Government, that he may seize the reins of authority, or cavils at public measures and policy that he may rise to distinction and office, has all the selfishness of a miser, and all the baseness of traitor." Those who would "destroy public confidence" in Confederate leaders would destroy the Southern cause. The very words "selfishness" and "baseness" recalled the political discourse of the 1790s, and in the midst of a bloody civil war, antiparty jeremiads left little room for legitimate opposition and no room for organized opposition.[40]

Calls for suppressing "treason" rested on the belief that government leniency toward Union men had already spread discord and discouraged enlistments. A Richmond editor declared himself tired of hearing about rights and privileges and insisted that the government use any available means to defeat the Yankees, including establishment of a military dictatorship.[41] Even during a war, however, the purpose of republican government remained the protection of liberty, and Governor John Gill Shorter of Alabama proclaimed that the machinery of state government would continue to safeguard the rights of citizens. Shorter regretted that men might "talk and bluster" about going back into the Union, but he refused to have anyone arrested who had not committed some overt act.[42]

These idealistic notions unfortunately ignored the reality of wartime politics. Patriotic enthusiasm quickly bred intolerance for dissent; political opposition was too readily seen as disloyalty. Worries about internal divisions, and especially about "spies" and "traitors," led Congress on February 27, 1862, to authorize the president to suspend the writ of habeas corpus in areas of the Confederacy threatened by enemy invasion. McClellan's army was on the Peninsula so Davis immediately suspended the writ in Richmond, Petersburg, and several Virginia towns. In the next few months, he added counties in western Virginia and East Tennessee, along with coastal districts in South Carolina. Yet the president was well aware of how sensitive Southerners would react to such an encroachment on traditional liberties. He refused to suspend the writ throughout the Confederacy, carefully weighing the claims of military necessity and political expediency.[43]

Historians have pointed out that Davis's approach to this issue illustrates his essential caution, conservatism, and commitment to states' rights. Although the president could be a stickler for constitutional procedures, he also realized the difficulty of expanding national authority in a society obsessed with individual liberty.[44] More than timidity, indecisiveness, or lack of imagination, the president's behavior showed an intelligent awareness of the central and sometimes contradictory values of Confederate politics. Stressing the homogeneity of interests in the Confederacy while easing the fears of highly individualistic and parochial Southerners presented a formidable challenge to his political leadership.

In the spring of 1862, however, ardent nationalists appeared to be in the ascendancy. Even the doctrinaire George Fitzhugh maintained that traditional and institutional checks on the exercise of arbitrary power would prove far more effective than easily evaded constitutional checks and balances. Despite the military emergency, the Confederacy remained much freer than the United States, where newspapers were routinely suppressed and the jails overflowed with political prisoners.[45] In April, Congress moved to reassure nervous citizens that the government would act with restraint by restricting the suspension of habeas corpus to cases involving arrests made by Confederate authorities and keeping the suspension in force for only thirty days after the beginning of its next session.[46]

This temporary abridgment of civil liberty had sailed through Congress and divided the president's critics. Those who had scolded the administration for lethargy welcomed habeas corpus suspension and conscription as signs of a more vigorous policy. Others worried that a dangerous precedent had been set. Perhaps Confederate troops in Richmond had intimidated the Congress, and in any case the Southern people appeared too willing to surrender ancient liberties.[47] Led by the *Charleston Mercury*, several South Carolina radicals accused Congress of bowing to presidential dictation. Military despotism threatened the nation, and both the executive and legislative branches were ignoring constitutional restrictions. "The forms of republicanism have been retained, while the sacred rights of holy liberty have been banished," a Memphis editor declared.[48]

But with the public far more worried about McClellan's army on the outskirts of Richmond than about executive tyranny, the Congress and the president had at last responded to the military and political crisis. Their actions on conscription and habeas corpus, however, had been bold on their face but cautious in substance. If the Confederacy managed to survive (by no means a sure bet), then debate over the South's complex experiment in libertarian nationalism would continue. The military fruits of conscription and to a lesser extent from suspending habeas corpus would be immediate and fairly obvious; the political costs would be far more uncertain and troublesome.

When Johnston withdrew his forces back up the Virginia Peninsula in May, newspaper strategists and political generals offered various suggestions to repel the Yankee invaders. If Davis would just order this, or some general would just do that, or if just the right commander were appointed . . . free advice was never in short supply. Constant retreating and Fabian tactics sapped confidence in Confederate leaders.[49]

After Johnston was seriously wounded at the battle of Seven Pines, the appointment of Robert E. Lee to command the defense of Richmond presaged a more aggressive strategy. Davis greatly respected Lee's military judgment, but in other ways also the Virginian was an ideal commander for a large and important army. Unlike Johnston, Lee usually rose above the politics of command; equally important, he could handle the president's prickly pride by avoiding any show of personal ambition. Rebuffing all overtures from the administration's congressional foes, he never became a political threat to Jefferson Davis, and his reserved dignity reminded Richard Taylor and other Confederate officers of George Washington.[50] He therefore appeared the perfect general for a revolution against politics. From June 25 through July 1, an impressive performance during the Seven Days campaign made him the toast of the Confederacy.

As prospects in the East improved, elsewhere matters drifted or deteriorated. After the retreat from Shiloh, Confederate fortunes in the West had gone from gloomy to grave. Davis could not understand why Beauregard—who now held the late Albert Sidney Johnston's command—had abandoned the important rail center at Corinth, Mississippi, and he soon found an excuse to place the troublesome Creole on the shelf. His subsequent appointment of Braxton Bragg to command the Western Department of the Confederate army infuriated Beauregard and his friends, making them implacable and dangerous enemies.[51]

Yet in the midst of these military crises, the Confederate government had begun to show a certain maturity and, if not more efficient, had grown more centralized and powerful. A few visionaries even decided that states'-rights doctrines had outlived their usefulness. According to Arkansas editor John R. Eakin, "thinking men" had decided that the Confederacy badly needed a "strong and stable government, free from the fluctuations of popular caprice, and the arts of the demagogue." Conscription had pushed the government toward a centralization based on the British model, and Eakin even foresaw the possibility of electing the president and Senate for life.[52] Perhaps the ghost of Alexander Hamilton had appeared, but these same ideas had been rejected by the Constitutional Convention in 1787, and the creation of a consolidated state would have to proceed on a more republican basis.

The president's most ardent supporters deplored talk of dictatorship. Believing that the Confederacy was teaching the world a profound lesson in genuine republicanism, Senator Benjamin Hill of Georgia praised Davis for abiding by both the letter and the spirit of the Constitution. Although Edmund Ruffin often ranted against West Pointism and administration incompetence, he also lashed out against "lawless opposition" and efforts by anyone to "play the part of Bonaparte or Cromwell." Even Yancey, who was no friend of the president, applauded Davis for conscientiously performing his duties while avoiding the temptations of extralegal power.[53]

Even as McClellan threatened Richmond, the president's political allies counterattacked against early administration critics. Just as Washington had been unjustly assailed during the American Revolution, so Davis had received too little credit for establishing a new and viable government. Errors had been made, but what president could measure up to the standards of perfection set by the chronic faultfinders? Angrily denying the label "administration organ" (despite receiving the public printing contract from the Confederate government), the *Richmond Enquirer* increasingly defended Davis on most issues. Senator Robert W. Barnwell of South Carolina deplored Rhett's slanders against the president. Another Charleston editor lauded Davis as "our Moses . . . leading us through the wilderness of revolution and war, to Canaan, the promised land of independence and prosperity."[54]

The most fanatical anti-Davis men tried to identify themselves with the sacred cause of Southern freedom while lambasting the administration. "Davis's supreme imbecility has well nigh undone us," raged Congressman Laurence Keitt. "You cannot find a more signal failure in history." Drawing the usual contrast between a virtuous people and a weak-kneed government, Keitt claimed that a "great leader would [already] . . . have carried us to victory."[55] Blustering Bob Toombs, who if anything was unhappier in the army than he had been in the cabinet, talked of launching another revolution to put the Confederacy back on its proper course.[56] On one well-oiled occasion, Louis Wigfall spouted that "Jeff Davis ought to be hung in Richmond." Yet the politically independent Wigfall did not let personal hatreds cloud his judgment. Even though he questioned the president's capacity to lead, he helped push the administration's conscription bill through Congress and generally worked to strengthen the government's hand.[57]

Wigfall's confusing behavior illustrates an important dilemma for Confederates—especially for those who had fervently sought the destruction of the old Union. A war for national independence demanded the exercise of government power, but a revolution against politics—including antiparty rhetoric, denunciations of demagoguery, and attacks on all sorts of political practices—only added to public skepticism of politicians. Especially when the war was going badly, citizens berated their leaders for too much talk and too little action but remained fearful of the many potential abuses of political power. The supposed prevalence of office-seeking and corruption further eroded public confidence and even fostered a sort of civic anomie. James Henry Hammond maintained that he had "long seen causes . . . at work in America that corrupted its institutions and demoralized and enfeebled its men, stripping them of every high quality, moral, mental and physical," but the deterioration had proceeded far more rapidly than he had expected.[58] Confederates still yearned for political salvation, a formula to restore the purer republicanism of the eighteenth century, an escape from the evils of party. Although political purification was not the raison d'être for Confederate independence, it remained central to all plans for the Southern nation's political future.

As several states prepared to hold elections, a Shreveport editor ritualistically intoned against those who would "fatten upon the spoils of the public." Doubting that the masses were capable of self-government, he argued for a government run by the planting interest, duly noting that Washington, Jefferson, Madison, Monroe, and Jackson had all been planters.[59] Such blunt assertions of class hegemony were rare in the Confederacy, but this editorial reveals a persistent uncertainty, a grasping for answers to knotty political questions. If the planters did not govern, who would? If a Southern bourgeoisie existed, it was hardly large or unified enough to take control. In the long run, the war might force a reordering of class relations and a redefining of political legitimacy.

In the short term, the states experimented with new constitutional forms that indirectly affected the balance of political power. The purpose of these changes was to streamline and energize state governments while minimizing internal divisions and of course avoiding the curse of partisanship. A tense triangular relationship, however, developed among the secession conventions (many of which had continued to meet for more than a year after the war began), the governors, and the legislatures. The rush of events between the election of delegates and the decision for secession had caused the conventions either to lag behind or run ahead of public opinion. The North Carolina convention's Unionist majority did not reflect the transformation of public sentiment after Lincoln's call for troops. In contrast, the South Carolina convention marked the full flowering of radical politics. Delegates boasted of their commitment to sacred principle and their indifference to politics and place-hunting. A few ideologues still favored reopening the African slave trade, and as late as September 1862 Rhett offered a resolution prohibiting the admission of free states to the Confederacy.[60]

The South Carolina convention had also created an executive council to advise Governor Francis Pickens and in effect watch over him. The executive council consisted of the governor, the lieutenant governor, and three members chosen by the convention, thus turning the governorship into a nearly useless and inconvenient appendage of state government. The three appointed members—James Chesnut, Jr., Isaac Hayne, and William H. Gist—took control of financial, police, and military affairs.[61]

This would-be revolutionary junta so provoked Pickens that he considered resigning, but the council soon became as unpopular as the hapless governor. The *Charleston Courier* lambasted it as a "secret conclave of five dictators" that ought to be dissolved along with the convention that had so brazenly usurped legislative authority.[62] When editors criticized the council for being undemocratic, they came dangerously close to repudiating Calhoun's old notion of a sovereign convention, but opposition to the council (and to the convention itself) had grown too powerful to worry about ideological consistency. South Carolinians turned the same libertarian arguments against their own leaders that they had used against both the United States and—more recently—the Confederate governments.

Sensing a shift in public sentiment, the governor's friends held several meetings in Edgefield District to denounce the convention. In the fall elections, voters chose a new legislature with a majority hostile to the council and the convention.[63] This bitter factional battle originated in South Carolina's antiparty tradition, but it also reflected the organizational chaos of Confederate politics. Because there was little chance of a powerful leader emerging to become a Confederate Calhoun, South Carolinians continued to bicker among themselves over military appointments and broad constitutional questions. The state's governors were ineligible for reelection, and Pickens believed that this restriction prevented men of "talent and character" from serving. In his opinion, the governor should appoint more administrative officers such as sheriffs and tax collectors so South Carolinians could nullify the effects of "low electioneering." This call for political purity, however, was largely beside the point. Although a special committee of twenty-one appointed by the convention issued a report defending the decisions of the executive council, the legislature abolished the body shortly after Pickens left office.[64]

Inevitably, Confederate politics began to shape state politics, and fierce state loyalties and libertarian convictions fragmented national politics. Loose and temporary alliances began forming as state leaders dealt with the Davis administration and the myriad local issues growing out of the war. Nowhere was this situation more evident than in North Carolina. Shortly after the presidential election, William W. Holden began organizing both Democratic cooperationists and former Whig opponents into a

Conservative party dedicated to preserving liberty against secessionist centralizers.[65]

In 1862, any party in North Carolina that condemned conscription would be popular. Conservatives appealed to white men fearful of enslavement to a consolidated government and sensitive to any apparent encroachment on their vaunted liberties. In addition, their equally firm conviction that the president had proscribed conservatives showed how patronage and political opportunism had become entangled in the defense of republican principles.[66]

For their part, secessionist Democrats adopted the nonpartisan label "Confederate." In February, several newspapers began trumpeting the gubernatorial candidacy of railroad president William Johnston, who had been informally nominated at a Charlotte meeting. A secessionist and lifelong Whig, Johnston apparently hoped to lure old party friends away from the Conservatives.[67] Conservative leaders met in Raleigh in April and nominated Zebulon B. Vance of Buncombe County for governor. Only thirty-two years old, a large man of around 230 pounds with massive shoulders and arms, Vance was physically impressive but had limited political experience. As a Whig Unionist and a colonel in the Confederate army, Vance could appeal to loyal men of various stripes who had grown dissatisfied with the state and Confederate administrations.[68]

Holden disingenuously denied organizing opposition to the administrations in either Richmond or Raleigh but at the same time labeled the Confederate party "destructives." In contrast to Vance's moderation, Holden continued to flay the Davis government for "partyism, favoritism, inefficiency, and misrule" and tried to turn the gubernatorial election into a referendum on Confederate war policies. Conservative candidates for the state legislature denied partisan motives and claimed to represent the people against the spoilsmen.[69]

Vance, who considered Holden's editorials in the *Standard* "too ultra," appeared temperate and calm. Realizing he could count on the Unionist vote, he adopted a conciliatory approach to the secessionists, hoping that Holden would soft-pedal his attacks on Davis and conscription. "Moderation, no partyism, harmony and deprecation of strife constitute our true tactics," he wisely observed. His acceptance letter stressed duty, honor, and civil religion along with antiparty sentiments and political harmony. Vance claimed to prefer remaining in the army but would serve if the people so decided. Relying on divine providence and "sincerely deprecating the growing tendency toward party strife . . . which every patriot should shun in the presence of the common danger," this Tar Heel Cincinnatus hoped for a "unity of sentiment and fraternity of feeling . . . [that] can enable us to prosecute this war for liberty and independence."[70]

There was little campaigning. Vance remained with his regiment, Johnston did no stumping, and interested voters had to rely on newspapers. For the so-called Confederates (mostly Democratic secessionists) the contest boiled down to a question of patriotism. Traditionally, of course, candidates had to prove their loyalty to Southern interests, and the politics of slavery was far from dead, especially in local contests. The friends of Captain Jabez Hunt of the Second North Carolina Cavalry, who was running for a Guilford County seat in the legislature, for instance, hotly denied that he was an "abolition candidate."[71] Statewide, Confederates stressed their commitment to Southern independence and blasted Vance as Holden's stalking-horse. Vance would supposedly kowtow to submissionists, and reports of peace meetings were already reaching North Carolina troops.[72]

Like several other states, North Carolina permitted its soldiers to vote in the field. Legislative candidates sent campaign letters to Confederate officers, and informal stump speaking enlivened camp routine. Many enlisted men, however, knew little about the election, did not bother to cast ballots, or believed that officers were trying to control their votes. Despite some irregularities, Vance won nearly two-thirds of the soldier vote.[73]

He ran even stronger at home, capturing almost three-fourths of the civilian vote to hand Johnston and the badly organized Confederate party a stunning defeat. Holden crowed that the people had repudiated place hunters in a "spontaneous uprising" to defend republican liberty. This was no doubt a bitter pill for the Democratic secessionists, but it was a clear victory neither for Holden nor for disaffected North Carolinians. As the *Richmond Enquirer* perceptively noted, there was no reason to regret Vance's election, only the partisanship that animated his followers.[74]

The meaning of partisanship in this context, however, was unclear. Divisions over secession had been more important than party in determining the results. Old Unionist strongholds favored Vance, and he carried many traditionally Whig counties. Yet he also made inroads in Democratic areas. In many ways, Holden's jerry-built Conservative party—perhaps best exemplified by Holden's cooperation with some of his bitterest antebellum foes—had begun to break down traditional voting patterns. At the same time, this election signified growing class tensions in the state as well as widening political divisions between slaveholding and nonslaveholding districts.[75] A vigorous democratic politics had survived though both sides increasingly resorted to antiparty rhetoric. Indeed, the experience of North Carolina shows that the entire Confederacy had not embraced antiparty ideology. Old political habits died hard, and despite their public posture, the Conservatives often behaved like a political party.

The campaign also marked the emergence of a brilliant political centrist and the Confederacy's most remarkable politician. Never a cat's-paw for Holden or anyone else, Vance steered a moderate and independent course through the treacherous shoals of Confederate and state politics. After his election on August 4, he moved quickly to dampen the highly partisan atmosphere of the recent campaign. Though not averse to using patronage, he tried to appease secessionists by fervently supporting the war and opposing any reconstruction schemes.[76] Throughout the war, political savvy would be Vance's most impressive characteristic.

By the summer of 1862, Confederate politics had undergone a perceptible shift. National preservation seemed to require conscription and the suspension of habeas corpus, even though these measures raised serious questions about the very nature of the Confederate experiment. Davis's critics had grown bolder, but there had been no political realignment, no movement toward party formation. Spurred by increasing dissatisfaction with Confederate policies and military losses, libertarian politics posed a serious challenge to a political culture based on national unity and class harmony. Yet even the rise of political opposition and the development of an alternative political culture took place within an antiparty framework.

Internal Stresses of War

I n the early fall of 1862, as Confederate military prospects improved, dissension abated. Taking little comfort in this temporary lull, however, Davis complained to Congress about the "unexpected criticism" of conscription. "Only by harmonious as well as zealous action" can a "government as new as ours . . . fulfill its duties," he warned. Why he should have been surprised at opposition to a draft is not clear, but his frustration in dealing with governors and other disputatious politicians was beginning to show. Just as he stressed the need for unity, the president also asserted the power of the Confederate government to demand sacrifices from its citizens. State-mandated draft exemptions, for instance, could "render the Confederacy an impracticable form of Government."[1]

Military necessity, national unity, and political expediency all militated against defiance of Confederate laws. Dissenters risked being labeled traitors: their challenge was to attack the administration without assailing the government, to criticize policies without becoming factious, to protest without forming an opposition party. In this way, libertarian ideologues could use controversies over conscription, civil liberties, and even military strategy to create an alternative political culture within an antiparty framework.

Despite the repulse of McClellan during the Seven Days campaign and the slackening of Federal offensives in the West, the manpower demands of the Confederate army became even more voracious. In addition to the heavy losses on the Virginia Peninsula, Lee's masterful attack on John

Pope at Second Manassas, the subsequent invasion of Maryland, and the bloody draw at the battle of Antietam proved to be extremely costly. Whether the Confederate draft could replace these enormous casualties (conservatively estimated at more than forty thousand men) was by no means clear. Conflicts with state officials continued to delay the law's execution, and many conscripts had deserted.

When the second session of the First Congress opened on August 18, Davis proposed raising the draft age to forty-five. This latest challenge to traditional liberties aroused surprisingly little opposition, sailing through both the House and Senate, with venomous Davis critic Louis T. Wigfall strongly in favor.[2]

Even in areas far removed from immediate danger, a dramatic shift in political attitudes had taken place. Although Caleb Herbert, the most extreme states'-rights man among Texas congressmen, warned that his state might have to secede from the Confederacy and hoist the Lone Star flag to resist conscription, two of his colleagues, Franklin B. Sexton and Malcolm Graham, replied that Texans understood the necessity for a draft and deplored constitutional quibbling. Such words would have shocked Southerners just a few months earlier, but the course of the war had clearly strengthened the hands of the centralizers. Even Senator Williamson S. Oldham, as doctrinaire as anyone on questions of state sovereignty, offered only perfunctory protests and wisely tried to the shift the discussion into a debate on military strategy.[3] Only one other senator (James L. Orr of South Carolina) joined Oldham in voting against the second Conscription Act.

Despite continuing skepticism and worries about military despotism, the debate in Congress increasingly centered on the operation rather than the legitimacy of a draft. Shortly after the initial adoption of conscription in April 1862, Congress had provided exemptions for public employees, mail carriers, river pilots, railroad workers, ministers, teachers, printers, and even apothecaries. Widespread abuses arising from this law did not prevent Congress from expanding the list in October to include millers, tanners, saltmakers, and shoemakers. It required two and one-half finely printed pages to list all the exempted classes. Requests for additional occupational exemptions, however, still poured into Congress, and each member, it seemed, had one or more pet categories, leading wags to suggest that lawmakers had exempted more able-bodied men than had been drafted. In responding to legitimate requests for allocating skilled manpower, Congress had created a legal and political nightmare.[4]

The law's unwieldiness prompted criticism, but the appearance of class favoritism stirred more serious discontent. The most controversial provision exempted the owner or overseer on plantations with twenty or more slaves. Derisively dubbed the "twenty nigger law," this measure was a response to numerous pleas from plantation owners, governors, and frightened citizens. The Senate narrowly defeated an amendment that would have required the Confederate government to enforce state laws mandating the presence of one able-bodied white man on any farm or plantation with as few as ten slaves.[5] From the beginning of the secession crisis, there had been apprehension about slave discipline, but the war had made it more difficult than ever for communities to maintain effective slave patrols.

However many times congressmen or newspaper editors might explain the necessity for assuring proper supervision of slaves, they had trouble convincing the yeomen and their hard-pressed families. In denouncing the exemption of overseers, many state politicians could not resist what one dismayed editor termed "the appeal of the demagogue." The North Carolina legislature, for example, adopted a resolution calling for the immediate repeal of that exemption and sharply criticizing Congress for granting special favors to the privileged and neglecting the welfare of the state's poorer citizens. In December, Senator James Phelan of Mississippi informed Davis that exempting slaveholders had demoralized the soldiers and encouraged draft resistance.[6]

Despite these objections, quick action by Congress in passing the second Conscription Act and the exemption bill signaled widespread support for or at least acquiescence in a draft. Even Rhett refused to nitpick over details. Editor John M. Daniel of the *Richmond Examiner* scolded Congress for timidity, scorning abstract appeals to individual liberty as disguised cowardice and greed.[7]

With the notable exception of Joe Brown and, to a lesser extent, Zebulon Vance, the state governors either strongly endorsed the draft or kept reservations to themselves. Governor John Milton of Florida considered the constitutionality of conscription a purely judicial matter and not a "question of political power between the Confederate and State Government." Debating political theories would "defeat the purposes of the Government of our choice, administered by statesmen of our own selection."[8]

In another remarkable display of political harmony, Yancey delivered a rousing speech to the Alabama General Assembly in early December during which he upheld congressional authority to place every available man in the field. Defending the exemption of overseers, he argued that sustaining agricultural production helped everyone and that well-managed slaves would be an asset to the Confederacy.[9] Thus the traditional emphasis on the harmony of interests and the absence of class conflict had been extended beyond local communities to buttress the exercise of national power. Yancey's arguments showed how proponents of conscription turned political and military necessity into a virtue—at least for the time being.

Cooperation from most of the state governors and some support from the Yanceys, the Daniels, and on rare occasions even the Rhetts could not of course erase doubts about Davis's leadership. Although agreeing with the president about the need to extend the draft, Senator Wigfall was fast becoming one of the administration's harshest critics. A Texas colleague considered Wigfall "a desperate man—a tyrant at heart, yet a man of wonderful ability." Besides his obvious influence in the Senate, Wigfall had important friends in both the eastern and western armies. An intimate of Joe Johnston and several other Confederate generals, Wigfall devoted much of his considerable energy and not inconsiderable intelligence to the politics of command. By late 1862, he had concluded that the great fool Davis was trying to be both president and general in chief, a task that would have daunted Napoleon.[10] Although Wigfall was unwilling and temperamentally unable to mend fences, he recognized that Davis commanded considerable support. So though he continued to rage against the president in hotel lobbies, at receptions, and in secret Senate sessions, he avoided a public break.

With a solid political base in Congress, a still friendly press, and a few battlefield victories, and despite the cavils of chronic complainers such as Wigfall, Toombs, Rhett, or Holden, Davis appeared to be riding high. Yet much of the president's support was tenuously conditional, ebbing and flowing with each change in the economic and military situation. As people began to feel financially strapped and once the war started going badly, opposition to the administration, often expressed in remarkably ideological terms, would grow apace.

A politics of individual liberty was beginning to resonate among Southerners having second thoughts about the costs of the war. Confederate identity became the broad issue in this running discussion over the shape and future of the Southern nation. Constitutional purists had watched with horror as conscription was extended and Congress debated renewing the suspension of habeas corpus. Apparently, freedom was being sacrificed on the altar of military necessity. Defenders of traditional liberties blamed the president, Congress, and many generals for losing faith in the people.[11] The great nightmare of these constitutional fundamentalists was that the Confederates might win the war but lose the republic.

Declarations of martial law by Braxton Bragg in Atlanta and Earl Van Dorn in Mississippi confirmed these fears. A Tennessee editor who had recently fled to Grenada, Mississippi, after the fall of Memphis, compared Van Dorn's order to an "imperial ukase from the Emperor of all the Russians." According to Louisiana governor Thomas O. Moore, who generally cooperated with Confederate officials, "no free people can or ought to submit" to such an illegal decree.[12] These military edicts proved especially embarrassing to congressmen who had voted for the suspension of habeas corpus.

The issue of martial law was a godsend to Davis's libertarian opponents. The necessity for such a step was by no means clear—some generals seemed more interested in suppressing newspaper criticism than in rounding up spies or traitors. Moreover, condemning the policy was politically safer than opposing conscription, which, unlike martial law, seemed essential for the success of Confederate arms. Even though the suspension of habeas corpus was primarily aimed at men using every legal trick to avoid conscription, many ardent Confederates hesitated to support blanket declarations of martial law. "More monstrous usurpations never were practiced by any of the Stuarts," Yancey fumed. "This is ... West Point despotism." The Southern nation stood in danger of embracing the heretical doctrines of its enemies, of becoming like the hated Lincoln or his evil genius Secretary of State William H. Seward. The Confederate Senate easily passed a resolution declaring that "martial law is unknown to the Constitution." Confederates who were particularly obsessed with threats to republican liberty asserted that Congress should have restored habeas corpus. The Federalism of the "elder Adams" had so taken hold of the Confederate government, the *Examiner* warned, that in "escaping one despotism, we rush heedlessly into the open jaws of another."[13]

Whatever political and ideological consistency these arguments may have had, they ignored the reality of draft evasion. Senator Robert W. Barnwell believed that congressional opposition to conscription had encouraged people to defy the law in Georgia and South Carolina. "If we are overrun," he told Wigfall, "politicians will have to answer for it." Indeed, those who had escaped the draft now busily hounded congressmen for bombproof public offices. Senator Clay concluded that the Confederate government was too weak to protect loyal persons or punish treason in northern Alabama. Maybe suspension of the writ and martial law were necessary even if they embodied "Federalist" notions of constitutional construction. In words that sounded like vintage John Marshall, a Confederate district judge in Mississippi offered a classic justification for expanded military authority: "When a power is granted, you grant the means necessary to carry the power into effect. When you grant to Congress the power to declare War, it is a mockery unless you grant the means to carry it on in the most efficient and energetic manner. . . . I have seen enough here to convince me that the civil authorities are wholly unfit to deal with a large class of offenders. . . . To say that the military shall not punish them is virtually to say that they shall go unpunished."[14]

Yet Davis himself balked at such broad constitutional construction. In a general order issued on September 12, he voided all proclamations of martial law made by Confederate generals. The following day, a report of the House Judiciary Committee commended the president for respecting the constitutional distinction between suspending habeas corpus and declaring martial law. His gingerly approach had been politically necessary and certainly well-timed. Davis wanted Congress to renew the suspension of habeas corpus, and the Judiciary Committee obliged by reporting out a new and clearer statute.[15] After considerable wrangling, Congress agreed to a second suspension. This law applied only to arrests made by Confederate authorities for offenses against the Confederate government. Like the first suspension, it would expire thirty days after the beginning of the next session of Congress (around mid-February 1863).[16]

By placing a time limit on the suspension, Congress had in essence postponed making a final decision, and this caution reflected a basic ambiguity in Confederate thinking. Public acceptance of emergency war legislation carried important qualifications. Politicians had to search for a compromise between the extreme centralizers and fanatical defenders of individual liberty. The perennial tension between freedom and responsibility caused the more thoughtful members of Congress to pause over hard choices touching fundamental freedoms. Even after he voted against the suspension of habeas corpus, Texas congressman Franklin B. Sexton second-guessed himself: "There are cases in these times when it should be suspended yet it is a dangerous thing to tinker with. I am willing to give the power to the President *but not to anybody else*. I am not sure, but we can get along *without* suspending it."[17] This confusion was understandable because dissatisfaction with Confederate war policies was disrupting state politics. The politics of national unity had begun losing ground to the politics of liberty in Georgia and North Carolina. Nationalists emphasized political and social harmony, the evils of subjugation, and the virtues of the Confederate system and Confederate leaders; the libertarians worried about the dangers of concentrated power, distrusted Confederate leaders, and claimed to be purer republicans than their more pragmatic opponents. As Brown, to some degree Vance, and other politicians took up the libertarian cause, an alternative political culture began to emerge.

Unhealed wounds from antebellum party battles, deep divisions over secession, and bitter disputes over the conduct of the war, along with persistent Confederate-Conservative divisions, helped account for continuing political conflict in North Carolina, but explaining the appeal of libertarian politics in Georgia is more difficult. Like North Carolinians, Georgians had been badly divided over secession, and except for the coastal areas, neither state had yet faced a serious threat of invasion and occupation. In addition, the weight of Confederate financial and military exactions fell hard on both the Georgia and North Carolina economies. But even more than for North Carolina, in Georgia the secession debates had cut across party lines and had been especially disruptive for Democrats. Moreover, since the Compromise of 1850 and even before, Georgians had acquired the habit of following a handful of prominent political leaders on national questions. Yet secession and war had not fostered political unity and had instead arrayed powerful politicians—many with forceful and eccentric personalities—against each other. As the war dragged on, Howell Cobb, Ben Hill, and a host of newspaper editors generally supported the Davis administration, while Toombs, the Stephens brothers, and Joe Brown led the opposition. Both principles and pragmatism induced administration critics to embrace a libertarian political credo.

For Brown, martial law and the suspension of habeas corpus were no less destructive of liberty than conscription. More ominously still, the people had submitted to usurpations "without murmur, much less resistance." Confederates had "much more to apprehend from military despotism than from subjugation by the enemy," the governor informed Vice-President Stephens. Although Brown is often considered a political opportunist, in this instance his beliefs squared with his actions.[18]

After unsuccessfully appealing to Vance for cooperation in resisting administration policies, Brown tried to draw the president into another dispute over conscription. The governor declared that the most oppressive acts of the United States government before the war had never "struck a blow at constitutional liberty as has been stricken by the conscription acts." Georgians had "entered into the revolution free men . . . [and] will refuse to yield their sovereignty to usurpation." Deferring to legislative authority when it served his purpose, he refused to allow the enrollment of conscripts until the General Assembly convened in November.[19]

In his message to the legislature, Brown declared that the draft laws treated free people like "chattels"—a telling analogy in a slave society. Yet his other arguments fell flat. A long and tedious discourse on the superiority of volunteers over conscripts, yet another tendentious discussion of the term "militia," and a final warning against the conscription of state officials made Brown's message stale and repetitious.[20] All the stock appeals were there, but they did not add up to much of a case. The usually astute Brown had failed to strike the right chord.

His political enemies in Georgia took advantage of this lackluster performance by dismissing the message as thinly disguised demagoguery. "The personal ambitions of politicians [i.e., Brown]," a Savannah editor asserted, were the sole cause of the controversy between Georgia and the Confederate government. The governor also lacked reliable political allies. Although Linton Stephens damned conscription during the legislative session with all the vigor Brown could have wished, his brother Aleck would not openly criticize the president. Even Robert Toombs, who normally would have joined anyone in condemning the administration, accused the governor of violating individual rights in a proclamation against whiskey distilling, a proposal for a new cotton tax, and the confiscation of salt from supposed speculators.[21]

The anti-Brown majority in the legislature took little notice of the governor's message. Although Senator George Gordon of Chatham County conceded that the draft laws undermined state sovereignty, he advised the people to submit out of necessity. Citizens could still criticize Confederate policies, the Virginia and Kentucky Resolutions remained sacred documents, and the founding fathers had never endorsed conscription, but Georgians should not defy the law.[22] Gordon and others were clearly searching for an elusive middle ground, some way to sustain the Southern nation and to preserve traditional freedoms at the same time. For such moderates, both the politics of unity and the politics of liberty contained their own charms and pitfalls.

The election of a new Confederate senator (to fill the seat Toombs had refused to accept) marked the culmination of this uncertainty and confusion in Georgia politics. Neither Brown nor his opponents had enough votes to dictate the outcome, and the selection of Herschel V. Johnson did not entirely please either the governor or the president. Johnson shared many of Brown's fears. "I look with concern and apprehension at the obvious tendency to absolutism," he wrote shortly after the passage of the second Conscription Act. Yet he believed Davis to be a "pure patriot," who "would shrink from . . . [despotism] with horror." In assessing the rival claims of nationalists and libertarians, Johnson adopted a philosophical attitude. Revolutions naturally led to centralization, and wars inevitably produced autocratic tendencies. "The sword can win victories and carve our way to independence. But independence is not good government. It is simply, separate nationality. Good government is the offspring of wise statesmanship *not of the sword*. The sword is the emblem of despotism, unless it be required to lay all its trophies on the altar of the Constitution." The critical questions then became whether a republic would survive the revolution and, conversely, whether a pure republic could win a revolutionary war.

Johnson understood this dilemma and ruminated on the intractable difficulty of reconciling these contradictory goals. "I pray for success; I hope for success; I do not expect success." Gloomy about military prospects and the Davis administration's defensive strategy, he nevertheless refused to criticize the government openly for fear of encouraging division and party spirit among the people.[23]

Johnson's moderation—in reality a painful ambivalence—made him a logical compromise candidate in a deeply divided General Assembly. Some legislators believed that opposition to conscription should be a litmus test for any would-be Confederate senator, but others blocked attempts to draw ideological lines. For men like Linton Stephens, Johnson had taken the correct constitutional position on conscription, but his refusal to attack Davis also won him friends among administration supporters. In an early December speech in Milledgeville, Johnson called for an end to political bickering and carefully downplayed the dangers of military despotism that had so alarmed him just two months earlier. Johnson regretted that people believed he was "going to Richmond to make war on Davis" when he was instead steering a middle course between the Georgia dissidents and the Confederate administration.[24]

Johnson's election was probably heartening to Georgia supporters of the Confederate administration, and they quickly went on the political offensive. In a lengthy address to the General Assembly on December 11, 1862, the state's other Confederate senator, Benjamin H. Hill, decried the natural tendency to blame the chief executive for problems and dismissed such criticism as the wailing of disappointed office-seekers. He then offered a powerful defense of conscription. If the Confederacy could not draft its citizens, it had no real government: "Men owe obligations as well as possess rights." The national government could not afford to wait for volunteers. Scoffing at the charge that conscription had turned Jefferson Davis into a military dictator, Hill exalted the president as a model of republicanism. Like Washington, Davis had "refused to exercise any power not expressly authorized by law."

With unmistakable references to Joe Brown, Hill saved his most devastating remarks for administration critics and turned libertarian fears against the opposition. History proved "that they find most fault with power in others, who themselves exercise ungranted powers most freely." Such ambition led Caesar, Cromwell, and Bonaparte to "trample upon the liberty they swore to defend, and grasp empire." As for the hoary maxim about vigilance and liberty, Hill sharply denied "that eternal vigilance means perpetual snarling, snapping, fault finding, and complaining." Let pothouse politicians carp; Confederate soldiers would stand behind the president. Hill wrapped his argument in antipolitical ideology by appealing to general distrust of politicians. Recent attacks on the Confederate government did not stem from any real threats to liberty but from "passion, personal ambition, and party maneuver."[25] Hill had given the most eloquent expression yet to the central values of the Confederacy's political culture of national harmony.

His telling remarks may also have given pause to ardent libertarians elsewhere. To cite the best example, many North Carolinians had expected Zeb Vance to follow Brown's lead in attacking conscription and the administration. Instead, his inaugural address in September had been a rousing summons to repel the invaders. Deploring disaffection, the governor bluntly inquired if there were "any in our midst who still look back to the fleshpots of vassalage, and for the sake of peace, would leave their children a heritage of shame, to feed upon the bitter husks of subjugation." Whatever objections might be raised against conscription, the people should obey the law. Having gone this far, Vance then slyly backtracked. Citizens should not surrender their liberties to cries of military necessity nor permit the gradual erosion of their freedoms. Like Herschel Johnson, Vance skillfully placed himself between the forces of national consolidation and the libertarian opposition.[26]

But North Carolinians were far from putting the bitterness of the recent election campaign behind them, and the state remained an exception to the rule in a largely antiparty political culture. The Conservative majority in the legislature elected the prominent Whig William A. Graham to the Confederate Senate, chose longtime Unionist Jonathan Worth as state treasurer, and gave the state printing contract back to Holden. Vance's supporters sometimes acted as a political party while cleverly calling for unity and deploring political proscription. Urging the appointment of Conservatives and still accusing the "destructives" of attempting to monopolize public offices, Holden nevertheless denied seeking vengeance against political opponents or weakening the nation.[27]

The anguished howls of the recently defeated Confederate party suggested otherwise as their delight with Vance's conciliatory inaugural address quickly turned to dismay. Watching the legislature purge Johnson supporters, former Whig Kenneth Rayner—who had once had a street brawl with Holden—claimed that he had never witnessed such "intolerance" even "in the worst days of party bitterness." The desperate Confederates even resorted to what once would have been considered dangerous appeals to class. One Raleigh editor chastised the legislature for spending most of its time distributing patronage and refusing to cooperate with Confederate military authorities. "Remember these things on your return," he advised the soldiers. "You are sacrificed that able-bodied magistrates, skulking militia officers, and rich men, who have purchased substitutes, may remain in their comfortable homes."[28] Both parties considered their opponents the special beneficiaries of economic and political privilege, and, more alarming to the true believers in republicanism, both fished in the treacherous waters of military politics.

As a former Confederate colonel, Vance was in a good position to build political support in the army and soon took up an issue dear to soldiers and their families. Conscripts complained that the War Department did not allow them to choose their own regiments, often scattering relatives, neighbors, and friends among several brigades. Regimental organization had reinforced localism and had shielded recruits from some of the impersonal realities of large organizations. Recognizing the political wisdom of keeping these soldiers (and voters) happy, Vance vigorously objected to the arbitrary assignment of draftees. The hostility of Vance and other governors to professional soldiers reflected the parochialism of their constituents along with prevailing prejudice against a "standing army."

When his protests were ignored, Vance pointedly informed the president that recent state elections had proven that the "original advocates of secession no longer hold the ear of our people." To sustain the war effort, the government had no choice but to conciliate former Union men. "If, on the contrary, West Point generals, who know less of human nature than I do of military science, are to ride roughshod over the people, drag them from their homes and assign them . . . to strange regiments and strange commanders . . . I must be compelled to decline undertaking a task [i.e., enforcing the Conscription Acts] which will certainly fail." Davis probably winced at such advice, though he shared Vance's hope that "party distinctions . . . would be buried in the graves of the gallant men who have fallen in the defense of their birthright."[29] With varying emphases on customary privileges, community rights, and republican principles, both Davis and Vance appealed to notions of public virtue dating back to the American Revolution.

The governor also tried to prevent Confederate conscription from encroaching too much on local prerogatives and preferred having militia rather than Confederate troops round up deserters and draft evaders. But his cooperation had distinct political limits. Vance denounced military arrests of civilians and called on Confederate authorities to respect writs of habeas corpus issued by state and local judges. Otherwise, freedom in the Southern republic might be lost forever.[30] The governor well understood the appeals of both national unity and individual liberty.

Despite Vance's historical reputation as an obstructionist and a thorn in Jefferson Davis's side, the governor was essentially moderate. He remained a sensitive barometer of North Carolina's continuing uncertainties about the war. Vance criticized specific features of conscription and other violations of civil liberties but refused to break with the Confederate administration.[31] Less inclined than Brown to lengthy disputes and rambling discourses on liberty, Vance nonetheless must have seemed cussedly independent to both Holden and Davis.

Despite the president's commitment to a politics of national unity, his official family was less than harmonious. Rumors of a falling-out between Davis and Vice-President Stephens, yet another cabinet crisis, continuing dissatisfaction over military appointments, and nagging problems of command in the western theater all created serious internal divisions. Even with the growing centralization of the Confederate government, the lack of political cohesion in the absence of parties made the Richmond government appear fragmented and indecisive.

In early 1862, Tom Cobb—with his usual penchant for exaggeration and paranoia—claimed that Vice-President Stephens was "openly opposing the administration and trying to get up an opposition party."[32] Stephens was doing no such thing, but he clearly had become disenchanted with Davis. As several Stephens biographers have pointed out, Davis and Stephens were too much alike to get along. Stiff, intense, and often ill, both men took their own opinions and themselves far too seriously. They both deplored compromise, and the word "conciliatory" was not in their vocabularies. If Davis had all the cold formality of a George Washington, Stephens sometimes resembled crusty old John Adams. Like the imperious New Englander, the Georgian often deprecated the arts of the politician and shunned any sacrifice of principle. The presence of both Davis and Stephens in Richmond symbolized the ostensible triumph of an austere antiparty ideology—both men were firmly convinced that they were rising above petty political considerations—but did not indicate any basic agreement on policy questions or ideology.[33]

Davis saw himself as the epitome of Confederate nationalism, whereas the prickly Stephens exemplified the politics of individual liberty. Despite his penchant for abstractions, Stephens's passions were local and particular. For the vice-president's heart was always in his Crawfordville, Georgia, home with his family, friends, slaves, his beloved dog Rio, and most of all his brother Linton, whose views were even more extreme than his own. Stephens hated wartime Richmond and much preferred the quiet repose of Liberty Hall, where, always on the alert for threats to freedom, he could contemplate his own political rectitude.

Stephens had become especially alarmed about conscription and habeas corpus. By late August 1862, he was pressing friends in Congress to speak out against these ruinous and unnecessary measures.[34] Pessimism about Confederate prospects added to his natural melancholy, and Linton's even grimmer views deepened his gloom. The declarations of martial law truly appalled him. "Better in my judgment that Richmond should fall and the enemy's armies should sweep our whole country from the Potomac to the Gulf, than that our people should submissively yield obedience to one of these edicts of our generals," he wrote in a moment of pique. Though couched in the language of republican liberty with its emphasis on civilian control over the military, his criticisms sounded increasingly captious and extreme. Stephens dismissed arguments of military necessity as "specious, insidious . . . the tyrant's plea." Most troubling was that no one heeded these wonderfully logical warnings, that too few people, including those who should have known better, could sense the danger. Congress-men were "ignorant of principles—lamentably ignorant"; sound constitu-tional arguments made no impression on "these children in politics and statesmanship."[35]

In utter exasperation, Stephens finally wrote two letters to the *Augusta Constitutionalist* (one under his own name) advising Georgians that their sole military obligation was to their own state.[36] Yet his obsession with principle, his aversion to compromise, and his abhorrence of political ma-neuver required him to abdicate the leadership of any political revolt against Davis. Like most Confederates, Stephens refused to countenance, much less join or organize, an antiadministration party. With his beloved ideals intact, he remained somehow above the fray.

Political dissension, however, was not always so ideological or so idealis-tic. Struggles over principles often degenerated into squabbles over office. Accused of nepotism, favoritism, and pig-headedness by disappointed sup-plicants from every faction, the president seemed to confront some pa-tronage muddle nearly every day. Unwilling to delegate authority to the secretary of war, he spent long hours reviewing military appointments, a procedure that caused frustrating delay.[37]

General questions of patronage often spilled over to involve the army because military cliques and political factions had become hopelessly en-tangled. Generals and aspiring generals usually had influential and insis-tent political friends who never ran short of ink or nerve. Even at the state level, libertarian politics and localism became intertwined with broader critiques of Confederate strategy. Cries that North Carolinians should command North Carolina regiments, that Mississippians should lead Mis-sissippians, and so on, intensified. Yancey offered a bill that would have required the president to appoint brigadier generals from the states in proportion to the number of their regiments in Confederate service. Ac-cording to the Alabama senator, too many defensive-minded Virginians had received important commands. The Senate overwhelmingly rejected Yancey's mathematically equitable but militarily naive proposal.[38] Yet he had made an important political point. As long as the army was organized by regiments raised in states and communities, political pressure to place hometown or home state residents in command of these troops would persist.

State politicians also regularly criticized the president for appointing too many old army and War Department cronies, including Northern-born generals of dubious ability and loyalty. These objections carried important political and even ideological overtones. Texas senator Williamson S. Old-ham later wrote that the president's "sycophancy to military men" caused the army "by degrees . . . [to lose] its republican character." Professional soldiers set themselves apart from the enlisted men, and the "idealistic young men of high social position," who at first had volunteered so enthusi-astically, became discouraged and abandoned the army for more lucrative civilian jobs.[39]

Geographical parochialism and attacks on professional soldiers—nota-bly Bragg—also influenced politics and strategy in the western theater, where the department organization system compounded these difficulties. Whatever the advantages of divided commands in assuring governors that their states were not being neglected, success depended on the compe-tence of the generals and their willingness to cooperate across departmen-tal lines. The establishment of department boundaries became crucial. Yet with the Federals threatening to move down the Mississippi River toward Vicksburg, the president kept Earl Van Dorn in charge of Confederate forces in Mississippi and placed the incompetent Theophilus H. Holmes in charge of the Trans-Mississippi Department. Divided responsibility for the defense of the most strategic area west of the Appalachian Mountains would bring delay, contention, and eventually disaster.[40]

Political considerations also militated against a unified, effective com-mand structure in the West. In Arkansas, for example, Governor Rector and his successor Harris Flanagin accused the Confederate government of abandoning their state. What they really wanted and what their congres-sional delegation made painfully clear to Davis in a stormy meeting in January 1863 was to bring Arkansas troops back home to defend the state. In an apt summary of the problem, the president remarked that the ex-istence of the country depended "on the complete blending of military strength of all the States into one united body, to be used anywhere and everywhere as the exigencies of the contest may require for the good of the *whole.*"[41] Yet Davis's department system had encouraged fragmenta-tion and parochialism while failing to placate the governors.

Separate, sometimes independent, commands also encouraged political and military intrigue; each general maintained close contact with his politi-cal supporters; some commanders kept the War Department in the dark about their plans. Military cliques flourished in the absence of strong polit-ical organizations. Though he remained on fairly good terms with his suc-cessor Braxton Bragg, Beauregard badly wanted to return west and had grown tired of his duties in Charleston, South Carolina. Fifty-nine congressmen signed a petition urging the president to restore Beauregard to a command in the West. Perhaps still seeing Beauregard as a political rival, Davis would have none of it. "If the whole world were to ask me to restore General Beauregard to the command which I have already given to General Bragg, I would refuse it," he told two Louisiana congressmen. Undaunted, Beauregard continued to offer suggestions for military operations to interested politicians and began courting Joe Brown and other governors. He even toyed with the possibility—widely bruited about in the newspapers and briefly discussed in Congress—of a negotiated peace. A conference between the Southern governors and their counterparts from the old Northwest might disorganize and demoralize the enemy, Beauregard suggested. In view of the South's dwindling resources, he was ready to "place more faith in diplomacy to end a war than in drawn battles." All the while, congressional allies sang his praises even as they damned Jefferson Davis.[42]

With Beauregard still on the shelf, hopes for turning the tide in the western theater rested on Braxton Bragg. Though a man of obvious talent, Bragg was also stubborn, contentious, and oddly indecisive in moments of crisis. Notorious for his harsh treatment of volunteers and a stickler for regulations, he seldom won the affection of either his generals or his troops. Bragg was sickly, thin, and a bit stooped in appearance; his thick black eyebrows and graying beard imparted a look of distinguished menace. In the summer of 1862, however, Bragg had seemed to be the only Confederate general in the western theater with any strategic imagination, and Davis had enormous confidence in him. In the face of hostile newspaper stories, Davis tried to reassure Bragg but in doing so revealed much about his own defensiveness and egotism: "You have the misfortune of being regarded as my personal friend and are pursued therefore with malignant censure by men regardless of truth and whose want of principle to guide their conduct renders them incapable of conceiving that you are trusted because of your known fitness for command, and not because of friendly regard. Revolutions develop the high qualities of the good and the great, but they cannot change the nature of the vicious and the selfish."[43] Clearly, the president was willing to assume considerable military and political risks for the sake of loyalty and to vindicate his own judgment.

After Bragg's unsuccessful invasion of Kentucky in the fall of 1862, there was hell to pay both in the West and in Richmond. Major General Edmund Kirby Smith declared that Bragg had "lost his mind"; Leonidas Polk and Major General William J. Hardee connived to have him removed from command. Kentucky generals, including the dashing raider John Hunt Morgan, bourbon-swilling John C. Breckinridge, and chronic complainer Humphrey Marshall, all joined what has been termed the "anti-Bragg bloc." Though not without friends in the army and even in Congress, Bragg had made some powerful political enemies or perhaps more accurately had whetted the appetite for blood among the anti-Davis crowd. Kentucky and Tennessee politicians despised him; Yancey, Wigfall, and others clamored to have him replaced with Joe Johnston or Beauregard; even some of the president's supporters recommended a new western commander.[44] Bragg's reputation also suffered when his performance was compared to that of the recently successful Lee, including the Virginian's stunning victory in December 1862 at the battle of Fredericksburg. Failures in the western theater seemed all the more glaring when contrasted with triumphs in the eastern theater.

The conduct of the war in the West came under careful and critical scrutiny from congressmen and other would-be strategists. Surprisingly, Texas senators Wigfall and Oldham wanted most of the troops in the Trans-Mississippi Department transferred to Bragg's army. Wigfall favored abandoning much of the territory west of the Mississippi River, though such a move would have found little favor in his own state. Such suggestions bespoke the influence of Beauregard and Johnston, who had long harped on the need for a concentration of forces in the western theater.[45] Those who pressed for this fundamental shift in strategy argued that national survival should overrule lesser and more parochial political concerns.

This debate over concentration, a year of bad news from the West, and mounting political pressure brought on another cabinet crisis. Secretary of War George W. Randolph agreed with Johnston about the need to transfer troops from Arkansas and Louisiana for the defense of Vicksburg but could not convince the president. In poor health and frustrated by working with Davis, he was apparently looking for an excuse to resign. As proud and uncommunicative as the president, Randolph had ruffled feathers in the War Department, in Congress, and in the state capitals. "I think we might as well drive out the common enemy before we make war on each other," he had once lectured Joe Brown. Randolph's efficiency and occasionally strong opinions also may have struck Davis as signs of a dangerous independence. Ironically, the president claimed to agree with Randolph about the need for cooperation between departments in the western theater. But on November 12, Davis sharply rebuked the secretary of war for exceeding his authority in ordering a transfer of troops from Holmes to Lieutenant General John C. Pemberton (who had replaced Van Dorn in Mississippi). On November 13, after a further exchange of notes—the two men never met to discuss their differences—Randolph resigned.[46]

Despite a sudden flurry of sympathy for Randolph from inveterate administration opponents, even the *Examiner* welcomed the appointment of Virginian James A. Seddon as the new secretary of war. Strangely enough, Seddon, who had twice been defeated for election to the Confederate Congress, quickly won approval from both friends and enemies of the administration. In frail health and with no experience in military affairs, Seddon was unlikely to challenge the president's views on army organization or strategy.[47]

Though he had moved rapidly and decisively in replacing Randolph with Seddon, Davis paid a political price. Almost as an afterthought, he had consulted with Wigfall and even broached the possibility of selecting Johnston or Major General Gustavus W. Smith. Unfortunately, Davis had already made up his mind when he spoke with Wigfall, and the Texan exploded when several newspapers announced the Seddon appointment prematurely.[48] This faux pas was for Wigfall the last straw. For many months the Texan had criticized the administration's military policies and appointments; he had agreed with Randolph and others about the need for a concentration of forces in the western theater and often had conferred with Joe Johnston about possible changes in command and strategy. He now openly and publicly expressed his opposition.

Davis himself had come to realize the need for greater coordination among the departments. Following Lee's retreat from Maryland after the battle of Antietam, he turned more of his attention to the West and especially Vicksburg. Recognizing the obvious lack of coordination between widely scattered armies, he decided to make a fateful experiment in organization. On November 24, Davis appointed Joe Johnston to overall command of the departments headed by Bragg and Pemberton—a huge expanse ranging from the Appalachians to the Mississippi River. Johnston accepted this assignment reluctantly, unsure about both the scope of his authority and the administration's views on the need for concentration.[49] This last matter was of course the very question that had driven Randolph from the cabinet, and Davis still appeared unwilling to give more than lip service to Johnston's recommendations.

Before accepting the assignment, Johnston had conferred extensively with Wigfall and perhaps other politicians. At a farewell breakfast shortly before the general's departure for the West, Yancey offered a champagne toast to "the only man who can save the Confederacy." Johnston quickly and somewhat disingenuously replied that it was Robert E. Lee who would lead the Southern nation to victory. Johnston left Richmond on November 29 and arrived on December 4 at his new headquarters in Chattanooga.[50]

Although the greatly outnumbered Pemberton appeared to be in desperate straits as General Ulysses S. Grant was preparing to advance toward Vicksburg, Davis still did not peremptorily order Holmes to cross the Mississippi River and suggested instead that troops be sent to Mississippi from Bragg's army encamped at Murfreesboro, Tennessee. To Johnston, this made no sense, but rather than telling Davis, he complained to Wigfall. The Texan immediately tried to convince Seddon that Holmes must move quickly to save Vicksburg and that any reinforcements sent from Bragg could not arrive in time. Political considerations, Wigfall stressed, must yield to military necessity.[51] The necessary order, however, was not issued, and Johnston never presented his case directly to his superiors.

After Bragg's retreat following the indecisive battle of Stones River at the beginning of 1863, Johnston again wrote to Wigfall about the impossibility of coordinating the movements of two widely scattered armies with vastly "different objects." Rightly concluding that he carried great responsibility with little real authority, he longed to escape from a clearly impossible situation.[52] But as always, Johnston expressed his opinions much more forcefully to his political friends than to the president or the War Department. And Johnston failed to exercise what authority he held or even take advantage of his ambiguous position as a more aggressive general might have done in part because he instinctively shrunk from taking risks or responsibility when his military reputation was at stake. Johnston did not trust Jefferson Davis, and the president was fast losing confidence in him. Neither man seemed capable of making a decision, and their mutual suspicions portended disaster. An ominous lethargy had settled over the western theater. Johnston stubbornly ignored Davis's suggestions and displayed a dangerous tendency toward self-pity. To prevent the Federals from advancing further toward Chattanooga while holding on to Vicksburg seemed impossible if not mutually exclusive goals. Seeing his task as hopeless, Johnston fretted but did not act.

Johnston's adamant refusal to supplant Bragg had surprised and appalled his political allies in Richmond. Certainly Wigfall and the anti-

Bragg forces in Congress suffered from their reliance on Johnston. For all the faultfinding and back-stabbing that had taken place during the second half of 1862, the president's opponents remained badly divided. They could snipe away at the administration, but their own disarray blunted their sharpest criticisms. Brown, the Stephens brothers, and Holden embraced the politics of individual liberty while on the other extreme Wigfall, Yancey, and even Rhett attacked the president for not being a forceful enough Confederate nationalist—especially in his military policies. These ideological and practical criticisms went off in too many contradictory directions to be effective and added to the basic fragmentation of rival political cultures, both devoted to the ideals of antiparty republicanism.

The controversies over conscription and the suspension of habeas corpus posed long-term threats to the Southern nation but had not yet galvanized the Confederate people into political action. Nor could the complex debate on strategy and the various intrigues involving Bragg and Johnston bring together a badly splintered opposition. If anything, military politics reinforced public skepticism of the political process. Their shared commitment to antiparty ideology along with fears of appearing unpatriotic prevented the president or his opponents from forming an effective political organization. In some ways, a divided and querulous opposition, however richly endowed with idiosyncratic talent, strengthened Davis's hand by its inability to challenge the administration effectively either in Congress or at the polls. Yet it also encouraged political deadlock both in Richmond and in the states. The stirrings of a peace movement along with growing signs of public disaffection would soon sharpen these political differences. National unity and individual liberty— these competing though sometimes overlapping visions of Confederate civic life—became the basis for the evolution of rival political cultures.

CHAPTER 9

The Two Political Cultures

Mr. Davis seems to have learned but one rule of government," novelist Augusta Jane Evans complained to Beauregard, "that laid down by Machiavelli in the celebrated sophistical dictum, 'the dissensions of great men contribute to the welfare of the state.'"[1] One suspects, however, that neither Evans nor Beauregard entirely grasped the irony in this bon mot. Whatever the effects on the Confederate state, Jefferson Davis had temporarily benefited from the "dissensions of great men."

Yet at the same time, the president remained a powerful symbol of Confederate nationalism—or at least Confederate nationalism as defined by the traditional Southern elite. Although by early 1863 Robert E. Lee too had become an icon in the Southern struggle for independence and had eclipsed Davis in popularity among soldiers and civilians, it was the president who had helped create the political culture of national unity whose basic features had now appeared. More broadly speaking, in speeches, textbooks, sermons, and family conversations, in public ceremonies, schoolrooms, churches, homes, and army camps, the Confederacy's core beliefs and values had emerged. These beliefs and values—along with libertarian alternatives—in turned shaped the content and tone of debate over public policy.

With the popular mood growing more optimistic, especially after Confederate victories at Fredericksburg and later at Chancellorsville, attacks on the administration seemed factious and selfish. Waspish editorials and the wailings of disenchanted office-seekers expressed a blind and often impotent fury. The wealthy Mississippi Whig James Lusk Alcorn, for instance, still bitterly resented being passed over for various military appointments. In a minor masterpiece of vituperation, Alcorn denounced Davis as a "miserable, stupid, one-eyed dyspeptic, arrogant tyrant who now occupies his cushioned seat at Richmond, draws his twenty-five thousand a year, and boasts of the future grandeur of the country which he has ruined, the soil which he has made wet with the tears of widows and orphans and the land which he has bathed in the blood of a people once free, but now enslaved. Oh, let me see him damned and sunk into the lowest hell."[2]

In Richmond, the third session of the First Confederate Congress (which opened on January 12, 1863) offered the president's critics an arena for venting their spleen. Yet between the lengthy speeches, Congress simply drifted, waiting for news from the battlefront. The initiative lay with Davis, but he no longer had either the popularity or the influence to control even this weak and divided Congress. The political stalemate gave the opposition an opportunity to coalesce. Though the process was at best incomplete and administration critics only partially united, they increasingly played the politics of liberty. This emotion- and tradition-laden set of beliefs focused on the defense of community and individual freedoms against centralization and executive tyranny. With the loss of so much Confederate territory and the virtual disappearance of states and despite victories by the Army of Northern Virginia, many Southerners could not look far beyond their town, county, or family.

The president's enemies tried to convince disheartened but still patriotic Southerners that the greatest threat to their long-cherished freedoms originated in the monarchical pretensions of Jefferson Davis. "Our President is aiming at the obtainment of power inconsistent with public liberty," the vice-president charged. Linton Stephens agreed, adding that West Point generals would destroy the character of free men by converting a conscript "into a machine." Calling for the Confederacy to rely on "citizen soldiers," he raised anew warnings against "standing armies" and laid claim to the traditions of 1776 for the libertarian extremists. The old cries against consolidation and despotism acquired new urgency. In rare agreement, both the *Richmond Examiner* and *Richmond Whig* asserted that the Confederacy's only hope rested in preserving a strictly republican government.[3] Yet attempting to paint Davis as a modern George III was rhetorical overkill, and even the president's bitterest enemies did not dare call for open resistance to executive usurpation.

During a western tour at the end of 1862, the president had responded to his libertarian critics by trying to reawaken Confederate patriotism. In defending conscription before the Mississippi legislature, Davis had gone to the heart of the problem. If the states provided for their own defense or obstructed the Confederate draft, chaos and disaster would surely follow. The president had called for greater cooperation between the Confederate and state governments. Boldly justifying the exemption of overseers, he had gamely tried to defuse the explosive question of class favoritism by pointing out how many wealthy Southerners had fought and died for their country.[4]

Although still describing the Confederacy as the last bastion of republican liberty, Davis increasingly emphasized Yankee barbarism. Rather than fighting simply to be left alone, Southerners fought to avoid enslavement. The president even dusted off a favorite argument of antebellum Southern intellectuals: that an irrepressible conflict between Northern and Southern civilizations had originated in clashes between Puritan and Cavalier in old England. If unselfish patriotism no longer sufficed, then perhaps blind hatred would rekindle the Southern fighting spirit.[5] Returning from his western journey, Davis again invoked the heritage of 1776. Praising the noble Virginians' tradition of defending liberty, he compared them to their eighteenth-century forebears. "You have shown yourself in no respect to be degenerate sons of your fathers," he noted, using a popular rhetorical formula. "You have fought mighty battles, and your deeds of valor will live among the richest spoils of Time's ample page." But the American Revolution had been fought against a "manly foe," not against the "offscourings of the earth." Thus tying a defense of Southern republicanism to the new emphasis on Yankee atrocities, he launched into a soon-to-be familiar litany on murdered prisoners, plundered civilians, and various other outrages. He increasingly described the differences between the two sides in terms of moral absolutes and played on public fears of defeat and especially of Northern despotism.[6]

On January 12, 1863, Davis elaborated on these themes in a lengthy message to Congress. Given the desperate need for national unity, the president naturally praised Southerners for affording "another example of the impossibility of subjugating a people determined to be free." Davis depicted Washington, D.C., as the center of a merciless despotism where the crimes of "Beast" Benjamin F. Butler and other petty tyrants received neither punishment nor rebuke. And the crowning infamy had occurred only a few days earlier, when Lincoln had issued a final Emancipation

Proclamation. This infamous decree was clearly intended to incite servile insurrection, to encourage slaves to murder their masters, to turn the rich farmlands of the South into a barren waste ruled over by a semibarbaric and treacherous people.[7] Never again would Davis so forcefully tap both the ideological and emotional roots of Confederate nationalism. His message aptly summed up the powerful appeal of a political culture based on national unity and increasingly on fear.

Even some of his harshest critics were impressed. Alexander Stephens found much to praise in Davis's latest effort. Texas congressman Franklin Sexton was even more enthusiastic, calling the president's message "the best state paper I have ever read." Taking their cues from Davis, Confederate propagandists added considerable detail to his already lengthy catalog of Northern sins. From the days of the "bigoted Pilgrim fathers," wrote a South Carolina pamphleteer, the Yankees had displayed the "envy, hatred, jealousy, and all uncharitableness, dissimulation, cunning, cupidity, and hypocrisy" that had eventually destroyed the once glorious Union. Their long history of religious persecution and deep involvement in the African slave trade made them consummate hypocrites. No mean trick was too low—including flooding the Confederacy with counterfeit currency and robbing helpless women and children—to accomplish their goal of crushing the South and extinguishing liberty's flickering flame.[8]

Such calls for a revitalized fighting spirit shored up public support for Jefferson Davis. Even while Brown and Vance were challenging the administration's interpretation of the conscription laws, their legislatures adopted resolutions expressing confidence in the president's leadership.[9] Many Southerners still saw Davis as a Confederate Washington even though agreement on the nature and meaning of Confederate republicanism remained elusive.

The concept of nation was still troublesome, especially for old fire-eaters. "We have no 'National life,'" Yancey informed his fellow senators. "The sole province of this government, its sole province, is to defend Constitutional government." By this he meant a government based on state and individual liberty. The danger was that the people would too readily surrender their rights to an all-powerful central government rather than undertaking the "onerous and trying duties of self-government." In a burst of hyperbole typical of libertarian fanatics, Yancey issued a somber warning: "Far better, if the people are to be governed by despotism, if free, Constitutional government is to be overthrown, that it be by the hands of an open enemy. . . . There is hope for a people who are crushed by superior power in their brave struggle for the right. There is no hope for a people so destitute of courage, and virtue, and wisdom, as to flee to a despotism of their own."[10] These sentiments, when contrasted with Davis's public statements, encapsulated the fundamental conflict between the rival political cultures. Each defined the essence of the Confederacy in strikingly different language and ideas.

Ultimately, political socialization is vital to the survival of any political system, but the war truncated and muddled the process. The disruption of families, schools, and churches made it much more difficult to transmit values and beliefs to young people coming of age in the 1860s. The "rising generation" could no longer gradually acquire a set of political convictions because the war diverted attention and energy away from the traditional rhythms and events of public life.[11]

Creating a republic of course involved acculturating young people (and their elders) into a complex system of rights and responsibilities. From the late eighteenth century onward, those interested in cultivating republicanism—whether politicians, intellectuals, teachers, or ministers—had stressed the need to inculcate a respect for virtue into the next generation. For Confederates, this meant first establishing national unity based on a sense of political and social distinctiveness. Southerners still used the word "revolution" gingerly, and the phrase "conservative revolution" neatly captured the dilemma of political leaders trying both to maintain and transform a political system. In this context, giving birth to a new political culture meant applying lessons from the past (to purify political practices) and fulfilling the promise of a revolution against politics.[12]

Normally fathers would initiate young men into the political culture. But with so many men in the army and with public events impinging so much on daily life, women not only began paying more attention to public questions but also played a larger role in the political socialization of their children.[13] In the absence of competing sources of information, families dominated political education. As in many "traditional" societies, localism and rural isolation reinforced lessons learned in the home. Confederate children acquired basic knowledge about national identity and recognized the names of a few Southern leaders, but the absence of political parties and prevailing prejudices against politics in general may have limited their political sophistication.[14]

Because of their small size and largely private character, Southern schools had not usually exerted much influence on the political socialization of the average child. But there were few other sources of political information (besides the ubiquitous newspapers) so formal education probably shaped the political views of the leadership class. Modern studies have downplayed the importance of formal courses and textbooks in forming young people's political attitudes, but forceful teachers and copybook maxims may have carried much more weight in the overwhelmingly rural South. Likewise, the highly decentralized system of education bolstered traditional notions of individual rights and community authority.[15]

During their first years in school, modern children gain a rudimentary knowledge of politics. They quickly learn about the presidency though the legislative process seems hazy; government appears generally benevolent if not infallible. In the mid-nineteenth-century South, however, the discussion of secession in homes and classrooms must have given some children ambivalent attitudes about political efficacy.[16] Even though schools generally instill an unsophisticated nationalism in their pupils, wartime teachers faced the challenge of redefining national allegiance and introducing new patriotic symbols to often distracted children. The flag and songs of a new nation had to replace the old ones; American history became an Old Testament prelude to the New Testament story of a Southern Confederacy developing under providential protection.

To break free of tradition without abandoning it was as tricky for the cultural nationalists as for the political nationalists. The fire-eaters had long lamented the South's dependence on Northern textbooks and Yankee teachers, but the movement for Southern textbooks and Southern teachers had met with little success in the antebellum decades. Secession and war guaranteed that education would receive little public attention and less money, but establishing "Confederate" schools became a test of Southern character. "Unless the present generation be morally great it is in danger of being overcome," intoned North Carolina education pioneer Calvin H. Wiley.[17] Such variations on the standard Confederate jeremiad leavened calls for Southern educational independence.

In the schoolroom, Southerners might at last throw off the shackles of Yankee cultural hegemony. Although teachers were exempt from the draft, many had volunteered, and Southern educators called on women to serve the new republic by entering the classroom.[18] But the sheer size of the task was daunting. In the midst of a costly and devastating civil war, Southerners would have to train a generation of teachers and write new textbooks to provide a genuinely Confederate education. Only then, claimed one Texas politician, could parents free their children "from the baleful influence of the Helperites, socialists, and abolitionists."[19] Such extreme statements ignored not only practical questions but also the larger problem of teaching Southerners of all ages allegiance to a new nation. In the schoolroom as in the legislative chamber, the content of Southern nationalism remained ill-defined and its strength uncertain.

Throughout the war, several publishers trumpeted the virtues of their supposedly Confederate textbooks. Teachers' conventions solemnly resolved to use only Southern texts, and in Richmond, Raleigh, Greensboro, Charleston, Augusta, Macon, and Mobile, the presses rolled. In many cases, however, the differences between Northern and Southern schoolbooks were only cosmetic—tacking a Confederate preface onto a book that had been in common use throughout the country for many years. Declarations of literary independence belied the imitative, derivative character of works in which writers did little more than add a few "Confederate" names to arithmetic problems or grammatical exercises. An ersatz nationalism with inflated claims of launching what one writer called an "intellectual revolution" characterized these hastily prepared textbooks, blurring the line between patriotism and profiteering.[20]

The typical new Southern textbook offered basic lessons in political socialization. Elementary geography and spelling books briefly described the workings of the executive and legislative branches, and a few introduced their students to various forms of government, often as a prelude to a lesson in the virtues of republicanism.[21] Although the authors were less concerned than those of modern texts with presenting a friendly, personal view of government, they idealized the political process. The Texas legislature, according to one widely used text, was a body of men meeting "to consult together for the good of the state."[22] Because most Southern children attended school for only a few years, the scattered references to government in these elementary texts, along with whatever material the teachers added, constituted their only formal introduction to civics. The absence of information about sales and classroom adoption makes it impossible to measure the influence of these works on political attitudes and behavior.

The most distinctive feature of these Confederate textbooks was their unabashed defense of slavery. Much of the impetus for educational independence had originated in fears that antislavery sentiments might creep into Southern classrooms. Yet even during the 1850s, Southern texts had not sold especially well, and at the beginning of the war there were complaints that Southern schoolchildren still used works "infested with abolitionism."[23] Many reading, spelling, and geography books that appeared during the war tried to rectify the problem by excising subversive passages or adding appropriate glosses.

Authors offered simple lessons in proslavery orthodoxy by filling their books with suitable Scripture passages. The texts tried to settle any youthful qualms about the institution by reassuring schoolchildren that a slave society represented the epitome of Christian civilization.[24] Although these books could hardly present proslavery ideology in all its rich complexity, they occasionally touched on racial and historical justifications for slavery. In a geography text with a strong missionary theme, Marinda Moore described Africans as "slothful and vicious," the miserable descendants of Noah's accursed son Ham. In contrast, the black slaves in America were well clothed, fed, and "better instructed than in their native country."[25]

These texts depicted slavery as the black race's natural and inevitable condition. The lesson for Southern schoolchildren was clear: any mawkish sympathy for the slave's plight was foolish and misguided. In a brief colloquy designed to allay lingering moral doubts, one elementary reader presented a slave appropriately named "Tom" who assures his young mistress that he has no desire to be free, that he is fit only for physical labor, and that his master cares for all his needs. Yet even in this passage, paternalism barely masked the reality of exploitation, and Southern educators sometimes pressed their case too far. The bolder their assertions the more doubts were raised about unresolved moral dilemmas. A group of North Carolina teachers maintained that Southerners must write their own schoolbooks to uphold their "peculiar social system" that was so "obnoxious to the phariseeism of the world." Not satisfied with merely establishing the legitimacy of slavery, they vowed to spread the proslavery argument around the globe.[26] Such universalist claims, however, could not hide the moral and intellectual isolation of the Confederacy in an antislavery world and may not even have convinced the brighter schoolchildren.

The same could be said for the scattered textbook references to Confederate nationalism. Authors generally touted their works as part of a larger crusade for literary and cultural independence, but like many secessionists, these cultural nationalists spent much more time and effort excoriating Yankee influences than defining the Confederate republic. The fear of cultural dependence hardly helped clarify matters. Regional chauvinism—best expressed in arithmetic books whose story problems emphasized Northern cowardice and cupidity—only made Southerners seem like swaggering braggarts.[27] What might be called "negative nationalism" could not build a strong sense of cultural identity.

The divisive influence of state pride even cropped up in Confederate textbooks. Rather than delineating a unified Confederate national character, Marinda Moore contrasted the brave and chivalrous South Carolina gentry with the state's largely ignorant poor people. She tactlessly argued that South Carolina slaves were treated more harshly than slaves in other states. The Virginia elite, by contrast, came off as ideal gentlemen and slaveholders. Most of these cultural stereotypes may have seemed harmless if a bit misplaced in an elementary geography book, but Moore also made the damaging admission that many North Carolinians had refused to fight for the Confederacy. She might dismiss this as the cowardice of poor and ignorant men, but she revealed in a most unexpected way the growing disaffection in the Tar Heel State.[28]

To what standard were Confederate children expected to conform? In alluding to draft resistance, Moore by implication introduced the politics of liberty, but most Confederate texts obviously promoted a nationalism based on a simple, unexamined allegiance. Whatever their weakness in defining Southern distinctiveness, the elementary texts at least presented the Confederate flag accompanied with a few lines of patriotic poetry.[29] That most writers had trouble going much beyond such basic symbols of a new political culture again suggests the amorphous and often contradictory character of Confederate nationalism.

Like Jefferson Davis, Southern educators increasingly extolled Confederate virtues by excoriating Yankee vices. Abraham Lincoln, according to one commonly used text, was a weak-kneed man who allowed the abolitionists to control his administration. "If the rulers of the United States had been good Christian men," this same author informed her young readers, "the present war would not have come upon us. The people sent bad men to Congress, and they were not willing to make just laws, but were selfish, and made laws to suit themselves." This introduction to antipolitical ideology sharply differentiated between republican rectitude and political iniquity while asserting that Southern leaders embodied the higher values of disinterested public service. A new reader for Texas schoolchildren contrasted the "martial pomp" of Lincoln's inauguration with the Confederate ceremony's "republican simplicity." But by the time this work appeared in 1863, Davis was no longer simply a Confederate Washington. The author admitted that the president had his faults but maintained that no one else could have done any better in the difficult task of leading a great "revolution."[30] Qualified praise for the president could hardly have aroused much enthusiasm when children could hear their parents bemoan his shortcomings.

Instead of positively defending the Southern cause, most authors harped on the theme of Yankee malevolence. "A despotism is a tyrannical, oppressive government," Robert Fleming wrote. "The administration of Abraham Lincoln is a despotism." Schoolchildren studied about Northern "infidelity and reckless puritanical fanaticism" and how secession has "shorn the United States of nearly all its greatness and prosperity." Such statements along with boiled-down secessionist rhetoric were no doubt far too abstract to capture most pupils' imaginations. Some authors stressed the suffering of Southerners living in occupied territory, but they could not be too graphic with young students. Moore, however, did tell her readers that God would soon wreak vengeance on the men who had caused all this misery.[31] One wonders how children reacted to such bloodcurdling prophecies.

A cynic might have added that the real question was whether God would uphold the self-righteous because most Southern textbooks were hardly modest or self-effacing in their claims for Confederate purity. To study republican government in its ideal form, schoolchildren need look no farther than the Confederate States of America. Nor did textbook writers shy away from discussing the Confederacy as a slaveholders' republic. Echoing Alexander Stephens, John Rice considered slavery the foundation of national prosperity: "Under the influence of slavery, which is the corner stone of her governmental fabric . . . the Confederate States has [sic] just commenced a career of greatness, to be rapidly augmented by the development of her vast agricultural and mineral resources . . . while the industry and genius of her citizens will soon rate her second to no nation in . . . manufactures of raw material of her own production."[32]

Despite obvious hubris and continued reliance on anti-Yankee propaganda, Confederate success remained contingent on public rectitude. The voters needed to select the best men for all offices, and in turn the politicians should "feel their dependence under God, on the will of a free and virtuous people." Thus Robert Fleming urged students to fulfill their solemn responsibility for preserving freedom. Even with the "good and wise" leadership of Jefferson Davis and other pious leaders, Marinda Moore conceded, the Confederacy would remain a "sad country." The nation's struggles placed a particular burden on the younger generation. "Then remember, little boys," she advised, "when you are men, never to vote for a bad man to govern the country."[33] Such counsel—reminiscent of election day sermons in Puritan New England and eighteenth-century discussions of popular virtue—prepared young people for more sophisticated Confederate jeremiads.

These themes easily dovetailed into a broader civil religion that continued the process of political socialization for devout adults. Preachers admitted their role as propagandists but also sought to convince their congregations that the establishment of national independence depended on divine favor. With more fervor than accuracy, W. T. D. Dalzell thanked God for the "unanimity which has characterized men of all shades of opinion previous to this struggle; and the total obliteration of party feelings and party names, uniting to sustain the administration."[34]

By 1863, however, the Almighty's purposes were no longer self-evident. The clergy increasingly reverted to old evangelical formulas, modifying early versions of the Confederate jeremiad. In a commencement address on March 29, James W. Miles prayed that the Confederates would fight for more than "selfish independence." Even when Southern armies prevailed, all could be lost if a struggle of "sectional parties" that had destroyed the old Union divided the new nation. Yet Miles held out the possibility of salvation. Despite the present darkness, Southerners had a priceless opportunity to establish a government that "is harmonized by the true relations of capital and labor" under providential protection.[35] National unity and social peace would characterize a people living according to the Lord's will. The Yankees could not destroy the Confederacy unless Southerners became apostates to their own traditions.

Unfortunately, the people of the Confederacy were fallible human beings. The list of their sins steadily lengthened, threatening to bring down divine wrath upon the fledgling nation. Moral lassitude and debauchery stalked the land, and war meted out punishments for people who had forgotten the ways of the Lord. Early in the war, an Augusta preacher accused the Southern people of pride, covetousness, selfishness, heedlessness, and disobedience. Like many others, he referred to the classic warnings from Jeremiah. Not only had the people persisted in violating God's holy ordinances, they had also tried to conceal their own guilt behind their neighbors' shortcomings. According to a Baptist editor, murmuring against Confederate leaders had even reached the point of giving comfort to the enemy.[36]

Calls to end factiousness went unheeded because self-interest overshadowed the common interest. Fat profits and bank deposits betokened an uncontrollable greed that could allow the suffering of soldiers' families to be viewed with cold indifference. Instead of blaming Jefferson Davis or the Congress, one need look no farther than the Southern people themselves to explain massive suffering. Appeals for Christian asceticism accompanied pleas for republican simplicity.[37] Yet the search for virtue in the midst of a civil war was frustrating, and Christians wondered whether there were enough righteous people left to forestall the Lord's anger.

Rather than examining their own lives, many Confederates looked for scapegoats and discovered an ancient one: foreign-born Jewish merchants. Henry S. Foote denounced "shylocks," *Examiner* editorials deplored "synagogue" influences, and Texas vigilance committees harassed Jewish businessmen. Although this anti-Semitism was episodic and some Confederates pointed out that Christians were as likely as Jews to engage in speculation, prejudice intensified when public officials failed to curb extortion.[38]

Resentment flared against rich men who had dodged the draft while continuing to live off the fat of a rapidly shrinking land, and demands for action grew. Although he was more than willing for the government to intervene in other areas of the economy, Jefferson Davis held that the iron laws of supply and demand would ultimately determine the prices of scarce commodities and he only weakly suggested that the states might try to curb speculation.[39] The governors, though more responsive to the public outcry, were equally at a loss to prevent hoarding and price gouging. "Merchants and tradesmen . . . are entitled to the fostering care of the government," Alabama governor A. B. Moore admitted early in the war, but when scarce commodities were stockpiled, soldiers and their families should be protected from becoming the "prey of such harpies." Most states adopted generally unenforceable laws against extortion and monopoly, and proposals for price controls got nowhere.[40]

Failure to take more than symbolic action against speculators further embittered class relations. Condemnations of extortion easily led to more general attacks on the wealthy. Exemption laws, the notorious stinginess of large planters, and class favoritism in the army and government all evoked indignation. These economic and political tensions not only heightened disaffection and encouraged desertion but also became linked to criticism of military leadership. "Aristocratic" West Pointers lorded it over the common soldiers, callously ordering the bodies of dead enlisted men dumped into shallow mass graves.[41] The impoverishment of the yeomanry, and eventually of many planters, fatally weakened the social fabric and placed enormous strains on the political system.

What most angered the poor was the contempt and indifference of the wealthy and their political representatives. When women, men, and children took to the streets of Richmond in the spring of 1863 demanding bread, too many congressmen dismissed them as ordinary thieves. Contemptuous of ragged looters, they denied that the rampage had anything to do with hunger. Edmund Ruffin described the rioters as mostly "prostitutes and low foreigners" and regretted that soldiers had not fired on them.[42] Ruffin's reaction illustrates the reluctance of Confederate leaders to tackle welfare problems. The national government provided limited assistance to destitute families, yet staggering needs for relief along with hyperinflation made even relatively large state appropriations seem niggardly. Local governments and private groups simply could not take up the slack.[43]

Rapidly spreading poverty exacerbated class conflict as desperate people considered desperate actions. A Georgian proposed that a secret organization seize supplies from "extortioners" at "reasonable" prices and threatened to take what was needed at gunpoint. In the midst of this crisis, Confederate leaders displayed an appalling lack of political sensitivity. Alabama congressman William P. Chilton opposed increasing soldiers' pay because they were "not fighting for money, but for freedom and glory"; Henry C. Chambers of Mississippi added that a patriotic soldier never worried about his pay.[44]

Perhaps these politicians could not comprehend that the large gulf between the comfortable and the downtrodden posed a serious threat to the political system. School lessons about unity, patriotism, and Confederate virtue seemed irrelevant. Persistent assertions that God was on their side could not prevent Southerners from taking to heart the jeremiads' darker prophecies. The wicked prospered, and the virtuous poor starved. The natural pessimism of an evangelical culture deteriorated into a dangerous fatalism.[45] The myth of class harmony was shattering into a thousand pieces. Rumors of peace and continued debate over highly divisive questions would eventually strengthen the appeal of a libertarian political culture.

Despite these economic and social cleavages and persistent talk of peace, a phenomenon largely tied to the vicissitudes of battle, in the spring of 1863, public support for administration policies and for the war itself held steady. Victory—as shown by Confederate triumphs at Fredericksburg and Chancellorsville and also by Grant's failure to take Vicksburg—was still possible and therefore what mattered were military campaigns. Rhett declared that only the army and navy could save the Confederacy. Brigadier General Howell Cobb, one of the president's most loyal Georgia friends, agreed that "the delusion of an early peace" could be "disastrous if not counteracted." Cobb proposed calling out all men up to forty-five years of age and placing the exempts in a reserve corps.[46] Military and political necessity seemed to open the way for more vigorous measures to strengthen that Davis administration's hand. The persistence of antiparty attitudes further splintered an opposition already divided between peace men such as Congressman William W. Boyce of South Carolina, die-hard Confederates such as Rhett and Wigfall, and libertarian fanatics such as Holden.

Tenuous national unity heartened administration supporters and encouraged some discussion of the Confederacy's political future. In an early 1863 speech appropriately titled "Social and Political Quicksands," Alabama congressmen Jabez Lamar Monroe Curry asserted that frequent elections turned representatives into "sycophants who seek popularity." To prevent the growth of the public vices that commonly beset republics, Curry proposed establishing colleges, academies, and schools to train young men and women. The next generation needed to understand that the Confederacy cherished education, slavery, constitutionalism, and Christianity. Surprisingly, the press and even other politicians offered similar definitions of Southern republicanism. Editors denounced partisanship more strongly than ever though they seldom avoided their usual editorial feuds. Even Confederates who admitted the advantages of political parties in peacetime—and they were rarities—deplored organized opposition during a war.[47]

Evidence of traditional political maneuvering often occasioned considerable soul-searching. As they worried about the economic and political health of their republic, argued about such questions as conscription and habeas corpus, or reacted to the latest news from the battlefields, Confederates could never agree whether the Southern people had lost their virtue or unscrupulous politicians had robbed them of their liberties. Should the voters be trusted to elect the president or should the states restrict the franchise? Preachers added their voices to the more secular jeremiads against political parties. The Reverend Joseph Stiles warned that demagoguery was "one of the direst evils of our land" because selfish politicians pursued "personal preferment." Party measures would yet ruin the country if unscrupulous men garnered votes from the "weakest and vilest by a shameless course of seduction, flattery and bribery, falsehood and dissipation." Stiles vividly described the results: "What peril to the foundations of the government when the masses, trained by the arts of the seducer, are ever ready to move at his will."[48] By defining political machination as a national sin, such statements further discouraged effective opposition to government policies.

The pervasiveness of such views inevitably made politicians wary of appearing factious. Again Herschel Johnson served as a bellwether. Hostile to the various conscription and habeas corpus measures but still unwilling to attack the president openly, Johnson resisted the formation of pro- and antiadministration parties in Georgia. "For the success of the cause in which we are engaged is paramount," he advised Linton Stephens, "and it could not fail to be seriously damaged by party strife." Patriotic duty required continued support for the president. "If forced to take sides in such a division [between Davis and his opponents]," Johnson concluded, "I should affiliate with the party sustaining the administration."[49] Yet even had the president's critics been more united, the rules of the Confederate political game would have hampered their efforts.

Confident of public support—as least while military prospects remained favorable and perhaps persuaded by their own rhetoric of national unity—administration supporters boldly reopened the habeas corpus question. Because the previous suspension expired in February, Congressman Ethelbert Barksdale of Mississippi introduced a new bill authorizing the president to suspend the writ anywhere in the Confederacy. Although Davis had seldom used the previous law, Congress was more reluctant than ever to grant him this authority. Wary of voter reaction in an election year, a majority decided to dodge the question.[50]

In contrast to conscription or debates over fiscal matters such as taxation and currency, the habeas corpus bill brought together more of the president's critics, from fire-eaters to Whigs to peace men, than any other issue. Rhett charged that the bill "converts the president into a despot and the people into his subjects and slaves of his will and pleasure." Congressional secrecy—which allowed nameless politicians to act without fear of public scrutiny—accounted for this latest outrage. The *Richmond Whig*, the leading editorial voice of Confederate conservatives, used precisely the same arguments. In the *Raleigh Standard*, Holden as usual excelled in antiadministration invective.[51]

More significant and despite the president's recent efforts to cultivate public support and exploit simple patriotism, the politics of liberty was gaining momentum. Even editors who had generally supported the president charged that the Barksdale bill would extinguish liberty throughout the Confederacy. "Despotism" became the favorite cry in Richmond and the state capitals, and politicians catered to fears of usurpation. A Mississippi Whig foresaw the death of Southern republicanism and warned that the people of his state would soon be reduced to the "condition of serfs."[52]

The renewed debate over habeas corpus raised hard questions about the future for the adherents of both political cultures. Because so many compromises in principle had already been made in the interest of national unity, many Confederates welcomed the chance to stand firm against new encroachments on individual freedom. Libertarians offered their own jeremiads on a Southern nation falling prey to tyranny. Supporters of the habeas corpus bill recognized the power and even the legitimacy of these arguments. Liberty, as defined by an important editorial in the *Richmond Enquirer*, included both national independence and the equality of all citizens before the law. The Confederate government needed extraordinary powers during wartime and had used this authority with remarkable restraint, but some people seemed less fearful of Yankee subjugation than of minor abuses by their own government. Better to achieve national independence under a Confederate king, the editor concluded, than be ruled by Lincoln.[53]

In a more sophisticated defense of administration policies, Frank Alfriend—editor of the *Southern Literary Messenger*, friend of the president, and later his biographer—tried to analyze the social basis for Confederate nationalism. Describing the Confederacy as a political democracy with a social aristocracy, he deplored tyranny or special privilege but favored rule by a wise, educated elite. A patriarchal society required a patrician government. Recognizing inherent tensions between slavery and democracy along with the volatility of a large white working class, Alfriend believed that Confederates should avoid industrialization and remain an agricultural people.[54] In a sense, unity and independence depended on the soundness of Thomas Jefferson's agrarian version of republicanism.

Even such arid logic and rarefied abstractions had important practical consequences. The problem of military manpower, accentuated by heavy casualties in the spring and summer campaigns, challenged both political cultures and raised questions that continued to eat away at the very foundations of the Confederate social order. For Davis, the demands of the army came first no matter what the political consequences.[55] In an ironic and tragic sense, the president had risen above democratic politics to the point of appearing oblivious to the people's needs. Under intense and immediate public pressure, state leaders paid more attention to welfare problems and remained highly protective of local interests. Ideally, governors worked with Confederate authorities while preserving their own prerogatives, and no one performed this political high-wire act better than Zeb Vance. With a mix of parochialism and patriotism, the politically sure-footed governor carefully balanced the politics of national unity against the politics of individual liberty.

Vance proudly maintained that he had always cooperated with Confederate authorities in meeting their legitimate demands. "I have not belonged to that class of politicians who made the 'night (and day) hideous' with cries for States' rights," he informed one Confederate general. Yet the governor strongly defended draft exemptions for militia officers and state officials and also well understood the political limits of cooperation. In a sometimes sharply worded correspondence with Major General D. H. Hill, Vance promised to help deal with desertion but observed that the "worst thing which could now happen to the state would be for me to lose . . . popularity with the people. . . . I have been . . . able to coax them into many things which I believe few others could have done."[56]

The governor's moderation contributed to a slow realignment in North Carolina politics that solidified his position while dividing the Conservative party. Congressman Burgess Gaither applauded Vance's stand against a "consolidated military despotism," but other Conservatives questioned the purity of his principles. Meanwhile, ardent Confederates renewed the "no party" cry even as Vance began to distance himself from the more extreme anti-Davis folks. Holden, the most prominent example of an alienated libertarian leader, remained mired in past politics—and the distant past at that. In classical eighteenth-century language, he argued that the Conservatives were the only legitimate party because the Confederates (or "destructives") represented a "faction" of place hunters.[57]

Ideological differences within the Conservative party and growing signs of political restlessness elsewhere showed that the politics of liberty had also become in part the politics of class. The exemption of overseers continued to stir resentment among the yeomanry and poor whites. The "twenty nigger law," grumbled one Alabamian, helped only the "negro aristocracy." "For God's sake," thundered a Georgia enlisted man, "don't tell the poor soldier who now shivers in a Northern wind while you snooze in a feather bed, that it is just and right that the men, whom Congress has exempted, should enjoy ease at home, amassing untold riches, while he must fight, bleed and even die for their ten negroes." Warnings of a possible revolution if the wealthy continued to neglect their less fortunate neighbors became commonplace, and political dissidents began to exploit class bitterness. The mythical organic unity of a slave society lay in shambles. "We are not willing to see any one white child starve to death on account of this war," Holden proclaimed, "while the negroes are fat and sleek."[58]

Vance deplored such subversive remarks, but Joe Brown fanned the flames of class warfare. Although Confederate privates received only eleven dollars per month in depreciated currency, he complained, "a large proportion of the wealthy class of people have avoided the fevers of the camp and the dangers of the battlefield, and have remained at home in comparative ease and comfort with their families." Denouncing the Conscription Acts as "grossly unjust and unequal," the governor recommended both strong measures against speculators and the doubling of soldiers' salaries.[59] Such proposals contradicted Brown's earlier statements on slavery and class harmony, but he well understood Georgians' sufferings and fears. And of course, he was unwilling to sacrifice political advantage to political consistency.

Appeals to class interests shocked administration supporters and many opposition leaders as well. Once "demagogues" stirred up the poor against the rich, the Southern social fabric would unravel. Those who most fervently espoused national harmony considered talk of class divisions specious and disingenuous. Furious when his own overseer was drafted, Florida governor John Milton claimed that overseers were poor men protecting white families of all classes against the danger of slave violence. Other Confederates fell back on the notion of *Herrenvolk* democracy long popular with proslavery apologists. "Slavery makes the poor man respectable," a Georgia editor asserted. "It gives the poor an elevated position in society that they would not otherwise have."[60]

Although in May 1863 Congress restricted the exemption of overseers to farms or plantations owned by "a minor, a person of unsound mind, a *femme sole*," or a man serving in the armed forces, the debate over class favoritism did not end. Yancey and Senator Benjamin Hill of Georgia believed Congress should protect the agricultural interest against the siren song of yeoman radicalism. Unsupervised slaves would not work and would endanger every Southern community. Denying any irreconcilable class differences between slaveholders and nonslaveholders, Wigfall appealed to ancient notions of social unity.[61] Faith in the organic nature of

Southern society persisted, at least among the Southern elite, despite the strident class rhetoric and much contrary evidence.

In addition to the continuing bitterness over the overseer exemption, many Confederates began to see each new economic law passed by Congress as class legislation. The expansion of national authority challenged traditions of community and individual rights or appeared to require less than equitable sacrifices from Confederate citizens.[62] Ideology and self-interest became hopelessly entwined as rich and poor reacted strongly to perceived injustices perpetrated by politicians who would either sacrifice the principles of Southern republicanism to supposed military necessity or leave the common people to the tender mercies of corrupt officials and heartless extortioners.

Besides the obviously important monetary and fiscal policies, new economic regulations stirred controversy. The discouragement of cotton planting touched a tender nerve among those who coveted the planters' long-established independence and power. To tell Southerners what to grow in their fields infuriated men (and some women) used to lording it over their households and cutting a proud figure in their neighborhoods. In the spring of 1863, when Congress adopted a weak resolution urging reduced production of staple crops such as cotton and tobacco, Davis called for increased food production to feed the hungry armies. Even these mild palliatives sparked new fears of centralization, and the usually cooperative John Milton raised constitutional objections.[63]

Talk of peace along with Confederate military success in the spring of 1863 encouraged planters to grow more rather than less cotton. Yeomen criticized wealthy slaveholders who still cultivated staple crops while refusing to help feed soldiers' families. Angry denunciations from neighbors and even suggestions from friends to cut back cotton production had not prevented the fiery Toombs from defying the government and anyone else who dared suggest what he should plant on his land.[64]

The tax in kind generated even more anger and opposition. When Confederate officials seized produce and livestock from farmers and planters, they trampled on both individual liberty and community autonomy. Public meetings in several North Carolina counties denounced the new levy as "unconstitutional, anti-republican and oppressive."[65] The choice of words was hardly surprising in a political culture devoted to protecting traditional freedoms and among a people long taught to be watchful for the first signs of tyranny. These protests also showed the alarming strength of local, libertarian opposition to Confederate policies.

Impressment of food and clothing caused even more serious disaffection. Army foraging parties became symbols of all that had gone wrong with the war, and protests reverberated with the catchphrases of libertarian politics. Impressment appeared little better than official robbery, a despotic milking of the people's substance by an oppressive government. Impressment threatened to reduce once proudly independent citizens to vassalage. In response to public outcries, many state legislatures passed laws prohibiting irregular seizures of goods and hamstringing legal ones.[66] More informal threats of defiance were far from idle ones.

Opposition to impressment of slaves was more narrowly focused but just as intense because those most affected tended to be powerful and articulate. Confederates viewed slaves not only as symbols of wealth and status but also as vital to the domestic economy and to their new republic's identity. For the government to interfere with the property rights of slaveholders made Confederate leaders—especially to libertarian fanatics—seem little better than Yankee despots. Impressment undermined the intimate relationship between masters and slaves, striking at the heart of the Southern domestic order. As Wigfall sadly observed, many Southerners seemed more willing to give up their sons than their slaves.[67]

By the spring of 1863, economic weaknesses, unpopular policies, and class divisions had accentuated differences between the two political cultures. Confederate leaders had tried to construct a political culture around national unity. In schools and in textbooks, children studied the central tenets of a social order grounded in political and class harmony with slavery as a cornerstone. Yet idealized definitions of Confederate nationalism often clashed with the daily reality of selfishness, speculation, and general sinfulness. According to Confederate jeremiads, the Southern people were paying a high price for their relentless pursuit of individual and political advantage. Internal divisions over conscription, habeas corpus, and more general constitutional questions not only undermined national unity but to more fervent defenders of Confederate policies also marked a national declension. Worthless currency, unjust taxes, and even impressment became the fitting rewards for a people who had strayed from the path of republican righteousness.

In the midst of this travail, politically conscious and active Southerners struggled with competing visions of their political future. The advocates of centralization argued military necessity and beat the drums for patriotic sacrifice. Indeed, the expansion of government authority in a nation supposedly committed to states' rights had been nothing short of extraordinary, and Confederate officials not only directly intervened in Southern economic life but also adopted military and other policies that affected the daily lives of most citizens.[68] But what appeared like a remarkable achievement to Jefferson Davis and to later historians spelled danger to many Confederates. With great vehemence, the spokesmen for individual and community liberty presented what they considered the only reasonable and principled alternative to the twin dangers of Yankee oppression and Confederate despotism: the rights of individuals, communities, and states must be maintained at all costs. For these politicians and their constituents, any new sacrifices of principle would make the Southern nation no longer worth saving. But as these two political cultures developed in a complex counterpoint, military decisions made in Richmond and on battlefields threatened to upset all political calculations.

CHAPTER 10

Spring and Summer
of Discontent

I n the spring of 1863, P. G. T. Beauregard's fancy turned to strategy. Still nursing wounds from his quarrels with Davis, he remained restless and unhappy in Charleston. Only by planning Confederate offensives in distant theaters could he still feel part of the real war. His fertile imagination overflowed with schemes for moving troops here, concentrating forces there, and especially for a massive counterattack in the western theater.

Beauregard must have looked longingly on the western command that Joe Johnston found so exasperating. Mutual distrust of the president and shared political connections now made these frustrated generals natural allies. Eager to share with Johnston some "general views on the coming summer campaign," Beauregard again proposed a concentration of forces. If twenty-five or thirty thousand men could be sent to Bragg, the Army of Tennessee could crush General William S. Rosecrans and then move toward Memphis to cut Grant's communication and supply lines along the Mississippi River. By the time he sent a copy of this plan to Wigfall, Beauregard had become even more expansive and less realistic. He talked of liberating Tennessee, Louisiana, Mississippi, and Arkansas; even Kentucky and Missouri seemed within his grasp. Beauregard asked that Johnston and Wigfall present his views in Richmond because the War Department would never listen to him.[1] Even the aggressive Wigfall must have shaken his head over the sheer impracticality of this scheme.

Whatever their military shortcomings, Beauregard's plans made a certain political sense. The Federal occupation of large parts of the western Confederacy had been militarily and politically disheartening. In this spring of grand designs and high hopes, the conflict between Lee and the "western concentration bloc" was coming to a head with the president caught in the middle. For despite the great distance separating them, the Mississippi and Virginia theaters were inextricably linked in a grand strategic tug-of-war. Not only would army and theater commanders have their say, but so would their political allies in Congress and the state capitals.

Amid this general clamor, a fragile national unity had become increasingly dependent on the limited successes of Confederate armies. The rhythms of politics followed the rhythms of war though Confederates of various stripes remained firmly committed to antiparty beliefs, and the revolution against politics continued. In the wake of defeats, violations of fundamental freedoms become intolerable, and libertarian politics showed increasing force and vitality. On the other end of the political spectrum, some fervid Confederate nationalists stepped up their attacks on the president and his policies, pushing for even more centralization. In the absence of political parties, bitter and often highly personal factiousness came to characterize the Confederacy's public life.

In addition to Beauregard, other Confederate generals dreamed of a decisive stroke to change the course of the war. After the dramatic victory at the battle of Chancellorsville and despite the death of Stonewall Jackson, Lee contemplated another invasion of the North. Any plan for an offensive offered Davis an opportunity temporarily to silence critics who had long called for carrying the war to the enemy, but such schemes also had serious drawbacks. The weakened Confederacy could not realistically launch ambitious campaigns. Whether to send more troops to Vicksburg, or strengthen the Army of Northern Virginia, or reinforce Bragg—any decision carried great risk. Yet a strictly defensive posture perhaps carried unacceptable political costs. Enormous public confidence in Lee and his army along with growing impatience with an administration that seemed too passive forced the president's hand.

And it was certainly easier to plan an offensive in the East than to deal with intractable problems in the West. While other generals contemplated grand offensives, Joe Johnston was immobilized. Refusing to confide in either the president or the War Department, Johnston seemed jealous of Lee and even made uncharitable remarks about the late Stonewall Jackson. All the while administration officials fretted about Johnston's lethargy in Mississippi and worried that he had no plan for defending Vicksburg. Johnston and Davis both appeared indecisive and had become so suspicious of each other's motives that candor and cooperation were impossible.[2] Communication at the highest level of the Confederate command structure had broken down at the worst possible moment.

Nervous Mississippians complained that Pemberton was as inactive as Johnston, but Davis refused to prod him.[3] On the evening of April 16, 1863, Union gunboats and transports ran the Vicksburg batteries. Johnston, finally ordered to Mississippi by Davis, arrived in Jackson on May 13 to find Grant's army planted between Pemberton and the Mississippi capital. Grant first drove Johnston's forces out of Jackson and then turned on Pemberton at Champion's Hill and the Big Black River. After a hasty retreat, Pemberton's forces were bottled up in Vicksburg.

Rather than marching toward the city to lift the siege, Johnston asked for more troops and got into a dispute with Davis about the number of men in his command. Secretary of War Seddon proposed that two divisions from the Army of Northern Virginia be sent west, but Lee convinced Davis and the cabinet to approve an offensive into Maryland and Pennsylvania. Promised reinforcements for Vicksburg from the Trans-Mississippi failed to appear. Grant was adding to his already superior numbers, and Johnston seemed paralyzed by indecision. As usual he failed to inform the government of his plans. The surrender of Vicksburg on July 4 marked the logical culmination of a campaign characterized by extraordinary indecisiveness. The Northern-born Pemberton received much of the blame. According to one influential Mississippian, Pemberton "has entirely lost the confidence of the country and the Army . . . his capacity for usefulness . . . is *utterly destroyed*."[4]

But as the political repercussions from the Vicksburg disaster reverberated throughout the summer and fall, criticism of Pemberton quickly turned into attacks on Davis. Wigfall and Johnston's other congressional allies rallied their forces against the president, and in many ways Davis's critics—whatever their real opinions of Johnston—used the general as a political cat's-paw. One War Department official suspected that Johnston had "more real popularity in the country than the President has." Displaying his usual loyalty to a faithful subordinate, Davis defended Pemberton, blamed Johnston for the loss of Vicksburg, and ignored his own responsibility for creating an unwieldy command structure. In a long letter, Davis pointedly reminded Johnston that he had been given control over both Bragg's and Pemberton's armies and therefore could have transferred troops from Bragg to Pemberton at any time. The president denied that the government had failed to provide the general with either the necessary men or the authority to coordinate a defense of the Mississippi River line. This nearly fifteen-page indictment infuriated Johnston. As proud and touchy as the president, he sent a lengthy reply disputing Davis's points in tedious detail. After reading Johnston's account of the controversy, Wigfall relished the prospect of exposing the "stupidity of Davis" by publishing the correspondence between Johnston and the War Department. Hoping for vindication by a court of inquiry, Johnston energetically gathered documents. After several delays, the War Department abruptly dropped the investigation, thereby preventing a dramatic showdown between Johnston, Pemberton, and Davis.[5]

Even before Vicksburg surrendered, friendly editors and politicians had spearheaded Johnston's defense. With material supplied by Wigfall or perhaps Clement Clay, they denounced the president for not granting Johnston enough discretionary authority and placing too much responsibility in Pemberton's incompetent hands.[6] Whether Johnston's would-be allies really understood or appreciated their man is another question. Wigfall and the others may well have believed that the western theater had been neglected, they may have had some grasp of the principle of concentration, but they seemed more eager to attack the administration than to promote Johnston's strategic views.

This controversy and its political fallout became linked to the ill-starred Gettysburg campaign. Skeptical from the outset about another invasion of the North, generals such as Beauregard and James Longstreet had preferred sending more troops either to Bragg or to Pemberton. Aside from the practical difficulties of such a proposal, it was unlikely that the administration would overrule Lee's judgment. Riding a wave of public acclaim after Chancellorsville, Lee could do no wrong in the eyes of Jefferson Davis and his advisers.[7]

After three days of heavy fighting at Gettysburg, a final murderous assault on an impregnable Federal line, and casualties the Confederates could ill afford, Lee graciously admitted his tactical mistakes but acknowledged no strategic errors.[8] During and after the campaign, several Confederate generals raised serious objections to the so-called raid into Pennsylvania. Even the usually temperate Wade Hampton described Gettysburg as a "terrible and *useless* battle." Longstreet—perhaps to justify his own lackluster performance on July 2 and 3—maintained that the Confederates should have tried to flank General George G. Meade's army and was furious that Davis and others would brook no criticism of Lee.[9]

The retreat from Pennsylvania and the loss of Vicksburg opened up the president and his allies to more blistering criticism. According to the acerbic Toombs, Lee lacked "sufficient genius to command an invading army" and was barely competent to hold a strong defensive position. To Wigfall, the Gettysburg fiasco proved that Lee should be removed and that Davis's mind was "unsettled." Some of these attacks, however, smacked of cheap hindsight with a sizable dose of inconsistency. For men like Rhett, who had been screaming for an offensive for more than a year and had welcomed the first reports of Lee's move into Pennsylvania, to claim that they had always favored sending reinforcements to the western theater was disingenuous at best.[10] Confusion and dismay after Vicksburg and Gettysburg showed how dangerously interwoven military and political disaffection had become. Congressmen regularly aired their differences over various command disputes, debate over strategy often became highly politicized, and soldiers (from generals to privates) could not ignore the political turmoil in Richmond and in the states.

Explanations for the recent disasters often reverted back to longstanding controversies that had pitted the Davis administration against its libertarian critics. Robert Toombs blamed the draft for demoralizing the people. "When we began to hunt up men with dogs like the Mexicans," he wrote in his usual hyperbolic style, "they necessarily became as worthless as Mexicans." Enforcing the conscription acts had become nearly impossible, and Lee's losses were irreplaceable. Heavy casualties, economic hardships, and general disillusionment all led to draft evasion. Lee reported that many recent conscripts and even veterans had gone home, and other generals feared that many others would follow their example.[11]

Evaders and deserters scrambled for legal protection. In the absence of a Confederate supreme court, the state courts had to decide the legal questions surrounding the draft and generally upheld the constitutionality of the conscription acts. Their rulings had far-reaching political implications. In two decisions involving petitions for writs of habeas corpus, the Virginia Supreme Court declared conscription essential for the preservation of liberty. "The obligation of the citizen to render military service is a paramount social and political duty. It is a matter in which the whole body politic is interested." Not only did the court tie liberty to conscription, but it gave concise and eloquent expression to the Confederate ideal of social harmony. Rights were balanced by responsibilities; society had certain claims on the most independent-minded individuals. Such reasoning was bound to discomfit traditional defenders of liberty by its imaginative linking of freedom to national authority. These decisions strengthened appeals to patriotic unity, pleased the War Department, and removed a potentially powerful pretext for defying Confederate authority.[12]

When the Georgia Supreme Court upheld the constitutionality of conscription, a political fire storm erupted. While Joe Brown arraigned the justices for succumbing to pressure from Confederate officials, legislators generally defended the judiciary. An Atlanta editor compared Brown's statements to the proclamations by Northern governors against the *Dred Scott* decision and criticized him for inconsistently upholding individual liberties. Brown might protest against conscription but did not hesitate to seize private property for public use or to prohibit whiskey distilling. Davis supporters and moderates welcomed the court's decision, and even some critics of conscription were not entirely displeased. Herschel Johnson rejoiced that the people could now "rally in unbroken phalanx to our common flag" and that the court's action had further discouraged the formation of pro- and antiadministration parties in Georgia.[13] Support for, or at least acquiescence with, government war policies along with antiparty ideology remained important elements of Confederate nationalism, but now they depended more than ever on evidence that the Southern nation could survive militarily. Some favorable news from the battlefields—and it was needed soon—was absolutely essential to maintain a political culture of national unity.

This was especially true in North Carolina, where the state government had seemingly become the center of opposition to the Confederate administration. In contrast to other states, the North Carolina judiciary came to the aid of reluctant conscripts, thereby giving added impetus to the politics of liberty. When Secretary of War Seddon refused to recognize the validity of writs of habeas corpus issued by state courts against Confederate officers, Chief Justice Richmond M. Pearson solemnly warned that judicial independence was in jeopardy. Not to be outdone in defending civil liberties, Vance pressed the War Department to abide by state court decisions.[14]

When, in a series of cases heard shortly before Gettysburg, Pearson ruled that state courts held concurrent jurisdiction with Confederate courts in habeas corpus cases, claimants for exemptions flocked to the chief justice for relief.[15] In both Richmond and Raleigh, Pearson had become a symbol of unyielding resistance to centralization.

For Vance, these rulings presented a thorny problem. Though denying interference with the judiciary and citing his own patience in the face of adverse court decisions, the governor protested against releasing men accused of murdering two militia officers. Dismayed by Vance's apparent abandonment of libertarian principles, Pearson charged that the state courts "lay prostrate" before Confederate authorities. Convinced that the other two supreme court justices had been pressured to overturn his decisions, Pearson dismissed Vance as a "young and inexperienced" executive. The governor tried to ease the judge's fears by promising that militia officers would respect the court's rulings.[16] Unable to mollify either the doctrinaire libertarians or the uncompromising centralizers, Vance maintained his delicately balanced position between the "destructives" and the Holden Conservatives.

But whether the governor's political center would hold in the aftermath of Vicksburg and Gettysburg was doubtful. A new wave of desertions from North Carolina regiments threatened to spread disloyalty in the state. Some ardent Confederates blamed Justice Pearson's decisions; others pointed to supposedly treasonous editorials in Holden's *Standard*.[17] Ominously, calls for peace grew more insistent and more politically charged, threatening to sweep away Vance's moderate coalition in a tide of disaffection.

Beginning in late July, nearly one hundred meetings were held in at least thirty counties. Peace petitions—reportedly printed in Holden's office—denounced Confederate violations of civil liberties and called for a new convention to protect the people's rights and interests either by opening negotiations with the Northern states or by withdrawing North Carolina from the Confederacy.[18]

Few North Carolinians publicly admitted favoring reconstruction, and most people still claimed to be loyal Confederates, but disaffection had reached dangerous levels. Recent defeats, one alarmist warned, might well bring on emancipation, black jurors, integrated schools, and, worst of all, "amalgamation and Yankee free-lovism." After seeing two Union flags raised near Asheville, a Confederate soldier described the area as a "free state of Reconstructionists, Abolitionists, and Tarheel Extortioners." Both these statements illustrate how the peace movement aroused racial and class anxieties. Holden blasted speculators and accused wealthy secessionists of desperately hanging on to their slaves. Some Confederates feared that poor whites would take advantage of political upheaval to seize their neighbors' property.[19]

If stories about increasing desertions demoralized civilians, reports of peace meetings back in North Carolina might have a similar effect on the soldiers. The first newspaper reports, however, seemed to enrage rather than dishearten the troops. Although officers may have dominated political discussions, the anger expressed was largely genuine and spontaneous. Meetings in several regiments denounced the peace movement and even called for suppressing the *Raleigh Standard*.[20] Many Confederates viewed Holden as the evil genius of a political counterrevolution.

As early as mid-June, the *Standard* had urged both sides to lay down their arms. "If they [the people] want continued, wasting, bloody war, let them say so," Holden declared less than three weeks after Gettysburg, "if they want peace, let them say so, and let them state the terms on which they would have it." Even a restoration of the Union would be preferable to subjugation.[21] Holden stopped short of calling for reconstruction, but his opponents logically concluded that he favored peace at any price, and his name became a byword for disloyalty throughout the Confederacy.[22]

Responding to rumors that the "Tory" Holden was in secret contact with the Yankees and probably egged on by nervous advisers, Jefferson Davis confidentially asked Vance what to do about this reported sedition. Ignoring hints for joint action, Vance deemed it "impolitic" to move against Holden or his newspaper and noted that opposition to Confederate policies stemmed from legitimate grievances. Yet delaying a confrontation with Holden carried risks. The editor remained a potent force, and some observers even believed that most North Carolinians now favored peace even if it meant reconstruction. At the same time, aggravated soldiers talked of driving Holden from the state or lynching him; in Virginia, Edmund Ruffin was amazed that there had been no "popular violence" against the *Standard*.[23]

This reference to the Anglo-American tradition of the "people out of doors" came only eight days before the political powder keg exploded. On the evening of September 9, Georgia troops from General Henry L. Benning's brigade broke into the *Standard* offices. Divided into squads and apparently directed by a major, the men threw type into the street, emptied kegs of ink, and scattered papers everywhere, but surprisingly left the printing presses intact. Vance himself finally dispersed them and escorted Holden to the governor's mansion for a glass of brandy. The following morning, a second mob—Holden sympathizers this time—ransacked the office of the rabidly secessionist *Raleigh State Journal*.

These attacks caused momentary panic in both Raleigh and Richmond but also illustrated once again the antiparty character of the two political cultures. Neither Holden nor his enemies recognized the legitimacy of political opposition. Wartime bloodlust and antiparty ideology made opponents turncoats or worse and offered a convenient excuse for lawlessness; at the same time, a "standing army" threatened to tyrannize the people. As Alabama soldiers angrily talked of stringing up Holden, Vance begged Davis to keep Confederate troops from passing through Raleigh. If officers failed to control their men, the governor warned, North Carolina soldiers would be called home. "Anarchy or despotism" loomed, he told Davis, "when armed soldiers, led by their officers, can with impunity outrage the laws of a State." Despite threats and counterthreats, an uneasy peace held, and the *Standard* soon resumed publication.[24] Vance had adroitly come to Holden's defense without embracing the peace movement or allowing his rival to gain the upper hand in Conservative party infighting.

At a late July meeting in Richmond, Davis apparently conceded that Vance would have to deal with the peace movement in his own way. Convinced that Holden was "for submission, reconstruction, or anything else that will put him back under Lincoln and stop the war," the governor also suspected that his erstwhile political ally meant to "punish his old friends and collaborators the secessionists." Ordinary citizens must have found this political maneuvering hopelessly confusing. Some believed that Vance supported the peace movement wholeheartedly while others expected the governor to crush "disloyalty" in the state.[25]

Vance doubted Holden's claim that four-fifths of the people favored reconstruction but nevertheless recognized the peace movement's broad appeal as well as the desperation of the "destructives." Vance feared that "men who see nothing but party advantage" were trying to "array Holden against myself." Yet the governor fundamentally disagreed with Holden and declared that it would be better to have his "right arm drop from the socket" than take North Carolina out of the war. Some Conservatives even feared that the governor was lining up with the secessionists.[26] Though not exactly waffling, Vance refused to be hurried into hasty new political arrangements.

In words that would have pleased Jefferson Davis, Vance informed one supporter that a peace such as Holden sought would bring emancipation and confiscation. Even when the enemy controlled large portions of the South, the people should present a united front. Otherwise, disaffection and talk of a counterrevolution would only encourage repression. A new suspension of habeas corpus would then be likely, and that would be the death knell of civil liberties. To Vance, only a strong Conservative party rallying the people to the Confederate cause offered any hope. Yet he also realized that stopping the peace meetings while preserving essential freedoms and avoiding violence would be tricky. The governor's dilemma did not go unnoticed, and friends of the Davis administration slowly began to realize that Vance was no longer—if he had ever been—Holden's puppet.[27]

Whiggish Conservatives played an important role in these shifting political alliances, and Vance listened carefully to their counsel. The highly respected former governor William A. Graham advised against a strong condemnation of the peace movement, suggesting instead a moderately phrased call for patriotic revival. Leaders such as Graham sought to check the tide of disaffection while maintaining their political independence from the Davis administration and from the state's original secessionists. Some former Whigs admitted that Holden's course had encouraged desertion but speculated that their old Democratic opponents might be promoting a rift between the editor and the governor for their own benefit. State treasurer Jonathan Worth—a Unionist Whig who sympathized with but could not embrace the peace movement—perceptively observed that Vance still hated the secessionists but had "less horror of war" than many Conservatives. Convinced that a majority of the people favored peace but also aware that Holden had not squarely faced the reconstruction issue, Worth sadly noted that most politicians, editors, and preachers still favored fighting to the "last man and last dollar."[28]

Perhaps a bit uncertain of his political strength and wary of a showdown, Vance and his closest advisers met with Holden in early September. The governor worried about growing support for an immediate peace but believed that "the brains are largely with us." Graham saw no reasonable alternative to sticking with the Confederate government. Holden reluctantly agreed to stop agitating the peace question but refused to discourage peace meetings and was shocked by Vance's newfound enthusiasm for the war.[29] The meeting ended inconclusively. Vance had made small concessions while Holden had been less than conciliatory; the peace movement would continue to drive the two apart.

In a proclamation on September 7, the governor cautioned North Carolinians against the folly of seeking to "cure the evils of one revolution by plunging the country into another." Though keeping his pledge not to condemn or suppress the peace meetings, he slyly courted the "destructives" (who had no realistic political alternative). Encouraging editor Edward J. Hale of the *Fayetteville Observer* to attack Holden, Vance privately hinted that he had not been all that displeased by the mob assault on the *Standard* office. So successful was the governor in moving away from the Holden faction that fears persisted he would go too far in conciliating the "destructives."[30] Vance seemed to have carried the Conservative party back toward the political center while winning over old political enemies.

Even one of the governor's friends, however, admitted that isolating Holden would not end either party strife or disaffection. The real cause of North Carolina's troubles, Albert Smedes observed, was "in the stomach rather than in the hands or hearts of our people." Because only the wealthy slaveholders (and not all of them) were able to afford many necessities of life and extortioners were piling up profits, the people would listen to Holden or anyone else who claimed to stand for peace and economic justice.[31] Class resentment remained a political trump card.

The Conservatives had failed to build a stable and well-organized political coalition; this so-called party was fast becoming a mere bagatelle to be fought over by the Vance and Holden factions. The fragmentation and personal bitterness that now characterized North Carolina public life was rapidly spreading into other parts of the Confederacy. The recent military disasters and the Confederacy's staggering financial problems prompted Southerners to indulge in a politics of recrimination in which Vance occupied the political center but listed toward the political culture of national unity and Holden represented the extreme development of libertarian political culture.

Political discourse throughout the steadily shrinking Confederacy acquired a sharp and sometimes jagged edge. National unity and social harmony were becoming more elusive; demagoguery and thwarted ambition embittered politicians and further divided an already fractured political system. Practice never quite caught up with ideology in the revolution against politics. Old habits died hard, and even in the midst of a military crisis the distribution of political loaves and fishes made for selfish posturing and occasionally nasty quarrels. Political patronage, warned one minister, was a "pestilent evil of the times." The civil administration of the Confederate states was still a favorite target for critics who stridently condemned the reign of supposedly incompetent spoilsmen.[32]

For those who feared the continuation of old-fashioned political jobbery, the Montgomery, Alabama, post office was a case in point. When Jefferson Davis ignored senatorial courtesy in appointing a postmaster, Yancey and Clay strenuously objected. Unappreciative of Clay's usually dependable support for the administration, Davis proudly defied what he termed senatorial "dictation." According to capital gossip that Clay passed on to Yancey, the president had also chosen an inspector general of hospitals who was "deaf as a horse-block and near seventy years old." Clay believed that he had done everything possible to soothe the president's prickly sensibilities, but Yancey had little patience with diplomacy. Unable to obtain an officer's commission for his son, he decided that a "conscientious difference of opinion with the President upon some points of administration" had caused much rancor and that Davis's appointments were "dictated mostly by personal hostility to me." The president hotly replied that the animosity originated with the senator, whose "opposition to my Administration . . . was not of that measured kind that results from occasional differences of opinion." Yet Davis sought a legal opinion from Attorney General Watts about making an appointment to the Montgomery post office while Congress was in recess—a petty maneuver whose political motive was transparent. This bickering began in May and continued into July while Yancey was slowly and painfully dying from a bladder infection.[33] The absence of parties to mediate such conflicts made them acrimonious and especially personal. Anyone reading the exchange of correspondence could reasonably conclude that old Washington patronage battles continued in Richmond and that the crusade to banish the place hunters had stalled.

Yet such an assessment would be premature because editors, preachers, and even some politicians exaggerated the extent of such conflicts in the Confederacy. For all its bitterness, the dispute over the Montgomery post office was unusual. Davis and his critics seldom quarreled over minor offices. In addition to constitutional restrictions and antiparty ideology, the war itself discouraged the normal skirmishes over civil appointments. Instead, the president and his opponents more often squabbled over military appointments and policies. These disputes frequently degenerated into barbed exchanges as both sides resorted to personal invective and eagerly sought to avoid responsibility for Confederate military failures.

A month after the fall of Vicksburg, the *Richmond Examiner* published a "letter" from Mississippi that bore the earmarks of a John M. Daniel editorial. It described the president as "serene upon the frigid heights of an infallible egoism" and "wrapped in sublime self complacency."[34] In some quarters, criticism of Davis degenerated into a blind, unreasoning hatred. Toombs excoriated the president as a "stupid, malignant wretch" who had led the nation to the brink of ruin. Besides his visceral hostility toward

Davis, Toombs firmly believed that the "road to liberty for the white man does not lie through slavery [to a powerful central government]." Defining the patriot's stark choice as "resistance or acquiescence," he decided that manly protest would do much less harm to the Southern cause than supine agreement. Excitable Linton Stephens sputtered that the country might need a Brutus against the "mad, infatuated . . . bloated piece of incompetence . . . [and would-be] tyrant" Davis.[35] But what could a Toombs or a Stephens do other than rail? The very legalism of the Southern mind, notably its commitment to a constitutional republic, made a coup—military or otherwise—unthinkable. Rhett vainly hoped that Congress would stand up to the great despot and even suggested impeachment. Clay and Wigfall tried to arrange a secret meeting of senators to discuss a course of action but found no takers.[36]

Eighteenth-century warnings about "cabals" appeared increasingly relevant, but such factiousness by its very nature failed either to attract much of a following or to coalesce public dissatisfaction into effective opposition. The despair after Gettysburg and Vicksburg, the early stirrings of a peace movement, and constant bickering in Richmond and the state capitals had less impact because it occurred in a political culture hostile to political organization and to politicians.

With demoralization rampant but unfocused by the late summer of 1863, a surprising resurgence of patriotism swept through the South. There was some sense that the public had simply grown weary of so much criticism of the Confederate government—no matter how well founded. Governors meeting in the Trans-Mississippi and the eastern Confederacy called for continuing the war until independence had been won. Distinguishing between his opposition to Davis and his loyalty to the cause, Wigfall hoped that the people would "realize . . . that their interests are identical with those of their government." Perennial optimists found many though not always convincing reasons for confidence in the future. The *Charleston Courier* asserted that Lee had really defeated Meade at Gettysburg, crowed over some minor Confederate victories elsewhere, exaggerated the strength of a Northern peace party, expected great benefits from English-built ironclads, praised the work of Confederate privateers, claimed that malaria was a natural ally in the Mississippi River Valley, and even reported that bumper crops of corn and wheat could feed Southerners for the next three years.[37] Reaching for any hopeful sign, grasping at the thinnest of straws, and distorting events were all signs of desperate efforts to lift sagging morale.

Indeed, Confederate nationalism too often remained a negative ideology with editors, politicians, and preachers all raising the "no reconstruction cry." The only alternative to continued war was emancipation and the enslavement of white Southerners to Yankee masters. In a fast-day sermon, the Reverend John Renfroe invoked the once powerful images of social harmony: "In our country, color is the distinction of classes—the only real distinction. Here the rich man and poor man, and their families are equal in every important respect." The war had caused some economic leveling, but it had also exacerbated class conflict and made the quondam elite nervous and testy. Fear became a substitute for hope. Absent soldiers must return to their regiments, the president warned, or face "subjection, slavery, and utter ruin of yourself, your families, and your country."[38] Victory, in other words, remained very much within the Confederacy's grasp if only the people would put forth one final effort.

The growing debate between still fervent patriots and those who had simply given up also illustrated the complex evolution of rival political cultures. Despite the relative constancy of beliefs and values, political culture is not static. Events can reinforce prevailing attitudes, but they also can shatter or transform them.[39] In the Confederacy, the often pessimistic worldview of classical republicanism and the jeremiad's traditional formulas became more closely related, and the deepening gloom affected the ardent nationalists as much as their libertarian opponents. The novelist Augusta Evans prayed that Southerners could learn from the history and ruin of past republics. Convinced that the Confederacy was plagued by corruption and demagoguery, she feared that without restrictions on the franchise, either anarchy or the "iron heel of despotism" would surely follow.[40]

Such laments naturally occurred when suffering, despair, and malaise prevailed. Beyond the usual warnings against decadence and ambition, ministers and some politicians again used civil religion to explain their nation's unhappy condition. It had been easy in 1861 to view the sectional conflict as a contest between innocent Southerners and evil Yankees, but by 1863 the theological picture was murky. Carping criticism had become commonplace, and the people had grown more selfish. Although faith in Confederate righteousness survived, Georgia bishop Stephen Elliott admonished Southerners to ponder their own sins of "complaining and murmuring" against the government. Early victories had made Southerners too proud and boastful, Jefferson Davis declared, even as their "love of lucre" had turned them into "worshipers of gain." Confederates therefore deserved the divine chastisement of defeat and conquest. Only through "humble supplications" and acknowledgment of God's sovereignty could they regain divine favor.[41]

Perhaps the president himself had become the suffering servant who would atone for the nation's sins. Ill and wracked by pain, Davis was often bedridden and unable to work for days at a time. Yet he husbanded his remaining strength to stir citizens to renewed commitment. Worried that some states might adopt the "suicidal" course of seceding from the Confederacy, Davis, like many other public officials, exploited fears of subjugation by evoking a litany of horrors. Freeborn Southerners losing their liberty forever to Yankee despotism became a powerful theme in Confederate propaganda.[42]

Still seeing himself as the exemplar of patriotic self-sacrifice and maybe also secretly relishing the martyr's role, Davis had not lost confidence in his own abilities. If some of his public statements sounded fatalistic, privately he remained convinced of his rectitude and wisdom. "I am no stranger to the misrepresentation of which malignity is capable," he told the beleaguered Pemberton. Doing one's duty seldom won acclaim, and opponents usually misread one's motives. In fact, Davis's critics worried that too many people still had faith in the chief executive. Especially dismayed by resolutions of support adopted in regimental meetings, Rhett asserted that "the country has tried the policy of a blind subserviency to President Davis, and it has brought us . . . to the verge of ruin." More galling yet, influential senators such as Barnwell and Hunter appeared blind to Davis's faults. Wigfall despaired that such men would ever "awake from their fatal slumber."[43] Indeed, the reservoir of patriotic devotion to Davis as the great symbol of the Confederate revolution was remarkable.

The summer military crisis brought new calls for a stronger assertion of executive authority. One War Department official wanted the president to take the field himself with Bragg and Johnston as corps commanders. This bizarre proposal revealed again the persistent hope that some bold stroke could reverse the string of recent defeats. More soberly, the *Richmond Enquirer* called for a "military monarchy" to supplant a Congress too preoccupied with army patronage and protecting draft evaders. Davis could then suspend the writ of habeas corpus and silence irresponsible newspaper criticism. Even the moderate Howell Cobb suggested to Alexander Stephens (of all people!) that the Confederacy needed a dictator.[44] Such proposals represented the extreme development of a political culture based on class, social, and civic harmony.

Talk of dictatorship also showed how little Davis had done to organize political support for his administration. Even those who favored a stronger presidency made only the vaguest suggestions for strengthening the office and did not appear ready to suspend the Constitution. And the unbending defenders of civil liberty made little effort to rally their forces, much less create an organized opposition. In avoiding the evils of political parties (though hardly eliminating factionalism, patronage, and other political vices), the revolution against politics—on its own terms—had been a qualified success.

Yet to many historians, the absence of a party system has seemed a serious handicap to the Confederacy. So prevalent has this interpretation become that it now rests more on assumptions than on evidence, and the potential advantages of political parties have become truisms.[45] The main arguments are deceptively simple and plausible. Parties would have strengthened the political system by making dissent more cohesive and responsible. A well-organized opposition could have pressured Davis either to change his policies or give way to a more effective leader.[46] Yet new nations—especially those born in revolutions—hardly ever develop sophisticated political mechanisms in the short run and often not in the long run. Just as the war reinforced Southerners' already strong aversion to partisanship, so also it inhibited the development of a political party system.

Other historians have asserted that a party system would have somehow helped Jefferson Davis. If the administration had united its supporters into an effective political organization, more people might have rallied to the Confederate cause. An administration party might have had a cohesive voting bloc in Congress to push through necessary legislation. The development of a party system would have further centralized authority in the Confederacy by encouraging people to sacrifice their outmoded political principles.[47] As it was, however, Davis got most of what he wanted from Congress (at least until its final session) and had but one veto overridden.

Implicit in the case for the creation of Confederate political parties is the assumption that organized opposition somehow aided the Union war effort.[48] Precisely how the Democrats, not to mention the various Republican factions, strengthened the Northern government remains unclear. So, too, party considerations placed such sterling warriors as Benjamin F. Butler, John A. McClernand, and Nathaniel P. Banks in important commands; such military geniuses as George B. McClellan, John C. Frémont, and John Pope each had vociferous political supporters. Even in the North, the putative advantages of a party system remained mostly theoretical.

Wedded to the tradition of two-party politics, historians seem to think that the virtues of such a system are self-evident.

Even had the Confederates set out to build a party system, they would have faced insuperable difficulties. The disappearance of the second party system in the lower South and its disruption in the upper South along with the whipsaw effects of secession and war badly fragmented Southern politics. The disjointed opposition to the Davis administration hardly formed a basis for political organization. To convince such determined individualists as Rhett, Holden, Brown, Stephens, Wigfall, or Toombs to work together under extremely adverse conditions was unlikely at best. With some Confederates calling for a more powerful national government and others accusing the president of becoming a despot, the opposition was most likely to splinter into factions. Yet even creating a multiparty system in the Confederacy was improbable. Congressmen largely voted for their constituents' interests, and senators acted even more independently and erratically. Complex, temporary, and unstable voting blocs in Congress would not coalesce into parties.[49]

Too many politicians with too odd a mixture of opinions made it difficult even to conceive a viable political coalition that would have evolved into a party. The earlier destruction of the second party system (Democrats and Whigs) in the South had made the whole notion of party (and especially party discipline) anathema. So too secession had brought to the fore leaders who, as the cooperationists had often complained, were more capable of destroying a political system than of building one. The premium still placed on individual honor also encouraged a prickly independence that defied efforts at organization or even cooperation, and the same individual often displayed contradictory political tendencies. Thus Wigfall often voted to strengthen the Confederate government while privately spouting that someone should hang Jefferson Davis. Herschel Johnson, caught squarely between the Brown and anti-Brown factions in Georgia, both sustained and criticized the Confederate government. And it is impossible to classify the ardent Southern nationalist and Mississippi senator Albert Gallatin Brown either as an opponent or a supporter of Jefferson Davis.[50] In many ways, political idiosyncrasies became more pronounced under the strain of civil war.

Moreover, as the Confederacy shrank, the difficulties of political organization multiplied. Early in the war congressmen from Missouri and Kentucky represented shadow constituencies. The problem had grown considerably by 1863, when many congressional districts were under Federal occupation, their representatives elected by the scattered votes of refugees and soldiers. At the beginning of the Second Congress, members from occupied "external" districts voted much differently than members facing pressure from real constituents who had become sharply critical of government policies and often the war itself.[51]

It is tempting to speculate on how a Confederate political system might have developed if the war had continued for several more years or if independence had been won. Perhaps the secessionist-cooperationist split would have evolved into parties, but the longer the Confederacy survived the less likely was that possibility. The peace advocates might eventually have become better organized, but their success would work their undoing whether peace meant reconstruction or simply the restoration of the Union. Historians have more often argued that surviving Whig-Democrat rivalries could have laid the foundation for what might be called a neo–second party system in the postwar South, but antiparty ideology remained strong and the already tangled and jerry-built wartime political alliances had fatally weakened old partisan loyalties. Even those few contemporaries who thought that the South should eventually develop a party system worried about what one Virginian called "pot-house politicians and office-seeking demagogues."[52] Perhaps in a triumphant Confederacy, voters would select candidates of character and intelligence over the usual run of time-serving hacks, but only the most sanguine believed that Southerners could escape such inherent political evils.

Even in mid-1863, prominent politicians remained in fundamental disagreement over basic questions of political power. Competing national and libertarian political cultures offered alternative blueprints for the political future. Some Confederate leaders held to a national vision of a political system in which government exercised considerable power and the people trusted their rulers. Implicit here also was a faith in social hierarchy and a strain of elitism. Other politicians stressed the importance of individual and community liberty, showed signs of democratic rambunctiousness, displayed a persistently parochial outlook on the war, and most of all feared the abuse of political power. These libertarians sometimes played on class resentments with caustic egalitarian rhetoric.[53] Of course, these competing notions of political culture were not always clear-cut, and practical politicians such as Vance and even Davis appealed to conflicting political beliefs. Because both political cultures shared a commitment to antiparty ideology (and a suspicion of politics in general), they would not form the basis for a Confederate party system.

Because of the antiparty character of the rival political cultures, political debate would remain cacophonous and disorganized. Texas senator Williamson S. Oldham later claimed that he had "always expressed . . . opposition [to government policies] in secret and did all in my power to strengthen the Government in the confidence and support of the people." He refused to become a "factionist or partisan."[54] Politicians of his ilk remained as committed, at least in theory, to wartime unity, simple republicanism, and antiparty ideology as Jefferson Davis. For Confederates looking for historical inspiration, their pantheon of political heroes, including Washington, Jefferson, Jackson, and Calhoun, contained striking examples of leaders who had called for political purification and had remained deeply ambivalent and generally hostile to political parties. In the 1863 state and national elections as in past Confederate elections, the battles would be fought without political parties, and most Confederates still preferred it that way.

CHAPTER 11

The Elections of 1863 and Political Fragmentation

More than six months before the first state and Confederate elections of 1863, William Lowndes Yancey pondered the political future. Disenchanted with Jefferson Davis and fearful of "consolidated nationalism," he nevertheless opposed the formation of political parties. From his pristinely republican perspective, "good patriots" too often fell into "the error of approving palpable violations of personal rights and of state sovereignty." He urged Confederate citizens to elect officials who would embody a "strict adherence to constitutional government and rigid observance of the reserved rights of the states."[1] This highly abstract prescription for defending liberty guaranteed ineffective opposition and further political fragmentation. There was of course a certain consistency in this view. Among the sacred principles that Yancey would never sacrifice to the demands of expediency, his belief in the evils of political parties remained paramount.

By spring 1863 as both the military and political campaign seasons began, the Confederacy was returning to a preparty political system. The absence of parties and public suspicion of traditional political practices dampened public interest in elections, reduced participation, and allowed citizens to focus most of their attention on military affairs. The scattering of state and congressional elections from May to November prevented voters from expressing clear and timely preferences for candidates or policies. Local and state issues often dominated these contests, but national questions also intruded, and in some areas candidates even presented the voters with a fairly distinct choice between the two political cultures.

Because so many congressional districts were under Union occupation, their public officials chosen by the votes of refugees and soldiers, political disintegration closely followed the Southern nation's military and physical decline. Rather than a simple contest between supporters and opponents of Jefferson Davis, the elections of 1863 became a crazy quilt of idiosyncratic, almost apolitical contests conducted before a largely apathetic though sometimes angry electorate.[2] Rapidly shrinking (and too often vanishing) newspapers made it difficult to follow truncated political campaigns. In many areas, voters simply stayed home. In others they turned out incumbents or anyone associated with unpopular war policies. Elsewhere they rallied to the Confederate cause. The search for a political middle ground continued and became a dominant theme in these otherwise often incoherent electoral contests.

Even the normally lively gubernatorial battles were largely reduced to struggles among frustrated and uncertain politicians conducted before a largely indifferent electorate. Federal troops occupied large portions of several states still ostensibly in the Confederacy and threatened to occupy others. Many so-called campaigns must been barely noticeable to the electorate, and even in areas not under Federal control, conventions, ratification meetings, and stump speaking were rare.

Few were more sensitive to these shifting political tides than Joe Brown, but in Georgia political organization had also grown feeble. The once belligerent *Savannah Republican*, for instance, denied mounting any factious opposition to the governor.[3] Brown hesitated to seek a fourth term, and early in the year many of his friends assumed that he would step down. "I have not said publicly that I will not under any circumstances be a candidate for another term," he informed Alexander Stephens, and the double negative suggested his true intentions. Brown supposedly favored either Linton Stephens or Robert Toombs as possible successors. The latter suggestion smacked of disingenuousness—a dominant trait in Joe Brown's character. The governor knew as well as anyone else that Toombs's insistence on planting cotton when the armies needed food had seriously damaged his popularity. In addition, Toombs's opposition to Davis had blinded him to political reality; his denunciations of the administration bordered on the maniacal. Unable to control his temper (and apparently his drinking),

Toombs would neither trim his political sails nor seek the governorship—a post he considered insufficiently powerful to halt the country's drift toward military despotism. Because the equally fanatical Linton Stephens would also have been a weak candidate, Brown obviously left open the possibility of "reluctantly" seeking another term.[4] Ambition cloaked in the traditional garb of a properly republican diffidence toward office-seeking always suited him.

By spring, the governor had clearly recovered from his bruising battles with the legislature and probably relished the prospect of popular vindication; by April, he admitted that an outpouring of public support might persuade him to run again. One disgusted editor thought the governor was "coqueting," but what really angered the opposition was his popularity. In great frustration, the *Savannah Republican* accused Brown of "attempting to get up a war of classes" by slandering "the rich for the simple reason that the poor have more votes."[5]

The governor presented himself as the best friend of widows, orphans, and soldiers' families. He called for a raise in pay for Confederate privates from eleven dollars to twenty dollars a month; he minded such everyday concerns as salt and meat for civilians; he made sure Georgia troops had proper uniforms and sufficient rations.[6] Yet he also avoided alienating the planters by doggedly defending slavery even as he dramatically worked to safeguard Georgians from supposed Confederate usurpation. With a pro forma display of hesitation, in May Brown agreed to stand for reelection. Fearing the Davis administration might put up a candidate, he asked Vice-President Stephens (who often visited the Georgia army hospitals) to work on the soldier vote.[7]

The nature of Confederate politics again weakened the opposition. Without parties or regular nominating procedures, Brown's enemies had trouble establishing the legitimacy of any challenge to the popular governor. When a few newspaper editors informally pushed Whig Unionist Joshua Hill and others came out for wealthy planter Timothy Furlow, the public response was tepid. Playing on popular suspicion of office-seekers, Hill noted that he had taken no part in politics since secession. Trying to steer a middle course, he attacked original secessionists while insisting on the impossibility of reconstruction. The governor's friends naturally branded Hill a submissionist and claimed that Brown and Jefferson Davis were working together for an honorable peace. Despite being prone to harsh rhetoric, Brown was a canny politician and though a much more consistent libertarian and administration critic than Vance, he could on occasion move toward the political center. Such legerdemain, however, was unnecessary because, as Brown remarked, Hill's candidacy "falls quite stillborn."[8]

The governor's supporters viewed the nomination of Furlow, a secessionist and Davis supporter who favored conscription, as a ploy to deadlock the election and throw it into a hostile legislature. In his only campaign letter, Furlow sounded a note of pragmatic nationalism: "This is no time for factious opposition or grudging support to the Administration. If we fail it matters not whether in strict accordance with the letter of the Constitution—if we succeed, not one among the happy thousands will stop his strains of praise and shouts of joy to enquire if it was all done according to the requirements of the Constitution."[9] Thus the colorless Furlow did little more than reiterate the hoary plea of military necessity.

The shotgun attacks on Brown indicated a desperate search for a political strategy but also showed how fragmented Georgia politics had become. Neither Hill, Furlow, nor their supporters could land an effective blow against the governor. Warnings about the dangerous precedent of a fourth term or complaints about Brown's supposed egotism fell flat. Some editors denounced the governor for shielding "pet militia officers" from the draft, but with Davis supporter Howell Cobb (recently promoted to major general) in command of the District of Georgia, such charges lost much of their force.[10] Some critics zeroed in on Brown's chief vulnerabilities: demagoguery and factious opposition to the Confederate government. "Brown is constitutionally . . . an oily flatterer of the masses," claimed a Milledgeville editor. Others worried that the governor was arraying the rich against the poor.[11] Although exaggerated, these accusations showed growing fear even among pro-Confederate Georgians that the war was destroying the foundations of Southern society—including slavery. The inherent tensions between elitism and popular participation that had long characterized Southern politics threatened to degenerate into bitter recrimination and class warfare.

Brown skillfully avoided such dangerous issues. Suddenly downplaying his differences with the Confederate administration, he adamantly opposed any reconstruction of the old Union. The governor dreaded the growth of disaffection in Georgia and moved quickly to denounce submissionist movements. Like many other politicians critical of the Confederate government, he spurned even the suggestion of organized opposition.[12]

Brown could afford to stand above the fray. The weakness of the opposition, voter apathy, and his enormous popularity turned the contest into a rout. With turnout down more than 20 percent from the presidential election of 1860, Brown captured over 58 percent of the vote while Hill won nearly 27 percent and Furlow finished a distant third with less than 15 percent; the soldier vote was even more lopsided in Brown's favor.

Hill's total in part reflected the growth of war weariness, but Brown's campaign maneuvering makes the results hard to interpret. Many of the disaffected may well have voted for Brown because of his well-known opposition to conscription, and some former Whigs may have voted for Hill out of political habit. The low total for Furlow reflected his obscurity and was not necessarily a bad sign for Davis. Given Brown's moderate tone during the campaign, many administration supporters may have simply preferred Brown to the outright Unionist Hill and realized that in any case Furlow had no chance. Yet the governor's persistent criticism of Confederate policies also played well with the voters, and one hostile editor hoped that, with the election over, Brown would discourage class warfare.[13] Besides being a tribute to the governor's popularity and political skills, the results also showed how national questions such as conscription and the Davis administration's record could influence state contests.

Elections elsewhere showed a similar pattern but were also provincial affairs whose outcomes often turned on local issues or old political quarrels. In South Carolina, where the legislature still elected the governor, the controversies over the convention and executive council refused to die. With no opportunity for the voters to express their wishes, politicians engaged in the infighting characteristic of this least democratic Southern state whose cliquish rivalries seemed increasingly irrelevant. Anxious to get rid of the incumbent, Francis Pickens, but also unwilling to elect anyone associated with the hated executive council, lawmakers chose a dark horse, Milledge Luke Bonham. A former brigadier general and a member of the Confederate Congress, Bonham would prove neither a forceful nor a distinguished governor.[14] Whether the choice had a wider significance to anyone outside a coterie of politicians in Columbia, South Carolina, was doubtful.

The gubernatorial race in Virginia attracted equally little attention. In a state where party and secession battles had continued up to the eve of the fighting, old wounds festered. Admitting the near morbidity of Democrats in Virginia, the *Richmond Examiner* charged that the Whigs (with help from former Know-Nothings) were plotting to win the governorship, control the legislature, and elect a Whig senator.[15] It was a strange way to describe what appear to be commonplace political activities, but this language resonated with the fear of "cabals" so prevalent in the early republic and reflected the desperation of the increasingly unpopular Virginia secessionists.

To disunionist Democrats, the revolution against politics had gone off course and the process of political purification remained sadly incomplete. Any effort to revive a system of caucus nominations for governor—suggested by at least one newspaper—would lead to the same corruption that had destroyed the Union. Citing the most frightening example imaginable, John M. Daniel warned that Virginia politics might soon sink to New York's level. Talk of dividing the offices between the two parties was too obviously self-serving for the weaker Democrats, but the *Richmond Enquirer* endorsed a Whig, George Munford, for the governorship.[16] All these machinations came to naught. In May, the eccentric anti–West Point brigadier general William "Extra Billy" Smith won an election characterized by considerable apathy. A Unionist Democrat acceptable to Whig conservatives, Smith appeared to embody a belated effort at political unity. Virginians who bothered to vote largely ignored partisan editorials and chose a man who would steadily if unspectacularly sustain the Confederate cause in the state. Though not exactly a triumph for Davis (who might have preferred that John Letcher serve another term), the results had certainly not weakened the Confederate government.

Despite reports of disaffection, the president still had considerable support, even in areas supposedly neglected by the Confederate administration. By the spring of 1863, Texas Confederates were jittery. Around San Antonio, "traitors" and "deserters" had reportedly swept loyal men from many local offices. Although ill health prevented him from running for governor, Sam Houston contemptuously denounced "Jeffy Davis" as a would-be "emperor." A perennial gubernatorial candidate, Thomas Jefferson Chambers, entered the race, perhaps spurred by Davis's refusal to appoint him a brigadier general. Accusing the administration of neglecting coastal defense and not choosing enough Texans for military commands, Chambers hardly concealed his thwarted ambition. Denying the need for a confrontation with Confederate authorities, he nevertheless vowed to send no more Texas troops outside the state.

Despite his own checkered war record, Chambers blasted his principal opponent, Pendleton Murrah, for cowardice and Unionism. Murrah in turn denounced Chambers as a wealthy Gulf Coast planter but said little else. Fewer than twenty thousand people voted, and Murrah won handily. Admitting in his inaugural address to having some differences with the Davis administration, Murrah nevertheless hoped that Texans would distinguish between real dangers of usurpation and technical problems in the execution of the laws to avoid making such "irregularities" a basis for "faction."[17] The victory for Murrah, apparently a cautious and colorless moderate, could only have pleased Davis, considering the problems that would have arisen with Chambers or, still worse, Houston in office.

Hostility to incumbents also grew as the effects of the war and suspicion of politicians continued to disrupt normal voting patterns. In Mississippi, for instance, animosity to Governor John J. Pettus centered on military appointments, local defense, and what one editor deemed Pettus's mulish stubbornness. But as in other states, traditional procedures for selecting candidates and campaigning had broken down. Suggestions were made that county meetings be held to choose delegates for a state convention. This presumably bipartisan assembly could then unite on one able gubernatorial candidate and thus avoid "the trickery and chicanery" characteristic of party conventions.[18] Unable to agree on nominating procedures, however, politicians and newspaper editors acted on their own but still shunned any political organization.

With twelve gubernatorial candidates, not only had Mississippi reverted to a highly personal, preparty politics shaped by local elites, but there were no clearly defined "factions." The three leading candidates were a strange group. Whig Unionist A. M. West so deprecated partisanship and ambition that he would not even say whether he was a candidate. Reuben Davis, who ran as an uncompromising critic of the president, represented the fire-eater element but seemed more animated by his hatred of Jefferson Davis than by any desire for the governorship. Squarely in the political center was Charles Clark, a former Whig turned Democrat, whose name appeared only in newspaper cards. Although Reuben Davis campaigned in the army camps, Clark won 70 percent of the vote.[19] The fragmentation of politics had again led to a triumph of sorts for moderation, but the military situation in Mississippi was so desperate after the fall of Vicksburg that the political impact of Clark's victory was minimal.

The apparent upheaval in neighboring Alabama potentially held far greater significance. Governor John Gill Shorter was too closely associated with unpopular war policies such as slave impressment to be a strong candidate for reelection. Peace meetings spread across northern Alabama and even into army camps. Whigs, Unionists, and various dissenters rallied to the enigmatic Thomas Hill Watts, then serving as attorney general in Davis's cabinet. Watts, who was rumored to be a reconstructionist, declined to campaign but agreed to serve if elected. He never denied being a peace candidate, and thousands of disgruntled Democrats in the northern counties deserted Shorter. Statewide, Watts won nearly three-fourths of the vote.[20]

As a Unionist Whig who had turned fervent secessionist after Lincoln's election, Watts had a mixed record, and his silence during the campaign only added to the confusion. Shorter's defeat, one editor raged, meant the beginning of a "regular demagogical reign . . . quietly inaugurated by the doubting, the despondent, the croakers, and the dissatisfied." After the election, however, Watts toured the northern part of the state strongly disavowing any reconstructionist sympathies. He promised to "build up a *wall of fire* between Yankeedom and the Confederate states, there to burn, for ages, as a monument to the folly, wickedness, and vandalism of the puritanic race."[21] Though no Joe Brown, Watts was something of an opportunist, and his politics often baffled supporters and opponents alike.

All in all, the Davis administration could live with the results of these gubernatorial elections. The voters rejected secessionist incumbents and peace candidates alike, generally preferring moderates. Some contemporaries and later historians detected a revival of Whiggery in both the state and congressional elections, but many of these men were chosen more for their centrist politics than because of old party ties. The multiplication of candidates, the absence of nominating conventions, limited campaigning, and the vicissitudes of military occupation greatly reduced political activity. Antiparty sentiments dovetailed with wartime necessity and mounting despair; in these state contests, neither administration supporters, peace advocates, nor political moderates showed any inclination for organization or energetic canvassing.

All these tendencies appeared in House and Senate elections to the Second Congress, but the often tangled relationship of local and state politics to Confederate politics added some new twists. In the absence of political parties, the "no party" cry remained a useful tactic. With secessionists and especially fire-eaters on the defensive as the war dragged on, Democrats naturally spurned party labels. "Harmony of feeling, Co-operation in action among our people of all classes and callings" were essential, claimed North Carolinian Thomas Ruffin. Yet Whiggish conservatives also deplored partisanship, especially in districts long controlled by their opponents.[22] This pragmatism (or if one prefers, opportunism) strengthened antiparty appeals, but such statements also carried considerable conviction. However reluctant some Confederates might be to give up old partisan feelings, their aversion to the evils of organized partisanship had become a central political conviction.

Even in Virginia, where the second party system had survived as long as in any Southern state, the war, suspicion of old-fashioned politics, and factional divisions made the election of a Confederate senator difficult—and a cynic might say meaningless. Early on, old-line Whigs pushed several candidates while disingenuously accusing Democrats of using "defunct party considerations" to keep their people in office. When editor Robert Ridgeway extolled the virtues of Whig Unionist William C. Rives, the *Richmond Examiner* denounced the "active intrigue" to perpetuate old party divisions. Editor Daniel need not have worried because the Whig party had ceased to exist as an organized political force. Unable to agree on a candidate and divided along east-west sectional lines, the remnants of Whiggery and the equally disorganized Democrats created a deadlock in the legislature that was broken only after exhausting debate and many ballots, when Whig Allen T. Caperton from the western section of the state prevailed by the thinnest of margins.

With Democrat Robert M. T. Hunter already in office, the parties had seemingly divided the Senate seats and had achieved a tenuous political harmony, despite some lingering hostilities. "Parties may be dead, but their worst prejudices have not been permitted to die with the organizations," the *Richmond Enquirer* groused. Yet this pro-Davis newspaper welcomed the election of Caperton—a man who thoroughly disliked the president—while the antiadministration *Examiner* was lukewarm. Such confusion further demonstrated how rapidly the old party organizations had broken down in the face of war, demands for national unity, and the crusade for political purification. Agreeing with Edmund Burke, editor O. Jennings Wise of the *Enquirer* warned that parties too often degenerate into narrow and selfish "factions."[23]

This assertion reflected contemporary opinion and broadly anticipated historical assessments of the Confederate Congress. Complaints about ineptitude and inertia in Richmond had become endemic, extending far beyond the usual carping of people accustomed to viewing politicians with a jaundiced eye. Many Southerners continued to believe—with some justification—that the best talent had gone into the army. Herschel Johnson described the Senate as a "weak body, scarcely equal, certainly not superior to the Georgia State Senate."[24] To be fair, most citizens probably knew little about the Congress or their representatives. Few newspapers carefully covered congressional proceedings, especially after paper shortages and war news crowded out political material. Editorial writers preferred to lambaste Congress generally rather than investigate the shortcomings of individual members. But even with limited information, many Southerners decided that their congressmen were useless rascals.

When incumbency was more often a liability than an asset, as in the 1861 elections, many congressional candidates preferred to run on their military rather than their political records. Charles J. Munnerlyn sought reelection from Georgia's Second District on an ardently nationalistic platform. His strongest opponent, William E. Smith, agreed that the Confederate government remained "our only means of salvation." Captain Smith, however, had lost his right leg at Oak Grove during the Seven Days campaign and won easily, with Munnerlyn finishing a distant third.[25]

In striking contrast to 1861, army officers running for Congress no longer aroused fears of "military despotism." Instead, they faced charges of simple opportunism. Shortly after his second defeat for a Confederate Senate seat, William C. Rives appeared conspicuously with some home guard units at Gordonsville, Virginia. Much to the disgust of Edmund Ruffin and other fire-eaters, this most reluctant of secessionists then won an uncontested congressional election in the Albemarle district. Suspicion of candidates exploiting a modest military record for political gain proved once again how deeply antipolitician sentiments had become ingrained in Confederate political thinking. Some candidates, a Georgia editor grumbled, enlisted in the army "simply to make capital to be used as a stepping stone in their hunt after office."[26] At a time when every able-bodied man was needed, resigning a commission to take a seat in Congress seemed unpatriotic.

Yet attempts to convert a military record into political capital did not always succeed. After his election to the First Congress from Virginia's Tenth District, Alexander R. Boteler strongly supported the Davis administration while also serving as a colonel on Stonewall Jackson's staff. In a bitter election campaign, Boteler used quotations from one of the late general's letters commending his service, but his opponent, Colonel Frederick W. Holliday, who commanded a regiment in the famous Stonewall Brigade, charged that the excerpts were bogus and that Boteler had merely taken a bombproof staff position. Boteler responded with a few choice words from the great Stonewall: "I am not willing to believe that Colonel Holliday is so wanting in patriotism as to consent to leave the army, where his services are so valuable, and go to Congress and take a seat where he has never been tried." This ploy indicated a desperate attempt by Boteler to shore up his apparently waning support in the army.[27] Holliday easily won both the soldier and civilian vote and proved even more willing than Boteler to vote increased authority for the Confederate government.

Few congressional races, however, centered on such a narrow question, nor did they necessarily reveal much about public sentiment on the war. In several districts, "national" issues or even war-related ones were surprisingly absent. Following antebellum practice, some counties took their turn sending a representative to Congress; in others, up-country and low-country rivalries persisted.[28] Despite the unpopularity of incumbents in a society with a paucity of political information, simple name recognition produced votes and eased sectional divisions within districts. Several newspapers urged reelection of incumbents simply to avoid disunity and partisanship; keeping experienced candidates would ensure continuity and internal harmony. Reverting to a more classical republican stance and even quoting Washington, a Mississippi editor advised citizens to elect the "best men" to Congress, in essence calling for a return to an eighteenth-century political system dominated by an elite group of "notables."[29]

Informal nominations also showed the prevalence of preparty political practices. As in the 1861 elections, would-be congressmen typically declared their candidacy with a public letter or card. Expected to shun vain ambition, candidates seldom admitted actively seeking the office but promised to serve if elected. For well-known politicians, the process could be complicated. Some Georgians had suggested that Toombs challenge an administration supporter for a congressional seat, but his considerable abilities had been almost subsumed by intemperate opposition to the president. Toombs reportedly preferred to "be under the domination of Lincoln than the arbitrary rule of Jeff Davis."[30] Still hoping to win a Senate seat, he disdained running for Congress; for Toombs, a prickly sense of personal honor often stood in the way of political success. And given the nature of Confederate politics, supporters were unlikely to launch an organized effort on his behalf.

Incumbents generally relied on brief announcements, but in a few districts, their challengers received more carefully orchestrated nominations. A convention in Georgia's First District selected wealthy planter Thomas Butler King to run against Congressman Julian Hartridge and issued an address to the voters attacking Congress and its secret sessions. Using the typical bromides, King reluctantly agreed to accept the honor but offered only general comments on the need for seasoned statesmanship during the present crisis.[31] Fighting for his political life against an experienced and well-known opponent, Hartridge eked out a narrow victory.

Other political veterans did not fare so well, and the 1863 elections produced a large turnover in Congress. In many cases, it was difficult to separate hostility toward experienced congressmen from more generally antipolitical attitudes. Even the generally pro-Davis *Charleston Courier* praised Georgia voters for ousting nine of ten incumbents. Too many congressmen had lost touch with their constituents, the editor believed, and he welcomed the appearance of "new men freshly informed from the people." The Confederacy could ill-afford the temporizing and caution of old Washington-trained politicians unsuited for leading a revolution. "Let a few rulers feel the rough handling of the public," an Alabamian declared, and Confederate patriots would show "enemies at home . . . that we are 'terribly in earnest.' "[32]

Yet the appearance of many lesser-known candidates only boded greater political instability. "Nearly every voter has lost a son, a brother, or seen them come home cripples," one perceptive editor observed, "and is glad to gratify his humor" in a protest vote against the incumbent. During the American Revolution, frightened conservatives had worried that "when the pot boils, the scum will rise." To some nervous Confederates, the new Southern nation appeared to be repeating the history of other revolutionary republics. In Alabama, secessionist Democrats charged Whig party "hacks" with deliberately nominating unknowns in congressional and state legislative races.[33] Peace and antiadministration candidates ran negative campaigns against vulnerable opponents. Taking advantage of public disaffection, they suddenly emerged from obscurity as defenders of the disenchanted.

Haphazard election procedures also contributed to voter apathy and helped inexperienced (and less wealthy) candidates. Newspapers rarely endorsed anyone. Because of the paper shortage, a Chattanooga editor refused to print candidates' letters because he could not see how these notices served any public purpose. In some areas, there was no canvassing; extensive speaking schedules were rare. By holding congressional elections between May and November, the states further diffused public interest. The results sometimes trickled in, and newspapers published incomplete returns or none at all.[34]

In many places, the quietest elections in anyone's memory passed virtually unnoticed. Light turnouts were the rule even in states still under

Confederate control. Unopposed candidates, limited newspaper coverage, a host of war-related distractions, and public revulsion against politics all discouraged participation.[35] The results suggested more than merely the electorate's apathy or disillusionment and raised new doubts about political legitimacy. The old mixture of local elites and democratic politics persisted, but the war had nearly destroyed public life in some states and produced political and legal anomalies everywhere. As early as 1861, John M. Daniel had questioned whether the legislature should appoint representatives from districts occupied by Federal armies and had proposed setting up polls in Richmond, where refugees could cast their ballots. This soon became standard procedure for state and Confederate elections. In Virginia, South Carolina, and Georgia, voters could mail in their ballots, but those residing outside the Confederate lines generally could not vote.[36] To offset the likely small turnout in states where several districts were occupied, some legislatures adopted a general ticket system that allowed a voter to cast a ballot for the state's entire congressional delegation.[37] Practical necessity in this case won out over traditional notions of representation.

Even in districts under Confederate control, soldiers' ballots could be decisive. South Carolina allowed polls to be opened at any camp where there were two or more Palmetto State soldiers. Though battle-hardened veterans probably would not have tolerated much canvassing in camp and little took place, candidates portrayed themselves as the best friend of the common soldier and his family.[38]

General tickets along with the votes of refugees and soldiers determined the outcome of congressional elections in states and parts of states under Union control. Delegations elected by people who had already sacrificed much for the Confederacy usually supported more Draconian war measures.[39] The absence of parties made these changes in election procedures all that much more important and further discouraged organized opposition. Congressmen from occupied districts naturally stressed national and political harmony, but in elections held any distance from the Union lines, notably in Georgia and North Carolina, the politics of liberty and calls for peace had a much greater influence on the results.

Although the point has often been exaggerated or distorted and the complexities of Confederate politics deserve attention for their own sake and not merely as barometers on the course of the war, the 1863 elections became in some places a referendum on secession and the Davis administration. Original secessionists often fared badly. In sections of North Carolina and Alabama, anyone remotely connected with disunion received few votes.[40] This resurgence of "conservatism"—or perhaps more accurately, latent cooperationism—signaled more a repudiation of secessionist leaders than outright opposition to the war. In August 1863, the Alabama legislature overwhelmingly elected Robert Jemison—the leading cooperationist in the secession convention—to Yancey's vacant Senate seat. This seemed an ironic event, to be sure, but Jemison proved to be a loyal Confederate. Despite opposition to certain taxes and a belief that some conscripts should remain under state control, Jemison favored extending the draft. Shortly after being elected, he called for burying past differences because the Southern people must fight or be "consigned to political degradation and doomed to a social equality with their slaves."[41] Jemison's class interests as a planter did not necessarily mesh with those of his erstwhile supporters so his election added little impetus to the peace movement.

The cooperationist strength in North Carolina made the Conservative party so dominant in several congressional districts that the so-called destructives offered virtually no opposition. Instead, the appearance of out-and-out peace candidates divided Conservatives, a rift that became more serious as Vance began to break away from Holden.[42] Even where Democratic secessionists remained competitive, incumbents faced stiff challenges from confident Conservatives.

Archibald Arrington had only narrowly defeated Josiah Turner for the Fifth District seat in 1861, and by the summer of 1863 he was in trouble. Having supported all necessary measures to strengthen the government and belatedly endorsed a pay raise for soldiers, he lamely admitted having made a mistake in voting for the overseer exemption. Turner capitalized on the unpopularity of "destructive" leaders by accusing able-bodied secessionists of dodging military service and unabashedly appealing to class resentments against wealthy speculators.[43] Despite his extremist rhetoric and ill-concealed peace views, Turner won easily. In a district with a large slave population and a tradition of voting Democrat, the secessionists should have been able to put up a better fight.

Most conservative candidates, however, were much more moderate than Turner and even faced charges of truckling to "destructives." Conservative Whig William N. H. Smith had been an effective and popular congressmen in North Carolina's First District. Running for reelection as both a staunch Confederate and defender of Tar Heel interests, Smith denounced disloyalty but also condemned the tax in kind and the overseer exemption. His opponent, Edward Warren, accused Smith of neglecting the soldiers' welfare and being indifferent to peace negotiations. Warren did everything but endorse the peace meetings and obviously tried to woo disaffected Conservatives.[44] Smith won because of his strong appeal to mainstream Conservatives in a traditionally Whig district.

In addition to the impact of the war in particular areas, old rivalries became entangled in Confederate politics, catching candidates in a crossfire of local and national questions. Fighting for his political life in Alabama, Senator Clement C. Clay worried that angry voters would cast all the "president's especial friends" from office, and candidates running against pro-Davis congressmen did drag the president's record into the campaign. Incumbents with antiadministration voting records had a double advantage. In the Confederate hinterlands, hostility to the government led to greater insistence on protecting state and local interests. Disaffected Texans, for instance, objected to their boys being sent across the Mississippi River to die for no good purpose.[45]

There were several political casualties among the president's prominent supporters. James Phelan faced strong but ill-defined opposition. A fervent Southern nationalist who had supported the most vigorous war measures, including the impressment of cotton, Phelan embodied Confederate patriotism. But after the fall of Vicksburg and the ensuing conservative reaction in Mississippi, Davis's friends were on the defensive. Because the Democrats could not unite on a candidate, the legislature took thirty-eight ballots to elect Whig cooperationist J. W. C. Watson.[46] Although Phelan's defeat hurt the president, Watson was no reconstructionist and eventually supported the suspension of habeas corpus and arming slaves.

If Confederate questions sometimes influenced the course of state politics, state factional rivalries fostered further debate over Confederate political values. Turmoil in Alabama centered on Senator Clay's checkered career. His prominence as a planter, lawyer, and states'-rights Democrat could not compensate for his political liabilities. An administration loyalist and Confederate nationalist but also a friend of Yancey and Wigfall and a critic of presidential appointments, Clay was ill-suited for the tumult of wartime politics. A guardian of fiscal integrity, he had opposed a four-dollar-a-month pay raise for Confederate soldiers and had claimed that the state and national governments provided enough food and clothing for the troops. Apparently little concerned for soldiers' families, he paid more attention to the plight of government clerks and tactlessly complained about his salary as a Confederate senator. A self-proclaimed model of republican purity, he preferred to vote "according to the dictates of my own judgment, and have the approval of my conscience, which every honest man prefers to the applause of the multitude."[47]

At first Clay was oblivious to antiadministration sentiment in Alabama and would not actively campaign to keep his Senate seat. Agreeing to serve if reelected, he tried to prevent "the revival of old party or personal antagonisms, division and discord" and promote "that harmony of feeling and unity of action so necessary to the successful prosecution of the war."[48] He said he was "sick of the selfishness, corruption, demagogism, and bigotry which characterize so large a portion of those in office" and claimed to prefer retirement to private life. Clay expressed the hopes of those Southerners who longed for a restoration of a more elitist government. He had little faith in democratic politics, failing to find "enough intelligence and integrity in the country to appreciate and sustain men who act only from a high sense of duty without regard to personal ends."[49]

In many ways, Clay was too much like Jefferson Davis. For all his highmindedness, he could never forget either his ambition or his sensitivity to criticism. Shortly after Alabama's August elections, he spent four days in Montgomery sizing up prospects. According to Clay, his great rival Congressman J. L. M. Curry had privately argued against a Senate bill for an army pay increase but then had opportunistically introduced the same bill in the House. Convinced that Curry "shall profit by his perfidy to me" and had yielded to the "popular clamor," Clay tried to gather evidence from Wigfall, Benjamin Hill, and other senators.[50]

All his efforts were for naught. After deadlocking on Clay, Curry, and Douglas Democrat J. J. Siebels, the legislature finally chose Whig jurist R. W. Walker on the twentieth ballot.[51] Clay's family and friends applauded his principled resistance to public pressure. Wigfall believed that "the Presidency itself, my dear friend, is not too high for your aspiration" and predicted that Clay could win four times as many votes as Davis. Clay's defeat, Rhett concluded, was another sign that "those who made this revolution do not direct it."[52] Yet for all the reports of disaffection, both Clay and Curry had lent unstinting support to Confederate war policies, and Walker would often vote to uphold or even expand Confederate authority. As in Mississippi, divisions among Democratic secessionists had opened the door for the election of a moderate Whig.

Centrist politics, however, carried risks because the peace issue strengthened the libertarians. "The country will never have peace till all the illiberal brainless rule-or-ruin set" are defeated, declared one Georgia editor. Peace candidates and reconstructionists gained influence, alarming even such Conservative party stalwarts as North Carolina's William A. Graham. In some areas, incumbent congressmen dared not defend conscription because voters had given up on the war. Louisiana's Fourth District congressman Lucius J. Dupré downplayed prospects for a negotiated peace and advised the people to place their faith in the army. He barely eked out a plurality against two opponents.[53]

Some Conservative party candidates in North Carolina unabashedly called for ending a war they saw as futile. Veteran Whig James T. Leach argued that the tax in kind, the overseer exemption, and secret sessions of Congress all signified a central government grown too powerful and arrogant. Leach also proposed raising a Confederate private's pay from eleven to thirty dollars a month. With the endorsement of Holden and local peace groups, Leach easily defeated three opponents to capture the seat in the traditionally Democratic and heavily slaveholding Third District. The *Richmond Enquirer* denounced Leach as a "traitor" and suggested that he should have run for the Federal instead of the Confederate Congress.[54]

To outsiders, most North Carolina Conservatives sounded like Leach, but the party still covered a wide spectrum. Incumbent Allen T. Davidson had condemned Confederate encroachments on civil liberties but by 1863 sounded much too moderate for the mountainous Tenth District. To make matters worse, fellow Conservative John D. Hyman badly wanted Davidson's seat even though they agreed on most issues and refused to approve peace meetings. A third Conservative candidate, George W. Logan, was a Unionist who had never embraced the Confederate cause, a staunch peace man, and a reconstructionist. Because neither Hyman nor Davidson would withdraw from the race, Logan won a fluke victory.[55]

Yet it was just such surprises that placed a small but vocal group of disaffected representatives in the new Congress. Divisions among administration supporters and, in North Carolina, Conservative factionalism had played into the hands of peace candidates. Ironically, the election of these congressmen decreased the likelihood of an effective, organized opposition. Men such as Leach and Logan had little in common with an ardent nationalist such as Wigfall, the conservative Stephens brothers, the fire-eating Rhett, or Brown and Vance. Even in Georgia and North Carolina, where opposition to the war had reached startling proportions and titanic struggles between the forces of national unity and the defenders of individual liberty were being waged, the political center did not disappear.

As Confederate patriotism revived in the late summer and fall of 1863, several congressmen and other politicians vigorously defended government policies and even praised the president. The recent military setbacks made political harmony essential; the present crisis was no time for "party divisions," declared William E. Smith. Although challenging an incumbent in Georgia's Second District, Smith called for continuing the war until the last Yankee had been driven from the South. The Confederate government remained the people's only hope for salvation.[56]

But remnants of partisanship and, paradoxically, prevailing antiparty attitudes weakened efforts to unite the president's supporters. Everyone in the Confederacy was a states'-rights Democrat, the *Richmond Enquirer* boldly (and inaccurately) declared. Because it had no place for labels, dead issues, or ancient quarrels, the Confederacy would have no parties. The people, according to this leading voice of old-line Democracy, should vote for simon-pure Confederates. In North Carolina, a committee led by former attorney general Bragg worked to counter antiwar protests.[57] Yet such patriotic political organizations emerged stillborn. Administration allies relied on public loyalty and specific appeals to antipolitical values in a society where the myth of public harmony still held sway.

Moreover, even friendly congressmen would not always stand by the president. David W. Lewis, the most consistent Confederate nationalist among Georgia congressmen, admitted that Davis had made mistakes. Yet he denied that the president lusted after power and praised the administration's military policies. Lewis's balanced position, designed to allay suspicions of toadyism and respond to antiadministration sentiment, still did not prevent his defeat at the hands of the relatively obscure John Shewmake. The right combination of independence and loyalty was elusive, and in some districts, centrist candidates ran against each other, only adding to voters' confusion.[58]

Besides drawing subtle distinctions between their positions and unpopular administration policies, Davis supporters generally wrapped themselves in patriotism. "The cause of the President is the cause of liberty and the cause of the country," declared Warren Akin in announcing his candidacy in Georgia's Tenth District. Carping against the administration could only pave the way for abolitionist rule, and Akin warned voters they would live like slaves if the war was lost.[59] Akin defeated incumbent Augustus R. Wright, who had backtracked on his earlier commitment to expanding the government's war powers.

For fervent Confederate nationalists, striking just the right note before a confused, often disheartened, and occasionally angry electorate was a tricky business. Although by 1863, Georgia voters still preferred "patriotic" candidates, cooperating too much with the Davis administration courted political ruin. Proud of his loyalty to the president, Congressman Augustus Holmes Kenan offered the stock pleas for public unity and also criticized governors (e.g., Brown) who hindered the enforcement of Confederate laws. Kenan, however, had become overconfident. Brown's friends persuaded Colonel Clifford Anderson to enter the race, and Kenan went down to defeat.[60] Yet Anderson was no enemy of Jefferson Davis, and in Congress he followed an independent course. By the fall of 1863, what was most impressive was not the spread of disaffection but the persistence of loyalty to the Confederate government and to the president. The politics of national unity held its own against the politics of liberty.

Whatever the issue—Davis, peace, or various war measures—the contests often broadened into a debate over fundamental political values: competing political cultures and differing visions of the Confederate future. Voters in Arkansas's Second District had a starkly clear choice. Incumbent Grandison D. Royston had supported Davis down the line. His opponent, Augustus H. Garland, dismissed Royston's pleas for unity as a crude effort to stifle discussion and destroy liberty. Viewing conscription as unnecessary and demoralizing, Garland denounced the suspension of habeas corpus as a threat to fundamental freedoms. In their scramble for patronage, Garland maintained, original secessionists had deliberately underestimated the costs of war. He furthermore charged Royston with using his office to protect his own property from impressment and his son from the draft. After a bitter campaign during which Garland stumped the district, Royston became the only Arkansas congressman defeated for reelection. Once in office, however, Garland moved toward the political center and, except on the habeas corpus question, stood by the president.[61] As is true of many other congressional races, the historian is at a loss to decide what the voters wanted or expected from Garland. By 1863, many Confederates were hedging their bets, unwilling to trust either administration or peace candidates.[62]

Yet definitions of moderation were ever-changing. The military and political situation was too unstable for politicians to feel any sense of security or to rely on time-tested appeals. Conservative party candidates William Preston Bynum and James Graham Ramsay harshly criticized Congressman William Lander of North Carolina's Eighth District. Lander had the misfortune to represent largely secessionist constituents who had lost faith in the Southern cause. His enemies saw him as a "last man, last dollar" destructive.

Lander had generally supported the president, had voted for conscription, but had also opposed "wrong" and "unjust" exemptions. After Bynum reluctantly withdrew from the race, Ramsay proudly pointed to his Unionist background and called for peace negotiations. Expressing strong opposition to conscription, exemption, impressment, the tax in kind, and the suspension of habeas corpus, he promised, like many another aspiring politician, to clean up the mess in Richmond. He did not, however, favor a state convention to take North Carolina out of the Confederacy and tried to appeal to all factions in the Conservative party by condemning the conscription acts but opposing their repeal. Some voters saw Ramsay as a peace candidate while others viewed him as a patriotic bulwark against reconstruction. His growing reticence during the campaign may also have contributed to a narrow 149-vote victory over Lander.[63] Once elected, Ramsay joined the peace-at-any-price faction. In his district, the political center barely survived past election day.

Depending on the area and the politicians involved, political moderation could be sincere, pragmatic, or opportunistic, and it was often difficult to distinguish among these categories. All three characteristics shaped the factional quarrels among North Carolina Conservatives. As an immediate secessionist who had expressed doubts about conscription, Congressman Thomas S. Ashe had not shown enough political independence to be classified as a Conservative. Ashe appeared with peace candidate Samuel H. Christian in a series of joint discussions and claimed to be picking up support despite Christian's "miserable demagogism." Ashe received no help from Governor Vance, worried that he had not distanced himself far enough from the Davis administration, and wondered if a stronger stand for peace negotiations might help. Disgusted with the political process and alarmed at the spread of disloyalty, he sounded panicky: "Are we to have a counter revolution and Jacobinism rampant in the land urging a war of extermination against all who have property and intellect?"[64] Perhaps unintentionally, Ashe gave voice to the fears of traditional Southern leaders who worried about their waning political influence and the rise of relatively unknown rivals. Ashe's vacillation probably hurt his chances, and Christian won the election. Vance generally favored moderate Conservatives who had been original Unionists but were not peace candidates. Sometimes he sought a rapprochement with the more reasonable secessionists; at others times he seemed more interested in conciliating Whig conservatives. Such complex maneuvering made the Conservative party center harder and harder to define.

In Georgia, the forces of moderation were considerably stronger. As early as March 1863, it appeared that the erratic Toombs would seek Herschel Johnson's Senate seat. Entering the contest as a matter of principle, Toombs promised to "offer whatever resistance I can to the ruin of the revolution and destruction of public liberty." He relished the prospect of striking a blow against Davis and received quiet support from the always formidable Joe Brown.

But Herschel Johnson was no administration lap dog, and his support for Confederate war policies had always been thoughtful and qualified. To many politicians, including Georgia's other senator, Ben Hill, as well as some who detested the president, the steady Johnson seemed preferable to the mercurial Toombs, whose attacks on the Confederate government had gone to embarrassing lengths. Johnson easily won reelection on the third ballot but refused to crow. Ever the conciliator and admitting his opponent's "great talents," he agreed with other Georgians that Toombs had "for a long time been in a frame of mind to make him a very dangerous man."[65] Toombs's defeat signified many politicians' preference and continuing search for some middle ground.

By November, when all the returns were in, assessing the various state and Confederate elections was not much easier. Administration alarmists worried that the next Congress would be filled with reconstructionists and even feared that Vance might patch up his differences with Holden.[66] Though several obscure and disaffected politicians would serve in the Second Congress, their inexperience in Richmond made them less effective and dangerous than many contemporaries had predicted. This "upheaval of political elements," as one editor termed the elections, did not presage a counterrevolution.[67]

Although the newcomers often represented disaffected constituents, they proved to be surprisingly moderate and in any event were unlikely to work effectively in a Congress now divided into several small factions—if faction is not too strong a word to describe these inchoate and temporary groupings. Historians have shown how the proportion of Whigs increased dramatically, but the meaning of this simple fact is elusive.[68] Were Whigs more likely to be elected to Congress because they were Whigs, because they had often been cooperationists, because some were peace candidates, or simply because the voters took out their frustrations on incumbents? Perhaps Whig cooperationists won because their hesitancy to approve secession in 1861 made them appear wiser in 1863. But just as in the New South, reports of Whiggery's revival in the Confederacy proved either exaggerated or misleading. The Whigs' own antiparty heritage prevented the rebirth of their old, jerry-rigged coalition. By 1863 party labels meant less and less even for veteran politicians.

It is equally tempting to treat these elections as a simple referendum on Jefferson Davis. By the most conservative estimates, antiadministration forces picked up at least a dozen seats in the Second Congress. More telling, the most reliable votes for the government now came from representatives and senators from states wholly or partially under Federal control who felt virtually no pressure from constituents.[69] State and local issues, however, often influenced the outcome of many races in what remained of the Confederacy, and the victory of a Whig conservative or antiadministration candidate did not always mean disaffection. Divisions among proadministration forces, contests with multiple candidates, and the often ambiguous records and campaign tactics of the winners made the triumph of antiadministration politicians less sweeping than might at first appear. Once elected, these new congressmen never formed a cohesive voting bloc; some moved toward the political center while others became either determined peace men or simply uncompromising opponents of expanded Confederate power. The surviving antiadministration fire-eaters led by Wigfall could never work effectively with the newcomers. A disenchanted and often apathetic electorate had mumbled a garbled and sometimes contradictory message. Showing some lingering party loyalties, voters seemed to favor centrist candidates, but then war had a way of undermining moderation and giving voice to extremists, and many politicians were obviously worried about being caught in a sea change. Conservative antidemocratic elites still sought to rein in democratic rambunctiousness. Volatility and a deepening suspicion of politicians, parties, and politics now characterized a political culture rent into warring factions—and competing political cultures—but also searching for ways to reconcile the often contradictory values of nationalism and liberty.

CHAPTER 12

Factious Politics

I n early 1864, while listening to Clement Clay, John C. Breckinridge, James L. Orr, Judah P. Benjamin, and Robert M. T. Hunter discuss the Confederacy's plight at a Richmond dinner party, Mary Chesnut drew the obvious conclusion: "We are rattling down hill—and nobody to put on the brakes." Yankee armies swallowed up more and more Confederate territory, and many Southern soldiers had gone home to protect their families. Orr blamed "a weak and incompetent President and an imbecile cabinet" for these disasters; others pointed to halfhearted patriots such as Vice-President Stephens and various anti-Davis congressmen. Taking a more philosophical tack, conservative North Carolinian David Schenck concluded that the Confederacy would soon become yet another failed republic because "God seems to have forsaken the nation."[1]

Whether the explanation lay in human weakness, fate, or divine judgment, to such Cassandras, the Confederate nation seemed poised on the brink of a great abyss. For the first nine months of 1864, however, campaigns and battles left the outcome of the war in doubt, and many Confederates thought and acted as if their nation still had a future. All the while, cries for peace, attacks on the government, calls for patriotic revival, and new clashes between nationalists and libertarians further strained the ligaments of Confederate civic life.

Hopes raised and then dashed contributed to a slowly spreading malaise. In the summer and fall of 1863, Davis had considered ordering a concentration of forces to drive back the Federals in Tennessee, but plans for a

Confederate offensive never materialized. After a resounding victory at Chickamauga Creek, Bragg's siege of Chattanooga became another occasion for bickering and back-stabbing in the Army of Tennessee. Several generals petitioned the War Department for Bragg's removal, and the general's chief of staff, William W. Mackall, worried that Davis would "indulge like a spoiled child his prejudices" and stick with Bragg, if only to avoid appointing Joe Johnston to command.[2] Finally grasping the seriousness of the situation, the president headed west for a conference with Bragg and his generals.

Howell Cobb, who like others had received disturbing reports from the Army of Tennessee and who well understood the political pressure to reinstate Johnston as well as the president's continuing hostility to "old Joe," claimed that Bragg had "not a single friend" among his generals. Even the president's military aide, James Chesnut, Jr., admitted that "every honest man he saw out west thought well of Joe Johnston" though as Mary Chesnut wryly commented, Johnston's "hatred of Jeff Davis amounts to a religion. With him it colors all things."[3]

Meeting with senior officers of the Army of Tennessee on October 9, the president soon learned that hostility to Bragg ran much deeper than he had imagined. Davis was unwilling to reward the generals who had plotted against Bragg or to appoint Beauregard to the command, and he rejected James Longstreet's suggestion of Johnston as a possible replacement. Several months after these meetings, Senator Orr compared Davis's attachment to Bragg to "the blind and gloating love of a mother for a deformed and misshapen offspring."[4] Although corps commanders were reshuffled, Davis had not resolved the Army of Tennessee's command problems.

When a Federal assault on November 25 drove the Confederates off Missionary Ridge and handed Bragg a stunning defeat, whole regiments panicked, and the Army of Tennessee retreated some thirty miles to Dalton, Georgia. Denunciations of Bragg and calls for Joe Johnston's return reached a crescendo.[5] Finally realizing the impossibility of his position, Bragg asked to be relieved; Davis agreed but soon brought him to Richmond as a military adviser.

Sidestepping a presidential request to go west himself, Lee at first recommended Beauregard but, receiving no encouragement, then gingerly suggested Johnston for command of the Army of Tennessee. Influential members of Congress and several generals also lobbied for Johnston. Bowing to political and military pressure, Davis reluctantly made the appointment.[6] Perhaps Davis's congressional enemies had been using the general to get at the president, but Johnston himself had never favored Bragg's removal and, for all his whining, was much less an intriguer than his congressional friends or many Army of Tennessee generals. Indeed, Johnston's supporters were a diverse lot that barely deserved the label "faction."

What Davis wanted and what many Confederates hoped for was an offensive to relieve the pressure on Georgia and recapture at least part of Tennessee, but Johnston was not suited for such an undertaking. As Alexander Stephens rightly observed, Johnston "will not fight unless he feels assured of victory," though Stephens believed that "our ultimate success depends as much on not fighting as fighting." From a much different perspective, Mary Chesnut agreed that "politicians and men with no stomach for fighting . . . found it easier to *cuss* Jeff Davis and laud Joe Johnston and stay at home than to go to the front with a musket."[7]

Johnston's appointment did not ease pressure on Davis. In Richmond, Howell Cobb found much more congressional opposition to the administration than he had expected. "Patriotism and policy," he believed, "both demand that the President should be sustained and his hands strengthened in fighting the revolution." Yet invoking the need for national unity had little effect. Even after Bragg's dismissal from command, Cobb acknowledged that "the state of feeling between the President and Congress is bad, indeed could not be much worse." He still vainly hoped that Lee, Johnston, and Beauregard could work together.[8]

Johnston welcomed the new command as a way to vindicate his military record but was as paranoid as ever about his relations with the government and especially the president. Johnston was taciturn by nature, and his fears of intrigue and back-stabbing made him even more reluctant to share his plans with Richmond. So while the president and others pushed for an offensive campaign, Johnston pursued a Fabian strategy and never lacked excuses for avoiding battle.[9] The old command problems in the Army of Tennessee persisted along with often petty disputes between generals and politicians that had already caused many needless delays, defeats, and deaths.

This politics of grand strategy weakened the president without necessarily strengthening or unifying his enemies. While Davis tried to prod Johnston into taking the offensive, the general's caution alarmed his most loyal political friends. Wigfall was disappointed that Johnston had not pushed for Bragg's removal and was much more interested than Johnston in putting political heat on the administration and personally embarrassing Davis. Johnston doubted that the senator had worked hard enough either to defend his reputation or to pressure the War Department into reinforcing the Army of Tennessee.[10]

Political fragmentation and division now extended throughout the army and the civil administration. Both the president and his critics would attempt to rally their forces and ultimately define the heart and soul of the Southern nation. Although a growing peace movement along with old political grievances eventually divided would-be defenders of individual liberty and community rights, criticism of the president intensified. Attacks from several directions further discouraged the formation of parties or even well-defined factions. Ambition and personal hostility added to the excesses of debate, though nagging, fundamental questions kept cropping up in the midst of political disorder, financial chaos, and military crisis. Strong personalities and sensitive egos account for some of this chronic factiousness, but basic differences in political principle were also involved.

On his trip to Bragg's headquarters in October 1863, Davis traveled through a divided nation filled with increasingly fearful and disheartened people. Yet for all his faults, the president (along with Lee) remained the personification of the Confederate nation. Comparisons to George Washington may not still have carried much weight, but Davis was determined to sustain public morale in a dark hour. Exhorting the soldiers in the Army of Tennessee, he declared that Southerners were fighting for the "freedom, equality, and State sovereignty" that had been "purchased by the blood of your revolutionary sires." The only alternative to a continued war for independence was a "slavish submission to despotic usurpation." In a clear though belated effort to boost public confidence and support for his administration, the president made several brief speeches along a route that took him from Chattanooga through Selma, Meridian, Mobile, Montgomery, Atlanta, Macon, Savannah, and finally to Charleston. Welcomed there by, of all people, Rhett and Beauregard, Davis tactlessly impugned the opposition's judgment and motives, saying that such croakers were "not worthy of the Confederate liberty for which we are fighting."[11]

Even when he tried, the president had difficulty being conciliatory, but then he never understood how anyone could doubt his selfless devotion to the cause. Davis stood as a defender of both national unity and civil liberty without addressing the inherent tension between them. For him there was no tension: only a strong national government could fight a successful war, and such centralization was necessary for a victory that would ensure the survival of basic freedoms in a Southern republic. Nor did he comprehend his critics' warnings (which he dismissed as hypocritical cant) of despotism and their questioning of both his judgment and motives.

After returning to Richmond on November 9, Davis abandoned the role of patriotic exhorter. His long and uninspiring annual message read like an administrative report garnished with rationalizations and wishful thinking on financial and military affairs. Even the obligatory descriptions of Northern barbarities fell flat, and his call for more sacrifice and national unity sounded more ceremonial than inspirational.[12] In fragile health as usual, Davis became increasingly preoccupied and depressed, often riding a horse through the suburbs of Richmond to collect his thoughts. Varina Davis still held receptions at which the president tried to appear in good spirits. But listening to his "melancholy cadence" one evening, Mary Chesnut found the conversation inexpressibly sad.[13]

In February 1864, Davis admitted to Congress that "discontent, disaffection and disloyalty" prevailed among those who had "enjoyed quiet and safety at home," while others sacrificed everything for the cause. Peace meetings and outright Unionism heartened Yankees, comforted traitors, reconfirmed the fears of the fainthearted, and discouraged patriots.[14] Calls for renewed commitment became in effect pleas to sustain the president against his unrelenting critics. If Davis remained at the "sacred center" of the Confederate cause, the nation's failings became his own. Well might he remember the biblical exhortation "every one to whom much is given, of him will much be required." The early comparisons to Washington had created unrealistic expectations and naturally led to frustration and criticism whenever the war was going badly.

Yet it is easy to exaggerate the extent of opposition to the administration and forget that Davis retained considerable public trust. In state after state and usually by lopsided votes, legislatures passed resolutions expressing undiminished confidence in him. In Georgia and South Carolina, where prominent politicians continued to assail the administration, legislators at least went through the motions of sustaining the president.[15]

His apologists lauded Davis as a wise and self-sacrificing patriot. A Georgian issued a lengthy pamphlet attacking Edward A. Pollard with as much vitriol as the *Richmond Examiner* usually directed against the government. Emphasizing the president's vast experience and praising his military judgment, this writer argued that unfair criticism was inevitable during a long war and that it was "absurd to expect that President Davis should escape what a Washington received."[16]

Both the substance and the symbols of these arguments exposed old difficulties in defining Confederate nationalism. The real question was whether the mass of white Southerners would remain true to the cause. Was the government unworthy of the people or were the people unfit to build a model republic? "The noisy are silent, the faint of heart begin to despair, and the disloyal . . . grow bold in the presence of national ills." Despite this gloomy assessment, Zebulon Vance still believed that "the great mass . . . continue hopeful and earnest," determined to preserve their liberties from the scourge of abolition, confiscation, and "vassalage." For Vance as well as for more extreme libertarians, the people remained steadfast despite the Confederate administration's incompetence. But even the strongly anti-Davis *Richmond Whig* held that too many Southerners supported the Confederacy with empty words instead of tangible deeds. Such contradictory attitudes toward the relative virtues of the people and their rulers reflected persistent tensions between democratic and elitist elements in Confederate political culture. An Atlanta editor described Southerners as "hereditary, organic Republicans" but irrevocably hostile to Northern "barbarian Democracy"; they were "an aristocracy in arms" fighting to uphold the Cavalier tradition.[17] In the haze of nostalgic romanticism and questionable history, "national unity," "social harmony," "liberty," and "state sovereignty" easily became rationalizations for special privilege and planter domination.

Proslavery ideologues saw the Confederacy as part of an Anglo-Saxon crusade to civilize Africans, preserve local self-government, and fulfill the promises of free trade. Even Alexander Stephens argued that the loss of cities or territory meant little so long as Southerners recalled the suffering of their ancestors in the revolutionary war and remembered that a liberty-loving people would ultimately triumph.[18] Although privately Stephens conveyed no such optimism, he still rejected the siren call of reunion. In many ways opposition to reconstruction became Confederate nationalism's lowest common denominator.

This flimsy basis for patriotism produced more self-deception than national strength. Confederate leaders made herculean efforts to show that the heroic sacrifices made by men, women, and children would lead to a glorious victory for independence. A congressional address, drafted by lame-duck congressman J. L. M. Curry, sounded confidently defiant: "The unanimity and zeal with which the separation [of the Union] was undertaken and perfected, finds no parallel in history. The people rose *en masse* to assert their liberties and protect their menaced rights." A fabled social and political unity made the Southern revolution safely conservative. "This Government is a child of law instead of sedition, of right instead of violence, of deliberation instead of insurrection. Its early life was attended by no anarchy, no rebellion, no suspension of authority, no social disorders, no lawless disturbances. Sovereignty was not for one moment in abeyance. The utmost conservatism marked every proceeding. . . . No attempt was made to build on speculative principles."[19] Yet these words also echoed old fears of Jacobinism, of a revolution that would destroy the foundations of the Southern social order, and their mystical and mythic appeal ignored the political and class divisions caused by the war.

This conservative ideology rested firmly on antipolitical foundations. A joint congressional resolution adopted in January 1864 urged the people to make a "magnanimous surrender of all personal and party feuds" and to spurn "every exhibition of factious temper." In part simply wartime rhetoric, the sort of appeal that could be expected when Northern armies were pressing on several fronts, such denunciations of partisanship were, however, more than empty words. Although the *Richmond Whig* offered a rare defense of the necessity for political parties as a counterweight to a "one-man power," most of the president's foes denied being "factious" and showed no interest in political organization. For moderates such as Herschel Johnson, antiparty ideology remained central to the Southern cause, and neither fanatical nationalists nor rabid libertarians disagreed.[20]

The various "factions" all shared to a greater or lesser degree a strong animus against political parties. Hence the best strategy for Davis's opponents was to exploit fears of consolidation. Although the president's critics have often been described as peevish and impractical fanatics, they believed important principles were at stake in their battles with the administration. Several editors again warned that the president was becoming a dictator—and with congressional acquiescence. Perhaps, some mused, the Confederate Constitution had sown the seeds of tyranny by creating a powerful executive. These comments denoted much more than the paranoid rantings of anti-Davis zealots, and the fears expressed were not entirely groundless. Some impatient Confederates did long for more decisive leadership, for a strong man who could carry them to victory without being hamstrung by constitutional technicalities or timid congressmen. Richmond insiders even speculated that the president's recent tour of the West was a prelude to dictatorship.[21]

Public disappointment with a seemingly impotent Congress also fueled talk of dictatorship. One editor playfully suggested limiting all floor speeches to ten minutes. Davis supporters naturally accused opposition congressmen of petty obstructionism, but administration critics agreed that Congress had too many weak and mediocre members. Washington-trained "party hacks" dominated Congress, the *Richmond Examiner* complained, and "the routine of caucus-holding, log-rolling, wire-pulling politicians is worse than useless in a revolution." By 1864 the paper asked what right a "rump" House with many members representing no real constituency had to enact legislation. Congressmen from occupied districts were too susceptible to executive influence to act with independence and integrity.[22]

Yet despite grumbling about what Rhett called "rulers without responsibility" meeting in secret sessions, the president received most of the political abuse. Even his halting efforts to shore up morale received criticism. Laurence Keitt accused Davis of exuding false confidence while Confederate territory was being lost and the government tottered toward bankruptcy.[23] Of course, the war was going badly and personal animosities exacerbated political disputes, but there were significant differences between what Davis and his critics considered vitally important questions. Such firmly held convictions naturally fostered ideological rigidity. The defense of individual, community, and state liberties grew ever more shrill and fanatical. Doctrinaires such as Robert Toombs still insisted that independence be purchased without the smallest sacrifice of liberty. Constitutional fundamentalism stirred paranoia about military despotism. Despite his repudiation of both the peace men and reconstructionists, recently elected Alabama governor Thomas Hill Watts insisted on "strict construction" as a bulwark against oppression. To true believers, the Southern people had become ideologically lax. Place hunters had acceded to any latitudinarian innovations so long as they could partake in the "corruptions of an overshadowing patronage," a Richmond editor lamented.[24] The more desperate the circumstances, the more tenaciously some Confederates clung to their notions of political purity.

An obsession with individual liberty not only encouraged disaffection but also raised disturbing questions about class relations. As inflation and food shortages ravaged the Confederate home front during the winter of 1863–64, resentment against the rich and against speculators mounted. Senator Albert Gallatin Brown of Mississippi denounced skulkers who had taken advantage of the exemption and substitution laws: "They have reaped when they have not sown, consumed when they have not produced," and now they jammed the streets and theaters of the great cities, sauntering about free of care, reveling in their wealth and cleverness. These social parasites must certainly "offend the war-worn and scar-covered soldier by exhibiting their fashionable clothes in contrast with his dirty rags."[25]

Such inflammatory remarks from so loyal a politician made even the president's most vehement critics wary of unleashing yeoman and poor white anger. So appeals for patriotism and national unity also contained appeals for class harmony. Setting class against class was by definition traitorous; the cry of a "rich man's war and a poor man's fight" was especially subversive. Throughout the war, according to the *Richmond Whig*, wealthy planters had served alongside their humbler neighbors in the Confederate army. White men of all classes loved liberty and would sacrifice anything to defend Southern rights. Even Joe Brown, who had employed class rhetoric during the recent gubernatorial campaign, warned that the poor would suffer most from the abolition of slavery because the wealthy could flee the country, forcing the yeomen and their families to "submit to negro equality."[26]

Such statements betrayed considerable nervousness because Confederate leaders could no longer be certain that racism would override class interests. The danger was that the nonslaveholding majority would turn against the slaveholding secessionists. With his usual candor and perception, James Henry Hammond admitted that "the poor hate the rich and make war on them every where, and here especially with universal suffrage." Little wonder, then, that social and economic resentments poured out. "This war is based on the principal fact of the inequality of mankind," Hammond mused, "for policy we say races, in reality, as all history shows it is . . . classes." Fearing upheaval from below, Hammond prayed that the Confederacy could safeguard slaveholders' interests and not give in to demagogues. On this score at least, he might have rested easy; most politicians hesitated to incite class warfare. A congressional address issued in early 1864 asserted that "all vocations and classes contributed to the swelling numbers [of the Confederate armies]. Abandoning luxuries and comforts to which they had been accustomed, they submitted cheerfully to the scanty fare and exactive service of the camps." War had become the great leveler, joining all Southerners in a grand crusade for liberty and for the "protection of their altars and firesides."[27] Or so Confederate propagandists asserted.

But economic disruption had already shattered such old myths, and the peace movement sometimes appealed directly to class interests. The most disaffected were willing to barter slavery for European recognition or give up the institution in negotiations between Southern and Northern states.[28] This linking of abolition to peace greatly alarmed defenders of Southern orthodoxy. To Howell Cobb, the path of duty was clear: "We must all be free, or all be slaves. We must all live or all perish."[29] Yet cries for peace naturally undermined social and political harmony and raised disturbing questions for the immediate future.

Discussion of a possible peace settlement became more divisive than earlier debates over public policy, accentuated the clash between the political cultures, but paradoxically divided the libertarians. Some North Carolina dissidents linked agitation for peace to a broader defense of liberty by playing on general fears of centralized power. "Destructives" in the state legislature, one peace advocate claimed, believed that "Jeff Davis is a god and . . . can do no wrong." In both the Congress and the states, the supine tools of an executive tyrant would do anything to protect their master from the people's righteous indignation.[30]

The prospect of the states setting peace terms or withdrawing from the Confederacy raised tough constitutional questions and hardly offered acceptable conditions for ending the war. On New Year's Day 1864, a "hill country" correspondent wrote to Vance that at least four out of five Southerners favored peace "on *any terms* that are *honorable*." The meaning of honor, however, was elastic. Even though most North Carolinians would have preferred the establishment of Southern independence, many were ready to accept a reconstruction of the Union. Holden and Congressman-elect James T. Leach called for a state convention, presumably to arrange an armistice preliminary to peace negotiations. Whether such a convention would take North Carolina out of the Confederacy was unclear; Holden denied that it would and even held out hope that slavery might be preserved. Leach went a step farther, arguing that North Carolina had a perfect right to leave the Confederacy when the people "could hear the clanking of the chains that are being forged to bind us."[31] Although Leach made no explicit reference to a natural right of revolution, he implied that the popular will should override decisions made by elected officials.

Did this mean general insurrection, political anarchy, or merely the disintegration of public authority? Even peace advocates were not yet ready to secede from the Confederacy and feared a civil war in North Carolina. Debates in Congress over extending conscription and suspending habeas corpus greatly alarmed Conservative leaders but failed to clarify the party's position on peace negotiations.[32]

Fearing prolonged and bloody internal strife, a newly established "Confederate" newspaper in Raleigh frantically warned of a possible "counter-revolution" against the national government. Secessionists also turned strict constructionism against the erstwhile defenders of liberty by denying the state's authority to negotiate on its own. For all their cleverness, political reality made these arguments largely beside the point. "Talking about it and ridiculing the [peace] movement," Kenneth Rayner conceded, "are about as vain and insufficient . . . as reading the riot act to an infuriated mob."[33] The tide seemed to be running against the "destructives," who sounded increasingly fatalistic.

The more cautious Conservatives worried about stirring up armed resistance to the Confederate government. Though favoring peace negotiations, state treasurer Jonathan Worth refused to countenance desertion. But disaffection in the state was bound to affect Tar Heel soldiers, especially when newspapers and letters from home reported widespread anti-war sentiment. In a sermon preached at the execution of twenty-two deserters in Brigadier General Robert F. Hoke's brigade, John Paris claimed that the peace meetings and class resentments aroused by editors and preachers had led these unfortunate souls to forget their duty to the nation. With a bow toward Confederate civil religion, he maintained that deserters were seldom pious because Christianity and patriotism were inseparable.[34]

Such assertions may have reassured nervous Confederates and even caused members of the Conservative party to rethink their positions. Congressman John A. Gilmer, a Whig Unionist who had once been offered a post in Lincoln's cabinet, deprecated talk of a convention and urged Governor Vance to repudiate Holden. The people must keep up the fight because "to doubt is to be damned." Such moderates saw reconstruction as no better than subjugation and hoped to continue the war without sacrificing fundamental liberties.[35] This delicate balance between patriotism and dissent suggested how fragile the Conservative party coalition had become.

As moderates struggled to define their position, the peace question became more divisive. Edward J. Hale still feared that Holden and other peace advocates were conspiring to seize control of the Conservative party from more cautious leaders such as Vance and William A. Graham.[36] So in the absence of a powerful secessionist or "destructive" party, North

Carolina's self-styled defenders of constitutional liberty continued to fight among themselves. With Holden openly calling for a state convention and sounding the tocsin against the Confederate government, even Conservatives who sympathized with the peace meetings felt painfully ambivalent. Jonathan Worth hesitated to embrace separate state action and hoped for a peace settlement that would preserve slavery. Others worried that Governor Vance would break with Holden too quickly or even conciliate the "destructives."[37] Conservatives of all stripes faced decisions with crucial but unpredictable consequences as events in Richmond and on the battlefields forced them to reassess their political loyalties and even their ideological commitment to a libertarian political culture.

Caught in the shifting political currents, Vance hoped to buy time by appealing to Davis for another peace initiative. With his usual condescension, the president replied that the governor could not realize the obstacles or the efforts the administration had made to open peace negotiations. Another attempt would "invite insult and contumely" because Lincoln still insisted on emancipation—a condition that all loyal people found unacceptable. Instead, Davis hoped that Vance would suppress the peace meetings in North Carolina.[38] To do so would mean condemning the peace movement and breaking with Holden, but separate state action was equally unacceptable. Confronting such a choice sorely tested Vance's considerable political talents.

At the beginning of 1864 and probably earlier, the governor had decided to assert his leadership. Rather than endorse a state convention, he would "see the Conservative party blown into a thousand atoms and Holden and his understrappers in hell." Using a favorite nationalist analogy, he argued that Confederate fortunes were no more desperate than those of the revolutionary forefathers in 1780–81. To abandon the cause now would dishonor both himself and the state.[39] Vance had moved away from the extreme libertarians in the Conservative party but could not be sure of winning control from Holden and the peace faction.

The winter months between the 1863 elections and the convening of the first Congress's final session had been a period of reassessment, reflection, and complex maneuvering. During this seasonal lull in the war, the peace question dominated political discussion. The symbiotic relationship between the rival political cultures, based on a mutual hostility to political organization, gave civic life a certain ideological tension. Spring brought a resumption of fighting and renewed controversy over public policy. Fear of the future, a longing for peace, political recrimination, class bitterness, and fundamental philosophical differences would all shape the course of Confederate politics.

Even casual students of Confederate politics find the controversies over conscription and habeas corpus, to cite the two most obvious examples, repetitious, endless, and pointless. Yet to contemporaries these acrimonious and sometimes arid disputes had great significance. Even in the early months of 1864, they exposed unresolved questions about the legitimacy of political power and also showed how the nationalist and libertarian political cultures differed over the central purpose of the Confederate experiment. These debates gave more tangible meaning to competing notions of national strength, individual liberty, community harmony, and class equity.

On February 17, the last day of its lame-duck session, Congress lowered the minimum age for conscription to seventeen and raised the maximum age to fifty. Some members would have gone farther. Wigfall favored drafting everyone between sixteen and sixty, and Brown of Mississippi proposed a levee en masse along with tough economic controls that would have stretched congressional war powers to the breaking point.[40] The real test, however, was whether exemptions would be limited. Unfortunately, too many influential people had vested interests in the status quo. Newspaper editors, for example, wanted to preserve their exempt status; state officials favored conscripting Confederate clerks but not their own employees.[41]

Davis sought broad authority to detail men for specific jobs and thus end the unwieldy system of class exemptions. In the House, William Porcher Miles of South Carolina argued for expanded executive authority to allocate manpower more efficiently. Libertarians remained unconvinced. Henry Foote predicted that guillotines would be set up for anyone who dared criticize the government and maintained that granting the president the power to detail men would only open up new "fountains of influence and corruption." Though brief and desultory, these exchanges showed that many politicians remained uncertain about how much more the public was willing to sacrifice, and this encouraged splitting the difference between nationalists and libertarians. The new conscription act allowed the president and secretary of war to draft men and then designate them for war-related jobs, but it retained many class exemptions. This measure was not entirely satisfactory to either side, but it placed Davis's leadership at the center of debate. A South Carolina editor declared that "President Davis is an honest man and pure patriot, and will never abuse power placed in his hands." Such reasoning appalled libertarians, especially when this same editor, citing Roman precedents, suggested that the country might soon have to make Davis a dictator.[42]

The adoption of this halfway measure energized the political opposition. By March the vice-president was saying publicly what he had long maintained privately: conscription was as useless as it was dangerous, as unnecessary as it was unconstitutional. Correctly predicting that this latest act would add few men to the Confederate army, Stephens condemned the draft as "radically wrong in principle." As might be expected, Toombs carried the argument beyond its logical limit. In a remarkably intemperate speech to some Georgia state troops, Toombs urged them to resist executive and congressional usurpation. "I ask for no mutiny," he added disingenuously, "unless it should be necessary in defense of Constitutional rights."[43]

Continued fears of centralization and frustration over recent military setbacks, notably the loss of Chattanooga, along with growing signs of financial weakness, led Congress to consider radically altering the relationship between the president, the cabinet, and the Senate. Despite his voting record favorable to the administration, Senator Robert W. Johnson of Arkansas introduced a bill on December 10, 1863, limiting cabinet terms to two years. The president could reappoint a cabinet member but only with the Senate's consent. Denying that his proposal infringed on the president's constitutional authority, Johnson maintained that few nominees would be rejected. Instead, such a measure would ensure that incompetent officials could not hold on to their positions indefinitely. Fearing that the president might be tempted to form a "federal" party, pointedly referring to the example of Alexander Hamilton, and warning about cabinet "oligarchs," Johnson strongly appealed to antipolitical values, particularly public hostility to ambitious officeholders.[44]

Johnson's bill, if passed, would provide a way at last for administration opponents to strike directly at Davis's authority and especially at his insistence on retaining unpopular and inept officials. Because the president and his cabinet seemed "impervious" to public opinion, the *Richmond Examiner* declared that Congress needed to rid the country of "stupidity, incompetence, or corruption." Other editors seized the high ground of political principle—in favor of efficiency and accountability—rather than explicitly attacking Davis or his advisers.[45]

In a sense this proposal was a logical culmination of the assault on executive patronage launched at Montgomery and expressed in several provisions of the Confederate Constitution. But to administration supporters, any restriction on the terms of cabinet members would cripple the president. Once one cut through the republican theory (and cant) about reining in executive authority, the political reality was obvious. Davis refused to dismiss controversial cabinet members so the Congress would in essence force them out of office without going through the cumbersome impeachment process. Echoing James Madison, the editor of the *Richmond Dispatch* denounced Johnson's bill for violating the separation of powers and spreading that disease often fatal to republics, the spirit of "faction." Legislative usurpation became the administration's rallying cry, and rumor had it that Davis would resign if Johnson's bill passed.[46] Ironically, such a step would have moved the Confederacy closer to becoming a parliamentary system, but after a long debate the bill died at the end of the session. The president could still count on enough votes in Congress to block hostile legislation, and his critics remained deadlocked and disorganized, unable to do much before the newly elected Second Congress convened in May.

Perhaps emboldened by his opponents' disarray, the president asked for another suspension of habeas corpus. To many devoted Confederates the need was obvious: judges released conscripts; peace men and other traitors spouted their venom with impunity; deserters roamed the countryside with little fear of capture. From all parts of the Confederacy came requests for action against a host of malcontents, dissidents, and turncoats.[47]

A newly established pro-Davis newspaper in North Carolina ran a series of editorials discussing English precedents. Given their passion for constitutional debate, some Southerners reveled in the legal fine points. Historical arguments became closely connected to pragmatic ones; after all, many ancient republics had suspended civil liberties during national emergencies. Albert Gallatin Brown predicted that all liberties would be lost if the Yankees won the war: "If I cannot save everything, I will save that which is the most valuable." Failing to acknowledge how closely this logic paralleled Abraham Lincoln's, Brown maintained that the real danger to liberty came from Washington, not from Richmond. Confederates could restrict civil liberties temporarily because they could trust Jefferson Davis. Those who argued that the president would abuse such authority, claimed the *Richmond Dispatch*, were the "real revolutionaries" who would subvert the Constitution.[48] These contentions were disparate, disingenuous, and even contradictory. The plea from necessity was not entirely convincing and hardly addressed the ideological objections.

The opposition naturally tried to shift the debate away from the present emergency toward a broader consideration of political theory. In the fashion of eighteenth-century pamphleteers and revolutionaries, they called for a return to "first principles." Grounding their case in a purified (and in many ways rarefied) vision of republicanism, they sounded increasingly doctrinaire. The habeas corpus issue raised again basic questions about the Confederacy's political future, and devoted libertarians saw little point living in a nation where sacred rights could be routinely abrogated through appeals to supposed military necessity. Even the triumph of Confederate arms should not be purchased by sacrificing fundamental rights.

Unfortunately, the Confederate Congress discussed the matter in secret session where members could express their views without worrying about the political consequences. By mid-February, the House overwhelmingly and the Senate much more narrowly had passed a new bill suspending the writ of habeas corpus until ninety days after the beginning of the next congressional session. Unlike previous laws, this one spelled out the constitutional justification and listed cases in which the writ could be suspended. These naturally included espionage and treason but more ominously encompassed "advising or inciting others to abandon the Confederate cause."[49] Did this provision outlaw peace meetings or even pessimistic letters written to soldiers? Even as Congress was debating habeas corpus and wrapping up the work of its lame-duck session, the public protests had begun.

Adopting a properly funereal tone, the opposition mourned the death of constitutional rights. Even before the habeas corpus bill had received final approval, Vice-President Stephens despaired of the Confederacy's future: "Constitutional liberty will go down," he advised a Georgia friend, "never to rise again on this continent, I fear. This is the worst that can befall us. Far better that our country should be overrun by the enemy, our cities sacked and burned, and our land laid desolate, than that the people should thus suffer the citadel of their liberties to be entered and taken by professed friends." Even questions of national survival mattered little if the very soul of the Confederacy was in mortal danger. Stephens's exposition of constitutional liberty showed why this technical question generated such heated debate. In part, opponents of the habeas corpus bill feared expanded executive authority. A Richmond editor drew the appropriate lesson: "History points to no instance where such enormous power has not been enormously abused."[50] In a broader sense, however, principled statesmen dared not allow any encroachment on sacred freedoms, and no other question could be of greater importance.

After all, the threat of dictatorship loomed. With the writ suspended, libertarians argued, any citizen could be locked up on the mere whim of the president or the secretary of war, thus transforming a republic into a despotism. Denying any particular animus against Jefferson Davis, they maintained that even a George Washington could not be trusted with such vast authority.[51] State politicians feared that suspension of the writ also meant the imposition of martial law with generals riding roughshod over civil officials. Beginning in late 1863, several legislatures adopted resolutions either protesting or attempting to impede the suspension of the writ, and there was even talk of nullification.[52]

As the rhetoric heated up on both sides, moderates were frightened by the possibility of armed resistance. Rumors of a counterrevolution suggested that the political center was being swallowed up by the extremes. Admitting his own opposition to suspending habeas corpus, Vance advised the president to refrain from using "this great power." Bristling at the governor's renewed complaints on patronage matters, Davis mistook Vance's position on habeas corpus for the "rhetoric" of the *Raleigh Standard*. Yet several of the president's most loyal friends in Congress had voted against the habeas corpus bill and warned him against arresting citizens who had committed no indictable crime. Feeling the heat from the uncompromising defenders of states' rights and individual liberty, Vance, Herschel Johnson, and other centrist politicians hoped the government would tread lightly, but their criticism of the administration did not translate into support for the peace movement.[53]

And despite these heated disagreements—intensified in the case of Toombs and others by personal hatred of the president—antipartyism exerted a powerful influence on both political cultures. Suspicion of politicians and their intrigues remained a core value of the Southern nation. For the most part, even fanatical libertarians rejected any notion of organized opposition to the government. Many Confederates who had reservations about conscription and suspension of habeas corpus refused to join the disaffected. Pointing to his own votes against administration measures, Herschel Johnson told Stephens that he nevertheless felt compelled to uphold the laws. He believed that there was now room for only one party, "the party of the country." After all, the Federals were preparing to move toward Atlanta. Like many other moderates in states threatened by Northern armies, he equated factiousness with disloyalty. Dissenters too often forgot the war's central purpose: the creation of an independent Southern nation. "This is no time to cavil about nice questions of constitutional construction when we are waging a terrible war in defense of individual and civil liberty," declared Mississippi governor Charles Clark. Steadfast Confederate nationalists portrayed themselves as the true defenders of traditional freedoms while arguing that the Christian's duty to obey elected leaders remained in force. Deploring disunity, ministers urged their parishioners to consider carefully before making thoughtless complaints. Baptist elder Thomas S. Dunaway warned that the "criticisms and strictures which we sometimes hear on the conduct of our able and patriotic Chief Magistrate, and our leaders, civil and military, are as injurious as they are ludicrous."[54]

In light of Confederate civil religion and orthodox republicanism, public virtue remained both the key to national survival and its greatest question mark. Prayers offered for the president or various generals would be unavailing if a stiff-necked people constantly bemoaned their fate and lost faith in the cause. Georgia bishop Stephen Elliott feared that Southerners might "conquer" themselves through endless carping and internal strife. During any revolution, it was natural for people to lose their early enthusiasm, to become critical of the powers that be, to long for peace, and eventually to flirt with treason. "Learn who are worthy to carry on this war; who are eager and earnest for the work of the Lord," Elliott advised his fellow citizens. After all, fainthearted Tories during the American Revolution had even cast aspersions on Washington. Confederate diplomat L. Q. C. Lamar argued that the "violent party contests" of the past had ignored the "question of virtue and ability and patriotism in our public men." Yet many of these assessments of national character seemed flimsy or transitory, heavily dependent on how the war was going. When victories, or at least what passed for victories, came in the spring and summer of 1864, confidence in popular virtue ran high. In June, the Confederate Congress boldly declared that the Yankees could never conquer eight million free men determined to preserve their liberties.[55]

The opposition also wrestled with questions about public virtue and warned that official propaganda might inure people to centralized tyranny. To libertarians the danger arose not from decadent people longing for the fleshpots of the old Union but from false prophets preaching blind support for the government. Congressman John Gilmer admired the president's patriotism but noted that he "is but a man, liable to error, and susceptible to flattery," and "his agents have been as worthless and corrupt as they are avaricious and tyrannical." Even the Alien and Sedition Acts paled in comparison to the enormities of martial law. Better to stand for states' rights and individual liberty than to succumb to what one editor called the "fiction" that the president, like a divinely anointed monarch, could do no wrong. But instead congressmen met in secret to pass legislation that forged sturdier chains of despotism for the Southern people. According to opposition political theory, Confederate citizens were honest but misguided and needed to shake off their lethargy.[56]

For months after the lame-duck session of Congress adjourned, libertarian extremists painted the political future in the darkest hues. Rhett would not have granted the angel Gabriel as much authority as Congress had conferred on Jefferson Davis. Convinced that he had been right all along in his doubts about the president, the Carolina firebrand had nearly lost hope that Southerners would defend their rights against executive usurpation.[57]

But no matter how much his enemies might fulminate against Davis, no one suggested a reasonable alternative. Few politicians believed that Stephens would be any better, and by this time the vice-president's devotion to the cause was in serious doubt. Wigfall hoped the Senate would reject Davis's foolish appointments and make him assume the responsibility for military defeats. The Texan also called for creating a post of commander in chief to prevent new strategic blunders.[58] The fiercely proud Wigfall was blasting Davis for egotism. Emotional intensity and intemperate wrath characterized such attacks on the president. Men like Wigfall and Toombs and to a lesser extent Stephens and Joe Brown were like caged animals eager to strike out in frustration or even in blind rage.

The tone of the opposition, combined with its largely negative character, its hostility to party organization, and its highly individualistic and idiosyncratic composition, substantially reduced its power. If the president and his administration often seemed adrift and unable to exert strong leadership in military, political, or financial affairs, the opposition (including but not confined to the ardent libertarians) also lacked organization, direction, and energy. Antiparty politics could not end factiousness, and the ideal of national unity would be elusive so long as strong-willed politicians remained committed to fixed ideological positions.

CHAPTER 13

Principle, Power, Politics, and Peace

During the spring of 1864, politicians, editors, and ordinary citizens continued to debate old questions—including conscription and habeas corpus—in tiresomely repetitive ways. Many of these discussions seemed irrelevant and even harmful because in the next several months, everything would depend on the army and the people. The fate of the Confederate nation would be decided on the battlefield and on the home front, but political leaders had to respond to both military and morale crises, and as they did so, they joined political ideology to immediate questions of political power.

As the peace movement gained support, nationalists and libertarians alike had to consider the practical consequences of their philosophical commitments. In both Georgia and North Carolina—more than ever the centers of political conflict in a shrinking Confederacy—the anti-Davis and peace elements sometimes cooperated, but factionalism within the political opposition remained a debilitating force. Highly charged disputes over peace and liberty also helped determine the political futures of Joe Brown and Zeb Vance.

In Richmond, Jefferson Davis remained at the center of political conflict. Still the most powerful spokesman for Confederate nationalism, the president would make his last great effort to rally public support for the war effort and for his administration. Unresolved problems of strategy and command would distract his attention and strengthen the political opposition, but he would still manage to keep the peace movement in check and somehow hold the nation together. The interplay of state and national politics, always strongly influenced by the ebb and flow of the armies, fostered a continued search for some middle ground but also brought forth efforts to break the political deadlock between the rival political cultures.

In Georgia political opposition to the Confederate government had grown bolder and more strident, and political principles had become entangled in a bitter struggle over political power. No one embodied the contradictory characteristics of ideologue and opportunist better than Joe Brown. Shortly after the 1863 election, the governor raised again the question of Georgia troops selecting their own officers. As before, Brown cloaked his arguments in the garb of states' rights, but his long, contentious letters to Richmond failed to conceal his obsession with the preservation of his own political prerogatives.[1]

For the governor's friend Vice-President Stephens, a fixation on principle hardened by intense opposition to administration policy remained a driving force. All of Stephens's biographers have noted how he made a fetish of "liberty." His sense of personal rectitude and perhaps his chronic ill health added to this streak of self-righteous stubbornness.[2] To Stephens and his brother Linton, political timing and other pragmatic considerations mattered little. Principle was everything, and the dangers were real. In one of his barely coherent tirades against the president, Linton had even talked of the need for a Brutus. Yet what many contemporaries and historians have labeled "fanaticism" followed logically from classical republican ideology; the rhetoric of the 1760s survived into the 1860s. In words that could have easily been written by James Otis or Sam Adams, South Carolinian J. Barrett Cohen warned the vice-president that the Confederacy faced a greater threat from internal than from external enemies. "The encroachments on liberty are gradual, the people become accustomed to their yoke and by degrees are prepared to bear heavier burdens. Never in the history of the world has power thus acquired been voluntarily surrendered, seldom have popular rights been reestablished without the cost of much precious blood." It therefore became "the duty of every freeman to watch closely his liberties and to guard them jealously from all encroachments."[3] Resistance was the only logical response to executive and congressional tyranny.

Brown and the Stephens brothers claimed to fear military despotism and dictatorship, but Brown paid more attention to the politics of liberty than to constitutional purity. After consultation with the Stephens brothers, on March 10, he sent a lengthy message to the General Assembly. In a highly abstract analysis of recent history, he described the signs of a deep-laid conspiracy to destroy states' rights and individual liberty: "Almost every act of usurpation of power, or of bad faith, has been conceived, brought forth and nurtured in *secret session*." To grant the Confederate government the power to detail men was the "essence of military despotism."

The heart of the message centered on what the governor considered the two most pressing issues facing Georgia and the Confederacy. In suspending habeas corpus on the *"pretext* of a necessity,*"* Congress had "struck a fell blow at the liberties of the people" by establishing what amounted to a Confederate "star chamber." Brown's rhetoric implied the necessity for resistance, but he went no farther than urging the law's repeal. Turning to the peace question, he proposed that after each important Confederate battlefield victory the Davis administration should offer to begin negotiations.[4] He had repeated old arguments, mixing exaggeration with impractical solutions, but whatever its defects, the message showed that ideology and politics would thrust Brown to the forefront of any opposition movement.

That Brown was transparently ambitious, that Linton Stephens and Bob Toombs loathed Davis, and that the vice-president still sulked over losing influence in Richmond is undeniable. But for the Stephens brothers, political principles were not easily disposable commodities. More than many Confederates, they held to a pure vision of an alternative political culture based not on an amorphous, artificial nationalism but on a genuine, organic tradition of state, community, and individual liberties. Liberty was their polestar, and their notions of liberty were closely connected to the seasonal rhythms of country life—the free and easy relations with kinfolk, the respect of neighbors, the command of slaves. Suspension of habeas corpus meant giving away something too priceless to be sacrificed, and the possibility of peace held out at least a glimmering hope of preserving what they held most dear, the conservative dream of living one's life in a stable and familiar world. That this dream was a delusion hardly made it less real or their commitment to a vanishing way of life less sincere or less tragic.

Jefferson Davis understood all this, but now his nationalism had become more important than his commitment to the idealized liberty of classical republicanism, and the views of his Georgia supporters had evolved in a similar fashion. In an address to the General Assembly in Milledgeville, Howell Cobb, who had often clashed with the vice-president and detested Brown, defended Congress and the president while upholding the suspension of habeas corpus and other recently enacted measures. As the commander of Confederate troops in Georgia, he appeared insensitive to the opposition's passionate commitment to liberty. During the debate on the habeas corpus and peace resolutions introduced by Linton Stephens, Cobb had free access to the House and Senate floor—a dangerous mixing of civil and military authority, according to republican political theory. Privately, he cursed Brown as a "tory" and a "traitor" who should be hanged.[5] Yet Cobb, like Brown, never lost sight of the political stakes involved in this highly charged debate and was eager to reduce the governor's political influence in Georgia.

Joining Cobb in lobbying against resolutions they considered incendiary, Confederate senator Ben Hill assured Aleck Stephens that the president would use his emergency powers sparingly and that the passage of the congressional habeas corpus act by itself should be enough to discourage traitors. Hill disingenuously claimed to agree with Stephens and Brown on the issues involved but at the same time refused to attack the president. Citing the moderation of men such as Vance in North Carolina, Hill hoped that the Georgians would not cause more division in Confederate ranks.[6] Like his colleague Herschel Johnson, Hill was searching for a political common ground, but his words papered over real ideological and political differences.

For Alexander Stephens, any accommodation would only weaken the republic, and he therefore had no choice but to break publicly with the Confederate administration and the president. In an extraordinary three-hour speech to the legislature on the evening of March 16, the vice-president carefully outlined his position. Allowing Davis to make "arbitrary arrests" and to draft state officials conferred on him more power than the English Parliament had ever bestowed on the king. History proved the dangers of such unchecked authority.

Although most of Stephens's speech was taken up with painstakingly dry constitutional arguments, he briefly acknowledged the political stakes involved. The Confederate government intended to suppress the peace meetings in North Carolina, he warned, and "put a muzzle upon certain presses" (i.e., the *Raleigh Standard*) in order to control elections in that state. Doubtless most Tar Heels remained loyal, but if there were traitors there, they could easily be arrested without suspending the writ. Using a favorite analogy of the states'-rights forces, Stephens urged Georgians to protest the latest threat to liberty just as the Virginia and Kentucky legislatures had remonstrated against the Alien and Sedition Acts. The remedy for usurpation remained a pristinely traditional and republican one, thus allowing Stephens to stand as a guardian of both liberty and the Confederacy.

Echoing Patrick Henry by asserting that life without liberty was worse than death, Stephens concluded his address with a stark but moving peroration. The Southern people should never view liberty as "subordinate to independence" because the cry of "independence first and liberty second" was a "fatal delusion." For Stephens, the essence of patriotism, the heart of the Confederate cause, rested on an unyielding commitment to traditional rights.[7] In this idealist vision of politics, military necessity, pragmatism, and compromise meant nothing.

Although some editors and many citizens welcomed Stephens's speech, in Georgia and across the Confederacy there was far more criticism than praise. That Stephens had joined the "factious" and opportunistic Brown greatly disappointed his longtime admirers. Naturally the president's friends roundly condemned the speech as both doctrinaire and divisive, but even the *Richmond Examiner* chastised the vice-president for not realizing that the press was as free as ever to criticize the government and that the Confederacy had done a remarkable job of safeguarding civil liberties in wartime.[8]

The address signally failed to win over moderates. Even before he had seen a full text, Herschel Johnson deplored its "rashness" and maintained that the real threat to liberty came from the Northern armies and "counterrevolutionaries" in Georgia and North Carolina. After carefully reading Stephens's speech, Johnson concluded that his friend had "allowed your antipathy to Davis to mislead your judgment." The greatest danger was that the "schism at home will extend to the army." Saddened and baffled that Johnson could not grasp the horror of suspending habeas corpus, Stephens denied personal hostility to the president or any interest in forming an antiadministration party. Yet he readily admitted regarding Davis as "weak and vacillating, timid, petulant, peevish, obstinate, but not firm" and had even come to doubt the man's "good intentions." Convinced that the president aimed at dictatorship, Stephens felt enough "hostility and wrath . . . to burst ten thousand bottles."[9]

A closer look at Linton's resolutions, however, indicated that the Stephenses had not entirely abandoned their Whiggish dread of political upheaval. Based on traditional libertarian arguments, the resolutions calmly asserted that restoring the writ of habeas corpus would encourage Northern opposition to Lincoln. Like Brown's message, the so-called peace resolutions included a long historical defense of the Southern cause and then called for a "just and honorable" peace based on the principles of the American Revolution. Despite their general and innocuous wording, the habeas corpus resolutions barely squeaked through the legislature. Even some Davis men could endorse the vaguely worded peace resolutions, and they were adopted by roughly two-to-one majorities in both houses.[10] As it turned out, the political symbolism of the resolutions far exceeded their bland substance.

The legislative session had satisfied no one, and tempers grew short. Brown was accused of bribing legislators with low-priced cotton cards and the opportunity to exchange depreciated Confederate currency for more valuable Georgia treasury notes. Hotly refuting these charges, friendly editors defended the governor. Melodramatic as usual, Toombs stood willing to "give Mr. Davis an early opportunity to make me a victim by advising resistance, resistance to the death, to his law." The would-be martyr now compared the president to a Roman emperor and could only hope that courageous men such as Brown and Aleck Stephens would stand against the tide of consolidation and preserve an undefiled republic. The Georgia movement, one South Carolinian enthused, "will tend to purify an atmosphere reeking with the filth of political corruption."[11]

Such rhetoric heightened the contrast between the two political cultures. The vice-president continued to fume about violations of individual liberty and deeply regretted that Congress had not fought harder against suspending habeas corpus. In that fashion, "this monster evil . . . might have been expelled and driven from our Eden!" This assertion, however, revealed a fundamental contradiction in opposition thinking. These politicians idealized free and independent citizens but also complained of the Southern people's willingness to fit their necks to a tyrant's yoke. Even after the legislature had adopted his resolutions, Linton Stephens doubted that members had enough courage to save the Confederacy from "absolutism" because pusillanimous politicians were always cowed by executive power.[12]

There was widespread criticism of the opposition movement for being irresponsible and factious. Some editors described Alexander Stephens as "vindictive" and "malignant." Brown, however, was the chief culprit. This "aspiring demagogue," who numbered disloyal croakers among his faithful friends, the *Edgefield Advertiser* declared, "deserves the infamy of a traitor."[13] In Georgia and across the Confederacy, Stephens's and Brown's names became synonymous with irresponsible factiousness.

These controversies inevitably spilled over into the army, where both sides assiduously courted support. Atlanta reporter Henry Watterson arranged for the distribution of excerpts from the vice-president's speech to Georgia soldiers. At a cost of over three thousand dollars, the governor sent copies of this document and the Stephens resolutions to the clerk of courts in each county and to the captains in every Georgia regiment.[14]

Despite these efforts, several regimental meetings adopted resolutions condemning political dissension in general and Brown in particular. The governor detected the hand of his old enemy Cobb in the controversy, and the general undoubtedly influenced several brigades. Brown accused officers of angling for promotions by supporting the Davis administration but was confident that enlisted men remained true defenders of liberty. According to Linton Stephens, most soldiers on both sides now favored a negotiated peace, and only West Pointers and unscrupulous profiteers wished to continue the war.[15]

There is little doubt that military pressure stalled Brown's anti-Davis offensive and gave the president's friends renewed confidence. Speaking at the Athenaeum in Atlanta, on April 14, 1864, L. Q. C. Lamar roundly criticized the Georgia opposition and especially Joe Brown. In a rousing defense of the Davis administration and Congress, he exposed a large hole in libertarian thinking: "The doctrine that no power must be exercised which is liable to abuse would put an end to all human government."[16] The activities of Hill, Lamar, and Cobb infuriated Brown, and he accused Cobb of seeking the presidency by organizing a "Consolidation party" in the legislature. In an exchange of harsh invective, Brown even suggested that Cobb had shown physical cowardice in the face of the enemy.[17] Brown's frustration was transparent. The legislature remained hostile, and neither the habeas corpus nor the peace resolutions had exactly been telling blows against the Davis administration.

The Georgia movement had foundered on the deep political divisions in the state and its failure to generate popular enthusiasm by speaking to people's tangible needs. The Stephens brothers had placed too much emphasis on legalisms to make a successful appeal to the Georgia yeomanry. Brown balked at stirring class resentments and presented his opinions far more vigorously in correspondence than in public statements. After the legislature adopted a resolution expressing confidence in Jefferson Davis, the governor petulantly refused to send it along to Richmond.[18] Yet Brown and his supporters would not join the North Carolina peace movement. Without an endorsement of separate state action, their position remained nebulous because they could not work with the Davis administration nor could they give up on the Confederacy. Their opposition proved far more divisive than effective.

Through all the talk of constitutionalism, there persisted a parochialism that could not be concealed behind a smoke screen of high principle; or perhaps localism and libertarianism were simply inseparable. Ambition, patronage, and the interests of cliques both inside and outside the army continued to make Confederate politics fractious. To whatever degree Confederates embraced the antiparty ideals of eighteenth-century republicanism, longing for an idyllic past or searching for a somehow pristine politics had not eliminated office-seeking or the desire for political power. From Richmond, to the state capitals, to the armies themselves, a persistent contentiousness characterized public life.

The question of drafting state officials was a case in point. Beginning in 1863, several state legislatures passed laws shielding civil officials and militia officers from conscription. North Carolina specifically protected justices of the peace, county trustees, county solicitors, registers, tax collectors, deputy sheriffs (one per county), deputy clerks (one for each court), coroners, constables, militia and home guard officers, mayors, and police. If this list seemed comprehensive, it was. When Mississippi lawmakers attempted to identify those officials *not* exempted, they could only come up with commissioners of relief, liquor dispensers, asylum trustees, overseers of roads, and deputy clerks of court. State courts generally upheld the constitutionality of these statutory limitations on national authority. North Carolina Supreme Court justice William H. Battle, who had sided with the Davis administration in various habeas corpus cases, nevertheless ruled that the Confederate government could not draft state officials because doing so would destroy the state government.[19]

With courthouse rings and local nabobs still wielding considerable power in the states, exempting various minor officials made political sense. So when a Vance or a Brown proclaimed dedication to constitutional principle, they also curried favor with the influential and wealthy men who dominated county government. Small wonder that governors routinely asserted their right to define which officials could not be spared.[20] Many of their "vital" services were of course political ones.

So, too, the persistent conflict over habeas corpus was as much a struggle over power as over principle. And if the libertarians strongly defended individual, local, and state autonomy, the more extreme nationalists favored an unprecedented expansion of centralized power. Many advocates of habeas corpus suspension now embraced constitutional theories that would have horrified them only a few years earlier. Congressman William C. Rives of Virginia eloquently discussed the evolution of constitutional interpretation and chastised men like Alexander Stephens for sanctifying musty precedents and fossilizing the legal process—a curious line of reasoning for a onetime Unionist Whig. But party labels had lost much of their meaning and force. Although the Mississippi legislature had called for repealing the habeas corpus act, the staunch Democrat Albert Gallatin Brown refused to recognize the right of instruction and urged the people to secure the independence of the Southern states before arguing about states' rights.[21]

If for nationalists, Jefferson Davis remained the Confederate Washington, to libertarians he seemed more like George III. Fear of power, along with a certain nostalgia for a loosely knit federal system resembling the old Articles of Confederation, contributed to the harsh, sometimes personal, attacks on the president. The rumors grew wilder. Davis was a traitor at heart; he had become a worse despot than the Russian czar; his family was profiting from the blockade. The *Richmond Examiner* even opposed an appropriation of additional money for light and fuel in the executive mansion: "Here is a door which opens on the universe of corruption."[22] Yet the authority of this would-be tyrant appeared to be declining, and he seemed to be losing control over military strategy.

A still unsettled and often chaotic command structure, along with Davis's often prickly relations with several generals, meant that military policy often lacked both direction and forcefulness. With Bragg gone and Johnston in command, morale in the Army of Tennessee improved, but old problems persisted. Informing Wigfall that rumors about his reluctance to launch an offensive were false, Johnston blamed the government's failure to send reinforcements and claimed that the army remained loyal to him despite the lack of support from "our high civil functionaries."[23] Even with growing public impatience and demands for a more aggressive strategy, the general retained powerful friends in Richmond and throughout the Confederacy.

During the spring and summer of 1864, Johnston typically kept his own counsel. The closer the Army of Tennessee moved to Atlanta, the greater the pressure on him not only to reveal his plans but to act. His suggestion for a cavalry raid against Sherman's supply lines had merit, and his Fabian policy—if carried on long enough without abandoning too much territory—

might have encouraged Northern peace men and even made the Northern presidential election a much closer contest. But time was running out.

Ben Hill and several congressmen tried to impress upon Johnston the necessity of holding Atlanta. On hearing rumors that the president was again thinking about taking the field, Johnston snapped, "I know Mr. Davis thinks he can do a great many things other men would hesitate to attempt. For instance, he tried to do what God failed to do. He tried to make a soldier of Braxton Bragg, and you know the result. It couldn't be done." Forgetting for the moment his own longtime support for Bragg, Johnston felt pressed not only by Sherman but by his critics in Richmond and his own generals.[24]

Unfortunately, he had not been able to end the notorious factionalism in the Army of Tennessee. Recently appointed corps commander John B. Hood, for example, complained about Johnston's unwillingness to fight. According to the aggressive and impetuous Hood, who never gave much thought to logistics, terrain, or planning, Johnston had missed several opportunities to destroy Sherman's army. Likewise, in a letter to the president, Lieutenant General William Hardee exaggerated the army's recent losses and implied that Johnston would retreat indefinitely.[25]

When Davis learned from Bragg and Ben Hill that Atlanta might soon be evacuated, he decided that Johnston had to go. Davis asked Lee's opinion on a replacement and specifically inquired about Hood. With his usual circumspection, Lee expressed regret over Johnston's evident shortcomings, and his endorsement of Hood ("good fighter, very industrious on the battlefield, careless off") was qualified at best. With no way of assessing Hood's ability to command an army, Lee simply commended his former subordinate's "gallantry, earnestness, [and] zeal." On July 17, 1864, the adjutant general sent the order relieving Johnston and appointing Hood the new commander of the Army of Tennessee.[26]

With the enemy on their doorsteps, the Georgians were caught in the middle. Whoever was in command, the Army of Tennessee needed reinforcements to stop Sherman. The Brown faction naturally accused the Davis administration of neglecting their state in favor of Virginia, but even Howell Cobb was shaken by news of Johnston's removal. Admitting that Johnston might have abandoned Atlanta, Cobb nevertheless retained some "confidence" in him and regretted the change in command.[27]

Indeed, despite his lackluster performance, Johnston still had a surprising number of ardent admirers. His departure was but the latest example of what the *Examiner* termed the government's tendency to "paralyze military genius," and Jefferson Davis was squarely to blame for the troubles in the Army of Tennessee. Some politicians could barely express their outrage, and Wigfall advised Hood not to accept the command. Quickly moving to supply the "facts" to friendly congressmen, Johnston claimed that Sherman had advanced toward Atlanta more slowly than Grant had moved toward Petersburg. With some justification, he accused Bragg and Hood of undermining his command.[28] Yet everyone recognized the real target of these attacks, and for Jefferson Davis the political costs were substantial.

The continuing woes in the Army of Tennessee had taken their toll on public confidence without giving Confederates any more appreciation for the war's larger picture. During Johnston's retreat toward Atlanta, state politicians still insisted on defending their own bailiwicks (and prerogatives). Although Davis could survive disparate and disorganized opposition, disaffection grew along with cries for peace. As the Confederacy shrank, citizens' sense of the cause more than ever narrowed to their own states and communities. This contraction of civic vision was more than a crabbed libertarianism; it represented an increasingly widespread disillusionment with the Confederate experiment.

In North Carolina, the peace forces had begun to gather strength against a governor who had mastered the rules of the Confederate political game. "The future darkens, and I can see no ray of hope. It is now apparent that North Carolina must soon look to herself. The power that made war can alone close it. The power of the sovereign States. Our next elections will turn on the question of a State convention. You well know where to find me on such a question."[29] Thus William W. Holden outlined to fellow Conservative Thomas Settle what would become the central theme in North Carolina and indeed in Confederate politics. At the beginning of 1864, Holden appeared a curious mix of dissent, cantankerousness, and ambition. His self-confidence, however, would betray him, and his political instincts would fail. Holden overestimated the strength of the peace movement, underestimated Zebulon Vance, and overplayed his political hand.

Despite their growing reputation for disloyalty, North Carolinians remained more divided than disaffected. According to one Tar Heel stationed in Virginia, "ignorant persons advise desertion" and had "been instructed by the pernicious teachings of Holden and others." Like other die-hard Confederates, he considered leaders of the peace movement nothing but traitors. Similar denunciations of "Tories" contained hints of class anxiety. David Schenck described the Unionists as "contemptible either by their ignorance, or generally, by their vicious character, such as never dared speak in times of peace."[30] So the peace movement not only threatened to destroy the Confederacy but also to unleash a political and social revolution in the states. Holden and his followers had raised the political stakes by their strong appeal to the disgruntled and at the same time aroused class anxieties among many members of both the Confederate and Conservative parties.

At the end of 1863 and the beginning of 1864, North Carolinians already anticipated a gubernatorial contest fought out on the peace question. Charging that subversive resolutions were being drafted in Holden's office for distribution to various counties, Vance encouraged editorial denunciations of "cowardly traitors." While strongly defending individual rights in speeches and state papers, the governor privately disparaged "platitudes" about civil liberty and military despotism.[31]

Politically, Vance was in an enviable position. Original secessionists might have to support him because they detested Holden. Moderate secessionists and Unionist Whigs alike favored a thorough canvass of the state to stop Holden, but such a strategy was tricky. On the one hand, Vance needed to court old political enemies who still saw him as little better than Holden, but on the other hand he wanted to retain the support of the more conciliatory peace men.[32]

In a brief campaign swing through the up-country in February, the governor condemned any movement to take North Carolina out of the Confederacy. If Lincoln refused to offer acceptable peace terms, the war would continue. Otherwise, peace meant nothing but subjugation, emancipation, and confiscation. Even though the war had been "badly managed," he still called for national unity. These hard truths met a lukewarm reception, but Vance was a vigorous campaigner, and his speeches often approached two hours in length.[33] The governor, crowed the *Raleigh Confederate*, had scotched a "dangerous movement" in the state. At many stops, the governor's humor and sly demagoguery made him a favorite with the crowds. As one observer noted, Vance seemed to be winning over the best of the Conservative party and leaving the worst elements with Holden.[34]

Yet Vance dared not embrace the secessionist Democrats too closely. During the late winter and early spring, the convention movement and Holden's editorials seemed to strike a responsive chord in North Carolina. Third District congressman James T. Leach introduced resolutions in Congress calling for a ninety-day armistice as a preliminary to a negotiated peace. By summer, he was supporting Holden and denouncing Vance.[35] Leach's cousin and fellow congressman James M. Leach followed a slightly different course. He favored a peace based on Confederate independence, disavowed submissionism, and refused to criticize Vance. To clarify his position further, he asked newspapermen to distinguish carefully between James M. Leach and James T. Leach in their reports.[36] And it was just such subtleties that produced cracks in the peace movement.

There were degrees of disaffection—some Conservatives pressed peace resolutions while others urged delay. In the spring, legislative candidates might boldly endorse a peace platform, but by early summer, with Lee holding off Grant in Virginia, they were scrambling to explain away disloyal-sounding statements. Even so staunch a Conservative and peace advocate as state treasurer Jonathan Worth insisted that North Carolina remain in the Confederacy.[37]

Rumors flew that the Davis administration intended to arrest Holden or at least suppress his newspaper. As a protest against the recently passed habeas corpus act, in late February, Holden suspended publication of the *Standard*; on March 3, he announced his candidacy for governor. Charging that Vance had abandoned the Conservative party for Davis and the "destructives" (thus becoming a latter-day John Tyler), Holden portrayed himself as the only true defender of civil liberties. In April, he resumed publication of the *Standard* with a clarion call for a state convention. But even a sympathetic observer admitted that Holden lacked Vance's "spirit, coolness, and singleness of purpose." He had never been an effective public speaker and stayed in Raleigh throughout the canvass.[38] Holden obviously felt betrayed by his onetime protégé, had given up on the Confederacy, and assumed that support for a convention would mushroom on its own.

According to the governor's friends, without the *Raleigh Standard* there would have been no peace meetings or political disaffection. Holden had become an agitator who, despite protestations to the contrary, was nothing but a submissionist, a men who would sell his soul for patronage or Yankee gold. In a letter to Vance written toward the end of the canvass, one irate citizen suggested that "you ought to have hung Holden long ere this." The very bitterness of such attacks also indicated fear that Holden might have considerable support; in early March, some advisers pressed Vance to defend states' rights more emphatically.[39]

Early reports of Holden's political strength, however, were highly exaggerated, and his desperation led to intemperate attacks on Vance. The governor had supposedly made a secret deal with "destructives" in North Carolina and elsewhere to destroy the Conservative party; he had reportedly skimmed money from the state's blockade running. Such wild charges did Holden little good and likely weakened his candidacy. Only a few prominent Conservatives endorsed him, and by summer he faced the prospect of a crushing defeat.[40]

Given their obvious advantages, the Vance forces took the political high road with appeals to patriotism and calls for an end to party squabbling. The governor cleverly played the middle against the extremes. Some editors even had a kind word or two for Jefferson Davis, but Vance also arranged for the publication of recent correspondence, in which he had advised Davis against suppressing dissent, to shore up his reputation as a staunch libertarian and to show that he had pressed the administration to make new peace offers. Secessionist Democrats admitted they had no choice but to support Vance, and many peace men gave him the benefit of the doubt.[41] This strategy drew careful distinctions between the candidates while keeping Vance's base of support as broad as possible. The governor was confident of his popularity both in the army and among former Whigs, who were the backbone of the Conservative party. Assured of support from many secessionists, the governor urged Secretary of War Seddon to suspend conscription in the mountain counties.[42]

In a message to a special session of the legislature on May 17, Vance criticized impressment, conscription, and the suspension of habeas corpus. Using conventional libertarian rhetoric, he was obviously bolstering his reputation as a defender of North Carolina interests against the encroachments of Confederate centralization. Yet he also denounced calls for a separate peace and again pointed to the dangers of internal strife. Striking a careful balance between national unity and individual liberty, the message was a finely crafted statement of centrist politics. Moderate without being bland, it carried a properly thoughtful and principled tone.[43] The legislature adopted resolutions echoing Vance's sentiments and offering an "indignant rebuke of every exhibition of factious temper." Shaken by what amounted to a stunning setback for the peace faction, Holden began backtracking from his support for separate state action.[44] Through carefully controlled criticism of the Davis administration and a generally conciliatory approach to the more moderate peace supporters, Vance had isolated the Holden faction.

The slow and reluctant conversion of Democratic secessionists heartened Vance but at the same time complicated the race for many Conservatives. Jonathan Worth's ambivalence toward the contest was typical. In a letter of July 7, he denied any hostility to Holden and even complained that Vance's reelection would strengthen the secessionists. He also feared that "the most reliable and zealous supporters of Gov. V. are the most ultra fire-eaters." Less than a week later, Worth noted that he would vote for Vance and still held out hope that conservative Whigs could moderate the governor's course. Although unwilling to endorse the governor publicly, Worth implicitly conceded that Holden had no chance of winning the governorship.[45] Many other North Carolinians shared his reluctance and fatalism, but their votes counted for Vance all the same.

As the campaign progressed, Holden appeared more like a dangerous extremist. Many North Carolina Conservatives and other Confederates who had no love for the Davis administration deprecated calls for a separate peace and dreaded the demoralizing effects of the convention movement. Internal divisions and disloyalty might yet ignite a civil war in North Carolina that would bring on emancipation and a racial Armageddon.[46] In late July, the *Raleigh Daily Confederate* carried screaming reports about the Heroes of America—a secret society of supposed Yankee collaborators pledged to vote for Holden. The origins of this group were murky, but it apparently was active in heavily Quaker counties and expressed great hostility to wealthy secessionists. Holden's connection to the Heroes was tenuous to say the least, and many "confessions" printed by pro-Vance editors were unsubstantiated.[47]

Yet the loyalty question surely helped Vance with the army vote. Not only did the several newspapers warn soldiers that Holden stood for subjugation and emancipation, but during the spring Vance visited North Carolina troops in their Virginia camps. On one occasion when Lee was present, the governor regaled his audience with Tar Heel anecdotes and warned of a counterrevolution if Holden were elected. Confederate officers often blamed Holden for public disaffection and claimed that only the most degraded conscripts would oppose Vance.[48]

Beginning in April, army meetings condemned the peace movement and called for Vance's reelection. Though worried about how the home folk would vote, many officers expressed great faith in their men's "loyalty." In reporting some forty-nine votes for Vance from one company in the First North Carolina Battalion of Sharpshooters, an enthusiastic soldier scrawled "Hurrah for Vance" across the bottom of the returns.[49] Holden had some support among the enlisted men, but his strength was hard to measure. If increases in desertion during the summer of 1864 were an accurate gauge, the peace movement might be gaining converts.

After hearing Vance address one North Carolina regiment, Private George Williams decided the governor was losing ground: "He wants to fight until hell freezes and then on the ice and we are not willing to fight so long as that think Mr. Holden is not for fighting that long and he is our choice by a large majority." Some soldiers reported that peace meetings had demoralized their comrades and that Holden might carry several regiments. The *Raleigh Standard* accused Vance supporters of intimidation and reminded voters to fold their tickets so no one could see them. Shortly before the election, Holden claimed that Confederate conscription officers were either arresting or refusing to detail his supporters.[50]

Back in North Carolina, reports of men being "forced" to vote for Vance in several counties appeared immediately after the election. Because the Vance ticket was yellow and the Holden ticket white it was hard to conceal one's allegiance. Confederate troops also may have crowded the polls to cow Holden supporters. According to some outraged observers, attractive women visiting the camps and hospitals tore up Holden tickets and tried to drum up support for Vance, but these accusations also suggested desperate efforts by the Holden forces to explain away their own poor showing.[51]

Whatever truth there was to these charges, and Holden voters may have been intimidated in some western counties, the election turned into a rout. Vance won an impressive victory: over 77 percent of the total vote and nearly 88 percent of the army vote. Secessionist Democrats along with many Conservatives supported the governor. Old party divisions had virtually disappeared; Holden had been crushed if not silenced. Secessionists could now cooperate with Vance and even declare an end to partisan warfare.[52]

Vance rejoiced that the people had rejected the siren call of a state convention and was heartened by the "unparalleled unanimity at the polls." Yet he also admitted that from the beginning politicians had been much more enthusiastic about the war than the people ever were and he could never stop second-guessing North Carolina's reluctant departure from the Union.[53] The election results showed that the strength of his political coalition depended on the ability of Confederate armies to hold on and the willingness of the Confederate administration to conciliate its more reasonable critics. By the time of the gubernatorial election, Petersburg was under siege, Atlanta had fallen, and Major General Philip H. Sheridan was advancing against Lieutenant General Jubal Early in the Shenandoah Valley. Perhaps Vance's triumph had only delayed the spread of disloyalty in North Carolina. Equally ominous, Holden now openly stated that reconstruction was preferable to subjugation and called for immediate peace negotiations.[54]

Loyal Confederates might celebrate the Vance victory as a stern rebuke to would-be traitors and unprincipled politicians, but the landslide also proved that the war had finally destroyed the customary patterns of political behavior in North Carolina. Old party loyalties may not have been dead, but they had become hopelessly confused. Democrats and Whigs alike had supported Vance, and if the governor was now the undisputed leader of the Conservative party, that coalition now included everyone from original secessionists to cooperationists to moderate peace advocates. The election results also signified a peculiar triumph for the contradictory values—unity and liberty—of the two political cultures even as the political center became harder to define. Indeed, Vance's victory was largely a personal one and a rebuke to Holden because the governor made no effort to bring his supporters into any moderate political organization. In many ways, the Conservative party survived in name only.

By late summer and fall, the limits of military endurance had nearly been reached; bad news from Georgia and the Shenandoah Valley along with a bloody stalemate at Petersburg resulted in cries for peace. The disheartened looked for threads of hope even as they lashed out in frustration against state and Confederate politicians. Yet even Joe Brown hesitated to organize a peace party in Georgia, spurned overtures for a parley with Sherman, refused to call a state convention, and firmly opposed a separate peace.[55]

In what remained of the Confederacy, the spread of disaffection and the formation of secret societies did not mean that the peace movement had become either more organized or more effective. For one thing, there was no agreement on acceptable terms. Could several states negotiate with their Northern counterparts? Would such discussions lead to a recognition of Southern independence, reconstruction, emancipation, or some unanticipated result? As Herschel Johnson pointed out, the Northern government had spurned all previous overtures and would not likely offer any terms save subjugation and confiscation.[56] So at the very time when war weariness was becoming widespread, uncertainty and disorganization left the Confederate government firmly in control of any diplomatic initiatives. The breakdown of parties and hostility to politicians weakened the opposition and the peace movement far more than it did the Davis administration.

Even veteran politicians found it impossible to build a workable political alliance in the face of antiparty attitudes and broad disagreement over the terms of an acceptable peace. In June 1864, Graham, Herschel Johnson, James L. Orr, newly elected South Carolina congressman William W. Boyce, and several others met in Richmond to discuss the peace question. Their determination to seek a settlement recognizing Southern independence differed little from the president's position. They papered over serious differences among themselves but suggested no practical means for achieving their goal.

Unhappy with such timidity and convinced that the Davis administration would yet ruin the country, Boyce sought assistance from Alabama, North Carolina, and Georgia congressmen as well as from Stephens, Brown, and Toombs. On September 29, the South Carolinian laid out his views in a public letter to the president. Warning that the Confederacy was steadily sinking toward "military despotism," Boyce called for an immediate armistice and a convention of Northern and Southern states to negotiate a settlement. The response was disappointing. Public meetings in South Carolina adopted resolutions condemning Boyce as a reconstructionist. For once, even the *Charleston Mercury* and the *Charleston Courier* agreed: a convention would mean capitulation to the Yankees.[57]

Despite its broad general appeal, Boyce's widely circulated letter caused considerable confusion. An Alabama editor hoped that calling a convention might divide the North and in any case would do no harm. Yet he also believed that the states could do nothing, that the president would do nothing, and that it was up to Congress to pursue peace negotiations. One wildly optimistic Georgian conceded that the Confederacy probably could not hang on to (as if it had ever controlled) Missouri, Kentucky, or Maryland.[58] Because the success of any diplomatic maneuver often depends on small details, Confederates naturally spent considerable time discussing the fine points of Boyce's proposal. There were obvious constitutional difficulties with states discussing peace terms and in effect usurping the national government's diplomatic authority. But for the Stephens brothers and others who favored a convention of the states, this question cut in a different direction. The vice-president maintained that the individual states would have to ratify any agreement reached by a convention. Firmly committed to state sovereignty, he also believed that a state could secede from the Confederacy. To deny such a right, his brother Linton declared, "is cant invented to serve the purpose of usurpation and consolidation."[59]

These arguments revealed the inextricable link between the peace movement and the politics of liberty. Even in desperate times, libertarians clung to their faith in constitutional procedures and could never quite admit that the times were so out of joint that what they considered vitally important legal points might appear perversely irrelevant to their despairing fellow citizens. Even the most fervent peace advocates could not escape these ideological snares. Such procedural debates divided the peace movement and weakened opposition to the Davis administration's war policies.

Despite sagging morale, public skepticism about any negotiated settlement remained strong. Many patriots still believed that only Southern arms could bring a just peace—that the Confederacy must still rely on the generalship of Lee or Hood.[60] Denunciations of the idea of a separate peace spread across the political spectrum. Allies of the Davis administration as well as chronic malcontents attacked the convention movement. Several editors dismissed the Boyce letter and other peace initiatives as thinly disguised proposals for reconstruction. According to one Georgian, only a tenth of the people would support such propositions, and the loyal majority favored fighting on to the "bitter end."[61] The vehemence of these responses, however, showed how many Confederates feared that Boyce and other peace advocates were gaining support.

These worries caused some inveterate opponents of the Davis administration to denounce the convention movement in unmeasured language. Boyce had advanced a "monstrous proposal," claimed the *Richmond Examiner*. Peace overtures would be seen as signs of weakness, and in any case Southerners could never rely on the promises of Northern Democrats. The *Charleston Mercury* even accused the vice-president of constitutional apostasy. To Rhett, any attempt to draw a historical parallel between the Constitutional Convention of 1787 and a proposed convention of the states would be as illogical as it was subversive.[62]

"Subversive" was the right word because behind the peace movement there were growing signs of class bitterness. In Richmond, reports circulated of cabinet members and other high officials dining on expensive delicacies while soldiers' families starved. The wealthy had their sons detailed to farms or plantations, leaving the poor and sickly to man the Petersburg trenches. Mary Chesnut wryly suggested that certain members of Congress be shot from cannon as the British had done with the sepoys in

India.[63] Talk of class warfare would only cause more divisions in the peace movement.

With Sherman's army in Atlanta, the Davis administration found little comfort in the opposition's apparent disarray. The president was clearly worried about the spread of disloyalty and hurriedly undertook another speaking tour to bolster public morale. Arriving at Macon, Georgia, with no advance notice on September 22, he spoke to a hastily assembled crowd. Davis asserted that Sherman could not possibly maintain such a long line of communication and would soon have to withdraw from Georgia just as Napoleon had retreated from Russia. After offering this wildly optimistic prediction, the president turned on his critics. The defense of Georgia had not been neglected whatever that "miserable man" (Joe Brown) might say. With still another jolting change of theme, Davis made a most damning admission. In a statement that must have shocked the audience, he disclosed that some two-thirds of all Confederate soldiers on the rolls were absent without leave.[64] The president's astonishing performance did little to bolster public confidence, and anyone reading newspaper accounts of the speech would have every reason to despair of the Confederacy.

At Montgomery, Alabama, Davis presented a much different address. Summoning all able men to "the front," he maintained that recent military setbacks should only lead to redoubled determination. In a later speech at Augusta, Georgia, the president offered a more detached, historical analysis of the crisis. Despite limited resources, the Confederacy had created an army and had "stemmed the tide of invasion." Denying once again that the Southern people were radical revolutionaries, Davis recalled the conservative foundations of Confederate nationalism. "We are not engaged in a Quixotic fight for the rights of man; our struggle is for inherited rights." The cause remained grounded in the local and the particular as opposed to the universal and the ideological. In a convoluted passage, Davis hinted that the people should support him and the generals regardless of their mistakes.[65] This forlorn appeal to both nationalists and libertarians was awkward at best and certainly came too late.

The president was unfortunately delivering several different messages to several different audiences, and his analysis of the conflict had become as fragmented as Confederate politics itself. Traveling to Columbia in the heart of South Carolina, Davis may well have dimly perceived the failure of this last push to rekindle patriotism. Desperation gave his words a dangerously unrealistic quality. Promising that Sherman would be defeated and Lee would hold on to Petersburg, he claimed that the government was well able to supply the army and that the Southern countryside held "teeming evidences of plenty." Downplaying general hardship and ignoring chronic food shortages, he once more recalled the tradition of the revolutionary fathers, whose patriotic examples might still fire Southern hearts. But by this time, despair and exhaustion were taking their toll on the president. Toward the end of his speech in Columbia, Davis sounded alternately resigned and exasperated. If the worst should happen, "it is the fate of all human designs," and in any event, Southerners were determined to "live or die free." In a singularly inappropriate conclusion to an overlong speech, Davis sarcastically proposed that armchair military critics should now head for the front, where their superior wisdom would surely bring victories. Although a vast throng crowded around to shake the president's hand, careful listeners must have been shaken by the speech's dissonant elements, and the aftermath was equally disturbing. The generosity of Columbia's upper crust allowed the president and his party to sip sixty-year-old Madeira while eating boned turkey with truffles accompanied by stuffed tomatoes and stuffed peppers.[66] This was no time for Davis to appear oblivious to the desperate straits of ordinary citizens.

The anomaly illustrated the nagging contradictions between an official ideology of shared sacrifice and the reality of class stratification. Even what one observer described as the president's forceful and measured tone of address suggested the dignity of a haughty planter, not the fire of a revolutionary leader. And perhaps Davis's unbending commitment to his own vision of Confederate nationalism—raised to a level of high abstraction—made his rhetoric seem cold, brittle, and abstruse. Critics considered the entire tour, and especially the Macon speech, demoralizing. Even sympathetic commentators believed that the president's statements had revealed too much about the Confederacy's serious weaknesses.[67]

Yet for all his clumsiness and uncertainty, Davis remained a respected if not exactly beloved leader, and continuing public support for the president along with still intense antiparty feelings frustrated the opposition. Administration critics complained that Davis benefited from a subservient, hireling press. Herschel Johnson assumed that some editors "trim their course to suit what they may suppose will please the administration or to obtain patronage or retain what they have." Perhaps Johnson was simply amazed that the president seemed to be holding his own against spreading disaffection and disloyalty. Even Robert Toombs considered Davis "impregnable on the peace issue." Temporarily muting his differences with the administration during a swing through eastern and southern Texas,

Louis Wigfall defended conscription, impressment, and recently enacted tax measures.[68] Some Confederates even discovered grounds for hope in the military situation. By late September and early October, Lee had prevented Grant from breaking through at Petersburg and Hood was maneuvering to cut Sherman's supply line from Chattanooga.

But many Confederates realized that they were experiencing a lull before the military campaign season began again in earnest. Whether the greatly outnumbered Lee could hold off Grant and what if anything might halt or even delay Sherman's advance through Georgia were the great unresolved questions. And Early's forces in the Shenandoah Valley had been hit hard by Sheridan. At best, political demoralization had abated only temporarily, and the tone of public life deteriorated. In Richmond, rumors spread of a counterrevolution. Although even the Rhetts deplored loose talk of coups and dictatorships, a disheartened North Carolinian wrote to Stephens that the president's "life was a burden to the Confederacy and a curse to our people."[69]

Such ugly remarks suggested how far the level of discourse had plummeted. The decline of civility, the unraveling of the social, economic, and political fabric of a young nation both appalled and fascinated Confederates. Factionalism in the military high command combined with the intense and often destructive political conflicts in Richmond, Georgia, and North Carolina widened the gap between the political cultures but also increased demands for at least a show of public harmony. Zebulon Vance and his supporters perhaps believed they had discovered the proper balance between the extremes, but even centrist politics showed signs of disintegration and the peace movement was far from dead.

CHAPTER 14

National Identity, the Political Cultures, and War's End

On October 26, 1864, Jefferson Davis issued a proclamation calling for a day of national worship, but whether God still considered Southerners His chosen people had become a deeply troubling question. Although the president affirmed his faith in divine protection, he also acknowledged that "our sins have merited and received grievous chastisement." There was still time for the people to repent, offer God the glory for any victories, and win back the Almighty's indispensable favor. Indeed, in the midst of demoralization and the distractions of camp life, religious revivals continued in the Confederate armies during the winter and spring.[1] National sin offered a convenient theological explanation for the anguish and despair of the war's final months.

In the tradition of evangelical Protestantism, ministers regularly lashed their congregations about their individual and collective transgressions. Increasingly, however, the jeremiads revealed cleavages over the nature of Confederate political culture. Alabama Episcopal bishop Richard Wilmer claimed that "the leveling doctrines of human equality, which tend downward to the gulf of Atheism, are disappearing before the stern reality that some men are 'born to honor.' "[2] This defense of hierarchy ignored the class resentments and social divisions that had disrupted military and civilian life. Wilmer's words sounded quaintly anachronistic and suggested the persistence of dangerous delusions.

Political opposition, and especially libertarian politics, had called into question old myths of economic, social, and political harmony. But political conflicts had not fostered political organization. Instead, the military crisis, bitter quarrels between the president and Congress, and even arguments about the future of slavery created a politics of recrimination. The political turmoil caused by the clash of political cultures and especially by the peace question remained heavily ideological but also involved no small amount of personal acrimony, all within an antiparty framework.

Although Davis's recent tour had temporarily stymied the convention movement, the approach of the Northern presidential election brought new hopes for a negotiated settlement. Worrying that too many Southerners might still place their trust in foreign intervention or promises offered by Northern Democrats, Bishop Stephen Elliott of Georgia argued that Lincoln's reelection was a "necessity for our deliverance." Only the Yankee president's "fanaticism" combined with "such fury as Grant's, such cruelty as Butler's, such fanaticism as Sherman's . . . [could] revive our courage, and reanimate our efforts."[3] For all its sincere patriotism, this strange argument showed a tenuous grasp of military and political reality.

At the other extreme, some Confederates saw the nomination of George B. McClellan and the Democrats' peace platform as a godsend. A hopeful Mississippian foresaw a peace settlement restoring confiscated property, preserving slavery, extending the Missouri Compromise line, repealing the emancipation measures, and providing "equality under the old Constitution."[4] Some Georgia leaders speculated that Lincoln's defeat could compensate for Confederate economic and military weaknesses. Vice-President Stephens and others talked vaguely of state sovereignty as a basis for peace. Yet the terms of any negotiated settlement remained as nebulous as ever. Did McClellan's Southern supporters favor a reconstruction of the Union? Would state conventions dismantle the Confederacy before McClellan could even be inaugurated? What about the future of slavery?[5] Few Confederates had clear answers to these questions, and in any case, Lincoln's reelection appeared inevitable after the fall of Atlanta.

McClellan's defeat forced the Georgia opposition's political hand. In an impassioned message to the legislature, Joe Brown finally came out for a convention of the states. "Confederate independence with centralized power without State sovereignty and Constitutional and religious liberty, would be very little better than subjugation," he thundered. People on both sides should pressure their governments to stop the bloodshed because "statesmen terminate wars by negotiation." As the Georgia legislature debated peace resolutions, more meetings were held, and rumors spread that counties were seceding from the Confederacy. Yet Lincoln's reelection probably weakened the peace movement and temporarily stifled the anti-Davis faction. The Georgia legislature voted down all peace resolutions by solid majorities in both houses and in effect rebuffed Brown again.[6] Despite the Confederacy's desperate circumstances, political support for the national government held steady.

Even in North Carolina, the peace movement appeared to be losing ground. Though secessionists worried that Vance would conciliate the disaffected, the battle still raged between the "crookeds" (Vance supporters) and the "straights" whose doctrinaire views on civil liberties and peace had given North Carolinians a reputation for disloyalty. In another setback for the Holden faction, the General Assembly elected moderate Whig Thomas S. Ashe, who in 1863 had been defeated for reelection to Congress by a peace candidate, to the Confederate Senate.[7]

As in Georgia, the legislature rejected all peace proposals. Even William A. Graham, who deplored Davis's foot-dragging on peace negotiations, feared that a convention of the states would only divide Confederates and strengthen the enemy. Although Holden was rumored to be planning a call for a state convention in May to bring North Carolina back into the Union, he still would not publicly endorse a separate peace. Vance spurned overtures from Joe Brown for fear of precipitating "another revolution." Believing that Davis would soon seek peace on some reasonable basis, Vance suggested that Georgia defer to North Carolina and Virginia rather than negotiating directly with the Federals.[8]

Outside Georgia and the Holden strongholds in North Carolina, proposals for a convention of the states attracted little support. Aside from constitutional problems, an irregularly negotiated peace settlement threatened to revolutionize Southern society. Anything short of Confederate independence would be "dishonorable," declared Florida governor John Milton, because the Yankees would destroy the entire "social fabric." Enemy armies threatened not only to conquer the South but also to reshape class and race relations. Louisiana governor Henry Watkins Allen warned that black men would soon be sitting in the Northern Congress and cabinet.[9] Only the survival of the Confederate nation could prevent the moral and political contamination of the South. There must be no reunion with

Massachusetts "fanaticism" and John Brown supporters, declared Alabama governor Thomas Hill Watts.[10]

The peace movement never became organized enough to exert widespread and effective political pressure. Although more former Whigs and Unionists sat in the Second Congress, representatives from occupied districts and states served as a counterbalance. Defeatism occasionally cropped up in floor debates and private discussions, but there remained a grim determination to see the war through to its ineluctable end.[11]

Of course, peace resolutions—some drafted with the help of the vice-president—were never in short supply. On November 19, 1864, a brief debate in the House set the tone for the rest of the session. According to James T. Leach, a "great hue and cry" had been raised because Joe Brown and Alexander Stephens "dared to differ from the anointed [Davis]." If members considered such sentiments "treason," Leach asked the "poor privilege of being hanged for it." In aping Patrick Henry, Leach appealed to the central values of libertarian politics. But talk of peace and reconstruction angered many loyal Confederates. Waller R. Staples of Virginia, a former Whig who had usually opposed administration policies, castigated Leach for fearing "Confederate consolidation" more than "Yankee despotism."[12]

The more prominent Leach's role in the debate, the less likely that Congress would act. Perhaps realizing his own impotence and under attack from several newspapers, Leach lashed out at his critics and even suggested that the government break up the offices of the *Richmond Examiner* and "hang them [the editors] by the neck until they were DEAD, DEAD, DEAD!" When Leach introduced peace resolutions vaguely based on a recognition of property rights and the reserved rights of the states, only two of his North Carolina colleagues opposed tabling the motions. One of them, Josiah Turner, Jr., privately admitted that he would not have supported Leach's resolutions had they come to a vote.[13]

Turner wanted the president to appoint thirteen commissioners (one for each state represented in the Confederate Congress) to negotiate with Northern representatives. North Carolinians did not oppose the government, he asserted, only the Davis administration. To the president's friends, this was a distinction without a difference. Ethelbert Barksdale of Mississippi noted that Confederate peace overtures had already been rebuffed and introduced a resolution defiantly calling on the people to persevere in their fight for national independence. Many administration critics agreed. The horrors of military occupation and reconstruction, most congressmen sadly conceded, left only one choice—to continue fighting until the Lincoln government offered reasonable terms of settlement.[14]

On January 12, 1865, Congressman Jehu A. Orr of Mississippi—a Confederate nationalist who had often criticized Davis and had conferred with Alexander Stephens—reported a resolution out of the House Committee on Foreign Affairs calling on the president to appoint three commissioners from each house to begin informal talks with the Lincoln administration. In a close vote, the House postponed consideration of Orr's resolutions.[15] What Congress expected from the president or from any negotiations with the Federals was not clear. Daniel C. de Jarnette of Virginia speculated that the Northern government would recognize Confederate independence in exchange for a joint expedition to drive the French out of Mexico.[16] This chimera cropped up in newspapers, diaries, and letters all over the Confederacy for the next several months, producing little besides turgid discussion of the Monroe Doctrine.

More than ever Congress became a great cave of the winds, with currents blowing in many directions. Williamson S. Oldham of Texas, a longtime administration opponent and states'-rights doctrinaire, deprecated talk of conventions and even claimed that the Confederacy had enough men, arms, and ammunition to carry on the war indefinitely. Subjugation would mean government by a "triumvirate consisting of the whining, canting, hypocritical Yankee, the red republican, infidel German, and the superior of the trio, the African negro." Southerners would suffer the "outrage and violation of their mothers, sisters, wives, and daughters, by brutalized negro soldiers, stationed in every town and city and quartered in the houses of the people to keep them in subjection and crush out the spirit of liberty." This statement of cultural chauvinism showed how the peace movement had failed to capture the libertarian opposition. Even the North Carolina delegation—the most disaffected in the entire Congress—split evenly over whether to support the convention movement.[17] The politics of peace had become the politics of fragmentation, dividing politicians who had once cooperated against the Confederate government and further weakening the political opposition. Congress refused to tie Davis's diplomatic hands but also failed to strengthen his political and military hands.

Instead of a last united effort against a common enemy, the war's final winter and spring brought a bitter reprise of shopworn debates on familiar political and military questions accompanied by a good deal of finger-pointing and invective. In the midst of all this factiousness, remarkably vigorous discussion took place about the nature of Confederate republicanism. At the same time, however, both nationalists and libertarians were frustrated by the breakdown of strategy and command.

Alarming rates of desertion made the demand for soldiers more urgent than ever and encouraged desperate proposals. Writing to a South Carolina country newspaper, "Peter the Hermit" recommended a "levee en masse" of all arms-bearing citizens to stop Sherman's inexorable march toward Savannah. Howell Cobb proposed forming new regiments to foster the spirit of volunteering—as if regimental organization mattered any longer. Many Southerners had given up on conscription, and the states increasingly looked to their own resources for local defense. South Carolina made all whites between the ages of sixteen and sixty subject to state service, an implicit threat that no more troops would be furnished for the Confederate army. The Georgia legislature, at the prompting of Joe Brown, insisted that the president accept battalions and regiments with elected officers. Finding that the "whole body politic is diseased," the governor remained obsessed with keeping Georgia soldiers under his control and limiting Davis's military authority.[18]

The president again called for an end to all class exemptions, asked for the power to detail men "essential to public service," and urged Congress to act quickly. Instead, lawmakers dawdled, restored previously eliminated exemptions, and refused to expand the president's power to detail men. Joe Brown blasted Davis for trying to "muzzle" both press and pulpit and promised to interpose the Georgia militia against "external assaults and internal usurpations." Edmund Ruffin feared that granting the president more discretion over manpower would "open a flood-gate for favoritism and falsehood and corruption." The *Richmond Examiner* even accused Davis of using the power to detail men for civilian employment to build up a "political party."[19] The political opposition remained sensitive to any sign of executive despotism and as committed as ever to antiparty ideology.

Congressional consideration of yet another habeas corpus bill (eventually passed by the House but blocked in the Senate) only added to these fears. The libertarian rhetoric grew more apocalyptic. Dire warnings about the death of the Constitution and the steady approach of tyranny gave this latest round of discussions a hyperbolic and almost surreal quality as Sherman prepared to march through the Carolinas and Grant tightened his grip on Petersburg. In language reminiscent of the 1790s, Virginian John H. Gilmer compared recent violations of civil liberties in the

South to the horrors of the French Revolution. Relying on several quotations from Edmund Burke, he foresaw a "death struggle for liberty" in which the Southern people might become "slaves" to their own government.[20] The words came from another century, but they evoked powerful fears in a slaveholders' republic.

National loyalty seemed to be fast disappearing as politicians scrambled to placate their angry constituents and perhaps preserve some remnants of their own power. Even South Carolina firebrands had turned lukewarm; in the birthplace of secession, talk of launching a counterrevolution showed how much Confederate and even state authority had evaporated. Newly elected Governor Andrew G. Magrath tried to persuade Joe Brown that the states could still lead the Confederate nation to victory, but only four days later he wrote to Jefferson Davis that a "paralysis of despair" had inundated every state, and "a chill will attend every effort, with which in vain you will attempt to remove or dispel the gloom." Those who believed that the army would survive the vast invasion "argue from their hopes, not from facts."[21] The painful process of coming to grips with the possibility (if not the certainty) of defeat prompted wishful thinking and self-deception, a curious amalgam of ambivalence, pain, and delusion, with an occasional dash of optimism.

In this psychologically charged atmosphere, people still had great faith in Lee, but Jefferson Davis was in danger of losing his status as the great symbol of the Confederate nation. Even members of the administration grumbled that the president had no policy, drifted from crisis to crisis, and listened to no one. His unwavering commitment to the cause ironically made him seem out of touch with the suffering, depressed, and disheartened populace.[22] Although he tried to be cordial with his political supporters, the president grew testy when anyone failed to share his optimism about Confederate prospects—including his peculiar notion that lost territory meant nothing because the Confederacy had no "vital points." Increasingly, the president hammered at his critics. The "brains and the heart of the country" should be represented in Congress, Davis believed, but the "bad conduct of those . . . [in official] position" had made it nearly impossible to "cultivate confidence and animate patriotism." Tired of hearing about soldiers reading the *Examiner* or the *Mercury*, Davis vetoed a law that provided for mailing newspapers to army camps postage free, but Congress for once overrode him. Increasingly, the president blamed others, especially Congress, for the nation's problems.[23]

The war brought out both the best and the worst in Jefferson Davis, magnifying both his strengths and weaknesses. Few dared question his patriotism, but the president could never separate himself from his nation, and his poor health made it more difficult to be flexible about policies or persons. The war had ravaged Davis and his family in many ways, but it did not do much to change Davis's personality, habits, or political attitudes. By so strongly identifying himself with the cause and failing to understand, much less benefit from, even the mildest criticisms, Davis lost the capacity to learn from experience. Instead of mellowing with age, he ossified; rather than becoming wiser, he became the brittle symbol of a collapsing revolution.

These final months accentuated reactionary tendencies in Confederate political thought. Perhaps republican government had failed, or maybe the Southern nation needed a monarch to counter the deadly heresy of political equality that had destroyed Rome, Greece, and France. Despite the reverence for constitutional limitations, states' rights, and popular sovereignty—all exemplified in a government resting on public consent—strict construction carried to extremes might undo the Confederate experiment. Irritated by what he deemed the hypocritical "men of the old federal school" raising the cry of "states' rights," Davis worried that supposed defenders of liberty would now "sink the States by the process of disintegration into imbecility and ultimate submission to Yankee despotism."[24]

Yet at the Confederacy's eleventh hour, a common but increasingly thin thread held together the nationalist and libertarian political cultures. That thread was antiparty ideology. Parties, Alexander Stephens still maintained, "are the curse and bane of republics." Jefferson Davis was equally convinced that "faction has done much to cloud our prospects and impair my power to serve the country." The president and vice-president would certainly have disagreed over who was to blame for keeping alive party spirit in the Confederacy, but they remained committed to the vision of the Southern nation's founding fathers. This is not to say that antiparty ideology held equal sway in both political cultures. Calls for unity came more naturally to ardent nationalists, and the persistent revulsion against political maneuvering made supporting the president easier. According to one editor, the "opposition [was] contemptible in numbers" and included not "one single man eminent for virtue and talent." From this perspective, Davis remained a model republican statesman, safeguarding the people's liberties from the Northern aggressors.[25] However adamantly they objected to such descriptions of the president, the libertarians and peace faction could not bring themselves to organize an opposition party.

But if Davis was to remain the Confederate Washington (or even share that distinction with Lee), he had to exert greater control over military strategy and personnel. In the winter and spring of 1865 that had become nearly impossible. During his recent speaking tour, Davis had consulted with John B. Hood about plans for an offensive into Tennessee. As usual, however, Hood ignored logistics and even avoided contact with his titular superior Beauregard; his divided and inefficient command was incapable of planning a campaign that required near perfect execution.[26]

Deciding that his officers and enlisted men had become enervated by entrenchments and had shown signs of cowardice, the intrepid Hood soon tested their courage by ordering a suicidal frontal assault on a strong Federal position at Franklin, Tennessee. He then marched his battered legions toward Nashville, where murderous Federal attacks destroyed the Army of Tennessee. Though he would later try to shift the blame to others, Hood at first took full responsibility for these disasters but grew increasingly withdrawn. At Columbia, South Carolina, in early February 1865, Mary Chesnut watched him gazing vacantly into a fire, "his face livid, spots of perspiration on his head. He was back evidently in some moment of his bitter trial . . . the fields of dead at Franklin—the panic at Nashville." Others too had seen the general's "agonized expression" and worried that he might be losing his mind.[27] Yet Hood was not the most important casualty of this ill-starred campaign.

After all, it was Davis who had removed Johnston, had appointed Hood, and had approved the movement into Tennessee. Frustration and despair made the president an easy target for scathing criticism, but the Tennessee debacle intensified military parochialism. Governor Magrath insisted that Joe Johnston be sent to Charleston and that men from Lee's army be transferred to that besieged city. Several prominent politicians, including Davis supporters William Porcher Miles and Robert Barnwell, accused the administration of doing nothing to prevent Sherman from plundering their state. Magrath tried to patch together with three neighboring governors a joint eleventh-hour defense policy relying on untrained militia.[28] Such desperate expedients plotted a mad course toward military decentralization. Had the war lasted into the summer, the Confederate government's ability to command its own regiments might have evaporated. The defiant attitudes of several governors raised serious doubts about national power and legitimacy.

These centrifugal impulses worked against a centripetal force moving to concentrate strategic authority in Robert E. Lee's hands. Many congressmen wanted the Virginian appointed general in chief to reduce Davis's influence over command and strategy, and several administration supporters agreed. Though confidants gingerly suggested that he had been overworking himself, the president bristled at such advice. "If I were Mr. Davis," a sympathetic senator remarked, "I would die or be hung before I would submit to the humiliation." The Senate ended up recommending Lee's elevation to general in chief, and the president could acquiesce because of his confidence in Lee and because the general had never shown any political ambition.[29] Davis's political base, especially in Congress, was clearly eroding; more ominous, his power as commander in chief was in danger of evaporating.

All the while in the wings lurked his nemesis Joe Johnston. From the day Hood had taken over the Army of Tennessee, Johnston's friends had been clamoring for his restoration to command and the smashup in Tennessee only made them more insistent. Wigfall talked wildly of deposing Davis and making Johnston military dictator—a ludicrously unsuitable role for a general who had so often dodged responsibility. Yet Wigfall's bluster was more a slap at Davis than a tribute to Johnston, who himself deplored congressional interference with military appointments.[30] Actually, both the general and the president were caught in a political dilemma. Resolutions for restoring Johnston to command of the Army of Tennessee's battered remnants easily passed the House and Senate, but Johnston thought it might be too late to save the situation or even vindicate his reputation.[31]

Confronted with a strongly worded petition on Johnston's behalf signed by fifteen Confederate senators, Lee still balked at playing military politics. Claiming that the senators overestimated his authority as general in chief, Lee hid behind legalisms. Angered by the congressional resolutions, Davis drafted a detailed critique of Johnston's military record, a full account of the general's delays, retreats, excuses, and obsessive secrecy. "My opinion of Gen. Johnston's unfitness for command," the president declared, "has ripened ... into a conviction so settled, that it would be impossible for me again to feel confidence in him as the commander of an army in the field." On February 21, however, Lee requested Johnston's appointment and assumed responsibility himself. Johnston complained that his new command offered "no hope of success." Displaying a pettiness equal to the president's, he considered Davis's mortification over the appointment "sufficient revenge."[32] Coming less than a week after Sherman's army had burned Columbia, South Carolina, Johnston's appointment was more symbolic than substantive. Military success, or even cooperation between field commanders and the government, was out of the question in this poisoned atmosphere. As desertions increased, morale plummeted, cries for peace almost became catatonic despair, and Confederate leaders contemplated policies that would strike at the heart of national identity.

The old saw about desperate times and desperate measures was especially apropos in the winter and spring of 1865. Proposals for conscripting and even emancipating slaves were last-gasp expedients, but they were far more than that. They raised anew important questions about the nature of the Confederacy and about Southern distinctiveness. Confederates still struggled over defining their republic, still weighed the claims of unity and liberty, and, curiously enough, still pondered the political future—a future seemingly fraught with still more revolutionary upheaval.

From the war's beginning, a few scattered suggestions for enrolling black men in the armies had horrified most white people. "We would as soon see them as guests at our table, or marrying our children," a Shreveport editor shuddered. "Negroes, by nature, are perfidious and treacherous—to make good servants of them, they must be kept down—nothing like equality or intimacy with them can be allowed."[33] By 1863, the voracious demands for manpower had forced more Confederates to think about the unthinkable. After Vicksburg and Gettysburg, editors in Alabama and Mississippi broached the idea of conscripting slaves.[34] Most politicians withheld judgment or denied the necessity for even considering such a dangerous experiment.

But as Confederate losses mounted, so did pressure to confront this tough issue. On January 2, 1864, Major General Patrick Cleburne, a first-rate division commander, and several other officers in the Army of Tennessee circulated a memorandum calling for the enrollment of black soldiers. Predicting that the war would "exhaust the white race," Cleburne also proposed legal recognition of slave marriages and gradual emancipation. His views were politically naive and bound to cause alarm. One of his fellow generals denounced Cleburne's suggestions as "monstrous" and "revolting to Southern sentiment, Southern pride, and Southern honor."[35] Such a visceral reaction revealed the primary and most explosive question. Enrolling slaves in the army might not make abolition inevitable, but it clearly would bring the Confederacy much closer to general emancipation.

Yet by October 1864, the pro-Davis *Richmond Enquirer* was urging

Congress to purchase 250,000 slaves, emancipate them, and train them as soldiers.[36] William W. Holden asked how such a proposal could be made in the Christian nineteenth century. The very notion of slave soldiers unnerved many Confederates. One Virginia editor confessed himself "completely dumbfounded" at a proposition "so strange" and "so completely destructive of our liberties."[37] Arming slaves meant elevating them to the level of their masters.

Confederate leaders responded cautiously to what many considered an absurd proposition. At a conference in Augusta, Georgia, the governors of Virginia, North Carolina, South Carolina, Georgia, and Alabama discussed but would not endorse the enlistment of slave soldiers. Thomas H. Watts told the Alabama legislature that enrolling black troops would be "utterly indefensible in principle and policy." Still wary of Holden, Vance maintained that the war could be won only by the "blood of white freemen."[38] Their political timidity aside, the governors clearly dreaded the revolutionary consequences of arming black men, and moderates such as Vance still saw slavery as vital to the Confederate republic.

So did Jefferson Davis. Although the president had shown considerable flexibility on many questions involving national authority, he approached the question of arming slaves with great trepidation. In a message to Congress on November 7, 1864, Davis proposed that the government use more slaves as army laborers and even suggested emancipation as a reward for "faithful service." He also maintained that the time had not arrived for the "dangerous expedient" of drafting slaves, though significantly he left the possibility open by noting that if subjugation ever became likely, black troops would become a necessity.[39] His position reflected a certain political realism and also shows how painfully ambivalent most Confederate leaders were about this issue.

Nor was Congress inclined to discuss the question at any length. Davis's critics naturally condemned the message. Many misinterpreted it as a call for emancipation, and most Confederates hesitated to make such a revolutionary break with their past. Mississippi congressman Henry C. Chambers, an ardent and volatile Southern nationalist who had killed his 1861 congressional opponent in a duel fought with rifles at fifty paces, proposed rounding up white deserters and making one last appeal to public patriotism. "The negro race was ordained to slavery by the Almighty," Chambers declared. "Emancipation would be the destruction of our social and political system. God forbid that this Trojan horse should be introduced among us."[40] No one challenged this argument, and those who favored enrolling slave soldiers dared not press for a vote.

First and last, emancipation became the sticking point. Offering slaves liberty as a reward for faithful military service would mean that the abolitionists had been right all along. "Freedom would prove a great curse to them [the slaves]," claimed one South Carolina editor. Emancipation would be no "boon" for black men, Mississippi governor Charles Clark agreed. "Steady, firm, but kind discipline, such as good masters enforce, is all that is required." Such strained logic had long been part of proslavery ideology, and as the debate dragged on, the arguments grew more bizarre. "Certainly negro slaves have a far stronger interest in defending a country where they have a master and protector and an assured home," one Richmond editor confidently asserted, "than one in which they would be left exposed, without defense, to the cruel benevolence of Yankee abolitionists." Slavery so benefited both races, Congressman John D. C. Clinton of Tennessee added, that, as an enlistment bounty, white soldiers should be given title to any slaves who themselves became soldiers.[41] In this world of fantasia, black soldiers would preserve and actually strengthen slavery!

Much of this discussion was beside the point because the best case for mustering slaves into the army rested on narrowly pragmatic grounds: better to sacrifice slavery than to lose the war. Proponents of black enlistment prided themselves on their realism. Even if the slaves had to be freed, claimed Virginia's governor William F. Smith, everyone would "cheerfully put the negro into the army rather than become a slave himself to our hated and vindictive foe." By defining the choice as black soldiers or white slavery, Smith and others appealed to traditional notions of white republican liberty. How much weight such arguments carried is difficult to gauge, but even practical considerations often degenerated into speculative musings.[42]

Whatever the relative strength of ideological and more hardheaded considerations, military opinion was crucial. In his usual straightforward manner, Robert E. Lee expressed confidence in the slaves' fighting abilities and informed Mississippi congressman Ethelbert Barksdale that the military situation required the use of black troops. But military reality kept getting tangled up in Confederate ideology. Lee admitted favoring a "well-digested plan of gradual and general emancipation"; though he did not elaborate, his statements sent shock waves through the South. That General Lee favored enlisting slaves was enough to convince many reluctant Confederates, but others decided that his military genius did not extend into the political arena. The *Charleston Mercury* groused that Lee had never been committed to slavery because he was a "hereditary Federalist."[43]

Setting aside the emancipation question, many Confederates still doubted black men's capacity to serve in the army. "If slaves will make good soldiers our whole theory of slavery is wrong," Howell Cobb observed with unintended irony. "Freed from restraint," they would become "licentious and fanatical," warned Virginia congressman Thomas Gholson. Nor were military men entirely persuaded by Lee or other generals. Writing to an Alabama newspaper, Charles Langdon claimed that enrolling blacks would be "degrading to our white soldiers" and would "demoralize the army." As a North Carolina enlisted man put it, "I did not volunteer my services to fight for a free negroes country but to fight for A free white mans free country and I do not think I love my country well enough to fight with black soldiers."[44]

In sharp contrast to Lee's sanguine expectations, opponents believed that slaves would likely desert to the enemy at the first opportunity. To assume otherwise, according to Edmund Rhett, would suppose that blacks lacked "even the common instincts of a monkey." After talking with his own slaves, James Chesnut, Jr., concluded that they might have fought for the Confederacy early in the war but now realized that in any case they would soon be free. The real danger would be that old Southern bugaboo servile insurrection. "Every woman and child in the Confederacy," North Carolina congressman Josiah Turner, Jr., told his wife, should recoil in horror at any effort to arm slaves.[45] The greatest nightmares of the slaveholding South were about to materialize as the war threatened to unleash a horde of Nat Turners on defenseless white families. The terrors of emancipation and race war made other objections pale in comparison.

There was, however, more at work here than mere fear. Confederate leaders could never separate slavery from national identity or their political culture. Both states' rights and Southern rights had long been used to defend a slaveholding society from a hostile world. In another long diatribe against supposed executive usurpation, Robert Barnwell Rhett pointed out the absurdity of strict constructionists sanctioning interference with slavery. If brave soldiers now had to fight alongside their slaves, the cause was lost anyway. After years of defending the rights of slaveholders to carry their slaves into distant territories such as Kansas, it would be shameful, hypocritical, and dishonorable to abandon slavery under the guise of military necessity.[46] Slavery remained an indispensable element of Confederate identity. To destroy or even seriously weaken the institution would sound the Southern nation's death knell. Southern independence without slavery was therefore inconceivable. This powerful commitment to slavery weakened the peace movement and blinded many conservatives to emancipation's usefulness as a diplomatic bargaining chip.[47]

In a more narrowly political sense, slavery was intrinsic to Southern republicanism. Confederates still believed that because slavery divided society into two great classes, political distinctions among white men were unnecessary. Slavery not only reduced the natural conflict between capital and labor but, as Calhoun had often argued, was essential for white liberty. In language that hearkened back to the late eighteenth century, prominent Presbyterian divine Benjamin M. Palmer proclaimed that the Southern states held the fate of republican government in their hands. Emancipation would signal the failure of republican government on the North American continent—and throughout the world.[48] Despite this almost messianic rhetoric and the obvious disproportion between Confederate goals and Confederate resources, the defensiveness, insecurity, and panic apparent here reflected the high stakes involved in the debate. Slavery remained vital to white Southerners' sense of themselves as a people and in many ways central to both the nationalist and libertarian political cultures. For this reason, even those who favored arming slaves were not prepared to sacrifice slavery.

Many editors, politicians, and ministers declared that nonslaveholding whites would suffer most from emancipation because they would have to compete with blacks for their daily bread. The debate over slave soldiers, however, proved that attempts to uphold race unity while downplaying class divisions were breaking down. The shrillest objections often came from the planters, and even those who conceded the military necessity for arming blacks usually refused to countenance emancipation. Many slaveholders seemed more willing to sacrifice their sons than their slaves, observed Georgia congressman Warren Akin. "The love of money has been the greatest difficulty in our way to independence."[49] Even with the Confederacy in its death throes, quondam aristocrats clung to their fortunes and tried to hold on to their slaves as the last remnants of status. Questions of race, class, and privilege shattered the veneer of Confederate unity but also reaffirmed that slavery remained at the heart of Confederate society.

The will-o'-the-wisp dream of a military triumph with slavery intact still lived. Even if slaves became soldiers, many Southerners believed that the government could avoid emancipating them or their families. Shibboleths of the proslavery argument prevented many Confederates from realistically assessing their political future. This was the logic of desperation, reflecting a refusal to choose between independence and slavery—if such a choice was still available. Nationalists might be able to accept the idea of slaves as soldiers but often could not face the idea of emancipation; libertarians generally rejected the whole idea of arming black men because they worried either about the rights of slaveholders or about the racial feelings of the common soldiers. In a more general sense, these arguments marked a continuation of the debate about the legitimate power of the Confederate government. But these persistent clashes between the political cultures (and the question of slave soldiers) also became entangled with the peace question.

After the quixotic visit of veteran Jacksonian politico Francis P. Blair, Sr., to Richmond in January 1865, prospects for a negotiated peace suddenly improved. Davis appointed Vice-President Stephens, Senator Robert M. T. Hunter of Virginia, and Assistant Secretary of War John A. Campbell to parley with the Federals aboard a steamer in Hampton Roads off Fort Monroe, Virginia. On February 3, Lincoln and Seward met informally with the three Confederate representatives but still insisted on a restoration of the Union and held out the possibility of gradual emancipation. This was exactly what Davis had expected, and he was pleased that Stephens had now seen Northern intransigence firsthand.[50] The president might temporarily silence the Georgia opposition, play for time, and hope for a miracle.

Unofficial reports on the Hampton Roads conference in Southern newspapers sparked a final patriotic revival. Robert Toombs defiantly asserted that "we have resources enough to whip *forty* Yankee nations." There was no more talk of exchanging emancipation for independence; the Southern people must carry the fight to victory or face subjugation. "There are no peace men among us now!" the *Richmond Sentinel* screamed.[51] Yet the appearance of unity was deceiving. Not only did many of the disaffected remain hostile to the president, but this sudden harmony did not signify a reconciliation of the two political cultures.

Ignoring persistent divisions, Davis tried to take advantage of the peace movement's temporary embarrassment by appealing directly to Confederate citizens. Despite bitter cold and four inches of snow on the ground, on the evening of February 6, ten thousand people, many spilling out into the streets, filled the African Church in Richmond. The president appeared exhausted and feeble, his voice halting and uncertain, but the enthusiastic crowd kept shouting for him to "go on." All hopes for a negotiated settlement on reasonable terms had been dashed by Northern obstinacy, he declared. Adopting an unusually conciliatory tone, he advised that "if there had been mistakes in the past, let us accept them as lessons of wisdom for the future." This eloquent call for unity was unfortunately followed by a remarkable flight of fancy. "We may believe," Davis promised, "that before the next summer solstice falls upon us, it will be the enemy who will be asking us for conferences and concessions." This statement rested on no firmer grounds than vain hopes that "half the absentees" would return to Lee's army and that miraculously Sherman might be stopped.[52]

Contemporaries deemed the speech an extraordinary performance, and even Pollard thought it the best Davis had ever made. Most striking, however, was what the president had not said. Even at this late date, his support for enrolling slaves in the army could only be implied. His faith in the cause had become truly blind. The president, under great physical strain, seemed to have no idea how to proceed.

Patriotism had become tinged with uncertainty and doubt, riddled by unresolved ideological and practical questions. On February 9 at a noontime meeting in the African Church, Judah Benjamin bluntly asked where were the men necessary to defend Richmond and the rest of the Confederacy. A member of the audience shouted, "Put in the niggers," and some people cheered. Lincoln could not have continued the war without black soldiers stolen from the South, Benjamin replied quickly, and the Confederate government should "say to every negro who wishes to go into the ranks, on condition of being free, 'go and fight you are free.'" If Virginia would take the lead, twenty thousand slave soldiers could soon man the Petersburg trenches. This appeal combined unrealistic expectations about recruiting, arming, and training black troops with the realistic acknowledgment that there were not enough white men left to hold off the enemy.[53]

Though Benjamin appeared to deal forthrightly with emancipation, he had finessed the question. His suggestions rested on the dubious assumption that slaves would fight for their masters *and* for freedom; he also had ignored the possible necessity for a draft and appeared oblivious to strong opposition from slaveholders. Nor had he acknowledged the continuing divisions among Confederate leaders. Sharing the platform with Benjamin and other dignitaries was Robert M. T. Hunter. The influential and ambitious Virginian delivered a spread-eagle oration, damning Lincoln and calling for a patriotic revival. Yet he also strongly defended slavery and glumly forecast that a Union victory would mean "three millions of slaves loosed in the midst of Southern society; we ourselves slaves, and our slaves freedmen."[54] The audience must have marveled at the remarkable divergence of views expressed at a meeting ostensibly held to cement national unity.

The meaning of loyalty had become muddled. The peace men in Congress were not united on a policy, had grown strangely apathetic, and seemed to be losing political ground. As prospects for a negotiated peace dimmed, Josiah Turner, Jr., wearily longed for home and wrote vaguely to his wife of "plans for the deliverance of the country, rather for saving a part of the ship wreck." So powerful had the political reaction become, however, that several peace initiatives died aborning. On March 14, Congress adopted a resolution calling for the continued prosecution of the war and promising to enact all measures needed for victory.[55]

Not quite all measures because Southern politicians still refused to give up on slavery. Louis T. Wigfall, whose Confederate nationalism was as strong as anyone's, had steadily condemned any talk of emancipation. "The time had come," he roared on the Senate floor, to settle whether "this was to be a free negro country, or a free white man's country." For Southerners to arm slaves would be like England abolishing the "landed aristocracy and put[ting] into their place a market-house mob." The Confederacy should never become another Santo Domingo—a reference sure to strike fear in the heart of any right-thinking Confederate.[56] The most reactionary elements of proslavery ideology now welled to the surface; Confederate leaders were paralyzed by fear of social revolution.

Many libertarians, whether they were peace men or not, shared Wigfall's apprehensions and seemed no more willing to sacrifice slavery. A prime example was North Carolina senator William A. Graham, who from the beginning had denounced all schemes for arming slaves as "insane proposals" and had curtly declined an invitation to address the war meeting at the African Church. Convinced that Confederate forces could never stop Sherman, and with no faith left in Davis, Graham nevertheless remained an orthodox Confederate. Citing the *Dred Scott* decision to support his racial views, he believed that enrolling blacks in the army would mean the "dissolution of the Confederacy." He still hoped for a negotiated peace that would preserve slavery, at least in the short term.[57]

These statements by Wigfall and Graham show why enacting a bill to make slaves soldiers was so difficult and why Congress moved so slowly on the question. The House narrowly agreed (by a vote of forty to thirty-seven) to a cautious proposal introduced by Mississippian Ethelbert Barksdale. If approved by the Senate, this measure would have authorized placing slaves in "companies, battalions, regiments, and brigades" and would have allowed the president to draft slaves if necessary. The bill, however, made no mention of emancipation.[58]

The Senate was even more reluctant to enter this political and ideological thicket. Although Albert Gallatin Brown offered a straightforward bill that would have emancipated slave soldiers as a reward for faithful service, Williamson S. Oldham countered with a watered-down measure similar to the Barksdale bill. Under his proposal, slaves could become soldiers only with their owners' consent, and the "social and political status of the slave population" would still be determined by the states. Constitutionalism, states' rights, and a tenacious commitment to slavery characterized the ensuing debate. On February 21 (the day after the House passed the Barksdale bill), the Senate voted eleven to ten to postpone consideration of Brown's proposal indefinitely.[59]

This disappointing anticlimax did not, however, settle the question. At the urging of Governor Smith and mindful of General Lee's opinion, the Virginia legislature quickly adopted a resolution calling for the enlistment of black troops and instructing the state's Confederate senators to vote for Oldham's bill. With greater or lesser grace, Richmond editors also fell into line—though both the Virginia legislature and the newspapers dodged the emancipation question.[60]

So did the senators. Hunter worried that so much agitation had demoralized the people, and he raised a host of practical and philosophical objections. But in the end, Hunter and his Virginia colleague Allen T. Caperton followed their legislature's instructions and provided the votes necessary for Senate passage (by a nine-to-eight margin) of a revised version of the Barksdale bill. It would be easy to exaggerate the significance of this long-delayed halfway measure. The new law restricted the president to conscripting "not more than twenty-five percent of the male slaves between the ages of eighteen and forty-five" in any state. Congress further declared that the act did not "authorize a change in the relation which the said slaves shall bear toward their owners, except by consent of the owners and of the States in which they may reside, and in pursuance of the laws thereof." In effect, the measure provided for a double veto on emancipation by both the slaveholders and the state governments. Although the president later made sure War Department regulations provided that slaves could be enrolled only if their masters consented to their freedom, how this would have worked out in practice will never be known.[61]

Frustrated and angry but unwilling to acknowledge the role of his own indecisiveness, Davis lashed out at Congress, chastising lawmakers for adopting slave conscription too late and for creating too many draft exemptions. After issuing this tactless rebuke, he begged congressmen to deliver morale-building speeches in their states and home districts. Praying that the Southern people would be "united in a common and holy cause," he invoked God's blessing and implied that only divine assistance could preserve the nation. Whether this last remark was mere formality or a last bow to Confederate civil religion, Jefferson Davis had struck a fatalistic note.[62]

This message incensed many senators, and the moderate Thomas J. Semmes of Louisiana apparently drafted the sternly worded rejoinder. The delay in passing the slave soldier bill was hardly surprising because the president had never sent a message to Congress explicitly calling for such a measure. "If loss of time be a vice inherent in deliberative assemblies, promptitude is a great virtue in Executive action," the report noted tartly. Davis had merely caused more "dissension and discord" with his ill-timed lecture to Congress. After reading both documents, Robert Toombs concluded that the president had "made a bold lick for the dictatorship" but the Senate had "struck him a blow from which he will never recover." Nothing could save the Confederacy now but the overthrow of Davis, Toombs blustered. Other alarmists remained wary of executive usurpation.[63]

At this point, neither the libertarians nor the nationalists seemed capable of grasping reality and instead clung to the hoary tenets of their proslavery credo. Graham suggested that masters could refuse to hand over their bondsmen to the government without violating the law. Those who favored enlisting black soldiers were equally adamant about limiting the new policy's convulsive effects. According to the proadministration *Richmond Enquirer*, to make slaves into soldiers did not require freeing them because medieval serfs had long provided military service to their lords. Many Confederates rejoiced that Congress had neither revolutionized the relationship between master and slave nor violated the Constitution.[64]

The past several months of crisis had strangely redounded to Jefferson Davis's benefit. He had stood ready to do whatever was necessary to defend the cause without becoming too directly entangled in the debate over slave conscription. A political culture of national unity had survived; the last patriotic revival had contained heavy doses of antiparty rhetoric. The *Raleigh Confederate* sharply denounced a supposed Wigfall-led "cabal" that was plotting to overthrow the president. The collapse of hopes for a negotiated peace and the debates in Congress over drafting slaves had confounded and further divided the libertarian opposition. The peace movement was clearly foundering, and everyone seemed to be waiting to see what the opening of the spring campaign season would mean to the armies. Yet Davis seemed to be living in a fantasy world. After Lee had been forced to abandon Richmond, he still talked about the advantages of interior lines. The president advised the people that, "relieved from the necessity of guarding cities and particular points," the army could freely "move from point to point" and take advantage of the people's "unquenchable resolve" to be free. The president's patriotism had become almost completely detached from military reality.[65] He could not see or would not admit that his beloved Confederacy had entered its death throes.

Mary Chesnut gloomily wrote that "our world has gone to destruction," and South Carolina senator James L. Orr believed that the Confederacy had "failed through the egotism, the obstinacy, and the imbecility of Jefferson Davis." A group of patriotic Virginians still hoped that "citizens in their comfortable homes, exempt from the privations and perils of the field, should be willing to exercise the severest self-denial" and donate their surplus provisions for the soldiers. But even this last appeal to class unity suggested the persistence of selfishness and aristocratic hauteur. So in the Confederacy's final days, a muted political conflict persisted. Less than a month before the Army of Northern Virginia surrendered, the *Richmond Sentinel* began publishing brief election announcements. The editor saw this activity as a healthy exercise of Anglo-Saxon liberty and an important sign that the Southern people were not yet subjugated.[66]

The hope for political harmony persisted, the passion for white liberty would endure, but because the Confederacy itself died, the revolution against politics failed. Even had the Southern nation survived, Confederate leaders had not been able to resolve the chronic tensions and contradictions between unity and liberty. Nor had they been able to realize their dreams for a purified political culture embodying their own ideals of white republicanism. Yet like the Confederate government and like the Rebel armies, the political revolution had its moments of triumph. Although signs of party spirit sometimes cropped up along with many of the same political practices that had supposedly destroyed the old Union, both the nationalists and the libertarians had refused to form political parties and for all their factiousness had been faithful to their antiparty creed. Although historians have deplored the absence of a party system in the Southern nation, many Confederates would have considered this a welcome sign of political health and perhaps a considerable accomplishment at the end of a bloody and unsuccessful war for national independence.

T he surrender of the armies and the death of the Southern nation did not put an end to Confederate politics. The years after the war brought long and sometimes angry debates over the might have beens, a battle of memoirs, and a minute and often embittered reexamination of strategy and tactics. Political memory, however, was often narrowly selective. The arrest and imprisonment of Jefferson Davis began his slow transformation from all-purpose scapegoat to Lost Cause martyr. In the eventual apotheosis of the Confederate president, his memorialists would remember him as a man with faults and prejudices but also as a leader who had sacrificed his health and shown an unbending devotion to the cause.[1] The image of the steadfast patriot dominated as fading recollections of wartime controversies made Davis seem more victim than villain.

When postwar discussions of the Confederate experience grew more sophisticated, states' rights and wartime dissension became handy explanations for Confederate defeat. Even Davis recalled telling a senator during the war that "Died of a Theory" might be the Southern nation's most suitable epitaph. Ben Hill agreed that demoralization, stimulated by malcontents, had seriously weakened the cause. Many former Confederates sadly remembered the divisiveness of leaders such as Joe Brown and Alexander Stephens. The hapless Braxton Bragg believed that too many "old, trading politicians and demagogues" had served in the Confederate government, busily "dividing spoils not yet secured." Zeb Vance repeated the common wartime assertion that all the best talent had gone into army and again expressed doubts that nonslaveholders had ever had their hearts in the war.[2] These early assessments anticipated later and more complex explanations for Confederate defeat and established a long-term historiographical agenda.

But they also anticipated a major problem with modern analyses of Confederate weaknesses that try to make the outcome of the war seem inevitable by ignoring military turning points.[3] Indeed, what remains most remarkable about the Confederacy was not its internal weaknesses—political, social, or economic—but its staying power and especially the ability of so many men and women to endure and make sacrifices. The political controversies discussed in this volume, to cite just one example of an internal factor, did not destroy the Southern nation, and if anything the political culture of national unity, with its patriotic appeals and symbols, was a source of strength.

The Confederate Constitution stood as a source of pride, a perfection of republicanism rightly understood. Building on the work of the American founding fathers, the delegates to the Montgomery convention had applied the lessons of recent political history. The result had been a new organic law reflecting widespread hostility to executive patronage, congressional logrolling, and political parties. From these beginnings there grew a nationalist political culture—perhaps best reflected in the quiet dignity of the 1861 state and national elections—that emphasized the importance of political and social unity. Beyond the narrowly political realm, many preachers and educators promoted the values of this political culture in churches and schoolrooms. By early 1862, the Confederate administration stood ready to adopt necessary war measures without caviling over traditional fear of centralized authority. In turn, antiparty ideology, along with deep-seated suspicions of many long-standing political practices, made the libertarian opposition much less effective and less dangerous to the Confederate cause than it might have been otherwise. As old party labels lost their hold on the electorate, the absence of effective organization and even consistent voting patterns in the 1863 elections exemplified success—however compromised and qualified by individual politicians and their constituents—for the revolution against politics.

At the same time, the gap between political theory and political practice sometimes remained wide. Indeed, the Confederacy's internal bickering, which historians have found so exasperating and often pointless, should not be used to explain the outcome of the war but rather should serve as a window through which to examine the political nature of the Southern revolution. Besides the obviously personal and sometimes petty acrimony between defenders of the rival political cultures and especially between Davis and his critics, there were serious ideological differences among Confederate leaders, sometimes reflected in the political behavior of ordinary citizens, but certainly central to understanding the political aspects of this experiment in nation building. The debates over conscription and habeas corpus, the two most obvious examples, deserve to be taken seriously in their own right, and not simply as sources of internal division, because for contemporaries they raised vital questions about what the Confederacy was all about. Would the expansion of national authority destroy the heart and soul of the Southern nation? Could the Confederate government preserve the liberty of states, communities, and individuals in the midst of a bloody civil war? Would ideological inconsistency and compromise lead to victory or simply destroy virtue? Many wartime political controversies stemmed from unresolved political disputes going back to the Montgomery convention, to the secession debates in the states, or even to the antebellum period.

And just as internal factors are not sufficient explanations for the outcome of the war, so also a focus on strategy, military leadership, and battles has sometimes obscured the significance and accomplishments of the revolution against politics. In the process of creating and sanctifying the myth of the Lost Cause, it was easy to neglect wartime disputes over political leadership and public virtue. This process in turn conflated the two political cultures. Confederate soldiers had fought both for a unified nation and for state, community, and individual liberty. Though true in a general sense, such an assertion not only conveniently ignores the central importance of slavery but also fails to take into account basic philosophical differences between the rival political cultures. However tedious and often petty wartime debates over issues ranging from conscription to impressment to habeas corpus to taxation may seem today, many Confederates at the time considered these issues critical to their own sense of purpose and national identity.

Historians would eventually examine wartime politics, but they would do so primarily to explain Confederate defeat and probe the weaknesses of Southern nationalism. Yet Confederate politics merits attention on its own terms regardless of the war's outcome. During the secession crisis, Southern politicians and many of their constituents began to debate and define their core political values. Civil religion, slavery, organic unity, ambivalent attitudes about democracy, and most notably antiparty ideology all became part of this emerging Confederate political culture. Old partisan feuds and the war itself shaped the evolution and bifurcation of Confederate politics. Politicians who best represented the political cultures of national unity and liberty shared many of these common political assumptions and beliefs but also tried to pull the Confederate revolution in different directions. At the same time, moderates such as Zeb Vance and Herschel Johnson searched for a reasonable and workable political center even though their efforts were undermined by lost battles, economic suffering, class resentments, growing cries for peace, and in the end a spiritual fatalism. The simultaneous discussion of peace terms and the possible enrollment of slaves as soldiers marked the final clash between the political cultures by placing the Confederate administration and its critics, as well as the political centrists, to the ultimate test. Ideology, practicality, power, individualism, and slavery all came together in one final struggle over the meaning of the Confederate experience.

Competing and sometimes contradictory political values long survived the war, and again their significance goes far beyond historical explanations for Confederate defeat. The premium placed on internal harmony and white liberty is essential for understanding the politics of Reconstruction. The Southern leadership class emerged from the war with a deep mistrust of politics and parties. Even the process of rejoining the national Democratic party was not smooth, and many politicians supported the party from a narrowly sectional perspective.[4] Thus the political values that were so central to the Confederate experience remained important in Southern politics long after the Confederate republic had disappeared.

Abbreviations

ADAH	Alabama Department of Archives and History, Montgomery
BTHC	Barker Texas History Center, University of Texas, Austin
Duke	Duke University, William R. Perkins Library, Durham, North Carolina
Emory	Emory University, Robert W. Woodruff Library, Atlanta, Georgia
GDAH	Georgia Department of Archives and History, Atlanta, Georgia
JCC	*Journal of the Confederate Congress*
LC	Library of Congress, Manuscripts Division
NCDAH	North Carolina Division of Archives and History, Raleigh
OR	*War of the Rebellion: Official Records of the Union and Confederate Armies*
SCL	South Caroliniana Library, University of South Carolina, Columbia
SHC	Southern Historical Collection, University of North Carolina, Chapel Hill
SHSP	*Southern Historical Society Papers* (proceedings of the Confederate Congress)
UG	University of Georgia Library, Special Collections, Athens
UVa	Alderman Library, University of Virginia, Charlottesville

Chapter 1

1. DuBose, *Yancey*, p. 376.

2. Ibid.

3. For the role of unspoken assumptions and persistent cultural characteristics in defining a political culture, see Formisano, *Transformation of Political Culture*, p. 4; Sidney Verba, "Comparative Political Culture," in Pye and Verba, *Political Culture and Political Development*, pp. 518–21; Inglehart, "Renaissance of Political Culture," pp. 1228–29.

4. Any definitions of political culture must begin with the classic and still useful work of Lucien Pye and Sidney Verba; see Pye, "Political Culture and Political Development," in Pye and Verba, *Political Culture and Political Development*, p. 7; Verba, "Comparative Political Culture," pp. 529–43.

5. Potter, *South and the Sectional Conflict*, pp. 67–83; Potter, *Impending Crisis*,

pp. 462–78. The disunity among the fire-eaters over defining Southern nationalism is fully explored in Eric H. Walther's fine new book, *The Fire-Eaters*. Professor Walther generously allowed me to read this work in manuscript.

6. Russell, *My Diary North and South*, pp. 106, 130–31. For stimulating, provocative, but not entirely persuasive attempts to develop the themes briefly noted by Wigfall and Rhett into coherent definitions of Southern distinctiveness, see Emory M. Thomas, *Confederate Nation*, pp. 21–28, and Anne Norton, *Alternative Americas*, pp. 99–112.

7. Channing, *Crisis of Fear*, pp. 146–47. See also the useful analysis of the inherent tensions between radical politics and cultural conservatism in Geertz, *Interpretation of Cultures*, pp. 311–26.

8. Barnwell, *Love of Order*, pp. 25–26; Barney, *Secessionist Impulse*, pp. 50–100; Wooster, *People in Power*, pp. 25–42; Kruman, *Parties and Politics in North Carolina*, pp. 45–54; Bailey, *Class and Tennessee's Confederate Generation*, pp. 20–76.

9. Baker, *Affairs of Party*, p. 10; Barnwell, *Love of Order*, p. 29; Hahn, *Roots of Southern Populism*, pp. 113–16.

10. Sydnor, *Development of Southern Sectionalism*, pp. 282–93; Wooster, *Politicians, Planters, and Plain Folk*, pp. 123–29; Cooper, *South and Politics of Slavery*, pp. 23–26; Eggleston, *Rebel's Recollections*, pp. 37–39.

11. Cooper, *South and the Politics of Slavery*, pp. 26–42; Thornton, *Politics and Power in a Slave Society*, pp. 59–78; Clarence Norton, *Democratic Party in Ante-Bellum North Carolina*, pp. 38–40; Ford, *Origins of Southern Radicalism*, pp. 99–144; J. William Harris, *Plain Folk and Gentry in a Slave Society*, pp. 94–120.

12. For a revisionist analysis that calls for a greater awareness of party loyalties in the antebellum South and downplays the importance of slavery, see Lucas, "'To Carry Out Great Fundamental Principles,'" pp. 1–22. Lucas, however, focuses on the 1830s and 1840s, neglects the persistence of antiparty ideas in the South, and does not carry his discussion into the 1850s.

13. Clarence Norton, *Democratic Party in Ante-Bellum North Carolina*, pp. 31–38; Kruman, *Parties and Politics in North Carolina*, pp. 29–37, 40–42; Thornton, *Politics and Power in a Slave Society*, pp. 118–28, 160–62; Watson, *Jacksonian Politics and Community Conflict*, pp. 60–81, 297–300.

14. Phillips, *Course of the South to Secession*, p. 131; White, *Rhett*, pp. 136–37, 160.

15. For a stimulating discussion of so-called National Democrats in Southern politics that nevertheless exaggerates both their importance and their commitment to party values, see Joel Silbey, "The Southern National Democrats, 1845–1861," in Silbey, *Partisan Imperative*, pp. 116–26.

16. The very tradition of sectional compromise also encompassed highly ambivalent attitudes about political parties. See Knupfer, *Union as It Is*, pp. 80–82.

17. For the social and cultural dimensions of honor, see Wyatt-Brown, *Southern Honor*. Noticeably absent from Wyatt-Brown's brilliant book is a thorough discussion of the relationships among honor, slavery, and politics. For these dimensions, see Cooper, *South and the Politics of Slavery*, pp. 69–74, 370–71.

18. James Henry Hammond, "Slavery in Light of Political Science," in E. N.

Elliott, *Cotton Is King and Proslavery Arguments*, pp. 637–39. An excellent treatment of the relationships among Southern rights ideology, fear of abolition, white unity, and partisanship is in Thornton, *Politics and Power in a Slave Society*, pp. 204–11, 348–65.

19. Basic problems are addressed in two classic historiographical essays: Shalhope, "Toward a Republican Synthesis," pp. 49–80, and Shalhope, "Republicanism and Early American Historiography," pp. 334–56. For purposes of the present study, Daniel T. Rodgers's observation that republicanism often loses its clarity and power outside its eighteenth-century context is especially apropos because in many ways Southern nationalism was a backward-looking ideology ("Republicanism," pp. 11–38).

20. William C. Harris, *Holden*, pp. 51–52; Greenberg, *Masters and Statesmen*, pp. 15–22; Anne Norton, *Alternative Americas*, pp. 124–31.

21. Nagel, *One Nation Indivisible*, pp. 246–51; Greenberg, *Masters and Statesmen*, pp. 65–84.

22. Ford, *Origins of Southern Radicalism*, pp. 348–73; Anderson, *Imagined Communities*, pp. 15–16. For alternative interpretations maintaining that Southerners felt guilty about the contradictions between their ideology and their practice, or that they failed to defend "absolute slavery," or that republicanism in a slave society fostered its own ambiguities and tensions among Democrats and Whigs, see Emory M. Thomas, *Confederate Nation*, p. 21; Greenberg, *Masters and Statesmen*, pp. 85–103; J. William Harris, *Plain Folk and Gentry in a Slave Society*, pp. 125–26. Without much consideration of political attitudes, Larry E. Tise offers a fine analysis of the connections between what he calls "conservative republicanism" and proslavery ideology (*Proslavery*, pp. 347–62).

23. Kruman, *Parties and Politics in North Carolina*, pp. 3–6; Thornton, *Politics and Power in a Slave Society*, pp. 348–65.

24. Greenberg, *Masters and Statesmen*, pp. 3–15; Carpenter, *South as a Conscious Minority*, pp. 34–126; Thornton, *Politics and Power in a Slave Society*, pp. 98–116.

25. Formisano, "Political Character, Antipartyism, and the Second Party System," pp. 683–709; Howe, *Political Culture of American Whigs*, pp. 3, 51–55; Kruman, *Parties and Politics in North Carolina*, pp. 36–40. The persistence of antiparty attitudes in the North might at first appear to present some problems for this interpretation of Southern and later Confederate political culture, but I am not addressing the age-old question of Southern distinctiveness and am only arguing that suspicion of politics and politicians was stronger in the South and had a large influence in shaping Southern political developments during the Civil War.

26. This analysis suggests why some historians have emphasized the comparative youth of many secessionists. For politicians coming of political age in the 1850s, attachment to a party system was especially weak. For helpful insight on political generations, see Samuel P. Huntington, "Generations, Cycles, and Their Role in American Development," in Samuels, *Political Generations and Political Development*, pp. 9–27.

27. Phillips, *Course of the South to Secession*, p. 130; Ford, *Origins of Southern*

Radicalism, pp. 183–217, 282–307, 338–48; Barney, *Road to Secession*, pp. 86–100, 114–22.

28. Greenberg, *Masters and Statesmen*, pp. 45–64; Wyatt-Brown, *Yankee Saints and Southern Sinners*, pp. 187–88.

29. Thornton, *Politics and Power in a Slave Society*, pp. 80–98, 211–12, 223–38; Spain, *Political Theory of Calhoun*, pp. 109–15.

30. Scarborough, *Diary of Edmund Ruffin*, 1:66, 222–23.

31. Walther, *Fire-Eaters*; Thornton, *Politics and Power in a Slave Society*, pp. 78–80; J. William Harris, *Plain Folk and Gentry in a Slave Society*, pp. 128–32; Greenberg, *Masters and Statesmen*, pp. 124–46.

32. Scarborough, *Diary of Edmund Ruffin*, 1:24; Summers, *Plundering Generation*, pp. 281–96. Summers's first-rate analysis of corruption also contains many important insights for students of Confederate political history and wartime propaganda.

33. Scarborough, *Diary of Edmund Ruffin*, 1:226–27; Crenshaw, *Slave States in the Election of 1860*, pp. 203–4.

34. Dumond, *Southern Editorials on Secession*, pp. 28–29; Crenshaw, *Slave States in the Election of 1860*, p. 66; Barney, *Road to Secession*, p. 139.

35. Dumond, *Southern Editorials on Secession*, p. 139; Channing, *Crisis of Fear*, p. 224.

36. Escott, *After Secession*, pp. 21–24; James Henry Hammond to Isaac W. Hayne, September 19, 1860, William Porcher Miles to Hammond, August 5, 1860, Hammond Papers, LC.

Chapter 2

1. Reese, *Proceedings of the Virginia State Convention*, 1:200–201; *Richmond Daily Dispatch*, February 14, 1861.

2. Phillips, *Correspondence of Toombs, Stephens, and Cobb*, p. 535; *Richmond Daily Whig*, January 22, 1861; Dumond, *Southern Editorials on Secession*, pp. 284–85; Charles D. Trenholm to William Porcher Miles, January 22, 1861, Miles Papers, SHC.

3. Shugg, "Suppressed Co-operationist Protest," pp. 202–3; *To the People of Virginia*, broadside.

4. Reese, *Proceedings of the Virginia State Convention*, 1:178–81, 2:106–7; Thomas J. Kirkpatrick to Alexander H. Stephens, March 2, 1861, Stephens Papers, LC; Reynolds, *Editors Make War*, p. 185; Virginia, *Documents*, no. 1 (1861), p. viii.

5. *Charleston Mercury*, January 22, 1861.

6. Isaac W. Hayne to James Henry Hammond, April 15, 1860, M. L. Hammond to James Henry Hammond, March 28, 1860, Hammond Papers, LC; *Charleston Mercury*, January 17, 1861; Elmore Diary, November 13, 1860, SCL; Crabtree and Patton, *"Journal of a Secesh Lady,"* p. 37.

7. Crofts, *Reluctant Confederates*, pp. 111–14; Blackford, *Mine Eyes Have Seen the Glory*, p. 147; Greenawalt, "Unionists in Rockbridge County," p. 82.

8. David Y. Thomas, *Arkansas in War and Reconstruction*, p. 42; Richard M. Johnston and Browne, *Stephens*, p. 369; Candler, *Confederate Records of Georgia*, 1:71.

9. Ash, *Middle Tennessee Society Transformed*, p. 70; Roark, *Masters without Slaves*, pp. 2–3; Amelia Williams and Barker, *Writings of Sam Houston*, 8:227.

10. Michael P. Johnson, *Toward a Patriarchal Republic*, pp. 28–34; Laurence Keitt to William Porcher Miles, October 3, 1860, Miles Papers, SHC.

11. Freeman, *Lee*, 1:421; Roark, *Masters without Slaves*, pp. 4–5; Oakes, *Ruling Race*, p. 238; Bleser, *Hammonds of Redcliffe*, p. 88.

12. Michael P. Johnson, *Toward a Patriarchal Republic*, pp. 52–58; Herschel V. Johnson to Alexander H. Stephens, December 22, 1860, Johnson Papers, Duke; Phillips, *Correspondence of Toombs, Stephens, and Cobb*, pp. 504–5; Cleveland, *Stephens*, pp. 695–713; Hayes, *Historical Evolution of Modern Nationalism*, p. 91.

13. James Henry Hammond to William Gilmore Simms, November 10, 1860 [misfiled in 1861], Hammond Papers, LC; C. R. Hauleite to Alexander H. Stephens, December 1, 1860, Willis Strickland to Stephens, February 4, 1861, Stephens Papers, LC.

14. *Raleigh Weekly Standard*, April 10, 1861; Michael P. Johnson, *Toward a Patriarchal Republic*, pp. 110–12; Inscoe, *Mountain Masters*, p. 234; Bettersworth, *Confederate Mississippi*, p. 15.

15. Candler, *Confederate Records of Georgia*, 1:65. Again it is important to note that secessionists used similar arguments for quite different purposes. According to Georgia's governor Joseph E. Brown and other disunionists, the Lincoln administration—not Southern nationalists—would create a monarchy or some sort of consolidated despotism (*OR*, ser. 4, vol. 1, p. 18); William R. Smith, *History and Debates of the Convention of Alabama*, p. 267.

16. Shugg, *Origins of the Class Struggle in Louisiana*, p. 167; Inscoe, *Mountain Masters*, pp. 231–32; Frontis W. Johnston, *Vance Papers*, p. 95.

17. For a perceptive, though somewhat overdrawn, analysis of these problems in one North Carolina county, see Durrill, *War of Another Kind*, pp. 3–4, 24–39.

18. *Raleigh Weekly Standard*, February 27, 1861; Inscoe, *Mountain Masters*, pp. 232–33; Frontis W. Johnston, *Vance Papers*, p. 78.

19. Alexander H. Stephens, *Recollections*, pp. 326–27; Brown Diary, January 1, 1861, SHC; Max Williams and Hamilton, *Graham Papers*, 5:233; Reese, *Proceedings of the Virginia State Convention*, 2:722–23. For an excellent analysis of how upper South Unionists in particular considered secession a psychological contagion, see Crofts, *Reluctant Confederates*, pp. 114–17.

20. For a more elaborate discussion of this point, see Frontis W. Johnston, *Vance Papers*, pp. 71–73.

21. Dougan, *Confederate Arkansas*, pp. 40–41; Brown Diary, January 25, 1861, SHC; Phillips, *Correspondence of Toombs, Stephens, and Cobb*, pp. 492–93, 496, 498–99.

22. Oliphant, Odell, and Eaves, *Letters of Simms*, 4:261; William R. Smith, *History and Debates of the Convention of Alabama*, pp. 43–49.

23. Alfred P. Aldrich to James Henry Hammond, November 25, 1860, Hammond Papers, LC.

24. James Henry Hammond to Alfred P. Aldrich et al., November 8, 1860, Hammond Papers, LC. See also the excellent analysis of conservative fears of a democratic revolution in Michael P. Johnson, *Toward a Patriarchal Republic*, pp. 94–101.

25. For an example of the attention given to old problems while neglecting questions about the political future of the Southern states, see Robert Toombs's speech to the Georgia secession convention, *OR*, ser. 4, vol. 1, pp. 81–85.

26. Useful general comments about dealing with both external and internal enemies in a crusade for "national salvation" are in Koon, *Believe, Obey, Fight*, p. xvii.

27. *OR*, ser. 4, vol. 1, pp. 1–2; Crofts, *Reluctant Confederates*, pp. 117–22; Bertram Wyatt-Brown, "Honor and Secession," in Wyatt-Brown, *Yankee Saints and Southern Sinners*, pp. 197–204.

28. Michael P. Johnson, *Toward a Patriarchal Republic*, pp. 34–39. For a brilliant analysis of the political dynamics involved in the ideology of secession, see Ford, *Origins of Southern Radicalism*, pp. 338–73.

29. In exploring political symbolism during the secession crisis, I have relied heavily on the theoretical insights in Edelman, *Politics as Symbolic Action*, pp. 12–24.

30. Planters' Convention, Memphis, *Report of Select Committee Appointed by the Planters' Convention*, pp. 2–7; "National Characteristics: The Issues of the Day," *De Bow's Review* 30 (January 1861): 42–53; Mary Ezell Diary, June 8, 1861, in Conigland Papers, SHC.

31. Coulter, *Confederate States of America*, pp. 11–13; *Proceedings of the Mississippi Convention*, pp. 79–82.

32. Mayes, *Lamar*, p. 637; Daniel, "Southern Presbyterians in the Confederacy," p. 232; Barney, *Road to Secession*, pp. 132–33; Oliphant, Odell, and Eaves, *Letters of Simms*, 4:346.

33. Candler, *Confederate Records of Georgia*, 1:47; Crofts, *Reluctant Confederates*, pp. 90–103; *Memphis Daily Appeal*, March 17, 1861.

34. *Richmond Daily Examiner*, May 11, 1861; Reese, *Proceedings of the Virginia State Convention*, 1:73–74.

35. See the still useful categorization of political cultures in Elazar, *American Federalism*, pp. 90–102.

36. *Journal of the Convention of Florida*, p. 4; *Alabama Senate Journal* (1861), pp. 6–7; Bragg Diary, January 11, 1861, SHC; Cleveland, *Stephens*, pp. 163–68; Long, "Unanimity and Disloyalty in Secessionist Alabama," pp. 257–73.

37. *Richmond Daily Dispatch*, March 30, 1861; Oliphant, Odell, and Eaves, *Letters of Simms*, 4:300. The interpretation presented here of the antiparty nature of secession relies heavily on the first-rate account in Holt, *Political Crisis of the 1850s*, pp. 220–22, 238–44.

38. Holt, *Political Crisis of the 1850s*, pp. 230–37; Candler, *Confederate Records of Georgia*, 1:86, 103–4, 129, 157–82; *Florida Senate Journal* (1860), p. 4.

39. Michael P. Johnson, *Toward a Patriarchal Republic*, pp. 39–46; *Raleigh*

Semi-Weekly Register, April 3, 1861; Dumond, *Southern Editorials on Secession*, p. 285. This is not to say, however, that some politicians may well have expected little change in the way they conducted business. See Thornton, *Politics and Power in a Slave Society*, pp. 425–26.

40. For provocative and differing interpretations of the role of party in the upper South, see Holt, *Political Crisis of the 1850s*, pp. 244–59; Crofts, *Reluctant Confederates*, pp. 130–63; Kruman, *Parties and Politics in North Carolina*, pp. 196–200; Mering, "Persistent Whiggery in the Confederate South," pp. 123–43.

41. Crofts, *Reluctant Confederates*, pp. 254–88; *Raleigh Weekly Standard*, February 13, 1861; J. William Harris, *Plain Folk and Gentry in a Slave Society*, pp. 132–39.

42. For evidence of the persistence of party in some areas, notably in the tendency of former Whigs to vote for cooperationist candidates, see Crofts, *Reluctant Confederates*, pp. xvi–xix, 37–65; Alexander, "Persistent Whiggery in the Confederate South," pp. 306–7; Kruman, *Parties and Politics in North Carolina*, pp. 180–81, 208–21.

43. Crofts, *Reluctant Confederates*, pp. 164–94; McCrary, Miller, and Baum, "Class and Party in the Secession Crisis," pp. 429–57; Wooster, *Secession Conventions of the South*, pp. 115–20; Woods, *Rebellion and Realignment*, pp. 161–62.

44. Jones and Rogers, "Montgomery as the Confederate Capital," pp. 51–52; Ringold, *Role of the State Legislatures in the Confederacy*, pp. 9–12; *Florida Senate Journal* (1862), pp. 41–47.

45. Walter L. Fleming, *Civil War and Reconstruction in Alabama*, pp. 34–38; *Atlanta Southern Confederacy*, September 5, 1861; *Raleigh Semi-Weekly Register*, September 11, 1861; Hamilton, *Ruffin Papers*, 3:185–86.

46. William R. Smith, *History and Debates of the Convention of Alabama*, pp. 117–18.

47. For examples, see *Journal of Both Sessions of the Convention of Arkansas*, pp. 122–23; *Official Journal of the Convention of the State of Louisiana*, pp. 17–18; *Journal of the Convention of Florida*, pp. 28–30; William R. Smith, *History and Debates of the Convention of Alabama*, pp. 55–56; *Journal of the [Mississippi] Convention January 1861*, p. 16. In Texas, the only Deep South state to hold a ratification election, the secession ordinance won approval by a roughly three-to-one margin. See Winkler, *Journal of the Secession Convention of Texas*, pp. 48–49, 90, 113–15, 184; Buenger, *Secession and the Union in Texas*, pp. 147, 174.

48. Rodgers, *Contested Truths*, pp. 96–97; Dougan, *Confederate Arkansas*, pp. 39–40; Tyson, *Ray of Light*, pp. 14–96.

49. *Richmond Daily Whig*, January 2, 12, 28, 1861; *Shreveport Southwestern*, February 27, 1861; Rainwater, *Mississippi*, p. 215; *Raleigh Weekly Standard*, January 23, 1861.

50. Barney, *Secessionist Impulse*, p. 303; Rainwater, *Mississippi*, pp. 212–14; William R. Smith, *History and Debates of the Convention of Alabama*, pp. 91–117, 445–47. In states with cooperationist majorities, secessionists were not above putting their own twist on popular sovereignty arguments. The *Richmond Enquirer*, long the editorial voice of Jackson Democrats in Virginia, defended the right of the

people to "instruct" their representatives through public meetings (March 26, 1861).

51. Herschel V. Johnson, "Autobiography," p. 325; Max Williams and Hamilton, *Graham Papers*, 5:234–36; Robert H. Taylor, *Speech*, broadside.

52. Although my own analysis differs in detail and emphasis, see the fine treatment of upper South Unionism in Crofts, *Reluctant Confederates*, pp. 104–6, 189–90, 195–253, 289–352.

53. *Mobile Daily Advertiser and Register*, December 23, 1860; William R. Smith, *History and Debates of the Convention of Alabama*, pp. 24–30, 68–75.

54. Herschel V. Johnson, "Autobiography," pp. 323–24; *Richmond Daily Whig*, January 30, 1861; Raper, *Holden*, pp. 37–38; Reynolds, *Editors Make War*, pp. 171–73.

55. Bragg, *Louisiana in the Confederacy*, pp. 182–83; Schenck Books, December 10, 1861, SHC; Max Williams and Hamilton, *Graham Papers*, 5:311–40; *Raleigh Weekly Standard*, December 18, 1861. To strengthen the conservatives in their continuing warfare with the original secessionists, Holden issued a pamphlet edition of Graham's address. See Max Williams and Hamilton, *Graham Papers*, 5:352; Graham, *Speech of Honorable William A. Graham on Test Oaths and Sedition*.

56. Escott, *Many Excellent People*, pp. 28–31; Kruman, *Parties and Politics in North Carolina*, pp. 189–96; *Raleigh Weekly Standard*, February 20, 1861; Max Williams and Hamilton, *Graham Papers*, 5:386–87.

57. Ringold, *Role of State Legislatures in the Confederacy*, pp. 61–64; Escott, *Many Excellent People*, p. 40; *Raleigh Semi-Weekly Register*, February 13, 1861. The disruption of financial markets and a critical shortage of hard currency forced the Alabama legislature to allow several banks to suspend specie payments temporarily. By the end of 1861, lawmakers agreed that this suspension could continue until one year after the conclusion of the war (*Alabama Acts, Called Session* [1861], pp. 11–12; *Alabama Acts, Second Called Session* [1861], pp. 20–22).

58. Max Williams and Hamilton, *Graham Papers*, 5:345–46; Hamilton, *Ruffin Papers*, 3:187; Schenck Books, February 1, 1862, SHC. North Carolina eventually adopted a debtor relief measure.

Chapter 3

1. *Journal of the Convention of Florida*, p. 105.

2. Roark, *Masters without Slaves*, pp. 14–21; *Journal of Both Sessions of the Convention of Arkansas*, p. 63; Dougan, *Confederate Arkansas*, pp. 63–64; *Journal of the Convention of Alabama*, pp. 178–84; Faust, *Creation of Confederate Nationalism*, pp. 33–40.

3. Despite differences in interpretation, I have relied heavily on the stimulating analysis in Michael P. Johnson, *Toward a Patriarchal Republic*, pp. 124–78.

4. Michael P. Johnson, *Toward a Patriarchal Republic*, pp. 179–87; *Savannah Republican*, June 24, 28, 1861; Avery, *History of Georgia*, p. 207; McCash, *Cobb*, pp. 235–36.

5. Henry Thomas Shanks, "Conservative Constitutional Tendencies of the Virginia Secession Convention," in Green, *Essays in Southern History*, pp. 28–33.

6. *Richmond Daily Dispatch*, June 18, 1861.

7. Shanks, "Conservative Constitutional Tendencies," pp. 35–36; *Richmond Daily Examiner*, June 24, 1861.

8. Shanks, "Conservative Constitutional Tendencies," pp. 33–45; Scarborough, *Dairy of Edmund Ruffin*, 2:167–71, 176; *Richmond Daily Whig*, July 8, November 22, 23, 28, 30, December 4, 1861; *Richmond Daily Dispatch*, November 30, 1861.

9. Scarborough, *Diary of Edmund Ruffin*, 2:184–85; *Richmond Daily Whig*, December 7, 14, 19, 30, 1861, January 10, 1862; Shanks, "Conservative Constitutional Tendencies," pp. 45–48.

10. DeLeon, *Four Years in Rebel Capitals*, pp. 23–24; Charles R. Lee, *Confederate Constitutions*, pp. 51–55; *Mobile Daily Advertiser*, February 15, 1861; *Atlanta Gate-City Guardian*, February 20, 1861.

11. Coulter, *Confederate States of America*, p. 22; Russell, *My Diary North and South*, p. 121; Cleveland, *Stephens*, p. 725; Alexander H. Stephens, *Constitutional View*, 2:325–26; Woodward, *Mary Chesnut's Civil War*, pp. 6–7.

12. Useful profiles of delegations and individual members are in Charles R. Lee, *Confederate Constitutions*, pp. 21–50; Yearns, *Confederate Congress*, pp. 7–10.

13. Charles R. Lee, *Confederate Constitutions*, pp. 55–59; *Journal of the Convention of Florida*, pp. 108–9; Mayes, *Lamar*, p. 637; Carpenter, *South as a Conscious Minority*, pp. 211–25; *Charleston Daily Courier*, January 29, February 4, 1861.

14. Von Barnes to Alexander H. Stephens, February 9, 1861, Stephens Papers, LC; Reese, *Proceedings of the Virginia State Convention*, 4:382; William H. Trescot to Howell Cobb, February 2, 1861, Cobb Papers, UG; *Rome* (Ga.) *Weekly Courier*, February 8, 1861.

15. Howell Cobb to A. R. Wright, February 18, 1861, Stephens Papers, LC; White, *Rhett*, pp. 194–95; *Charleston Mercury*, February 8, 1861; Laurence Keitt to James Henry Hammond, February 13, 1861, Hammond Papers, LC.

16. DeLeon, *Four Years in Rebel Capitals*, pp. 24–25; Yearns, *Confederate Congress*, p. 12; Jones and Rogers, "Montgomery as the Confederate Capital," p. 12.

17. *New Orleans Daily Picayune*, February 5, 1861; Hull, "Correspondence of Cobb," pp. 161–62; *Atlanta Southern Confederacy*, April 2, 1861; Schenck Books, March 18, 1861, SHC; *Rome* (Ga.) *Weekly Courier*, March 1, 1861.

18. Faust, *Creation of a Confederate Nation*, pp. 1–19. Yet focusing on the weaknesses of Confederate nationalism can still be a fruitful approach in the hands of a skillful historian. For the best recent example, see Royster, *Destructive War*, pp. 172–92.

19. Nevins, *Statesmanship of the Civil War*, pp. 67–95; Nichols, *Blueprints for Leviathan*, pp. 233–43; Kenneth M. Stampp, "The Southern Road to Appomattox," in Stampp, *Imperiled Union*, pp. 246–69; Beringer et al., *Why the South Lost*, pp. 66–75.

20. David M. Potter, "The Historian's Use of Nationalism and Vice Versa," in Potter, *South and the Sectional Conflict*, pp. 34–67; Fehrenbacher, *Constitutions and Constitutionalism in the Slaveholding South*, pp. 59–61.

21. William R. Taylor, *Cavalier and Yankee*, pp. 261–97.

22. Oakes, *Ruling Race*, pp. 239–41; Emory M. Thomas, *Confederacy as a Revolutionary Experience*, pp. 1–2; Easterby, *South Carolina Rice Plantation*, pp. 175–76; *New Orleans Daily Picayune*, July 4, 1861.

23. *JCC*, 1:33; Hayes, *Historical Evolution of Modern Nationalism*, pp. 10–11, 30; Kohn, *Idea of Nationalism*, pp. 8–9. For a different interpretation of Confederate claims to 1776, see Royster, *Destructive War*, pp. 175–77.

24. Rodgers, *Contested Truths*, p. 136; Thornton, *Politics and Power in a Slave Society*, pp. 213–27; Hunt, *Politics, Culture, and Class in the French Revolution*, pp. 19–51; Koon, *Believe, Obey, Fight*, pp. 19–21.

25. Bilbo, *Past, Present, and Future of the Confederacy*, pp. 5–12.

26. *Journal of the Convention of South Carolina*, p. 4.

27. Cleveland, *Stephens*, pp. 724–25; Pollard, *Southern History of the War* [First Year], 1:98–99; *Richmond Daily Examiner*, March 6, 1861; Robert C. Tucker, *Political Culture and Leadership in Soviet Russia*, p. 8. For perceptive and differing approaches to the question of whether the Confederates were launching a conservative or a reactionary revolution, see Emory M. Thomas, *Confederacy as a Revolutionary Experience*, pp. 133–34; Emory M. Thomas, *Confederate Nation*, pp. 222–23; Michael P. Johnson, *Toward a Patriarchal Republic*, pp. 106–7; Faust, *Creation of Confederate Nationalism*, p. 21.

28. Patrick, *Davis and His Cabinet*, p. 15; *Milledgeville Southern Federal Union*, March 5, 1861.

29. George Fitzhugh, "The Revolutions of 1776 and 1861 Contrasted," *Southern Literary Messenger* 37 (November and December 1863): 718–26; Analytica, *Problem of Government*, pp. 4–23; Coulter, *Confederate States of America*, pp. 62–67.

30. "The Union: Its Benefits and Dangers," *Southern Literary Messenger* 32 (January 1861): 1–4; Woodward, *Mary Chesnut's Civil War*, p. 161.

31. "Past and Present," *De Bow's Review* 30 (February 1861): 187–98.

32. *Plan of a Provisional Government for the Southern Confederacy*, pp. 3–6; Charles R. Lee, *Confederate Constitutions*, pp. 60–69.

33. Charles R. Lee, *Confederate Constitutions*, pp. 82–84; *JCC*, 1:896.

34. The most recent study argues that the Confederate Constitution was first and foremost an embodiment of state sovereignty growing out of the Federalist versus Anti-Federalist debates of the 1780s and heavily dependent on John C. Calhoun's political theories (DeRosa, *Confederate Constitution*).

35. Fitts, "Confederate Convention: Constitutional Debate," pp. 195–96; *Charleston Mercury*, February 4, 1861.

36. John R. Horsey to William Porcher Miles, December 10, 1860, Miles Papers, SHC; Hull, "Correspondence of Cobb," p. 174; *Raleigh Semi-Weekly Register*, March 6, 1861.

37. *Charleston Mercury*, February 16, 1861; Cobb, *Substance of an Address*, pp. 2–4; Fitts, "Confederate Convention: Constitutional Debate," pp. 199–200.

38. Takaki, *Pro-slavery Crusade*, pp. 228–30; Potter, *Impending Crisis*, pp. 398–401.

39. William R. Smith, *History and Debates of the Convention of Alabama*, pp. 194–211, 228–65.

40. *Journal of the [Mississippi] Convention January 1861*, p. 78; *Official Journal of the Convention of Louisiana*, pp. 28–30; Candler, *Confederate Records of Georgia*, 1:708–10; *Edgefield* (S.C.) *Advertiser*, February 20, March 13, 1861; *OR*, ser. 4, vol. 1, pp. 41–42; Sitterson, *Secession Movement in North Carolina*, p. 222; Raphael Semmes to Alexander H. Stephens, January 25, 1861, Stephens Papers, LC; *Paulding* (Miss.) *Eastern Clarion*, March 22, 1861; *Savannah Republican*, January 24, 1861; *Milledgeville Southern Federal Union*, January 29, 1861.

41. Sitterson, *Secession Movement in North Carolina*, pp. 177–78; *Richmond Daily Whig*, January 3, 1861; Greenawalt, "Unionists in Rockbridge County," p. 96; Frontis W. Johnston, *Vance Papers*, pp. 80–81; Tolbert, *Papers of Ellis*, 2:564–65.

42. William H. Trescot to Howell Cobb, February 2, 1861, Cobb Papers, UG; *JCC*, 1:35–36, 869; *Raleigh Weekly Standard*, March 13, 1861.

43. *Charleston Mercury*, February 12, 1861; "The New Republic," *Southern Literary Messenger* 32 (May 1861): 392–94; Oliphant, Odell, and Eaves, *Letters of Simms*, 4:329–30.

44. Cleveland, *Stephens*, pp. 721–23. For perceptive discussions of this point, see Escott, *After Secession*, pp. 227–50, and Schott, *Stephens*, p. 334.

45. *OR*, ser. 4, vol. 1, pp. 4–11, 19; Winkler, *Journal of the Secession Convention of Texas*, pp. 16–17; Daniel, *Richmond Examiner during the War*, pp. 17–18.

46. Michael P. Johnson, *Toward a Patriarchal Republic*, pp. 46–52; William H. Holcombe, "The Alternative: A Separate Nationality, or the Africanization of the South," *Southern Literary Messenger* 32 (February 1861): 81–88; Cornwall Book, January 4, 1861, SHC.

47. [Miles], *The Relation between the Races at the South*, p. 3. Faust, *Creation of Confederate Nationalism*, pp. 58–81.

48. Candler, *Confederate Records of Georgia*, 2:118–25.

49. Spratt, *Philosophy of Secession*, pp. 1–2; Bland, *Southern Document*, p. 5; Candler, *Confederate Records of Georgia*, 1:54–55; *Annual Cyclopedia* (1861), p. 13; *South Carolina Senate Journal* (1861), pp. 23–25.

50. Wight, "Letters of Northrop," p. 462; Roark, *Masters without Slaves*, pp. 21–24; Hahn, *Roots of Southern Populism*, pp. 86–91.

51. Shore, *Southern Capitalists*, pp. 79–92; Hamilton, *Ruffin Papers*, 3:109; J. Henly Smith to Alexander H. Stephens, November 16, 1860, B. C. Warner to Stephens, August 1, 1861, Stephens Papers, LC.

52. Max Williams and Hamilton, *Graham Papers*, 5:205–6; "The African Slave Trade," *Southern Literary Messenger* 33 (August 1861): 105–13.

53. Oliphant, Odell, and Eaves, *Letters of Simms*, 4:335–36; *JCC*, 1:861–62; Fitts, "Confederate Convention: Constitutional Debate," p. 198.

54. Hull, "Correspondence of Cobb," p. 255; *JCC*, 1:885–86, 895; Charles R. Lee, *Confederate Constitutions*, pp. 112–16.

55. This point is strongly and persuasively argued in Emory M. Thomas, *Confederate Nation*.

56. Cleveland, *Stephens*, pp. 719, 727.

57. Charles R. Lee, *Confederate Constitutions*, pp. 98–100.

58. *JCC*, 1:875; Charles R. Lee, *Confederate Constitutions*, pp. 103–7; Cleveland, *Stephens*, pp. 720–21.

59. An Alabaman, "The One Great Cause of the Failure of the Federal Government," *Southern Literary Messenger* 32 (May 1861): 329–34; *Atlanta Gate-City Guardian*, February 21, 1861.

60. Fitts, "Confederate Convention: Constitutional Debate," p. 193; Carpenter, *South as a Conscious Minority*, pp. 254–60.

61. Fehrenbacher, *Constitutions and Constitutionalism in the Slaveholding South*, p. 64; Donald Nieman, "Republicanism, the Confederate Constitution, and the American Constitutional Tradition," in Hall and Ely, *Uncertain Tradition*, pp. 207–13. Nieman's essay offers an analysis far superior to previous interpretations of the Confederate Constitution.

62. Fitts, "Confederate Convention: Constitutional Debate," p. 204; Pollard, *Echoes from the South*, p. 193.

63. Robert H. Smith, *Address to Citizens of Alabama*, pp. 5–14.

64. Benjamin H. Hill, Jr., *Hill*, p. 253; *Richmond Daily Examiner*, March 16, 1861; Reese, *Proceedings of the Virginia State Convention*, 2:32–34; James Henry Hammond to John D. Ashmore, April 2, 1861, Hammond Papers, LC.

65. *Huntsville* (Ala.) *Independent*, April 20, 1861; *Mobile Daily Advertiser*, March 17, 1861; *Atlanta Southern Confederacy*, April 5, 1861; *Charleston Daily Courier*, March 16, April 4, 1861; Patrick, *Davis and His Cabinet*, p. 321.

66. *Mobile Daily Advertiser*, February 14, April 2, 1861; *Raleigh Weekly Standard*, March 27, June 5, 1861; *Shreveport Southwestern*, March 27, April 3, 1861; *Natchez Daily Courier*, March 19, 1861.

67. Dick, *To the Freemen of the Sixth Congressional District*, broadside; *Raleigh Weekly Standard*, March 6, 1861; Reese, *Proceedings of the Virginia State Convention*, 1:368–69, 2:315–16, 3:631.

68. *New Orleans Daily Picayune*, March 21, 1861; *Montgomery Daily Advertiser*, April 7, 1861; *Address to the People of Texas*, pp. 1–12; *Atlanta Southern Confederacy*, April 12, 1861; Kendall, "Interregnum in Louisiana," pp. 322–24.

69. William R. Smith, *History and Debates of the Convention of Alabama*, pp. 323–65; *Official Journal of Proceedings of the Convention of Louisiana*, pp. 69–70; *Journal of the State Convention [Mississippi]*, pp. 26, 36; *Proceedings of the Convention of Florida*, pp. 32–33; Candler, *Confederate Records of Georgia*, 1:458–62; Winkler, *Journal of the Secession Convention of Texas*, pp. 232–34; *Journal of the Convention of the People of North Carolina*, pp. 17–18; *Journal of the Convention of Arkansas*, pp. 182–83.

70. *Journal of the Convention of South Carolina*, pp. 207, 214–15, 229, 236–38, 243–49; *Atlanta Southern Confederacy*, April 3, 1861; *Charleston Mercury*, April 5, 1861.

71. William R. Smith, *History and Debates of the Convention of Alabama*, pp. 223–27; McCash, *Cobb*, pp. 219–23; *Richmond Daily Dispatch*, December 4, 1861; "What of the Confederacy?—The Present and Future," *De Bow's Review* 31 (December 1861): 519–21; Lonn, *Foreigners in the Confederacy*, pp. 384–416; Charles-

ton *Mercury*, August 15, 1862, January 21, 1863; Frank H. Alfriend, "The Great Danger of the Confederacy," *Southern Literary Messenger* 37 (January 1863): 39–43; Stiles, *National Rectitude*, pp. 32–34.

72. *JCC*, 1:872–73; Myers, *Children of Pride*, p. 725; Jacobs, *Sermon, for the Times*, pp. 2–3; Tupper, *Thanksgiving Discourse*, p. 8; Palmer, *National Responsibility before God*, pp. 11–16; Elliott, *God's Presence with the Confederate States*, pp. 11–13.

73. See, for example, Emory M. Thomas, *Confederate Nation*, pp. 58–66; Beringer et al., *Why the South Lost*, pp. 75–81. More recently Don Fehrenbacher has cogently argued that the derivative character of the Confederate Constitution is hardly evidence of a weak commitment to Southern nationalism (*Constitutions and Constitutionalism in the Slaveholding South*, pp. 62–63).

74. Again see Nieman, "Confederate Constitution," pp. 201–3, 215–19, for an excellent analysis that differs in emphasis from that offered here.

75. Nieman, "Confederate Constitution," p. 204, and Fehrenbacher, *Constitutions and Constitutionalism in the Slaveholding South*, pp. 65–66.

76. For contrasting views on the meaning of antiparty thought in the Confederacy and its effect on constitution making, see Nieman, "Confederate Constitution," pp. 204–7, and Luraghi, *Rise and Fall of the Plantation South*, p. 85.

Chapter 4

1. *JCC*, 1:77.

2. Scarborough, *Diary of Edmund Ruffin*, 1:551.

3. Lipset, *First New Nation*, pp. 16–23; Hunt, *Politics, Culture, and Class in the French Revolution*, pp. 87–119; Agulhon, *Marianne into Battle*, pp. 11–37.

4. Hull, "Correspondence of Cobb," pp. 160, 164; M. W. Boyer to Robert M. T. Hunter, February 5, 1861, Hunter Papers, UVa.; Schott, *Stephens*, p. 327; *Milledgeville Southern Federal Union*, February 12, 1861.

5. William H. Trescot to Howell Cobb, February 2, 1861, Cobb Papers, UG; Phillips, *Correspondence of Toombs, Stephens, and Cobb*, pp. 536–37; Hull, "Correspondence of Cobb," p. 164.

6. Crist and Dix, *Davis Papers*, 7:25.

7. Rowland, *Davis*, 8:461–63; R. W. Barnwell to James Lawrence Orr, February 9, 1861, Orr and Patterson Family Papers, SHC; Reese, *Proceedings of the Virginia State Convention*, 1:74.

8. *Charleston Mercury*, February 6, 1861; William Henry Trescot to William Porcher Miles, February 6, 1861, Miles Papers, SHC; Dodd, *Davis*, p. 220; Cauthen, *South Carolina Goes to War*, p. 86; Woodward and Muhlenfeld, *Private Mary Chesnut*, p. 85.

9. Phillips, *Correspondence of Toombs, Stephens, and Cobb*, pp. 537–38; Hull, "Correspondence of Cobb," pp. 168, 171–72; Richard M. Johnston and Browne, *Stephens*, pp. 389–91; Alexander H. Stephens, *Constitutional View*, 2:329–33.

10. DeLeon, *Belles, Beaux, and Brains of the 60's*, p. 101; Richard Taylor, *Destruction and Reconstruction*, pp. 26–28.

11. One enthusiastic Georgia editor predicted that Davis and Stephens would end the abuses of the old political system by erecting a new political order based on virtue (*Atlanta Gate-City Guardian*, February 13, 1861).

12. Alexander H. Stephens to Richard M. Johnston, February 2, 1861, quoted in Richard M. Johnston and Browne, *Stephens*, pp. 383–84; Stephens to James P. Hambleton, February 22, 1861, Hambleton Papers, Emory; Howell Cobb to his son, February 10, 15, 1861, Cobb Papers, UG; Hull, "Correspondence of Cobb," pp. 168–69, 175. See also the fine analysis of Stephens's dilemma in Thomas E. Schott's superb biography, *Stephens*, pp. 325–33.

13. Varina Davis, *Davis*, 2:18–19; Coulter, *Confederate States of America*, pp. 26, 113; Rowland, *Davis*, 5:47–48.

14. The best descriptions of Davis's physical appearance in Montgomery are Russell, *My Diary North and South*, pp. 124–25; DeLeon, *Four Years in Rebel Capitals*, p. 25. For useful later descriptions, see Charles M. Blackford, *Letters from Lee's Army*, p. 86; Sorrel, *Recollections of a Confederate Staff Officer*, p. 63; John B. Jones, *Rebel War Clerk's Diary*, 1:36–37; Schenck Books, June 21, 1861, SHC.

15. Charles R. Lee, *Confederate Constitutions*, pp. 79–80; Robbins, "Confederate Nationalism," pp. 8–11; Woodward and Muhlenfeld, *Private Mary Chesnut*, p. 12; Ellen N. Jackson to Mary H. Noyes, February 19, 1861, Jackson Papers, ADAH.

16. Crist and Dix, *Davis Papers*, 7:46–51. For insightful discussion of Davis as an orator and spokesman for Southern nationalism, see Wiley, *Road to Appomattox*, pp. 17–20; Vandiver, *Their Tattered Flags*, pp. 35–36; Escott, *After Secession*, pp. 38–53; Vandiver, "Davis," pp. 15–16.

17. DeLeon, *Four Years in Rebel Capitals*, pp. 25–26, 153–54; Varina Davis, *Davis*, 2:40; Varina Davis to Virginia Clay, May 10, 1861, Clay Papers, Duke; Vandiver, *Davis and the Confederate State*, pp. 17–22; Patrick, *Davis and His Cabinet*, pp. 17–22, 43–45; Eaton, *Southern Confederacy*, pp. 49–53; William C. Davis, *Davis*, pp. 310–20.

18. Varina Davis, *Davis*, 2:163; Pollard, *Davis*, pp. 102–8; Escott, *After Secession*, pp. 256–74; David M. Potter, "Jefferson Davis and the Political Factors in Confederate Defeat," in Donald, *Why the North Won the Civil War*, pp. 100–109; William C. Davis, *Davis*, pp. 388–93; Coulter, *Confederate States of America*, p. 108; Wiley, *Road to Appomattox*, pp. 20–25, 40–42; Beringer, "Jefferson Davis's Pursuit of Ambition," pp. 5–38.

19. Hull, "Correspondence of Cobb," pp. 181, 234. Historians have long argued that the fire-eaters felt excluded from the new government. But this was by no means the case. Yancey, Wigfall, and Keitt, to name the three most conspicuous examples, did not experience the alienation felt by Rhett. For the most recent statement of what has become a stock and highly embroidered tale of a "conservative" takeover of the Confederate movement, see Freehling, *Road to Disunion*, pp. 3–7.

20. Vandiver, *Their Tattered Flags*, p. 25; Patrick, *Davis and His Cabinet*, pp. 49–50.

21. DeLeon, *Belles, Beaux, and Brains of the 60's*, pp. 83–84; Thompson, *Toombs*, pp. 165, 172–74; Patrick, *Davis and His Cabinet*, pp. 82–85.

22. Robert Barnwell Rhett, Jr., "The Confederate Government at Montgomery," in Robert U. Johnson and Buel, *Battles and Leaders*, 1:104–5; Pollard, *Davis*, pp. 174–75.

23. DeLeon, *Four Years in Rebel Capitals*, pp. 33–34; John B. Jones, *Rebel War Clerk's Diary*, 1:38; King, *Wigfall*, pp. 127–28.

24. Patrick, *Davis and His Cabinet*, pp. 245–46; *JCC*, 1:105–6; DeLeon, *Belles, Beaux, and Brains of the 60's*, pp. 83–84; Woodward and Muhlenfeld, *Private Mary Chesnut*, pp. 16–17, 31.

25. DeLeon, *Belles, Beaux, and Brains of the 60's*, pp. 90–91; Proctor, *Not without Honor*, pp. 132, 137.

26. Russell, *My Diary North and South*, p. 127; Wright, *Southern Girl in '61*, p. 30; Alfriend, "Social Life in Richmond," p. 384; Fremantle, *Three Months in the Southern States*, p. 207; Patrick, *Davis and His Cabinet*, pp. 156–57; John B. Jones, *Rebel War Clerk's Diary*, 1:38; Meade, "Benjamin and Davis," p. 474.

27. DeLeon, *Four Years in Rebel Capitals*, pp. 26, 31–32; Woodward and Muhlenfeld, *Private Mary Chesnut*, pp. 6–7, 13–14.

28. Howell Cobb to his son, February 15, 1861, Cobb Papers, UG.

29. Woodward, *Mary Chesnut's Civil War*, pp. 17, 49; Russell, *My Diary North and South*, p. 118; Hull, "Correspondence of Cobb," pp. 257–58.

30. McCash, *Cobb*, pp. 244–45; Hull, "Correspondence of Cobb," pp. 240–41, 313; L. Fouchie to Howell Cobb, February n.d., 1861, Leander M. Crook to Cobb, February 7, 1861, Cobb Papers, UG.

31. *Richmond Daily Whig*, March 5, 1861; *Natchez Daily Courier*, March 27, 1861; Christopher G. Memminger to William Porcher Miles, May 23, 1861, Miles Papers, SHC; J. Henly Smith to Alexander H. Stephens, May 16, 1861, Stephens Papers, LC.

32. The best accounts of the Confederate decisions on Fort Sumter (and Fort Pickens) are McWhiney, *Southerners and Other Americans*, pp. 72–82; Current, *Lincoln and the First Shot*, pp. 126–53; McPherson, *Battle Cry of Freedom*, pp. 272–73.

33. Richardson, *Messages and Papers*, 1:81–82.

34. Faust, *Creation of Confederate Nationalism*, pp. 22–29; Silver, *Confederate Morale and Church Propaganda*, pp. 42–59; *JCC*, 1:237–38.

35. Silver, *Confederate Morale and Church Propaganda*, pp. 25–41; Myers, *Children of Pride*, pp. 694–95, 709.

36. [Barten], *Sermon Preached in St. James' Church*, pp. 5–12; Ann Hardeman Diary, April 30, 1861, in Stuart Papers, MDAH; McGuire, *Diary of a Southern Refugee*, p. 110; Cornwall Book, May 2, 1861, SHC.

37. Richardson, *Messages and Papers*, 1:103–4.

38. Armstrong, *"The Good Hand of God Upon Us,"* pp. 6–7; De Veaux, *Fast-day Sermon*, p. 10; Augustus B. Longstreet, *Fast-day Sermon*, pp. 4–12. For the typology of the jeremiad, see Bercovitch, *American Jeremiad*.

39. *Atlanta Southern Confederacy*, March 6, 26, June 28, 1861; *Mobile Daily Advertiser*, March 29, 1861; J. Henly Smith to Alexander H. Stephens, July 15, 1861, Stephens Papers, LC; Wight, "Letters of Northrop," p. 463; Bilbo, *Past, Present, and Future of the Confederacy*, pp. 23–25.

40. McMillan, *Disintegration of a Confederate State*, p. 22; Dubay, *Pettus*, pp. 97–98, 106–7, 110–11; Fox-Genovese and Genovese, *Fruits of Merchant Capital*, pp. 255–56.

41. Boney, *Letcher*, pp. 121–22; John B. Jones, *Rebel War Clerk's Diary*, 1:33; *Richmond Daily Examiner*, May 17, June 29, August 29, 1861; *Richmond Enquirer*, May 14, 1861; *Proceedings of the Virginia State Convention*, 4:599–628. For similar criticism of the Arkansas convention, see *Des Arc* (Ark.) *Semi-Weekly Citizen*, May 17, 1861.

42. *Annual Cyclopedia* (1861), p. 539; Tolbert, *Papers of Ellis*, 2:697–704; *Raleigh Semi-Weekly Register*, May 8, 1861. For an excellent discussion of politics in this early period, see Kruman, *Parties and Politics in North Carolina*, pp. 201–8, 223–25.

43. *Raleigh Semi-Weekly Register*, May 11, 1861; Max Williams and Hamilton, *Graham Papers*, 5:254–55; *Journal of the Convention of North Carolina* (First Session), pp. 119–28.

44. Hamilton, *Correspondence of Worth*, 1:141–42, 144, 157–58; Max Williams and Hamilton, *Graham Papers*, 5:248–50, 257.

45. John B. Jones, *Rebel War Clerk's Diary*, 1:41; *Charleston Mercury*, May 22, 1861.

46. McCash, *Cobb*, p. 250; Palmer, *National Responsibility before God*, pp. 16–19.

47. Robbins, "Confederate Nationalism," p. 56; Richard M. Johnston to Alexander H. Stephens, September 15, 1861, Stephens Papers, LC; Henry S. Foote, *War of the Rebellion*, pp. 354–55; R. T. Scott to Clement Claiborne Clay, October 11, 1861, Clay Papers, Duke; *Richmond Enquirer*, June 4, 1861; *Richmond Daily Whig*, July 4, 1861.

48. Monroe, "Early Confederate Patronage," pp. 51–61; Todd, *Confederate Finance*, pp. 2–11; Parish, *American Civil War*, p. 213.

49. Eric L. McKitrick, "Politics and the Union and Confederate War Efforts," in Chambers and Burnham, *American Party Systems*, pp. 132–33; Van Riper and Scheiber, "Confederate Civil Service," pp. 448–70; Capers, *Memminger*, pp. 325–39; Reagan, *Memoirs*, p. 147; Trexler, "Davis and the Confederate Patronage," pp. 49–58.

50. Schwab, *Confederate States*, pp. 6–18; Todd, *Confederate Finance*, pp. 25–48, 64–65, 85–102.

51. See the sometimes harsh but generally persuasive critique of Confederate fiscal policies in Ball, *Financial Failure and Confederate Defeat*, pp. 23–33, 200–223.

52. Herschel V. Johnson to James Henry Hammond, August 29, 1861, Hammond Papers, LC.

53. Herschel Johnson to Alexander H. Stephens, May 8, 1861, Johnson Papers, Duke; Myers, *Children of Pride*, p. 695; Russell, *My Diary North and South*, p. 178;

Daniel, *Richmond Examiner during the War*, pp. 14–15; Woodward, *Mary Chesnut's Civil War*, p. 83.

54. Robert Barnwell Rhett, Jr., to George W. Bagby, June 17, 1861, Bagby Papers, Duke; White, *Rhett*, pp. 207–8; *Memphis Daily Appeal*, July 23, 1861; *Richmond Daily Enquirer*, July 12, 1861.

55. James Henry Hammond to Jefferson Davis, May 26, 1861, [not sent], Hammond Papers, LC; Richard M. Johnston and Browne, *Stephens*, p. 401; Roland, *Confederacy*, p. 53.

56. Plato, *Republic*, p. 275.

57. Woodward and Muhlenfeld, *Private Mary Chesnut*, p. 74; Durrill, *War of Another Kind*, pp. 40–67; *Baton Rouge Advocate*, n.d., in *Shreveport Southwestern*, May 1, 1861; Escott, *After Secession*, pp. 94–99; *OR*, ser. 4, vol. 1, pp. 318–19.

58. Rowland, *Davis*, 5:104; Richardson, *Messages and Papers*, 1:119–20.

59. Roman, *Beauregard*, 1:77–78.

60. Ibid., pp. 81–113; Woodward and Muhlenfeld, *Private Mary Chesnut*, p. 102; Pollard, *Davis*, p. 141.

61. T. Harry Williams, *Beauregard*, pp. 96–98; Daniel, *Richmond Examiner during the War*, pp. 18–19; Rowland, *Davis*, 5:120–21; Roman, *Beauregard*, 1:125–26; Woodward, *Mary Chesnut's Civil War*, p. 129; *OR*, ser. 1, vol. 2, p. 504; *Richmond Daily Enquirer*, September 18, 1862.

62. Fremantle, *Three Months in the Southern States*, p. 117; Freeman, *Lee's Lieutenants*, 1:111–12; Richard Taylor, *Destruction and Reconstruction*, pp. 42–44.

63. Woodward and Muhlenfeld, *Private Mary Chesnut*, p. 91; Govan and Livingood, *Different Valor*, pp. 70–71, 225; Joseph E. Johnston to Jefferson Davis, June 25, 1861, Davis Papers, Emory.

64. Crist and Dix, *Davis Papers*, 7:335; Rowland, *Davis*, 5:119, 132; Joseph E. Johnston, *Narrative of Military Operations*, pp. 70–73. The most judicious accounts of this episode are McMurry, "'The Enemy at Richmond,'" pp. 5–7; William C. Davis, *Davis*, pp. 356–61; and Symonds, *Johnston*, pp. 125–29.

65. Roman, *Beauregard*, 1:131–51; Gustavus W. Smith, *Confederate War Papers*, pp. 14–40; Joseph E. Johnston, *Narrative of Military Operations*, pp. 75–77.

66. Anne Norton, *Alternative Americas*, pp. 123–24; Augustus R. Wright to Alexander H. Stephens, September 15, 1861, Stephens Papers, LC; *Richmond Daily Whig*, September 11, 1861.

67. McWhiney, *Southerners and Other Americans*, pp. 90–104; Thomas G. Rhett to William Porcher Miles, August 13, 1861, Miles Papers, SHC. Even those who had received appointments remained dissatisfied. In Pensacola, Florida, Braxton Bragg assumed that his military ability would not win promotions but self-righteously pledged to "continue a soldier until the political demagogues are all killed off." Because of a long acquaintance with Davis and other leaders of the Southern revolution, Kentucky general Humphrey Marshall kept asking for an independent command and especially resented serving under the Whig "traitor" George Crittenden (Whittington, "Thomas O. Moore," pp. 30–31; Marshall to Alexander H. Stephens, November 30, December 14, 1861, February 22, 1862, Stephens Papers, Emory).

68. For example, Louisiana governor Thomas O. Moore informed Davis in early

September 1861 that he agreed with many citizens who opposed sending any more troops out of his state because of the sorry condition of local defense (Crist and Dix, *Davis Papers*, 5:331).

69. *OR*, ser. 1, vol. 3, pp. 710–11, vol. 6, p. 301, ser. 4, vol. 1, pp. 419–20, 474–75; Crist and Dix, *Davis Papers*, 7:246. For fuller discussions of local defense, military appointments, and states' rights, see Owsley, *State Rights in the Confederacy*, pp. 5–31, 77–149, and William C. Davis, *Davis*, pp. 341–43.

70. Woodward and Muhlenfeld, *Private Mary Chesnut*, pp. 85, 109, 119, 121–22; James Henry Hammond to "Dear Major," August 11, 1861, Hammond to Herschel V. Johnson, September 2, 1861, Hammond Papers, LC; *Charleston Mercury*, August 28, 1861; Marszalek, *Diary of Emma Holmes*, p. 91.

71. Woodward and Muhlenfeld, *Private Mary Chesnut*, p. 100; Woodward, *Mary Chesnut's Civil War*, pp. 86, 143; King, *Wigfall*, pp. 126–32.

72. King, *Wigfall*, pp. 132–35; Hull, "Correspondence of Cobb," pp. 312–13; Russell, *My Diary North and South*, p. 87.

73. *Richmond Daily Examiner*, August 6, 1861.

74. Wadley Diary, July 28, 1861, SHC. For the importance of symbolic leadership in establishing political legitimacy and in solidifying a political culture, see Edelman, *Politics as Symbolic Action*, pp. 31–44; Edelman, *Symbolic Uses of Politics*, pp. 76–81.

Chapter 5

1. See the still useful analysis of the relationship between values, behavior, and political culture in Sidney Verba, "Comparative Political Culture," in Pye and Verba, *Political Culture and Political Development*, pp. 513–18.

2. *Richmond Daily Whig*, August 26, 1861.

3. *Charleston Mercury*, October 22, 1861; *Richmond Daily Whig*, September 9, 1861.

4. *South Carolina Senate Journal* (1862), pp. 11–12.

5. Jean H. Baker, "The Ceremonies of Politics: Nineteenth Century Rituals of National Affirmation," in Cooper, *Master's Due*, pp. 161–65, 169–78; Baker, *Affairs of Party*, pp. 261–304.

6. *OR*, ser. 4, vol. 1, pp. 337–38.

7. *Richmond Daily Examiner*, September 16, 18, 1861.

8. *Memphis Daily Appeal*, September 24, 1861; *Jackson Weekly Mississippian*, October 9, 1861; *Savannah Republican*, September 24, 1861; *Raleigh Weekly Standard*, September 18, 1861; *Richmond Daily Whig*, September 24, 1861; *Richmond Daily Enquirer*, September 16, 24, 1861.

9. Herschel V. Johnson to Alexander H. Stephens, September 23, 1861, Johnson Papers, Duke; L. Basil Frisch to Alexander H. Stephens, September 11, 1861, Richard F. Lyon to Stephens, September 19, 1861, Stephens Papers, LC; *Atlanta Southern Confederacy*, September 24, 1861.

10. *New Orleans Daily Picayune*, October 23, 1861; *Raleigh Weekly Standard*,

August 21, 1861; *Richmond Daily Examiner,* October 17, 1861; *Memphis Daily Appeal,* September 17, 1861; *Richmond Daily Dispatch,* November 6, 1861; *Richmond Daily Enquirer,* August 26, 1861; Phillips, *Correspondence of Toombs, Stephens, and Cobb,* p. 577.

11. *Richmond Daily Enquirer,* September 16, 1861; Dougan, *Confederate Arkansas,* p. 81; *New Orleans Daily Picayune,* September 15, 26, 1861. Only in North Carolina did the choice of electors generate any controversy. A slate of eight secessionist Democrats and four Unionist Whigs ran against a ticket of four secessionist Democrats, three Unionist Democrats, and five Unionist Whigs gotten up by William W. Holden, editor of the *Raleigh Standard.* Much to Holden's dismay, the voters appeared indifferent, turnout was low, and his slate was badly defeated (*Raleigh Semi-Weekly Register,* October 12, 1861; Kruman, *Parties and Politics in North Carolina,* pp. 229–30; *Raleigh Weekly Standard,* October 9, November 6, 27, 1861; William C. Harris, *Holden,* pp. 11–12). Some disgruntled South Carolina radicals denounced the president but received little encouragement from most citizens. The *Charleston Courier* and several country newspapers disavowed the *Mercury*'s extremism and strongly endorsed the administration (Benjamin Franklin Arthur to ?, October 23, 1861, Arthur Papers, SCL; Woodward and Muhlenfeld, *Private Mary Chesnut,* pp. 166, 169–70, 183; *Edgefield* [S.C.] *Advertiser,* October 2, 1861).

12. *Richmond Daily Dispatch,* October 17, 1861; *Raleigh Weekly Standard,* October 23, 1861; *Richmond Daily Whig,* October 16, 1861; *New Orleans Daily Picayune,* November 6, 1861; *Paulding* (Miss.) *Eastern Clarion,* November 1, 1861.

13. *Des Arc* (Ark.) *Weekly Citizen,* October 30, 1861; *Memphis Daily Appeal,* October 22, 1861; *Jackson Weekly Mississippian,* September 24, 1861.

14. John B. Jones, *Rebel War Clerk's Diary,* 1:89; *New Orleans Daily Picayune,* November 8, 1861; *Edgefield* (S.C.) *Advertiser,* November 6, 1861.

15. *Richmond Enquirer,* October 1, 1861; *Richmond Daily Whig,* November 1, 1861; *Richmond Daily Examiner,* October 7, 1861.

16. *Richmond Daily Enquirer,* October 14, 22, 1861; *Edgefield* (S.C.) *Advertiser,* October 16, 30, 1861; *Richmond Daily Whig,* September 27, 1861.

17. *Raleigh Weekly Standard,* October 2, 1861; *Richmond Enquirer,* October 1, 1861; *Richmond Daily Whig,* October 4, 1861; Scarborough, *Diary of Edmund Ruffin,* 2:157.

18. *Richmond Daily Whig,* October 18, 29, November 1, 1861.

19. *Richmond Daily Enquirer,* October 23, 1861; Goode, *Recollections of a Lifetime,* p. 76. A similar approach by Thomas F. Goode in the Fifth Congressional District of Virginia failed against the popular Thomas S. Bocock, who served as speaker of the Confederate House of Representatives throughout the war. Bocock attacked Goode for trying to hold two offices at the same time. Forced on the defensive, Goode finally promised to resign his commission if elected to Congress, but the damage had already been done (*Richmond Daily Whig,* October 9, 1861; *Richmond Daily Enquirer,* October 22, 23, 1861).

20. *Atlanta Southern Confederacy,* September 24, October 9, 1861; Herbert Fielder to Joseph E. Brown, September 14, 1861, Brown Papers, Duke.

21. *Raleigh Weekly Standard*, June 12, 1861; *Raleigh Semi-Weekly Register*, September 14, 1861. See the fine analysis in Kruman, *Parties and Politics in North Carolina*, pp. 225–26. Editors seemed more likely to endorse candidates in some of the country districts. See *Edgefield* (S.C.) *Advertiser*, October 9, 1861; *Rome* (Ga.) *Weekly Courier*, September 7, 1861.

22. Neely, Holzer, and Boritt, *Confederate Image*, p. 6. For a striking contrast, see the partisan editorials, reports of ratification meetings, excerpts from stump speeches, and even an advertisement for dollar portraits of Democratic gubernatorial candidate Horatio Seymour in the *Albany* (N.Y.) *Atlas and Argus*, November 1, 1862. Northern papers also reported campaigns and elections outside their states in vastly more detail than their Confederate counterparts. See the analysis of the New York elections in *Baltimore American and Commercial Advertiser*, November 6, 1862.

23. *Richmond Daily Whig*, October 11, 29, 1861; *Des Arc* (Ark.) *Weekly Citizen*, October 23, 1861; Dougan, *Confederate Arkansas*, p. 81.

24. *Jackson Weekly Mississippian*, September 17, November 4, 1861; *Des Arc* (Ark.) *Weekly Citizen*, September 11, 1861.

25. *Richmond Daily Enquirer*, September 16, October 11, 1861.

26. *Memphis Daily Appeal*, September 11, 1861; *New Orleans Daily Picayune*, October 12, 1861; *Richmond Daily Whig*, September 26, 1861; Barrow, *Remarks on the Present War*, p. 2.

27. *Richmond Daily Whig*, October 11, 1861; Bilbo, *Past, Present, and Future of the Confederacy*, pp. 25, 43–47.

28. *Savannah Republican*, October 15, 1861; *Greensboro* (Ala.) *Beacon*, October 25, 1861; Yearns and Barrett, *North Carolina Civil War Documentary*, p. 310.

29. *New Orleans Daily Picayune*, October 8, 1861. One Georgia editor suggested that the congressional elections be an "old-fashioned honest scrub race" in which any man could enter and citizens could vote for anyone, including themselves (Coulter, *Confederate States of America*, p. 114).

30. *Jackson Weekly Mississippian*, October 30, 1861; *Raleigh Weekly Standard*, September 4, October 16, 1861; Robbins, "Confederate Nationalism," p. 45; Martin J. Crawford to Alexander H. Stephens, September 26, October 14, November 3, 1861, Stephens Papers, LC; *New Orleans Daily Picayune*, October 12, 13, 1861; *Richmond Daily Enquirer*, September 24, 1861.

31. *Des Arc* (Ark.) *Weekly Citizen*, September 25, 1861; *Richmond Daily Examiner*, October 22, November 4–6, 13, 1861; Scarborough, *Diary of Edmund Ruffin*, 2:162; *Rome* (Ga.) *Weekly Courier*, October 4, 1861.

32. *Edgefield* (S.C.) *Advertiser*, October 23, 1861; *Richmond Daily Enquirer*, September 24, October 11, 19, 1861; William H. Thomas, *To the Freemen of the Tenth Congressional District*, broadside; *Richmond Daily Whig*, October 21, 1861; Dougan, *Confederate Arkansas*, pp. 81–82.

33. *Richmond Daily Examiner*, October 2, 8, 1861; J. W. Ellis to Thomas D. McDowell, September 18, 1861, McDowell Papers, SHC.

34. *Richmond Enquirer*, October 1, 1861; *Richmond Daily Whig*, February 10, 1862.

35. Max Williams and Hamilton, *Graham Papers*, 5:298–99; *Raleigh Weekly Standard*, October 30, 1861; Yearns, *Confederate Congress*, p. 44.

36. *Des Arc* (Ark.) *Weekly Citizen*, October 30, 1861; *Raleigh Weekly Standard*, October 16, 1861; R. T. Scott to Clement Claiborne Clay, October 11, 1861, Clay Papers, Duke; Yearns, *Confederate Congress*, pp. 44–45.

37. *Richmond Daily Whig*, October 25, 1861. Generalizations about candidates' announcements are based on the following: *John Perkins to Voters of 6th Congressional District* [La.], broadside, October ?, 1861, Perkins Papers, SHC; Edward R. Hord, *Dear Sir*, broadside; *Richmond Enquirer*, October 1, 12, 1861; *Raleigh Semi-Weekly Register*, September 14, 1861; *Richmond Daily Dispatch*, October 17, 1861; *Raleigh Weekly Standard*, October 2, 1861.

38. *Richmond Daily Whig*, November 19, 1861; Robbins, "Confederate Nationalism," pp. 39–41; Schenck Books, June 1, 1861, SHC.

39. M. Gordon M'Cabe, "Political Corruption," *Southern Literary Messenger* 34 (February and March 1862): 81–89; Virginius, "Treating at Election-Time," ibid., pp. 154–56; "Thoughts Suggested by the War," *De Bow's Review* 31 (September 1861): 302.

40. *Richmond Daily Whig*, October 1, 1861; *Paulding* (Miss.) *Eastern Clarion*, September 6, 1861; *Richmond Enquirer*, October 4, 1861.

41. *Nashville Christian Advocate*, n.d., quoted in *Southern Cultivator* 19 (November 1861): 293; Henry H. Tucker, *God in the War*, p. 20; J. Henry Smith, *Sermon Delivered at Greensboro*, p. 10.

42. Schenck Books, November 7, 1861, SHC; *Shreveport Southwestern*, July 24, October 23, 1861; A. J. Gattarray to Thomas D. McDowell, September 30, 1861, McDowell Papers, SHC; Scarborough, *Diary of Edmund Ruffin*, 2:288.

43. For examples of the fragmentary returns that appeared at the time, see *New Orleans Daily Picayune*, November 7, 1861; *Richmond Daily Whig*, November 7, 1861; *Edgefield* (S.C.) *Advertiser*, November 13, 1861. See the useful analysis of the North Carolina vote in Kruman, *Parties and Politics in North Carolina*, pp. 229–30. Some states allowed soldiers to vote in their camps, but there was some confusion over how—and even if—their ballots would be counted. See Flournoy, *Calendar of Virginia State Papers*, 11:192–93; Ringold, *State Legislatures in the Confederacy*, pp. 69–70; *Edgefield* (S.C.) *Advertiser*, November 27, 1861.

44. See the thorough and helpful discussion of these issues in Alexander and Beringer, *Anatomy of the Confederate Congress*, pp. 43–44.

45. *Mississippi House Journal* (1861–62), pp. 52–54; Absalom Dantzler to Susan Dantzler, November 10, 1861, Dantzler Papers, Duke.

46. Tabulations made from Alexander and Beringer, *Anatomy of the Confederate Congress*, pp. 47–48, 354–89, but do not include Kentucky and Missouri, which did not officially secede but later received representation in the Confederate Congress.

47. *Florida Senate Journal* (1861), pp. 93–101, 111–14, 124–26, 136–39, 180–84, 270. There is also some evidence that legislators were reluctant to select men with too much Washington experience. In Louisiana, wealthy lawyer-planter and secessionist Whig Edward Sparrow, who had never been elected to a state or national

office, beat out veteran political operator (and current secretary of war) Judah P. Benjamin. For the other Senate seat, the legislature chose Thomas Jenkins Semmes, a secessionist Democrat with little legislative experience (*Louisiana Senate Journal* [1861], pp. 19–21).

48. Dougan, *Confederate Arkansas*, p. 83.

49. R. T. Scott to Clement Claiborne Clay, October 11, 1861, J. W. Withers to Clay, November 29, 1861, J. W. Bradford to Clay, December 1, 1861, Clay Papers, Duke; Nuermberger, *Clays of Alabama*, pp. 187–90.

50. *Richmond Daily Examiner*, December 9, 1861, January 20, 21, 23, 24, 1862; *Richmond Daily Whig*, December 28, 1861, January 1, 2, 8, 1862; *Richmond Enquirer*, January 10, 1862; *Virginia Senate Journal* (1861–62), p. 102; Younger, *Inside the Confederate Government*, p. 22. The Virginia legislature did preserve some semblance of political balance by selecting western Whig William Ballard Preston for the other Senate seat.

51. James Henry Hammond to John D. Ashmore, April 2, 1861, Hammond Papers, LC; A. P. Aldrich to Milledge Luke Bonham, August 28, October 2, 1861, Bonham Papers, SCL; Woodward, *Mary Chesnut's Civil War*, pp. 215, 254; White, *Rhett*, pp. 218–20.

52. *Atlanta Southern Confederacy*, October 22, 1861; *Georgia Senate Journal* (1861), pp. 104–8; Herschel Johnson to E. A. Cochran, October 31, November 17, 26, 1861, Johnson to James H. Hook, November 20, 1861, Johnson Papers, Duke.

53. T. J. Smith to Alexander H. Stephens, November 29, 1861, A. H. Kenan to ?, March 23, 1862, Stephens Papers, LC; Avery, *History of Georgia*, p. 222; Phillips, *Correspondence of Toombs, Stephens, and Cobb*, p. 608; Phillips, *Toombs*, pp. 240–42.

54. Schenck Books, August 16, 1861, SHC.

55. *Shreveport Southwestern*, September 18, 1861; *New Orleans Daily Picayune*, November 3, 1861.

56. Thomas J. Chambers, *To the People of Texas*, broadside; Lubbock, *To the Voters of the State of Texas*, broadside; Raines, *Six Decades in Texas*, pp. 322–24; Ralph A. Wooster, "Texas," in Yearns, *Confederate Governors*, p. 198.

57. Dubay, *Pettus*, pp. 104–5, 112–13; Bettersworth, *Confederate Mississippi*, pp. 30–36; *Paulding* (Miss.) *Eastern Clarion*, August 9, September 6, 1861.

58. Dubay, *Pettus*, p. 114; *Jackson Weekly Mississippian*, August 13, September 4, 18, 1861; *Paulding* (Miss.) *Eastern Clarion*, September 6, 1861; *Mississippi House Journal* (1861–62), pp. 38–39.

59. Thornton, *Politics and Power in a Slave Society*, pp. 437–41; *Troy* (Ala.) *Southern Advertiser*, April 9, 1861; *Florence* (Ala.) *Gazette*, July 3, 1861; *Montgomery Daily Advertiser*, March 19, 23, 1861; *Alabama Senate Journal* (First Regular Session, 1861), pp. 91–92; McMillan, *Disintegration of a Confederate State*, pp. 30–33.

60. For a useful description of Brown, see Bass, "Georgia Gubernatorial Elections," pp. 170–71. The standard biography is Parks, *Brown*.

61. Candler, *Confederate Records of Georgia*, 3:23–28; *OR*, ser. 4, vol. 1, pp. 424, 466, 477–78.

62. Parks, *Brown*, pp. 156–58; *Milledgeville Southern Federal Union*, March 19, June 25, July 2, 9, 16, 1861.

63. Avery, *History of Georgia*, pp. 207–8; Peterson Thweatt to Alexander H. Stephens, August 19, 1861, Stephens Papers, LC; Phillips, *Correspondence of Toombs, Stephens, and Cobb*, p. 574.

64. *Atlanta Southern Confederacy*, August 13, 15, 1861; *Milledgeville Southern Federal Union*, August 20, 27, 1861.

65. Phillips, *Correspondence of Toombs, Stephens, and Cobb*, pp. 560, 568; *Savannah Republican*, July 18, 1861.

66. Bass, "Georgia Gubernatorial Elections," pp. 172–77; *Savannah Republican*, September 7, 1861; Parks, *Brown*, pp. 158–61.

67. *Rome* (Ga.) *Weekly Courier*, September 13, 1861; *Milledgeville Southern Federal Union*, September 17, 1861; Peterson Thweatt to Alexander H. Stephens, September 17, 1861, Stephens Papers, LC; Myers, *Children of Pride*, p. 746; Parks, *Brown*, pp. 161–64.

68. *Atlanta Southern Confederacy*, September 14, 1861; *Savannah Republican*, September 16, 23, 1861; *Rome* (Ga.) *Weekly Courier*, September 26, 1861; Richard Peters to Alexander H. Stephens, September 26, 1861, E. L. Thomas to Stephens, September 30, 1861, R. S. Burch to Stephens, October 1, 1861, Stephens Papers, LC.

69. *Atlanta Southern Confederacy*, September 24, 1861; Phillips, *Correspondence of Toombs, Stephens, and Cobb*, pp. 577, 580; *Milledgeville Southern Federal Union*, October 22, 1861.

Chapter 6

1. *Richmond Daily Whig*, November 14, 18, 1861; *Memphis Daily Appeal*, December 1, 1861.

2. Marten, *Texas Divided*, pp. 35–36; Thomas V. Moore, *God Our Refuge and Strength*, pp. 11–12.

3. E. A. Nisbet to Alexander H. Stephens, February 6, 1862, Stephens Papers, LC; Hamilton, *Ruffin Papers*, 3:282; *Charleston Mercury*, January 23, 1862; Woodward, *Mary Chesnut's Civil War*, p. 204; Jesse P. Rice, *Curry*, pp. 39–40.

4. *Richmond Daily Whig*, November 15, 1861; McCash, *Cobb*, p. 283; *OR*, ser. 4, vol. 1, pp. 708–11.

5. Thomas J. Devine, *Speeches Delivered*, pp. 3, 22.

6. Richardson, *Messages and Papers*, 1:141; *Richmond Daily Whig*, November 13, 1861; Raper, *Holden*, p. 41; Barrow, *Remarks on the Present War*, p. 4.

7. *OR*, ser. 1, vol. 7, pp. 742–45, 763–64, 785; J. A. Stewart to Alexander H. Stephens, November 5, 1861, Stephens Papers, LC; Max Williams and Hamilton, *Graham Papers*, 5:357–58; Worley, "Arkansas Peace Society," pp. 445–56; Rector, *Message of Gov. Henry M. Rector, November 6, 1861*, p. 9.

8. Hamilton, *Thomas Ruffin Papers*, 3:215–16; Yearns and Barrett, *North Carolina Civil War Documentary*, pp. 310–11.

9. Max Williams and Hamilton, *Graham Papers*, 5:347–51, 305–9; Hamilton, *Reconstruction in North Carolina*, p. 38.

10. Candler, *Confederate Records of Georgia*, 2:83–89, 149–69, 171–82; *Acts of Georgia* (1862), p. 141; *Milledgeville Southern Federal Union*, December 24, 1861; Avery, *History of Georgia*, pp. 212–21; J. Henly Smith to Alexander H. Stephens, December 16, 1861, Stephens Papers, LC.

11. *OR*, ser. 1, vol. 6, pp. 762–63.

12. Bragg Diary, January 17, 1862, SHC.

13. Rowland, *Davis*, 5:146–47, 150–51, 156–57, 164–66; Eggleston, *Rebel's Recollections*, pp. 168–69; John B. Jones, *Rebel War Clerk's Diary*, 1:89; *Richmond Daily Whig*, November 7, 1861; T. Harry Williams, *Beauregard*, pp. 105–8; Crist and Dix, *Davis Papers*, 7:399–401.

14. *OR*, ser. 1, vol. 2, pp. 511–12; Rowland, *Davis*, 5:159; Dodd, *Davis*, p. 281.

15. Richardson, *Messages and Papers*, 1:137; Pollard, *Lost Cause*, p. 153.

16. Daniel, *Richmond Examiner during the War*, pp. 23–24; Phillips, *Correspondence of Toombs, Stephens, and Cobb*, pp. 577–79; *Charleston Mercury*, September 6, 28, 1861; Reuben Davis, *Recollections of Mississippi and Mississippians*, pp. 431–33; James Henry Hammond to M. C. M. Hammond, November 15, 1861, Hammond Papers, LC.

17. Phillips, *Correspondence of Toombs, Stephens, and Cobb*, pp. 575–76; Connelly and Jones, *Politics of Command*, pp. 82–86.

18. For a critical assessment of Confederate strategy and command, see Woodworth, *Davis and His Generals*, pp. 26–70.

19. *OR*, ser. 1, vol. 7, p. 820. For a warning about the danger of such a proposal, see "Confederate Republicanism or Monarchy," *De Bow's Review* 32 (January and February 1862): 113–19.

20. *OR*, ser. 1, vol. 8, p. 701; Robert H. Smith to his wife, December 11, 1861, Smith Papers, SHC; Castel, *Price*, pp. 66–67; Shalhope, *Price*, pp. 192–98.

21. Herschel Johnson to Alexander H. Stephens, December 3, 1861, Johnson Papers, Duke; John B. Jones, *Rebel War Clerk's Diary*, 1:104; Emory M. Thomas, *Confederate Nation*, p. 142; Robert H. Smith to his wife, December 7, 1861, Smith Papers, SHC.

22. Bragg Diary, January 22, 1862, SHC; Frank Moore, *Rebellion Record*, 4:192.

23. *SHSP* 44 (1923): 13–14; *OR*, ser. 4, vol. 1, p. 771; *JCC*, 1:845–46; *New Orleans Daily Picayune*, February 27, 1862.

24. Richardson, *Messages and Papers*, 1:217–18.

25. For a useful discussion of the differences between ideological and pragmatic political styles that has some application to the Confederacy, see Sidney Verba, "Comparative Political Culture," in Pye and Verba, *Political Culture and Political Development*, pp. 544–50.

26. For helpful theoretical suggestions, see Geertz, *Interpretation of Cultures*, pp. 3–30; Jean H. Baker, "The Ceremonies of Politics: Nineteenth-Century Rituals of National Affirmation," in Cooper, *Master's Due*, pp. 165–69; Hunt, *Politics, Culture, and Class in the French Revolution*, pp. 12–14; Robert C. Tucker, *Political Culture and Leadership in Soviet Russia*, pp. 3–5.

27. On the role of governing elites in establishing national symbols, see Clifford Geertz, "Centers, Kings, and Charisma: Reflections on the Symbolics of Power," in Geertz, *Local Knowledge*, p. 124.

28. For descriptions of the inauguration, see Bragg Diary, February 22, 1862, SHC; *SHSP* 44 (1923): 38–39; Pollard, *Davis*, pp. 197–98; Putnam, *Richmond during the War*, p. 106; DeLeon, *Four Years in Rebel Capitals*, pp. 163–64; Reuben Davis, *Recollections of Mississippi and Mississippians*, pp. 429–30.

29. Richardson, *Messages and Papers*, 1:183–88.

30. John B. Jones, *Rebel War Clerk's Diary*, 1:111; Fleet and Fuller, *Green Mount*, p. 108; *Raleigh Weekly Standard*, February 26, 1862; McGuire, *Diary of a Southern Refugee*, p. 94.

31. *Richmond Daily Dispatch*, February 22, 1862; *JCC*, 1:845; *New Orleans Daily Picayune*, February 22, 1862.

32. Bragg Diary, February 21–22, 1862, SHC; Stephen Elliott, *"New Wine Not to Be Put into Old Bottles,"* pp. 8–18.

33. J. Henly Smith to Alexander H. Stephens, December 16, 1861, Stephens Papers, LC; Eaton, *Southern Confederacy*, pp. 54–56; Boney, *Letcher*, p. 168; Vandiver, *Their Tattered Flags*, p. 175; Alexander H. Stephens, *Constitutional View*, 2:464–65.

34. Alexander and Beringer, *Anatomy of the Confederate Congress*, pp. 56–58. For anyone interested in the Confederate Congress and especially in a detailed study of roll-call voting, this quantitative analysis is indispensable.

35. Yearns, *Confederate Congress*, pp. 13–15; Nichols, *Blueprints for Leviathan*, pp. 14–15; DeLeon, *Four Years in Rebel Capitals*, pp. 88–89; *Richmond Enquirer*, September 3, 1862.

36. Alexander and Beringer, *Anatomy of the Confederate Congress*, pp. 30–31; Coulter, *Confederate States of America*, p. 140; *Milledgeville Southern Federal Union*, March 25, 1862; *Milledgeville Southern Recorder*, March 18, 1862; *Savannah Republican*, March 19, 1862; *Richmond Sentinel*, April 21, 1863; James T. Harrison to Regina Harrison, January 8, 1862, Harrison Papers, SHC; Schwab, *Confederate States*, p. 182.

37. *Charleston Mercury*, December 27, 1861, January 31, June 13, 1862; Pollard, *Davis*, p. 309; Coulter, *Confederate States of America*, pp. 140–41.

38. Richard M. Johnston and Browne, *Stephens*, p. 415; Cauthen, *South Carolina Goes to War*, pp. 207–9.

39. *Charleston Mercury*, February 18, March 7, 1862; *Richmond Daily Whig*, March 10, 1862.

40. Marszalek, *Diary of Emma Holmes*, p. 125; *Edgefield* (S.C.) *Advertiser*, February 28, 1862.

41. Myers, *Children of Pride*, pp. 850–51; Matthews, *Statutes at Large of the Confederate States of America*, 1st Cong., 2d sess., resolutions 2 and 3; *SHSP* 44 (1923): 54, 62–64.

42. In examining the politics of military strategy, I have especially benefited from the original and stimulating assessments in Stephenson, "Theory of Jefferson Davis," pp. 73–90, and Escott, *After Secession*, pp. xi–xii, 54–58, 62–67.

43. Bragg Diary, February 10, 15, 1862, SHC; Rowland, *Davis*, 5:193, 195–97.

44. Richardson, *Messages and Papers*, 1:189–91; Bragg Diary, February 25, 1862, SHC; Vandiver, *Rebel Brass*, pp. 21–22. Contemporaries and historians analyzed the departmental command system and its weaknesses along with Davis's strategy of defense and dispersal without paying much attention to the political necessity for these measures. See Oldham, "Memoirs," pp. 203–16, BTHC; Archer Jones, *Confederate Strategy*, pp. 16–32; Connelly and Jones, *Politics of Command*, pp. 87–103.

45. Connelly, *Army of the Heartland*, p. 138; Connelly and Jones, *Politics of Command*, pp. 49–86.

46. Woodworth, *Davis and His Generals*, p. 89; Rowland, *Davis*, 5:215–19; Richardson, *Messages and Papers*, 1:215–16.

47. Patrick, *Davis and His Cabinet*, pp. 298–99; *Richmond Daily Examiner*, February 24, 1862; *Richmond Daily Whig*, November 27, 1861, February 22, 1862.

48. *JCC*, 2:74.

49. *SHSP* 44 (1923): 175–77; Henry S. Foote, *War of the Rebellion*, pp. 351–57; Meade, *Benjamin*, pp. 201–29; Wise, *End of an Era*, p. 176.

50. John B. Jones, *Rebel War Clerk's Diary*, 1:89, 96–97; Milledge Luke Bonham to William Porcher Miles, December 7, 1861, Miles Papers, SHC; Evans, *Benjamin*, p. 145.

51. *JCC*, 2:73–74.

52. Bragg Diary, February 25, March 17, 1862, SHC; Patrick, *Davis and His Cabinet*, pp. 54–57; *Richmond Daily Examiner*, March 21, 1862; Woodward, *Mary Chesnut's Civil War*, pp. 288–89.

Chapter 7

1. Bragg Diary, March 19, 1862, SHC.

2. Kemp P. Battle, "A Secret Session of the North Carolina Secession Convention of 1862," *SHSP* 23 (1885): 315–18; Hamilton, *Correspondence of Worth*, 1:164; Rowland, *Davis*, 5:229–30; Bragg Diary, February 5, 1862, SHC.

3. Kibler, *Perry*, pp. 363–65; Brown Diary, April 14, June 21, 1862, SHC.

4. Andrews, "Confederate Press and Public Morale," pp. 445–65; Coulter, *Confederate States of America*, pp. 493–500. For a helpful discussion of the role of newspapers in nation building, see Anderson, *Imagined Communities*, pp. 37–40.

5. *Charleston Mercury*, April 5, 1862; Scarborough, *Diary of Edmund Ruffin*, 2:229.

6. *Charleston Mercury*, March 4, 22, 25, 26, 1862; Robert Barnwell Rhett to Milledge Luke Bonham, February 11, 1862, Bonham Papers, SCL; Taylor, "Boyce-Hammond Correspondence," pp. 352–53; Peterson Thweatt to Alexander H. Stephens, March 10, 1862, Stephens Papers, LC; Woodward, *Mary Chesnut's Civil War*, p. 318; Daniel, *Richmond Examiner during the War*, p. 44; Hamilton, *Ruffin Papers*, 3:227.

7. Taylor, "Boyce-Hammond Correspondence," pp. 349, 351; James Henry Ham-

mond to William Gilmore Simms, March 24, 1862, Hammond Papers, LC; Hull, "Correspondence of Cobb," p. 291.

8. *New Orleans Daily Picayune*, March 2, 4, 1862; Mary Ezell Diary, March 12, 1862, in Conigland Papers, SHC; *Milledgeville Southern Federal Union*, April 1, 1862.

9. Coulter, *Confederate States of America*, p. 146; Eaton, *Davis*, pp. 213–15; Wiley, *Road to Appomattox*, pp. 25–36; Roland, *Confederacy*, pp. 133–34.

10. Pierce, *The Word of God a Nation's Life*, pp. 14–15; Grayson, *Witness to Sorrow*, pp. 186–87, 190; *Richmond Daily Examiner*, March 26, 1862.

11. Wylie W. Mason to C. C. Clay, Jr., February 14, 1862, Clay Papers, Duke; Rowland, *Davis*, 5:337; Phillips, *Correspondence of Toombs, Stephens, and Cobb*, p. 592.

12. *Atlanta Southern Confederacy*, February 7, 1862; Brown Diary, February 8, 1862, SHC; Trexler, "Davis and the Richmond Press," p. 186; Richard M. Johnston to Alexander H. Stephens, January 8, 1862, Stephens Papers, LC; *Charleston Mercury*, January 25, 1862.

13. John T. Morgan to C. C. Clay, Jr., February 17, 1862, Clay Papers, Duke; DuBose, *Yancey*, pp. 667–68.

14. *Richmond Daily Whig*, February 21, 1862; Taylor, "Boyce-Hammond Correspondence," pp. 349–50; *Charleston Mercury*, February 26–27, 1862; *Savannah Republican*, June 23, 1862.

15. *OR*, ser. 1, vol. 10, pt. 2, p. 314; *SHSP* 44 (1923): 132–35; Dougan, *Confederate Arkansas*, p. 88.

16. A useful summary of the Shiloh campaign from a strategic perspective is in Woodworth, *Davis and His Generals*, pp. 86–108.

17. Whittington, "Thomas O. Moore," p. 16; Woodward, *Mary Chesnut's Civil War*, p. 330.

18. Symonds, *Johnston*, pp. 132–39; Rowland, *Davis*, 5:208–9; Freeman, *Lee's Lieutenants*, 1:137–47; Govan and Livingood, *Different Valor*, pp. 98–103.

19. Rowland, *Davis*, 5:222.

20. Ibid., pp. 242–43; *Richmond Daily Examiner*, May 6, 1862; *Milledgeville Southern Federal Union*, May 13, 1862; Woodward, *Mary Chesnut's Civil War*, pp. 331–32; Gustavus W. Smith, *Confederate War Papers*, pp. 328–29.

21. James A. Nisbet to Alexander H. Stephens, February 6, 1862, Stephens Papers, LC; Myers, *Children of Pride*, pp. 845–46; Archer Jones, *Confederate Strategy*, pp. 45–50; E. D. Tracy to C. C. Clay, February 22, 1862, Clay Papers, Duke.

22. For the need for scholars of political culture to explore the relationship between political culture and public policy, see the excellent suggestions in Richard L. McCormick, "The Social Analysis of American Political History," in McCormick, *Party Period and Public Policy*, pp. 116–33.

23. Robbins, "Confederate Nationalism," p. 96; Bragg Diary, March 7, 1862, SHC.

24. Richardson, *Messages and Papers*, 1:205–6.

25. Robbins, "Confederate Nationalism," pp. 96–98; *SHSP* 45 (1925): 26–28, 161; *JCC*, 2:253–54, 5:228; Alexander and Beringer, *Anatomy of the Confederate Congress*, pp. 114–15.

26. Matthews, *Statutes at Large of the Confederate States of America*, 1st Cong., 1st sess., ch. 31 (1862), pp. 29–33.

27. *Charleston Mercury*, April 3, 1862; McCash, *Cobb*, p. 282; *Atlanta Southern Confederacy*, April 20, 1862.

28. *Rome* (Ga.) *Weekly Courier*, April 29, 1862; Schenck Books, April 23, 1862, SHC; Albert B. Moore, *Conscription and Conflict in the Confederacy*, pp. 21–23; *Milledgeville Southern Recorder*, April 22, 1862; *Washington* (Ark.) *Telegraph*, May 7, 1862.

29. Woodward, *Mary Chesnut's Civil War*, p. 326; *Raleigh Weekly Standard*, April 9, 23, 1862; J. William Harris, *Plain Folk and Gentry in a Slave Society*, p. 148; Coulter, *Confederate States of America*, pp. 390–91.

30. Brown Diary, July 6, 1862, SHC; R. C. Puryear to Henry T. Clark, April 23, 1862, Clark Papers, Duke.

31. For the traditional argument that states' rights seriously weakened and eventually destroyed the Southern nation, see Owsley, *State Rights in the Confederacy*, pp. 1–2. For recent attempts to minimize the effects of states' rights on the Confederate war effort, see Beringer et al., *Why the South Lost*, pp. 203–8, and Scarboro, "North Carolina and the Confederacy," pp. 133–34. For a sophisticated approach emphasizing the efforts made by Jefferson Davis to build a Southern nation in the face of powerful state, local, and class interests, see Escott, *After Secession*, pp. 76–93.

32. *Milledgeville Southern Federal Union*, April 8, 22, 1862; Virginia, *Documents*, no. 1 (Extra Session, 1862), pp. iii–v; Boney, *Letcher*, p. 162; Herschel Johnson to Alexander H. Stephens, May 4, 1862, Johnson Papers, Duke. That the Confederate states in fact made considerable strides toward centralization proves that these libertarian fears had some legitimate basis. See the extended analysis of Confederate "statism" in Bensel, *Yankee Leviathan*, pp. 94–237.

33. Parks, *Brown*, p. 210; *OR*, ser. 4, vol. 1, pp. 1082–85.

34. N. N. Wates to Colonel M. Boyd, May 5, 1862, Brown Papers, Duke; Brown to Alexander H. Stephens, May 7, 1862, Stephens Papers, Emory; Candler, *Confederate Records of Georgia*, 3:224–25, 228–29.

35. *OR*, ser. 4, vol. 1, pp. 1116–20, 1133–38, 1156–69, vol. ·2, pp. 2–3, 10–13; *Atlanta Southern Confederacy*, June 20, 1862; J. Henly Smith to Alexander H. Stephens, June 21, 1862, Stephens Papers, LC; *Milledgeville Southern Recorder*, July 1, 1862; Pollard, *Southern History of the War* [Second Year], 1:374; *Rome* (Ga.) *Weekly Courier*, May 15, June 26, 1862. Vice-President Stephens and his friends agreed with Brown over both the meaning of the term "militia" and the threat to constitutional liberty posed by conscription but (as yet) refused to come out in open opposition to the administration (Alexander H. Stephens to Thomas W. Thomas, June 23, 1862, Peterson Thweatt to Stephens, May 11, 1862, Stephens Papers, LC).

36. Armistead, *Soldiers of Our Army*, p. 3; *OR*, ser. 4, vol. 1, pp. 847–52, 918–21.

37. Richardson, *Messages and Papers*, 1:122, 184.

38. *Shreveport Southwestern*, February 5, 1862; *Memphis Daily Appeal*, January 17, 1862; *Richmond Daily Dispatch*, January 13, 1862; Daniel, *Richmond Ex-*

aminer during the War, pp. 35–37. For useful discussion, see Mathis, "Freedom of the Press in the Confederacy," pp. 633–48.

39. Lipset, *First New Nation*, pp. 36–45; Litt, *Political Culture of Massachusetts*, p. 59.

40. Thornwell, *Our Danger and Our Duty*, pp. 8–9; *New Orleans Daily Picayune*, April 4, 1862.

41. *Memphis Daily Appeal*, August 14, 1861; *New Orleans Daily Picayune*, March 12, 1862; *Richmond Daily Dispatch*, April 1, 1862.

42. *OR*, ser. 4, vol. 1, p. 772; John Gill Shorter to General L. M. Jenkins, December 19, 1861, Shorter to Sheriff of Walker County, Alabama, December 23, 1861, Shorter Letterbooks, ADAH.

43. Richardson, *Messages and Papers*, 1:219–27, 259–60; Robbins, "Confederacy and the Writ of Habeas Corpus," pp. 83–86.

44. On the tensions between centralization and states' rights, see the excellent discussions in Escott, *After Secession*, pp. 70–76, and Beringer et al., *Why the South Lost*, pp. 218–26. For a more traditional view of how preserving civil liberties weakened the Confederate war effort, see David Donald, "Died of Democracy," in Donald, *Why the North Won the Civil War*, pp. 84–88.

45. George Fitzhugh, "Conduct of the War and Reflections on the Times," *De Bow's Review* 33 (May–August 1862): 33–42; *Richmond Enquirer*, March 20, 1862.

46. Alexander and Beringer, *Anatomy of the Confederate Congress*, pp. 116–69; Matthews, *Statutes at Large of the Confederate States of America*, 1st Cong., 1st sess., ch. 44, p. 40.

47. John B. Jones, *Rebel War Clerk's Diary*, 1:120; *Memphis Daily Appeal*, April 20, 1862.

48. *Charleston Mercury*, April 22, 1862; Cauthen, *South Carolina Goes to War*, pp. 204–5; Oldham, "Memoirs," p. 157, BTHC; *Memphis Daily Appeal*, March 30, 1862.

49. Robert Toombs to Julia Toombs, May 13, 19, 1862, Toombs Papers, UG; Woodward, *Mary Chesnut's Civil War*, pp. 361, 391–92; Pollard, *Southern History of the War* [Second Year], 1:379–82; Varina Howell Davis to William Preston Johnston, June 5, 1862, Johnston Papers, Tulane University.

50. Richard Taylor, *Destruction and Reconstruction*, pp. 111–12.

51. Roman, *Beauregard*, 1:396–413; P. G. T. Beauregard to Thomas Jordan, July 12, 1862, Beauregard Papers, Duke.

52. Robbins, "Confederate Nationalism," p. 106; *Washington* (Ark.) *Telegraph*, May 14, June 18, 1862.

53. *Richmond Daily Enquirer*, July 9, 1862; Scarborough, *Diary of Edmund Ruffin*, 2:331; DuBose, *Yancey*, pp. 677–79.

54. *Richmond Daily Enquirer*, May 3, 7, June 26, August 27, 1862; Robert Barnwell Rhett, Jr., to Robert W. Barnwell, May 22, 1862, Rhett Papers, SCL; *Charleston Daily Courier*, May 22, 1862.

55. Laurence Keitt to James Henry Hammond, June 14, 1862, Hammond Papers, LC; *Charleston Mercury*, May 13, 1862; Daniel, *Richmond Examiner during the War*, pp. 52–53.

56. Phillips, *Correspondence of Toombs, Stephens, and Cobb*, p. 595; A. L. Alexander to Edward Porter Alexander, May 23, 1862, Alexander Papers, SHC; Woodward, *Mary Chesnut's Civil War*, p. 352.

57. Woodward, *Mary Chesnut's Civil War*, p. 359; Wigfall to Clement Claiborne Clay, May 16, 1862, Clay Papers, Duke; Russell, *My Diary North and South*, pp. 87–88; Pollard, *Davis*, p. 226; DeLeon, *Belles, Beaux, and Brains of the 60's*, p. 100; King, *Wigfall*, pp. 136–42.

58. Dubay, *Pettus*, p. 132; James Henry Hammond to Laurence M. Keitt, June 27, 1862, Hammond to William Gilmore Simms, June 27, 1862, Hammond Papers, LC.

59. *Shreveport Southwestern*, June 11, 1862.

60. J. H. Thornwell, "The State of the Country," *De Bow's Review* 30 (April 1861): 4–5; *Journal of the Convention of South Carolina*, pp. 412–13, 425.

61. *Journal of the Convention of South Carolina*, pp. 307–8, 365–69, 376, 378–79; Edmunds, *Pickens*, pp. 150–72; Cauthen, *South Carolina Goes to War*, pp. 139–62; White, "Fate of Calhoun's Sovereign Convention," pp. 757–71.

62. Woodward, *Mary Chesnut's Civil War*, pp. 275, 287, 301; I. W. Hayne to Francis W. Pickens, March 5, 1862, Pickens Papers, Duke; *Charleston Daily Courier*, May 15, 1862.

63. *Edgefield* (S.C.) *Advertiser*, April 9, May 21, August 13, 1862; *Charleston Mercury*, May 3, 1862; One of the People [pseud.], *To the Honorable Chief Justice and Judges of the State*, pp. 1–7; Grayson, *Witness to Sorrow*, pp. 238–41; James Henry Hammond to William Gilmore Simms, August 29, 1862, Hammond Papers, LC; Kibler, *Perry*, pp. 354–55.

64. *South Carolina Senate Journal* (1862), pp. 20–22, 29–37; South Carolina, *Convention Documents*, pp. 5–7. In Arkansas, Governor Henry M. Rector battled with a three-member military board. The governor became very unpopular when he temporarily moved the state government from Little Rock during a Federal invasion. After many fellow Democrats broke with Rector, the state convention called another gubernatorial election for the fall of 1862. Rector charged both the convention and the courts with usurping legislative authority in ordering an election. Portraying himself as the victim of "political filth . . . scraped up by party scavengers," he accused his enemies of toadying for "everything Confederate" in their lust for public printing contracts. "Wire pullers," he said, had forced an election contrary to the people's wishes. Former Whig Harris Flanagin, backed by "Family" Democrats and conservatives easily defeated Rector by a more than two-to-one margin (*Message of Gov. Henry M. Rector, November 6, 1861*, pp. 9–10; Dougan, *Confederate Arkansas*, pp. 75–80, 94–96; *Washington* (Ark.) *Telegraph*, September 17, 1862).

65. Kruman, *Parties and Politics in North Carolina*, pp. 230–32; William C. Harris, *Holden*, pp. 113–14.

66. Augustus S. Merrimon to Kemp P. Battle, April 10, 1862, Battle Family Papers, SHC.

67. Kruman, *Parties and Politics in North Carolina*, p. 232.

68. William C. Harris, *Holden*, pp. 115–17; Kruman, *Parties and Politics in North Carolina*, pp. 232–33.

69. *Raleigh Weekly Standard*, June 4, 18, 25, July 30, 1862.

70. *Raleigh Weekly Standard*, May 14, 28, 1862; Vance to George Little, June 1, 1862, Little-Mordecai Collection, NCDAH; Frontis W. Johnston, *Vance Papers*, pp. 145–46.

71. Cole, *A Card*, broadside.

72. *Raleigh Semi-Weekly Register*, May 7, June 14, 18, 21, 1862; Hamilton, *Ruffin Papers*, 3:253–54, 256–57; Schenck Books, August n.d., 1862, SHC; Max Williams and Hamilton, *Graham Papers*, 5:516.

73. Hamilton, *Correspondence of Worth*, 1:117–79; James W. Eason to Thomas D. Snead, August 3, 1862, Snead Papers, Duke; Kruman, *Parties and Politics in North Carolina*, p. 237.

74. *Raleigh Weekly Standard*, August 20, 1862; Max Williams and Hamilton, *Graham Papers*, 5:413–14; *Richmond Daily Enquirer*, August 15, 1862.

75. Though differing somewhat, my interpretation rests on the fine analysis of the election returns in Kruman, *Parties and Politics in North Carolina*, pp. 237–39, and Baker, "Class Conflict and Political Upheaval," pp. 163–72.

76. *Raleigh Weekly Standard*, August 20, 1862; Max Williams and Hamilton, *Graham Papers*, 5:401; Frontis W. Johnston, *Vance Papers*, pp. 153–54, 160–62, 167–68.

Chapter 8

1. Richardson, *Messages and Papers*, 1:234–35; *OR*, ser. 4, vol. 2, pp. 73–75.

2. Yearns, *Confederate Congress*, pp. 60–73; Matthews, *Statutes at Large of the Confederate States of America*, 1st Cong., 2d sess., ch. 15, pp. 61–62; Albert B. Moore, *Conscription and Conflict in the Confederacy*, pp. 114–39; King, *Wigfall*, pp. 142–46.

3. *SHSP* 45 (1925): 213–16; Estill, "Diary of a Confederate Congressman," pt. 1, pp. 277–78; Oldham, *Speech of W. S. Oldham, of Texas, upon the Bill to Amend the Conscript Law*, pp. 1–16; Oldham, "Memoirs," pp. 147–51, BTHC.

4. Albert B. Moore, *Conscription and Conflict in the Confederacy*, pp. 52–82, 140–61; Matthews, *Statutes at Large of the Confederate States of America*, 1st Cong., 2d sess., ch. 45, pp. 77–79; Oldham, "Memoirs," pp. 151–52, BTHC; Estill, "Diary of a Confederate Congressman," pt. 1, p. 287. See the excellent discussion of exemption bills as examples of logrolling in Alexander and Beringer, *Anatomy of the Confederate Congress*, pp. 109–10. The draft law also affected political behavior. Candidates of military age had to explain why they were running for office instead of serving in the army. Some candidates even claimed that their physical infirmities made them better qualified for public office. See Sullivan, *To the Voters of the 6th Judicial District*, broadside; *Edgefield* (S.C.) *Advertiser*, October 1, 1862, April 13, 1864; *Washington* (Ark.) *Telegraph*, September 24, 1862.

5. *JCC*, 2:310–11.

6. Reuben Davis, *Recollections of Mississippi and Mississippians*, pp. 433–36; *Troy* (Ala.) *Southern Advertiser*, November 26, 1862; *Washington* (Ark.) *Tele-*

graph, December 17, 1862; *North Carolina Laws* (1862–63), pp. 49–50; *OR*, ser. 1, vol. 17, pt. 2, pp. 790–92.

7. *Charleston Mercury*, July 30, 1862; *Richmond Daily Examiner*, September 3, 1862.

8. *South Carolina Senate Journal* (1862), pp. 12–13; *Alabama Senate Journal* (1862), pp. 17–19; *Florida Senate Journal* (1862), pp. 33–35.

9. DuBose, *Yancey*, pp. 672–75; *Montgomery Daily Advertiser*, December 21, 1862.

10. Estill, "Diary of a Confederate Congressman," pt. 1, p. 281; Woodward, *Mary Chesnut's Civil War*, p. 433; Wigfall to Clement C. Clay, Jr., December 11, 1862, Clay Papers, Duke; Wright, *Southern Girl in '61*, p. 90. For a careful account of how Wigfall and Joe Johnston became allied against Davis, see Symonds, *Johnston*, pp. 174–84.

11. Henry Wayne to Alexander H. Stephens, September 6, 1862, Stephens Papers, LC; Oldham, "Memoirs," pp. 190–95, BTHC.

12. *Memphis Daily Appeal*, August 21, 1862; Whittington, "Thomas O. Moore," pp. 12–14. In a September 12, 1862, letter, Moore apologized to the president for the strong language he had used earlier.

13. *Milledgeville Southern Federal Union*, September 9, 1862; Yancey, *Speeches*, pp. 24–25; *SHSP* 47 (1930): 89–92; *JCC*, 2:382; *Richmond Daily Whig*, October 11, 1862; *Richmond Daily Examiner*, September 11, 1862.

14. R. W. Barnwell to Louis T. Wigfall, November 5, 1862, Wigfall Papers, BTHC; *OR*, ser. 4, vol. 2, pp. 141–42; Alexander M. Clayton to Jefferson Davis, September 8, 1862, quoted in Robbins, "Confederate Nationalism," pp. 70–71.

15. Robbins, "Confederate Nationalism," pp. 71–72; *JCC*, 5:373–77.

16. Matthews, *Statutes at Large of the Confederate States of America*, 1st Cong., 2d sess., ch. 51, p. 84.

17. *Chattanooga Daily Rebel*, November 9, 1862; Estill, "Diary of a Confederate Congressman," pt. 1, p. 288.

18. Phillips, *Correspondence of Toombs, Stephens, and Cobb*, pp. 605–6.

19. Schott, *Stephens*, p. 362; *OR*, ser. 4, vol. 2, pp. 128–31.

20. Candler, *Confederate Records of Georgia*, 2:283–85.

21. *Savannah Republican*, November 21, 1862; Bryan, *Confederate Georgia*, p. 40; Phillips, *Correspondence of Toombs, Stephens, and Cobb*, p. 609.

22. *Georgia Senate Journal* (1862), 189–91; Gordon, *Speech of Hon. George A. Gordon of Chatham, on the Constitutionality of the Conscription Laws*.

23. Herschel V. Johnson to A. E. Cochran, October 8, 22, 1862, Johnson Papers, Duke.

24. Avery, *History of Georgia*, pp. 250–51; *Atlanta Southern Confederacy*, December 7, 1862; Herschel Johnson to Alexander H. Stephens, December 24, 1862, quoted in Flippin, *Johnson*, p. 224.

25. Benjamin H. Hill, Jr., *Hill*, pp. 256–72.

26. North Carolina, *Executive and Legislative Documents* (1862–63), no. 18, pp. 1–10; *Raleigh Semi-Weekly Register*, September 10, 14, 1862.

27. *Journal of the Convention of the People of North Carolina* (2d sess.), pp. 37–

38; *Raleigh Weekly Standard*, November 26, December 24, 1862. I am again indebted to the fine analysis in Kruman, *Parties and Politics in North Carolina*, pp. 239–40.

28. Hamilton, *Ruffin Papers*, 3:271–72; *Raleigh Semi-Weekly Register*, November 26, 1862, February 21, 1863; Yearns and Barrett, *North Carolina Civil War Documentary*, pp. 313–14.

29. Frontis W. Johnston, *Vance Papers*, pp. 250–53; *OR*, ser. 4, vol. 2, pp. 146–47, 154.

30. Albert B. Moore, *Conscription and Conflict in the Confederacy*, pp. 281–84; North Carolina, *Executive and Legislative Documents* (sess. 1862–63), no. 1, pp. 12–14.

31. For a useful analysis of Vance as a moderate, see Beringer et al., *Why the South Lost*, pp. 209–12.

32. Hull, "Thomas R. R. Cobb," p. 289.

33. For the origins of the Stephens-Davis feud, see the fine account in Schott, *Stephens*, pp. 326–65, the still useful treatment in Rabun, "Stephens and Davis," pp. 290–321, and the stimulating revisionism in Brumgardt, "Confederate Career of Alexander Stephens," pp. 64–81.

34. Alexander H. Stephens, *Constitutional View*, 2:500–501, 568–75; Stephens to Linton Stephens, August 27, 1862, quoted in Richard M. Johnston and Browne, *Stephens*, pp. 417–18.

35. Stephens to Richard M. Johnston, September 1, 1862, and Stephens to Linton Stephens, September 7, 1862, quoted in Richard M. Johnston and Browne, *Stephens*, pp. 419–21.

36. Stephens to Linton Stephens, August 31, 1862, and Memorandum of conversation between Stephens and Richard M. Johnston, winter 1862, quoted in Richard M. Johnston and Browne, *Stephens*, p. 418; Schott, *Stephens*, pp. 361, 426.

37. John B. Jones, *Rebel War Clerk's Diary*, 1:205; King, *Wigfall*, pp. 158–60; Richard Taylor, *Destruction and Reconstruction*, pp. 20–21; Younger, *Inside the Confederate Government*, p. 34.

38. Jesse P. Rice, *Curry*, p. 41; Frontis W. Johnston, *Vance Papers*, pp. 355–58; Yancey, *Speeches*, pp. 42–51; *JCC*, 2:315.

39. John B. Jones, *Rebel War Clerk's Diary*, 1:178; Coulter, *Confederate States of America*, pp. 374–77; Oldham, "Memoirs," pp. 175–78, BTHC.

40. Woodworth, *Davis and His Generals*, pp. 108–24; Connelly and Jones, *Politics of Command*, pp. 170–200; Vandiver, *Rebel Brass*, pp. 23–43.

41. Brown Diary, July 18, 1862, SHC; Rector, *Message of Henry M. Rector Nov'r 1862*, pp. 4–7; Rowland, *Davis*, 5:248–49, 457–62.

42. Roman, *Beauregard*, 1:414–19; P. G. T. Beauregard to Joseph E. Brown, October 31, 1862, Governors' Correspondence (Brown), GDAH; Villeré, *Review of Certain Remarks Made by the President*, pp. 3–28.

43. Fremantle, *Three Months in the Southern States*, p. 145; Richard Taylor, *Destruction and Reconstruction*, p. 117; Rowland, *Davis*, 5:312–13. The fairest assessment of Bragg's strengths and weaknesses is McWhiney, *Bragg*, pp. 389–92.

44. Heth, *Memoirs*, p. 168; Connelly and Jones, *Politics of Command*, pp. 62–82;

McWhiney, *Bragg*, pp. 326–33; James Henry Hammond to William Gilmore Simms, January 1, 1863, Hammond Papers, LC; Gustavus A. Henry to Louis T. Wigfall, October 25, 1862, Wigfall Papers, BTHC; E. S. Dargan to Jefferson Davis, November 7, 1862, Davis Papers, Duke.

45. *SHSP* 47 (1930): 51–52; Oldham, "Memoirs," pp. 30–38, 216–77, BTHC; Connelly and Jones, *Politics of Command*, pp. 111–20.

46. Younger, *Inside the Confederate Government*, pp. 30–31; Estill, "Diary of a Confederate Congressman," pt. 1, p. 276; Patrick, *Davis and His Cabinet*, pp. 120–31; Shackelford, *Randolph*, pp. 143–50; Woodworth, *Davis and His Generals*, pp. 179–80.

47. *Richmond Daily Examiner*, November 14, 20, 1862; Fremantle, *Three Months in the Southern States*, p. 215; John B. Jones, *Rebel War Clerk's Diary*, 1:191–92.

48. Reagan, *Memoirs*, pp. 161–62. There was also increased grumbling in the War Department that Davis had grown more stubborn, aloof, and isolated from anyone who might challenge his pet notions (John B. Jones, *Rebel War Clerk's Diary*, 1:184; Younger, *Inside the Confederate Government*, p. 34).

49. Govan and Livingood, *Different Valor*, pp. 162–65; Joseph E. Johnston, *Narrative of Military Operations*, pp. 148–50; Connelly, *Autumn of Glory*, pp. 32–36. The most judicious account of the Johnston-Davis relationship is McMurry, "'The Enemy at Richmond,'" pp. 9–11.

50. Louis T. Wigfall to Clement C. Clay, Jr., December 11, 1862, Clay Papers, Duke; Symonds, *Johnston*, pp. 179–80. Wigfall may have been more interested in getting rid of Bragg and attacking Davis than in helping Johnston. Johnston clearly used Wigfall to promote the ideas of the "western concentration bloc" in Congress (Connelly and Jones, *Politics of Command*, pp. 120–21).

51. Wright, *Southern Girl in '61*, pp. 98–100; Wigfall to Seddon, December 8, 1862, Wigfall Papers, BTHC.

52. John B. Jones, *Rebel War Clerk's Diary*, 1:232; Wright, *Southern Girl in '61*, pp. 106–8, 121–23.

Chapter 9

1. Evans to Beauregard, March 17, 1863, quoted in Govan and Livingood, *Different Valor*, p. 184.

2. Pereyra, *Alcorn*, pp. 39–72; Rainwater, "Letters of Alcorn," p. 204.

3. Alexander H. Stephens to Linton Stephens, January 29, April 7, 1863, quoted in Richard M. Johnston and Brown, *Stephens*, pp. 434–35, 441; Linton Stephens to Alexander H. Stephens, February 9, 1863, Stephens Papers, LC; *Richmond Daily Whig*, February 5, 1863; Daniel, *Richmond Examiner during the War*, pp. 74–75. I am greatly indebted to Marc Kruman's excellent analysis of the "politics of liberty" in North Carolina. He rightly observes that images of republican liberty permeated public and private discourse and cannot therefore be dismissed as "propaganda" (*Parties and Politics in North Carolina*, pp. 242–43).

4. Dodd, *Davis*, p. 299; Frank Moore, *Rebellion Record*, 6:294–301.

5. For a fine, though somewhat different, treatment of the shifting themes in Davis's public speeches, see Escott, *After Secession*, pp. 179–85.

6. Rowland, *Davis*, 5:390–91. For the use of images and metaphors to arouse popular passions, either with appeals to fundamental anxieties or by reducing complex questions to simple struggles between good and evil, see Edelman, *Politics as Symbolic Action*, pp. 65–70.

7. Richardson, *Messages and Paper*, 1:277, 289–93.

8. Alexander H. Stephens to Linton Stephens, January 18, 1863, quoted in Richard M. Johnston and Browne, *Stephens*, p. 431; Estill, "Diary of a Confederate Congressman," pt. 1, p. 290; *The Confederate. By a South Carolinian*, pp. 3–102.

9. *North Carolina Laws* (1862–63), pp. 43–44; *Acts of Georgia*, (1862–63), p. 235; *OR*, ser. 1, vol. 17, pt. 2, p. 789.

10. DuBose, *Yancey*, pp. 682–83.

11. For useful definitions of political socialization, see Langton, *Political Socialization*, pp. 4–5; Easton and Dennis, *Children in the Political System*, pp. 7, 47–69; Koon, *Believe, Obey, Fight*, p. xv.

12. For a description of the types of political socialization (maintaining, transforming, creating), see Dawson and Prewitt, *Political Socialization*, pp. 29–36.

13. For the growing interest of women in political and military affairs, see Rable, *Civil Wars*, pp. 144–51.

14. For the general role of families in political socialization, see Paul Allen Beck, "The Role of Agents in Political Socialization," in Renshon, *Handbook of Political Socialization*, pp. 122–27; Dawson and Prewitt, *Political Socialization*, pp. 105–26. For the types and limits of political information acquired in the home, see Easton and Dennis, *Children in the Political System*, pp. 73–110. Unfortunately, much of the literature on political socialization focuses on how parents transmit party affiliation to their children. In the 1850s, this became more important in the Northern states because of weak party competition in the Southern states, especially in the lower South. See Langton, *Political Socialization*, pp. 21–51; Baker, *Affairs of Party*, pp. 27–70; William E. Gienapp, "'Politics Seem to Enter into Everything': Political Culture in the North, 1840–1860," in Maizlich and Kushma, *Essays on American Antebellum Politics*, pp. 32–66.

15. Jennings and Niemi, *Political Charter of Adolescence*, pp. 181–206; Langton, *Political Socialization*, pp. 84–119; Beck, "Role of Agents in Political Socialization," pp. 127–31; Easton and Dennis, *Children in the Political System*, p. 275.

16. Easton and Dennis, *Children in the Political System*, pp. 111–41; Dawson and Prewitt, *Political Socialization*, pp. 146–67. See the valuable discussion of citizenship training in Northern schools in Baker, *Affairs of Party*, pp. 71–107.

17. McCardell, *Idea of a Southern Nation*, pp. 177–226; Frontis W. Johnston, *Vance Papers*, pp. 232–34.

18. Draft exemptions for teachers were necessary, claimed one writer, so that badly needed Southern textbooks could be written. These new works would be a "sure defense of our children against the poisonous flood of Yankee school books and Yankee literature" and would "save them from mental vassalage to the nation

whose principles and tenets we hate with a perfect hatred" (Junius [pseud.], *Conscription of Teachers*, p. 5).

19. *Address to the People of North Carolina*, pp. 1, 6, 9–11; Hollins Institute, *Education of Teachers in the South*, pp. 5–24; Thomas J. Chambers, *To the People of Texas* [giving his platform], p. 2. The reference is to Hinton Rowan Helper, a North Carolinian émigré living in New York and author of *The Impending Crisis* (1857). In this book that shook the foundations of the Southern social order, Helper argued that slavery had impoverished nonslaveholding whites and retarded Southern economic growth.

20. Thomas, "Rebel Nationalism," pp. 343–55; Carroll, "Sterling, Campbell and Albright," pp. 169–98; Coulter, *Confederate States of America*, pp. 517–19; Worrell, *Principles of English Grammar*, p. iii; Roswell C. Smith, *Smith's English Grammar*, p. 5; Smythe, *Our Own Primary Grammar*, p. iii.

21. [Richard A. Smith], *Confederate Spelling Book*, p. 5; Robert Fleming, *Elementary Spelling Book*, pp. 58–60; Stewart, *Geography for Beginners*, pp. 36–38.

22. Easton and Dennis, *Children in the Political System*, pp. 287–88; *New Texas Primary Reader*, p. 55.

23. Ezell, "Southern Education for Southrons," pp. 303–27; "Future Revolution in Southern School Books," *De Bow's Review* 30 (May and June 1861): 606–14.

24. Richard Sterling, *Our Own Third Reader*, pp. 211–22; Robert Fleming, *Elementary Spelling Book*, pp. 5, 72, 94–95.

25. Marinda Moore, *Geographical Reader*, pp. 10–11.

26. John H. Rice, *System of Modern Geography*, p. 8; Lander, *Verbal Primer*, p. 27; *Address to the People of North Carolina*, p. 11.

27. Bingham, *Grammar of the Latin Language*, p. iv; Allen M. Scott, *New Southern Grammar*, p. iv; Yearns and Barrett, *North Carolina Civil War Documentary*, pp. 233–34; Joynes, *Education after the War*, p. 13; *Proceedings of the Convention of Teachers of the Confederate States*, p. 8; Silver, "Propaganda in the Confederacy," pp. 495–96. For the broader use of Yankee stereotypes in Confederate thought, see Royster, *Destructive War*, pp. 180–85.

28. Marinda Moore, *Geographical Reader*, pp. 13, 20–21.

29. *Southern Pictorial Primer*, p. 17; *Pictorial Primer*, p. 19. Such symbols of nationalism also became important outside the classroom. Flags, poems, songs, and pictures of Davis and various military leaders appeared throughout the South, and some efforts were made to establish July 4 and Washington's birthday as Confederate holidays (Coulter, *Confederate States of America*, pp. 70–72). Yet the Confederate revolution did not last long enough to create a sophisticated iconography that would shape political values. See Koon, *Believe, Obey, Fight*, p. xvii; Hunt, *Politics, Culture, and Class in the French Revolution*, pp. 52–86.

30. Marinda Moore, *Geographical Reader*, pp. 13–14; Marinda Moore, *Dixie Speller*, p. 33; *New Texas Reader*, pp. 126–31.

31. Robert Fleming, *Elementary Spelling Book*, p. 97; John H. Rice, *System of Modern Geography*, p. 51; Marinda Moore, *Geographical Reader*, p. 26.

32. Baird, *Confederate Spelling Book*, p. 185; John H. Rice, *System of Modern Geography*, pp. 12, 21.

33. Robert Fleming, *Elementary Spelling Book*, p. 90; Marinda Moore, *Geographical Reader*, pp. 14–15.

34. Silver, *Confederate Morale and Church Propaganda*, pp. 59–63; W. M. Burwell to Alexander H. Stephens, March 6, 1862, Stephens Papers, LC; Dalzell, *Thanksgiving to God*, p. 9.

35. Miles, *God in History*, p. 24. For an unconvincing argument that the jeremiad was an almost exclusively New England phenomenon and not a part of Southern evangelical culture, see Anne Norton, *Alternative Americas*, pp. 5–7.

36. Silver, *Confederate Morale and Church Propaganda*, pp. 64–76; J. S. Lamar, *Discourse Delivered*, pp. 8–13; *Tuskegee* (Ala.) *South Western Baptist*, November 6, 1862. For a penetrating analysis that strongly emphasizes the importance of economic sins in Confederate jeremiads, see Faust, *Creation of Confederate Nationalism*, pp. 29–33, 41–57.

37. Reiger, "Deprivation, Disaffection, and Desertion in Confederate Florida," p. 281; Gordon, *"What Will He Do with It?,"* pp. 9–27; *Edgefield* (S.C.) *Advertiser*, December 24, 1862.

38. Coulter, *Confederate States of America*, pp. 226–29; Pollard, *Southern History of the War* [Second Year], 1:587; Marten, *Texas Divided*, pp. 91–93; *Richmond Daily Dispatch*, February 6, 1864. Politically astute Jews defended themselves from these crude attacks but also wisely condemned speculators and anyone who would take advantage of the poor (Michelbacher, *Sermon Delivered*, pp. 3–14).

39. John B. Jones, *Rebel War Clerk's Diary*, 2:271; Ada Sterling, *Belle of the Fifties*, pp. 194–95; Rowland, *Davis*, 5:425–26.

40. *OR*, ser. 4, vol. 1, pp. 701–2, 739; Joseph E. Brown to O. R. Broyles, January 22, 1865, Broyles Papers, Duke; Ringold, *Role of the State Legislatures in the Confederacy*, pp. 72–76; Emory M. Thomas, *Confederate State of Richmond*, pp. 148–49; John B. Jones, *Rebel War Clerk's Diary*, 2:67; *Richmond Daily Dispatch*, October 22, 1863.

41. Escott, *After Secession*, pp. 99–134; Escott, *Many Excellent People*, pp. 59–84; Martin, *Desertion of Alabama Troops*, pp. 121–59; Bailey, *Class and Tennessee's Confederate Generation*, pp. 77–104.

42. Rable, *Civil Wars*, p. 110; Estill, "Diary of a Confederate Congressman," pt. 2, pp. 46–47; Scarborough, *Diary of Edmund Ruffin*, 2:621.

43. See the important analysis of welfare policies in Escott, *After Secession*, pp. 135–44.

44. Campbell, *To the People of Fannin*, pp. 1–7; *SHSP* 45 (1925): 189–90.

45. For the importance of fatalistic attitudes, see Sidney Verba, "Comparative Political Culture," in Pye and Verba, *Political Culture and Political Development*, pp. 522–25.

46. *Charleston Mercury*, February 13, 1863; Howell Cobb to Robert M. T. Hunter, March 5, 1863, Hunter Papers, UVa.

47. Jesse P. Rice, *Curry*, p. 43; Coulter, *Confederate States of America*, p. 114; *Tuskegee* (Ala.) *South Western Baptist*, April 23, 1863; *Washington* (Ark.) *Telegraph*, July 1, 1863.

48. *Richmond Daily Whig*, January 12, 1863; *Tuskegee* (Ala.) *South Western Baptist*, April 30, 1863; Stiles, *National Rectitude*, pp. 26–27.

49. Herschel Johnson to A. E. Cochran, March 4, 1863, Johnson Papers, Duke; Johnson to Linton Stephens, March 4, 1863, Stephens Papers, LC.

50. Robbins, "Confederate Nationalism," p. 75; Owsley, *State Rights in the Confederacy*, pp. 171–76.

51. *Charleston Mercury*, March 12, April 18, 1863; *Richmond Daily Whig*, March 3, 1863; *Raleigh Weekly Standard*, March 11, May 6, 1863.

52. *Montgomery Daily Advertiser*, March 8, 1863; *Memphis Daily Appeal*, March 16, 1863; Collier, *Correspondence and Remarks on Two Occasions*, pp. 15, 22, 24–32; Davenport, "Essay on Habeas Corpus in the Judge Sharkey Papers," pp. 243–46.

53. *Richmond Daily Enquirer*, March 20, 1863.

54. Frank H. Alfriend, "A Southern Republic and a Northern Democracy," *Southern Literary Messenger* 37 (May 1863): 283–90.

55. For a highly critical account of administrative bungling and indifference to the problems of ordinary citizens, see Escott, *After Secession*, pp. 145–59.

56. Seddon to Vance, March 26, 1863, Vance to Seddon, April 22, 1863, Davis to Vance, May 22, 1863, Vance Letterbooks, NCDAH; *OR*, ser. 4, vol. 2, pp. 465–66; Bridges, *Lee's Maverick General*, pp. 180–81.

57. B. S. Gaither to Zebulon Vance, April 24, 1863, C. D. Smith to Vance, March 12, 1863, Vance Papers, NCDAH; Max Williams and Hamilton, *Graham Papers*, 5:463–64, 471–72; *Raleigh Weekly Standard*, March 4, April 22, 1863.

58. E. G. Richards to C. C. Clay, Jr., February 19, 1863, Clay Papers, Duke; *Atlanta Southern Confederacy*, October 30, 1862; Yearns and Barrett, *North Carolina Civil War Documentary*, p. 98; *Raleigh Weekly Standard*, July 1, 1863. Yet racial considerations sometimes banked the fires of class conflict. "We have but little interest in the value of slaves," D. W. Siler informed Governor Vance, but "we are opposed to Negro equality." In the fight for white supremacy, even people in the mountainous western counties "are willing to spare the last men, down to the point where the women and children begin to suffer for food and clothing . . . rather than be equalized with an inferior race" (*OR*, ser. 1, vol. 18, pp. 772–73).

59. Candler, *Confederate Records of Georgia*, 2:433–37.

60. John Milton to Howell Cobb, May 22, 1863, Cobb Papers, E. Merton Coulter Collection, UG; *Florida Senate Journal* (1863), pp. 12–16; *Atlanta Southern Confederacy*, October 25, 1862.

61. Matthews, *Statutes at Large of the Confederate States of America*, 1st Cong., 3d sess., ch. 80, pp. 158–59; William L. Yancey, Speech in the Confederate Senate, February 16, 1863, Yancey Papers, ADAH; *SHSP* 48 (1941): 105–9. By taxing overseers and forcing planters to sell surplus produce to soldiers' families at official prices, the government tried with only limited success to reduce these class tensions (Bensel, *Yankee Leviathan*, pp. 183–84).

62. For good discussions of economic centralization in the Confederacy, see Escott, *After Secession*, pp. 58–61; and Beringer et al., *Why the South Lost*, pp. 212–18.

63. Yearns, *Confederate Congress*, p. 131; Richardson, *Messages and Papers*, 1:331–35; *OR*, ser. 4, vol. 2, p. 488.

64. Phillips, *Correspondence of Toombs, Stephens, and Cobb*, pp. 613–14; Roark, *Masters without Slaves*, pp. 62–67; Thompson, *Toombs*, pp. 186–87; *Rome* (Ga.) *Weekly Courier*, July 4, 1862.

65. Stephenson, *Day of the Confederacy*, pp. 92–93.

66. James Henry Hammond to William Gilmore Simms, August 24, 1864, Hammond Papers, LC; *Jackson* (Miss.) *Daily Southern Crisis*, February 21, 1863; *OR*, ser. 4, vol. 2, pp. 943–44; *North Carolina Laws* (Adjourned Session 1863), p. 19; Ringold, *Role of the State Legislatures in the Confederacy*, pp. 32–33; DeRosa, *Confederate Constitution*, pp. 115–18; Owsley, *State Rights in the Confederacy*, pp. 228–54.

67. Richard F. Lyon to Alexander H. Stephens, August 23, 1862, Stephens Papers, LC; Faust, *Hammond*, p. 369; Roark, *Masters without Slaves*, pp. 79–80; Owsley, *State Rights in the Confederacy*, pp. 254–65.

68. See the fine analysis of Confederate achievements in Emory M. Thomas, *Confederate Nation*, and Emory M. Thomas, *Confederacy as a Revolutionary Experience*.

Chapter 10

1. *OR*, ser. 1, vol. 23, pt. 2, pp. 836–38.

2. Richard Taylor, *Destruction and Reconstruction*, pp. 44–45; Younger, *Inside the Confederate Government*, p. 50, 72; Fremantle, *Three Months in the Southern States*, pp. 125, 220.

3. Rowland, *Davis*, 5:464–65. For the Vicksburg campaign, see the trenchant analysis in Woodworth, *Davis and His Generals*, pp. 200–221.

4. Crabtree and Patton, *"Journal of a Secesh Lady,"* pp. 427–28; Augusta J. Evans to J. L. M. Curry, July 15, 1863, Curry Papers, LC; Rowland, *Davis*, 5:580–82; Francis W. Pickens to Louis T. Wigfall, July 28, 1863, Wigfall Papers, BTHC.

5. Lydia Johnston to Charlotte Wigfall, August 2, 1863, Wigfall Papers, LC; Younger, *Inside the Confederate Government*, p. 83; Rowland, *Davis*, 5:556–63; Joseph E. Johnston, *Narrative of Military Operations*, pp. 211–55; Symonds, *Johnston*, pp. 219–26; King, *Wigfall*, pp. 179–82; Joseph E. Johnston to Louis T. Wigfall, August 12, September 15, 1863, Wigfall Papers, BTHC.

6. *Montgomery Daily Advertiser*, June 10, 1863; *Richmond Daily Examiner*, June 10, 1863; Scarborough, *Diary of Edmund Ruffin*, 3:503–4; Pollard, *Southern History of the War* [Third Year], 2:70–71, 88–89.

7. *OR*, ser. 1, vol. 23, pt. 2, p. 839; Longstreet, *From Manassas to Appomattox*, p. 331. Postmaster General Reagan also favored sending troops to Pemberton, but Davis and the rest of the cabinet approved Lee's proposal (Reagan, *Memoirs*, pp. 120–23). For a controversial, overstated, but also useful reassessment of Lee's generalship that argues for a more defensive strategy in the eastern theater, see Nolan, *Lee Considered*, pp. 59–106.

8. Freeman, *Lee's Dispatches*, pp. 108–10; Fremantle, *Three Months in the Southern States*, p. 269.

9. Wright, *Southern Girl in '61*, pp. 142–43; *OR*, ser. 1, vol. 28, pt. 2, pp. 173–74; Piston, *Lee's Tarnished Lieutenant*, pp. 62–68.

10. Robert Toombs to Linton Stephens, July 19, 1863, Stephens Papers, Emory; Louis T. Wigfall to C. C. Clay, Jr., August 13, 1863, Clay Papers, Duke; *Charleston Mercury*, July 30, 1863.

11. Phillips, *Correspondence of Toombs, Stephens, and Cobb*, pp. 628–29; Dowdey and Manarin, *Wartime Papers of Lee*, p. 591; *OR*, ser. 1, vol. 25, pt. 2, pp. 746–47.

12. *Opinion of the Supreme Court of Virginia*, pp. 3–22; *Selected Cases Supreme Court of Alabama*, pp. 637–67; *Supreme Court of Texas on the Constitutionality of the Conscript Laws*, pp. 4–19.

13. Albert B. Moore, *Conscription and Conflict in the Confederacy*, p. 170; Waddell, *Biographical Sketch of Linton Stephens*, pp. 246–48; Avery, *History of Georgia*, pp. 249–50; *Atlanta Southern Confederacy*, November 19, 1862; Herschel Johnson to James S. Hook, November 14, 1862, Johnson Papers, Duke.

14. Max Hamilton and Williams, *Graham Papers*, 5:439–41; Zebulon Vance to James A. Seddon, May 22, 1863, Vance Letterbooks, NCDAH; *OR*, ser. 1, vol. 51, pt. 2, p. 714.

15. *Cases at Law, Supreme Court of North Carolina, June Term, 1863*, pp. 1–73, 168–74, 186–96.

16. Vance to Pearson, October 7, December 26, 1863, Pearson to Vance, December 7, 1863, January 11, 1864, Vance Letterbooks, NCDAH.

17. Daniel H. Hill to Zebulon Vance, June 15, 1863, Vance Papers, NCDAH; Schenck Books, June 11, 1863, SHC; Bardolph, "Inconstant Rebels," pp. 183–85; Zebulon Vance to James A. Seddon, July 26, 1863, Vance Letterbooks, NCDAH.

18. Max Hamilton and Williams, *Graham Papers*, 5:517; *Raleigh Weekly Standard*, August 5, 1863; Hamilton, *Correspondence of Worth*, 1:245; Kruman, *Parties and Politics in North Carolina*, pp. 248–52.

19. J. Devereau to Edward J. Hale, August 19, 1863, ?, Raleigh, N.C., to Hale, August 29, 1863, P. W. Starbuck to Hale, August n.d., 1863, Hale Papers, NCDAH; A. W. King to Alexander H. Stephens, September 15, 1863, Stephens Papers, LC; William C. Harris, *Holden*, pp. 127–31; Escott, *Many Excellent People*, pp. 45–47; Calvin H. Wiley to Zebulon Vance, August 22, 1863, Vance Papers, NCDAH.

20. L. C. Edwards to Edward J. Hale, August 26, 1863, Hale Papers, NCDAH; *Richmond Daily Enquirer*, August 13, September 2, 1863; William C. Harris, *Holden*, p. 138. Holden charged that "destructive" leaders had organized these meetings and that many officers and at least three-fourths of the enlisted men agreed with the *Standard*'s editorial stance (*Raleigh Weekly Standard*, August 19, 1863).

21. William C. Harris, *Holden*, pp. 131–35; *Raleigh Weekly Standard*, July 22, 29, 1863.

22. Schenck Books, September 11, 1863, SHC; W. G. Harris to Edward J. Hale, August 24, 1864, Hale Papers, NCDAH; *Raleigh Semi-Weekly Register*, July 22, August 5, 1863; *Washington* (Ark.) *Telegraph*, August 26, 1863.

23. *OR*, ser. 1, vol. 18, pp. 1052–53, 1092, vol. 51, pt. 2, pp. 739–40; Hamilton, *Correspondence of Worth*, 1:253–55; Kenzer, *Kinship and Neighborhood in a Southern Community*, p. 81; Scarborough, *Diary of Edmund Ruffin*, 3:129.

24. Raper, *Holden*, p. 49; *OR*, ser. 1, vol. 29, pt. 2, p. 710, vol. 51, pt. 2, pp. 763–65, 770–71, 777–78; *Raleigh Weekly Standard*, October 7, 1863; Hamilton, *Correspondence of Worth*, 1:260–62; George Little to Edward J. Hale, September 21, 1863, Hale Papers, NCDAH. For the best account of the attack on the *Standard* office, see William C. Harris, *Holden*, pp. 139–40.

25. Zebulon Vance to Edward J. Hale, August 11, 1863, Frederick Fitzgerald to Hale, July 24, 1863, Hale Papers, NCDAH; Joseph G. Michaux to his brother, August 23, 1863, Michaux-Randolph Papers, NCDAH. Although he downplays the real differences between Vance and Holden, Marc Kruman provides an excellent account of the early stages of their falling-out (*Parties and Politics in North Carolina*, pp. 249–52).

26. Zebulon Vance to Edward J. Hale, July 26, 1863, Hale Papers, NCDAH; B. F. Moore to William W. Holden, January 20, 1866, Moore and Gatling Papers, SHC; Hamilton, *Correspondence of Worth*, 1:247–48.

27. Zebulon Vance to John H. Haughton, August 17, 1863, Vance to Col. Byrum, August 26, 1863, Vance Papers, NCDAH; *Richmond Daily Dispatch*, August 8, 1863.

28. Max Williams and Hamilton, *Graham Papers*, 5:521–22, 527–28; Hamilton, *Correspondence of Worth*, 1:256–58.

29. Zebulon Vance to Edward J. Hale, September 7, 1863, Hale Papers, NCDAH; Max Williams and Hamilton, *Graham Papers*, 5:529–31; William W. Holden to B. F. Moore, August 2, 1866, Moore and Gatling Papers, SHC; Boyd, *Memoirs of W. W. Holden*, pp. 24–25.

30. *OR*, ser. 4, vol. 2, pp. 794–96; Vance to Edward J. Hale, September 11, 20, 1863, T. P. Devereux to Hale, September 21, 1863, Kemp P. Battle to Hale, September 16, 1863, Hale Papers, NCDAH; H. A. Gilliam to David Miller Carter, September 7, 1863, Carter Papers, SHC.

31. Albert Smedes to Edward J. Hale, August 31, 1863, Hale Papers, NCDAH.

32. Stiles, *National Rectitude*, p. 27; Pollard, *Southern History of the War* [Second Year], 1:635–36.

33. DuBose, *Yancey*, pp. 743–49; William L. Yancey to Clement C. Clay, Jr., May 13, 1863, Clay Papers, Duke; Rowland, *Davis*, 5:498, 528–30; Patrick, *Opinions of the Confederate Attorneys General*, pp. 261–65.

34. Rowland, *Davis*, 5:590–92; *Mobile Weekly Advertiser and Register*, August 22, 1863; C. C. Clay, Jr., to Louis T. Wigfall, August 5, 1863, Wigfall Papers, BTHC; Wigfall to Clay, August 13, 1863, Clay Papers, Duke; *Richmond Daily Examiner*, August 5, 1863.

35. Robert Toombs to Linton Stephens, July 19, 1863, Stephens Papers, Emory; Phillips, *Correspondence of Toombs, Stephens, and Cobb*, p. 629; Schott, *Stephens*, p. 385.

36. *Charleston Mercury*, September 5, 1863; Shelby Foote, *Civil War*, 2:648; Nuermberger, *Clays of Alabama*, pp. 221–22. A disgruntled Georgian who had lost

three sons in the war warned Davis that he might soon lose his office or even his head (John B. Jones, *Rebel War Clerk's Diary*, 2:51).

37. Dougan, *Confederate Arkansas*, pp. 103–4; Candler, *Confederate Records of Georgia*, 2:777–80; John Rutherford et al. to Alexander H. Stephens, July 27, 1863, Stephens Papers, LC; Coulter, *Confederate States of America*, p. 105; *Charleston Daily Courier*, July 23, August 8, 1863.

38. *Memphis Daily Appeal* (then published in Atlanta), August 21, 1863; J. W. Warren to Alexander H. Stephens, September 5, 1863, Stephens Papers, LC; Renfroe, *"The Battle Is God's,"* pp. 17–18; Richardson, *Messages and Papers*, 1:329–31.

39. See the useful discussion of these points in Eckstein, "Culturalist Theory of Political Change," pp. 793–804, and Howe, *Political Culture of American Whigs*, p. 2.

40. Augusta J. Evans to J. L. M. Curry, July 15, 1863, Curry Papers, LC.

41. Leroy M. Lee, *Our Country—Our Dangers—Our Duty*, pp. 20–21; Stephen Elliott, *Ezra's Dilemma*, pp. 6–26; Richardson, *Messages and Papers*, 1:328. By this time, days of fasting, humiliation, and public prayer elicited as much cynicism as piety. John M. Daniel thought such rituals smacked of Yankee Puritanism and preachers meddling in politics. Virginia senator Robert M. T. Hunter noted sardonically that "the parsons tell us every Sunday that the Lord is on our side. I wish, however, he would show his preference for us a little more plainly than he has been doing lately" (Daniel, *Richmond Examiner during the War*, pp. 112–14; Woodward, *Mary Chesnut's Civil War*, p. 505).

42. Fremantle, *Three Months in the Southern States*, p. 211; Richard M. Johnston and Browne, *Stephens*, pp. 447–48; Stephenson, *Day of the Confederacy*, p. 95; Rowland, *Davis*, 5:548–50. Although Paul Escott makes Confederate ideology in this period appear too negative, his analysis of the efforts of Davis and other leaders to rekindle patriotism is superb (*After Secession*, pp. 190–93).

43. Younger, *Inside the Confederate Government*, p. 86; Rowland, *Davis*, 5:587–88; *Edgefield* (S.C.) *Advertiser*, September 16, 1863; Renfroe, *"The Battle Is God's,"* p. 26; *Charleston Mercury*, September 23, 1863; Louis T. Wigfall to C. C. Clay, Jr., August 13, 1863, Clay Papers, Duke.

44. Younger, *Inside the Confederate Government*, pp. 100–101; *Richmond Daily Enquirer*, August 10, 1863; *Richmond Daily Whig*, July 18, 1863; Howell Cobb to Alexander H. Stephens, September 1, 1863, Stephens Papers, LC. Cobb's letter must have nearly given Stephens apoplexy, but in an earlier letter, the vice-president had already offered his assessment of the dictatorship question. Not for a minute would he confer such broad powers on the most honorable of the founding fathers—much less on Jefferson Davis. He tartly stated his "inexpressible repugnance" to an idea that could only bring on a "lamentable catastrophe" (Stephens to Cobb, August 29, 1863, Stephens Papers, Emory).

45. For examples of how casually scholars treat this assumption, see Parish, *American Civil War*, p. 199; Nieman, "Republicanism, the Confederate Constitution, and the American Constitutional Tradition," in Hall and Ely, *Uncertain Tradition*, p. 219.

46. David M. Potter, "Jefferson Davis and the Political Factors in Confederate

Defeat," in Donald, *Why the North Won the Civil War*, pp. 110–12; Emory M. Thomas, *Confederate Nation*, p. 140.

47. See the useful discussions of these points in McPherson, *Battle Cry of Freedom*, pp. 689–91, and Parish, *American Civil War*, pp. 218–25. Conversely, there is considerable evidence that the absence of organized opposition helped Davis and his supporters strengthen the Confederate state (Bensel, *Yankee Leviathan*, pp. 230–33).

48. Potter, "Davis and Confederate Defeat," p. 111; Eric L. McKitrick, "Politics and the Union and Confederate War Efforts," in William N. Chambers and Burnham, *American Party Systems*, pp. 120–21. Also implicit in this argument, as Richard Bensel has pointed out, is the odd notion that the lack of organization somehow strengthened opponents of the Davis administration (*Yankee Leviathan*, p. 229).

49. McKitrick, "Politics and the Union and Confederate War Efforts," pp. 142–46. The influence of antebellum party affiliation and secession positions became more important after the 1863 elections, but even in the most desperate of times, nothing resembling clear party divisions appeared in Congress. See the cogent analysis of voting patterns in Alexander and Beringer, *Anatomy of the Confederate Congress*, pp. 330–45. Traditional party allegiances survived longer in North Carolina than in any other state, though even there, the war and the peace movement made for some bizarre alliances (Kruman, *Parties and Politics in North Carolina*, p. 222).

50. King, *Wigfall*, pp. 183–84; Herschel V. Johnson, "Autobiography," p. 333; Ranck, *Albert Gallatin Brown*, pp. 239–46.

51. For the soldier vote, see Ringold, *Role of State Legislatures in the Confederacy*, pp. 69–70. For differences between "internal" and "external" congressmen, see Alexander and Beringer, *Anatomy of the Confederate Congress*, pp. 66–68.

52. B. R. Welford, "Parties and Partyism," *De Bow's Review* 35 (July and August 1864): 71–79. For an informative consideration of possible political alignments in a longer-lived Confederacy, see Beringer, "Unconscious 'Spirit of Party' in the Confederate Congress," pp. 312–28.

53. For helpful general discussions of how political culture evolves, see Litt, *Political Culture of Massachusetts*, p. 81; Lucien Pye, "Political Culture and Political Development," in Pye and Verba, *Political Culture and Political Development*, pp. 8–24; Eckstein, "Culturalist Theory of Political Change," pp. 789–94.

54. Oldham, "Memoirs," p. 3, BTHC.

Chapter 11

1. William L. Yancey to C. W. Jones et al., October 8, 1862, Yancey Papers, ADAH.

2. Although the South's traditional political leadership class still controlled public policies at the national and state levels, the Confederate elite became increas-

ingly fragmented between ultra nationalists such as Wigfall, Davis supporters, libertarians, various moderates, and political trimmers. See Kavanagh, *Political Culture*, pp. 20–27.

3. *Savannah Republican*, December 6, 1862.

4. Peterson Thweatt to Alexander H. Stephens, January 20, 31, March 21, 1863, Stephens Papers, LC; Phillips, *Correspondence of Toombs, Stephens, and Cobb*, pp. 610–11, 614, 619.

5. Peterson Thweatt to Alexander H. Stephens, June 6, 1863, Stephens Papers, LC; *Savannah Republican*, May 25, 1863; *Atlanta Southern Confederacy*, April 9, 1863; Bryan, *Confederate Georgia*, p. 38.

6. *Milledgeville Confederate Union*, March 24, April 23, May 5, 1863. For the importance of rewards for loyalty in establishing political legitimacy, see Lipset, *First New Nation*, pp. 45–60. I have found very useful Paul Escott's two somewhat different interpretations of Brown's political success in *After Secession*, pp. 159–66, and "Georgia," in Yearns, *Confederate Governors*, pp. 70–82.

7. Phillips, *Correspondence of Toombs, Stephens, and Cobb*, pp. 617–19.

8. *Annual Cyclopedia* (1863), pp. 447–48; *Milledgeville Confederate Union*, August 25, September 1, 1863; Phillips, *Correspondence of Toombs, Stephens, and Cobb*, p. 628.

9. *Milledgeville Southern Recorder*, September 1, 15, 1863.

10. Bryan, *Confederate Georgia*, p. 46; *Savannah Republican*, August 6, 1863; Howell Cobb to Lucy Ann Cobb, September 9, 1863, Cobb Papers, UG.

11. *Savannah Republican*, September 11, 1863; *Milledgeville Southern Recorder*, September 8, 22, 29, 1863.

12. Phillips, *Correspondence of Toombs, Stephens, and Cobb*, pp. 621–22; *Annual Cyclopedia* (1863), pp. 447–48; Candler, *Confederate Records of Georgia*, 2:470–73; *Milledgeville Southern Recorder*, September 15, 1863.

13. *Annual Cyclopedia* (1863), p. 448; Avery, *History of Georgia*, p. 261; *Milledgeville Southern Recorder*, November 3, 1863.

14. Cauthen, *South Carolina Goes to War*, pp. 162–63; Oliphant, Odell, and Eaves, *Letters of Simms*, 4:416–17.

15. *Richmond Daily Enquirer*, November 28, 1862; *Richmond Daily Examiner*, February 11, April 9, 1863.

16. *Richmond Daily Examiner*, April 27, May 27, 1863; *Richmond Daily Enquirer*, May 18, 1863; J. T. Ellis to Charles Munford, May 29, 1863, Munford-Ellis Family Papers, Duke.

17. *OR*, ser. 1, vol. 26, pt. 2, pp. 13–14; Rowland, *Davis*, 5:442–44; Thomas J. Chambers, *To the People of Texas* (broadside announcing his candidacy for governor); Kerby, *Kirby Smith's Confederacy*, pp. 153–54; Murrah, *Inaugural Address*, pp. 4–5.

18. Bettersworth, *Confederate Mississippi*, pp. 48–50; Bettersworth and Silver, *Mississippi in the Confederacy*, 1:107; *Jackson Daily Mississippian*, April 14, 21, 1863.

19. *Jackson Daily Mississippian*, May 5, 1863; Robert W. Dubay, "Mississippi,"

in Yearns, *Confederate Governors*, p. 127; Bettersworth, *Confederate Mississippi*, pp. 51–54.

20. McMillan, *Disintegration of a Confederate State*, pp. 52–55, 67–70; McMillan, *Alabama Confederate Reader*, pp. 236–37; *Greensboro* (Ala.) *Beacon*, June 3, 1863; Walker, "Shorter," p. 282; *Troy* (Ala.) *Southern Advertiser*, August 12, 1863; Fleming, "Peace Movement in Alabama," pp. 248–60.

21. *Troy* (Ala.) *Southern Advertiser*, August 12, 1863; *Mobile Weekly Advertiser and Register*, August 22, 1863; Robbins, "Confederate Nationalism," pp. 208–9; McMillan, *Disintegration of a Confederate State*, pp. 82–83.

22. Hamilton, *Ruffin Papers*, 3:327–29; *Charleston Mercury*, September 26, 1863; Brown Diary, November 4, 1863, SHC.

23. *Richmond Daily Whig*, January 3, 10, 16, 19, 1863; *Richmond Daily Examiner*, January 8, 19, 1863; *Virginia Senate Journal* (1862–63), pp. 210–14; *Richmond Daily Enquirer*, January 17, 19, 1863.

24. Daniel, *Richmond Examiner during the War*, pp. 111–12; Schwab, *Confederate States*, pp. 295–96; Herschel Johnson to A. E. Cochran, March 4, 1863, Johnson Papers, Duke.

25. *Milledgeville Southern Recorder*, August 25, 1863; Robbins, "Confederate Nationalism," p. 204. The third candidate in the race, James L. Seward, promised help for soldiers' families and a sounder financial policy (*Milledgeville Confederate Union*, August 18, 1863). Mark Blandford, whose right arm had been amputated, defeated an incumbent congressman in Georgia's Third District, and George Lester, who had lost an arm at the battle of Perryville, won in the Eighth District (Robbins, "Confederate Nationalism," p. 206).

26. Scarborough, *Diary of Edmund Ruffin*, 3:43; *Savannah Republican*, September 3, 1863.

27. Alexander Robinson Boteler, "To My Constituents of the 10th Congressional District," May 24, 1863, Boteler Papers, Duke; S. T. Holliday to Frederick W. Holliday, May 28, 29, June 1, 1863, U. C. Moore to Holliday, March 17, 1863, Holliday to Moore, March 27, 1863, Holliday Papers, Duke.

28. *Edgefield* (S.C.) *Advertiser*, January 21, 1863; Freeman, *Calendar of Confederate Papers*, pp. 265–66.

29. *Washington* (Ark.) *Telegraph*, July 22, 1863; *Shreveport Southwestern*, September 2, 1863; *Jackson Daily Mississippian*, April 22, 1863. For a fine discussion of the domination of early national politics by "notables," see McCormick, *Presidential Game*, pp. 41–116.

30. *Richmond Daily Whig*, April 3, 1863; M. C. Fulton to Alexander H. Stephens, August 2, 1863, C. H. Shockly to Stephens, July 11, 1863, C. P. Culver to Stephens, July 23, 1863, Stephens Papers, LC.

31. *Savannah Republican*, June 18, July 28, 1863.

32. *Charleston Daily Courier*, March 5, 1864; St. Paul, *Our Home and Foreign Policy*, pp. 8–12.

33. *Richmond Daily Examiner*, June 9, 1863; *Troy* (Ala.) *Southern Advertiser*, August 12, 1863; Yearns, *Confederate Congress*, pp. 55–56; McMillan, *Disintegra-*

tion of a Confederate State, pp. 80–82. In Alabama's Fourth District, J. L. M. Curry ran for reelection against Marcus H. Cruikshank. A peace advocate and reputed reconstructionist, Cruikshank declined a joint canvass and campaigned secretly, apparently in conjunction with a local peace society. Cruikshank's two-to-one margin of victory vindicated the strategy of running relatively obscure candidates in the most disaffected areas. Curry and his friends angrily blamed demagogism and universal suffrage for this stunning defeat. See Alderman and Gordon, *Curry*, pp. 168–70; Oldham, "Memoirs," pp. 62–63, BTHC; Martin, *Desertion of Alabama Troops*, pp. 110–12; Augusta J. Evans to J. L. M. Curry, October 16, 1863, Curry Papers, LC.

34. *Chattanooga Daily Rebel*, June 13, 1863; Yearns, *Confederate Congress*, p. 53. For an exception, see coverage of Augustus H. Garland's campaign in the Third District of Arkansas and the list of speaking engagements (*Washington* [Ark.] *Telegraph*, August 5, 19, 1863). When Unionist John B. Baldwin defeated former governor John Letcher in Virginia's Eleventh District, it took nearly a month for the returns to come in (Boney, *Letcher*, pp. 192–93).

35. *Charleston Mercury*, October 21, 1863; John B. Jones, *Rebel War Clerk's Diary*, 1:334; *Richmond Daily Dispatch*, May 30, 1863; *Edgefield* (S.C.) *Advertiser*, October 14, 1863.

36. *Richmond Daily Examiner*, December 12, 1861; *North Carolina Laws* (Called Session 1863), p. 4; Yearns, *Confederate Congress*, p. 43; Matthews, *Statutes at Large of the Confederate States of America*, 1st Cong., 3d sess., ch. 79, pp. 157–58; Kerby, *Kirby Smith's Confederacy*, p. 152.

37. Matthews, *Statutes at Large of the Confederate States of America*, 1st Cong., 4th sess., ch. 38, p. 189; ibid., 2d Cong., 1st sess., ch. 15, pp. 257–58; Coulter, *Confederate States of America*, p. 54; *Louisiana Acts* (1863), p. 9; Yearns, *Confederate Congress*, p. 36.

38. *Laws of Florida* (1863), p. 8; *Laws of Mississippi, March and April 1864*, p. 35; *Acts of South Carolina* (1862), pp. 129–31; Fremantle, *Three Months in the Southern States*, p. 157; Harry T. Hays to Thomas J. Semmes, October n.d., 1864, Semmes Papers, Duke.

39. Yearns, *Confederate Congress*, pp. 53–54, 57–58; Robbins, "Confederate Nationalism," pp. 215–17; Alexander and Beringer, *Anatomy of the Confederate Congress*, pp. 201–35. Conversely, the refusal of the Alabama legislature to allow soldiers to vote by waiving residency requirements was blamed for the defeat of administration supporter J. L. M. Curry in his bid for reelection (McMillan, *Disintegration of a Confederate State*, p. 81).

40. James D. McIver to John McIver, August 14, September 1, 1863, McIver Papers, Duke; *Montgomery Advertiser*, n.d., in *Richmond Daily Enquirer*, August 10, 1863; Scarborough, *Diary of Edmund Ruffin*, 3:117–18.

41. *Alabama Senate Journal* (1863), pp. 29–30, 40–42.

42. See the fine analysis of North Carolina congressional races in Kruman, *Parties and Politics in North Carolina*, pp. 253–55.

43. A. H. Arrington, "To the Voters of the 5th Congressional District of North Carolina," n.d., Arrington Papers, SHC; Jonathan Worth to Josiah Turner, July 13,

1863, in Hamilton, *Correspondence of Worth*, 1:245; *Raleigh Weekly Standard*, October 14, 1863.

44. John Pool to George Pool, October 25, 1863, John Pool to G. W. Brooks, October 25, 1863, William N. H. Smith Papers, Duke; *Raleigh Weekly Standard*, October 14, 21, 28, 1863.

45. C. C. Clay, Jr., to Louis T. Wigfall, August 5, 1863, Wigfall Papers, BTHC; Robbins, "Confederate Nationalism," p. 197; Yearns, *Confederate Congress*, p. 56.

46. *Mississippi Senate Journal* (December 1862 and November 1863), pp. 141–52, 169–73; Bettersworth, *Confederate Mississippi*, pp. 54–59.

47. C. C. Clay, Jr., to Mr. Figures, October 30, 1862, Clay to Susanna Clay, November 11, 1863, Clay Papers, Duke.

48. DuBose, *Yancey*, 2:752; C. C. Clay, Jr., to John W. Payne, August 27, 1863, Clay Papers, Duke.

49. C. C. Clay, Jr., to Louis T. Wigfall, September 11, 1863, Wigfall Papers, BTHC.

50. C. C. Clay, Jr., to Virginia Clay, March 25, 1863, Clay to Benjamin Hill, November 14, 1863, Hill to Clay, November 19, 20, 1863, Clay Papers, Duke; Clay to Louis T. Wigfall, September 11, November 15, 1863, Wigfall Papers, BTHC.

51. *Alabama Senate Journal* (1863), pp. 138–43, 151–57, 160–62, 164–65.

52. J. Withers Clay to C. C. Clay, Jr., November 29, 1863, January 7, 1864, Louis T. Wigfall to Clay, April 12, 1864, Clay Papers, Duke; *Charleston Mercury*, November 30, 1863.

53. J. Henly Smith to Alexander H. Stephens, August 20, 1863, Stephens Papers, LC; Max Williams and Hamilton, *Graham Papers*, 5:531–32; Hamilton, *Correspondence of Worth*, 1:251; *Jackson* (Miss.) *Daily Southern Crisis*, March 23, 1863.

54. *Raleigh Weekly Standard*, August 12, 1863; James T. Leach, circular, "Fellow-Citizens of the Third Congressional District of North Carolina," September 17, 1863, Leach Papers, SHC; *Richmond Daily Enquirer*, September 12, 1863. Williamson R. W. Cobb won election as a peace candidate from Alabama's Third District but crossed into Federal lines, took an oath of allegiance to the United States, and was formally expelled from the Confederate House (*SHSP* 51 [1958]: 6–8, 310–11, 316–18).

55. Kruman, *Parties and Politics in North Carolina*, pp. 245–55; John Hyman to Zebulon Vance, May 25, 1863, A. T. Davidson to Vance, May 31, 1863, Vance Papers, NCDAH.

56. C. P. Culver to Alexander H. Stephens, July 23, 1863, Stephens Papers, LC; *Milledgeville Confederate Union*, August 18, 1863.

57. *Richmond Daily Enquirer*, May 28, 1863; Hamilton, *Reconstruction in North Carolina*, pp. 48–49; Schwab, *Confederate States*, p. 209.

58. *Milledgeville Southern Recorder*, July 7, 1863; Robbins, "Confederate Nationalism," pp. 204–5, 212.

59. *Milledgeville Confederate Union*, August 25, 1863; *Rome* (Ga.) *Weekly Courier*, September 4, 1863.

60. *Milledgeville Southern Recorder*, September 11, 1863; Peterson Thweatt to Alexander H. Stephens, October 10, 1863, Stephens Papers, LC; *Milledgeville*

Confederate Union, October 13, 1863. Many administration candidates had to fend off peace candidates, but Congressman Lewis M. Ayer in South Carolina's Third District, an ardent Confederate, faced a challenge for reelection from that most notorious Southern extremist, Robert Barnwell Rhett. Although Ayer, like Rhett, opposed any undue enlargement of national authority, he was sure that Rhett had entered the race only to embarrass Davis. By this time many South Carolinians had had their fill of Rhett's relentless agitation. After Ayer defeated Rhett by around five hundred votes, the *Mercury* compared the vanquished hero to the "Savior of the world [who] was rejected of men." With Davis's friend Robert W. Barnwell and Rhett's old enemy James L. Orr still in the Confederate Senate, his humiliation was complete (White, *Rhett*, pp. 232–34; *Charleston Mercury*, September 8, 1863; Cauthen, *South Carolina Goes to War*, pp. 205–6, 213; Roland, *Confederacy*, p. 145).

61. *Washington* (Ark.) *Telegraph*, September 30, October 21, 1863, January 27, 1864; Dougan, *Confederate Arkansas*, pp. 111, 123–24.

62. This moderation or ambivalence has been interpreted as evidence of "cognitive dissonance" as well as a weakened commitment to Confederate nationalism (Beringer et al., *Why the South Lost*, pp. 286–93). In many districts the voters seemed determined to renounce secessionists without renouncing the war. Yet a commitment to internal unity persisted along with an aversion to political organizations. Antiparty politics continued to link the two political cultures together in complex ways.

63. James G. Ramsay to F. E. Shober, October 9, 1863, William P. Little to Ramsay, November 12, 1863, J. H. King to Ramsay, September 22, 1863, M. L. Holmes to Ramsay, September 22, 1863, W. P. Bynum to Ramsay, August 24, 31, 1863, J. S. Maxwell to Ramsay, September 12, 1863, R. D. Whitley to Ramsay, September 14, 1863, L. S. Bingham to Ramsay, September 8, 1863, Ramsay Papers, SHC; Yearns and Barrett, *North Carolina Civil War Documentary*, pp. 314–17; *Raleigh Weekly Standard*, October 28, 1863; Kruman, *Parties and Politics in North Carolina*, pp. 252–54.

64. Thomas S. Ashe to Edward J. Hale, August 5, October 5, 15, 1863, Hale to Zebulon Vance, October 27, 1863, Hale Papers, NCDAH.

65. Herschel Johnson to Alexander H. Stephens, March 25, November 29, 1863, Johnson Papers, Duke; Phillips, *Correspondence of Toombs, Stephens, and Cobb*, p. 630; Joseph E. Brown to Stephens, November 10, 1863, Stephens Papers, Emory; *Savannah Republican*, November 13, 1863; Pearce, *Hill*, pp. 84–85; *Georgia Senate Journal* (Annual Session 1863), pp. 109–11.

66. Younger, *Inside the Confederate Government*, p. 119.

67. Alexander and Beringer, *Anatomy of the Confederate Congress*, pp. 25–29; Stephenson, *Day of the Confederacy*, p. 94.

68. For the debate on the "persistent Whiggery" thesis, see Alexander, "Persistent Whiggery in Alabama," pp. 35–52; Alexander, "Persistent Whiggery in the Confederate South," pp. 305–29; Mering, "Persistent Whiggery in the Confederate South," pp. 123–43.

69. For useful though contradictory analyses of the elections as indicators of

support or opposition to the Davis administration, see Yearns, *Confederate Congress*, p. 58; Escott, *After Secession*, p. 155; Robbins, "Confederate Nationalism," pp. 199, 217–18.

Chapter 12

1. Woodward, *Mary Chesnut's Civil War*, pp. 520, 550; *Richmond Daily Whig*, November 25, 1863; James L. Orr to James Henry Hammond, January 3, 1864, Hammond Papers, LC; Schenck Books, January 19, 1864, SHC.

2. Woodworth, *Davis and His Generals*, pp. 222–55; Woodward, *Mary Chesnut's War*, p. 469; McMurry, "'The Enemy at Richmond,'" pp. 17–18.

3. Howell Cobb to Mary Ann Cobb, October 5, 1863, Cobb Papers, UG; Woodward, *Mary Chesnut's Civil War*, p. 482.

4. Longstreet, *From Manassas to Appomattox*, pp. 465–67; Rowland, *Davis*, 6:54–56; Grady McWhiney, "Jefferson Davis and His Generals," in McWhiney, *Southerners and Other Americans*, p. 93.

5. Daniel, *Richmond Examiner during the War*, pp. 143–44; *Richmond Daily Whig*, November 28, 1863; *Alabama Acts* (1863), p. 219; Hamilton, *Ruffin Papers*, 3:348.

6. Dowdey and Manarin, *Wartime Papers of Lee*, p. 641; Govan and Livingood, *Different Valor*, pp. 236–39; *SHSP* 50 (1933): 21–22; *OR*, ser. 1, vol. 31, pt. 3, pp. 796–97; Connelly, *Autumn of Glory*, pp. 282–84.

7. Schott, *Stephens*, p. 389; Woodward, *Mary Chesnut's Civil War*, p. 517.

8. Howell Cobb to Mary Ann Cobb, December 10, 15, 17, 1863, Cobb Papers, UG.

9. Joseph E. Johnston to Louis T. Wigfall, December 27, 1863, February 14, 1864, Wigfall Papers, BTHC; Wright, *Southern Girl in '61*, pp. 161–62, 168–69; Brooks, "Howell Cobb Papers," pp. 367–68. For a judicious and persuasive interpretation of the relationship between Johnston and Davis, see McMurry, "'The Enemy at Richmond,'" pp. 18–31.

10. *OR*, ser. 4, vol. 3, pp. 31–32; Woodward, *Mary Chesnut's Civil War*, pp. 501, 583–84; King, *Wigfall*, pp. 194–97; Symonds, *Johnston*, p. 265.

11. Richardson, *Messages and Papers*, 1:336; Strode, *Davis*, 2:491. For a first-rate analysis of Davis's shifting defenses of Confederate nationalism, see Escott, *After Secession*, pp. 168–79, 193–95.

12. Richardson, *Messages and Papers*, 1:345–82.

13. John B. Jones, *Rebel War Clerk's Diary*, 2:125; Pryor, *Reminiscences of Peace and War*, pp. 263–64; A. H. Kenan to Alexander H. Stephens, February 8, 1864, Stephens Papers, LC; Woodward, *Mary Chesnut's Civil War*, p. 532.

14. Richardson, *Messages and Papers*, 1:395–400.

15. *South Carolina Senate Journal* (1863), pp. 85, 87, 100; *Laws of Texas* (1863), p. 52; *Acts of Georgia* (1863), pp. 100–101; *OR*, ser. 4, vol. 2, pp. 1052–54.

16. *Memphis Daily Appeal* (published in Atlanta), January 5, 1864; *Richmond Daily Dispatch*, January 13, 1864; Abrams, *Davis and His Administration*, pp. 5–15, 19–20.

17. North Carolina, *Executive and Legislative Documents* (Extra Sessions 1863–64), pp. 7–8; Dodd, *Davis*, p. 323; *Richmond Daily Whig*, February 24, 1864; Abrams, *Davis and His Administration*, pp. 16–18; *Address of the Atlanta Register*, p. 2.

18. *Address of the Atlanta Register*, pp. 4–10; Cleveland, *Stephens*, p. 763; *OR*, ser. 4, vol. 2, pp. 960–61.

19. *Address of the Atlanta Register*, pp. 1, 12–16; "Address of Congress to the People of the Confederate States," pp. 24–25.

20. Matthews, *Statutes at Large of the Confederate States of America*, 1st Cong., 4th sess., resolution 3, p. 238; *Raleigh Daily Confederate*, May 3, 1864; *Richmond Daily Dispatch*, December 18, 1863; *Richmond Daily Whig*, January 21, 1864; Daniel, *Richmond Examiner during the War*, pp. 150–51; Herschel Johnson to A. E. Cochran, November 22, 1863, Johnson to Alexander H. Stephens, November 29, 1863, Johnson Papers, Duke.

21. *Charleston Mercury*, January 5, 1864; *Richmond Daily Examiner*, January 13, 1864; *Memphis Daily Appeal* (published in Atlanta), January 16, 1864; John Scott, *Letters to an Officer in the Army*, pp. 13–82; Augusta J. Evans to J. L. M. Curry, January 27, 1864, Curry Papers, LC; Alexander H. Stephens to Richard M. Johnston, November 6, 1863, quoted in Cleveland, *Stephens*, pp. 176–77; *Atlanta Southern Confederacy*, February 2, 1864; *Petersburg Express*, January 27, 1864, quoted in Schwab, *Confederate States*, p. 211; John B. Jones, *Rebel War Clerk's Diary*, 2:89–90.

22. *Richmond Daily Enquirer*, January 1864; *Richmond Daily Dispatch*, December 5, 1863, January 20, 22, 1864; Coulter, *Confederate States of America*, pp. 144–45; Crabtree and Patton, *"Journal of a Secesh Lady,"* pp. 516–17; Woodward, *Mary Chesnut's Civil War*, p. 544; Alfred P. Aldrich to James Henry Hammond, February 15, 1864, Hammond Papers, LC; *Richmond Daily Examiner*, February 5, 20, 1864.

23. *Charleston Mercury*, November 28, January 26, 1864; Laurence Keitt to James Henry Hammond, December 11, 1863, Hammond Papers, LC.

24. *Annual Cyclopedia* (1863), pp. 207–8; *Memphis Daily Appeal* (published in Atlanta), January 22, 1864; Oldham, "Memoirs," p. 144, BTHC; *Alabama Senate Journal* (1863), pp. 192–206; *Richmond Daily Examiner*, February 6, 1864.

25. *Laws of Texas* (1863), p. 50; John B. Jones, *Rebel War Clerk's Diary*, 2:108; Albert G. Brown, *State of the Country*, pp. 2, 4–5.

26. Virginia, *Documents*, no. 1 (1863–64), pp. iii–viii; *Richmond Daily Whig*, November 13, 1863; Candler, *Confederate Records of Georgia*, 2:483–88.

27. *Charleston Mercury*, January 29, 1864; James Henry Hammond to James L. Orr, December 11, 1863, Hammond Papers, LC; "Address of Congress to the People of the Confederate States," p. 27.

28. James H. Harper to Alexander H. Stephens, January 5, 1864, William F. Samford to Stephens, January 4, 1864, Stephens Papers, LC.

29. Frank Moore, *Rebellion Record*, 8:341–45.

30. Max Williams and Hamilton, *Graham Papers*, 6:4–6, 27–31; M. Mosland to Zebulon B. Vance, January n.d., 1864, Martin Starbuck et al. to Thomas Settle, January 7, 1864, Settle to Starbuck et al., January 14, 1864, Settle Papers, SHC.

31. Yearns and Barrett, *North Carolina Civil War Documentary*, pp. 296–97; Hamilton, *Correspondence of Worth*, 1:282–84; Petition, n.d., 1864, enclosed in John Hyman to Vance, January 30, 1864, Vance Papers, NCDAH; *Raleigh Weekly Standard*, January 20, 1864; James T. Leach to *Raleigh Standard*, January 13, 1864, clipping, Leach Papers, SHC. For a somewhat different analysis of the convention movement, see Kruman, *Parties and Politics in North Carolina*, pp. 259–60.

32. Max Williams and Hamilton, *Graham Papers*, 6:3–4, 27; Hamilton, *Correspondence of Worth*, 1:286–87; *Raleigh Weekly Standard*, February 10, 1864; *OR*, ser. 1, vol. 51, pt. 2, pp. 815–16; O'Brien, *Legal Fraternity and the Making of a New South Community*, pp. 53–54; Yearns and Barrett, *North Carolina Civil War Documentary*, pp. 300–301.

33. *Raleigh Daily Confederate*, January 26, 29, 1864; Hamilton, *Ruffin Papers*, 3:367; Peter Mallett to Zebulon Vance, December 24, 1863, Vance Letterbooks, NCDAH.

34. Hamilton, *Correspondence of Worth*, 1:285–86; Paris, *A Sermon: Preached before Brig. Gen. Hoke's Brigade*, pp. 8–15.

35. Max Williams and Hamilton, *Graham Papers*, 6:22–24; John A. Gilmer to Zebulon Vance, January 5, 1864, Vance Papers, NCDAH; C. D. Smith to James G. Ramsay, November 17, 1863, Ramsay Papers, SHC.

36. Max Williams and Hamilton, *Graham Papers*, 5:543–44, 6:1–2, 16–21, 24–26.

37. William C. Harris, *Holden*, pp. 141–43; Hamilton, *Correspondence of Worth*, 1:297–98; J. McCormick to Zebulon Vance, November 28, 1863, Vance Papers, NCDAH.

38. *OR*, ser. 1, vol. 51, pt. 2, pp. 808–10, 813; George Davis to Edward J. Hale, January 15, 1864, Hale Papers, NCDAH; Max Williams and Hamilton, *Graham Papers*, 6:24; *Raleigh Daily Confederate*, January 28, 1864.

39. Zebulon Vance to Edward J. Hale, December 21, 1863, Hale Papers, NCDAH; *OR*, ser. 1, vol. 51, pt. 2, pp. 807, 817; Yearns and Barrett, *North Carolina Civil War Documentary*, pp. 308–9; Vance to David L. Swain, January 2, 1864, Swain Papers, SHC.

40. Yearns, *Confederate Congress*, pp. 86–88; Albert B. Brown, *State of the Country*, pp. 2–3.

41. [Gibbes], *Memorial*, pp. 1–4; *OR*, ser. 4, vol. 2, pp. 767, 856–58.

42. Albert B. Moore, *Conscription and Conflict in the Confederacy*, pp. 83–113; *SHSP* 50 (1953): 189–93; *Edgefield* (S.C.) *Advertiser*, February 3, 1864.

43. Cleveland, *Stephens*, pp. 761–67; *Montgomery Daily Mail*, April 16, 1864; Coulter, *Confederate States of America*, pp. 386–87.

44. Robert W. Johnson, *Speech of Mr. Johnson of Arkansas on Bill to Limit and Define Terms of Office*, pp. 3–19.

45. *Richmond Daily Examiner*, December 12, 1863, January 19, 1864; *Charleston Mercury*, January 25, 1864; *Atlanta Southern Confederacy*, February 3, 1864.

46. Younger, *Inside the Confederate Government*, p. 126; John B. Jones, *Rebel War Clerk's Diary*, 2:116, 132; *Richmond Daily Dispatch*, December 14, 1863; *Richmond Sentinel*, December 14, 1863; Woodward, *Mary Chesnut's Civil War*, p. 545.

47. D. K. McCrae to Edward J. Hale, January 16, 1864, Hale Papers, NCDAH; Younger, *Inside the Confederate Government*, pp. 137–38; Hamilton, *Ruffin Papers*, 3:373; *OR*, ser. 1, vol. 26, pt. 2, p. 285, vol. 28, pt. 2, pp. 272–74.

48. *Raleigh Daily Confederate*, February 11, 1864; Albert B. Brown, *State of the Country*, pp. 14–16; *Savannah Republican*, February 13, 1864; *Richmond Sentinel*, February 6, 1864.

49. *JCC*, 3:712, 6:764; Matthews, *Statutes at Large of the Confederate States of America*, 1st Cong., 4th sess., ch. 37, pp. 187–89.

50. Alexander H. Stephens to Richard M. Johnston, January 21, 1864, quoted in Richard M. Johnston and Browne, *Stephens*, p. 453; Stephens to Jefferson Davis, January 22, 1864, Davis Papers, Duke; *Richmond Daily Whig*, January 15, 1864. For a perceptive analysis of the relationship between Stephens and Davis on this question, see Schott, *Stephens*, pp. 395–96.

51. *Montgomery Daily Mail*, January 20, 1864; *Richmond Daily Dispatch*, January 12, 1864; *Richmond Daily Examiner*, January 9, 1864.

52. *Laws of Florida* (1863), pp. 55–56; *Laws of Mississippi, December 1862 and November 1863*, pp. 159–60; *North Carolina Laws* (Adjourned Session 1864), pp. 23–25; Sidney D. Brummer, "The Judicial Interpretation of the Confederate Constitution," in *Studies in Southern History and Politics*, pp. 129–311; Coulter, *Confederate States of America*, p. 394.

53. *Richmond Daily Whig*, January 1, 1864; *Memphis Daily Appeal* (published in Atlanta), January 4, 1864; *OR*, ser. 1, vol. 51, pt. 2, pp. 818–20; Herschel Johnson to Jefferson Davis, ca. February 27 and March 10, 1864, Davis Papers, Duke.

54. Herschel Johnson to Alexander H. Stephens, March 10, 1864, Johnson Papers, Duke; Marten, *Texas Divided*, pp. 49–50; *Mississippi Senate Journal* (1864), pp. 7, 14–15; Dunaway, *Sermon*, pp. 17–18. Class unity also remained central to arguments for political harmony with increasing emphasis on the costs of emancipation to nonslaveholding whites (*Raleigh Daily Confederate*, April 14, 1864).

55. Stephen Elliott, *Gideon's Water-Lappers*, pp. 15–20; Mayes, *Lamar*, pp. 653–56; Matthews, *Statutes at Large of the Confederate States of America*, 2d Cong., 1st sess., resolution 13, pp. 286–88.

56. Gilmer, *Substance of the Argument*, broadside; *Atlanta Southern Confederacy*, March 25, 1864; *Memphis Daily Appeal* (published in Atlanta), April 21, 1864.

57. Coulter, *Confederate States of America*, p. 394; *Charleston Mercury*, March 30, April 27, 1864; Robert Barnwell Rhett to Louis T. Wigfall, April 15, 1864, Wigfall Papers, BTHC; James Henry Hammond to Wigfall, April 15, 1864, Hammond Papers, LC.

58. King, *Wigfall*, pp. 191–93; Louis T. Wigfall to James Henry Hammond, [ca. March or April 1864], Hammond Papers, LC.

Chapter 13

1. Candler, *Confederate Records of Georgia*, 2:526–32, 673–76, 3:458–63; *OR*, ser. 4, vol. 2, pp. 1062–63; Phillips, *Correspondence of Toombs, Stephens, and Cobb*,

p. 632; Louise B. Hill, *Brown and the Confederacy*, p. 83; *Acts of Georgia* (1863), pp. 106–7.

2. Parks, *Brown*, pp. 277–78; J. William Harris, *Plain Folk and Gentry in a Slave Society*, pp. 163–66; Schott, *Stephens*, p. 360; Rabun, "Stephens and Davis," p. 321; Howe, *Political Culture of American Whigs*, pp. 254–59.

3. Andrew H. Dawson to Alexander H. Stephens, March 4, 1864, J. Barrett Cohen to Stephens, April 1, 1864, Stephens Papers, LC.

4. Candler, *Confederate Records of Georgia*, 2:595–655.

5. Schott, *Stephens*, p. 383; Howell Cobb to Mary Ann Cobb, January 9, 1864, Cobb Papers, UG; Parks, *Brown*, pp. 275–77; Phillips, *Correspondence of Toombs, Stephens, and Cobb*, p. 640.

6. Benjamin H. Hill to Alexander H. Stephens, March 2, 1864, Stephens Papers, Emory; Phillips, *Correspondence of Toombs, Stephens, and Cobb*, pp. 634–37.

7. Schott, *Stephens*, p. 407; Cleveland, *Stephens*, pp. 761–86.

8. For examples of support, see Schott, *Stephens*, p. 411; *Atlanta Southern Confederacy*, April 5, 1864; J. H. Linebaugh to Alexander H. Stephens, April 7, 1864, Stephens Papers, LC; Leroy P. Walker to Stephens, April 8, 1864, Stephens Papers, Emory. For examples of criticism, see *Savannah Republican*, March 28, 1864; Schott, *Stephens*, p. 412; *Richmond Daily Dispatch*, March 25, 1864; *Richmond Daily Enquirer*, May 2, 1864; *Richmond Daily Examiner*, April 19, 1864; Coulter, *Confederate States of America*, p. 138.

9. Herschel Johnson to Alexander H. Stephens, March 19, April 1, 6, 11, 1864, Johnson Papers, Duke; *OR*, ser. 4, vol. 3, pp. 278–81.

10. *OR*, ser. 4, vol. 3, pp. 234–37; Schott, *Stephens*, pp. 410–11; *Georgia House Journal* (Extra Session 1864), pp. 105–6, 118–19; *Georgia Senate Journal* (Extra Session 1864), pp. 98–99.

11. *Memphis Daily Appeal* (published in Atlanta), March 28, 30, 1864; *Milledgeville Confederate Union*, April 5, 1864; Coulter, *Confederate States of America*, p. 394; Phillips, *Correspondence of Toombs, Stephens, and Cobb*, pp. 637–39; J. Barrett Cohen to Alexander H. Stephens, April 21, 1864, Stephens Papers, LC.

12. Cleveland, *Stephens*, p. 793; *Milledgeville Confederate Union*, March 29, 1864; Waddell, *Biographical Sketch of Linton Stephens*, pp. 257–59.

13. *Milledgeville Southern Recorder*, April 19, 1864; Peterson Thweatt to Alexander H. Stephens, April 9, 1864, Stephens Papers, LC; Schott, *Stephens*, p. 411; Coulter, *Confederate States of America*, p. 541; *Edgefield* (S.C.) *Advertiser*, April 6, 1864.

14. Henry Watterson to Alexander H. Stephens, April 3, 1864, Stephens Papers, LC; Phillips, *Correspondence of Toombs, Stephens, and Cobb*, pp. 639–40.

15. Bass, "Attack upon the Confederate Administration in Georgia," pp. 246–47; *OR*, ser. 4, vol. 3, pp. 372–75; Phillips, *Correspondence of Toombs, Stephens, and Cobb*, pp. 641–43; *Milledgeville Confederate Union*, April 12, May 3, 1864; James A. Russ to Alexander H. Stephens, April 28, 1864, Stephens Papers, LC; Linton Stephens to Julia Toombs, March 30, 1864, Toombs Papers, UG.

16. Mayes, *Lamar*, pp. 646–53.

17. Phillips, *Correspondence of Toombs, Stephens, and Cobb*, p. 643; *OR*, ser. 4, vol. 3, pp. 417–22, 431–40, 455–57.

18. *Acts of Georgia* (1864), p. 154; Cleveland, *Stephens*, pp. 791–92.

19. *Acts of Georgia* (1863), p. 104; *Laws of Texas* (1864), p. 17; *Louisiana Acts* (1865), pp. 57–58; *North Carolina Laws* (Adjourned Session 1863), pp. 11–12; *Laws of Mississippi, August 1864*, pp. 54–55; Sidney D. Brummer, "The Judicial Interpretation of the Confederate Constitution," in *Studies in Southern History and Politics*, pp. 115–19; North Carolina, *Cases at Law, Decided at the Extra Term, Commencing on the 26th of October 1864*, pp. 13–18.

20. Candler, *Confederate Records of Georgia*, 2:683–87; Albert B. Moore, *Conscription and Conflict in the Confederacy*, pp. 251–54; Escott, *Many Excellent People*, p. 39; Lt. Col. G. W. Gray to Col. Peter Mallett, April 7, 1863, John Gill Shorter to Zebulon Vance, April 7, 1863, Vance to Col. T. P. August, March 20, 1863, Vance Letterbooks, NCDAH.

21. *SHSP* 51 (1958): 66–68, 109–13, 118–27; Murray, *Speech of Hon. John P. Murray of Tennessee, in Favor of Repealing the Act Suspending the Privilege of the Writ of Habeas Corpus*, pp. 1–8. A bill repealing the suspension of habeas corpus was tabled in the House. Despite the general trend toward weakening old party ties, former Whigs generally voted against suspension (*JCC*, 7:54; Alexander and Beringer, *Anatomy of the Confederate Congress*, pp. 173–200).

22. Taylor, "Boyce-Hammond Correspondence," p. 354; Younger, *Inside the Confederate Government*, p. 156; James Henry Hammond to William Gilmore Simms, June 12, 1864, Hammond Papers, LC; *Charleston Mercury*, June 27–29, 1864; *Richmond Daily Examiner*, June 7, 1864.

23. Joseph E. Johnston to Louis T. Wigfall, April 5, 30, 1864, Wigfall Papers, BTHC. The administration had in fact delayed sending reinforcements, and the president never issued direct orders transferring the necessary troops to Johnston's command. For careful analyses of western command problems in the spring and summer of 1864, see Woodworth, *Davis and His Generals*, pp. 260–304; and Symonds, *Johnston*, pp. 257–67.

24. *Memphis Daily Appeal* (published in Atlanta), June 16, 1864. See the excellent accounts of Johnston's plans and eventual removal in Shelby Foote, *Civil War*, 3:411–22; Connelly, *Autumn of Glory*, pp. 391–426; Symonds, *Johnston*, pp. 302–29.

25. *OR*, ser. 1, vol. 38, pt. 5, pp. 879–80; William J. Hardee to Jefferson Davis, June 22, 1864, Davis Papers, Emory.

26. Dowdey and Manarin, *Wartime Papers of Lee*, pp. 821–22; Hill, "Address," p. 498; Rowland, *Davis*, 8:349–54; *OR*, ser. 1, vol. 38, pt. 5, p. 885.

27. *Milledgeville Confederate Union*, September 13, 1864; Phillips, *Correspondence of Toombs, Stephens, and Cobb*, pp. 651–52; Howell Cobb to Mary Ann Cobb, July 19, 1864, Cobb Papers, E. Merton Coulter Collection, UG.

28. Woodward, *Mary Chesnut's Civil War*, pp. 633, 635; Daniel, *Richmond Examiner during the War*, pp. 211–12; *Montgomery Daily Mail*, July 21, 1864; Joseph E. Johnston to Louis T. Wigfall, August 27, 1864, Wigfall Papers, BTHC.

29. William W. Holden to Thomas Settle, December 22, 1863, Settle Papers, SHC.

30. Jimerson, *Private Civil War*, p. 190; John Francis Shaffner to Carrie Fries, February 4, 1864, Shaffner Papers, NCDAH; Schenck Books, February 19, 1864, SHC.

31. John D. Hyman to Zebulon Vance, February 17, 1864, Thomas L. Clingman to Vance, February 18, 1864, Vance Papers, NCDAH; David M. Carter to D. B. Perry, December 10, 1863, Carter Papers, SHC; D. W. Berringer to Edward J. Hale, November 17, 23, 1863, Vance to Hale, January 1, 9, February 4, 1864, Hale to William A. Graham, February 5, 1864, Hale Papers, NCDAH; Spencer, *Last Ninety Days of the War in North Carolina*, pp. 124–27; A. M. Gorman to J. D. Brown, February 3, 1864, Nancy Young Collection, SHC.

32. Zebulon Vance to Edward J. Hale, February 11, 1864, Hale Papers, NCDAH; William T. Dortch to Vance, March 5, 1864, Henry E. Coulton to Vance, February 14, 1864, Vance Papers, NCDAH; Max Williams and Hamilton, *Graham Papers*, 6:45–47; Rowland, *Davis*, 9:330–32.

33. Zebulon Vance to Edward J. Hale, February 28, 1864, Hale Papers, NCDAH; Glenn Tucker, *Vance*, pp. 361–66; *Raleigh Daily Confederate*, April 16, 1864; *Richmond Daily Dispatch*, March 10, 1864.

34. *Raleigh Daily Confederate*, March 2, 1864; Max Williams and Hamilton, *Graham Papers*, 6:31–33; Schenck Books, March 26, 1864, SHC.

35. James T. Leach to Zebulon Vance, March 5, 8, 1864, Vance Papers, NCDAH; *SHSP* 51 (1958): 130–31; *JCC*, 7:84–85; *Raleigh Weekly Standard*, July 6, 1864; Leach to ?, March 4, 1864, Leach to Voters of Third Congressional District, n.d., 1864, Leach to *Raleigh Standard*, clipping, n.d., 1864, Leach Papers, SHC.

36. *SHSP* 51 (1958): 16–19; James M. Leach, Broadside to the Voters of the Seventh Congressional District, April 5, 1864, Vance Papers, NCDAH.

37. Josiah Turner, Jr., to Sophia Turner, May 7, 1864, Turner Papers, SHC; William Henry Bagley to Adelaide Worth, February 1, June 8, 17, August 16, 1864, Worth Papers, SHC; Hamilton, *Correspondence of Worth*, 1:292–93.

38. Hamilton, *Correspondence of Worth*, 1:299–300; William W. Holden to Calvin J. Cowles, March 18, 1864, Holden Papers, NCDAH; William C. Harris, *Holden*, pp. 144–49; Raper, *Holden*, pp. 52–55; *Raleigh Weekly Standard*, April 6, 1864; Max Williams and Hamilton, *Graham Papers*, 6:33–36.

39. *Raleigh Daily Confederate*, March 7, 22, 1864; Alfred G. Forster to Zebulon Vance, March 13, 1864, John D. Hyman to Vance, March 19, 1864, Phi L. Carston to Vance, July 22, 1864, Vance Papers, NCDAH; McCrae and Gordon [*Raleigh Daily Confederate*] to Robert Franklin Hackett, March 23, 1864, W. W. Hampton to Hackett, April 17, 1864, Gordon and Hackett Family Papers, SHC.

40. Hamilton, *Ruffin Papers*, 3:381, 403–4; Max Williams and Hamilton, *Graham Papers*, 6:63; *Raleigh Weekly Standard*, May 25, 1864; William C. Harris, *Holden*, pp. 149–50; Hamilton, *Correspondence of Worth*, 1:303; J. B. Batchelor to Kemp P. Battle, April 15, 1864, Battle Family Papers, SHC; Hamilton, *Reconstruction in North Carolina*, p. 61.

41. *Raleigh Daily Confederate*, March 16, 22, April 8, 1864; Zebulon Vance to Edward J. Hale, March 20, 1864, Hale Papers, NCDAH; James M. Leach to Vance, April 27, 1864, Vance Papers, NCDAH; Hamilton, *Correspondence of Worth*, 1:309; Yearns and Barrett, *North Carolina Civil War Documentary*, pp. 319–20.

42. Zebulon Vance to Edward J. Hale, April 13, 1864, Hale Papers, NCDAH; Max

Williams and Hamilton, *Graham Papers*, 6:57–58; Vance to James A. Seddon, April 11, 1864, Vance Letterbooks, NCDAH.

43. North Carolina, *Executive and Legislative Documents* (Extra Sessions 1863–64), pp. 3–20.

44. *North Carolina Senate Journal* (1864), pp. 16–22; *North Carolina Laws* (Adjourned Session 1864), pp. 20–21, 25; *Raleigh Daily Confederate*, May 26, 1864; William C. Harris, *Holden*, p. 149.

45. William Robinson to Zebulon Vance, May 30, 1864, Vance Papers, NCDAH; Yearns and Barrett, *North Carolina Civil War Documentary*, p. 318; Charles Phillips to Kemp P. Battle, June 22, 1864, Battle Family Papers, SHC; Hamilton, *Correspondence of Worth*, 1:317–18, 321–23.

46. *Raleigh Daily Confederate*, April 2, 1864; Richmond M. Pearson to *Fayetteville Observer*, April 11, 1864, Pearson Papers, SHC; *Richmond Daily Examiner*, July 18, 1864; *Montgomery Daily Mail*, June 8, 1864; Collier Diary, June 17, 1864, SHC.

47. *Raleigh Daily Confederate*, July 19, August 16, 1864; Hamilton, "Heroes of America," pp. 11–19; Auman and Scarboro, "Heroes of America in Civil War North Carolina," pp. 327–63; Auman, "Neighbor against Neighbor," pp. 59–92.

48. *Raleigh Daily Confederate*, July 27, 1864; John Francis Shaffner to Carrie Fries, March 27, 1864, Shaffner Diary and Papers, NCDAH; Wesley N. Freedman to Joseph Cather, April 25, 1864, Cather Papers, NCDAH; L. S. Biddle to his father, April 11, 1864, Biddle Papers, Duke.

49. John Francis Shaffner to Carrie Fries, March 27, August 4, 1864, Shaffner Diary and Papers, NCDAH; *Raleigh Daily Confederate*, March 29 and April 1864; Kenzer, *Kinship and Neighborhood in a Southern Community*, p. 81; Election returns from Company A, First North Carolina Battalion of Sharpshooters, July 28, 1864, Pearson Papers, Duke.

50. George A. Williams to his father, April 5, 1864, Williams-Womble Papers, NCDAH; Joseph Leander Gash to his sister, June 18, 1864, Gash Family Papers, NCDAH; *Raleigh Weekly Standard*, July 13, 27, 1864.

51. *Raleigh Weekly Standard*, August 10, 1864; Durrill, *War of Another Kind*, pp. 213–15; William W. Holden to Calvin Cowles, July 19, 1864, Cowles Papers, NCDAH; *Raleigh Daily Confederate*, August 1, 1864; William Henry Bagley to Adelaide Worth, August 9, 1864, Worth Papers, SHC. Vance supporters claimed that most of intimidation came from the other side and that in some cases soldiers voted for Holden simply to spite their officers (J. L. Henry to Zebulon Vance, August 2, 1864, Vance Papers, NCDAH; Hamilton, *Ruffin Papers*, 3:412).

52. Kruman, *Parties and Politics in North Carolina*, p. 265; Baker, "Class Conflict and Political Upheaval," pp. 175–78; Hamilton, *Ruffin Papers*, 3:414; Henry Machen Patrick to Sue Patrick, August 13, 1864, Patrick Papers, NCDAH; *Raleigh Daily Confederate*, August 6, 1864.

53. North Carolina, *Executive and Legislative Documents* (Sessions of 1864–65), pp. 19–20; Zebulon Vance to David Swain, September 22, 1864, quoted in Coulter, *Confederate States of America*, p. 549.

54. William C. Harris, *Holden*, pp. 153–54.

55. Joseph E. Brown to Aaron Wilbur, September 22, 1864, Wilbur Papers, Emory.

56. Bettersworth, *Confederate Mississippi*, p. 210; *OR*, ser. 4, vol. 3, pp. 393–98; Bohannon, *Circular*, broadside; Marten, *Texas Divided*, pp. 36–37; Peterson Thweatt to Alexander H. Stephens, October 3, 1864, Stephens Papers, LC; Herschel Johnson to "Several Gentlemen in Middle Georgia," *Augusta Constitutionalist*, October 7, 1864, clipping in Johnson Papers, Duke.

57. Yearns, *Confederate Congress*, p. 176; W. W. Boyce to Alexander H. Stephens, August 24, 1864, Stephens Papers, Emory; *Raleigh Weekly Standard*, October 12, 1864; Cauthen, *South Carolina Goes to War*, pp. 217–20; *Charleston Mercury*, October 13, 1864; *Charleston Daily Courier*, October 22, 1864; Woodward, *Mary Chesnut's Civil War*, p. 656.

58. Nelson, *Bullets, Ballots, and Rhetoric*, pp. 134–46; *Montgomery Daily Mail*, October 18, 1864; Henry W. Hilliard to Alexander H. Stephens, September 10, 1864, Stephens Papers, LC.

59. Cleveland, *Stephens*, pp. 191–96; Alexander H. Stephens to Linton Stephens, October 9, 15, 1864, quoted in Richard M. Johnston and Browne, *Stephens*, pp. 473–74; Alexander H. Stephens to W. W. Boyce, October 13, 1864, Stephens Papers, Emory; Waddell, *Biographical Sketch of Linton Stephens*, pp. 281–86.

60. *Troy* (Ala.) *Southern Advertiser*, April 1, 1864; *Montgomery Daily Mail*, July 27, 1864; *Savannah Republican*, August 13, 1864; *Washington* (Ark.) *Telegraph*, October 19, 1864.

61. *Richmond Daily Dispatch*, October 19, 1864; *Montgomery Daily Advertiser*, September 20, October 23, 1864; *Richmond Daily Enquirer*, October 29, 1864; *Milledgeville Southern Recorder*, October 4, 1864.

62. *Richmond Daily Examiner*, October 14, 1864; *Charleston Mercury*, June 6, August 24, October 5, 1864.

63. Woodward, *Mary Chesnut's Civil War*, pp. 439–40. For rumors and reports that generated the cynicism described here, see *Charleston Daily Courier*, September 22, 1864; John B. Jones, *Rebel War Clerk's Diary*, 2:275, 279, 290, 339, 349.

64. Rowland, *Davis*, 6:341–44; Parks, *Brown*, pp. 299–300; *Raleigh Weekly Standard*, October 5, 1864.

65. Rowland, *Davis*, 6:345–47, 356–60.

66. Ibid., pp. 350–53, 355; Woodward, *Mary Chesnut's Civil War*, p. 651.

67. Schenck Books, September n.d., 1864, SHC; Scarborough, *Diary of Edmund Ruffin*, 3:584–85; *Montgomery Daily Mail*, September 27, 1864; *Milledgeville Confederate Union*, October 4, 1864; Benjamin H. Hill to Jefferson Davis, October 14, 1864, quoted in Pearce, *Hill*, p. 99.

68. *Raleigh Daily Confederate*, September 13, 1864; Herschel Johnson to Alexander H. Stephens, September 28, 1864, Johnson Papers, Duke; Phillips, *Correspondence of Toombs, Stephens, and Cobb*, pp. 652–53; King, *Wigfall*, p. 199.

69. *Richmond Daily Enquirer*, October 1, 1864; Eggleston, *Rebel's Recollections*, pp. 170–71; Max Williams and Hamilton, *Graham Papers*, 6:187–88; *Charleston Mercury*, November 27, 1864; Andrew H. H. Dawson to Alexander H. Stephens, October 6, 1864, Stephens Papers, LC.

Chapter 14

1. Richardson, *Messages and Papers*, 1:564–65; Bennett, *Narrative of the Great Revival in the Southern Armies*, pp. 401–27.

2. Dunaway, *Sermon*, pp. 3–19; Doggett, *The War and Its Close*, pp. 15–20; Wilmer, *Future Good*, pp. 15–20. For a perceptive discussion of slavery in this national soul-searching with a most useful analysis of the tension between conservatism and democracy in Confederate nationalism, see Faust, *Creation of Confederate Nationalism*, pp. 58–85.

3. Stephen Elliott, *Vain Is the Help of Man*, pp. 11–13.

4. Nelson, *Bullets, Ballots, and Rhetoric*; Max Williams and Hamilton, *Graham Papers*, 6:174–75.

5. Alexander H. Stephens to H. V. Hilliard, September 12, 1864, Stephens Papers, Emory; J. Henly Smith to Stephens, September 21, 1864, Stephens Papers, LC; John B. Jones, *Rebel War Clerk's Diary*, 2:283; *Annual Cyclopedia* (1864), pp. 199–200.

6. Candler, *Confederate Records of Georgia*, 2:735–52; J. William Harris, *Plain Folk and Gentry in a Slave Society*, pp. 181–82; Wiley, *Letters of Warren Akin*, pp. 70, 72; *Milledgeville Southern Recorder*, January 17, 1865; *Georgia Senate Journal* (1865), pp. 33–34.

7. *Raleigh Weekly Standard*, October 12, November 23, 1864; Max Williams and Hamilton, *Graham Papers*, 6:205–7; *Raleigh Daily Confederate*, December 5, 1864; John A. Gilmer to Zebulon Vance, November 23, December 6, 1864, Edward J. Hale to Vance, November 29, 1864, Vance Papers, NCDAH.

8. *Raleigh Daily Confederate*, December 15, 1864; Raper, *Holden*, p. 57; Max Williams and Hamilton, *Graham Papers*, 6:195–96; Vance to ?, January 2, 1865, Vance Papers, NCDAH; *OR*, ser. 1, vol. 46, pt. 2, pp. 1093–94.

9. Andrew G. Magrath to William H. Trescot, January 9, 1865, Magrath Papers, SCL; *OR*, ser. 1, vol. 53, pp. 395–96; *Florida Senate Journal* (1864), pp. 10–13; *Annual Message of Governor Henry Watkins Allen, January 1865*, pp. 18–19.

10. Virginia, *Documents* (1863–64), no. 15, p. 1; *Laws of Texas* (Second Extra Session 1864), pp. 20–22; Watts, *Governor's Message*, pp. 11–15. Brave words, however, could not stop peace meetings in north Alabama counties or prevent deserters from moving about the state with impunity. Support for the war had nearly evaporated in some areas. One editor claimed in the fall of 1864 that only Davis's visit to Montgomery had prevented the legislature from adopting peace resolutions (Martin, *Desertion of Alabama Troops*, pp. 112–20; McMillan, *Disintegration of a Confederate State*, p. 105).

11. See the careful analysis of voting behavior in Alexander and Beringer, *Anatomy of the Confederate Congress*, pp. 274–99.

12. Schott, *Stephens*, p. 433; *SHSP* 51 (1958): 311–12, 329–36.

13. *SHSP* 51 (1958): 353–54, 377–78; Josiah Turner to Sophia Turner, December n.d., 1864, Turner Papers, SHC. Even Henry Foote opposed separate state action. His resolutions calling for a convention of the states was tabled by a vote of sixty-three to thirteen (*SHSP* 51 [1958]: 409–10). In January 1865, Foote was arrested

near Fredericksburg, Virginia, supposedly trying to pass through the Federal lines on a private peace mission. An expulsion motion fell short of the required two-thirds majority, but the House censured him (John B. Jones, *Rebel War Clerk's Diary*, 2:385; *SHSP* 52 [1959]: 215–17).

14. *SHSP* 52 (1959): 12–14, 130–31; Speech of William E. Smith in Confederate Congress, n.d., 1865, Smith Papers, Duke.

15. *JCC*, 7:451–52; Schott, *Stephens*, p. 438.

16. De Jarnette, *Monroe Doctrine*, pp. 1–20.

17. Oldham, *Speech of W. S. Oldham of Texas Concerning Peace, Reconstruction, and Independence*, pp. 1–13; John A. Gilmer to Zebulon Vance, February 1, 1865, Vance Papers, NCDAH.

18. *Edgefield* (S.C.) *Advertiser*, November 23, 1864; Howell Cobb to Jefferson Davis, December 28, 1864, Davis Papers, Emory; *OR*, ser. 1, vol. 53, pp. 393–94; Stephenson, *Day of the Confederacy*, pp. 150–52; *Acts of Georgia* (1864–65), p. 84; Candler, *Confederate Records of Georgia*, 2:835–55.

19. Richardson, *Messages and Papers*, 1:491; Yearns, *Confederate Congress*, pp. 92–94; Candler, *Confederate Records of Georgia*, 2:792–98, 3:643–68; Scarborough, *Diary of Edmund Ruffin*, 3:686–87; *Richmond Daily Examiner*, December 16, 1864.

20. *JCC*, 7:329–50; Alexander H. Stephens to Linton Stephens, December 3, 24, 1864, quoted in Richard M. Johnston and Browne, *Stephens*, pp. 475–76; Echols, *Speech*, pp. 1–2; Gilmer, *Letter Addressed to Hon. W. C. Rives*, pp. 1–11. Several states tried to limit the power of Confederate officials to arrest private citizens by reaffirming the right of judges to issue writs of habeas corpus (*Laws of Florida* [1864], p. 28; *Louisiana Acts* [1865], p. 60; *Acts of Georgia* [1864–65], pp. 83–84).

21. Wesley, *Collapse of the Confederacy*, p. 90; Woodward, *Mary Chesnut's Civil War*, p. 694; Andrew G. Magrath to Joseph E. Brown, January 26, 1865, Magrath Papers, SCL; Magrath to Jefferson Davis, January 22, 1865, Davis Papers, Emory.

22. John B. Jones, *Rebel War Clerk's Diary*, 2:372; Younger, *Inside the Confederate Government*, pp. 186–87; Alexander T. B. Merritt to W. H. E. Merritt, January 17, 1865, Merritt Papers, Duke.

23. Richardson, *Messages and Papers*, 1:484–85; Wiley, *Letters of Warren Akin*, p. 75; Rowland, *Davis*, 6:418–21; William C. Davis, *Davis*, p. 582; Ramsdell, *Laws and Joint Resolutions of the Last Session of the Confederate Congress*, p. 28.

24. Schenck Books, December n.d., 1864, SHC; Stephenson, *Day of the Confederacy*, p. 185; Katharine M. Jones, *Ladies of Richmond*, pp. 267–68; Strode, *Davis: Private Letters*, p. 140.

25. Cleveland, *Stephens*, pp. 796–804; Phillips, *Correspondence of Toombs, Stephens, and Cobb*, pp. 661–62; *Richmond Sentinel*, January 7, 1865; Henry, *Speech*, pp. 1–13; *Richmond Daily Dispatch*, January 12, 1865; *Louisiana Acts* (1865), pp. 6–8.

26. Roman, *Beauregard*, 2:276–94; Max Williams and Hamilton, *Graham Papers*, 6:199–200; Woodworth, *Davis and His Generals*, pp. 290–331.

27. John B. Hood to Jefferson Davis, March 31, 1865, Davis Papers, Emory; Woodward and Muhlenfeld, *Private Mary Chesnut*, p. 222.

28. Andrew G. Magrath to Robert W. Barnwell, December 3, 1864, Barnwell to Magrath, January 9, 1865, William Porcher Miles to Magrath, January 15, 1865, Magrath to Zebulon Vance, January 11, 1865, Magrath Papers, SCL; McMillan, *Disintegration of a Confederate State*, pp. 114–15; Cauthen, *South Carolina Goes to War*, pp. 224–27.

29. Ballard, *Long Shadow*, pp. 13–17; Younger, *Inside the Confederate Government*, p. 190; William Nelson Pendleton to Jefferson Davis, December 26, 1864, Davis Papers, Emory; *JCC*, 4:453–58; Pollard, *Lost Cause*, p. 656.

30. Pollard, *Davis*, p. 384; Bleser, *Secret and Sacred*, pp. 298–99; Govan and Livingood, *Different Valor*, pp. 334–37; Woodward, *Mary Chesnut's Civil War*, pp. 698, 700–701; *Richmond Daily Whig*, January 9, 1865; *Richmond Daily Examiner*, December 21, 1864; Symonds, *Johnston*, p. 342.

31. Wade Hampton to Louis T. Wigfall, January 20, 1865, Joseph E. Johnston to Wigfall, February 12, 1865, Wigfall Papers, BTHC; Woodward and Muhlenfeld, *Private Mary Chesnut*, p. 225; *JCC*, 4:453–58, 7:463.

32. Petition of Confederate Senators to Robert E. Lee, February 4, 1865, Joseph E. Johnston to Louis T. Wigfall, March 14, 1865, Wigfall Papers, BTHC; Dowdey and Manarin, *Wartime Papers of Lee*, p. 894; Rowland, *Davis*, 6:491–503; Woodward, *Mary Chesnut's Civil War*, p. 725; Govan and Livingood, *Different Valor*, p. 346. For a fine account of the maneuvering for Johnston, see Connelly, *Autumn of Glory*, pp. 517–20.

33. Hay, "South and the Arming of the Slaves," pp. 36–39; *Shreveport Southwestern*, May 22, 1861.

34. Meade, *Benjamin*, pp. 289–91; Durden, *Gray and the Black*, pp. 30–34, 40–44.

35. Durden, *Gray and the Black*, pp. 54–67. Jefferson Davis ordered the Cleburne memorandum suppressed.

36. Durden, *Gray and the Black*, pp. 75–77, 79–80; *Richmond Daily Enquirer*, October 18, November 1, and passim, 1864.

37. Scarborough, *Diary of Edmund Ruffin*, 3:624; *Milledgeville Southern Recorder*, October 4, 1864; Durden, *Gray and the Black*, pp. 88–96.

38. Durden, *Gray and the Black*, pp. 99–100, 252–53; Watts, *Governor's Message*, p. 10.

39. Richardson, *Messages and Papers*, 1:493–96.

40. *Raleigh Weekly Standard*, November 9, 1864; Durden, *Gray and the Black*, pp. 106–12; *SHSP* 51 (1958): 275–76, 292–96; Thomas J. Chambers, *Policy of Employing Negro Troops*, pp. 1–7; Younger, *Inside the Confederate Government*, pp. 177–78.

41. Langdon, *Question of Employing the Negro as a Soldier*, pp. 9–11; *Mississippi Senate Journal* (1865), pp. 12–13; *Edgefield* (S.C.) *Advertiser*, November 23, 30, 1864, January 10, March 1, 1865; Durden, *Gray and the Black*, pp. 200–201; *SHSP* 52 (1959): 293–95.

42. John B. Jones, *Rebel War Clerk's Diary*, 2:353–54; Durden, *Gray and the Black*, pp. 143–47; Phillips, *Correspondence of Toombs, Stephens, and Cobb*, pp. 656–58; Wiley, *Letters of Warren Akin*, p. 94.

43. Wiley, *Letters of Warren Akin*, pp. 94, 116; Durden, *Gray and the Black*,

pp. 87–88, 206–9, 217, 235–36; Crabtree and Patton, *"Journal of a Secesh Lady,"* p. 651.

44. Durden, *Gray and the Black*, pp. 183–85; Gholson, *Speech*, pp. 3–20; Langdon, *Question of Employing the Negro as a Soldier*, pp. 11–13; J. Francis Maides to his mother, February 18, 1865, quoted in Bardolph, "Inconstant Rebels," p. 177.

45. *SHSP* 52 (1959): 289–93; Durden, *Gray and the Black*, pp. 156–58, 250–52; Edmund Rhett to William Porcher Miles, January 11, February 3, 1865, Miles Papers, SHC; Woodward, *Mary Chesnut's Civil War*, pp. 678–79; Josiah Turner, Jr., to Sophia Turner, February 11, 1865, Turner Papers, SHC.

46. Durden, *Gray and the Black*, pp. 97–99, 113–17; Langdon, *Question of Employing the Negro as a Soldier*, pp. 13–16; Gilmer, *Letter from John H. Gilmer to a Member of the Virginia Senate*, broadside, December 28, 1864.

47. Durden, *Gray and the Black*, pp. 117–19, 232–33; Scarborough, *Diary of Edmund Ruffin*, 3:692–93; Wesley, *Collapse of the Confederacy*, pp. 159–60; *Charleston Daily Courier*, January 24, 1865; Barney, *Flawed Victory*, p. 90; Collier, *Remarks on the Subject of Ownership of Slaves*, pp. 4–28. Although Zebulon Vance and others—including a fair number of clergy—argued that slavery needed reforming, the contention that Southerners could more easily give up on Confederate independence because of guilt about slavery is not persuasive (Zebulon Vance to Calvin H. Wiley, February 3, 1865, Wiley Papers, NCDAH; Beringer et al., *Why the South Lost*, pp. 357–67). For a balanced, first-rate analysis of slaveholders' guilt, see Foster, "Guilt over Slavery," pp. 665–94.

48. *Washington* (Ark.) *Telegraph*, January 18, 1865; Palmer, *Discourse before the General Assembly of South Carolina*, pp. 9–12; *Charleston Mercury*, January 26, 1865; Durden, *Gray and the Black*, pp. 180–81; William E. Smith, Speech in Congress on Arming Slaves, n.d., Smith Papers, Duke.

49. *Richmond Daily Dispatch*, January 30, 1865; Roark, *Masters without Slaves*, pp. 101–3; Shore, *Southern Capitalists*, pp. 92–95; Crabtree and Patton, *"Journal of a Secesh Lady,"* pp. 652–53; Durden, *Gray and the Black*, pp. 124–25, 174–76; Max Williams and Hamilton, *Graham Papers*, 6:190–91; Pollard, *Southern History of the War* [Last Year], 2:471–73; Wiley, *Letters of Warren Akin*, pp. 32–33.

50. See the detailed and perceptive analysis of the Hampton Roads conference in Schott, *Stephens*, pp. 440–48.

51. Shelby Foote, *Civil War*, 3:781–83; *Mississippi Senate Journal* (1865), pp. 13–14; Wiley, *Letters of Warren Akin*, p. 110; *Richmond Daily Dispatch*, February 10, 1865; Durden, *Gray and the Black*, pp. 187–88.

52. Pollard, *Davis*, pp. 470–72; John B. Jones, *Rebel War Clerk's Diary*, 2:411; Durden, *Gray and the Black*, pp. 188–90.

53. Durden, *Gray and the Black*, pp. 192–95; Evans, *Benjamin*, pp. 282–87. A few days later, the Senate deadlocked on a no-confidence resolution against Benjamin. The secretary of state drafted a letter of resignation, but Davis refused to accept it (Evans, *Benjamin*, pp. 289–91).

54. Durden, *Gray and the Black*, pp. 190–92; *Richmond Daily Dispatch*, February 10, 1865.

55. Josiah Turner, Jr., to Sophia Turner, February 19, 1865, Turner Papers, SHC;

Moore, "Rives Peace Resolution," pp. 155–60; Oldham, "Memoirs," pp. 302–5, BTHC; Ramsdell, *Laws and Joint Resolutions of the Last Session of the Confederate Congress*, pp. 134–35.

56. *SHSP* 52 (1959): 282–83, 322–24.

57. Max Williams and Hamilton, *Graham Papers*, 6:211, 228–31, 246, 252–54, 257.

58. Durden, *Gray and the Black*, pp. 210–11; *SHSP* 52 (1959): 329–31; *JCC*, 7:612–13.

59. *SHSP* 52 (1959): 300–306, 309–10, 325–26; *JCC*, 2:585.

60. *Richmond Daily Enquirer*, February 25, 1865; *Richmond Sentinel*, February 25, 1865; *Richmond Daily Whig*, February 20, March 3, 1865; *Richmond Daily Dispatch*, February 20, 1865; Preisser, "Virginia Decision to Use Negro Soldiers," pp. 105–13; Durden, *Gray and the Black*, pp. 210–11, 225–28, 236–39, 249–50.

61. *SHSP* 52 (1959): 453–56; *JCC*, 4:670–71; Durden, *Gray and the Black*, pp. 202–3; Escott, *After Secession*, p. 252. Davis later claimed that he had vigorously called for the passage of this bill, but he had certainly not done so publicly, and there is no contemporary evidence that he worked very hard to convince reluctant congressmen and senators (Jefferson Davis, *Rise and Fall of the Confederate Government*, 1:518–19). Throughout his superbly edited volume of documents, *The Gray and the Black*, Robert Durden stresses the centrality of emancipation and accuses historians of either misreading or ignoring Davis's role. Of course, Davis had hardly pursued a straightforward course, and Durden's subtitle, *The Confederate Debate on Emancipation*, is misleading. Confederates discussed emancipation, but even many who favored using black soldiers often avoided the question—the best evidence being the law passed by Congress. Paul Escott has rightly observed that even this late in the game, there was substantial resistance from politicians and slaveholders (*After Secession*, pp. 252–55).

62. Richardson, *Messages and Papers*, 1:544–51.

63. Durden, *Gray and the Black*, pp. 258–61; Younger, *Inside the Confederate Government*, pp. 258–61; Robert Toombs to General Gustavus W. Smith, March 25, 1865, Toombs Letter, UG; *Montgomery Daily Advertiser*, March 5, 1865; *Washington* (Ark.) *Daily Telegraph*, March 29, 1865.

64. Durden, *Gray and the Black*, pp. 181, 198–99; Max Williams and Hamilton, *Graham Papers*, 6:273–74; *Richmond Daily Enquirer*, March 13, 1865.

65. *Milledgeville Southern Recorder*, February 7, 1865; *Milledgeville Confederate Union*, February 28, 1865; *Richmond Sentinel*, March 1, 1865; Marszalek, *Diary of Emma Holmes*, p. 407; *Raleigh Daily Confederate*, April 1, 1865; Richardson, *Messages and Papers*, 1:568–70.

66. Woodward, *Mary Chesnut's Civil War*, p. 737; Hanna, *Flight into Oblivion*, p. 67; Hoge, *Appeal to the People of Virginia*, pp. 1–4; *Richmond Sentinel*, March 22, 1865.

Epilogue

1. For a representative postwar assessment of Davis, see Fenner, "Ninety-Third Anniversary of the Birth of Pres. Davis," pp. 21–23.

2. Jefferson Davis, *Rise and Fall of the Confederate Government*, 1:518–19; Hill, "Address," p. 500; Boom, "'We Sowed & We Have Reaped,'" p. 78; Vance, "Address," p. 517.

3. For a fine analysis of "contingency" in explaining Confederate defeat, see McPherson, *Battle Cry of Freedom*, pp. 857–59. For perceptive critiques of efforts to interpret Confederate defeat as "inevitable" while ignoring military events, see James M. McPherson, "American Victory, American Defeat," and Gary W. Gallagher, "'Upon Their Success Hang Momentous Interests': Generals," in Boritt, *Why the Confederacy Lost*, pp. 17–42, 81–108.

4. In the postwar South there remained a fundamental tension between official ideology and political practice. To stress the importance of unity and white liberty, for example, does not mean ignoring divisive influences in Southern society or the existence of articulate and sometimes powerful dissenting voices from groups ranging from Republicans, to various independent movements, to Populists.

Manuscripts

Alabama Department of Archives and History, Montgomery
    Thomas Jefferson Franklin Jackson Papers
    John Gill Shorter Letterbooks (Governors' Papers)
    William L. Yancey Papers
Barker Texas History Center, University of Texas, Austin
    Williamson S. Oldham, "Memoirs of Williamson S. Oldham"
    Louis T. Wigfall Papers (typescripts)
Duke University, William R. Perkins Library
    George William Bagby Papers
    Pierre Gustave Toutant Beauregard Papers
    Samuel Simpson Biddle Papers
    Alexander Robinson Boteler Papers
    Eliza Hall Gordon Boyles Papers
    Joseph E. Brown Papers
    Oze Reed Broyles Papers
    Henry Toole Clark Papers
    Clement Claiborne Clay Papers
    Absalom F. Dantzler Papers
    Jefferson Davis Papers
    William W. Holden Papers
    Frederick William Mackey Holliday Papers
    Herschel Vesparian Johnson Papers
    John McIver Papers
    Alexander B. Meek Papers
    William H. E. Merritt Papers
    Munford-Ellis Family Papers
    Richmond Mumford Pearson Papers
    Francis Wilkinson Pickens Papers
    Thomas Jenkins Semmes Papers
    William Ephriam Smith Papers
    William Nathan Harrell Smith Papers
    Thomas D. Snead Papers
    Alexander Hamilton Stephens Papers

Emory University, Robert W. Woodruff Library, Atlanta
  Jefferson Davis Papers
  James P. Hambleton Papers
  Alexander H. Stephens Papers
  Aaron Wilbur Papers
Georgia Department of Archives and History, Atlanta
  Governors' Correspondence (Joseph E. Brown)
University of Georgia Library, Special Collections, Athens
  Cobb-Erwin-Lamar Papers
  Howell Cobb Papers
  Howell Cobb Papers (E. Merton Coulter Collection)
  Robert Toombs Letter
  Robert Toombs Papers
Library of Congress
  J. L. M. Curry Papers
  James Henry Hammond Papers
  Alexander H. Stephens Papers
  Louis T. Wigfall Papers
Mississippi Department of Archives and History, Jackson
  Oscar J. E. Stuart Papers
Southern Historical Collection, University of North Carolina, Chapel Hill
  James Lusk Alcorn Papers
  Edward Porter Alexander Papers
  Archibald Hunter Arrington Papers
  Battle Family Papers
  Thomas Bragg Diary
  John W. Brown Diaries
  David Miller Carter Papers
  Elizabeth Collier Diary
  Edward Conigland Papers
  Susan Cornwall Book
  Gordon and Hackett Family Papers
  James Thomas Harrison Papers
  James Thomas Leach Papers
  Andrew Gordon Magrath Papers
  Peter Mallett Papers
  Thomas David Smith McDowell Papers
  Christopher Gustavus Memminger Papers
  William Porcher Miles Papers
  Moore and Gatling Papers
  Orr and Patterson Family Papers
  Richmond Mumford Pearson Papers
  John Perkins Papers
  Pettigrew Family Papers

James Graham Ramsay Papers
David Schenck Books
Thomas Settle Papers
Robert Hardy Smith Papers
Mary Stamps Papers
David L. Swain Papers
Josiah Turner, Jr., Papers
Sarah Wadley Diary
Jonathan Worth Papers
Nancy Young Collection
Howard Tilton Memorial Library, Tulane University, New Orleans
William Preston Johnston Papers
North Carolina Division of Archives and History, Raleigh
Joseph Cather Papers
Calvin J. Cowles Papers
Gash Family Papers
Governors' Papers and Letterbooks (Vance)
Edward J. Hale Papers
William Woods Holden Papers
Little-Mordecai Collection
Michaux-Randolph Papers
Henry Machen Patrick Papers
Patterson Papers
Shaffner Diary and Papers
Zebulon B. Vance Papers
Calvin H. Wiley Papers
Williams-Womble Papers
South Caroliniana Library, University of South Carolina, Columbia
Benjamin Franklin Arthur Papers
Louis Malone Ayer Papers
Milledge Luke Bonham Papers
Grace B. Elmore Diary, typescript
Andrew Gordon Magrath Papers
Robert Barnwell Rhett Papers
Alderman Library, University of Virginia, Charlottesville
Robert M. T. Hunter Papers

Confederate and State Documents

Confederate States of America

C.S.A. House. *Minority Report of the Committee on the Judiciary, on the Suspension of the Habeas Corpus*. Richmond: n.p., 1864.
——. *Report of the Committee on the Judiciary, Upon the Suspension of the Habeas Corpus*. Richmond: n.p., 1864.

Journal of the Congress of the Confederate States of America, 1861–1865. 7 vols. Washington, D.C.: Government Printing Office, 1904–5.

Matthews, James M., ed. *The Statutes at Large of the Confederate States of America.* Richmond: R. M. Smith, 1862–64.

Monroe, Thomas B. *Arkansas Contested Election. Johnson vs. Garland. Exposition and Argument by the Counsel of Mr. Johnson.* Richmond: n.p., 1862.

Proceedings of the Confederate Congress. *Southern Historical Society Papers,* vols. 44–52 (1923–59).

Ramsdell, Charles W., ed. *Laws and Joint Resolutions of the Last Session of the Confederate Congress. . . . Together with Secret Acts of Previous Congresses.* Durham, N.C.: Duke University Press, 1941.

Alabama

Alabama Acts, 1861–63.

Alabama Senate Journal, 1861–63.

Journal of the Convention of the People of the State of Alabama. Montgomery: Shorter and Reid, 1861.

Selected Cases . . . in the Supreme Court of Alabama, during the years 1861–'62–'63. Montgomery: Montgomery Advertiser and Book and Job Office, 1864.

Smith, William Russell. *The History and Debates of the Convention of the People of Alabama . . . January 7, 1861.* Montgomery: White, Pfister & Co., 1861.

Watts, Thomas H. *Governor's Message* [November 1864]. Montgomery: n.p., 1864.

Arkansas

Journal of Both Sessions of the Convention of the State of Arkansas. Little Rock: Johnson and Yerkes, 1861.

Rector, Henry M. *Message of Gov. Henry M. Rector to the General Assembly of Arkansas, . . . November 6, 1861.* Little Rock: Johnson and Yerkes, 1861.

——. *Message of Henry M. Rector to the General Assembly of . . . Arkansas . . . Nov'r 1862.* Little Rock: Johnson and Yerkes, 1862.

Florida

Florida Senate Journal, 1860–64.

Journal of the Proceedings of the Convention of the People of Florida . . . January 3, 1861. Tallahassee: Office of the Floridian and Journal, 1861.

Laws of Florida, 1863–64.

Proceedings of the Convention of the People of Florida . . . February 26, 1861. Tallahassee: n.p., 1861.

Georgia

Acts of Georgia, 1862–65.

Candler, Allen D., ed. *The Confederate Records of Georgia.* 5 vols. Atlanta: Charles P. Byrd, 1909–11.

Georgia House Journal, 1864–65.
Georgia Senate Journal, 1861–65.

Louisiana

Annual Message of Governor Henry Watkins Allen, to the Legislature of the State of Louisiana. Shreveport: Office of the Caddo Gazette, 1865.
Louisiana Acts, 1863, 1865.
Louisiana Senate Journal, 1861.
Official Journal of the Proceedings of the Convention of the State of Louisiana. New Orleans: J. O. Nixon, 1861.

Mississippi

Journal of the State Convention and Ordinances and Resolutions Adopted in January 1861. Jackson, Miss.: E. Barksdale, State Printer, 1861.
Journal of the State Convention, Ordinances and Resolutions Adopted in March 1861. Jackson, Miss.: E. Barksdale, State Printer, 1861.
Laws of Mississippi, 1863–65.
Mississippi House Journal, 1861–62.
Mississippi Senate Journal, 1861–65.
Proceedings of the Mississippi State Convention. Jackson, Miss.: Power & Cadwallader, 1861.

North Carolina

Cases at Law, Argued and Determined in the Supreme Court of North Carolina, at Raleigh, June Term, 1863. Raleigh: n.p., 1863.
Cases at Law, Decided at the Extra Term, Commencing on the 26th of October 1864, Extra Session—Fall Term, 1864. Raleigh: n.p., 1864.
Executive and Legislative Documents, 1861–65.
Journal of the Convention of the People of North Carolina. Raleigh: John W. Syme, 1862.
North Carolina Laws, 1861–64.
North Carolina Senate Journal, 1861–64.

South Carolina

Acts of South Carolina, 1862–63.
Convention Documents. Columbia: R. W. Gibbes, Printer, 1862.
Journal of the Convention of the People of South Carolina, Held in 1860, 1861, and 1862. Columbia: R. W. Gibbes, Printer, 1862.
South Carolina Senate Journal, 1861–63.

Texas

Inaugural Address of Gov. P. Murrah, Delivered November 5th, 1863. Austin: State Gazette Book and Job Office, 1863.

Laws of Texas, 1863–65.
The Supreme Court of Texas on the Constitutionality of the Conscript Laws.
  Houston: Telegraph Book and Job Establishment, 1863.
Winkler, Ernest William, ed. *Journal of the Secession Convention of Texas.*
  Austin: Austin Printing Company, 1912.

Virginia

Documents, 1861–65.
*Opinion of the Supreme Court of Appeals of Virginia in Regard to Liability to
  Military Service of the Principals of Substitutes.* Richmond: James E. Goode,
  1864.
Reese, George H., ed. *Proceedings of the Virginia State Convention of 1861.* 4
  vols. Richmond: Virginia State Library, 1965.
Virginia Senate Journal, 1861–65.

Newspapers and Periodicals

Atlanta Gate-City Guardian
Atlanta Southern Confederacy
Charleston Courier
Charleston Mercury
Chattanooga Daily Rebel
De Bow's Review
Des Arc (Ark.) *Weekly Citizen*
Edgefield (S.C.) *Advertiser*
Florence (Ala.) *Gazette*
Greensboro (Ala.) *Beacon*
Huntsville (Ala.) *Daily Confederate*
Huntsville (Ala.) *Gazette*
Huntsville (Ala.) *Independent*
Jackson (Miss.) *Daily Southern Crisis*
Jackson Mississippian
Memphis Daily Appeal
Milledgeville Confederate Union
Milledgeville Southern Federal Union
Milledgeville Southern Recorder
Mobile Weekly Advertiser and Register
Montgomery Daily Advertiser
Montgomery Daily Mail
Natchez Courier
New Orleans Daily Picayune
Paulding (Miss.) *Eastern Clarion*
Raleigh Daily Confederate
Raleigh Register

Raleigh Weekly Standard
Richmond Dispatch
Richmond Enquirer
Richmond Examiner
Richmond Sentinel
Richmond Whig
Rome (Ga.) *Weekly Courier*
Savannah (Ga.) *Republican*
Shreveport Southwestern
Southern Cultivator
Southern Literary Messenger
Troy (Ala.) *Southern Advertiser*
Tuskegee (Ala.) *South Western Baptist*
Washington (Ark.) *Telegraph*

Books, Pamphlets, and Broadsides

Abrams, A. *Davis and His Administration*. Atlanta: By the author, 1864.
Address of the Atlanta Register, to the People of the Confederate States. Atlanta:
    J. A. Sperry and Company, 1864.
Address to the People of North Carolina [signed by twelve North Carolina
    educators]. Raleigh?: n.p., 1861.
Address to the People of Texas. Austin: n.p., 1861.
Agulhon, Maurice. *Marianne into Battle: Republican Imagery and Symbolism in
    France, 1789–1880*. Cambridge: Cambridge University Press, 1979.
Alderman, Edwin A., and Armistead Churchill Gordon. *J. L. M. Curry: A
    Biography*. New York: Macmillan, 1911.
Alexander, Thomas B., and Richard E. Beringer. *The Anatomy of the Confederate
    Congress: A Study of the Influence of Member Characteristics on Legislative
    Voting Behavior, 1861–1865*. Nashville: Vanderbilt University Press, 1972.
Almond, Gabriel, and Verba, Sidney. *The Civic Culture: Political Attitudes and
    Democracy in Five Nations*. Princeton: Princeton University Press, 1963.
——, eds. *The Civic Culture Revisited*. Newbury Park, Calif.: Sage Publications,
    1989.
Amlund, Curtis Arthur. *Federalism in the Southern Confederacy*. Washington,
    D.C.: Public Affairs Press, 1966.
Analytica [pseud.]. *The Problem of Government in the Light of the Past, Present,
    and the Future*. Richmond: Published by the author, 1862.
Anderson, Benedict. *Imagined Communities: Reflections on the Origin and
    Spread of Nationalism*. London: Verso, 1983.
Andrews, J. Cutler. *The South Reports the Civil War*. Princeton: Princeton
    University Press, 1970.
Annual Cyclopedia and Register of Important Events, 1861–65. New York: D.
    Appleton, 1862–66.

Armistead, Robert H. *Soldiers of Our Army*. Richmond: Macfarlane and Fergusson, 1862.

Armstrong, George Dodd. *"The Good Hand of God Upon Us": A Thanksgiving Sermon Preached on Occasion of the Victory of Manassas, July 21st, 1861*. Norfolk, Va.: J. D. Ghiselin, Jr., 1861.

Ash, Stephen V. *Middle Tennessee Society Transformed, 1860–1870*. Baton Rouge: Louisiana State University Press, 1988.

Avery, Isaac W. *The History of the State of Georgia from 1850 to 1881*. New York: Brown and Derby, 1881.

Bailey, Fred Arthur. *Class and Tennessee's Confederate Generation*. Chapel Hill: University of North Carolina Press, 1987.

Baird, Washington. *The Confederate Spelling Book: Interspersed with Choice Reading Lessons in Poetry and Prose*. Macon, Ga.: Burke, Boykin, and Company, 1864.

Baker, Jean H. *Affairs of Party: The Political Culture of Northern Democrats in the Mid-Nineteenth Century*. Ithaca, N.Y.: Cornell University Press, 1983.

Ball, Douglas B. *Financial Failure and Confederate Defeat*. Urbana: University of Illinois Press, 1991.

Ballard, Michael B. *A Long Shadow: Jefferson Davis and the Final Days of the Confederacy*. Jackson: University Press of Mississippi, 1986.

Barney, William L. *Flawed Victory: A New Perspective on the Civil War*. New York: Praeger, 1975.

——. *The Road to Secession: A New Perspective on the Old South*. New York: Praeger, 1972.

——. *The Secessionist Impulse: Alabama and Mississippi in 1860*. Princeton: Princeton University Press, 1974.

Barnwell, John. *Love of Order: South Carolina's First Secession Crisis*. Chapel Hill: University of North Carolina Press, 1982.

Barrett, John G. *The Civil War in North Carolina*. Chapel Hill: University of North Carolina Press, 1963.

Barrow, Robert Ruffin. *Remarks on the Present War, by R. R. Barrow of Terrebone. The Objects of the Abolition Party*. New Orleans?: n.p., 1861.

[Barten, O. S.]. *A Sermon Preached in St. James' Church, Warrenton, Va., on the Fast-Day June 13, 1861*. Richmond: Enquirer Book and Job Press, 1861.

Bennett, William W. *A Narrative of the Great Revival Which Prevailed in the Southern Armies*. 1876. Reprint. Harrisonburg, Va.: Sprinkle Publications, 1989.

Bensel, Richard Franklin. *Yankee Leviathan: The Origins of Central State Authority in America, 1859–1877*. Cambridge: Cambridge University Press, 1990.

Bercovitch, Sacvan. *The American Jeremiad*. Madison: University of Wisconsin Press, 1978.

Beringer, Richard E., Herman Hattaway, Archer Jones, and William N. Still, Jr. *Why the South Lost the Civil War*. Athens: University of Georgia Press, 1986.

Bettersworth, John K. *Confederate Mississippi: The People and Policies of a Cotton State*. Baton Rouge: Louisiana State University Press, 1943.

Bettersworth, John K., and James W. Silver, eds. *Mississippi in the Confederacy.* 2 vols. Baton Rouge: Louisiana State University Press, 1961.

Bilbo, William N. *The Past, Present and Future of the Southern Confederacy: An Oration Delivered by Col. W. N. Bilbo in . . . Nashville, Oct. 12, 1861.* Nashville: J. D. W. Green, 1861.

Bingham, William. *A Grammar of the Latin Language for the Use of Schools with Exercises and Vocabularies.* Greensboro, N.C.: Sterling, Campbell, and Albright, 1863.

Blackford, Charles Minor, ed. *Letters from Lee's Army.* New York: Charles Scribner's Sons, 1947.

Blackford, L. Minor. *Mine Eyes Have Seen the Glory.* Cambridge, Mass.: Harvard University Press, 1954.

Bland [pseud.]. *A Southern Document. To the People of Virginia. The Great Issue! Our Relations to It.* Wytheville, Va.: D. A. St. Clair, 1861.

Bleser, Carol, ed. *The Hammonds of Redcliffe.* New York: Oxford University Press, 1981.

——. *Secret and Sacred: The Diaries of James Henry Hammond, a Southern Slaveholder.* New York: Oxford University Press, 1988.

Bluhm, Walter T. *Ideologies and Attitudes: Modern Political Culture.* Englewood Cliffs, N.J.: Prentice-Hall, 1974.

Bohannon, C. *Circular. Fellow-citizens and Soldiers of the 44th Senatorial District.* N.p.: n.p., 1864.

Boney, F. N. *John Letcher of Virginia: The Story of Virginia's Civil War Governor.* University, Ala.: University of Alabama Press, 1966.

Boritt, Gabor S., ed. *Why the Confederacy Lost.* New York: Oxford University Press, 1992.

Boyd, William K., ed. *Memoirs of W. W. Holden.* Durham, N.C.: Seeman Printery, 1911.

Bragg, Jefferson D. *Louisiana in the Confederacy.* Baton Rouge: Louisiana State University Press, 1941.

Breckinridge, Robert J. *To the Citizens and Soldiers of Kentucky.* Richmond: n.p., 1864.

Bridges, Hal. *Lee's Maverick General: Daniel Harvey Hill.* New York: McGraw-Hill, 1961.

Brown, Albert Gallatin. *State of the Country. Speech of Hon. A. G. Brown of Mississippi in the Confederate Senate, December 24, 1863.* Richmond?: n.p., 1863.

Brown, James R. *Debate on Endorsement. Speech of Hon. James R. Brown of the 39th Senatorial District. Delivered in the Senate, April 9, 1863.* Atlanta: Atlanta Intelligencer Steam Power Press, 1863.

——. *To the Voters of the 39th Senatorial District.* Canton, Ga.: n.p., 1862.

Bryan, T. Conn. *Confederate Georgia.* Athens: University of Georgia Press, 1953.

Buenger, Walter L. *Secession and the Union in Texas.* Austin: University of Texas Press, 1984.

Burr, Virginia Ingraham, ed. *The Secret Eye: The Journal of Ella Gertrude*

Clanton Thomas, 1848–1889. Chapel Hill: University of North Carolina Press, 1990.

Butler, Pierce. *Judah P. Benjamin*. Philadelphia: George W. Jacobs, 1906.

Campbell, William A. *To the People of Fannin*. Morganton, Va.?: n.p., 1862.

Capers, Henry D. *The Life and Times of C. G. Memminger*. Richmond: Everett Waddey Company, 1893.

Carpenter, Jesse T. *The South as a Conscious Minority, 1789–1861*. New York: New York University Press, 1930.

Carson, James Petigru. *Life, Letters and Speeches of James Louis Petigru, the Union Man of South Carolina*. Washington, D.C.: W. H. Lowdermilk, 1920.

Cassidy, Vincent H., and Amos E. Simpson. *Henry Watkins Allen of Louisiana*. Baton Rouge: Louisiana State University Press, 1964.

Castel, Albert. *General Sterling Price and the Civil War in the West*. Baton Rouge: Louisiana State University Press, 1968.

Cauthen, Charles Edward. *South Carolina Goes to War, 1860–1865*. Chapel Hill: University of North Carolina Press, 1950.

Chambers, H. C. *Policy of Employing Negro Troops. Speech of Hon. H. C. Chambers, of Mississippi*. Richmond?: n.p., 1864.

Chambers, Thomas Jefferson. *To the People of Texas* . . . [giving his platform]. Galveston: n.p., 1861.

———. *To the People of Texas* [announcing his candidacy for governor]. Austin?: n.p., 1863.

Chambers, William Nisbet, and Walter Dean Burnham, eds. *The American Party Systems: Stages of Political Development*. New York: Oxford University Press, 1967.

Channing, Steven A. *Crisis of Fear: Secession in South Carolina*. New York: Norton, 1970.

Cleveland, Henry. *Alexander H. Stephens, in Public and Private*. Philadelphia: National Publishing Company, 1866.

Cobb, Thomas Read Rootes. *Substance of an Address of T. R. R. Cobb, to His Constituents of Clark County, April 6, 1861*. N.p.: n.p., 1861.

Cole, B. L. *A Card* [in defense of Jabez Hunt, a candidate from Guilford County for a seat in the House of Commons of the legislature]. Greensboro, N.C.?: n.p., 1862.

Coleman, Kenneth. *Confederate Athens, 1861–1865*. Athens: University of Georgia Press, 1967.

Collier, Robert Ruffin. *Correspondence and Remarks on Two Occasions in the Senate of Virginia on the Subject of Martial Law*. Richmond: J. E. Goode, 1863.

———. *Remarks on the Subject of the Ownership of Slaves, Delivered by R. R. Collier of Petersburg, in the Senate of Virginia, October 12, 1863*. Richmond: James E. Goode, 1863.

The Confederate. By a South Carolinian. Mobile: S. H. Goetzel and Co., 1863.

Connelly, Thomas Lawrence. *Army of the Heartland: The Army of Tennessee, 1861–1862*. Baton Rouge: Louisiana State University Press, 1967.

———. *Autumn of Glory: The Army of Tennessee, 1862–1865*. Baton Rouge: Louisiana State University Press, 1971.

Connelly, Thomas Lawrence, and Archer Jones. *The Politics of Command: Factions and Ideas in Confederate Strategy.* Baton Rouge: Louisiana State University Press, 1973.

Cooper, William J., Jr. *Liberty and Slavery: Southern Politics to 1860.* New York: Knopf, 1983.

——. *The South and the Politics of Slavery, 1828–1856.* Baton Rouge: Louisiana State University Press, 1978.

Cooper, William J., Jr., et al. *A Master's Due: Essays in Honor of David Herbert Donald.* Baton Rouge: Louisiana State University Press, 1985.

Coulter, E. Merton. *The Confederate States of America, 1861–1865.* Baton Rouge: Louisiana State University Press, 1950.

——. *Travels in the Confederate States: A Bibliography.* Norman: University of Oklahoma Press, 1948.

——. *William G. Brownlow: Fighting Parson of the Southern Highlands.* Chapel Hill: University of North Carolina Press, 1937.

——. *William Montague Browne: Versatile Anglo-Irish American, 1833–1883.* Athens: University of Georgia Press, 1967.

Crabtree, Beth G., and James W. Patton, eds. *"Journal of a Secesh Lady": The Diary of Catherine Ann Devereux Edmondston, 1860–1866.* Raleigh: North Carolina Division of Archives and History, 1979.

Crandall, Marjorie L., ed. *Confederate Imprints: A Check List Based Principally on the Collections of the Boston Athenaeum.* 2 vols. Boston: Boston Athenaeum, 1955.

Crenshaw, Ollinger. *The Slave States in the Presidential Election of 1860.* Baltimore: Johns Hopkins University Press, 1945.

Crist, Lynda Lasswell, and Mary Seaton Dix, eds. *The Papers of Jefferson Davis.* 7 vols. to date. Baton Rouge: Louisiana State University Press, 1971–.

Crofts, Daniel W. *Reluctant Confederates: Upper South Unionists in the Secession Crisis.* Chapel Hill: University of North Carolina Press, 1989.

Culver, C. P. *A Scheme for the Relief of the Financial Embarrassments of the Confederate States.* Richmond: Geo. P. Evans and Co., 1863.

Current, Richard N. *Lincoln and the First Shot.* Philadelphia: J. B. Lippincott, 1963.

Curry, J. L. M. *Address of Congress to the People of the Confederate States.* Richmond: n.p., 1864.

——. *Civil History of the Government of the Confederate States, with Some Personal Reminiscences.* Richmond: B. F. Johnson, 1901.

Dalzell, W. T. D. *Thanksgiving to God. A Sermon Preached in St. Mark's Church, San Antonio, on Wednesday, 4th Feb., 1863.* San Antonio: Herald Book and Job Press, n.d.

Daniel, John M. *The Richmond Examiner during the War.* New York: Printed for the author, 1868.

Davis, Jefferson. *The Rise and Fall of the Confederate Government.* 2 vols. London: Longmans and Green, 1891.

Davis, Reuben. *Recollections of Mississippi and Mississippians.* Boston: Houghton Mifflin, 1889.

Davis, Varina Howell. *Jefferson Davis, Ex-President of the Confederate States of America: A Memoir by His Wife.* 2 vols. New York: Belford and Co., 1890.

Davis, William C. *Breckinridge: Statesman, Soldier, Symbol.* Baton Rouge: Louisiana State University Press, 1974.

——. *Jefferson Davis: The Man and His Hour.* New York: Harper Collins, 1991.

——. *Stand in the Day of Battle.* Garden City, N.Y.: Doubleday, 1983.

Dawson, Richard E., and Kenneth Prewitt. *Political Socialization.* Boston: Little, Brown, 1969.

Degler, Carl N. *Place Over Time: The Continuity of Southern Distinctiveness.* Baton Rouge: Louisiana State University Press, 1977.

DeJarnette, Daniel C. *The Monroe Doctrine. Speech of Hon. D. C. DeJarnette, of Virginia, in the Confederate House of Representatives, January 30th, 1865.* Richmond: n.p., 1865.

DeLeon, Thomas Cooper. *Belles, Beaux, and Brains of the 60's.* New York: G. W. Dillingham, 1909.

——. *Four Years in Rebel Capitals.* Mobile: Gossip Printing Company, 1890.

DeRosa, Marshall L. *The Confederate Constitution of 1861: An Inquiry into American Constitutionalism.* Columbia: University of Missouri Press, 1991.

De Veaux, T. L. *Fast-day Sermon, Preached in the Good Hope Church, Lowndes County, Alabama, Thursday, June 13th, 1861.* Wytheville, Va.: D. S. St. Clair, 1861.

Devine, Donald J. *The Political Culture of the United States: The Influence of Member Values on Regime Maintenance.* Boston: Little, Brown, 1972.

Devine, Thomas J. *Speeches Delivered on the 17th January 1862, in the Representative Hall, Austin Texas, by Thos. J. Devine and A. W. Terrell.* Austin: John Marshall and Co., 1862.

Dick, Robert P. *To the Freemen of the Sixth Congressional District . . . Speech of Robert P. Dick, of Guilford, in Convention, June 5th, 1861.* Greensboro, N.C.?: n.p., 1861.

Dodd, William E. *Jefferson Davis.* Philadelphia: George W. Jacobs and Company, 1907.

Doggett, David Seth. *The War and Its Close. A Discourse, Delivered in Centenary Church, Richmond, Va., Friday, April 8th, 1864.* Richmond: Macfarlane and Fergusson, 1864.

Donald, David, ed. *Why the North Won the Civil War.* Baton Rouge: Louisiana State University Press, 1960.

Dougan, Michael B. *Confederate Arkansas: The People and Policies of a Frontier State in Wartime.* University, Ala.: University of Alabama Press, 1976.

Dowd, Clement. *Life of Zebulon B. Vance.* Charlotte, N.C.: Observer Printing, 1897.

Dowdey, Clifford, and Louis H. Manarin, eds. *The Wartime Papers of R. E. Lee.* New York: Bramhall House, 1961.

Dubay, Robert W. *John Jones Pettus, Mississippi Fire-Eater: His Life and Times, 1813–1867.* Oxford: University Press of Mississippi, 1975.

DuBose, John W. *The Life and Times of William Lowndes Yancey.* 1892. Reprint. New York: Peter Smith, 1942.

Dumond, Dwight Lowell, ed. *Southern Editorials on Secession*. New York: Appleton-Century-Crofts, 1931.

Dunaway, Thomas Sanford. *A Sermon Delivered by Elder Thomas S. Dunaway of Lancaster County, Virginia, before Coan Baptist Church ... April 1864*. Richmond: Enquirer Book and Job Press, 1864.

Durden, Robert F. *The Gray and the Black: The Confederate Debate on Emancipation*. Baton Rouge: Louisiana State University Press, 1972.

Durrill, Wayne K. *War of Another Kind: A Southern Community in the Great Rebellion*. New York: Oxford University Press, 1990.

Easterby, J. H., ed. *The South Carolina Rice Plantation as Revealed in the Papers of Robert F. W. Allston*. Chicago: University of Chicago Press, 1945.

Easton, David, and Jack Dennis. *Children in the Political System: Origins of Political Legitimacy*. New York: McGraw-Hill, 1969.

Eaton, Clement. *A History of the Southern Confederacy*. New York: Macmillan, 1954.

———. *Jefferson Davis*. New York: Free Press, 1977.

Echols, Joseph H. *Speech of Hon. Joseph H. Echols*. Richmond: n.p., 1865.

Edelman, Murray. *Politics as Symbolic Action*. Chicago: Markham Publishing Company, 1971.

———. *The Symbolic Uses of Politics*. Urbana: University of Illinois Press, 1964.

Edmunds, John B., Jr. *Francis W. Pickens and the Politics of Destruction*. Chapel Hill: University of North Carolina Press, 1986.

Eggleston, George C. *A Rebel's Recollections*. Bloomington: Indiana University Press, 1959.

Elazar, Daniel J. *American Federalism: A View from the States*. 2d ed. New York: Harper & Row, 1972.

Elliott, E. N., ed. *Cotton Is King and Proslavery Arguments*. Augusta, Ga.: Pritchard, Abbott and Loomis, 1860.

Elliott, Stephen. *Ezra's Dilemma: A Sermon Preached in Christ Church, Savannah on Friday, August 21st, 1863*. Savannah, Ga.: Power Press of George N. Nichols, 1863.

———. *Gideon's Water-Lappers: A Sermon Preached in Christ Church, Savannah, on Friday, the 8th Day of April 1864*. Macon, Ga.: Burke, Boykin, and Company, 1864.

———. *God's Presence with the Confederate States: A Sermon Preached in Christ Church, Savannah, on Thursday, the 13th June*. Savannah, Ga.: W. Thorne Williams, 1861.

———. *"New Wine Not to Be Put into Old Bottles": A Sermon Preached in Christ Church, Savannah, on Friday, February 28th, 1862*. Savannah, Ga.: Steam Power Press of John M. Cooper and Company, 1862.

———. *"Vain Is the Help of Man": A Sermon Preached in Christ Church, Savannah, on Thursday, September 15, 1864*. Macon, Ga.: Burke, Boykin, and Company, 1864.

Eppes, Susan Bradford. *Through Some Eventful Years*. Gainesville: University of Florida Press, 1968.

Escott, Paul D. *After Secession: Jefferson Davis and the Failure of Confederate Nationalism*. Baton Rouge: Louisiana State University Press, 1978.

——. *Many Excellent People: Power and Privilege in North Carolina, 1850–1900*. Chapel Hill: University of North Carolina Press, 1985.

Evans, Eli N. *Judah P. Benjamin: The Jewish Confederate*. New York: Free Press, 1988.

Faust, Drew Gilpin. *The Creation of Confederate Nationalism: Ideology and Identity in the Civil War South*. Baton Rouge: Louisiana State University Press, 1988.

——. *James Henry Hammond and the Old South: A Design for Mastery*. Baton Rouge: Louisiana State University Press, 1982.

Fehrenbacher, Don E. *Constitutions and Constitutionalism in the Slaveholding South*. Athens: University of Georgia Press, 1989.

Fidler, William Perry. *Augusta Evans Wilson, 1835–1909*. University, Ala.: University of Alabama Press, 1951.

Fiedler, Herbert. *To the Voters of the Eighth Congressional District of Georgia, Cedar Town, Polk County, Ga. 1861*. N.p.: n.p., 1861.

Fleet, Betsy, and John D. P. Fuller, eds. *Green Mount: A Virginia Plantation Family during the Civil War*. Lexington: University of Kentucky Press, 1962.

Fleming, Robert. *The Elementary Spelling Book, Revised and Adapted to the Youth of the Southern Confederacy, Interspersed with Bible Readings on Domestic Slavery*. Atlanta: J. J. Toon and Co., Publishers, 1863.

Fleming, Walter L. *Civil War and Reconstruction in Alabama*. New York: Columbia University Press, 1905.

Flippin, Percy S. *Herschel V. Johnson of Georgia: State Rights Unionist*. Richmond: Dietz Printing Company, 1931.

Flournoy, H. W., ed. *Calendar of Virginia State Papers*. 11 vols. New York: Kraus Reprint, 1893.

Foote, Henry S. *War of the Rebellion or Scylla and Charybdis, Consisting of Observations upon the Causes, Course, and Consequences of the Late Civil War in the United States*. New York: Harper and Brothers, 1866.

Foote, Shelby. *The Civil War: A Narrative*. 3 vols. New York: Random House, 1958–74.

Ford, Lacy K., Jr. *Origins of Southern Radicalism: The South Carolina Upcountry, 1800–1860*. New York: Oxford University Press, 1988.

Forgie, George B. *Patricide in the House Divided: A Psychological Interpretation of Lincoln and His Age*. New York: Norton, 1979.

Formisano, Ronald P. *The Transformation of Political Culture: Massachusetts Parties, 1790s–1840s*. New York: Oxford University Press, 1983.

Fox-Genovese, Elizabeth, and Eugene D. Genovese. *Fruits of Merchant Capital: Slavery and Bourgeois Property in the Rise and Expansion of Capitalism*. New York: Oxford University Press, 1983.

Freehling, William W. *The Road to Disunion: Secessionists at Bay*. New York: Oxford University Press, 1990.

Freeman, Douglas Southall. *A Calendar of Confederate Papers*. Richmond: Confederate Museum, 1908.

——. *Lee's Lieutenants: A Study in Command*. 3 vols. New York: Charles Scribner's Sons, 1942–44.

——. *R. E. Lee: A Biography*. 4 vols. New York: Charles Scribner's Sons, 1934–36.

——, ed. *Lee's Dispatches: Unpublished Letters of General Robert E. Lee, C.S.A. to Jefferson Davis*. New York: G. P. Putnam's Sons, 1957.

Fremantle, Lieut. Col. *Three Months in the Southern States, April–June, 1863*. New York: John Bradburn, 1864.

Garland, Augustus Hill. *Contested Election from Arkansas between J. P. Johnson and A. H. Garland. Response by A. H. Garland to Petition of J. P. Johnson*. Richmond: Enquirer Book and Job Press, Tyler, Wise & Smith, 1862.

Garland, Augustus Hill. *Contested Election of Johnson vs. Garland. Speech of A. H. Garland before House of Representatives, April 4, 1862*. Richmond: n.p., 1862.

Geertz, Clifford. *The Interpretation of Cultures*. New York: Basic Books, 1973.

——. *Local Knowledge: Further Essays in Interpretative Anthropology*. New York: Basic Books, 1983.

Gholson, Thomas S. *Speech of Hon. Thos. S. Gholson, of Virginia, on the Policy of Employing Negro Troops, and the Duty of All Classes to Aid in the Prosecution of the War*. Richmond: George P. Evans and Co., Printers, 1865.

[Gibbes, Robert Wilson]. *Memorial. To the Honorable the Congress of the Confederate States of America*. N.p.: n.p., 1864?

Gilmer, John Harmer. *Letter Addressed to Hon. Wm. C. Rives, by John H. Gilmer, on the Existing Status of the Revolution*. Richmond?: n.p., 1864.

——. *Letter from John H. Gilmer to a Member of the Virginia Senate, on the Position and Duties of Virginia*. Richmond: n.p., 1864.

——. *Substance of the Argument Delivered by John H. Gilmer, before Judge J. B. Halyburton*. N.p.: n.p., 1864?

Goode, John. *Recollections of a Lifetime*. New York: Neale Publishing Company, 1906.

Gordon, George Anderson. *Speech of Hon. George A. Gordon, of Chatham, on the Constitutionality of the Conscription Laws ... December 9, 1862*. Atlanta: Printed at the Office of the Daily Intelligencer, 1862.

——. *"What Will He Do with It?" An Essay, Delivered in Masonic Hall, Savannah, on Thursday, October 27, 1863 ... for Wayside Home*. Savannah, Ga.: George N. Nichols, 1863.

Govan, Gilbert E., and James W. Livingood. *A Different Valor: The Story of Joseph E. Johnston, C.S.A.* Indianapolis: Bobbs-Merrill, 1956.

Graham, William Alexander. *Speech of Hon. William A. Graham, of Orange, in the Convention of North-Carolina, Dec. 7th, 1861, on ... Test Oaths and Sedition*. Raleigh: W. W. Holden, Printer, 1862.

Grayson, William J. *Witness to Sorrow: The Antebellum Autobiography of William J. Grayson*. Edited by Richard J. Calhoun. Columbia: University of South Carolina Press, 1990.

Green, Fletcher M. *Constitutional Development in the South Atlantic States, 1776–1860.* Chapel Hill: University of North Carolina Press, 1930.

——, ed. *Essays in Southern History Presented to James Gregoire de Roulhac Hamilton.* Chapel Hill: University of North Carolina Press, 1949.

Greenberg, Kenneth S. *Masters and Statesmen: The Political Culture of American Slavery.* Baltimore: Johns Hopkins University Press, 1985.

Hahn, Steven. *The Roots of Southern Populism: Yeoman Farmers and the Transformation of the Georgia Upcountry, 1850–1890.* New York: Oxford University Press, 1983.

Hall, Kermit L., and James W. Ely, Jr., eds. *An Uncertain Tradition: Constitutionalism and the History of the South.* Athens: University of Georgia Press, 1989.

Hamilton, James G. de Roulhac. *Reconstruction in North Carolina.* New York: Columbia University Press, 1914.

——, ed. *The Correspondence of Jonathan Worth.* 2 vols. Raleigh: State Department of Archives and History, 1909.

——. *The Papers of Thomas Ruffin.* 4 vols. Raleigh: Edwards and Broughton, 1918–20.

Hanna, A. J. *Flight into Oblivion.* Richmond: Johnson Publishing Company, 1938.

Harris, J. William. *Plain Folk and Gentry in a Slave Society: White Liberty and Black Slavery in Augusta's Hinterlands.* Middletown, Conn.: Wesleyan University Press, 1985.

Harris, William C. *Leroy Pope Walker: Confederate Secretary of War.* Tuscaloosa, Ala.: Confederate Publishing Company, 1962.

——. *William Woods Holden: Firebrand of North Carolina Politics.* Baton Rouge: Louisiana State University Press, 1987.

Harwell, Richard B., ed. *More Confederate Imprints.* 2 vols. Richmond: Virginia State Library, 1957.

Hayes, Carlton J. H. *The Historical Evolution of Modern Nationalism.* New York: Macmillan, 1931.

Hendrick, Burton J. *Statesmen of the Lost Cause: Jefferson Davis and His Cabinet.* New York: Literary Guild, 1939.

Henry, Gustavus Adolphus. *Speech of Hon. Gustavus A. Henry of Tennessee in the Senate of the Confederate States, November 29, 1864.* Richmond: n.p., 1864.

Heth, Henry. *The Memoirs of Henry Heth.* Edited by James L. Morrison. Westport, Conn.: Greenwood Press, 1974.

Hill, Benjamin H., Jr. *Senator Benjamin H. Hill of Georgia, His Life Speeches and Writings.* Atlanta: H. C. Hudgins, 1891.

Hill, Benjamin Harvey. *Speech of Hon. B. H. Hill, Delivered before the Georgia Legislature . . . on the Evening of 11th December, 1862, Milledgeville.* Milledgeville, Ga.: R. M. Orme and Son, Printers, 1863.

Hill, Louise Biles. *Joseph E. Brown and the Confederacy.* Chapel Hill: University of North Carolina Press, 1939.

Hoge, Moses D., et al. *Appeal to the People of Virginia, Richmond, February 22, 1865.* Richmond: n.p., 1865.

Hollins Institute. *The Education of Teachers in the South: Embracing a Letter from Prof. Edw'd Joynes to Joe P. Taloe*. Lynchburg: Virginian Power-Press Book and Job Office, 1864.

Holt, Michael F. *The Political Crisis of the 1850s*. New York: Wiley, 1978.

Hord, Edward R. *Dear Sir, June 6, 1861* [election circular]. Brownsville, Tex.?: n.p., 1861.

Howe, Daniel Walker. *The Political Culture of the American Whigs*. Chicago: University of Chicago Press, 1979.

Hunt, Lynn. *Politics, Culture, and Class in the French Revolution*. Berkeley: University of California Press, 1984.

Inscoe, John C. *Mountain Masters, Slavery, and the Sectional Crisis in Western North Carolina*. Knoxville: University of Tennessee Press, 1989.

Jacobs, Ferdinand. *A Sermon, for the Times: Preached in Farview Presbyterian Church, Perry County, Ala., . . . on Thursday, June 13, 1861*. Marion, Ala.: n.p., 1861.

Jennings, M. Kent, and Richard Niemi. *The Political Character of Adolescence: The Influence of Families and Schools*. Princeton: Princeton University Press, 1974.

Jimerson, Randall C. *The Private Civil War: Popular Thought during the Sectional Conflict*. Baton Rouge: Louisiana State University Press, 1988.

Johns, John E. *Florida during the Civil War*. Gainesville: University of Florida Press, 1963.

Johnson, Michael P. *Toward a Patriarchal Republic: The Secession of Georgia*. Baton Rouge: Louisiana State University Press, 1977.

Johnson, Robert Underwood, and Clarence Clough Buel, eds. *Battles and Leaders of the Civil War*. 4 vols. 1887–88. Reprint. New York: Castle Books, 1956.

Johnson, Robert Ward. *Speech of Mr. Johnson of Arkansas, in the C.S. Senate, February 9th, 1864, on Bill to Limit and Define the Terms of Office*. Richmond: James E. Goode, 1864.

Johnston, Frontis W., ed. *The Papers of Zebulon Baird Vance*. Raleigh: North Carolina Department of Archives and History, 1963.

Johnston, Joseph E. *Narrative of Military Operations during the Late War*. Bloomington: Indiana University Press, 1959.

Johnston, Richard M., and William H. Browne. *Life of Alexander H. Stephens*. Philadelphia: J. B. Lippincott, 1878.

Jones, Archer. *Confederate Strategy from Shiloh to Vicksburg*. Baton Rouge: Louisiana State University Press, 1961.

Jones, John Beauchamp. *A Rebel War Clerk's Diary at the Confederate States Capital*. 2 vols. Philadelphia: J. B. Lippincott, 1866.

Jones, Katharine M., ed. *Ladies of Richmond*. Indianapolis: Bobbs-Merrill, 1962.

Joynes, Edward Southey. *Education after the War. A Letter Addressed to a Member of the Southern Educational Convention, Columbia, S.C., 28th April, 1863*. Richmond: Macfarlane and Fergusson, 1863.

Junius [pseud.]. *Conscription of Teachers*. N.p.: n.p., n.d.

Kavanagh, Dennis. *Political Culture*. London: Macmillan, 1972.

Kenzer, Robert C. *Kinship and Neighborhood in a Southern Community: Orange County, North Carolina, 1849–1881*. Knoxville: University of Tennessee Press, 1987.

Kerby, Robert L. *Kirby Smith's Confederacy: The Trans-Mississippi South, 1863–1865*. New York: Columbia University Press, 1972.

Kibler, Lillian A. *Benjamin F. Perry, South Carolina Unionist*. Durham, N.C.: Duke University Press, 1946.

King, Alvy L. *Louis T. Wigfall, Southern Fire-eater*. Baton Rouge: Louisiana State University Press, 1970.

Knupfer, Peter B. *The Union as It Is: Constitutional Unionism and Sectional Compromise, 1787–1861*. Chapel Hill: University of North Carolina Press, 1991.

Kohn, Hans. *The Idea of Nationalism: A Study of Its Origins and Background*. New York: Macmillan, 1944.

Koon, Tracy H. *Believe, Obey, Fight: Political Socialization of Youth in Fascist Italy, 1922–1943*. Chapel Hill: University of North Carolina Press, 1985.

Kruman, Marc W. *Parties and Politics in North Carolina, 1836–1865*. Baton Rouge: Louisiana State University Press, 1983.

Lamar, J. S. *A Discourse Delivered in Christian Church on the Confederate Fast Day, Friday, Nov. 15th, 1861*. Augusta, Ga.: Printed at the Office of the Constitutionalist, 1861.

Lamar, Lucius Quintus Cincinnatus. *Speech of Hon. L. Q. C. Lamar, of Miss., on the State of the Country*. Atlanta: J. J. Toon and Co., Publishers, 1864.

Lander, Rev. S., A.M. *The Verbal Primer*. Greensboro, N.C.: Sterling, Campbell, and Albright, 1865.

Langdon, Charles C. *The Question of Employing the Negro as a Soldier. The Impolicy and Impracticality of the Proposed Measure Discussed*. Mobile: Advertiser and Register Steam Job Press, 1864.

Langton, Kenneth. *Political Socialization*. New York: Oxford University Press, 1969.

Lee, Charles R., Jr. *The Confederate Constitutions*. Chapel Hill: University of North Carolina Press, 1963.

Lee, Leroy Madison. *Our Country—Our Dangers—Our Duty. A Discourse Preached in Centenary Church, Lynchburg, Va., on the National Fast Day, August 21, 1863*. Richmond: Soldiers' Tract Associations, M.E. Church, South, 1863.

Lipset, Seymour Martin. *The First New Nation: The United States in Historical and Comparative Perspective*. New York: Basic Books, 1973.

Litt, Edgar. *The Political Culture of Massachusetts*. Cambridge, Mass.: MIT Press, 1965.

Longstreet, Augustus Baldwin. *Fast-day Sermon Delivered in the Washington Street Methodist Episcopal Church, Columbia, S.C., June 13, 1861*. Columbia: Townsend and North, 1861.

Longstreet, James. *From Manassas to Appomattox: Memoirs of the Civil War in America*. 1896. Reprint. Edited by James I. Robertson, Jr. Bloomington: Indiana University Press, 1960.

Lonn, Ella. *Desertion during the Civil War*. New York: Century Company, 1928.
——. *Foreigners in the Confederacy*. Chapel Hill: University of North Carolina Press, 1940.
Lubbock, Francis Richard. *To the Voters of Texas*. Houston?: n.p., 1861.
Luraghi, Raimondo. *The Rise and Fall of the Plantation South*. New York: Franklin Watts, 1978.
Maizlich, Stephen E., and Kushma, John J., eds. *Essays on American Antebellum Politics, 1840–1860*. College Station: Texas A&M University Press, 1982.
Marszalek, John F., ed. *The Diary of Miss Emma Holmes, 1861–66*. Baton Rouge: Louisiana State University Press, 1979.
Marten, James. *Texas Divided: Loyalty and Dissent in the Lone Star State*. Lexington: University Press of Kentucky, 1990.
Martin, Bessie. *Desertion of Alabama Troops during the Civil War*. New York: Columbia University Press, 1932.
Mayes, Edward. *Lucius Q. C. Lamar: His Life, Times and Speeches, 1825–1893*. Nashville: Publishing House of the Methodist Episcopal Church, South, 1896.
McCardell, John. *The Idea of a Southern Nation: Southern Nationalists and Southern Nationalism, 1830–1860*. New York: Norton, 1979.
McCash, William B. *Thomas R. R. Cobb, 1823–1862: The Making of a Southern Nationalist*. Macon, Ga.: Mercer University Press, 1983.
McCormick, Richard L. *The Party Period and Public Policy: American Politics from the Age of Jackson to the Progressive Era*. New York: Oxford University Press, 1986.
——. *The Presidential Game: The Origins of Presidential Politics*. New York: Oxford University Press, 1982.
McGuire, Judith White Borockenbrough. *Diary of a Southern Refugee*. 2d ed. New York: E. J. Hale and Son, 1867.
McMillan, Malcolm C. *The Disintegration of a Confederate State: Three Governors and Alabama's Wartime Home Front, 1861–1865*. Macon, Ga.: Mercer University Press, 1986.
——, ed. *The Alabama Confederate Reader*. University, Ala.: University of Alabama Press, 1963.
McPherson, James M. *Battle Cry of Freedom: The Civil War Era*. New York: Oxford University Press, 1988.
McWhiney, Grady. *Braxton Bragg and Confederate Defeat*. New York: Columbia University Press, 1969.
——. *Southerners and Other Americans*. New York: Basic Books, 1973.
Meade, Robert D. *Judah P. Benjamin: Confederate Statesman*. New York: Oxford University Press, 1943.
Michelbacher, Maxmillian J. *A Sermon Delivered on the Day of Prayer, Recommended by the President of the CSA, on the 27th of March, 1863*. Richmond: Macfarlane and Fergusson, 1863.
Miles, James Warley. *God in History. A Discourse Delivered before the Graduating Class of the College of Charleston, on Sunday Evening, March 29, 1863*. Charleston: Evans and Cogswell, 1863.

[——]. *The Relation between the Races at the South.* Charleston: Evans and Cogswell, 1861.

Mitchell, Memory F. *Legal Aspects of Conscription and Exemption in North Carolina, 1861–1865.* Chapel Hill: University of North Carolina Press, 1965.

Monroe, Thomas B. *Arkansas Contested Election. Johnson vs. Garland. Exposition and Argument by the Counsel of Mr. Johnson.* Richmond: n.p., 1862.

Moore, Albert Burton. *Conscription and Conflict in the Confederacy.* New York: Macmillan, 1924.

Moore, Frank, ed. *The Rebellion Record: A Diary of American Events.* 11 vols. New York: Putnam and Van Nostrand, 1861–68.

Moore, Marinda. *The Dixie Speller. To Follow the First Dixie Reader.* Raleigh: Branson and Farrar, 1864.

——. *The Geographical Reader, for the Dixie Children.* Raleigh: Branson, Farrar, and Co., 1863.

Moore, Thomas Verner. *God Our Refuge and Strength in This War. A Discourse before the Congregations of the First and Second Presbyterian Churches, on . . . Nov. 15, 1861.* Richmond: W. Hargrave White, 1861.

Murrah, Pendelton. *Inaugural Address of Gov. P. Murrah, Delivered November 5th, 1863.* Austin: State Gazette Book and Job Office, 1863.

Murray, John P. *Speech of Hon. John P. Murray, of Tennessee, in Favor of Repealing the Act Suspending the Privilege of the Writ of Habeas Corpus.* Richmond?: n.p., 1864?

Myers, Robert Manson, ed. *The Children of Pride.* New Haven: Yale University Press, 1972.

Nagel, Paul C. *One Nation Indivisible: The Union in American Thought, 1776–1861.* New York: Oxford University Press, 1964.

Neely, Mark E., Jr., Harold Holzer, and Gabor S. Boritt. *The Confederate Image: Prints of the Lost Cause.* Chapel Hill: University of North Carolina Press, 1987.

Nelson, Larry E. *Bullets, Ballots, and Rhetoric: Confederate Policy for the United States Presidential Contest of 1864.* University, Ala.: University of Alabama Press, 1980.

Nevins, Allan. *The Statesmanship of the Civil War.* New York: Macmillan, 1962.

The New Texas Primary Reader for the Use of Primary Schools. Houston: E. H. Cushing, Telegraph and Job Printing, 1863.

The New Texas Reader. Designed for the Use of Schools in Texas. Houston: E. H. Cushing, 1864.

Nichols, Roy F. *Blueprints for Leviathan: American Style.* New York: Atheneum, 1963.

Nolan, Alan T. *Lee Considered: General Robert E. Lee and Civil War History.* Chapel Hill: University of North Carolina Press, 1991.

Norton, Anne. *Alternative Americas: A Reading of Antebellum Political Culture.* Chicago: University of Chicago Press, 1986.

Norton, Clarence Clifford. *The Democratic Party in Ante-Bellum North Carolina, 1835–1861.* Chapel Hill: University of North Carolina Press, 1930.

Nuermberger, Ruth Ketring. *The Clays of Alabama: A Planter-Lawyer-Politician Family*. Lexington: University of Kentucky Press, 1958.

Oakes, James. *The Ruling Race: A History of American Slaveholders*. New York: Knopf, 1982.

O'Brien, Gail Williams. *The Legal Fraternity and the Making of a New South Community*. Athens: University of Georgia Press, 1986.

Oldham, Williamson Simpson. *Speech of Hon. W. S. Oldham, of Texas, on the Resolutions of the State of Texas, Concerning Peace, Reconstruction, and Independence*. Richmond: n.p., 1865.

——. *Speech of W. S. Oldham, of Texas, upon the Bill to Amend the Conscript Law, Made in the Senate, September 4, 1862*. Richmond: n.p., 1862.

Oliphant, Mary C. Simms, Alfred Taylor Odell, and T. C. Duncan Eaves, eds. *The Letters of William Gilmore Simms*. 5 vols. Columbia: University of South Carolina Press, 1952–56.

One of the People [pseud.]. *To the Honorable the Chief Justice and Judges of the State*. N.p.: n.p., 1861.

Owsley, Frank Lawrence. *State Rights in the Confederacy*. Chicago: University of Chicago Press, 1925.

Palmer, Benjamin Morgan. *A Discourse before the General Assembly of South Carolina, on December 10, 1863*. Columbia: Charles P. Pelham, State Printer, 1864.

——. *National Responsibility before God. A Discourse, Delivered on the Day of Fasting, Humiliation and Prayer . . . June 13, 1861*. New Orleans: Price-Current Steam Book and Job Printing Office, 1861.

Paris, John. *A Sermon: Preached before Brig. Gen Hoke's Brigade, at Kinston, N.C. on the 28th of February 1864*. Greensboro, N.C.: A. W. Ingold and Co., 1864.

Parish, Peter. *The American Civil War*. New York: Holmes and Meier, 1975.

Parks, Joseph H. *Joseph E. Brown of Georgia*. Baton Rouge: Louisiana State University Press, 1977.

Parrish, T. Michael, and Robert M. Willingham, Jr. *Confederate Imprints: A Bibliography of Southern Publications from Secession to Surrender*. Austin, Tex.: Jenkins and Foster, 1987.

Patrick, Rembert W. *Jefferson Davis and His Cabinet*. Baton Rouge: Louisiana State University Press, 1944.

——, ed. *The Opinions of the Confederate Attorneys General, 1861–1865*. Buffalo: Dennis and Co., 1950.

Pearce, Haywood J., Jr. *Benjamin H. Hill: Secession and Reconstruction*. Chicago: University of Chicago Press, 1928.

Pereyra, Lillian A. *James Lusk Alcorn: Persistent Whig*. Baton Rouge: Louisiana State University Press, 1966.

Phelan, James. *Speech of Hon. James Phelan, of Mississippi, on the Judiciary Bill*. Richmond: n.p., 186-.

——. *Speech of Hon. James Phelan, of Mississippi, on the Motion to Conscript "Justices of the Peace."* Richmond: Enquirer Book and Job Press, 1862.

Phillips, Ulrich B. *The Course of the South to Secession: An Interpretation.* 1939. Reprint. New York: Hill and Wang, 1964.

——. *The Life of Robert Toombs.* New York: Macmillan, 1913.

——, ed. *The Correspondence of Robert Toombs, Alexander H. Stephens, and Howell Cobb.* Washington, D.C.: American Historical Association, 1913.

The Pictorial Primer: Designed for the Use of Schools and Families. Richmond: West and Johnson, 1865.

Pierce, George Foster. *Sermons of Bishop Pierce and Rev. B. M. Palmer, Delivered before the General Assembly at Milledgeville, Ga., on Fast Day, March 27, 1863.* Milledgeville, Ga.: Boughton, Nisebey and Barnes State Printers, 1863.

——. *The Word of God a Nation's Life. A Sermon Preached before the Bible Convention of the Confederate States, Augusta, Ga., March 19, 1862.* Augusta, Ga.: Printed at the Office of the Constitutionalist, 1862.

Piston, William Garrett. *Lee's Tarnished Lieutenant: James Longstreet and His Place in Southern History.* Athens: University of Georgia Press, 1987.

Plan of a Provisional Government for the Southern Confederacy. Charleston: Steam-Power Presses of Evans and Cogswell, 1861.

Planters' Convention, Memphis. *Report of Select Committee Appointed by the Planters' Convention.* Memphis: n.p., 1862.

Plato. *The Republic of Plato.* Translated and edited by Francis MacDonald Cornford. New York: Oxford University Press, 1967.

Pollard, Edward A. *Echoes from the South.* New York: E. B. Treat, 1886.

——. *A Letter on the State of the War. By One Recently from the Enemy's Country.* Richmond: n.p., 1865.

——. *Life of Jefferson Davis with a Secret History of the Southern Confederacy, Gathered "Behind the Scenes in Richmond."* Philadelphia: Books for Libraries Press, 1869.

——. *The Lost Cause: A New Southern History of the War of the Confederates.* New York: E. B. Treat, 1867.

——. *Southern History of the War* [First, Second, Third, and Last Years]. 2 vols. New York: Fairfax Press, 1866.

Potter, David M. *The Impending Crisis, 1848–1861.* Completed and edited by Don E. Fehrenbacher. New York: Harper & Row, 1976.

——. *The South and the Sectional Conflict.* Baton Rouge: Louisiana State University Press, 1968.

Proceedings of the Convention of Teachers of the Confederate States Assembled at Columbia, South Carolina, April 28, 1863. Macon, Ga.: Burke, Boykin, and Co., 1863.

Proctor, Ben H. *Not without Honor: The Life of John H. Reagan.* Austin: University of Texas Press, 1962.

Pryor, Mrs. Roger A. *Reminiscences of Peace and War.* New York: Macmillan, 1904.

Putnam, Sallie. *Richmond during the War: Four Years of Personal Observation.* New York: G. W. Carleton, 1867.

Pye, Lucien, and Sidney Verba. *Political Culture and Political Development.* Princeton: Princeton University Press, 1965.

Rable, George C. *Civil Wars: Women and the Crisis of Southern Nationalism.* Urbana: University of Illinois Press, 1989.

Raines, C. S., ed. *Six Decades in Texas: Memoirs of Francis Richard Lubbock.* Austin: Ben C. Jones, 1900.

Rainwater, Percy Lee. *Mississippi: Storm Center of Secession, 1856–1861.* Baton Rouge: Otto Claitor, 1938.

Ramsdell, Charles W. *Behind the Lines in the Southern Confederacy.* Baton Rouge: Louisiana State University Press, 1944.

Ranck, James B. *Albert Gallatin Brown, Radical Southern Nationalist.* New York: D. Appleton-Century Co., 1937.

Raper, Horace W. *William W. Holden: North Carolina's Political Enigma.* Chapel Hill: University of North Carolina Press, 1985.

Reagan, John H. *Memoirs, with Special Reference to Secession and the Civil War.* Edited by Walter F. McCaleb. New York: Neale Publishing Company, 1906.

Remarks on the Policy of Prohibiting the Exportation of Cotton. By One of the People. Charleston: Steam-Power Press of Evans and Cogswell, 1861.

Renfroe, John J. D. *"The Battle Is God's." A Sermon Preached before Wilcox's Brigade, on Fast Day, the 21st of August, 1863, Near Orange Courthouse, Va.* Richmond: Macfarlane and Fergusson, 1863.

Renshon, Sidney. *Handbook of Political Socialization: Theory and Research.* New York: Free Press, 1977.

Reynolds, Donald E. *Editors Make War: Southern Newspapers in the Secession Crisis.* Nashville: Vanderbilt University Press, 1970.

Rice, Jesse Pearl. *J. L. M. Curry: Southerner, Statesman, and Educator.* New York: King's Crown Press, Columbia University, 1949.

Rice, John H. *A System of Modern Geography . . . Expressly for the Use of Schools and Academies in the Confederate States of America.* Atlanta: Franklin Printing House, Wood, Hanletter, Rice Co., 1862.

Richardson, James D., ed. *A Compilation of the Messages and Papers of Jefferson Davis and the Confederacy, Including Diplomatic Correspondence, 1861–1865.* 2 vols. Nashville: United States Publishing Company, 1905.

Ringold, May Spencer. *The Role of the State Legislatures in the Confederacy.* Athens: University of Georgia Press, 1966.

Roark, James L. *Masters without Slaves: Southern Planters in the Civil War and Reconstruction.* New York: Norton, 1977.

Robbins, John Brawner. "Confederate Nationalism: Politics and Government in the Confederate South, 1861–1865." Ph.D. dissertation, Rice University, 1964.

Robinson, William M., Jr. *Justice in Gray: A History of the Judicial System of the Confederate States of America.* Cambridge, Mass.: Harvard University Press, 1941.

Rodgers, Daniel T. *Contested Truths: Key Words in American Politics since Independence.* New York: Basic Books, 1987.

Roland, Charles. *The Confederacy.* Chicago: University of Chicago Press, 1960.

Roman, Alfred. *Military Operations of General Beauregard.* 2 vols. New York: Harper and Brothers, 1884.

Rowland, Dunbar, ed. *Jefferson Davis, Constitutionalist: His Letters, Papers and Speeches.* 10 vols. Jackson, Miss.: Mississippi Department of Archives and History, 1923.

Royster, Charles. *The Destructive War: William Tecumseh Sherman, Stonewall Jackson, and the Americans.* New York: Knopf, 1991.

Russell, William Howard. *My Diary North and South.* Edited by Eugene H. Berwanger. New York: Knopf, 1988.

Samuels, Richard J., ed. *Political Generations and Political Development.* Lexington, Mass.: Lexington Books, 1977.

Scarborough, William Kauffman, ed. *The Diary of Edmund Ruffin.* 3 vols. Baton Rouge: Louisiana State University Press, 1972–89.

Schott, Thomas E. *Alexander H. Stephens of Georgia: A Biography.* Baton Rouge: Louisiana State University Press, 1988.

Schwab, John C. *The Confederate States of America, 1861–1865: A Financial and Industrial History of the South during the Civil War.* New Haven: Yale University Press, 1901.

Scott, Allen M. *A New Southern Grammar of the English Language. Designed for the Use of Schools and Private Learners.* Memphis: Hutton and Frelign, Southern Publishing House, 1861.

Scott, John. *Letters to an Officer in the Army; Proposing Constitutional Reform in the Confederate Government after the Close of the Present War.* Richmond: A. Morris, 1864.

Secession: Considered as a Right in the States Composing the Late American Union of States. Jackson, Miss.: South-Western Confederate Printing House, 1863.

Shackelford, George C. *George Wythe Randolph and the Confederate Elite.* Athens: University of Georgia Press, 1988.

Shalhope, Robert E. *Sterling Price: Portrait of a Southerner.* Columbia: University of Missouri Press, 1971.

Shanks, Henry T. *The Secession Movement in Virginia, 1847–1861.* Richmond: Garrett and Massie, 1934.

Shore, Laurence. *Southern Capitalists: The Ideological Leadership of an Elite, 1832–1885.* Chapel Hill: University of North Carolina Press, 1986.

Shoup, F. A. *Policy of Employing Negro Troops.* Richmond: n.p., 1865.

Shugg, Roger W. *Origins of the Class Struggle in Louisiana: A Social History of White Farmers and Laborers during Slavery and After, 1840–1875.* Baton Rouge: Louisiana State University Press, 1939.

Silbey, Joel H. *The Partisan Imperative: The Dynamics of American Politics before the Civil War.* New York: Oxford University Press, 1985.

Silver, James W. *Confederate Morale and Church Propaganda.* Tuscaloosa, Ala.: Confederate Publishing Company, 1957.

Simpson, Craig A. *A Good Southerner: The Life of Henry A. Wise of Virginia.* Chapel Hill: University of North Carolina Press, 1985.

Sitterson, Joseph Carlyle. *The Secession Movement in North Carolina*. Chapel Hill: University of North Carolina Press, 1939.

Smith, Daniel E. H., et al. *Mason Smith Family Letters, 1860–1868*. Columbia: University of South Carolina Press, 1950.

Smith, Gustavus W. *Confederate War Papers*. New York: Atlantic Publishing, 1884.

Smith, J. Henry. *A Sermon Delivered at Greensboro, N.C. . . . on the 5th December 1861*. Greensboro: J. W. Albright, 1862.

[Smith, Richard McAllister]. *The Confederate Spelling Book*. 4th ed. Richmond: George L. Bidgood, 1865.

Smith, Robert Hardy. *Address to the Citizens of Alabama on the Constitution and Laws of the Confederate States of America*. Mobile: Mobile Daily Register Print, 1861.

Smith, Roswell Chamberlain. *Smith's English Grammar . . . Adapted to the Use of Schools in the Confederate States*. Richmond: George L. Bidgood, 1863.

Smythe, Charles W. *Our Own Primary Grammar for the Use of Beginners*. Greensboro, N.C.: Sterling and Campbell, 1861.

Sorrel, G. Moxley. *Recollections of a Confederate Staff Officer*. Jackson, Tenn.: McCowat-Mercer Press, 1958.

The Southern Pictorial Primer: Combining Instruction with Amusement and Designed for Use in Schools and Families. Richmond: West and Johnston, 1864.

Spain, August O. *The Political Theory of John C. Calhoun*. New York: Bookman Associates, 1951.

Spencer, Cornelia Phillips. *The Last Ninety Days of the War in North Carolina*. New York: Watchman Publishing Company, 1866.

Spratt, L. W. *The Philosophy of Secession; A Southern View, Presented in a Letter Addressed to the Hon. Mr. Perkins of Louisiana*. Charleston: n.p., 1861.

St. Paul, Henry. *Our Home and Foreign Policy*. Mobile: Office of the Daily Register and Advertiser, 1862.

Stampp, Kenneth M. *The Imperiled Union: Essays on the Background of the Civil War*. New York: Oxford University Press, 1980.

Stephens, Alexander H. *A Constitutional View of the War between the States*. 2 vols. Philadelphia: National Publishing Company, 1868–70.

——. *Recollections of Alexander H. Stephens*. 1910. Reprint. New York: Da Capo, 1971.

[Stephens, Linton]. *Resolutions on the Subject of Independence and Peace*. Macon, Ga.: n.p., 1865.

Stephenson, Wendell Holmes. *The Day of the Confederacy*. New Haven: Yale University Press, 1919.

Sterling, Ada, ed. *A Belle of the Fifties: Memoirs of Mrs. Clay of Alabama, Covering Social and Political Life in Washington and the South, 1853–66*. New York: Doubleday, Page, 1904.

Sterling, Richard. *Our Own Third Reader: For the Use of Schools and Families*. Greensboro, N.C.: Sterling, Campbell, and Albright, 1863.

Stewart, Kensey Johns. *A Geography for Beginners*. Richmond: J. W. Randolph, 1864.

Stiles, Joseph Clay. *National Rectitude the Only True Basis of National Prosperity: An Appeal to the Confederate States*. Petersburg, Va.: Evangelical Tract Society, 1863.

Strode, Hudson. *Jefferson Davis*. 3 vols. New York: Harcourt, Brace, and Company, 1955–64.

———, ed. *Jefferson Davis: Private Letters, 1823–1889*. New York: Harcourt, Brace and World, 1966.

Studies in Southern History and Politics Inscribed to William Archibald Dunning. New York: Columbia University Press, 1914.

Sullivan, C. J. *To the Voters of the 6th Judicial District*. N.p.: n.p., 1862.

Summers, Mark W. *The Plundering Generation: Corruption and the Crisis of the Union, 1849–1861*. New York: Oxford University Press, 1987.

Sydnor, Charles S. *The Development of Southern Sectionalism, 1819–1848*. Baton Rouge: Louisiana State University Press, 1948.

Symonds, Craig L. *Joseph E. Johnston: A Civil War Biography*. New York: Norton, 1992.

Takaki, Ronald T. *A Pro-Slavery Crusade: The Agitation to Reopen the African Slave Trade*. New York: Free Press, 1971.

Tatum, Georgia L. *Disloyalty in the Confederacy*. Chapel Hill: University of North Carolina Press, 1934.

Taylor, Richard. *Destruction and Reconstruction*. Edited by Richard Harwell. New York: Longmans, Green, 1955.

Taylor, Robert H. *Speech of Robert H. Taylor, Delivered in the House of Representatives, of the Texas Legislature*. Austin: n.p., 1861.

Taylor, William R. *Cavalier and Yankee: The Old South and the American National Character*. New York: George Braziller, 1961.

Terrell, A. W. *Oration Delivered on the Fourth Day of July, 1861 at the Capitol, Austin, Texas*. Austin: John Marshall and Co., 1861.

Thomas, David Y. *Arkansas in War and Reconstruction*. Little Rock: Arkansas Division, United Daughters of the Confederacy, 1926.

Thomas, Emory M. *The Confederacy as a Revolutionary Experience*. Englewood Cliffs, N.J.: Prentice-Hall, 1971.

———. *The Confederate Nation, 1861–1865*. New York: Harper & Row, 1979.

———. *The Confederate State of Richmond*. Austin: University of Texas Press, 1971.

Thomas, William H. *To the Freemen of the Tenth Congressional District*. N.p.: n.p., 1861.

Thompson, William Y. *Robert Toombs of Georgia*. Baton Rouge: Louisiana State University Press, 1966.

Thornton, J. Mills, III. *Politics and Power in a Slave Society: Alabama, 1800–1860*. Baton Rouge: Louisiana State University Press, 1978.

Thornwell, James Henley. *Our Danger and Our Duty*. Columbia, S.C.: Southern Guardian Steam-Power Press, 1862.

———. *The State of the Country: An Article Published from the Southern Presbyterian Review*. Columbia, S.C.: Southern Guardian Steam-Power Press, 1861.

Tise, Larry E. *Proslavery: A History of the Defense of Slavery in America, 1701–1840*. Athens: University of Georgia Press, 1987.

To the People of Virginia. Broadside. N.p.: n.p., 1861.

Todd, Robert Cecil. *Confederate Finance*. Athens: University of Georgia Press, 1954.

Tolbert, Noble J., ed. *The Papers of John Willis Ellis*. 2 vols. Raleigh: State Department of Archives and History, 1964.

Tucker, Glenn. *Zeb Vance: Champion of Personal Freedom*. Indianapolis: Bobbs-Merrill, 1965.

Tucker, Henry Holcombe. *God in the War. A Sermon Delivered before the Legislature of Georgia, in . . . Milledgeville, on Friday, November 15, 1861*. Milledgeville, Ga.: Boughton, Nisbet and Barnes, 1861.

Tucker, Robert C. *Political Culture and the Leadership in Soviet Russia*. New York: Norton, 1987.

Tupper, Henry Allen. *A Thanksgiving Discourse, Delivered at Washington, Ga, on Thursday, September 18, 1862*. Macon, Ga.: Burke, Reynolds, and Boykin, 1862.

Tyson, Bryan. *A Ray of Light; or, A Treatise on the Sectional Troubles, Religiously and Morally Considered*. Browner's Mills, N.C.: Published by the author, 1862.

Vandiver, Frank E. *Jefferson Davis and the Confederate State*. New York: Oxford University Press, 1964.

——. *Rebel Brass: The Confederate Command System*. Baton Rouge: Louisiana State University Press, 1956.

——. *Their Tattered Flags: The Epic of the Confederacy*. New York: Harper's Magazine Press, 1970.

——, ed. *The Civil War Diary of General Josiah Gorgas*. University, Ala.: University of Alabama Press, 1947.

Villeré, Charles J. *Review of Certain Remarks Made by the President When Requested to Restore General Beauregard to the Command of Department No. 2*. Charleston: Steam Power Press of Evans and Cogswell, 1863.

Waddell, James D., ed. *Biographical Sketch of Linton Stephens, Containing a Selection of His Letters, Speeches and State Papers*. Atlanta: Dodson and Scott, 1877.

Wallenstein, Peter. *From Slave South to New South: Public Policy in Nineteenth-Century Georgia*. Chapel Hill: University of North Carolina Press, 1987.

Walther, Eric H. *The Fire-Eaters*. Baton Rouge: Louisiana State University Press, 1992.

War of the Rebellion: A Compilation of the Official Records of the Union and Confederate Armies. 127 vols. Washington, D.C.: Government Printing Office, 1880–1901.

Warner, Ezra J., and W. Buck Yearns. *Biographical Register of the Confederate Congress*. Baton Rouge: Louisiana State University Press, 1975.

Watson, Harry L. *Jacksonian Politics and Community Conflict: The Emergence of the Second American Party System in Cumberland County, North Carolina*. Baton Rouge: Louisiana State University Press, 1981.

Wesley, Charles H. *The Collapse of the Confederacy*. Washington, D.C.: Associated Publishers, 1937.

White, Laura A. *Robert Barnwell Rhett, Father of Secession*. New York: Appleton-Century-Crofts, 1931.

Wiley, Bell I. *The Road to Appomattox*. Memphis: Memphis State College Press, 1956.

——, ed. *Letters of Warren Akin, Confederate Congressman*. Athens: University of Georgia Press, 1959.

Williams, Amelia, and Eugene C. Barker, eds. *The Writings of Sam Houston, 1813–1863*. 6 vols. Austin: University of Texas Press, 1938–43.

Williams, Max R., and J. G. de Roulhac Hamilton, eds. *The Papers of William Alexander Graham*. 6 vols. Raleigh: State Department of Archives and History, 1957–76.

Williams, T. Harry. *Beauregard: Napoleon in Gray*. Baton Rouge: Louisiana State University Press, 1954.

Wilmer, Richard Hooker. *Future Good—The Explanation of Present Reverses: A Sermon Preached at Mobile and Sundry Other Points in the State of Alabama during the Spring of 1864*. Charlotte, N.C.: Protestant Episcopal Church Publishing Association, 1864.

Winters, John D. *The Civil War in Louisiana*. Baton Rouge: Louisiana State University Press, 1963.

Wise, John S. *The End of an Era*. New York: Houghton Mifflin, 1900.

[Withers, Thomas Jefferson]. *"Cato" on Constitutional "Money" and Legal Tender in Twelve Numbers, from the Charleston Mercury*. Charleston: Steam Power Presses of Evans and Cogswell, 1862.

Woods, James M. *Rebellion and Realignment: Arkansas's Road to Secession*. Fayetteville: University of Arkansas Press, 1987.

Woodward, C. Vann, ed. *Mary Chesnut's Civil War*. New Haven: Yale University Press, 1981.

Woodward, C. Vann, and Elisabeth Muhlenfeld, eds. *The Private Mary Chesnut: The Unpublished Civil War Diaries*. New York: Oxford University Press, 1984.

Woodworth, Steven E. *Jefferson Davis and His Generals*. Lawrence: University Press of Kansas, 1990.

Wooster, Ralph A. *The People in Power: Courthouse and Statehouse in the Lower South, 1850–1860*. Knoxville: University of Tennessee Press, 1969.

——. *Politicians, Planters, and Plain Folk: Courthouse and Statehouse in the Upper South, 1850–1860*. Knoxville: University of Tennessee Press, 1975.

——. *The Secession Conventions of the South*. Princeton: Princeton University Press, 1962.

Worrell, Adolphus Spalding. *The Principles of English Grammar*. Nashville: Graves, Marks, and Company, 1861.

Wright, Mrs. D. Giraud. *A Southern Girl in '61*. New York: Doubleday, Page, 1905.

Wyatt-Brown, Bertram. *Southern Honor: Ethics and Behavior in the Old South*. New York: Oxford University Press, 1982.

——. *Yankee Saints and Southern Sinners*. Baton Rouge: Louisiana State
University Press, 1985.

Yancey, William Lowndes. *Speeches of William L. Yancey, Senator from the State
of Alabama; Made in the Senate of the Confederate States*. Montgomery, Ala.:
Montgomery Advertiser Book and Job Office, 1862.

Yates, Richard S. *The Confederacy and Zeb Vance*. Tuscaloosa, Ala.: Confederate
Publishing Company, 1958.

Yearns, Wilfred Buck. *The Confederate Congress*. Athens: University of Georgia
Press, 1960.

——, ed. *The Confederate Governors*. Athens: University of Georgia Press, 1985.

Yearns, Wilfred Buck, and John G. Barrett, eds. *North Carolina Civil War
Documentary*. Chapel Hill: University of North Carolina Press, 1980.

Younger, Edward, ed. *Inside the Confederate Government: The Diary of Robert
Garlick Hill Kean*. New York: Oxford University Press, 1957.

Articles

"Address of Congress to the People of the Confederate States of America."
Southern Historical Society Papers 1 (1876): 23–38.

Alexander, Thomas B. "Persistent Whiggery in Alabama and the Lower South,
1860–1867." *Alabama Review* 12 (January 1959): 35–52.

——. "Persistent Whiggery in the Confederate South, 1860–1877." *Journal of
Southern History* 27 (August 1961): 305–29.

Alfriend, Edward M. "Social Life in Richmond during the War." *Southern
Historical Society Papers* 19 (1891): 380–86.

Andrews, J. Cutler. "The Confederate Press and Public Morale." *Journal of
Southern History* 32 (November 1966): 445–65.

Auman, William T. "Neighbor against Neighbor: The Inner Civil War in the
Randolph County Area of Confederate North Carolina." *North Carolina
Historical Review* 61 (January 1984): 59–92.

Auman, William T., and David D. Scarboro. "The Heroes of America in Civil War
North Carolina." *North Carolina Historical Review* 58 (October 1981): 327–63.

Baker, Robin E. "Class Conflict and Political Upheaval: The Transformation of
North Carolina Politics during the Civil War." *North Carolina Historical
Review* 69 (April 1992): 148–78.

Bardolph, Richard. "Inconstant Rebels: Desertion of North Carolina Troops in the
Civil War." *North Carolina Historical Review* 41 (April 1964): 163–89.

Bass, James H. "The Attack upon the Confederate Administration in Georgia in
the Spring of 1864." *Georgia Historical Quarterly* 18 (September 1934): 228–47.

——. "The Georgia Gubernatorial Elections of 1861 and 1863." *Georgia Historical
Quarterly* 17 (September 1933): 167–88.

Beringer, Richard E. "Jefferson Davis's Pursuit of Ambition: The Attractive
Features of Alternative Decisions." *Civil War History* 38 (March 1992): 5–40.

——. "The Unconscious 'Spirit of Party' in the Confederate Congress." *Civil War History* 18 (December 1972): 312–33.

Bettersworth, John K., ed. "Mississippi Unionism: The Case of Reverend James A. Lyon." *Journal of Mississippi History* 1 (January 1939): 37–52.

Boney, F. N. "Governor Letcher's Candid Correspondence." *Civil War History* 10 (June 1964): 167–80.

——. "John Letcher's Secret Criticism of the Confederate Cabinet." *Virginia Magazine of History and Biography* 72 (July 1964): 348–55.

Boom, Aaron G., ed. " 'We Sowed & We Have Reaped': A Postwar Letter from Braxton Bragg." *Journal of Southern History* 31 (February 1965): 75–79.

Brooks, Robert P., ed. "Howell Cobb Papers." *Georgia Historical Quarterly* 6 (December 1922): 355–94.

Brumgardt, John R. "Alexander Stephens and the State Convention Movement in Georgia: A Reappraisal." *Georgia Historical Quarterly* 59 (Spring 1975): 38–49.

——. "The Confederate Career of Alexander H. Stephens: The Case Reopened." *Civil War History* 27 (March 1981): 64–81.

Carroll, Karen C. "Sterling, Campbell and Albright: Textbook Publishers, 1861–1865." *North Carolina Historical Review* 63 (April 1986): 169–98.

Current, Richard N. "The Confederates and the First Shot." *Civil War History* 7 (December 1961): 357–69.

Daniel, W. Harrison. "Southern Presbyterians in the Confederacy." *North Carolina Historical Review* 44 (Summer 1967): 231–55.

Davenport, F. Garvin, ed. "The Essay on Habeas Corpus in the Judge Sharkey Papers." *Mississippi Valley Historical Review* 23 (September 1936): 243–46.

——, ed. "Judge Sharkey Papers." *Mississippi Valley Historical Review* 23 (June 1933): 75–90.

Eckstein, Harry. "A Culturalist Theory of Political Change." *American Political Science Review* 82 (September 1988): 789–804.

Escott, Paul D. "Joseph E. Brown, Jefferson Davis, and the Problem of Poverty in the Confederacy." *Georgia Historical Quarterly* 61 (Spring 1977): 59–71.

Estill, Mary S., ed. "Diary of a Confederate Congressman, 1862–1863." Parts 1 and 2. *Southwestern Historical Quarterly* 28, 29 (April and July 1935): 270–301, 33–65.

Ezell, John S. "A Southern Education for Southrons." *Journal of Southern History* 17 (August 1951): 303–27.

Fahrner, Alvin A. "William 'Extra Billy' Smith, Governor of Virginia, 1864–1865: A Pillar of the Confederacy." *Virginia Magazine of History and Biography* 74 (January 1966): 68–87.

Fenner, Charles E. "The Ninety-Third Anniversary of the Birth of Pres. Davis." *Southern Historical Society Papers* 29 (1901): 1–33.

Fitts, Albert N. "The Confederate Convention: The Constitutional Debate." *Alabama Review* 2 (July 1949): 189–210.

——. "The Confederate Convention: The Provisional Constitution." *Alabama Review* 2 (April 1949): 83–101.

Fleming, Walter L. "The Peace Movement in Alabama during the Civil War." *South Atlantic Quarterly* 2 (April, July 1903): 114–24, 246–60.

Formisano, Ronald P. "Deferential-Participant Politics: The Early Republic's Political Culture, 1789–1840." *American Political Science Review* 68 (June 1974): 473–87.

——. "Political Character, Antipartyism and the Second Party System." *American Quarterly* 21 (Winter 1969): 683–709.

Foster, Gaines. "Guilt over Slavery: A Historiographical Analysis." *Journal of Southern History* 56 (November 1990): 665–94.

Greenawalt, Bruce, ed. "Unionists in Rockbridge County: The Correspondence of James Dorman Davidson Concerning the Virginia Secession Convention of 1861." *Virginia Magzaine of History and Biography* 73 (January 1965): 78–102.

Hall, Mark. "Alexander H. Stephens and Joseph E. Brown and the Georgia Resolutions for Peace." *Georgia Historical Quarterly* 54 (Spring 1980): 50–63.

Hamilton, James G. de Roulhac. "Heroes of America." *Publications of the Southern Historical Association* 11 (January 1907): 10–19.

——. "The State Courts and the Confederate Constitution." *Journal of Southern History* 4 (November 1938): 425–48.

Hay, Thomas R. "The Davis-Hood-Johnston Controversy in 1864." *Mississippi Valley Historical Review* 11 (June 1924): 54–84.

——. "The South and the Arming of the Slaves." *Mississippi Valley Historical Review* 6 (June 1919): 34–73.

Herd, Elmer Don, Jr., ed. "Laurence M. Keitt's Letters from the Provisional Congress of the Confederacy, 1861." *South Carolina Historical Magazine* 61 (January 1960): 19–25.

——. "Sue Sparks Keitt to a Northern Friend, March 4, 1861." *South Carolina Historical Magazine* 62 (April 1961): 82–87.

Hill, Benjamin H. "Address of Honorable B. H. Hill before the Georgia Branch of the Southern Historical Society at Atlanta, February 18, 1874." *Southern Historical Society Papers* 14 (1886): 484–505.

Huff, Leo. "The Martial Law Controversy in Arkansas, 1861–65: A Case History of Internal Confederate Conflict." *Arkansas Historical Quarterly* 37 (Summer 1978): 147–67.

Hull, Augustus Longstreet, ed. "The Correspondence of Thomas Read Rootes Cobb, 1860–1862." *Southern Historical Association Publications* 11 (May, July, November, 1907): 147–85, 233–60, 312–28.

——. "Thomas R. R. Cobb: Extracts from Letters to His Wife, February 3, 1861–December 10, 1862." *Southern Historical Society Papers* 28 (1900): 208–301.

Inglehart, Ronald. "The Renaissance of Political Culture." *American Political Science Review* 82 (December 1988): 1203–30.

Jennings, M. Kent, and Richard G. Niemi. "The Transmission of Political Values from Parent to Child." *American Political Science Review* 62 (March 1968): 169–83.

Johnson, Herschel V. "From the Autobiography of Herschel V. Johnson, 1856–1867." *American Historical Review* 30 (January 1925): 311–36.

Johnson, Ludwell H. "Jefferson Davis and Abraham Lincoln as War Presidents: Nothing Succeeds Like Success." *Civil War History* 27 (March 1981): 49–63.

Jones, James P., and William Warren Rogers, eds. "Montgomery as the Confederate Capital." *Alabama Historical Quarterly* 26 (Spring 1964): 1–125.

Kendall, Lane Carter. "The Interregnum in Louisiana in 1861." *Louisiana Historical Quarterly* 16 (October 1933): 639–69.

Kerby, Robert L. "Why the Confederacy Lost." *Review of Politics* 35 (July 1973): 326–45.

Kruman, Marc W. "Dissent in the Confederacy: The North Carolina Experience." *Civil War History* 27 (December 1981): 293–313.

Long, Durwang. "Unanimity and Disloyalty in Secessionist Alabama." *Civil War History* 11 (September 1965): 257–73.

Lucas, M. Phillip. " 'To Carry Out Great Fundamental Principles': The Antebellum Southern Political Culture." *Journal of Mississippi History* 52 (February 1990): 1–22.

Mathis, Robert Neil. "Freedom of the Press in the Confederacy: A Reality." *Historian* 37 (August 1975): 633–48.

McCrary, Peyton, Clark Miller, and Dale Baum. "Class and Party in the Secession Crisis: Voting Behavior in the Deep South, 1856–1861." *Journal of Interdisciplinary History* 8 (Winter 1978): 429–57.

McLean, Mrs. Eugene. "A Northern Woman in the Confederacy." *Harper's Monthly Magazine* 128 (February 1914): 440–51.

McMurry, Richard M. " 'The Enemy at Richmond': Joseph E. Johnston and the Confederate Government." *Civil War History* 27 (March 1981): 5–31.

Meade, Robert D. "The Relations between Judah P. Benjamin and Jefferson Davis." *Journal of Southern History* 5 (1939): 468–78.

Mering, John V. "Persistent Whiggery in the Confederate South: A Reconsideration." *South Atlantic Quarterly* 69 (Winter 1970): 123–43.

Miller, Robert D. "Samuel Field Phillips: The Odyssey of a Southern Dissenter." *North Carolina Historical Review* 58 (July 1981): 263–80.

Monroe, Haskell. "Early Confederate Political Patronage." *Alabama Review* 20 (January 1967): 45–61.

Moore, John Hammond. "The Rives Peace Resolution—March 1865." *West Virginia History* 26 (April 1965): 153–60.

Preisser, Thomas M. "The Virginia Decision to Use Negro Soldiers in the Civil War, 1864–65." *Virginia Magazine of History and Biography* 83 (January 1975): 98–113.

Rabun, James Z. "Alexander H. Stephens and Jefferson Davis." *American Historical Review* 58 (January 1953): 290–321.

——. "Alexander H. Stephens and the Confederacy." *Emory University Quarterly* 6 (October 1950): 129–46.

——. "A Letter for Posterity: Alexander Stephens to His Brother Linton, June 3, 1864." *Emory University Publications* ser. 8, no. 3 (1954): 12–24.

Rainwater, Percy L., ed. "Letters of James Lusk Alcorn." *Journal of Southern History* 3 (May 1937): 196–209.

Reid, Bill C. "Confederate Opponents of Arming the Slaves, 1861–1865." *Journal of Mississippi History* 22 (October 1960): 249–70.

Reid, Richard. "A Test Case of the 'Crying Evil': Desertion among North Carolina Troops during the Civil War." *North Carolina Historical Review* 58 (Summer 1981): 234–62.

Reiger, John F. "Deprivation, Disaffection, and Desertion in Confederate Florida." *Florida Historical Quarterly* 48 (January 1970): 279–98.

Richardson, Ralph. "The Choice of Jefferson Davis as Confederate President." *Journal of Mississippi History* 17 (July 1955): 161–76.

Robbins, John B. "The Confederacy and the Writ of Habeas Corpus." *Georgia Historical Quarterly* 55 (Summer 1971): 83–101.

Rodgers, Daniel T. "Republicanism: The Career of a Concept." *Journal of American History* 79 (June 1992): 11–38.

Scarboro, David D. "North Carolina and the Confederacy: The Weakness of States' Rights during the Civil War." *North Carolina Historical Review* 56 (April 1979): 133–49.

Shalhope, Robert E. "Republicanism and Early American Historiography." *William and Mary Quarterly* 39 (April 1982): 334–56.

——. "Toward a Republican Synthesis: The Emergence of Republicanism in American Historiography." *William and Mary Quarterly* 29 (January 1972): 49–80.

Shugg, Roger Wallace. "A Suppressed Co-operationist Protest against Secession." *Louisiana Historical Quarterly* 19 (January 1936): 199–203.

Silver, James W. "Propaganda in the Confederacy." *Journal of Southern History* 11 (November 1945): 487–503.

Stephenson, Nathaniel W. "The Question of Arming the Slaves." *American Historical Review* 18 (January 1913): 295–308.

——. "A Theory of Jefferson Davis." *American Historical Review* 21 (October 1915): 73–90.

Sumner, John Osborne, ed. "Georgia and the Confederacy." *American Historical Review* 1 (October 1895): 97–102.

Talmadge, John E. "Peace-Movement Activities in Civil War Georgia." *Georgia Review* 7 (Summer 1953): 190–203.

Taylor, Rosser H., ed. "Boyce-Hammond Correspondence." *Journal of Southern History* 3 (August 1937): 348–54.

Thomas, Emory. "Rebel Nationalism: E. H. Cushing and the Confederate Experience." *Southwestern Historical Quarterly* 73 (January 1970): 343–55.

Trexler, Harrison A. "The Davis Administration and the Richmond Press, 1861–1865." *Journal of Southern History* 16 (May 1950): 177–95.

——. "Jefferson Davis and the Confederate Patronage." *South Atlantic Quarterly* 28 (January 1929): 45–58.

——. "The Opposition of Planters to the Employment of Slaves as Laborers by the Confederacy." *Mississippi Valley Historical Review* 27 (September 1940): 211–24.

Vance, Zebulon B. "Address Delivered by Governor Z. B. Vance, of North

Carolina, before the Southern Historical Society, at White Sulphur Springs, West Virginia." *Southern Historical Society Papers* 14 (1886): 506–21.

Vandiver, Frank E. "Jefferson Davis—Leader without Legend." *Journal of Southern History* 43 (February 1977): 3–18.

Van Riper, Paul P., and Harry N. Scheiber. "The Confederate Civil Service." *Journal of Southern History* 25 (November 1959): 448–70.

Walker, Anne Kendrick. "Governor John Gill Shorter: Miscellaneous Papers, 1861–1863." *Alabama Review* 11 (October 1958): 267–85.

White, Laura A. "The Fate of Calhoun's Sovereign Convention in South Carolina." *American Historical Review* 34 (July 1929): 757–71.

Whittington, G. P. "Thomas O. Moore." *Louisiana Historical Quarterly* 13 (January 1930): 5–31.

Wight, Willard E., ed. "Some Letters of Lucius Bellinger Northrop." *Virginia Magazine of History and Biography* 68 (October 1960): 456–77.

Worley, Ted R. "The Arkansas Peace Society of 1861: A Study in Mountain Unionism." *Journal of Southern History* 24 (November 1958): 445–56.

"Yancey and Hill." *Southern Historical Society Papers* 19 (1891): 374–76.

Barnwell, Robert W.: at Montgomery convention, 49; on Davis as presidential prospect, 66; election to Senate, 103; criticism of Rhett, 148; on opposition to conscription, 158; criticizes Davis administration, 285

Barry, William T. S., 51

Barten, O. S., 76

Battle, William H., 262

Beauregard, P. G. T.: and First Manassas, 82; rank in Confederate army, 83; and Davis, 116–17; and western concentration bloc, 128–29; and quarrel with Benjamin, 130; removed from western command, 147; desire for western command, 168–69; and Brown, 169; strategic ideas, 195; on Gettysburg campaign, 198; possible appointment to western command, 237; and Davis in Charleston, 239

Benjamin, Judah P.: appointed attorney general, 73; and governors, 116; criticized by Reuben Davis, 117; early attacks on, 129–30; at Richmond dinner party, 236; on slave soldiers, 293; and 1861 Senate elections, 323–24 (n. 47); no-confidence resolution, 363 (n. 53)

Benning, Henry L., 202

Bensel, Richard Franklin, 345 (n. 48)

Blandford, Mark, 347 (n. 25)

Bocock, Thomas S., 119–20, 321 (n. 19)

Bonham, Milledge Luke, 130, 218

Boteler, Alexander R., 223–24

Boyce, William C., 134, 136, 187, 272–73

Bragg, Braxton: appointed to western command, 147; declares martial law, 158; described, 169; early opposition to, 169–70; and Johnston, 172–73, 265; and loss of Tennessee, 237–38; Johnston on, 264; on Confederate defeat, 299; and military appoint-

ments, 319 (n. 67); and Davis-Johnston dispute, 336 (n. 49)

Bragg, Thomas, 119, 128–29, 132, 231

Breckinridge, John C., 18, 170, 236

Brown, Albert Gallatin: elected to Senate, 100; ambivalent role in Confederate politics, 211; on exemption laws, 243–44; on expanding conscription, 248; on habeas corpus, 250, 263; on slave soldiers, 295

Brown, John W., 140

Brown, Joseph E.: and secession, 29; on slavery, 54; as presidential prospect, 65; on 1861 presidential election, 91; on 1861 congressional elections, 93; described, 106–7; and 1861 gubernatorial election, 106–8; and Confederate cause, 110; and military appointments, 115; and state arms, 116; early opposition to conscription, 141–43; as leader of Georgia opposition, 160–63; and Beauregard, 169; and Randolph, 170; as defender of soldiers' interests, 191; on state supreme court, 200; and 1863 state elections, 215–18; and 1863 congressional elections, 232; on class tensions, 244; and 1864 political conflict in Georgia, 256–62; and Atlanta campaign, 264; and peace sentiments in Georgia, 271; and Boyce, 272; and Davis's Macon speech, 274; endorses convention of the states, 278–80; and Georgia troops, 282; on Lincoln administration, 307 (n. 15); on nature of militia, 330 (n. 35); as politician, 346 (n. 6)

Brownlow, William G., 21

Bruce, Eli M., 136

Buchanan, James, 16–17

Buncombe County, N.C., 151

Burke, Edmund, 23, 283

Butler, Benjamin F., 176, 210

Bynum, William Preston, 233

Cabinet, 71–74, 249–50

Calhoun, John C., 13, 15, 70

Campbell, John A., 292

Caperton, Allen T., 222, 295

Chambers, Henry C., 186, 288–89

Chambers, Thomas Jefferson, 105, 219–20

Chancellorsville, battle of, 174, 186, 196, 198

Charleston, S.C., 180

Charleston Courier, 150, 207, 225, 272, 321 (n. 11)

Charleston Mercury: on Democrats, 18; on Montgomery convention, 44, 50; on slave trade, 53; and Confederate Constitution, 61; on Davis as presidential prospect, 66; early opposition to Davis, 86, 126, 133; on presidential election, 89, 321 (n. 11); and military offensive, 117; on Davis's character, 119; on congressional secrecy, 125; warns of military despotism, 146; on Boyce, 272; on Stephens, 273; on Lee and slave soldiers, 290

Charlotte, N.C., 151

Chatham County, Ga., 161

Chattanooga, Tenn., 249

Chesnut, James, Jr., 66, 103, 150, 237, 290

Chesnut, Mary Boykin: on Montgomery convention, 43, 73; on need for stronger leadership, 112; on Davis's early success, 130; on depression in Richmond, 236; on Johnston, 237–38; on Davis, 240; on Congress and peace, 273–74; on Hood, 285; on Confederacy's final days, 297

Chilton, William P., 186

Christian, Samuel H., 233–34

Civil liberties: in early Confederacy, 113–14, 144–46. *See also* Conscription; Habeas corpus

Clark, Charles, 220, 253, 289

Clark, Edward, 105

Clark, Henry T., 115, 133

Clark, John B., 127

Class tensions: in antebellum South, 8–9, 11–12; and secession, 25; early in war, 81–82, 133; and defense of planter interests, 149; in 1862 North Carolina gubernatorial campaign, 152–53; in Confederate textbooks, 182; during Civil War, 185–86; and overseer exemption, 190–92; and Confederate patriotism, 243–45; and peace movement, 273–74; and Confederate jeremiad, 277–78; and slavery, 340 (n. 58), 354 (n. 54); and taxation, 340 (n. 61)

Clausewitz, Karl von, 116

Clay, Clement C., Jr.: and Walker, 72; election to Senate, 101–2; on military appointments, 136; on weakness of Confederate government, 158–59; and defense of Johnston, 198; and Montgomery post office, 205–6; and 1863 elections, 228–29

Clay, Henry, 15

Cleburne, Patrick, 287

Clinton, John D. C., 289

Cobb, Howell: in antebellum politics, 14; on Montgomery convention, 44; on Confederate Constitution, 58; as presidential prospect, 65–67; on election of Stephens, 67; on patronage in Montgomery, 73; opposed to Brown, 108; address to Georgians, 119; farewell speech to Provisional Congress, 120; as Georgia political leader, 160; on peace movement, 187; on need for dictatorship, 209; command in Georgia, 217; on Bragg, 237; on dangers of subjugation, 245; and 1864 political conflict in Georgia, 257–58, 261; and Johnston's removal, 264; and limiting of exemptions, 282; on slave soldiers, 290

Cobb, Thomas R. R.: on secession, 24; on Montgomery convention, 45; on new Confederacy, 46; on Rhett, 51; on admission of nonslaveholding states, 56; and immigration, 62; and religion in Confederacy, 62; on presidential prospects, 65–66; on election of Stephens, 67; on Confederate patronage, 71; on patronage in Montgomery, 74; address to Georgians, 119; attack on Benjamin, 130; on Stephens's possible succession to presidency, 134; on disaffection of Stephens, 166

Cobb, Williamson R. W., 349 (n. 54)

Cognitive dissonance, 350 (n. 62)

Cohen, J. Barrett, 256

Columbia, S.C., 274

Compromise, sectional, 304 (n. 16)

Confederate Constitution, 4, 43–63; provisional, 50; and slave trade, 51–53; and slavery, 51–56; historical assessments of, 58–59, 62–63; contemporary assessment of, 59–63; ratification of, 60–62; on presidential elections, 89; and wartime debate, 111–12; and state sovereignty, 312 (n. 34)

Confederate nationalism: and Montgomery convention, 45–46; defined, 74–75; in schools and textbooks, 179–84; as negative ideology, 208; weaknesses of, 311 (n. 18)

Confederate party: and North Carolina politics, 151–52, 164

Congress: Provisional, 50–51; 1861 elections, 92–104; first session of permanent, 123–26; and conscription, 139–40; and occupied areas, 211–12; assessed, 222–23; criticized, 242–43; and peace resolutions, 280–81; chastises Davis, 296; roll calls, 327 (n. 34)

Connelly, Thomas, 128

Conscription: first measures, 138–43; and states' rights, 147; Davis and critics of, 154; second congressional act, 155–57; denounced by Brown, 161; ambivalent attitude of Vance toward, 163–65; problems of evasion, 199–200; in North Carolina courts, 200–201; 1864 debate on, 248–49; of state officials, 262; of slaves, 287–96; and militia, 330 (n. 35); and political candidates, 333 (n. 4)

Conservative party: and North Carolina politics, 150–52, 164, 190, 245–47

Constitutions, state, 39–43, 149–50

Cooper, Samuel, 83

Cooper, William J., Jr., 10

Cooperationists, 21–38, 92–104

Corinth, Miss., 128, 137, 147

Cornwall, Susan, 54

Corruption: in antebellum politics, 17; and secession, 22, 28–29; fear of in Confederate Constitution, 56; fear of in early Confederacy, 79; and elections, 98–99; feared by Hammond, 148–49

Cotton production, 192

Crawford, Martin J., 96, 119

Crittenden, George, 319 (n. 67)

Cruikshank, Marcus H., 348 (n. 33)

Curry, Jabez Lamar Monroe, 112–13, 187, 229, 241–42, 348 (nn. 33, 39)

Dalton, Ga., 237

Dalzell, W. T. D., 184

Daniel, John M.: on Virginia constitution, 41–42; on patronage, 77; early support for Davis, 81; on 1861 congressional elections, 97; on 1861 Senate elections, 102; attack on Benjamin, 130; and support for conscription, 156; attack on Davis after Vicksburg, 206; on 1863 Virginia elections, 219; on voting procedures, 226; on civil religion, 344 (n. 41)

Danton, Georges Jacques, 47

Davidson, Allen T., 230

Davis, Jefferson, 4; in antebellum Southern politics, 13–14; and reconstruction, 44, 74; on slavery, 53; as revolutionary leader, 64–65, 69, 274; elected Confederate president, 64–68; speech in Montgomery, 68; compared to Washington, 68–70, 87; background and description, 68–71; inaugurations, 69–70, 121–23; as administrator, 70–71; cabinet selections, 71–74; and defining of Confederate nationalism, 74–75; and civil religion, 76; and early Confederate patronage, 79–80, 135–36; early financial problems, 80; early military strategy, 81; early support for, 81; patriotic oratory, 82, 239–40; and First Manassas, 82–83; beginnings of quarrel with Johnston, 83–84; early military appointments, 84–85; early opposition to, 85–87, 133–34, 151–52; as candidate in 1861 presidential election, 90–91; opposition in North Carolina, 115; and governors, 116; and Beauregard, 116–17; and western command problems, 118–19, 171–72, 196–98, 236, 263–65; early optimism of, 120; early relations with Congress, 126, 130; and defense of territory, 127–29; response to early criticism, 128–29; anger of, 132; and defense of North Carolina, 133; relations with Congress, 134–35; and military appointments, 136; strategy in western theater, 136–37; strategy in eastern theater, 137–38; calls for conscription, 139–40, 142; and first habeas corpus suspension, 143–44; as would-be dictator, 147, 175, 209–10; debate between supporters and critics of, 147–49; complains about critics, 154; proposes second Conscription Act, 155; early political support for, 157–58; on martial law, 159;

early relationship with Vance, 165; relationship with Stephens, 166–67, 335 (n. 33); military appointments criticized, 167–69; and defense of Arkansas, 168; refusal to reappoint Beauregard, 169; and Bragg, 169–70; and Randolph, 170–71; clash with Wigfall over Seddon appointment, 171; criticized by Augusta Evans, 174; 1862 western tour, 176; 1863 message to Congress, 176–77; and economic regulation, 185; and democratic pressures, 189–90; defends Pemberton, 197–98; and disaffection in North Carolina, 202–4; and Montgomery post office, 205–6; mounting opposition to, 206–7; and Confederate jeremiad, 208–9; on dangers of subjugation, 208–9; and absence of political parties, 210–13; and Louis T. Wigfall, 211; and 1863 state elections, 218–21; and 1863 congressional elections, 226–32; 1863 western tour, 239; and political opposition, 242–45, 247, 255; and 1864 conscription debate, 248–49; and debate on cabinet, 249–50; and 1864 habeas corpus debate, 250–52; and 1864 political conflict in Georgia, 256–61; and libertarian opposition, 263; and 1864 North Carolina elections, 267–68; 1864 western tour, 274–75; proclamation of national fast day, 277; requests tougher conscription law, 282; in Confederacy's final days, 283–84; and antiparty ideology, 284; late-war military strategy, 285–86; and Lee, 286; on slave soldiers, 288, 364 (n. 61); and Hampton Roads conference, 292; and late patriotism, 292–93; chastises Congress, 296; on continuing war, 297; as Lost Cause martyr, 299; and Confederate nationalism, 316 (n. 16); and departmental command, 328 (n. 44);

and Moore, 334 (n. 12); stubborn-
ness, 336 (n. 48); and dispute with
Johnston, 336 (n. 49), 356 (n. 23); and
Confederate patriotism, 344 (n. 42);
and political parties, 345 (nn. 47–48);
visit to Montgomery, 360 (n. 10)
Davis, Reuben, 117, 220
Davis, Varina, 68, 70
De Bow's Review, 49, 98
De Jarnette, Daniel C., 281
DeLeon, Thomas Cooper, 70
Democracy: in antebellum South,
9–10; and secession, 25–27; and
Montgomery convention, 48–49; in
presidential elections, 89; hostility
to, 112–13; and early attacks on
Davis administration, 126; and con-
servative fears, 308 (n. 24)
Democratic party, 15–18, 31–32,
92–104
Desertion, 201, 246, 282
Devine, Thomas J., 113
Dick, Robert P., 60
Dictatorship, 147, 242–43, 344 (n. 44)
Douglas, Stephen A., 16, 18, 56
Dunaway, Thomas S., 253
Dupré, Lucius J., 230
Durden, Robert, 364 (n. 61)

Eakin, John R., 147
Early, Jubal A., 93, 271, 276
Economic regulation, 192–93
Edgefield, S.C., 150
Edgefield Advertiser, 260
Edwards, Weldon N., 33
Eggleston, George Cary, 9
Elections: 1860, 17–19; secession, 32;
and state constitutions, 41–42; and
Confederate Constitution, 58; 1861
presidential, 88–92, 316 (n. 11); 1861
congressional, 92–104, 321 (n. 19),
322 (nn. 21, 29), 323 (n. 43), 323–24
(n. 47), 324 (n. 50); 1861 state, 104–
10; general conditions of 1863, 214–
15; 1863 state, 215–21; 1863 congres-

sional, 221–35, 347 (n. 25), 347–48
(n. 33), 348 (nn. 34, 39), 349 (n. 54),
349–50 (n. 60); 1863 assessed, 234–
35; 1864 North Carolina gubernatorial, 267–71; Northern presidential,
278, 322 (n. 22); 1861 Arkansas
gubernatorial, 332 (n. 64)
Eliot, T. S., 137
Elliott, Stephen, 62, 123–24, 208, 253,
278
Emancipation, fear of, 54. *See also*
Slavery
Escott, Paul D., 344 (n. 42), 346 (n. 6),
364 (n. 61)
Evans, Augusta Jane, 174, 208
Exemption, 155–56, 190–92, 248, 262,
337 (n. 18)

Faust, Drew, 45
Fayetteville Observer, 204
Fehrenbacher, Don E., 46, 315 (n. 73)
Fielder, Herbert, 93
Fire-eaters, 7–8, 303–4 (n. 5), 316
(n. 19). *See also* Secessionists
Fitzhugh, George, 48, 145
Flanagin, Harris, 168, 332 (n. 64)
Fleming, Robert, 183
Florida: secession convention, 39–40;
and Confederate Constitution, 56;
and election of Davis, 64, 66; and
appointment of Mallory, 72; 1861
Senate elections, 101
Foote, Henry S., 129, 185, 248, 360–61
(n. 13)
Fort Donelson, Tenn., 120
Fort Henry, Tenn., 120
Fort Monroe, Va., 292
Fort Sumter, S.C., 317 (n. 32)
France: intervention in Mexico, 281
Franklin, Tenn., battle of, 285
Fredericksburg, battle of, 170, 174,
186
Frémont, John C., 210
Furlow, Timothy, 216–18

Gaither, Burgess, 35, 190

Garland, Augustus H., 232, 348 (n. 34)

Gartrell, Lucius J., 93

Geertz, Clifford, 121

George III, 135

Georgia: constitution, 40–41; and slave trade, 52; and election of Confederate president, 66–67; 1861 congressional elections, 93, 95–96; 1861 Senate elections, 101, 103–4; 1861 gubernatorial election, 106–7; 1861 clash between Brown and legislature, 115; and early opposition to conscription, 141–43; and opposition politics, 160–63, 177; court ruling on conscription, 200; 1863 state elections, 215–18; 1863 congressional elections, 223–26, 231–32, 234, 347 (n. 25); legislature supports Davis, 240; 1864 political conflict in, 256–62; peace movement in, 279

Gettysburg, campaign of, 198–99

Gholson, Thomas, 290

Gilmer, John A., 246, 254

Gilmer, John H., 282–83

Gist, William H., 150

Goode, John, 93

Goode, Thomas F., 321 (n. 19)

Gordon, George, 161

Graham, Malcolm, 155

Graham, William A.: and secession, 35–38; elected to Senate, 164; on peace movement in North Carolina, 204; on peace candidates, 230; and Conservative party, 246; on peace question, 272, 279; on slave soldiers, 295, 296

Grant, Ulysses S., 172, 282

Greensboro, N.C., 99, 180

Grenada, Miss., 158

Habeas corpus: early discussion of suspension, 113; first suspension, 143–44; and problem of martial law, 158–59; second suspension, 159–60; third

debate, 188–89; in state courts, 199–200; 1864 debate on, 250–52; and 1864 political conflict in Georgia, 257–60; and political power, 262–63; final debate in Congress, 282–83; and House vote, 356 (n. 21)

Hale, Edward J., 204, 246

Hamilton, Alexander, 147, 249

Hammond, James Henry: on class tensions, 12, 244; and secession, 18, 24, 26–27; and 1861 Senate elections, 103; Hampton Roads conference, 292

Hampton, Wade, 198

Hardee, William J., 169–70, 264

Harley, B. C., 96

Harris, Isham G., 85

Hartridge, Julian, 95, 224–25

Hayne, Isaac, 150

Helper, Hinton Rowan, 338 (n. 19)

Henry, Patrick, 259, 280

Herbert, Caleb, 155

Heroes of America, 269

Heth, Henry, 118

Hill, Benjamin: election to Senate, 103; opposed to Brown, 108; praises Davis, 147; as Georgia political leader, 160; address to Georgia legislature, 162–63; on overseer exemption, 191; and 1863 Senate elections, 234; and 1864 political conflict in Georgia, 258; and Johnston, 264

Hill, D. H., 190

Hill, Joshua, 216–18

Hillsboro, N.C., 114

Hoke, Robert F., 246

Holden, William W.: and antebellum republicanism, 13; and secession, 31, 36–37; on Montgomery convention, 53; on Confederate Constitution, 60; organizes North Carolina opposition, 150–52; and state printing contract, 164; as libertarian, 187; as defender of Conservative party principles, 190; on overseer exemption, 191; and disaffection, 201–5;

and 1863 congressional elections, 230; and results of 1863 elections, 234; and peace question, 245–47; and 1864 elections, 265–71, 358 (n. 51); and North Carolina peace movement, 279; on slave soldiers, 288; and publication of Graham speech, 310 (n. 55); on presidential electors, 321 (n. 11); and army meetings, 342 (n. 20); and differences with Vance, 343 (n. 25)

Holliday, Frederick W., 223–24

Holmes, Theophilus, 168, 171–72

Holt, Hines, 96

Honor, 11, 304 (n. 17)

Hood, John B., 264–65, 285–86

Hopkins, M. L., 95

Houston, Sam, 22, 219–20

Huger, Benjamin, 128

Hunt, Jabez, 152

Hunt, Lynn, 47, 65

Hunter, Robert M. T.: presidential ambitions, 17; as presidential prospect, 65; election to Senate, 102–3; as Davis supporter, 209; in Confederate Senate, 222; at Richmond dinner party, 236; and Hampton Roads conference, 292; on slave soldiers, 293–95; on civil religion, 344 (n. 41)

Hyman, John D., 230

Immigration: into Confederacy, 62

Impressment, 193

Inflation: in Richmond, 125

Iverson, Alfred, 103

Jackson, Thomas J., 130, 196, 223

Jamison, David F., 47

Jefferson, Thomas, 15, 47

Jemison, Robert, 227

Jeremiad: Confederate, 184–86, 317 (n. 38), 339 (n. 36); antiparty theme, 187–88; and liberty, 189; in 1863, 208–9; and political culture, 277; and New England, 339 (n. 35)

Johnson, Herschel V.: and Confederate finances, 80; early support for Davis, 81; opposition to political parties, 90, 252–53; on 1861 Senate elections, 103; on Davis administration, 119, 162; on conscription, 141, 200; elected to Senate, 162; antiparty stance, 188; ambivalent role in Confederate politics, 211; on Confederate Senate, 222; and 1863 Senate elections, 234; on habeas corpus, 252; and 1864 political conflict in Georgia, 258–59; and peace movement, 271; on peace question, 272; on the press and Davis, 274

Johnson, Robert W., 101, 249

Johnston, Albert Sidney, 83, 118, 128, 136, 137

Johnston, Joseph E.: and First Manassas, 82–83; beginnings of quarrel with Davis, 83–84; and Davis, 117, 336 (n. 49); and western concentration bloc, 128–29; quarrel with Benjamin, 130; and strategy in eastern theater, 137–38; as possible military dictator, 138; and Peninsula campaign, 146; appointed to western command, 171–72; on Lee, 172; and Bragg, 172–73; and Beauregard, 195; western command problems, 196–98, 237–39, 356 (n. 23); and Atlanta campaign, 263–65; restored to command, 286–87

Johnston, William, 151–52

Jones, Archer, 128

Jones, Charles C., Jr., 62

Jones, Charles Colcock, 75

Kean, Robert G. H., 102–3

Keitt, Laurence M.: and antebellum politics, 18, 23; and Montgomery convention, 44; on three-fifth clause, 56; opposition to Davis, 86, 148, 242; role in Confederacy, 316 (n. 19)

Kenan, Augustus Holmes, 232

Kentucky: Confederate collapse in, 120; in Confederate Congress, 127, 211; demands for an offensive in, 136

King, Thomas Butler, 224

Knoxville Whig, 21

Kruman, Marc W., 336 (n. 3), 343 (n. 25)

Lacy, J. Horace, 99

Lamar, L. Q. C., 253, 261

Lander, William, 233

Langdon, Charles, 290

Leach, James M., 267

Leach, James T., 230, 245, 266–67, 280

Lee, Robert E.: on secession, 23; rank in Confederate army, 83; as a general above politics, 146–47; and Second Manassas, 154–55; Johnston on, 172; as Confederate hero, 174; and western concentration bloc, 196; offensive plans, 197; and Gettysburg campaign, 198–99, 341 (n. 7); on conscription, 199; recommends Beauregard for western command, 237; on Johnston and Hood, 264; and Petersburg, 274; as general in chief, 285–86; on slave soldiers, 289–90, 295

Legitimacy: and Confederate politics, 4–5

Lester, George, 347 (n. 25)

Letcher, John, 77, 141, 143, 348 (n. 34)

Lewis, David W., 231

Liberty: in Southern political culture, 2; and conscription, 138–43; as focus for political dissent, 157–58; as foundation for alternative political culture, 160; Brown as defender of, 160–61; defined by Yancey, 177–78; as force in Confederate politics, 188–92; and economic regulation, 192–93; and opposition to Confederate policies, 243–44; and 1864 habeas corpus debate, 251–52; and public virtue, 253; and 1864 political conflict in Georgia, 256–62; and

localism, 262; and presidential power, 263; and peace movement, 272–73; in final debate on habeas corpus, 282–83; in North Carolina politics, 336 (n. 3). *See also* Habeas corpus

Lincoln, Abraham, 27–28, 143, 158, 182–83, 250, 278, 292

Logan, George W., 230

Longstreet, Augustus Baldwin, 76–77

Longstreet, James, 198, 237

Louisiana: and slave trade, 52; and Confederate Constitution, 60–61; 1861 congressional elections, 95; and defense of Vicksburg, 170; 1861 Senate elections, 323–34 (n. 47)

Loyalty oath, 36–37

Lubbock, Francis, 105

McAfee, Madison, 105

McClellan, George B., 138, 154, 210, 278

McClernand, John A., 210

McDowell, Irvin, 82

McFarland, William H., 96

McGuire, Judith, 123

Mackall, William W., 237

McMannen, John, 38

Macon, Ga., 180, 274

Madison, James, 250

Magrath, Andrew G., 283, 285

Mallory, Stephen R., 72, 129

Manassas, Va., 138; first battle of, 82–83; second battle of, 154–55

Marshall, Humphrey, 170, 319 (n. 67)

Marshall, John, 159

Martial law, 158–59, 166. *See also* Habeas corpus

Maxwell, Augustus E., 101

Meade, George G., 198

Memminger, Christopher G., 50, 72, 80

Memphis, Tenn., 195

Memphis Appeal, 29, 112

Merrimon, Augustus S., 114

Miles, James W., 184

Miles, William Porcher, 18–19, 248, 285

Milledgeville Southern Federal Union, 107, 141

Milton, John S., 39, 85, 116, 156, 279

Missionary Ridge, battle of, 237

Mississippi: and slave trade, 52; early disaffection in, 77; 1861 Senate elections, 100–101; 1861 gubernatorial election, 105–6; Davis addresses legislature, 176; 1863 gubernatorial election, 220; 1863 congressional elections, 224; exemption of state officials, 262; legislature on habeas corpus, 263

Mississippi River, 137, 168, 195, 198

Missouri: and western command, 118–19; in early Congress, 127; in Confederate Congress, 211

Mitchel, C. W., 101

Mobile, Ala., 180

Monetary policy: in early Confederacy, 80

Monroe Doctrine, 281

Montgomery, Ala., 53, 59, 64–70, 274, 360 (n. 10)

Moore, Andrew B., 30, 185

Moore, Bartholomew F., 38

Moore, Marinda, 181–83

Moore, Thomas O., 137, 158, 319–20 (n. 68), 334 (n. 12)

Moore, Thomas V., 112

Morgan, John Hunt, 170

Morgan, John T., 136

Munford, George, 219

Munnerlyn, Charles J., 223

Murfreesboro, Tenn., 172

Murrah, Pendleton, 219–20

Nashville, Tenn., 128, 285

Nashville Christian Advocate, 99

National Democrats, 304 (n. 15)

New Orleans Picayune, 46, 91, 123

Newspapers: in Confederacy, 133–34

Nieman, Donald, 314 (n. 61)

Nisbet, Eugenius A., 108–10, 112

North Carolina: and secession, 24–25, 36–37; and Confederate Constitution, 60; elections to Provisional Congress, 78; 1861 congressional elections, 94, 97; 1861 Senate elections, 101; early disaffection in, 114–15, 149–53; and Confederate military strategy, 127; Unionism in 1862, 133; and calls for repealing overseer exemption, 156; persistent political conflict in, 160; early Vance administration, 163–65; opposition and support for Davis, 177; teachers in support slavery, 181; in Confederate textbooks, 182; and tension between unity and liberty, 190–91; denunciations of tax in kind, 192–93; disaffection in, 200–205; 1863 congressional elections, 227–30, 232–34; and peace question, 245–48; exemption of state officials, 262; peace movement and 1864 gubernatorial election, 265–71, 358 (n. 51); peace movement in, 279–80; regimental meetings in, 342 (n. 20); party organization in, 345 (n. 49)

Oldham, Williamson S., 139, 155, 168, 170, 212, 281, 295

Orr, James L., 103, 126, 155, 236, 237, 272, 297

Orr, Jehu A., 281

Palmer, Benjamin M., 79, 291

Paris, John, 246

Patriotism, 207–8, 231–32, 239–42, 292–93

Patronage: and Confederate Constitution, 58; in Montgomery, 71, 73–74; in border states, 77–78; in early Confederacy, 79–80; continuing conflict over, 135–36; problems in Davis administration, 167; and civil religion, 205; in Alabama, 205–6

Peace movement, 186–87, 200–202, 229–31, 245–48, 255, 259–60, 265–74, 278–81, 292–94, 360 (n. 10)

Pearson, Richmond M., 200–201

Pemberton, John C., 171, 197, 341 (n. 7)

Perry, Madison, 85

Petersburg, Va., 145; siege of, 270–71, 274, 282

Pettus, John J., 105–6, 220

Phelan, James, 101, 156, 228

Pickens, Francis W., 54–55, 66, 89, 116, 149–50, 218

Pierce, George F., 135

Pillow, Gideon, 128

Plato, 81

Plural officeholding, 92

Political culture: in Confederacy, 1; defined, 3–4, 303 (n. 4); during revolutions, 47; changes in, 208; competing, 212–13; as source of Confederate strength, 300–301; role of unspoken assumptions, 303 (n. 3); values and behavior, 320 (n. 1); and public policy, 329 (n. 22)

Political leadership, 345–46 (n. 2)

Political parties: in antebellum South, 9–12; and secession, 31; in upper South, 309 (n. 40); persistence in secession debates, 309 (n. 42); in Confederacy, 345 (nn. 47–49)

Political socialization, 178–84, 337 (nn. 12, 14)

Polk, Leonidas, 128, 169–70

Pollard, Edward A., 240, 293

Pope, John, 155, 210

Potter, David, 3, 7, 46

Presidency, 57–58. *See also* Davis, Jefferson

Preston, William Ballard, 324 (n. 50)

Price, Sterling, 118, 129, 134

Propaganda, Confederate, 176–78, 187

Pryor, Roger A., 93, 96

Puryear, R. C., 140

Raleigh, N.C., 151, 180

Raleigh Confederate, 266, 269, 297

Raleigh Register, 78

Raleigh Standard: on habeas corpus, 188; and disaffection, 201–3, 205; and Georgia opposition, 258; suspended, 267; attack on Vance, 270; on presidential electors, 321 (n. 11)

Raleigh State Journal, 202

Ramsay, James Graham, 233

Randolph, George W., 130, 138, 170–71

Randolph, John, 13

Rayner, Kenneth, 164, 246

Reagan, John H., 72, 341 (n. 7)

Reconstruction: fears of, 44–45, 56, 74

Rector, Henry M., 101, 114, 168, 332 (n. 64)

Reid, Sam C., 95

Religion, civil: and secession, 30; and Confederate Constitution, 62; in Davis's first inaugural, 70; in new Confederacy, 75–77; and elections, 99; in early Confederacy, 123–24; and antiparty ideology, 135; during Civil War, 184–85; and patronage, 205; in 1863, 208–9; and desertion, 246; and public virtue, 253; in Davis proclamation, 277; and prayer days, 344 (n. 41)

Renfroe, John, 208

Republicanism, 305 (n. 19); in antebellum South, 12–16; in secession debates, 21, 23; at Montgomery convention, 48–49; and slavery, 54, 291; and Confederate Constitution, 63; in Confederate civil religion, 76–77; in Davis's inaugural address, 122; and habeas corpus, 251; in late-war debates, 281–87

Revolution: and Confederacy, 2, 23, 44–45, 47–48, 63, 78, 120, 312 (n. 27)

Rhett, Edmund, 7, 290

Rhett, Robert Barnwell: and antiparty ideology, 16; in 1860 elections, 17–18; and secession, 21; at Montgomery convention, 43; and Confederate Constitution, 50–51, 61; on slave trade, 53; as presidential prospect, 65, 67; on Davis as presidential prospect, 66; and early Davis administration, 71; on presidential election, 89; and 1861 Senate elections, 103; and opposition to Davis administration, 133–34; on conscription, 139; criticism of Davis, 148; opposes admission of free states, 149; support for second Conscription Act, 156; on Confederate army, 186–87; as Confederate nationalist, 187; on habeas corpus, 188; on Gettysburg campaign, 199; concerned about support for Davis, 209; on Clay's defeat, 229; and Davis in Charleston, 239; criticizes Congress, 242; and presidential power, 254; on convention of states, 273; on dictatorship, 276; on slave soldiers, 290–91; role in Confederacy, 316 (n. 19); and 1863 congressional elections, 350 (n. 60)

Rice, John, 183

Richmond, Va., 78–79, 121–22, 145, 180, 186

Richmond Dispatch, 41, 123, 250–51

Richmond Enquirer: on patronage, 77–78; on plural officeholding, 92; on 1861 Senate elections, 102; as defender of Davis, 148; on 1862 North Carolina gubernatorial election, 152; on liberty, 189; on dictatorship, 209; on 1863 Virginia Senate elections, 222; on James T. Leach, 230; on unity in 1863 elections, 231; on slave soldiers, 296

Richmond Examiner: on Virginia constitution, 41–42; on patronage, 77; early support for Davis, 81; early assessment of Davis, 86–87; on 1861 presidential election, 90; on 1861 congressional elections, 96–97; on 1861 Senate elections, 102; and mili-

tary offensive, 117; on congressional secrecy, 125; on Davis's relations with cabinet, 129; attack on Benjamin, 130; and opposition to Davis, 133; suggests a Continental Congress, 135; and support for conscription, 156; on martial law, 158; on Seddon, 171; defends republicanism, 175; and anti-Semitism, 185; attack on Davis after Vicksburg, 206; on 1863 Virginia elections, 218, 222; criticizes Congress, 242; on limiting cabinet appointments, 249; on Stephens's speech, 259; opposition to executive spending, 263; on Johnston's removal, 264–65; on Boyce, 273; opposes Davis detailing men, 282; on slave soldiers, 287–88

Richmond Sentinel, 292, 297

Richmond Whig: on constitutional change, 42; on early Confederate patronage, 79; and powerful presidency, 84; on 1861 presidential election, 88–89; on 1861 Senate elections, 102; on Confederate Constitution, 112; on suspending habeas corpus, 113; and Beauregard letter, 116; and Confederate Congress, 124–25; defends republicanism, 175; on habeas corpus, 188; on emptiness of Confederate patriotism, 241; on political parties, 242; on planters in war, 244

Ridgeway, Robert, 42, 88, 112, 222

Rives, William C., 222, 223, 263

Roanoke Island, N.C., 120, 126, 128–30, 133

Rodgers, Daniel T., 305 (n. 19)

Rosecrans, William S., 195

Royston, Grandison D., 232

Ruffin, Edmund: and antiparty ideology, 16; and corruption, 17; on Virginia constitution, 42; and election of Davis and Stephens, 64; on military despotism, 92–93; on 1861 congressional elections, 100; on Rhett, 133; on Richmond bread riot, 186; and *Raleigh Standard*, 202; on 1863 congressional elections, 221; on William C. Rives, 223; opposes granting Davis more power, 282

Ruffin, William K., 114

Russell, William Howard, 73–74

Saunders, George, 56

Savannah Republican, 18, 41, 107, 136, 215

Schenck, David, 69, 98, 104, 236, 266

Schools, 178

Scott, Winfield, 15

Secession, 20–38; as revolution, 6–7; and fear of the future, 24; and slavery, 24–25; and class tensions, 25; and democracy, 25–27; and sectional differences, 27–28; and corruption, 28–29; and need for unity, 30; and political parties, 30–31; elections, 32; conventions, 32–38; and sovereignty, 33–34; and children, 179; ideology of, 308 (n. 28); antiparty character of, 308 (n. 37); ratification election in Texas, 309 (n. 47); ratification of, 309–10 (n. 50)

Secessionists, 20–38, 92–104, 305 (n. 26)

Seddon, James A., 171, 197, 200

Semmes, Thomas J., 296

Seven Days campaign, 154

Seward, James L., 347 (n. 25)

Seward, William H., 158, 292

Sexton, Franklin B., 155, 159, 177

Seymour, Horatio, 322 (n. 22)

Shenandoah Valley, Va., 271, 276

Sheridan, Philip H., 270

Sherman, William T., 264–66, 274, 276, 282

Shewmake, John, 231

Shiloh, battle of, 136

Shorter, John Gill, 106, 139, 145, 220–21

Siler, D. W., 340 (n. 58)

Simms, William E., 127

Simms, William Gilmore, 26, 53, 56

Slavery: and antebellum political culture, 8–9; in antebellum Southern politics, 10–16; and secession, 24–25; and Confederate Constitution, 51–56; and Davis's first inaugural, 69–70; and yeoman soldiers, 81–82; and overseer exemption, 156, 190–92; in Confederate textbooks, 180–81, 183; and impressment, 193; and Confederate patriotism, 241; and debate over conscription, 287–96, 364 (n. 61); and guilt, 305 (n. 22), 363 (n. 47); and class tensions, 340 (n. 58); in final days of Confederacy, 360 (n. 2)

Slave trade, 21, 51–53, 149

Slidell, John, 95

Smedes, Albert, 205

Smith, Edmund Kirby, 169

Smith, Gustavus W., 171

Smith, J. Henly, 55, 143

Smith, J. Henry, 99

Smith, Robert Hardy, 59, 119

Smith, William, 92

Smith, William E., 223, 231

Smith, William F. "Extra Billy," 219, 289, 295

Smith, William N. H., 227–28

Soldier voting, 152

Soulé, Pierre, 95

South Carolina: antebellum politics in, 10; and Montgomery convention, 44; secession convention, 47–48; and Confederate Constitution, 61–62; and election of Confederate president, 66; and opposition to Davis, 85–86; 1861 Senate elections, 103; early support for Davis, 126; habeas corpus suspended in, 145; controversy over executive council, 149–50; in Confederate textbooks, 182; 1863 gubernatorial election, 218;

1863 congressional elections, 226, 350 (n. 60); legislature supports Davis, 240; disaffection in, 283; and 1861 presidential election, 321 (n. 11)

Southern distinctiveness, 304 (n. 6)

Southern Literary Messenger, 49, 98, 189

Southern nationalism. *See* Confederate nationalism

Sovereignty: in secession conventions, 33–34

Sparrow, Edward, 323–24 (n. 47)

Staples, Waller R., 280

States' rights: and Montgomery convention, 56–57; and cabinet selections, 71; and military appointments, 85; and wartime divisions, 112; and conscription, 141; possible obsolescence of, 147; as explanation for Confederate defeat, 299, 330 (n. 31)

Stay laws, 37–38

Stephens, Alexander H.: on secession, 21–23, 26; on Montgomery convention, 43; and reconstruction, 44; on slavery, 53; on admission of non-slaveholding states, 56; on fiscal policy, 56; on presidency, 58; elected vice-president, 64, 67–68; as presidential prospect, 65–67; described, 67; and Confederate finances, 80; and 1861 presidential election, 90–91; as supporter of Johnston, 117, 238; early loss of hope, 126; possible succession to presidency, 134; as Georgia political leader, 160; and Brown, 161; relationship with Davis, 166–67, 335 (n. 33); on Davis as usurper, 175; praises Davis, 177; attacks Davis, 207; and 1863 Georgia elections, 215–16; on ultimate Confederate triumph, 241; and 1864 conscription debate, 249; on 1864 habeas corpus suspension, 251; as alternative to Davis, 254; and 1864 political conflict in Georgia, 256–61;

and Boyce, 272; on peace movement, 272–73; and negotiated peace, 278, 280–81; and antiparty ideology, 284; and Hampton Roads conference, 292; on nature of militia, 330 (n. 35); on dictatorship, 344 (n. 44)

Stephens, Linton, 160, 161, 162, 256–61, 272

Stiles, Joseph, 187–88

Stones River, battle of, 172

Stuart, Alexander H. H., 41

Summers, Mark W., 306 (n. 32)

Symbolic leadership, 320 (n. 74)

Symbols: in Confederate political culture, 121, 337 (n. 6), 338 (n. 39)

Tariffs: and Confederate Constitution, 56

Taxation, 21, 37, 56, 80, 192–93, 340 (n. 61)

Taylor, Robert H., 35

Tennessee: 1861 Senate elections, 101; bridges burned in, 114; habeas corpus suspended in, 145; military problems in, 236–38

Terrill, A. W., 113

Texas: and appointment of Mallory, 72; 1861 gubernatorial election, 105; and conscription, 155; legislature in Confederate textbook, 180; anti-Semitism in, 185; 1863 elections, 219–20; secession ratification election in, 309 (n. 47)

Textbooks, 179–83, 337–38 (n. 18)

Thornwell, James Henley, 8, 144

Three-fifths clause: and Confederate Constitution, 55–56

Tise, Larry E., 305 (n. 22)

Toombs, Robert: on admission of non-slaveholding states, 56; on presidency, 58; as presidential prospect, 65–67; as secretary of state, 71–72; and Confederate finance, 80; and 1861 Senate elections, 103–4; and Brown, 108, 161; and military offen-

Whig party, 15, 26, 31–32, 40, 42, 92–104, 114, 129, 135–36, 218–21, 235

Wigfall, Charlotte, 86

Wigfall, Louis T.: idea of southern nation, 7; on presidential prospects, 65; and Walker, 72; early opposition to Davis, 86; as supporter of Johnston, 117; and western concentration bloc, 128; on conscription, 139, 248; sharply attacks Davis, 148, 157; opposition to Bragg, 170; and Seddon appointment, 171; and appointment of Johnston to western command, 171–72; as Confederate nationalist, 187; on impressment of slaves, 193; and Beauregard, 195; on Johnston and Vicksburg, 197–98; on Gettysburg campaign, 199; patriotic statements, 207; concerned about support for Davis, 209; ambivalent role in Confederate politics, 211; on Clay's defeat, 229; and anti-Davis forces, 235, 297; and Davis appointments, 254; and Hood, 265; defends government policies, 275–76; on making Johnston a dictator, 287; on slave soldiers, 294; role in Confederacy, 316 (n. 19); and Davis-Johnston dispute, 336 (n. 49)

Wiley, Calvin H., 179

Williams, George, 270

Wise, O. Jennings, 91, 222

Worth, Jonathan: on patronage, 78; chosen state treasurer, 164; on Vance and conservatives, 204; on peace question, 246–47, 267; on 1864 North Carolina elections, 269

Yancey, William Lowndes: and secession, 6–7, 35, 36; as presidential prospect, 65; election to Senate, 101–2; on military appointments, 136, 167; praises Davis, 147; supports conscription, 156–57; on martial law, 158; opposition to Bragg, 170; toast to Johnston, 171; as defender of liberty, 177–78, 214; on overseer exemption, 191; and Montgomery post office, 205–6; role in Confederacy, 316 (n. 19)

Yeomen, 55, 156, 192